Emilio J. Vazquez M.D.

$54.95

D1592433

GYNECOLOGICAL DECISION MAKING

Second Edition

CLINICAL DECISION MAKING™ SERIES

Consulting Editor
Ben Eiseman, M.D.

GYNECOLOGICAL DECISION MAKING

Second Edition

By the Staff of the Beth Israel Hospital, Boston

Emanuel A. Friedman, M.D., Sc.D.

Professor of Obstetrics and Gynecology
Harvard Medical School

Obstetrician-Gynecologist-in-Chief
Department of Obstetrics and Gynecology
Beth Israel Hospital
Boston, Massachusetts

Max Borten, M.D., J.D.

Associate Professor of Obstetrics and Gynecology
Harvard Medical School

Director, Division of Medical Gynecology
Department of Obstetrics and Gynecology
Beth Israel Hospital
Boston, Massachusetts

David S. Chapin, M.D.

Instructor in Obstetrics and Gynecology
Harvard Medical School

Director, Gynecology Service
Department of Obstetrics and Gynecology
Beth Israel Hospital
Boston, Massachusetts

1988

B.C. Decker Inc • Toronto • Philadelphia

Publisher

B.C. Decker Inc
3228 South Service Road
Burlington, Ontario   L7N 3H8

B.C. Decker Inc
320 Walnut Street
Suite 400
Philadelphia, Pennsylvania   19106

Sales and Distribution

United States and Possessions	**The C.V. Mosby Company** 11830 Westline Industrial Drive Saint Louis, Missouri 63146
Canada	**The C.V. Mosby Company, Ltd.** 5240 Finch Avenue East, Unit No. 1 Scarborough, Ontario M1S 5P2
United Kingdom, Europe and the Middle East	**Blackwell Scientific Publications, Ltd.** Osney Mead, Oxford OX2 OEL, England
Australia	**Harcourt Brace Jovanovich** 30–52 Smidmore Street Marrickville, N.S.W. 2204 Australia
Japan	**Igaku-Shoin Ltd.** Tokyo International P.O. Box 5063 1–28–36 Hongo, Bunkyo-ku, Tokyo 113, Japan
Asia	**Info-Med Ltd.** 802–3 Ruttonjee House 11 Duddell Street Central Hong Kong
South Africa	**Libriger Book Distributors** Warehouse Number 8 "Die Ou Looiery" Tannery Road Hamilton, Bloemfontein 9300
South America (non-stock list representative only)	**Inter-Book Marketing Services** Rua das Palmeiras, 32 Apto. 701 222--70 Rio de Janeiro RJ, Brazil

Gynecological Decision Making Second Edition   ISBN 1–55664–065–X

Library of Congress catalog card number: 83-70108

10 9 8 7 6 5 4 3 2 1

CONTRIBUTORS

DAVID B. ACKER, M.D.

Assistant Professor of Obstetrics and Gynecology, Harvard Medical School; Associate Chief, Department of Obstetrics and Gynecology, Beth Israel Hospital, Boston, Massachusetts

CATHERINE T. ALVAREZ, R.N.

Audit and Data Coordinator, Department of Obstetrics and Gynecology, Beth Israel Hospital, Boston, Massachusetts

BALMOOKOOT BALGOBIN, M.D.

Instructor in Obstetrics and Gynecology, Harvard Medical School; Clinical Director, Ambulatory Care Program, Department of Obstetrics and Gynecology, Beth Israel Hospital, Boston, Massachusetts

STEVEN R. BAYER, M.D.

Instructor in Obstetrics and Gynecology, Harvard Medical School; Director, Gynecologic Endocrinology Laboratories, Division of Reproductive Endocrinology and Infertility, Department of Obstetrics and Gynecology, Beth Israel Hospital, Boston, Massachusetts

MAX BORTEN, M.D., J.D.

Associate Professor of Obstetrics and Gynecology, Harvard Medical School; Director, Division of Medical Gynecology, Department of Obstetrics and Gynecology, Beth Israel Hospital, Boston, Massachusetts

LOUIS BURKE, M.D.

Associate Professor of Obstetrics and Gynecology, Harvard Medical School; Director, Colposcopy Unit, Department of Obstetrics and Gynecology, Beth Israel Hospital, Boston, Massachusetts

JEROLD M. CARLSON, M.D., M.P.H.

Instructor in Obstetrics and Gynecology, Harvard Medical School; Director, Geriatric Gynecology Unit, Department of Obstetrics and Gynecology, Beth Israel Hospital, Boston, Massachusetts

DAVID S. CHAPIN, M.D.

Instructor in Obstetrics and Gynecology, Harvard Medical School; Director, Gynecology Service, Department of Obstetrics and Gynecology, Beth Israel Hospital, Boston, Massachusetts

JOSEPH F. D'AMICO, M.D.

Instructor in Obstetrics and Gynecology, Harvard Medical School; Clinical Fellow, Reproductive Endocrinology and Infertility, Department of Obstetrics and Gynecology, Beth Israel Hospital, Boston, Massachusetts

MIGUEL DAMIEN, M.D.

Instructor in Obstetrics and Gynecology, Harvard Medical School; Clinical Fellow, Reproductive Endocrinology and Infertility, Department of Obstetrics and Gynecology, Beth Israel Hospital, Boston, Massachusetts

DAVID G. DIAZ, M.D.

Instructor in Obstetrics and Gynecology, Harvard Medical School; Clinical Fellow, Reproductive Endocrinology and Infertility, Department of Obstetrics and Gynecology, Beth Israel Hospital, Boston, Massachusetts

ALEXANDER M. DLUGI, M.D.

Assistant Professor of Obstetrics and Gynecology, Harvard Medical School; Director, In-Vitro Fertilization Program, Division of Reproductive Endocrinology and Infertility, Department of Obstetrics and Gynecology, Beth Israel Hospital, Boston, Massachusetts

EMANUEL A. FRIEDMAN, M.D., Sc.D.

Professor of Obstetrics and Gynecology, Harvard Medical School; Obstetrician-Gynecologist-in-Chief, Department of Obstetrics and Gynecology, Beth Israel Hospital, Boston, Massachusetts

LYNN H. GALEN, M.D.

Instructor in Obstetrics and Gynecology, Harvard Medical School; Director, Section on Fertility Control, Department of Obstetrics and Gynecology, Beth Israel Hospital and Obstetrician Gynecologist, East Boston Neighborhood Health Center, Boston, Massachusetts

VICKI L. HELLER, M.D.

Instructor in Obstetrics and Gynecology, Harvard Medical School; Associate in Obstetrics and Gynecology, Beth Israel Hospital and Obstetrician Gynecologist, East Boston Neighborhood Health Center, Boston, Massachusetts

HENRY KLAPHOLZ, M.D.

Assistant Professor of Obstetrics and Gynecology, Harvard Medical School; Assistant Director, Section on Maternal-Fetal Medicine, Department of Obstetrics and Gynecology, Beth Israel Hospital, Boston, Massachusetts

ERIC D. LICHTER, M.D.

Instructor in Obstetrics and Gynecology, Harvard Medical School; Coordinator, Emergency Unit, Obstetrics and Gynecology, Department of Obstetrics and Gynecology, Beth Israel Hospital, Boston, Massachusetts

CAROL LONDON, R.N.

Assistant Clinical Instructor, Boston University School of Nursing; Clinical Specialist in Sexually Transmitted Diseases, Beth Israel Hospital, Boston, Massachusetts

JANET L. MITCHELL, M.D., M.P.H.

Assistant Professor of Obstetrics and Gynecology, Harvard Medical School; Director, Ambulatory High-Risk Obstetrics Unit, Department of Obstetrics and Gynecology, Beth Israel Hospital, Boston, Massachusetts

JONATHAN M. NILOFF, M.D.

Assistant Professor of Obstetrics and Gynecology, Harvard Medical School; Director, Division of Gynecology, Deaconess Hospital and Associate in Obstetrics and Gynecology, Beth Israel Hospital, Boston, Massachusetts

JOHANNA F. PERLMUTTER, M.D.

Assistant Professor of Obstetrics and Gynecology, Harvard Medical School; Director, Section on Human Sexuality, Department of Obstetrics and Gynecology, Beth Israel Hospital, Boston, Massachusetts

BENJAMIN P. SACHS, M.B., B.S., D.P.H.

Associate Professor of Obstetrics and Gynecology, Harvard Medical School and Associate Professor, Harvard School of Public Health; Director, Section on Maternal-Fetal Medicine, Department of Obstetrics and Gynecology, Beth Israel Hospital, Boston, Massachusetts

MACHELLE M. SEIBEL, M.D.

Associate Professor of Obstetrics and Gynecology, Harvard Medical School; Director, Division of Reproductive Endocrinology and Infertility, Department of Obstetrics and Gynecology, Beth Israel Hospital, Boston, Massachusetts

LENARD R. SIMON, M.D.

Instructor in Obstetrics and Gynecology, Harvard Medical School; Director, Section on Gynecologic Oncology, Department of Obstetrics and Gynecology, Beth Israel Hospital, Boston, Massachusetts

Decision making in gynecology parallels that used in all other disciplines in medicine. The process is based on a sequence of data gathering that focuses on the presenting problem and that aims at progressive clarification of an underlying cause or a pathogenetic mechanism. This leads, in turn, to some insight into the nature of the condition for which the patient seeks help and which then serves as the basis for formulating and implementing a plan for therapy. The subsequent response to treatment is obviously important insofar as it confirms or refutes the appropriateness and the logic of the foregoing analysis; proof that it was correct generally comes from a good result, whereas failure suggests error. This second edition of *Gynecological Decision Making* attempts to provide guidelines to aid in this activity and thus offers a resource for practicing gynecologists, generalists, residents, and interns in training, as well as for medical students who might use the instruction when approaching a broad range of diagnostic and therapeutic issues relevant to this specialty.

An integral component of decision making is the dynamic interplay between the health provider and the patient. Therefore, in addition to a large number of topics on gynecological conditions not previously addressed in the earlier edition, we have added much new material pertaining to counseling, informed consent, and to medicolegal issues. Our intention is to make this volume even more practical than the previous one. To this end, not only has the text been completely rewritten and updated, but also some modifications have been made in the format. These changes are intended to facilitate use by the busy physician or student.

The book is divided into seven sections, beginning with general gynecological principles of screening and routine care, proceeding through evaluation by complaint or symptom and specific disorders, to diagnostic procedures, then to operative procedures and their complications; the concluding section is on medicolegal issues. Each topic is presented in two formats, a decision algorithm and a complementary annotated discussion that expands, elucidates, or explains the rationale for the branching. Each decision tree is introduced by a series of suggestions as to the kinds of background considerations to which one should be alert when dealing with the issue under investigation. Whereas in the prior edition of this book all needed laboratory studies were grouped together, we have now dispersed the listing of objective testing at various sites within the tree; these are based on a more appropriate and timely application of those assessments to specific problems. In general, the trees have been simplified in structure, yet made more complete in terms of comprehensive verbiage. Similarly, the explanatory notes have been redesigned so that they can be used almost independently of the trees. By making each statement essentially complete, we have tried to reduce or eliminate the difficulty that is so obviously inherent in using two interrelated, but incomplete sources of information for cross reference.

Although our intent here is to offer a practical and readily assimilable framework for use when evolving the thought processes necessary for constructing systematized plans for clinical evaluation, differential diagnosis, and therapy, we feel it imperative to emphasize that we do not believe the programmatic approaches espoused here to be the last (or only) word on the subject. They are neither fixed nor are they necessarily practiced everywhere. Programmatic approaches have proved useful in our hands, but we accept that equally effective programs are currently in effect elsewhere. Because so many major changes have been made in the substance of this book in the five years that have elapsed since publication of the first edition, the changing nature of the practice of this specialty is clearly demonstrated. Our objective, therefore, is more to teach techniques of organized and orchestrated thinking rather than to concentrate exclusively on the narrow perspective of concretizing a way to resolve a specific problem, no matter how important that is in the context of carrying out the activities of one's daily practice. Because the book is addressed to a range of practitioners, it assumes the reader has basic medical knowledge and skills. We have pointed out areas of interpretation and intervention that require highly sophisticated capabilities not ordinarily available to all practitioners, including many with gynecological training and experience, and not always available in all communities. Under such circumstances, recognizing one's limitations is important, and referral to physicians with the necessary expertise or to regional centers is urged. Such responsible conduct is in the interest of ensuring optimal care for one's patients.

Thanks are due to the contributing authors whose diligence and industry are rewarded by their justifiable pride in the results they have achieved; to my co-editors for their efforts in helping to produce such a comprehensive and homogeneous edition, especially Doctor Max Borten for his indefatigable energy and dedication; to Ms. Audrey Landay for her stellar typing and editing skills in the preparation of the manuscript; and to Ms. Cynthia McCann for her fine art contributions.

Emanuel A. Friedman, M.D., Sc.D.
Boston, Massachusetts

CONTENTS

GYNECOLOGICAL DISORDERS

COMPLICATIONS

MEDICOLEGAL ISSUES

INTRODUCTION

Formal clinical decision analysis is a newly developed scientific tool that systematically formalizes the nature of decisions, dissects their component parts, assesses the areas of uncertainty, and quantitates the costs (where quantifiable) of the several alternatives. Whereas this book neither incorporates this tool nor provides the data needed to achieve its aims, it gives the basic skeleton structure upon which decisions in gynecological practice can be based. The decision trees illustrate various types of logical sequences that impose measures to evaluate a problem and to identify those therapeutic or interventive options likely to yield the best results. They try to take into account both objective evidence and intangible uncertainties. This means balancing known or anticipated risks against benefits.

Every physician is confronted with the need to make clinical decisions many times each day, whether on trivial matters pertaining to minor patient complaints or to life-threatening conditions of major importance. The art of decision making is a combination of intuitive reasoning and a more formal application of cognitive scientific rationale. It is learned only by diligent effort. With growing utilization and experience, the astute physician acquires the capacity to reflect consciously on the available alternatives, to be alert to limitations inherent in information, to be receptive to new data as such are generated, to modify action or even change course when new developments indicate it is appropriate to do so, to painstakingly weigh the positive and negative consequences of an intervention (or delay), and to synthesize these considerations formally into a reasoned judgment. An especially important means for physicians to demonstrate and sharpen their skills in this regard lies in the written documentation of their thoughts. This not only serves to help the writer, who is thus forced to spell out the stepwise sequence of the decision making process, but it proves exceedingly useful for ancillary personnel as an educational device and informational source.

The substance of this book is a comprehensive series of algorithms relating to the spectrum of decisions that have to be made for gynecological patients in the course of clinical practice. Each constitutes a guide for making relevant decisions about the condition it addresses. In this regard, it provides a logical sequence of action, which usually leads to appropriate diagnosis and management. It helps focus diagnostic evaluations, thereby averting costly overutilization of resources, reducing delay in instituting needed care, and identifying the therapeutic program likely to provide maximum benefit. More than that, however, it is intended to help the physicians learn the aforementioned art of clinical decision making. While the decision trees, based on good clinical results, do give outlines of currently accepted practices at this institution, we suggest they should not be adhered to rigidly. Many special circumstances may pertain to a given patient and warrant the modifying of judgments and decisions. Such circumstances should be weighed by the physician to aid in making the necessary changes in the plan of management. Confidence, which is acquired by observing the effects of modifying the decision algorithm, will enhance one's ability in this developing skill, which can then be applied increasingly to other clinical activities. Moreover, as newer information and concepts are learned, one can much more readily incorporate them into one's clinical armamentarium and thus modify a clinician's activities with regard to decision making; accordingly, decisions are made in a meaningful fashion, rather than following a familiar sequence by rote.

To use any given paradigm, recognize that the flow is always downward. The circled letters within each decision tree refer to the explanatory comments, similarly designated, on the corresponding adjacent page. In the tree, the material presented immediately to the left reminds the clinician about any background information about which there should be concern. Generally, history, physical examination, and designated laboratory studies follow in sequence before any branching occurs. Relevant findings are stressed to help determine the differential diagnosis. With each subsequent branching, decisions are usually based on some additional observation or finding until the probable diagnosis is established, and treatment options are to be considered. Definitive operative diagnostic or therapeutic intervention is capitalized and boxed for emphasis. Thus characteristic findings are flagged for purposes of helping differentiate and focus increasingly on the nature of the problem, thereby refining the decision making process. At each step, bear in mind that one should be making a conscious judgment about relative risks and benefits. This will serve to solidify a very useful habit pattern for future clinical decision making.

Reference

Weinstein MC, Fineberg HV. Clinical decision analysis. Philadelphia: WB Saunders, 1980.

PERIODIC HEALTH EXAMINATION IN WOMEN

David B. Acker, M.D.

A. A periodic health assessment will provide the opportunity for the physician to function as a primary care provider to uncover clinically inapparent conditions. Additionally, timely and factual discussions or referrals for problems related to contraception (p 30), marital and sexual problems, sexually transmitted diseases (including AIDS), menopause (p 94), and adjustments to life crises will benefit the patient. Assess for socioeconomic factors that may affect the patient's well-being. Nutrition, smoking, and use of medicines, recreational drugs, and alcohol should also be explored. Gynecologists should also use the opportunity to teach their patients the technique of breast self-examination (p 10).

B. Risk factors requiring special attention include signs of emotional problems as manifested by sleeplessness, anorexia or other signs of depression, and adverse attributes such as drug abuse, low socioeconomic status, or malnutrition, plus multiple sexual partners, previous pelvic infection or use of an intrauterine device, and familial diseases such as breast cancer, hypertension, or diabetes. Be especially alert for nonspecific symptoms (malaise and fatigue, for example) that may be associated with collagen, cardiovascular, renal, or hematopoietic disease.

C. The general physical examination and detailed pelvic examination must be complete and well documented. It must include relevant observations such as blood pressure and weight measurements. Include evaluation of remote areas such as the eyegrounds for vascular problems, the neck for thyroid enlargement, and the rectum for stool guaiac testing. The spectrum of laboratory examinations to be undertaken will depend on the complaints, findings, and history disclosed, including smear and cervical cultures for gonorrhea, serologic test for syphilis, tine test for tuberculosis, complete blood count and anemia or coagulation studies, urinalysis and urine culture, glucose tolerance test, stool guaiac, and blood urea nitrogen, as indicated.

D. The gynecologist can do much to create a warm, nonthreatening, and respectful relationship with the adolescent, especially if she is not yet sexually active. This trusting relationship will facilitate return visits for specific complaints in the future, for appropriate birth control measures when coitus is anticipated, and for periodic check-up examinations.

E. An annual Papanicolaou smear (p 12) for cervical cytology should be considered an essential part of the examination for every adult woman. It is even called for among sexually active adolescents. Repetition annually runs counter to the three-year schedule recommended by the American Cancer Society, but it is felt to be justified because some women may experience rapid progression of cervical dysplasia and some Papanicolaou smears will prove to be falsely negative.

F. Mammography is very useful today for early detection of breast cancer. Involve the patient actively in a program of breast self-examination supplemented by periodic screening mammograms. While small lesions can sometimes be palpated by the patient, many cannot even though they may be detectable by mammography. Beginning between age 35 and 45 years, repeat the mammogram every one to two years until age 50 and annually after that. The fear of radiation exposure associated with this technique is unfounded given the small radiation dose (0.1 rad) and the high incidence of breast cancer in the population of women being studied. The recommendation is further supported by the fact that most cancers can be detected in an early stage (and therefore are potentially more likely to be curable) by mammography. Ultrasonography is not as reliable as mammography for the detection of nonpalpable malignancies but can better differentiate a solid from a cystic lesion (p 216).

References

Feig SA. Radiation risk from mammography: Is it clinically significant? Am J Radiol 143:469, 1984.

Foster RS, Costanza MC. Breast self-examination practices and breast cancer survival. Cancer 53:999, 1984.

Holland R, Mravunac M, Hendricks JHCL, et al. So-called interval cancer of the breast: Pathologic and radiologic analysis of sixty-four cases. Cancer 49:2527, 1982.

Richart RM, Barron BA. Screening strategies for cervical cancer and cervical intraepithelial neoplasm. Cancer 47:1176S, 1981.

Sickles EA, Filly RA, Callen PW. Benign breast lesions: Ultrasound detection and diagnosis. Radiology 151:467, 1984.

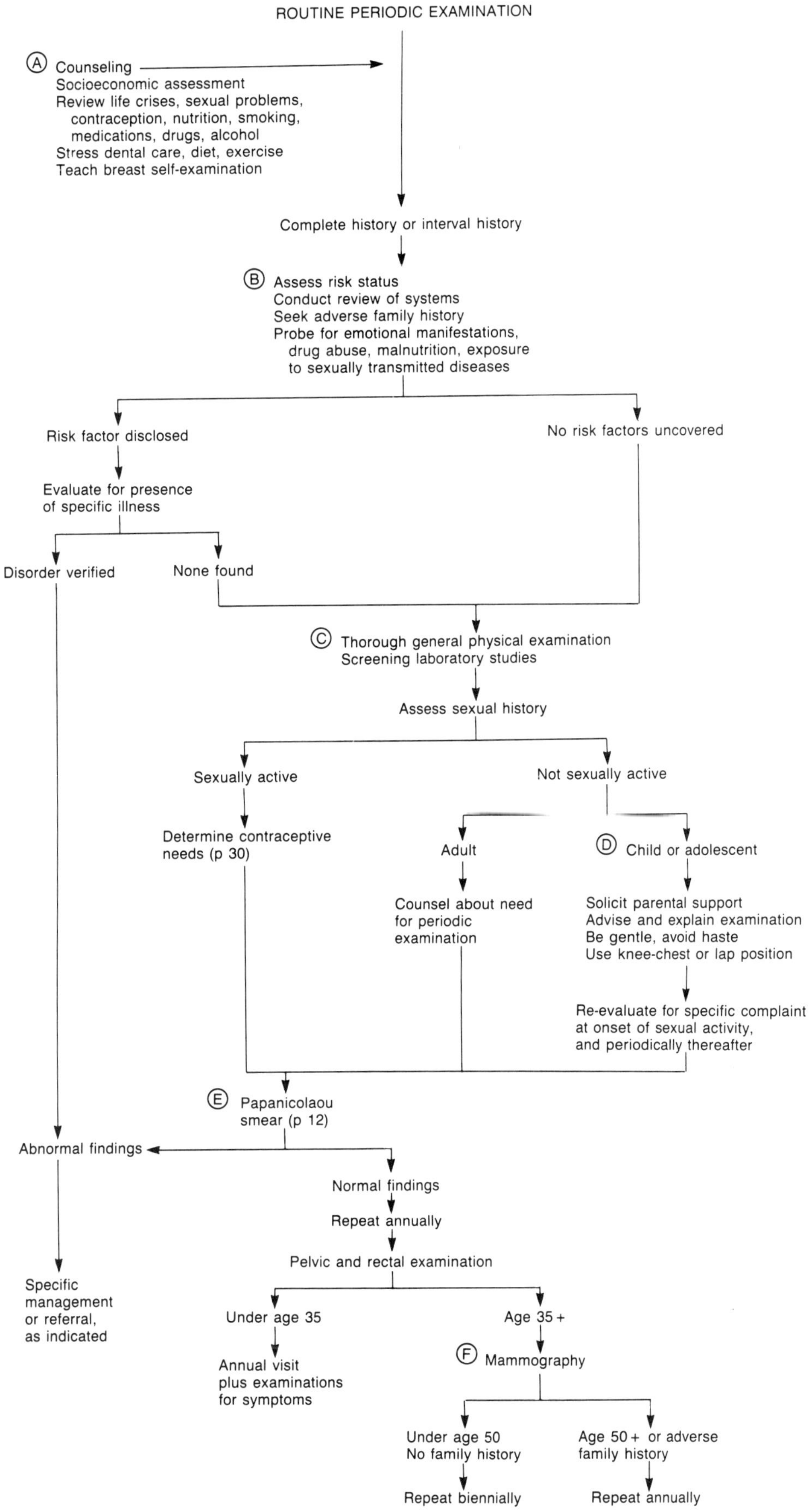

ROUTINE PERIODIC EXAMINATION

Ⓐ Counseling
   Socioeconomic assessment
   Review life crises, sexual problems,
     contraception, nutrition, smoking,
     medications, drugs, alcohol
   Stress dental care, diet, exercise
   Teach breast self-examination

Complete history or interval history

Ⓑ Assess risk status
   Conduct review of systems
   Seek adverse family history
   Probe for emotional manifestations,
     drug abuse, malnutrition, exposure
     to sexually transmitted diseases

Risk factor disclosed

No risk factors uncovered

Evaluate for presence
of specific illness

Disorder verified   None found

Ⓒ Thorough general physical examination
   Screening laboratory studies

Assess sexual history

Sexually active

Not sexually active

Determine contraceptive
needs (p 30)

Adult

Ⓓ Child or adolescent

Counsel about need
for periodic
examination

Solicit parental support
Advise and explain examination
Be gentle, avoid haste
Use knee-chest or lap position

Re-evaluate for specific complaint
at onset of sexual activity,
and periodically thereafter

Ⓔ Papanicolaou
   smear (p 12)

Abnormal findings ◄

Normal findings

Repeat annually

Pelvic and rectal examination

Specific
management
or referral,
as indicated

Under age 35

Age 35 +

Annual visit
plus examinations
for symptoms

Ⓕ Mammography

Under age 50
No family history

Age 50 + or adverse
family history

Repeat biennially

Repeat annually

3

GYNECOLOGICAL HISTORY

Henry Klapholz, M.D.

A. Family history is worth probing in detail because it can often provide insights into a background of risk factors pertaining to both medical and gynecological conditions. For example, one should be alert to the occurrence of pelvic malignancy, especially ovarian and breast cancer, in close female relatives. Leiomyoma uteri and endometriosis can also be familial. Recurrent abortion or infertility therapy in the mother of the patient may signal that in utero diethylstilbestrol (DES) exposure occurred. Ask about familial bleeding diathesis as well as prior blood loss problems associated with surgical procedures or trauma.

B. Obtain a history of all gynecological surgery, including for each operation the date, reason for and type of procedure, pathologic findings, and clinical result. It may be invaluable for assessing a current problem to acquire a copy of the actual operative note and the pathology report pertaining to relevant prior surgery.

C. Gather data on infertility and obstetrical performance and fetal wastage. The latter should survey the total number of pregnancies and delve into induced and spontaneous abortions, ectopic pregnancies, and premature and term births. Assess each viable pregnancy for gestational duration, labor abnormality, method and site of delivery, delivery and postpartum complications, and fetal outcome. The birth weight and current status of each child may prove significant. Record past breast or lactational disorders, such as nodules, cysts, biopsies, mastitis, and failure of puerperal lactation.

D. Take a detailed menstrual history, concentrating on regularity of the cycles, their length and duration, and the patterns of blood loss and pain. Attempt to quantitate the flow in terms of actual volume, if possible; a rough but useful method for assessing blood loss is the number of pads or tampons used per hour or day per cycle. Accuracy is limited, however, because women vary widely in how frequently they change pads and tampons, the frequency often being more related to meticulousness than to the amount of menstrual blood absorbed. Nonetheless, such counts can be very helpful in elucidating any meaningful change in the flow pattern. Especially note intermenstrual and postcoital bleeding. Information about the nature of dysmenorrhea, particularly if of recent onset, helps to differentiate pathologic entities.

E. The patient's contraceptive history can sometimes be of critical importance. Get a detailed account of oral contraceptives taken in the past; include dates and duration of their administration. Inquire about side effects, such as headache and nausea, and probe for thromboembolic complication, hypertension, and migraine. Pay special attention to previous or current use of an intrauterine device, noting its type, duration in place, and any problems potentially related to it. If no longer worn, determine why it was removed and whether there were any problems associated with its removal. Of major importance is a history of pelvic infection related to an intrauterine device.

F. Ascertain when the patient's last Papanicolaou smear was done, if she has had one, and whether there has been any prior abnormal report or biopsy finding. If cervical dysplasia, inflammation, or condyloma has been diagnosed in the past, it should be duly recorded. Any prior evaluation or treatment for cytologic abnormality is also noteworthy, including colposcopy, biopsy, or ablative cauterization.

G. The sexual history can be very important. If it discloses any homosexual or bisexual activity by her partner, it raises the specter of acquired immune deficiency syndrome (p 122). Similarly, sexual practice such as oral, anal, or urethral intercourse is important. Determine the age at first intercourse and number of sexual partners, if possible, for purposes of assessing risk status for cervical dysplasia (p 162).

H. With all the historic background data thus far amassed, one should be in a good position to evaluate the present illness by focusing one's attention principally on the kinds of disorders suggested by the risk factors uncovered. The focus generally becomes even sharper when the patient's specific complaints are taken into consideration. This will lead one into investigations that concentrate on elucidating specific problems related to a given organ (such as bladder, ovary, or vulva) or function (including endocrine, reproductive, or sexual). It will thus help to identify the disease state (i.e., inflammatory, neoplastic, or anatomic) in an expeditious and definitive manner.

References

Lee NC, Rubin GL, Ory HW, Burkman RT. Type of intrauterine device and the risk of pelvic inflammatory disease. Obstet Gynecol 62:1, 1983.

Lynch HT, Albano WA, Lynch JF, et al. Surveillance and management of patients at high genetic risk for ovarian carcinoma. Obstet Gynecol 59:589, 1982.

Piver MS, Barlow JJ, Sawyer DM. Familial ovarian cancer: Increasing in frequency? Obstet Gynecol 60:397, 1982.

Schmidt CL. Endometriosis: A reappraisal of pathogenesis and treatment. Fertil Steril 44:157, 1985.

Weckstein LN, Boucher AR, Tucker H, et al. Accurate diagnosis of early ectopic pregnancy. Obstet Gynecol 65:393, 1985.

GYNECOLOGICAL EXAMINATION

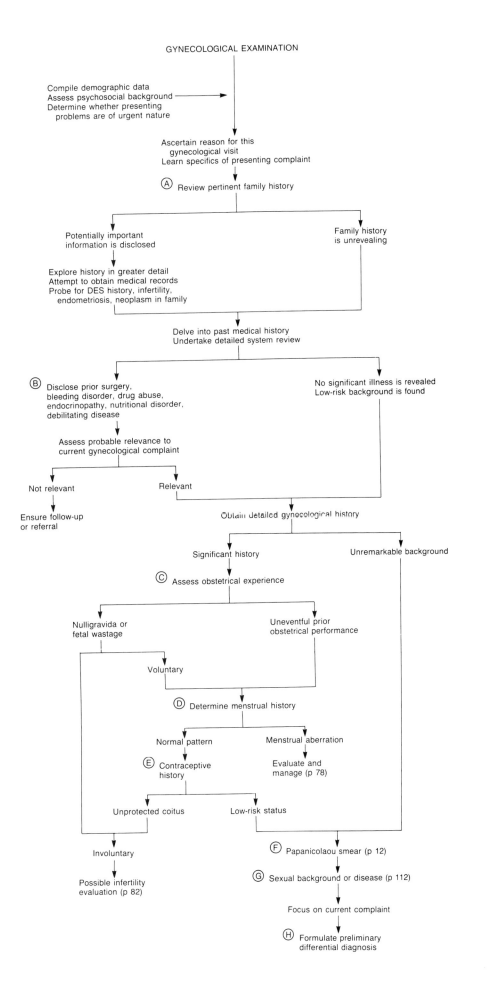

Compile demographic data
Assess psychosocial background
Determine whether presenting
    problems are of urgent nature

Ascertain reason for this
    gynecological visit
Learn specifics of presenting complaint

Ⓐ Review pertinent family history

Potentially important
information is disclosed

Family history
is unrevealing

Explore history in greater detail
Attempt to obtain medical records
Probe for DES history, infertility,
    endometriosis, neoplasm in family

Delve into past medical history
Undertake detailed system review

Ⓑ Disclose prior surgery,
bleeding disorder, drug abuse,
endocrinopathy, nutritional disorder,
debilitating disease

No significant illness is revealed
Low-risk background is found

Assess probable relevance to
current gynecological complaint

Not relevant

Relevant

Ensure follow-up
or referral

Obtain detailed gynecological history

Significant history

Unremarkable background

Ⓒ Assess obstetrical experience

Nulligravida or
fetal wastage

Uneventful prior
obstetrical performance

Voluntary

Ⓓ Determine menstrual history

Normal pattern

Menstrual aberration

Ⓔ Contraceptive
history

Evaluate and
manage (p 78)

Unprotected coitus

Low-risk status

Involuntary

Ⓕ Papanicolaou smear (p 12)

Possible infertility
evaluation (p 82)

Ⓖ Sexual background or disease (p 112)

Focus on current complaint

Ⓗ Formulate preliminary
differential diagnosis

5

PELVIC EXAMINATION

Henry Klapholz, M.D.

A. Essential prerequisites for an effective pelvic examination include a fully cooperative, informed, and relaxed patient. Anxiety can be allayed somewhat and cooperation facilitated by discussing the objectives and techniques beforehand and proceeding in a slow, deliberate, and reassuring manner. Explain each step in advance. Ensure comfortable positioning on the examining table. The presence of a female chaperone is prudent at all times regardless of the gender of the examiner. Choose the type of speculum according to anticipated needs. Use a vaginoscope for children and a pediatric speculum to examine virginal women. Extremely obese women and grand multiparas may require a large Graves speculum for adequate visualization because the vaginal walls tend to bow in and obstruct the view. In the course of the examination, be gentle, especially if structures are tender or there is involuntary guarding. It is much preferable to distract the patient's attention or formally elicit relaxation than to apply more intensive pressure and thereby

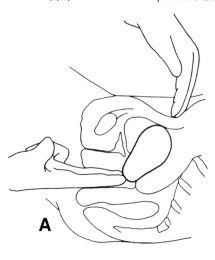

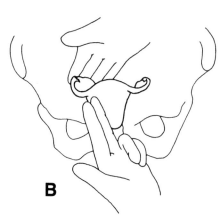

Figure 1 Bimanual palpation of the uterus, lateral view (A), with external fingers advancing uterus so that it can be palpated between the examining hands. Anterior view (B) illustrates abdominal hand insinuated behind right adnexa, which can then be more readily felt by internal fingers.

aggravate the situation. Give the patient the opportunity to slow or stop the examination whenever she desires. Do not rush the examination. One may use mirrors as an effective way to familiarize the patient with her intravaginal anatomy and the cytologic smear technique.

B. Most patients still desire adequate draping before and during the pelvic examination to minimize exposure. The contrary wishes of a small minority should be respected. Have the patient urinate to empty her bladder before the examination not only for the sake of comfort but to optimize one's ability to feel the pelvic organs. It is helpful to use a comfortably padded table with the head elevated about 20 degrees. Consider knee-chest position for a child. Older women and those with potential cardiac and respiratory embarrassment may require greater degrees of elevation. Do not leave a patient waiting in lithotomy position with her feet in stirrups. The stirrups should be cleaned between patients; if stirrup covers are used, change them between patients.

C. Examine the external genitalia carefully for lesions. If any are seen, apply the vital stain toluidine blue to help pinpoint areas of potential dysplasia for biopsy sampling. Look for evidence of vaginal discharge. Culture for gonorrhea and chlamydial infection; the latter requires vigorous scraping to include cervical cells because the organism cannot be cultured in a cell free environment. A hanging drop saline mount preparation is needed to examine for trichomonads, yeast, and the characteristic clue cells containing *Gardnerella* organisms.

D. Prewarm the speculum and keep it dry. Spread the labia and insert it gently without using lubricant that would distort the cell cytology. The speculum is usually best inserted at 90 degrees and then gently rotated to its final axial position as it is advanced. Cytologic study of exfoliated cells must be done if a year or more has elapsed since the last Papanicolaou smear (p 12). After examining the cervix and upper vagina and obtaining the necessary cultures and smears, slowly withdraw the speculum while simultaneously studying the exposed vaginal mucosa for any abnormality that may have been overlooked previously.

E. Gently insert the lubricated index and middle fingers of the gloved hand into the vagina and palpate using abdominal counterpressure with the opposite hand (Fig. 1). Specifically note the size, shape, consistency, and mobility of the cervix, uterine corpus, ovaries, and tubes; assess for tenderness elicited by compression or motion. Examine the vaginal walls for submucosal nodularity that could not be seen earlier on speculum examination. Abnormal findings will determine what additional evaluations will be needed. A palpable mass, for example, can be verified and its nature clarified by various noninvasive imaging techniques, including radiography, ultrasonography (p 216), and newer, more sophisticated procedures (p 218).

F. A pelvic examination cannot be considered complete

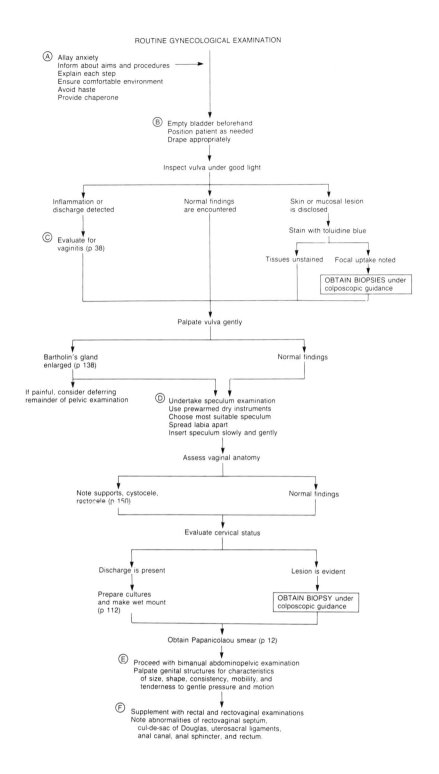

ROUTINE GYNECOLOGICAL EXAMINATION

Ⓐ Allay anxiety
Inform about aims and procedures
Explain each step
Ensure comfortable environment
Avoid haste
Provide chaperone

Ⓑ Empty bladder beforehand
Position patient as needed
Drape appropriately

Inspect vulva under good light

Inflammation or discharge detected | Normal findings are encountered | Skin or mucosal lesion is disclosed

Ⓒ Evaluate for vaginitis (p 38)

Stain with toluidine blue

Tissues unstained | Focal uptake noted

OBTAIN BIOPSIES under colposcopic guidance

Palpate vulva gently

Bartholin's gland enlarged (p 138) | Normal findings

If painful, consider deferring remainder of pelvic examination

Ⓓ Undertake speculum examination
Use prewarmed dry instruments
Choose most suitable speculum
Spread labia apart
Insert speculum slowly and gently

Assess vaginal anatomy

Note supports, cystocele, rectocele (p 150) | Normal findings

Evaluate cervical status

Discharge is present | Lesion is evident

Prepare cultures and make wet mount (p 112)

OBTAIN BIOPSY under colposcopic guidance

Obtain Papanicolaou smear (p 12)

Ⓔ Proceed with bimanual abdominopelvic examination
Palpate genital structures for characteristics
of size, shape, consistency, mobility, and
tenderness to gentle pressure and motion

Ⓕ Supplement with rectal and rectovaginal examinations
Note abnormalities of rectovaginal septum,
cul-de-sac of Douglas, uterosacral ligaments,
anal canal, anal sphincter, and rectum.

without supplementary rectovaginal and rectal examinations. They are done to assess the structures posterior to the vagina, looking for evidence of neoplasm, endometriosis, and infection. Keep in mind that the uterosacral ligaments and cul-de-sac of Douglas are much more readily accessible to palpation by way of the rectum than by the vagina.

References

Beard RW, Highman JH, Pearce S, Reginald PW. Diagnosis of pelvic varicosities in women with chronic pelvic pain. Lancet 2:946, 1984.

Broadmore J, Carr-Gregg M, Hutton JD. Vaginal examinations: Women's experiences and preferences. NZ Med J 99:8, 1986.

Slocumb JC. Neurological factors in chronic pelvic pain: Trigger points and the abdominal pelvic pain syndrome. Am J Obstet Gynecol 149:536, 1984.

Voss SC, Lacey CG, Pupkin M, Degefu S. Ultrasound and the pelvic mass. J Reprod Med 28:833, 1983.

EXAMINING THE CHILD

Johanna F. Perlmutter, M.D.

A. Other than the usual cursory neonatal examination to establish sexual phenotype and assure normal external genitalia, infants and children are seldom subjected to thorough gynecological examination. Most often, they are seen for vaginal discharge, itching, bleeding, or odor. Children frequently insert foreign bodies, including buttons and other small objects, into their vagina; after a time, symptoms develop from infection and ulceration. Be alert to the possible presence of sexually transmitted diseases, especially gonorrhea to which prepuberal children are especially sensitive. Although pelvic and abdominal tumors are rare in this age group, they do occur and should be searched for and aggressively evaluated because of their malignant potential. Bear in mind that a pelvic mass may represent a displaced kidney or hematocolpos (the latter in conjunction with imperforate hymen in adolescence). Moreover, a history of intrauterine exposure to diethylstilbestrol (DES) warrants examination after menarche for vaginal adenosis and clear cell vaginal adenocarcinoma. Remember to examine the breasts as well. An index of the adequacy of perineal hygiene can be readily perceived by noting fecal contamination of the vulva, especially in the folds of the labia, or residua of smegma. Excoriations should raise the suspicion of pruritus caused by infection, such as pinworms.

B. Be sure to tell the child what is about to be done before each step of the examination, demonstrating in advance whatever instrument is being used. In the knee-chest position, the vagina can generally be visualized without any aid because it distends spontaneously with air. One can usually see the cervix readily. A cotton-tipped swab may be all that is needed for obtaining a smear or culture. A foreign body, if present, is often apparent in the short vagina of the young child. A digital examination of the rectum, done slowly and gently with good lubrication, gives needed information about the uterus and adnexa. If necessary, use a vaginoscope to inspect the vagina and cervix directly. None of the available specula, including pediatric, otoscopic, and nasal varieties, are

as useful because they are too wide or too short to permit one to do an adequate examination. By contrast, a long, narrow vaginoscope is most effective for visualization and causes the least discomfort to the child. A topical anesthetic gel may have to be used, but is seldom really indicated. Similarly, sedation is not generally warranted, although it can be used in exceptional cases.

C. A pelvic examination need not be unpleasant for the child, although it often is, particularly if she or her mother has had prior unsatisfactory experiences. Too often the genital area is regarded as taboo and the anatomy poorly comprehended. The child may be embarrassed, fearful, apprehensive, and self-conscious about a stranger looking at or touching her in this area. It is important to try to allay these anxieties by having the parent present and spending as much time as necessary to establish good rapport with the child. Be patient, solicitous, and sensitive. If necessary, make another appointment for sequestered time outside of regular office hours to ensure against being rushed or interrupted. The time is well spent preparing the child. The parent can be of great assistance in helping to establish cooperation. Parental concerns should be assuaged as well; assurances may be needed about the fact that virginity will remain undisturbed because the hymen will not be adversely affected.

D. The standard dorsal lithotomy position used for the adult may be quite satisfactory for a child as well. It is perhaps most applicable for those approaching puberty. For children in the intervening age between infancy and adolescence, however, the knee-chest position may prove to be more utilitarian and easier for the child to accept and tolerate. Consider examining the small child or infant while she is semisitting in her parent's lap with her legs abducted gently to permit visualization and access for palpation (Fig. 1).

E. Very infrequently, it may be necessary to examine a child under anesthesia. Clearly, this would not be appropriate just for a routine examination, but it is indicated if there appears to be a potentially serious problem that warrants the associated risk and costs. It should be obvious that general anesthesia in a hospital setting should be strictly limited to those children who cannot be examined adequately in the office setting and who have manifestations that warrant it.

References

Capraro VJ, Rodgers DE, Rodgers BD. The gynecological examination for newborns, young children, and adolescents. Contemp Obstet Gynecol 20:43, 1982.

Cowell CA. The gynecologic examination of infants, children, and young adolescents. Pediatr Clin North Am 28:247, 1981.

Emans SJ, Goldstein DP. The gynecologic examination of the prepubertal child with vulvovaginitis: Use of the knee-chest position. Pediatrics 65:758, 1980.

Seymore C, Durant RH, Jay MS, et al. Influence of position during examination and sex of examiner on patient anxiety during pelvic examination. J Pediatr 108:312, 1986.

Figure 1 Examination of an infant or young child facilitated by placement in mother's lap facing examiner with legs supported in abducted position.

GYNECOLOGICAL EXAMINATION OF CHILD

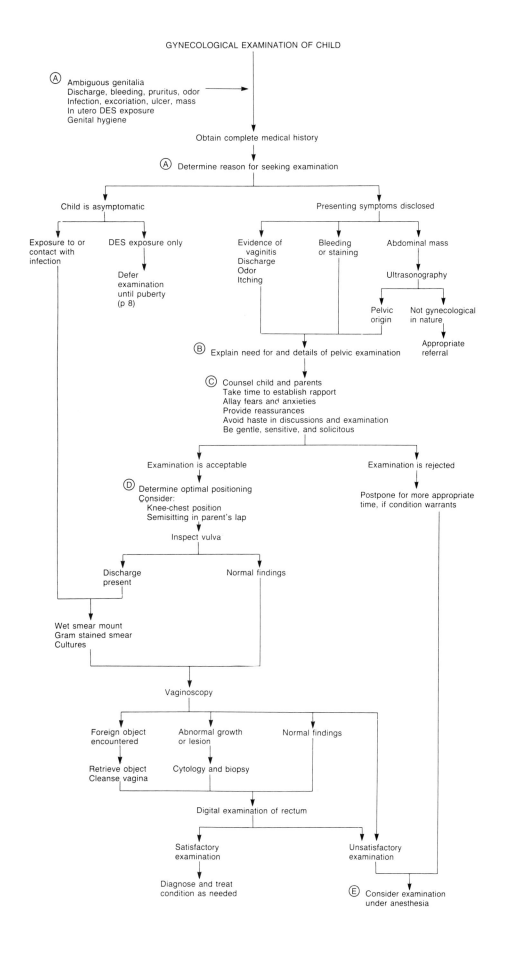

Ⓐ Ambiguous genitalia
Discharge, bleeding, pruritus, odor
Infection, excoriation, ulcer, mass
In utero DES exposure
Genital hygiene

Obtain complete medical history

Ⓐ Determine reason for seeking examination

Child is asymptomatic

Presenting symptoms disclosed

Exposure to or contact with infection

DES exposure only

Defer examination until puberty (p 8)

Evidence of vaginitis
Discharge
Odor
Itching

Bleeding or staining

Abdominal mass

Ultrasonography

Pelvic origin

Not gynecological in nature

Appropriate referral

Ⓑ Explain need for and details of pelvic examination

Ⓒ Counsel child and parents
Take time to establish rapport
Allay fears and anxieties
Provide reassurances
Avoid haste in discussions and examination
Be gentle, sensitive, and solicitous

Examination is acceptable

Examination is rejected

Ⓓ Determine optimal positioning
Consider:
Knee-chest position
Semisitting in parent's lap

Postpone for more appropriate time, if condition warrants

Inspect vulva

Discharge present

Normal findings

Wet smear mount
Gram stained smear
Cultures

Vaginoscopy

Foreign object encountered

Abnormal growth or lesion

Normal findings

Retrieve object
Cleanse vagina

Cytology and biopsy

Digital examination of rectum

Satisfactory examination

Unsatisfactory examination

Diagnose and treat condition as needed

Ⓔ Consider examination under anesthesia

9

BREAST EXAMINATION

Johanna F. Perlmutter, M.D.

A. It is of utmost importance for the gynecologist, who is often the only physician to see a woman over the course of her reproductive life, to be ever alert in order to detect breast cancer, which is one of the most common malignancies among women. Although occurring principally in the perimenopausal years, breast cancer can develop at any age. Flag cases at especially high risk by probing for a family history of breast carcinoma. The risk for a given individual is high if a close family member (mother or sister) has had breast cancer, and that risk is still further enhanced if more than one family member is affected. Familial cancer clusters should be considered very significant indicators of potential risk, warranting even closer attention than ordinarily. Women who have delayed their childbearing (or are nulliparous) should also be considered at risk because breast cancer is more likely to occur in them than in those women who conceived early and particularly in those who have nursed their infants. Even in the absence of any risk factor, however, every woman who presents for a check-up or for a gynecological complaint deserves the benefits of a thorough breast examination. They should also be encouraged to conduct regular self-examinations of the breast (see D) after every period or, if postmenopausal, at monthly intervals.

B. Carry out the breast examination under good illumination with the patient supine and then with her sitting facing the examiner. Inspect carefully, searching for dissimilarities between the two breasts. Note any changes in skin characteristics, such as pigmentation, inflammatory reaction, localized areas of venous engorgement, edema, or induration; characteristic peau d'orange appearance may represent lymphatic obstruction. Look for signs of nipple deviation, retraction, or fixation. Investigate by gentle palpation for any dominant mass. Supraclavicular and axillary palpation is also essential to detect lymph nodes, noting especially if they are matted or fixed. Systematically survey the breasts, examining the central periareolar area and each quadrant separately in sequence. Palpate with the flat of the fingers when the patient is in the supine position and bimanually when she is seated.

C. Pursue an aggressive program of evaluation without delay for any suspicious nodule discovered during a routine examination. This should especially apply to patients who fall into a high-risk category or if the mass shows characteristics that make it likely to be malignant, such as fixation to the overlying skin, the underlying pectoralis muscle, or the chest wall. Under such circumstances, it is always preferable to proceed with the evaluation than to hazard the possibility of overlooking a neoplasm. If it is unclear whether there is really a dominant mass, it may be acceptable to wait and repeat the examination after the next menstruation when conditions may be more optimal. Consider such delay if the patient falls into a low-risk category and the examination is being done premenstrually when the breasts tend to be somewhat congested and engorged. Excision biopsy should be undertaken for definitive histologic diagnosis of the nature of a solid mass. If the mass feels cystic, it should be aspirated (p 72). If the fluid obtained is serosanguineous, it should be sent for cytology. Any solid components remaining after aspiration require excisional biopsy.

D. Regular breast self-examination should be taught and stressed. Patients should be instructed in the proper method for examining their breasts. The examination should be done regularly after every period beginning with breast inspection under good light in a large mirror. Point out what to look for. Next, careful systematic palpation should be done, perhaps in the shower. With the right arm raised up behind the head, the fingers of the left hand can be used to assess the condition of the right breast and axilla (and vice versa for the left side). Stress the need for the patient to develop a sense of familiarity with the consistency and characteristics of her own breast so that she will be able to recognize any change.

E. Breast cancer screening is best done using low-dose soft tissue technique mammography. Newer techniques of contact thermography (with liquid crystal cholesteric plates) have not yet been fully investigated, but they show promise. Mammography may be helpful as a preliminary diagnostic tool for evaluating a suspicious breast mass. For screening purposes among women without a palpable mass or a risk factor, it is now generally recommended that mammography be started between age 35 and 45 years and repeated every one to two years. For high-risk women, by contrast, such screening should begin earlier, perhaps at age 30 to 35 years, and be repeated no less often than annually.

References

Foster RS, Costanza MC. Breast self-examination practices and breast cancer survival. Cancer 53:999, 1984.

Homer MJ. Mammographic detection of breast cancer. Clin Obstet Gynecol 25:393, 1982.

Nichols GP. Ingredients of survival: Breast self-examination. Obstet Gynecol 65:295, 1985.

Nyirjesy I, Billingsley FS. Detection of breast carcinoma in a gynecologic practice. Obstet Gynecol 64:747, 1984.

Vorherr H. Breast aspiration biopsy. Am J Obstet Gynecol 148:127, 1984.

ROUTINE GYNECOLOGICAL EXAMINATION

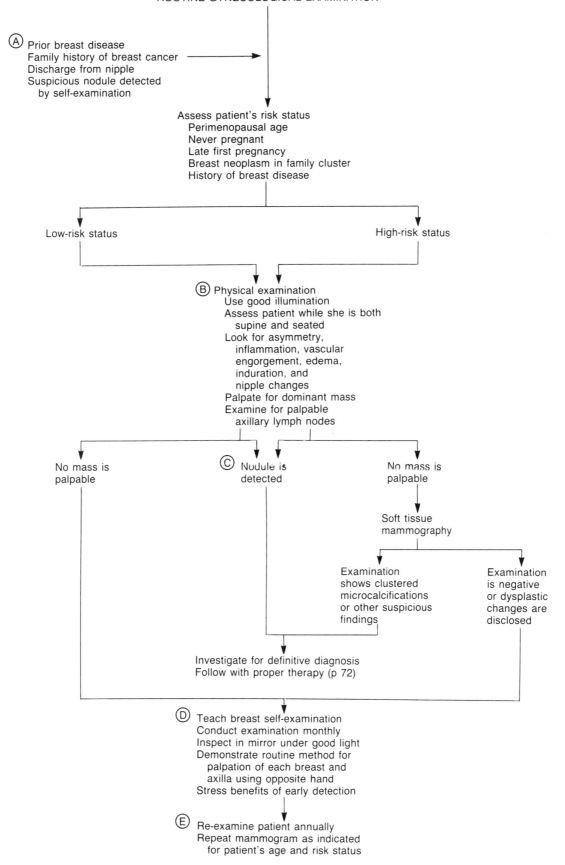

(A) Prior breast disease
Family history of breast cancer
Discharge from nipple
Suspicious nodule detected
  by self-examination

Assess patient's risk status
  Perimenopausal age
  Never pregnant
  Late first pregnancy
  Breast neoplasm in family cluster
  History of breast disease

Low-risk status   High-risk status

(B) Physical examination
  Use good illumination
  Assess patient while she is both
    supine and seated
  Look for asymmetry,
    inflammation, vascular
    engorgement, edema,
    induration, and
    nipple changes
  Palpate for dominant mass
  Examine for palpable
    axillary lymph nodes

No mass is   (C) Nodule is   No mass is
palpable   detected   palpable

                                        Soft tissue
                                        mammography

                    Examination   Examination
                    shows clustered   is negative
                    microcalcifications   or dysplastic
                    or other suspicious   changes are
                    findings   disclosed

Investigate for definitive diagnosis
Follow with proper therapy (p 72)

(D) Teach breast self-examination
Conduct examination monthly
Inspect in mirror under good light
Demonstrate routine method for
  palpation of each breast and
  axilla using opposite hand
Stress benefits of early detection

(E) Re-examine patient annually
Repeat mammogram as indicated
  for patient's age and risk status

CERVICAL CYTOLOGY

Johanna F. Perlmutter, M.D.

A. Cervical cytology of exfoliated cells is an inexpensive, painless, and effective screening technique for detecting precancerous dysplastic and overtly neoplastic lesions of the cervix and vagina. It may occasionally even disclose cancer of the endometrium, tube, or ovary. The frequency for repeating the smear is a matter of debate, but it is generally accepted that it should be done annually. This runs counter to the three-year interval recommended by the American Cancer Society; annual smears are justified in practice because there are false negative results (potentially delaying detection of a lesion) and some lesions develop and progress rapidly. Every adult female should have a Papanicolaou smear at regular intervals as part of her routine gynecological examination. This should apply even if she has no symptoms that could raise a suspicion of cervical dysplasia. Cervical cytology is especially important in patients who are at high risk for developing genital neoplasm (see H). It should be done even among teenagers who are sexually active because they have been shown to be at considerably increased risk for developing dysplastic lesions.

B. Proper technique requires one to expose the cervix well with a vaginal speculum. It should be inserted gently, without lubricant, if possible, because most lubricants tend to distort cell morphology, including hypotonic solutions (such as water) and lubricating jellies. A good light is essential to ensure the cervix is easily visualized. Try an electric heating pad to warm the speculum in advance yet keep it dry.

C. Use a saline moistened cotton swab placed in the endocervical canal and turned 360 degrees to provide an adequate sample of endocervical cells for study. Identify the squamocolumnar junction and obtain a sample of surface epithelial cells by vigorously scraping with an Ayer spatula or similar device. Quickly place each specimen on a separate area of a slide or preferably on two or more slides. The practice of using more than one slide has the advantage of ensuring that the cells will be fixed before the smear dries. It also permits one to identify the cells from each area separately.

D. Spread the material collected evenly and thinly to ensure the cytologist will be able to evaluate the cellular morphology optimally. Prevent cellular distortion and artifact in the smear, which could interfere badly with cytologic assessment, by placing the slide into a fixative solution (or spraying it with fixative) at once before the thin layer of smeared material has a chance to dry. Any delay is unacceptable.

E. Active vaginitis or cervicitis may interfere with cytologic interpretation. If the inflammatory reaction is intense, treat the infection first and then repeat the smear. The results are generally quite satisfactory and the delay is usually acceptable. If there is an apparent cancerous lesion that is grossly infected, however, immediate biopsy is clearly preferable. Do not delay definitive diagnosis.

F. An interval of six weeks is required before repeating the cytologic examination because it takes that long for epithelial cells to regenerate after they have been scraped off the surface. If repeated earlier, the smear may yield a false negative report based on reparative squamous metaplasia.

G. Seek a cytologic interpretation that provides a verbal description of the cell morphology. Reports that just give a numerical class are much less informative and may even be confusing. If the cytologic smear identifies dysplastic cells, one must pursue a histologic diagnosis by colposcopy and directed biopsies (p 214). Unless the report indicates the cytologic evaluation to have been inadequate (because of insufficient material or distortion), it is poor practice to repeat the smear to confirm the presence of dysplasia. If the next smear proves to be negative, it does not negate the potential significance of the previous one. It is more appropriate and prudent to proceed with a more definitive evaluation instead.

H. Women who have never been sexually active or who do not initiate intercourse until after age 18 years generally fall into a low-risk category for cervical cancer. While repeating smears for low-risk women annually may not be cost effective, the fact that cervical cancer may sometimes develop unexpectedly within a relatively short time after a negative smear supports the practice. Be alert to high-risk factors including coitus at an earlier age, multiple sex partners, and sexually transmitted disease, especially genital herpesvirus infection and condyloma acuminatum. It is essential to repeat the smear in women who present with these risk factors at least every year and to ensure that the technique and assessment are adequate to satisfy their screening needs.

References

Lunt R. Worldwide early detection of cervical cancer. Obstet Gynecol 63:708, 1984.

Nasiell K, Roger V, Nasiell M. Behavior of mild cervical dysplasia during long-term follow-up. Obstet Gynecol 67:665, 1986.

Reiter RC. Management of initial atypical cervical cytology: A randomized prospective study. Obstet Gynecol 68:237, 1986.

Sadeghi SB, Hsieh EW, Gunn SW. Prevalence of cervical intraepithelial neoplasia in sexually active teenagers and young adults. Am J Obstet Gynecol 148:726, 1984.

Wright VC, Riopelle MA. Age at beginning coitus versus chronologic age as a basis for Papanicolaou smear screening: An analysis of 747 cases of preinvasive disease. Am J Obstet Gynecol 149:824, 1984.

ROUTINE GYNECOLOGICAL EXAMINATION

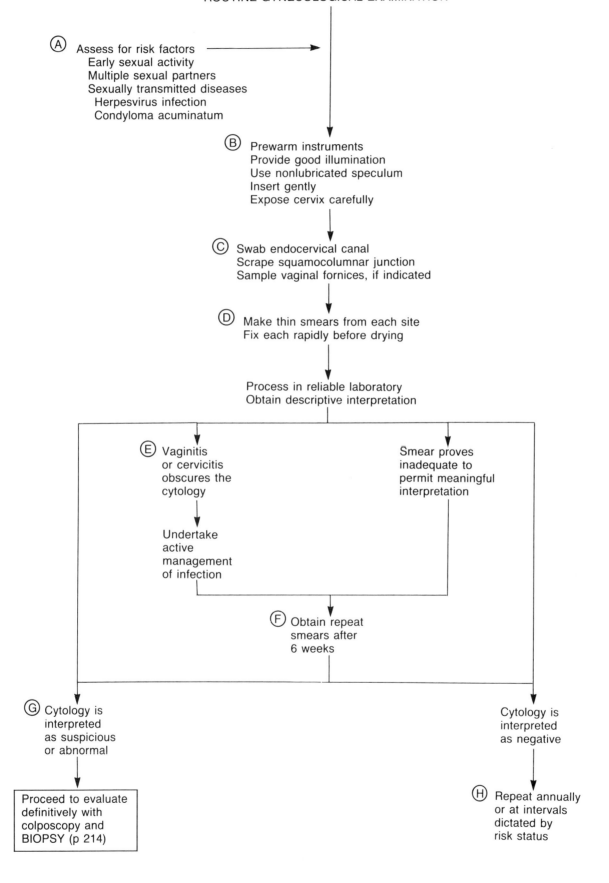

Ⓐ Assess for risk factors
    Early sexual activity
    Multiple sexual partners
    Sexually transmitted diseases
    Herpesvirus infection
    Condyloma acuminatum

Ⓑ Prewarm instruments
Provide good illumination
Use nonlubricated speculum
Insert gently
Expose cervix carefully

Ⓒ Swab endocervical canal
Scrape squamocolumnar junction
Sample vaginal fornices, if indicated

Ⓓ Make thin smears from each site
Fix each rapidly before drying

Process in reliable laboratory
Obtain descriptive interpretation

Ⓔ Vaginitis
or cervicitis
obscures the
cytology

Smear proves
inadequate to
permit meaningful
interpretation

Undertake
active
management
of infection

Ⓕ Obtain repeat
smears after
6 weeks

Ⓖ Cytology is
interpreted
as suspicious
or abnormal

Cytology is
interpreted
as negative

Proceed to evaluate
definitively with
colposcopy and
BIOPSY (p 214)

Ⓗ Repeat annually
or at intervals
dictated by
risk status

13

DIAGNOSIS OF PREGNANCY

David B. Acker, M.D.

A. In gynecological practice, pregnancy and pregnancy related complications frequently present with bizarre manifestations mimicking other disorders. This applies especially for patients with abnormal implantation sites (i.e., ectopic pregnancy, p 198), but even otherwise normal intrauterine pregnancy may yield signs and symptoms resembling those of other general medical or gynecological disorders. The classic symptoms of early pregnancy include cessation of menses; increased size and sensitivity of the breasts; altered skin pigmentation in the areolar area of the breasts, the linea nigra, and nevi; nausea with or without vomiting; urinary frequency; and fatigue. However, they are not consistent and do not necessarily appear in everyone. Vaginal bleeding at the time of implantation may resemble a normal or somewhat altered menstrual period. Subsequent bleeding associated with threatened or spontaneous abortion (p 74) may be indistinguishable from menorrhagia or metrorrhagia from other causes (p 80). Amenorrhea itself can be caused by a number of other conditions as well (p 56). Similarly, the pelvic pain that sometimes arises from a corpus luteum of early pregnancy must be differentiated from pain due to other adnexal disorders. Thyroid disease and pregnancy also share common manifestations, including skin and hair changes, altered temperature tolerance, thyroid bruit, fine tremor, wide pulse pressure, heart rhythm disturbances, pretibial edema, and menstrual aberrations. Such signs and symptoms, therefore, cannot be relied upon for purposes of diagnosing or ruling out pregnancy, although they should serve to alert one to the possibility.

B. Commercially available home pregnancy tests for use by the consumer herself cannot be considered to be as dependable as claimed. Experience shows particularly inaccurate results in the hands of teenagers or women with limited formal education. Even among intelligent educated women, reliability is poor, especially if the test is done too soon after a missed period. In practical terms, such home kits should not be used until at least six days have passed after the date on which the missed period was expected to begin. A positive test even as early as nine days after the missed period is not entirely accurate for predicting pregnancy (78 to 84 percent predictive), and negative tests at this time may give false reassurances in nearly half the cases (predictive value can be as low as 56 percent). Only if the test has been repeated at least one week later and is consistent in its results can it be relied upon for diagnosis.

C. The physical signs of gestation to look for when pregnancy is suspected relate primarily to size, shape, and consistency of the uterus, coloration and consistency of the cervix, and appearance of the vagina. The uterus tends to be enlarged, globular, and softened. Softening especially affects the isthmus (lower uterine segment) early in pregnancy so that the cervix feels structurally separate from the corpus. The cervix characteristically softens as well. Both cervix and vagina become congested and cyanotic, although this need not be apparent unless illumination is optimal. It is important to recognize that all these changes may occur even if the pregnancy implantation site is extrauterine.

D. Identification of the beating fetal heart provides clear-cut confirmation of pregnancy. Auscultation with the aid of a simple fetoscope or stethoscope (using the concave bell) cannot generally be reliably accomplished before 16 to 20 gestational weeks. Doppler instruments can usually detect fetal cardiac action by 12 to 14 weeks. This is facilitated if the examiner lifts the uterus into the abdomen by means of transvaginal digital pressure to make the fetus more accessible for examination. Real-time ultrasonography can discern fetal heart motion by six to eight weeks and a gestational ring as early as five to six weeks. Prior to this time, the radioimmunoassay determination of the beta-subunit of human chorionic gonadotropin (hCG) is most accurate, especially from about nine days after ovulation and fertilization (or three to five days before the onset of the next expected period). However, a positive test does not distinguish hydatidiform mole, ectopic pregnancy, or blighted ovum.

E. Although the most likely diagnosis will be an early intrauterine pregnancy, the physician must always be alert for signs, symptoms, and laboratory studies that may indicate an abnormality of pregnancy or pseudocyesis.

References

Cartwright PS, Victory DF, Wong SW, Dao AH. Evaluation of the new generation of urinary pregnancy tests. Am J Obstet Gynecol 153:730, 1985.

Doshi ML. Accuracy of consumer performed in-home tests for early detection of pregnancy. Am J Public Health 76:512, 1986.

Kadar N, Caldwell BV, Romero R. A method of screening for ectopic pregnancy and its indications. Obstet Gynecol 58:162, 1981.

Landesman R, Singh M, Saxena BB. Human chorionic gonadotropin assay sensitivity on screening for ectopic pregnancy. Am J Obstet Gynecol 155:681, 1986.

Nyberg DA, Filly RA, Mahony BS, et al. Early gestation: Correlation of hCG levels and sonographic identification. Am J Radiol 144:951, 1985.

PATIENT WITH SUSPICION OF PREGNANCY

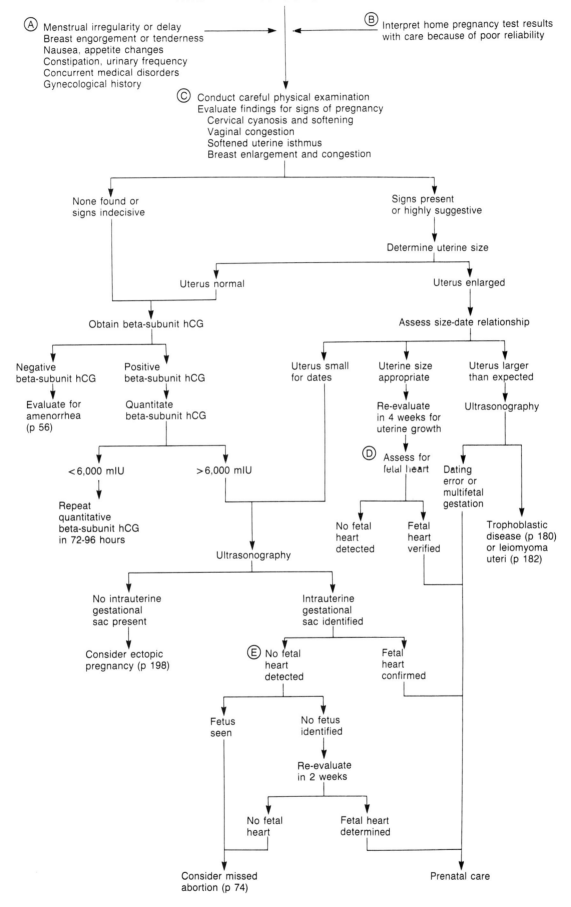

Ⓐ Menstrual irregularity or delay
Breast engorgement or tenderness
Nausea, appetite changes
Constipation, urinary frequency
Concurrent medical disorders
Gynecological history

Ⓑ Interpret home pregnancy test results
with care because of poor reliability

Ⓒ Conduct careful physical examination
Evaluate findings for signs of pregnancy
  Cervical cyanosis and softening
  Vaginal congestion
  Softened uterine isthmus
  Breast enlargement and congestion

None found or
signs indecisive

Signs present
or highly suggestive

Determine uterine size

Uterus normal

Uterus enlarged

Obtain beta-subunit hCG

Assess size-date relationship

Negative
beta-subunit hCG

Positive
beta-subunit hCG

Uterus small
for dates

Uterine size
appropriate

Uterus larger
than expected

Evaluate for
amenorrhea
(p 56)

Quantitate
beta-subunit hCG

Re-evaluate
in 4 weeks for
uterine growth

Ultrasonography

Ⓓ Assess for
fetal heart

Dating
error or
multifetal
gestation

<6,000 mIU

>6,000 mIU

No fetal
heart
detected

Fetal
heart
verified

Trophoblastic
disease (p 180)
or leiomyoma
uteri (p 182)

Repeat
quantitative
beta-subunit hCG
in 72-96 hours

Ultrasonography

No intrauterine
gestational
sac present

Intrauterine
gestational
sac identified

Consider ectopic
pregnancy (p 198)

Ⓔ No fetal
heart
detected

Fetal
heart
confirmed

Fetus
seen

No fetus
identified

Re-evaluate
in 2 weeks

No fetal
heart

Fetal heart
determined

Consider missed
abortion (p 74)

Prenatal care

15

PREOPERATIVE EVALUATION

Henry Klapholz, M.D.

A. Before one can undertake any surgical procedure, it is mandatory to discuss the problem at length with the patient, if the degree of urgency permits, and with a responsible relative, if indicated and permitted. A fully informed patient is essential (p 326). The discussion should review the diagnosis, rationale for the surgery, all alternative treatment options, and the material risks of the recommended operation as compared with other management regimens, including expectancy.

B. Undertake laboratory evaluation as indicated. A complete blood count will disclose anemia or leukocytosis. A urinalysis is needed to show proteinuria, glucosuria, hematuria, or infection. Determine serum electrolyte levels, including calcium, and obtain liver function tests if warranted by the history. A history of hepatitis necessitates screening for the hepatitis B associated antigen. Screening for HIV antibody is done if AIDS exposure is suspected (p 122). If a large blood loss is expected, carry out blood typing and an antibody screen in anticipation of the need to cross match blood expediently.

C. Cardiologic evaluation should be done if congenital or acquired heart disease is suspected. Examine for heart murmur or evidence of failure. Obtain electrocardiography at minimum and other tests when indicated. Give prophylactic antibiotics for organic valvular disease, including mitral valve prolapse, prior to major gynecological surgery. Assess and monitor pulmonary artery wedge pressure (by Swan-Ganz catheter) if indicated for incipient decompensation.

D. Evaluate pulmonary function and arterial blood gas levels in patients with chronic obstructive disease. Use incentive spirometry (Fig. 1) and intermittent positive pressure breathing and give bronchodilators before and after the operation. Try to get smokers to stop smoking well in advance. Consult with the anesthetist several days ahead to alert him or her to potential problems.

E. Schedule the surgery for diabetic patients for early in the day to ensure orderly mobilization of resources and optimum care. If they do not eat or drink for many hours before surgery, control of glucose metabolism can become very difficult. Check serum electrolyte levels, especially potassium, before surgery begins and monitor them frequently during insulin therapy. Give intravenous aqueous dextrose by continuous infusion supplemented periodically with increments of insulin as needed. Superimposed infection tends to increase insulin requirements. Thyroid function assessment is important whenever gland dysfunction is suspected.

F. Pay special attention to a history of bleeding with surgery. Evaluate for bleeding and clotting time, platelet count, prothrombin time, partial thromboplastin time, and fibrinogen. Remember that disseminated intravascular coagulation can occur with sepsis or carcinomatosis (p 208). Probe drug and medication history. Some drug use may affect anesthesia requirements (such as analgesics) and others may cause unanticipated bleeding (including inhibitors of prostaglandin synthesis). Corrections should be made, if possible, to avert complications as long in advance of the operation as possible.

G. Consider prophylactic anticoagulation for patients who are at risk of developing thromboembolism (p 20), beginning before surgery. Antiembolic stockings and a low-dose heparin regimen are beneficial for elderly, immobile, and obese patients as well as those who undergo prolonged surgery. Full anticoagulation may be needed in cases with prior thrombosis. Pneumatic boots promote lower extremity circulation.

H. Give antibiotics prophylactically for vaginal or abdominal hysterectomy, starting between one and four hours before surgery is scheduled to begin. It is unnecessary to continue the antibiotics beyond the first 24 hours after surgery. Cefazolin, 1 g every eight hours for three doses, is a useful regimen. If the patient becomes febrile postoperatively, a full work-up for infection should be done; stop the antibiotics and obtain all appropriate cultures. If it is felt necessary to shave the operative site, it should not be done until just before the operation. To do it earlier increases the risk of postoperative wound infection. A patient who is overtly septic before surgery should be started on a combination of antibiotics to cover a broad spectrum of bacterial organisms for at least six to eight hours. If surgery can be delayed safely, it should be deferred until the patient is stable. Evaluate for septic shock and manage aggressively (p 202).

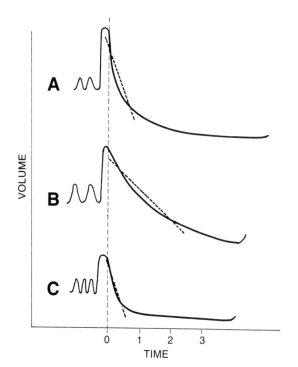

Figure 1 Spirometry recordings of respiratory volume against time in seconds, contrasting normal pulmonary function (A) with chronic obstructive lung disease (B) and restrictive disease (C).

CONSIDERATION OF SURGICAL PROCEDURE

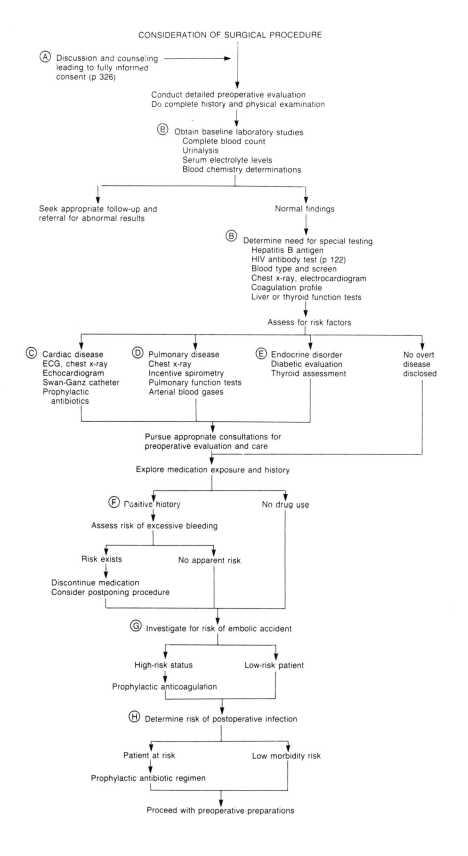

Ⓐ Discussion and counseling leading to fully informed consent (p 326)

Conduct detailed preoperative evaluation
Do complete history and physical examination

Ⓑ Obtain baseline laboratory studies
Complete blood count
Urinalysis
Serum electrolyte levels
Blood chemistry determinations

Seek appropriate follow-up and referral for abnormal results

Normal findings

Ⓑ Determine need for special testing
Hepatitis B antigen
HIV antibody test (p 122)
Blood type and screen
Chest x-ray, electrocardiogram
Coagulation profile
Liver or thyroid function tests

Assess for risk factors

Ⓒ Cardiac disease
ECG, chest x-ray
Echocardiogram
Swan-Ganz catheter
Prophylactic
antibiotics

Ⓓ Pulmonary disease
Chest x-ray
Incentive spirometry
Pulmonary function tests
Arterial blood gases

Ⓔ Endocrine disorder
Diabetic evaluation
Thyroid assessment

No overt
disease
disclosed

Pursue appropriate consultations for preoperative evaluation and care

Explore medication exposure and history

Ⓕ Positive history

No drug use

Assess risk of excessive bleeding

Risk exists

No apparent risk

Discontinue medication
Consider postponing procedure

Ⓖ Investigate for risk of embolic accident

High-risk status

Low-risk patient

Prophylactic anticoagulation

Ⓗ Determine risk of postoperative infection

Patient at risk

Low morbidity risk

Prophylactic antibiotic regimen

Proceed with preoperative preparations

References

Goldberger AL, O'Konski M. Utility of the routine electrocardiogram before surgery and on general hospital admission: Critical review and new guidelines. Ann Intern Med 105:552, 1986.

Pasulka PS, Bistrian BR, Benotti PN, Blackburn GL. The risks of surgery in obese patients. Ann Intern Med 104:540, 1986.
Platt R. Antibiotic prophylaxis in surgery. Rev Infect Dis 6:880S, 1984.
Savino JA. Del Guercio LRM. Preoperative assessment of high-risk surgical patients. Surg Clin North Am 65:763, 1985.

BOWEL PREPARATION

Henry Klapholz, M.D.

A. While intraoperative bowel injury cannot always be anticipated, it often can, especially in patients who are being operated on for extensive carcinoma, endometriosis, pelvic inflammatory disease or those with a history of multiple intra-abdominal surgical procedures or inflammatory bowel disease. Be alert to these conditions in order to identify those women in need of adequate preoperative preparation of the bowel for purposes of reducing luminal bacterial flora to a minimum. If suitably prepared beforehand, any injury to the bowel associated with entry into the lumen and spillage of its contents or requiring resection or repair can be handled with a minimum of risk and morbidity to the patient. Even though bowel preparation can be unpleasant, it has clear-cut compensating benefits. Consider formal bowel preparation before undertaking surgery, for example, in cases with endometriosis affecting the cul-de-sac, rectum, or small bowel; the operation can be expected to be a difficult dissection that could easily result in injury or require segmental bowel resection. Similarly, operating for ovarian neoplasm may involve a debulking procedure necessitating partial resection or repair of bowel. Preoperative colonoscopy, radiographic gastrointestinal series, and barium enema will often help determine the existence and extent of bowel involvement in advance. All cases of elective surgery in which injury may be anticipated should be prepared.

B. The lower bowel should be routinely emptied prior to any gynecological surgery, even if the procedure planned is a minor one or is expected to be entirely uncomplicated. This is done to avoid the mechanical problems created by a full rectum, potential fecal contamination of the operative field, and the discomfort of an obstipated patient early in her postoperative course. Preoperative cleansing of the rectum and sigmoid colon is generally done by means of an enema with phosphosoda (Fleet) or a normal saline solution. The use of soapsuds for the enema is decried because it exposes the patient to rare but nonetheless serious hazards, including potentially fatal soap embolization and anaphylactoid reaction. The use of tap water may result in excessive electrolyte depletion, especially in the elderly. Because electrolyte imbalance can also occur from phosphosoda enemas as well, they are contraindicated in patients at risk for hypernatremia, such as those with cardiac or renal decompensation.

C. For patients about to undergo emergency surgery, there may not be enough time available to prepare the bowel adequately. Moreover, it may be inappropriate to do so because the bowel may already be injured, inflamed, or obstructed. Giving an enema under these circumstances could aggravate the problem or even be catastrophic. If bowel involvement is unlikely, and time and circumstances permit, give one or more saline enemas to cleanse the rectosigmoid preoperatively.

D. Bowel preparation by a combination of mechanical flushing and antibiotics has been shown to be effective and beneficial in substantially reducing postoperative infectious morbidity. A utilitarian program begins three days prior to the date of the scheduled surgery with a low residue or clear liquid diet; a cathartic agent, such as bisacodyl (Dulcolax 1 tablet) is given simultaneously. On the next day, give magnesium sulfate (30 ml of 50 percent solution orally at 10 AM, 2 PM, and 6 PM) and saline enemas repeated until the returns are clear. Repeat the magnesium sulfate twice on the day before surgery (at 10 AM and 2 PM), adding neomycin sulfate and erythromycin (three doses of 1 g each by mouth). One may use an alternative antibiotic regimen, such as metronidazole 500 mg and gentamicin 80 mg three times per day for two days, beginning instead just before the surgical procedure. Empty the rectum by an enema on the morning before the surgery. The use of mechanical cleansing alone without antibiotic prophylaxis is not as effective as the combined treatment.

E. Another equally effective approach is whole bowel lavage. Consider giving a lavage of saline or saline plus mannitol administered via nasogastric tube at a rate of 3 liters per hour over a three-hour period. Such large volumes of isotonic saline effectively evacuate the bowel contents within a relatively short time after the lavage has begun without causing undue patient discomfort. Metoclopramide may also be given intravenously (10 mg) for purposes of stimulating peristalsis. The use of a large volume of a preparation containing polyethylene glycol plus balanced electrolytes for lavage (GoLytely), taken orally or by nasogastric tube, has been shown to provide a safe, comfortable means for effecting whole bowel emptying; it is associated with a lower incidence of infection than traditional methods. It is given in a schedule of 8 ounces every 10 minutes to a total 4 liters. Watery diarrhea usually commences within one hour.

References

Fleites RA, Marshall JB, Eckhauser ML, et al. The efficacy of polyethylene glycol-electrolyte lavage solution versus traditional mechanical bowel preparation for elective colonic surgery: A randomized, prospective, blinded clinical trial. Surgery 98:708, 1985.

Marti MC, Auckenthaler R. Antibiotic prophylaxis in large bowel surgery: Results of a controlled clinical trial. Surgery 93:190, 1983.

Panton ONM, Atkinson KG, Crichton EP, et al. Mechanical preparation of the large bowel for elective surgery: Comparison of whole-gut lavage with the conventional enema and purgative technique. Am J Surg 149:615, 1985.

Solhaug JH, Bergman L, Kylberg F. A randomized evaluation of single dose chemoprophylaxis in elective colorectal surgery: A comparison between metronidazole and doxycycline. Ann Clin Res 15:15, 1983.

PATIENT WITH INCREASED RISK OF BOWEL INJURY

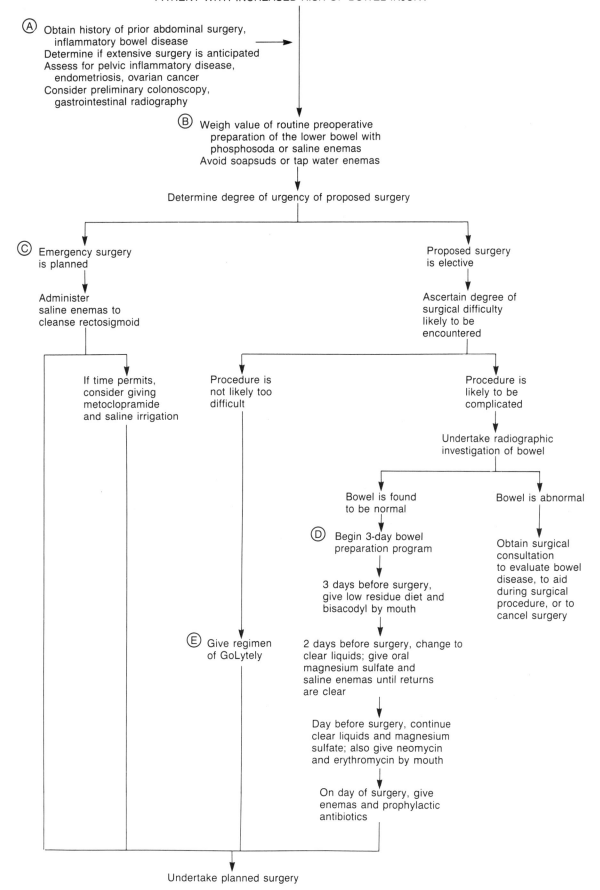

Ⓐ Obtain history of prior abdominal surgery,
   inflammatory bowel disease
   Determine if extensive surgery is anticipated
   Assess for pelvic inflammatory disease,
      endometriosis, ovarian cancer
   Consider preliminary colonoscopy,
      gastrointestinal radiography

Ⓑ Weigh value of routine preoperative
   preparation of the lower bowel with
   phosphosoda or saline enemas
   Avoid soapsuds or tap water enemas

Determine degree of urgency of proposed surgery

Ⓒ Emergency surgery
   is planned

Administer
saline enemas to
cleanse rectosigmoid

If time permits,
consider giving
metoclopramide
and saline irrigation

Procedure is
not likely too
difficult

Ⓔ Give regimen
   of GoLytely

Proposed surgery
is elective

Ascertain degree of
surgical difficulty
likely to be
encountered

Procedure is
likely to be
complicated

Undertake radiographic
investigation of bowel

Bowel is found
to be normal

Ⓓ Begin 3-day bowel
   preparation program

3 days before surgery,
give low residue diet and
bisacodyl by mouth

2 days before surgery, change to
clear liquids; give oral
magnesium sulfate and
saline enemas until returns
are clear

Day before surgery, continue
clear liquids and magnesium
sulfate; also give neomycin
and erythromycin by mouth

On day of surgery, give
enemas and prophylactic
antibiotics

Bowel is abnormal

Obtain surgical
consultation
to evaluate bowel
disease, to aid
during surgical
procedure, or to
cancel surgery

Undertake planned surgery

ANTICOAGULATION

Miguel Damien, M.D.

A. Anticoagulation therapy helps prevent venous thrombosis and pulmonary embolism. Heparin therapy should be considered prior to major gynecological surgery because nearly half develop thrombosis of leg veins. Risk factors are prolonged major or radical surgery, postoperative immobilization, advanced age, debilitation, obesity, cancer, leg edema, severe varicosities, radiation therapy, and prior thrombosis. Calf vein thrombosis may propagate to the popliteal or femoral vessels, from which pulmonary emboli may arise. This risk warrants prophylaxis in high-risk patients to avoid a life-threatening complication.

B. The incidence of deep vein thrombosis can be reduced five-fold in high-risk patients by low-dose heparin (5,000 units subcutaneously twice a day). In this regimen, heparin produces no measurable alteration of clotting and no increase in operative or postoperative bleeding. Heparin binds to antithrombin III; together they inhibit the activated coagulation factors XIIa, XIa, Xa, and thrombin. Low doses of heparin interfere with the early stages of coagulation before thrombin is formed, thereby preventing thrombus formation.

C. Postoperatively, pelvic thrombophlebitis (p 298) presents a number of difficult diagnostic and therapeutic problems. It poses a significant risk of pulmonary embolism to the affected patient (p 294). If the condition is suspected because of persistent fever, leg swelling, and pain, venography should be employed to confirm the diagnosis before the patient is committed to anticoagulation. Treatment includes local heat, elevation of the leg, rest, and anticoagulation with heparin. Avoid any form of massage that may dislodge a clot and lead to embolization. Pelvic venous thrombosis (p 298) is usually diagnosed by exclusion in a patient with persistent fever unresponsive to antibiotics. Pelvic vein ultrasonography is inconsistently helpful in confirming the diagnosis. Anticoagulation is usually started, regardless of test results, if the index of suspicion for pelvic vein thrombosis is high and other causes, such as infection, have been excluded. The dramatic results that are seen warrant this approach.

D. Continuous intravenous infusion of heparin is preferred because there are fewer bleeding complications than with an intermittent dosage schedule. Start with a loading dose of 5,000 to 10,000 units given as a bolus injection. Follow with 800 to 2,000 units per hour delivered by an infusion pump. The concentration of heparin should not exceed 20,000 units per liter of intravenous fluid because overinfusing a more concentrated solution is hazardous. Monitor the heparin therapy by partial thromboplastin time (PTT) determinations. Values 1.5 to 2.5 times the control PTT are generally appropriate. Measure PTT every four hours at first to help adjust the infusion rate. Daily monitoring is sufficient once a steady dose is achieved. Advise patients on heparin to report any signs of bleeding, the principal adverse effect. Uncommon side effects include acute and reversible thrombocytopenia, hypersensitivity or anaphylactic reaction, and osteopenia.

E. For long-term anticoagulation, start warfarin (Coumadin) after three days of effective heparin therapy. Begin the warfarin dosage at 10 to 15 mg orally every day for three to five days. Stop the heparin 48 hours after the prothrombin time reaches a therapeutic value. The daily maintenance dosage of warfarin is 2 to 15 mg, adjusted according to the prothrombin time, aiming at 2.0 to 2.5 times the control value. Reassess every two weeks. Keep the patient on warfarin for an additional three to six months, depending on the relative risk of embolism and hemorrhage for the patient being treated. Warfarin is much more convenient for long-term out-patient use than heparin. It interferes with the hepatic vitamin K-dependent carboxylation of prothrombin, factors VII, IX, X, and the anticoagulant proteins C and S.

F. Bleeding diathesis can complicate anticoagulant treatment. It is seen more often with heparin therapy than with warfarin. Protamine sulfate administered slowly by intravenous infusion will reverse the activity of heparin; the dose should not exceed 1,000 mg to avoid protamine sulfate from acting itself as an anticoagulant. Phytonadione (vitamin K) orally or intravenously will counteract the effect of prothrombin depressing drugs. If transfusion is required, fresh blood or fresh frozen plasma should be utilized.

References

Hattersley PG, Mitsouka JC, King JH. Heparin therapy for thromboembolic disorders: A prospective evaluation of 134 cases monitored by the activated coagulation time. JAMA 250:1413, 1983.

Hirsh J, Deykin D, Poller L. "Therapeutic range" for oral anticoagulant therapy. Chest 89:11S, 1986.

Levine MN, Raskob G, Hirsh J. Hemorrhagic complications of long-term anticoagulant therapy. Chest 89:16S, 1986.

Petitti DB, Strom BL, Melmon KL. Duration of warfarin anticoagulant therapy and the probabilities of recurrent thromboembolism and hemorrhage. Am J Med 81:255, 1986.

Shafer KE, Santoro SA, Sobel BE, Jaffe AS. Monitoring activity of fibrinolytic agents: A therapeutic challenge. Am J Med 76:879, 1984.

PATIENT BEING CONSIDERED FOR ANTICOAGULATION

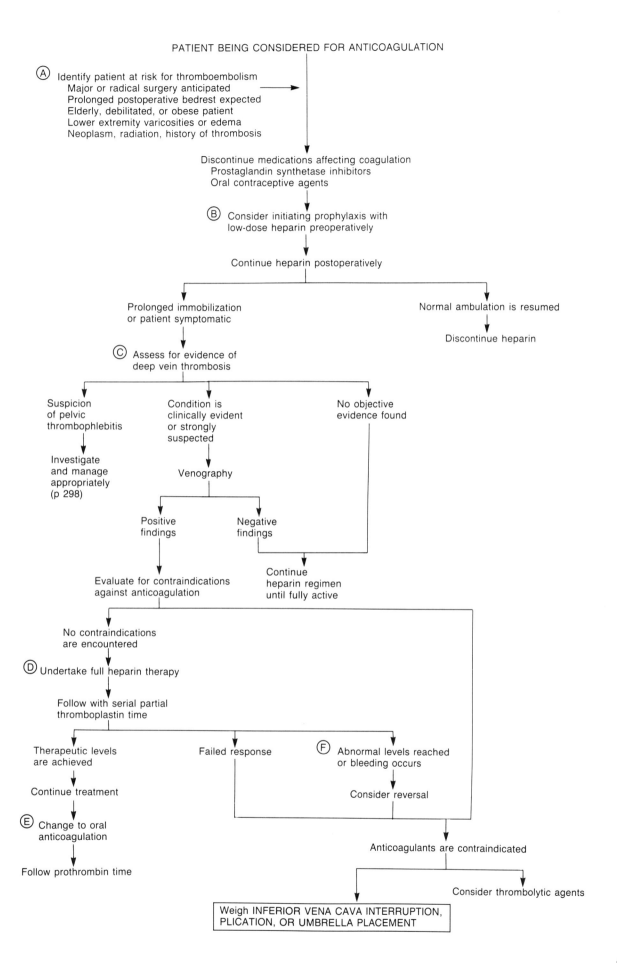

Ⓐ Identify patient at risk for thromboembolism
    Major or radical surgery anticipated
    Prolonged postoperative bedrest expected
    Elderly, debilitated, or obese patient
    Lower extremity varicosities or edema
    Neoplasm, radiation, history of thrombosis

Discontinue medications affecting coagulation
    Prostaglandin synthetase inhibitors
    Oral contraceptive agents

Ⓑ Consider initiating prophylaxis with
    low-dose heparin preoperatively

Continue heparin postoperatively

Prolonged immobilization
or patient symptomatic

Normal ambulation is resumed

Discontinue heparin

Ⓒ Assess for evidence of
    deep vein thrombosis

Suspicion
of pelvic
thrombophlebitis

Condition is
clinically evident
or strongly
suspected

No objective
evidence found

Investigate
and manage
appropriately
(p 298)

Venography

Positive
findings

Negative
findings

Continue
heparin regimen
until fully active

Evaluate for contraindications
against anticoagulation

No contraindications
are encountered

Ⓓ Undertake full heparin therapy

Follow with serial partial
thromboplastin time

Therapeutic levels
are achieved

Failed response

Ⓕ Abnormal levels reached
or bleeding occurs

Continue treatment

Consider reversal

Ⓔ Change to oral
anticoagulation

Anticoagulants are contraindicated

Follow prothrombin time

Consider thrombolytic agents

Weigh INFERIOR VENA CAVA INTERRUPTION,
PLICATION, OR UMBRELLA PLACEMENT

21

ELECTROLYTES

Henry Klapholz, M.D.

A. Patients with conditions likely to result in fluid and electrolyte imbalance need special attention pre- and postoperatively. Extensive surgery can be expected to result in major fluid losses or shifts. Electrolytic homeostasis is adversely affected by vomiting, diarrhea, bowel or wound drainage, and third space accumulation. Fluid administration can compound the problem if not given in appropriate amount and kind.

B. Obtain baseline laboratory assessments of serum sodium, chloride, carbon dioxide (bicarbonate), potassium, and glucose. Determine serum calcium and magnesium levels if prolonged parenteral support is needed. Confirm abnormal serum sodium determinations by computing the anion gap (see C) to ensure it is not specious. Assess for acidosis or alkalosis by determining arterial blood gas levels.

C. Calculate the anion gap as the difference between serum levels of the principal anions $(Na+K)$ and those of cations (HCO_3+Cl). Values seldom exceed 16, except with sodium-losing states. A gap of less than 9 suggests laboratory error. Replace sodium lost during prolonged nasogastric suction at 150 mEq per liter. Give up to 300 mEq per day for losses due to small bowel suction. An ileostomy stoma can lose as much as 150 mEq per day. Third space fluid accumulation may sequester up to 800 mEq per day. Estimate the sodium deficit by subtracting the serum sodium level from 140 and multiplying the difference by 0.3 and by the patient's weight in kilograms.

D. Although hyperglycemia is inversely related to sodium concentration, serum sodium is not significantly affected in most clinical circumstances. Every 100 mg rise per deciliter of glucose reduces sodium by 1.6 mEq per liter.

E. It is possible for hyponatremia to reflect an increase in total body water rather than actual sodium loss. Weigh the patient daily with a bed scale to detect major water loss or retention, and watch for decreased skin turgor, dry oral mucosa, and low blood pressure as indices of water loss. Give appropriate amounts of normal saline as indicated for such losses. Paradoxically, increased total body water may be seen with sodium loss in patients with salt-losing nephropathy or cardiac decompensation. Urine sodium concentrations above 22 mEq per liter reflect a syndrome of inappropriate antidiuretic hormone action requiring restriction of free water intake. Renal failure, congestive heart failure, and excess fluid administration yield low urinary sodium levels.

F. Determinations of arterial blood gas levels to disclose acid-base imbalances should be done for serum electrolyte or CO_2 abnormalities. The arterial pO_2 will help diagnose an adult respiratory distress syndrome.

G. Various nomographic aids are available for detecting mixed metabolic and respiratory derangements. The Siggaard-Andersen alignment nomogram is especially useful because it takes the buffering effect of hemoglobin into account.

H. Respiratory alkalosis, characterized by high pH with low pCO_2, usually reflects mechanical hyperventilation, pregnancy, or anxiety. It is corrected by reducing the ventilatory rate or applying a rebreathing apparatus. The high pCO_2 of metabolic alkalosis often results from excessive intake of antacids. Large amounts of hydrogen and potassium ion may be lost directly via nasogastric suction. Renal compensation by retaining potassium may aggravate the hydrogen losses and produce hypochloremic, hypokalemic alkalosis as a consequence.

I. Acidosis is identified by a low arterial blood pH. Respiratory acidosis, accompanied by high pCO_2, requires ventilatory assistance to help expel carbon dioxide. Seriously sick postoperative patients may need mechanical ventilation until they are functionally able to exchange gases properly. Metabolic acidosis, reflected by low pCO_2, demands investigation for diabetic ketoacidosis, lacticacidosis, or toxicity from such agents as aspirin and methanol. Most acidosis is a mixture of respiratory and metabolic forms. Calculate the amount of replacement bicarbonate by subtracting the serum level from 25 and multiplying by 0.3 and by the patient's weight in kilograms. Give 44 to 88 mEq (one or two ampules) at once and the rest over 24 to 48 hours.

References

Parker RT, Piscitelli J. Gynecologic surgery in the elderly patient. Clin Obstet Gynecol 29:453, 1986.

Roberts JP, Roberts JD, Skinner C, et al. Extracellular fluid deficit following operation and its correction with Ringer's lactate: A reassessment. Ann Surg 202:1, 1985.

Tweedle DE. Electrolyte disorders in the surgical patient. Clin Endocrinol Metab 13:351, 1984.

Twigley AJ, Hillman KM. The end of the crystalloid era? A new approach to perioperative fluid administration. Anaesthesia 40:860, 1985.

PATIENT IN PRE- OR POSTOPERATIVE STATUS

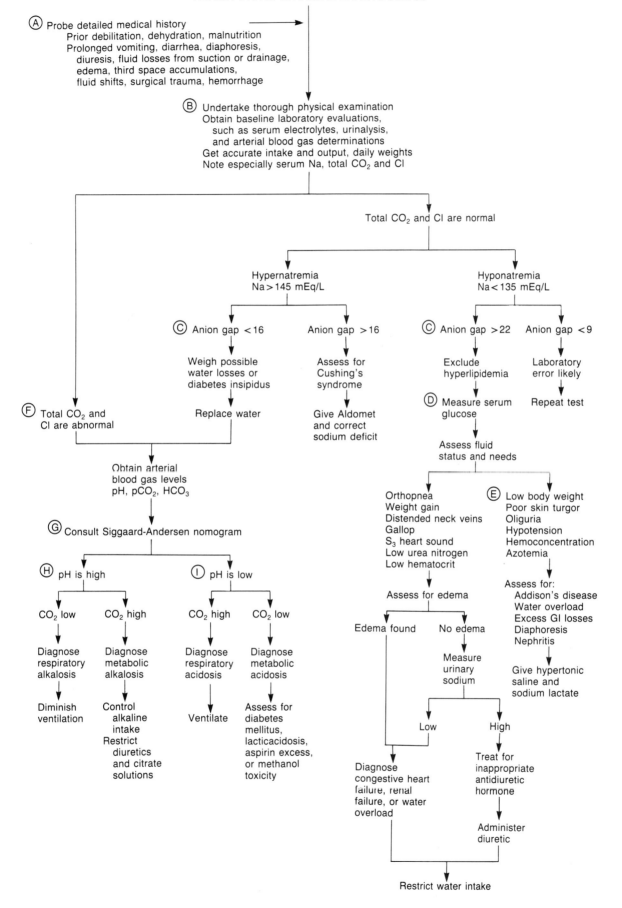

Ⓐ Probe detailed medical history
   Prior debilitation, dehydration, malnutrition
   Prolonged vomiting, diarrhea, diaphoresis,
     diuresis, fluid losses from suction or drainage,
     edema, third space accumulations,
     fluid shifts, surgical trauma, hemorrhage

Ⓑ Undertake thorough physical examination
   Obtain baseline laboratory evaluations,
     such as serum electrolytes, urinalysis,
     and arterial blood gas determinations
   Get accurate intake and output, daily weights
   Note especially serum Na, total CO_2 and Cl

Total CO_2 and Cl are normal

Hypernatremia
Na > 145 mEq/L

Hyponatremia
Na < 135 mEq/L

Ⓒ Anion gap < 16

Anion gap > 16

Ⓒ Anion gap > 22

Anion gap < 9

Weigh possible
water losses or
diabetes insipidus

Assess for
Cushing's
syndrome

Exclude
hyperlipidemia

Laboratory
error likely

Ⓕ Total CO_2 and
Cl are abnormal

Replace water

Give Aldomet
and correct
sodium deficit

Ⓓ Measure serum
glucose

Repeat test

Assess fluid
status and needs

Obtain arterial
blood gas levels
pH, pCO_2, HCO_3

Orthopnea
Weight gain
Distended neck veins
Gallop
S_3 heart sound
Low urea nitrogen
Low hematocrit

Ⓔ Low body weight
Poor skin turgor
Oliguria
Hypotension
Hemoconcentration
Azotemia

Ⓖ Consult Siggaard-Andersen nomogram

Assess for edema

Assess for:
   Addison's disease
   Water overload
   Excess GI losses
   Diaphoresis
   Nephritis

Ⓗ pH is high

Ⓘ pH is low

Edema found

No edema

CO_2 low

CO_2 high

CO_2 high

CO_2 low

Measure
urinary
sodium

Give hypertonic
saline and
sodium lactate

Diagnose
respiratory
alkalosis

Diagnose
metabolic
alkalosis

Diagnose
respiratory
acidosis

Diagnose
metabolic
acidosis

Low

High

Diminish
ventilation

Control
alkaline
intake
Restrict
diuretics
and citrate
solutions

Ventilate

Assess for
diabetes
mellitus,
lacticacidosis,
aspirin excess,
or methanol
toxicity

Diagnose
congestive heart
failure, renal
failure, or water
overload

Treat for
inappropriate
antidiuretic
hormone

Administer
diuretic

Restrict water intake

FLUID REPLACEMENT

Janet L. Mitchell, M.D., M.P.H.

A. Attention to fluid and electrolyte needs is essential in order to ensure homeostasis. While this applies mostly to the postoperative period, it is important under other circumstances as well, such as for any sick patient unable to take adequate fluids by mouth, as well as debilitated, dehydrated, ketoacidotic women and those with cardiac, renal, or neoplastic disease. Daily replacement is usually guided by totaling the measured fluid loss (urine, wound drainage, gastrointestinal suction, and diarrhea) and the estimated insensible loss (from lungs and skin). Insensible respiratory losses average 450 ml daily; they increase proportionally to the respiratory rate. Skin evaporation is about the same amount per day. Febrile patients can be expected to lose considerably more; estimate about 90 ml more per degree (centigrade) of fever per day. A hot, humid environment can cause liters of fluid to be lost by perspiration. Healthy patients can accommodate small to moderate deficiencies or excesses of administered fluids without any clinically apparent adverse effect. Large excesses, however, can lead to fluid overload cardiac decompensation; inadequate amounts lead to hypotension and poor tissue perfusion. Patients who need long-term fluid therapy, who have large fluid shifts or losses, or who have marginal heart or kidney function require the strictest attention to fluid balance.

B. Management of fluid replacement involves correcting the degree of deficiency or excess and anticipating dynamic needs based on continuing fluid losses or shifts. Give special consideration to any pre-existing or underlying condition that may predispose to a fluid or electrolyte imbalance. Use carefully documented intake and output recordings plus accurate daily body weight measurements to verify adequacy of replacement and to indicate the need for adjusting intake volume.

C. The urinary output is also useful as an index of renal function, reflecting adequacy of tissue perfusion. Output varies according to fluid intake and the capacity of the kidney to concentrate, but it should be at least 30 ml per hour. If less, consider the possibility of inadequate

circulatory or renal function. An indwelling bladder catheter may be needed to monitor urinary excretion during critical periods. Periodic urinalyses give valuable supplemental information on osmolality and specific gravity. Renal tubular damage can be recognized by production of small volumes of low osmolality urine. Clinical signs of poor tissue turgor, tachycardia, and hypotension reflect only the most severe forms of dehydration.

D. Consider giving an adequate fluid load by rapid administration of an isotonic intravenous solution (such as 0.9 percent saline or lactated Ringer's solution) to assess volume depletion as the cause of the oliguria, simultaneously monitoring central venous pressure to avoid overload. Hypovolemia is readily corrected in this manner. Failure to achieve good urinary output despite adequate fluid load and an elevated venous pressure warrants intravenous use of mannitol (100 ml, 20 percent), furosemide (40 to 100 mg), or albumin (100 to 300 ml, 25 percent).

E. Postoperative patients who are very ill and require prolonged parenteral fluid replacement must have their circulatory, pulmonary, and renal functions monitored almost continuously until stabilized. Fluid needs have to be adjusted to account for major losses due to febrile morbidity, drainage, and suction. In these cases, one cannot rely entirely on measurements of intake and output, even when assiduously obtained, because fluid needs may fluctuate widely and their ability to compensate for small to moderate fluid excesses or deficiencies is often very limited.

F. The central venous pressure (CVP) is simple and particularly useful for monitoring right atrial filling pressure (Fig. 1). It may be adequate for monitoring fluid administration and preventing fluid overload. The normal range is 5 to 12 cm of water. Be sure the catheter tip is properly located at or near the heart. For better assessment of left ventricular function, a Swan-Ganz catheter is preferable. It can measure the pulmonary capillary wedge pressure (normally 8 to 12 mm Hg) as well as cardiac output. It is sensitive to both fluid depletion and overload. Additional valuable information may be obtained from arterial blood gas and pH measurements. They are useful for detecting acidosis resulting from administering large volumes of fluid and for determining the adequacy of pulmonary perfusion and diffusion.

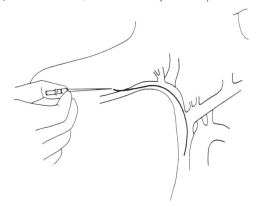

Figure 1 Central venous pressure catheter inserted into subclavian vein below the junction of the middle and inner third of the right clavicle aimed medially along the caudal surface of the clavicle. After the catheter is advanced into the superior vena cava and fixed by suture to the skin, the needle is removed and the catheter is attached to a water manometer.

References

Lattanzi WE, Siegel NJ. A practical guide to fluid and electrolyte therapy. Curr Probl Pediatr 16:1, 1986.

Orr JW Jr, Shingleton HM, Soong SJ, et al. Hemodynamic parameters following pelvic exenteration. Am J Obstet Gynecol 146:882, 1983.

Roberts JP, Roberts JD, Skinner C, et al. Extracellular fluid deficit following operation and its correction with Ringer's lactate: A reassessment. Ann Surg 202:1, 1987.

Skorecki KL, Brenner BM. Body fluid homeostasis in man: A contemporary view. Am J Med 70:77, 1981.

PATIENT WITH PROBABLE FLUID REPLACEMENT NEEDS

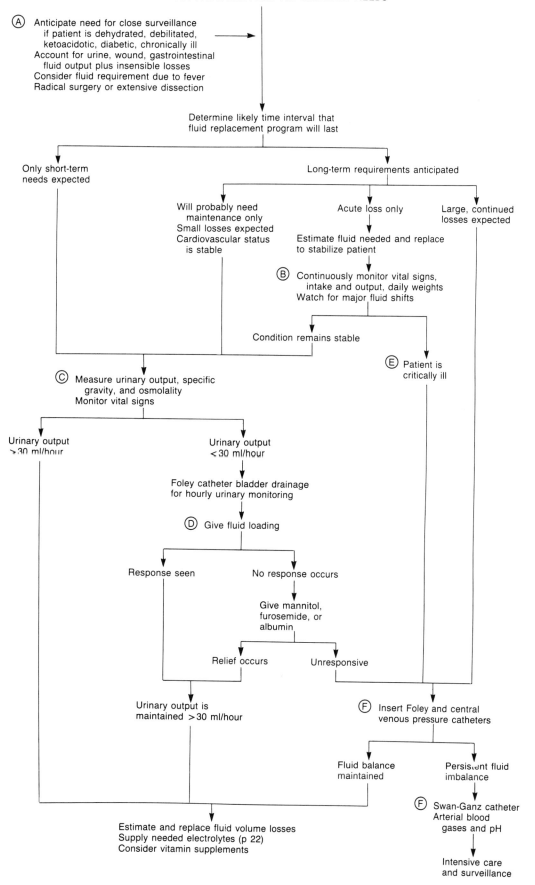

Ⓐ Anticipate need for close surveillance
if patient is dehydrated, debilitated,
ketoacidotic, diabetic, chronically ill
Account for urine, wound, gastrointestinal
fluid output plus insensible losses
Consider fluid requirement due to fever
Radical surgery or extensive dissection

Determine likely time interval that
fluid replacement program will last

Only short-term
needs expected

Long-term requirements anticipated

Will probably need
maintenance only
Small losses expected
Cardiovascular status
is stable

Acute loss only

Large, continued
losses expected

Estimate fluid needed and replace
to stabilize patient

Ⓑ Continuously monitor vital signs,
intake and output, daily weights
Watch for major fluid shifts

Condition remains stable

Ⓔ Patient is
critically ill

Ⓒ Measure urinary output, specific
gravity, and osmolality
Monitor vital signs

Urinary output
>30 ml/hour

Urinary output
<30 ml/hour

Foley catheter bladder drainage
for hourly urinary monitoring

Ⓓ Give fluid loading

Response seen

No response occurs

Give mannitol,
furosemide, or
albumin

Relief occurs

Unresponsive

Urinary output is
maintained >30 ml/hour

Ⓕ Insert Foley and central
venous pressure catheters

Fluid balance
maintained

Persistent fluid
imbalance

Estimate and replace fluid volume losses
Supply needed electrolytes (p 22)
Consider vitamin supplements

Ⓕ Swan-Ganz catheter
Arterial blood
gases and pH

Intensive care
and surveillance

PARENTERAL NUTRITION

Janet L. Mitchell, M.D., M.P.H.

A. Intravenous hyperalimentation is an effective means for providing nutritional support for patients who are unable to take oral feedings over long periods of time. It is especially helpful for ensuring against or correcting nitrogen deficiency that could predispose the postoperative gynecological patient to complications related to recovery and wound healing. It is recognized that hypoproteinemia is associated with a marked delay in antibody production.

B. Certain patients should be considered as candidates for total parenteral nutrition. They include especially those who have lost 10 percent or more of their body weight or who will be unable to begin adequate oral intake for seven days or more. Conditions that place patients at risk include sepsis and advanced malignancy. Other indications are enterovaginal or enterocutaneous fistulas and bowel obstruction. This form of treatment has greatly reduced mortality from external gastric or intestinal fistula. Sepsis affects intermediary metabolism to cause weight loss, diminished muscle mass, hypoalbuminemia, and increased urea excretion. Fever augments nitrogen demand by 5 to 8 percent per degree (centigrade). Sepsis is characteristically associated with negative nitrogen balance and impaired gluconeogenesis. There is generally no need for special nutritional care of the patient whose infection can be controlled in a week or less. By contrast, those with severe or prolonged sepsis must be maintained in balance by the intravenous administration of 30 to 40 kilocalories plus 0.3 g nitrogen per kilogram per day.

C. Assessing the patient's nutritional status is fundamental. Although there are very few good laboratory indices, anemia and hypoproteinemia tend to be most helpful. In addition, measure height, weight, total lymphocyte count, skin test antigens, and nitrogen balance. Serum albumin and transferrin levels serve as indicators of protein deficits. Determine urinary urea nitrogen and creatinine to assess nitrogen balance based on a 24-hour urine collection.

D. Provide replacement tailored according to the individual's needs. The nutritional requirements for parenteral nutrition are generally based on recommended daily allowances (RDA) for oral intake. They are age and weight dependent. For example, the average young adult should have 0.45 g protein per kilogram per day. Begin fatty acid replacement after two weeks on total parenteral nutrition. Give 2.4 mEq sodium and 2.0 mEq potassium per 100 calories intake per day along with a daily aliquot of 200 to 400 mg calcium and 300 mg phosphorus. Essential trace elements, such as zinc, copper, manganese, and iodine, are also needed. Most pharmacies stock standard formulations to simplify the process, but consultation with a parenteral nutrition team is advised.

E. Complications associated with total parenteral nutrition fall into four categories: technical, metabolic, septic, and respiratory. Some of the most common complications are pneumothorax, subclavian artery puncture, catheter malposition, hyperglycemia, and catheter sepsis. Moreover, long-term use of intravenous hyperalimentation catheters frequently causes thrombophlebitis at the site of implantation. It is very important, therefore, to take meticulous care of the indwelling central catheter. Use careful aseptic technique to insert it and apply an antimicrobial ointment on a sterile occlusive dressing to reduce the risks of secondary infection. Replace the tubing used for fluid administration every 48 hours. When the catheter is changed or removed, culture the tip for colonized organisms.

F. Home parenteral nutrition is possible, but rarely necessary, for the gynecological patient. Approximately two weeks are needed to educate the patient and her caretakers in sterile technique and proper handling of the intravenous line. The cost of total parenteral nutrition is 20 to 60 times greater than that of oral feedings. Home therapy is somewhat less expensive, but it is still very costly.

References

Daly JM, Long JM. Intravenous hyperalimentation: Techniques and potential complication. Surg Clin North Am 61:583, 1981.

Fabri PJ, Mirtallo JM, Ruberg RI, et al. Incidence and prevention of thrombosis of the subclavian vein during total parenteral nutrition. Surg Gynecol Obstet 155:238, 1982.

Hew LR, Deitel M. Total parenteral nutrition in gynecology and obstetrics. Obstet Gynecol 55:464, 1980.

Phillips CD. Total parenteral nutrition in acute illness. Anaesth Intensive Care 13:288, 1985.

PATIENT WITH PROBABLE NEED FOR PARENTERAL HYPERALIMENTATION

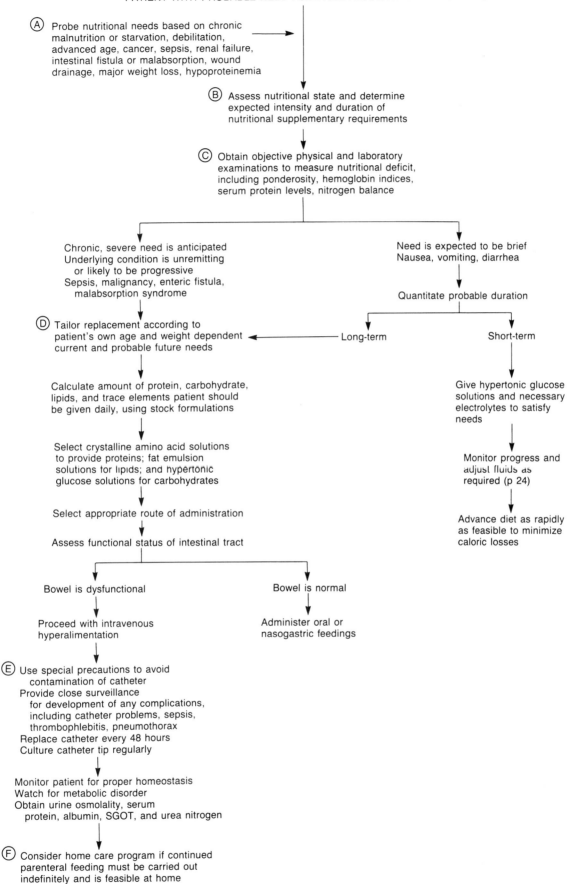

Ⓐ Probe nutritional needs based on chronic malnutrition or starvation, debilitation, advanced age, cancer, sepsis, renal failure, intestinal fistula or malabsorption, wound drainage, major weight loss, hypoproteinemia

Ⓑ Assess nutritional state and determine expected intensity and duration of nutritional supplementary requirements

Ⓒ Obtain objective physical and laboratory examinations to measure nutritional deficit, including ponderosity, hemoglobin indices, serum protein levels, nitrogen balance

Chronic, severe need is anticipated
Underlying condition is unremitting or likely to be progressive
Sepsis, malignancy, enteric fistula, malabsorption syndrome

Need is expected to be brief
Nausea, vomiting, diarrhea

Quantitate probable duration

Long-term

Short-term

Ⓓ Tailor replacement according to patient's own age and weight dependent current and probable future needs

Calculate amount of protein, carbohydrate, lipids, and trace elements patient should be given daily, using stock formulations

Select crystalline amino acid solutions to provide proteins; fat emulsion solutions for lipids; and hypertonic glucose solutions for carbohydrates

Select appropriate route of administration

Assess functional status of intestinal tract

Bowel is dysfunctional

Bowel is normal

Proceed with intravenous hyperalimentation

Administer oral or nasogastric feedings

Give hypertonic glucose solutions and necessary electrolytes to satisfy needs

Monitor progress and adjust fluids as required (p 24)

Advance diet as rapidly as feasible to minimize caloric losses

Ⓔ Use special precautions to avoid contamination of catheter
Provide close surveillance for development of any complications, including catheter problems, sepsis, thrombophlebitis, pneumothorax
Replace catheter every 48 hours
Culture catheter tip regularly

Monitor patient for proper homeostasis
Watch for metabolic disorder
Obtain urine osmolality, serum protein, albumin, SGOT, and urea nitrogen

Ⓕ Consider home care program if continued parenteral feeding must be carried out indefinitely and is feasible at home

HORMONE SUPPLEMENTATION

Jerold M. Carlson, M.D., M.P.H.

A. Although there are clinical profiles to help identify menopausal patients, it is nevertheless impossible to predict with accuracy which patients will definitely benefit from hormone replacement. Research data, however, have confirmed the efficacy of estrogen replacement therapy for three specific menopausal disorders, namely in providing temporary relief from vasomotor and urogenital symptoms and in long-term prevention of osteoporosis. Thus, effective treatment for vasomotor instability (hot flashes and flushes) involves use of estrogen preparation (natural and synthetic) administered either systemically or locally; alternatively, the patient can be treated with progesterone alone, with combinations of estrogens and progestins, with androgens, or with clonidine. Urogenital atrophy generally responds well to estrogen preparations, often used topically. Osteoporosis prevention requires long-term therapy consisting of a combination of various options including estrogens, estrogen-progestin, calcium supplementation, exercise, and possibly vitamin D and fluorides (p 96).

B. Each patient must be evaluated individually and carefully counseled about the risks, benefits, alternative options, and contraindications of hormonal replacement. The minimal essentials of the work-up include a complete history and physical examination, Papanicolaou smear, mammography, and basic laboratory evaluation as indicated to assess estrogen status (p 94).

C. There has been much controversy for several decades over whether it is appropriate to give estrogens on a prophylactic basis. It was initially advocated as a potential cure for all menopausal symptoms. This initial enthusiasm was tempered by the realization that unopposed estrogen administration was associated with the development of endometrial carcinoma. The risk of endometrial cancer, which is about 1 per 1,000 annually in untreated menopausal women, increases four to ten times in women who use unopposed estrogens. This risk has now been determined to be reduced to about the level expected in the untreated population by adding sequential progestin to the regimen. The minimum recommended progestin use is seven days for each cycle, but 10 to 14 days is still better for purposes of averting the cancer risk.

D. The advantages of any particular estrogen-progestin therapy over any other have not been conclusively demonstrated. As a general rule, one should aim to provide the lowest dosage effective for a particular problem. A typical regimen might include conjugated estrogen (Premarin) 0.625 mg daily from day 1 to day 25 plus a progestin (such as Provera) 10 mg on days 13 to 25. Estrogens may also be administered transdermally.

Patients who have an intact uterus should be warned of the possibility of withdrawal bleeding. If the goal of treatment is simply amelioration of hot flashes, then give lower doses of estrogen for a limited period of time. Patients who have impaired estrogen metabolism might require lower dosages. Adjust the dosage regimen, if possible, to provide symptom relief while minimizing side effects.

E. Estrogens have gained renewed popularity, but they are not totally innocuous. Known risks include gallbladder disease and hypertension. Endometrial hyperplasia and carcinoma are associated, as aforementioned, with use of unopposed estrogens. The long-term effects on the breasts in regard to carcinogenesis are unclear; short-term use appears to have no impact in this regard. Whether estrogens have any effect on carbohydrate intolerance is a matter of debate. There is probably no association with thromboembolic phenomena. The cardiovascular risk-benefit data are particularly inconclusive because of confounding by progestin use, smoking, and blood lipid changes. Nonetheless, patients on a long-term estrogen replacement regimen should be checked periodically for these potential effects. Moreover, estrogens should not be prescribed for patients with certain conditions that place them at special risk, unless there are overriding considerations to warrant such use.

F. Symptoms of estrogen replacement are often the same as those seen with the use of oral contraceptives, although the dose of estrogen given is much smaller for menopausal treatment. Effects include nausea, vomiting, headaches, breast tenderness, edema, weight gain, and vaginal mucorrhea. Premenstrual molimina may occur with progesterone use.

G. Routine endometrial sampling must be assessed annually on an individual basis, but any abnormal bleeding requires immediate and thorough evaluation.

References

Abbasi R, Hodgen GD. Predicting the predisposition to osteoporosis: Gonadotropin-releasing hormone antagonist for acute estrogen deficiency test. JAMA 255:1600, 1986.

Hammond CB, Maxson WS. Estrogen replacement therapy. Clin Obstet Gynecol 29:407, 1986.

Laufer LR, Erlik Y, Meldrum DR, Judd HL. Effect of clonidine on hot flashes in postmenopausal women. Obstet Gynecol 60:583, 1982.

Schiff I, Tulchinsky D, Cramer D, Ryan KJ. Oral medroxyprogesterone in the treatment of postmenopausal symptoms. JAMA 244:1443, 1980.

PATIENT WITH INDICATION FOR HORMONE REPLACEMENT

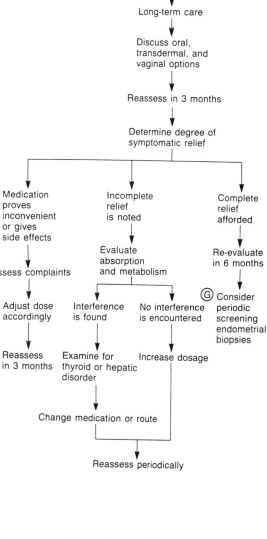

Ⓐ Medical and gynecological history
   Menstrual pattern
   Menopausal symptoms (p 94)
   Results of annual mammography and
      Papanicolaou cytology

Ⓑ Probe for contraindications against hormone use

Contraindications are recognized

No contraindications are disclosed

Ⓒ Counsel about risks, benefits, and
   alternatives of hormone administration

Patient declines
hormone therapy

Patient desires
and accepts therapy

Assess for hormone
deficiency symptoms

Assess expected duration
of hormone therapy program

Short-term

Ⓓ Administer estrogen-progestin

Reassess in 6 months

Ⓔ Adverse symptoms

Good effect

Discuss risks of
osteoporosis (p 96)

Long-term care

Discuss oral,
transdermal, and
vaginal options

Recommend program
of exercise, calcium
supplementation,
and vitamin D

Reassess in 3 months

Evaluate at regular
intervals for
persistence or
worsening of
symptoms

Determine degree of
symptomatic relief

Symptoms
subside

Symptoms
persist or
worsen

Ⓕ Medication
proves
inconvenient
or gives
side effects

Incomplete
relief
is noted

Complete
relief
afforded

Follow-up
care

Consider
transdermal
clonidine
Psychosocial
support

Assess complaints

Evaluate
absorption
and metabolism

Re-evaluate
in 6 months

Adjust dose
accordingly

Interference
is found

No interference
is encountered

Ⓖ Consider
periodic
screening
endometrial
biopsies

Reassess
in 3 months

Examine for
thyroid or hepatic
disorder

Increase dosage

Change medication or route

Reassess periodically

CONTRACEPTION

Johanna F. Perlmutter, M.D.

A. To help a patient or couple in a stable relationship to select the optimal contraception, one should explore details of the family and personal history to uncover potential risk factors. Information about a patient's prior experience with contraception will serve to evaluate her needs, acceptance, compliance, and fastidiousness as well as any adverse side effects and failure. Assess psychological and intellectual factors, particularly emotional maturity, stability, comprehension, and intelligence, to provide an index of the patient's probable ability to deal with a contraceptive method that may require special skill or continuing daily attention.

B. The history and physical examination may disclose conditions that contraindicate one or more contraceptive methods. The presence of a vaginal anomaly (such as duplication, septum, or stenosis) or a cervical deformation (hypoplasia or foreshortening) makes use of a diaphragm unlikely to be successful. Women with uterine retroversion can use a diaphragm with careful instruction to ensure proper placement. A contraindication to oral contraceptives precludes their use.

C. It is important to provide counseling for the patient who is seeking contraception to help her choose the method that will be most effective for her with the least likelihood of failure or adverse reaction. This applies even to the woman who comes requesting a specific method because she may not be sufficiently knowledgeable or well informed to have chosen wisely. Therefore, review all options available to her, weighing their relative efficacy and safety. Detail the side effects and complications that can be expected to arise in her case, particularly if she exhibits some recognized risk factor placing her at increased hazard.

D. Birth control pills can be used without any serious problems in most healthy women. Before prescribing oral contraceptive agents, however, one must first ensure that there are no high-risk problems to make their use inappropriate, such as prior thrombophlebitis or thromboembolic disorder, cardiovascular disease, estrogen-dependent neoplasm, and benign or malignant liver tumor. They must not be given if there is a possibility that the patient is pregnant.

E. Follow-up investigation is important and should first be undertaken within three months. At that time, obtain an interim history and carry out a physical examination. Evaluate for adverse effects. If the blood pressure is elevated or cardiovascular symptoms, such as chest pain, have developed, discontinue use of the pills. Such major effects warrant changing to another contraceptive method. Also note any side effects that are not life-threatening, such as breakthrough bleeding, so that one can adjust the type of pill and its dosage and thereby alleviate the symptom.

F. The only intrauterine device (IUD) currently available for use in the United States is Progestasert, which contains a reservoir of progesterone that is slowly released for its local effect on the endometrium. However, there are still many women who have copper-containing Cu-7 and Cu-T devices in place and some with Dalkon shields (even though they have been unavailable for clinical use for more than a decade). The use of IUDs is recognized to be associated with pelvic inflammatory disease (p 186), which is often indolent and subclinical in nature. The relative risk probably varies among the different devices; it is greatest with the Dalkon shield, for example, and magnified if the device has been in place for a prolonged period of time. IUD users at greatest risk are those who have had a prior pelvic infection or multiple sexual partners, but there is an intrinsic IUD risk entirely independent of these factors. One cannot insert an IUD unless there is clear-cut assurance that the patient understands the risks to which she is exposing herself and is mature and intelligent enough to understand and accept them. Be especially aware that if pregnancy should occur with an IUD in place, the patient may be at serious risk not only from spontaneous abortion but potentially fatal septic abortion (p 90).

G. Because rhythm techniques depend on abstention around the time of ovulation, successful contraception requires reliable information about ovulation timing. The failure rate by this method is intrinsically high even in women with regular periods, and it is considerably worse for those with irregular menstrual patterns. Withdrawal is a technique that involves interrupting coitus just prior to the male orgasm, but it is associated with both dissatisfaction and failure because sperm may be deposited intravaginally prior to ejaculation. The use of spermicidal preparations as gels or impregnated in a sponge placed in the vagina before intercourse does protect somewhat against pregnancy, but they are probably not nearly so effective as condoms, diaphragms, or birth control pills.

References

Cramer DW, Schiff I, Schoenbaum SC, et al. Tubal infertility and the intrauterine device. N Engl J Med 312:941, 1985.

Dickey RP. Managing Contraceptive Pill Patients. 3rd ed. Durant, OK: Creative Informatics, 1984.

Gregoire AT, Blye RT. Contraceptive Steroids: Pharmacology and Safety. New York: Plenum Press, 1986.

Klaus H. Natural family planning: A review. Obstet Gynecol Surv 37:128, 1982.

Kulig JW. Adolescent contraception: An update. Pediatrics 76:675, 1985.

Spellacy WN, Kerr DA, White B, et al. A family planning risk scoring system for health care providers. Obstet Gynecol 63:846, 1984.

PATIENT WITH DESIRE FOR CONTRACEPTION

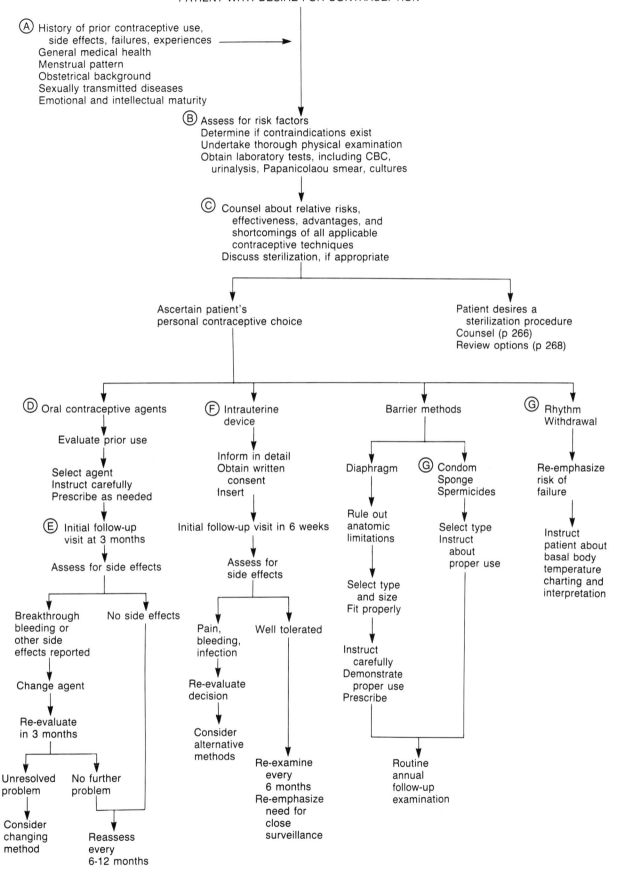

A History of prior contraceptive use,
   side effects, failures, experiences
   General medical health
   Menstrual pattern
   Obstetrical background
   Sexually transmitted diseases
   Emotional and intellectual maturity

B Assess for risk factors
   Determine if contraindications exist
   Undertake thorough physical examination
   Obtain laboratory tests, including CBC,
   urinalysis, Papanicolaou smear, cultures

C Counsel about relative risks,
   effectiveness, advantages, and
   shortcomings of all applicable
   contraceptive techniques
   Discuss sterilization, if appropriate

Ascertain patient's
personal contraceptive choice

Patient desires a
sterilization procedure
Counsel (p 266)
Review options (p 268)

D Oral contraceptive agents

Evaluate prior use

Select agent
Instruct carefully
Prescribe as needed

E Initial follow-up
visit at 3 months

Assess for side effects

Breakthrough
bleeding or
other side
effects reported

No side effects

Change agent

Re-evaluate
in 3 months

Unresolved
problem

No further
problem

Consider
changing
method

Reassess
every
6-12 months

F Intrauterine
device

Inform in detail
Obtain written
consent
Insert

Initial follow-up visit in 6 weeks

Assess for
side effects

Pain,
bleeding,
infection

Well tolerated

Re-evaluate
decision

Consider
alternative
methods

Re-examine
every
6 months
Re-emphasize
need for
close
surveillance

Barrier methods

Diaphragm

G Condom
Sponge
Spermicides

Rule out
anatomic
limitations

Select type
Instruct
about
proper use

Select type
and size
Fit properly

Instruct
carefully
Demonstrate
proper use
Prescribe

Routine
annual
follow-up
examination

G Rhythm
Withdrawal

Re-emphasize
risk of
failure

Instruct
patient about
basal body
temperature
charting and
interpretation

BLOOD REPLACEMENT

Janet L. Mitchell, M.D., M.P.H.

A. Think about the procedure being contemplated and any special problems that are likely to be encountered in order to be able to advise the patient in advance about potential blood replacement needs and to prepare for the eventuality of transfusions during or following the surgery. Certain operations can be anticipated to require blood because large blood losses are common, such as radical cancer surgery or cases requiring extensive dissection for inflammatory disease or endometriosis. Before deciding to transfuse blood, weigh the risk and benefits carefully. Clearly, if blood transfusions have to be given as a life-saving measure, there is seldom any risk not worth accepting. By contrast, it is often unnecessary to give blood to a patient whose cardiovascular system is stable and whose blood loss is only moderate and well controlled. This applies especially for patients who are given just a single unit transfusion; it is difficult to justify exposing them to the risks of the transfusion for the negligible benefit a single unit of blood could offer. Bear in mind that, despite the recent advances in blood banking, transfusions still carry some risk (see C). Moreover, because the supply of blood is limited, it is essential to use it judiciously. Institutional policy should openly address the issue of patients whose religious beliefs interdict use of blood or blood products, clearly enunciating refusal to comply or concur in whole or in part in the event of a life-threatening hemorrhage. Such patients must understand and accept a practice involving the administration or withholding of blood in an extreme emergency.

B. Because nearly all blood banks are able to expedite blood availability, a typing and screening procedure for antibodies, rather than a formal full cross matching of the units of actual blood that might be needed for transfusion, is generally adequate for most gynecological procedures. This eliminates the necessity to reserve blood that may not have to be utilized. The limited supply is thus less likely to become outdated. By averting unnecessary blood bank activities, one thereby reduces patient care costs as well.

C. Patients who will be undergoing elective procedures some time in the future should be encouraged to predeposit autologous blood by donating one or more units for storage. Autologous blood cannot introduce a transmissible infection to the patient or cause allo-immunization. It is considered the safest choice for transfusion. Patients who refuse blood in any form on religious grounds, however, will not even consider this as an acceptable option.

D. The risks of blood transfusion are basically of two types: those caused by transfusing incompatible blood and those involving transmission of disease. Patients receiving incompatible blood may experience manifestations that range from chills, fever, or hives to potentially fatal vascular collapse or disseminated intravascular coagulation (DIC). The most commonly transmitted disease is hepatitis, although human immune deficiency virus (HIV), the AIDS virus, is also of concern (p 122). Blood banks routinely test for both viruses today, but the tests have only a 96 to 98 percent sensitivity. Thus, although there is very good reassurance that transfused blood is free of these viruses, one cannot be entirely sure. Patients who have received blood transfusions should be offered the opportunity of long-term screening for early signs of the aforementioned diseases.

E. Special precautions must be taken in the event large volumes of blood are required to care for patients with massive hemorrhage from an intra-abdominal or retroperitoneal catastrophe, such as ruptured tubal or cornual pregnancy or uncontrolled intraoperative bleeding. Physicians tend to underestimate intraoperative blood loss by 15 to 40 percent. The incidence of hepatitis is directly related to the number of units transfused. Massive transfusions are also associated with decreased platelets, DIC, reduced capacity to deliver oxygen to the tissues, acid-base imbalance, citrate toxicity, hypothermia, and pulmonary insufficiency. Congestive heart failure from fluid overload is not uncommon; the best guide for the patient who requires large transfusion volumes is the pulmonary capillary wedge pressure measurement obtained by means of a Swan-Ganz catheter.

References

Hill ST, Lavin JP. Blood ordering in obstetrics and gynecology: Recommendations for the type and screen. Obstet Gynecol 62:236, 1983.

Koziol DE, Holland PV, Alling DW, et al. Antibody to hepatitis B core antigen as a paradoxical marker for non-A, non-B hepatitis agents in donated blood. Ann Intern Med 104:488, 1986.

Patten E, Alperin JB. Type and screen: A safe and effective preoperative blood ordering policy with emphasis on its use in obstetrics and gynecology. Am J Obstet Gynecol 142:563, 1982.

Toy PT, Strauss RG, Stehling LC, et al. Predeposited autologous blood for elective surgery: A national multicenter study. N Engl J Med 316:517, 1987.

PATIENT WITH POSSIBLE NEED FOR BLOOD TRANSFUSION

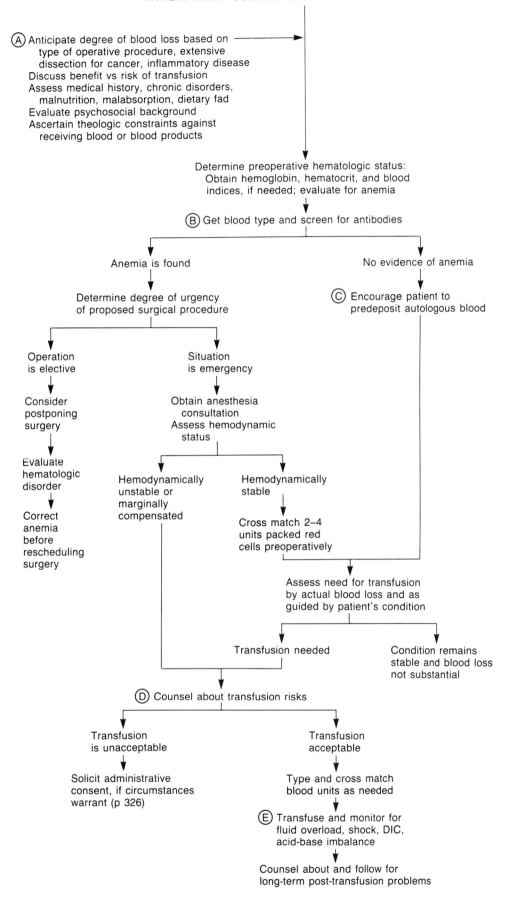

Ⓐ Anticipate degree of blood loss based on
    type of operative procedure, extensive
    dissection for cancer, inflammatory disease
Discuss benefit vs risk of transfusion
Assess medical history, chronic disorders,
    malnutrition, malabsorption, dietary fad
Evaluate psychosocial background
Ascertain theologic constraints against
    receiving blood or blood products

Determine preoperative hematologic status:
    Obtain hemoglobin, hematocrit, and blood
    indices, if needed; evaluate for anemia

Ⓑ Get blood type and screen for antibodies

Anemia is found

No evidence of anemia

Determine degree of urgency
of proposed surgical procedure

Ⓒ Encourage patient to
predeposit autologous blood

Operation
is elective

Situation
is emergency

Consider
postponing
surgery

Obtain anesthesia
consultation
Assess hemodynamic
status

Evaluate
hematologic
disorder

Hemodynamically
unstable or
marginally
compensated

Hemodynamically
stable

Correct
anemia
before
rescheduling
surgery

Cross match 2–4
units packed red
cells preoperatively

Assess need for transfusion
by actual blood loss and as
guided by patient's condition

Transfusion needed

Condition remains
stable and blood loss
not substantial

Ⓓ Counsel about transfusion risks

Transfusion
is unacceptable

Transfusion
acceptable

Solicit administrative
consent, if circumstances
warrant (p 326)

Type and cross match
blood units as needed

Ⓔ Transfuse and monitor for
fluid overload, shock, DIC,
acid-base imbalance

Counsel about and follow for
long-term post-transfusion problems

33

BLADDER CARE

Vicki L. Heller, M.D.

A. The time it should take for normal bladder function to return postoperatively will dictate whether urinary drainage is needed. Try to anticipate the need so as to forewarn the patient. If there is little intraoperative dissection in the area of the bladder, most patients will void spontaneously, thus averting the risks of catheterization. In the immediate postoperative period, constant bladder drainage does have the advantage of providing a means for careful evaluation of fluid status, and it may, therefore, be indicated on that basis. Few patients subjected to an uncomplicated pelvic operation require drainage for more than 24 hours. The more paraurethral and paravesical dissection done, the greater the delay in return of function. Patients operated on for correction of urinary stress incontinence generally require several days with an indwelling catheter. Extensive pelvic dissection can disturb urinary innervation from either edema or direct nerve damage, resulting in prolonged (rarely permanent) bladder dysfunction. Surgery involving bladder or urethra generally requires prolonged drainage for two or more weeks to avoid stress on the healing wound. Pre-existing bladder dysfunction aggravates the problem. A previously distended bladder is likely to become hypotonic after surgery and will require a longer drainage period until function returns. Pre-existing detrusor dysfunction will persist or even worsen.

B. Suprapubic catheterization carries the least risk of infection and is the treatment of choice for long-term catheterization. It should also be considered if the risk of infection is significant. A disadvantage is that the soft tubing used may become accidentally occluded. A special advantage is the capability to occlude drainage intermittently by means of a three-way stopcock for voiding trials (see D). Once effective bladder emptying is achieved transurethrally, the suprapubic catheter can be removed.

C. Care must be taken to prevent catheter obstruction, which can result in bladder overdistension leading to possible vesical rupture or hydronephrosis. Voiding around a catheter can indicate blockage. If this is not corrected by flushing the tubing gently or by changing the catheter, consider the possibility of a urinary fistula (p 274).

D. A successful voiding trial is one in which spontaneous voiding occurs with essentially complete emptying. It should not be followed by a sensation of incomplete emptying. Measure the postvoid residual volume in patients with inadequate voiding volumes, defective urinary sensation, recurrent failed voiding trials, or following prolonged bladder drainage. A residual of less than 100 ml is acceptable. Subsequent residual volumes are likely to be smaller. A large residual requires re-instituting continuous drainage. If urinary output is low, carefully evaluate for disturbed fluid status, continuity of upper urinary tracts, renal function, or antidiuretic hormone effect.

E. Prophylactic antibiotics have not proved useful for preventing bladder infection in catheterized patients. Their use may give rise to resistant organisms. Urine culture should be obtained prior to removing a catheter that has been in place for more than 24 hours and in patients who require intermittent transurethral catheterizations. In the case of prolonged drainage, surveillance with cultures at regular intervals will help diagnose infection early and identify the offending organism to ensure that an appropriate antibiotic is instituted.

F. Prolonged catheterization can lead to painful bladder spasms requiring spasmolytics or urinary analgesics. There are conditions for which one might consider some form of substitute for prolonged catheterization. Patients with severe neurologic dysfunction, for example, could be managed by intermittent manual compression of the bladder or catheterization. These techniques can be performed by well motivated patients. They can also mechanically assist themselves to void by positional change, such as leaning forward.

G. Medications with anticholinergic or sympatholytic effects tend to relax detrusor function while enhancing urinary sphincter contraction, thereby sometimes causing urinary retention. Conversely, parasympathomimetic drugs effect stronger contraction of the bladder and sympatholytics relax the sphincter. These agents can sometimes be used to treat patients who are persistently unable to void.

References

Bhatia NN, Bergman A. Urodynamic predictability of voiding following incontinence surgery. Obstet Gynecol 63:85, 1984.

Broberg C. Catheter drainage after gynecologic surgery: A comparison of methods. Am J Obstet Gynecol 149:18, 1984.

Galicier C, Richet H. A prospective study of postoperative fever in a general surgery department. Infect Control 6:487, 1985.

Schaeffer AJ. Catheter-associated bacteriuria. Urol Clin North Am 13:735, 1986.

Tammela T, Konturi M, Lukkarinen O. Postoperative urinary retention: I. Incidence and predisposing factors. Scand J Urol Nephrol 20:197, 1986.

POSTOPERATIVE PATIENT IN NEED OF BLADDER CARE

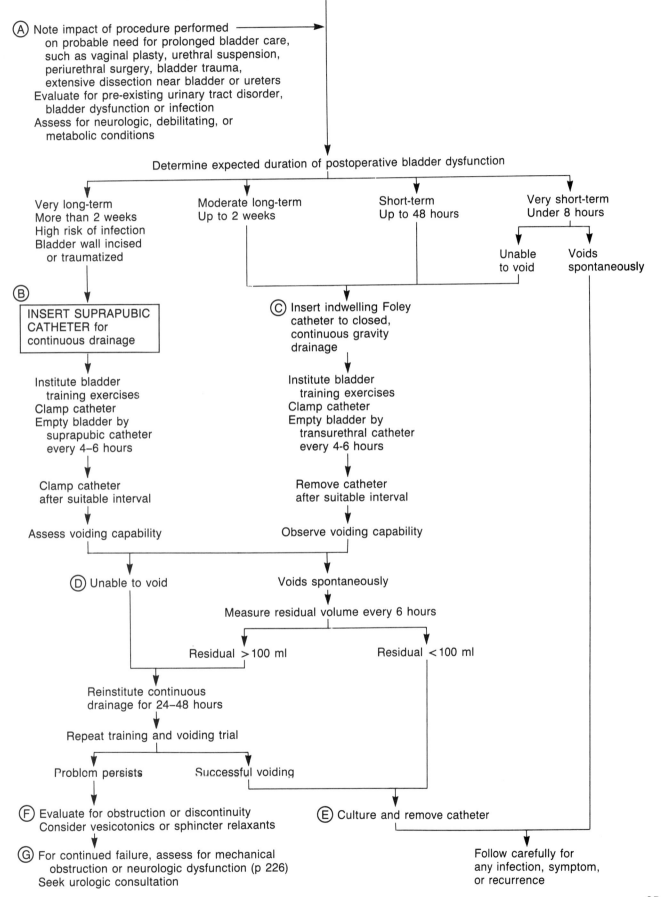

Ⓐ Note impact of procedure performed
    on probable need for prolonged bladder care,
    such as vaginal plasty, urethral suspension,
    periurethral surgery, bladder trauma,
    extensive dissection near bladder or ureters
  Evaluate for pre-existing urinary tract disorder,
    bladder dysfunction or infection
  Assess for neurologic, debilitating, or
    metabolic conditions

Determine expected duration of postoperative bladder dysfunction

Very long-term   Moderate long-term   Short-term   Very short-term
More than 2 weeks   Up to 2 weeks   Up to 48 hours   Under 8 hours
High risk of infection
Bladder wall incised   Unable   Voids
  or traumatized   to void   spontaneously

Ⓑ
INSERT SUPRAPUBIC   Ⓒ Insert indwelling Foley
CATHETER for   catheter to closed,
continuous drainage   continuous gravity
                               drainage

Institute bladder   Institute bladder
  training exercises   training exercises
Clamp catheter   Clamp catheter
Empty bladder by   Empty bladder by
  suprapubic catheter   transurethral catheter
  every 4–6 hours   every 4-6 hours

Clamp catheter   Remove catheter
  after suitable interval   after suitable interval

Assess voiding capability   Observe voiding capability

        Ⓓ Unable to void   Voids spontaneously

                                Measure residual volume every 6 hours

                    Residual >100 ml   Residual <100 ml

            Reinstitute continuous
              drainage for 24–48 hours

            Repeat training and voiding trial

        Problem persists   Successful voiding

Ⓕ Evaluate for obstruction or discontinuity   Ⓔ Culture and remove catheter
  Consider vesicotonics or sphincter relaxants

Ⓖ For continued failure, assess for mechanical   Follow carefully for
    obstruction or neurologic dysfunction (p 226)   any infection, symptom,
  Seek urologic consultation   or recurrence

35

CARE OF DRAINS

Lynn H. Galen, M.D.

A. Drains are employed therapeutically to evacuate collections of blood, lymph, serous secretions, and purulent material or prophylactically to prevent such collections. In radical pelvic surgical cases, drains significantly reduce postoperative morbidity due to the anticipated accumulations of exudation from the denuded tissue surfaces left after extensive dissection. Drains are especially valuable for a leaking or ruptured pelvic abscess or a case in which it is necessary to leave overtly necrotic tissue in place. Drainage is not a substitute for good surgical technique requiring delicate tissue handling, anatomic dissection, careful apposition of tissue layers, closure of dead space, minimizing tissue damage and foreign material, and most important of all, meticulous hemostasis.

B. Choose the drain that best suits the purpose intended. Passive drains, such as the Penrose drain, function by providing a path for passive outflow of accumulated fluid. While they are soft and avoid erosion of surrounding structures, they are inefficient and have the distinct disadvantage of allowing retrograde migration of bacteria to the operative site. Use them principally for draining pus and necrotic debris. Sump pump (suction) and closed drainage systems function by providing continuous negative pressure. Their effectiveness is not dependent on the patient's position for proper functioning and they are less vulnerable to bacterial colonization of the drainage tubing. Closed drainage systems have particular merit for wounds with a large potential dead space because they help to keep tissues apposed while draining fluid.

C. An abdominal cavity drain should be led out through a separate stab wound incision, never through the abdominal incision itself (Fig. 1). In making the stab incision, take care to avoid injuring the inferior or superior epigastric arteries. Place it 2 to 3 cm from the wound edge, if feasible, to facilitate access should hemorrhage occur. The drain site may be located above or below a transverse incision to bring it in closest proximity to the intraperitoneal area being drained. Use the most direct route to avoid kinking and enhance drainage. Situate the proximal tip so that it will not abut bowel, blood vessels, or any abdominal viscera. Transvaginal drains offer no special benefit except for retroperitoneal drainage of the potential space above the vaginal cuff after hysterectomy.

D. To prevent occlusion of the catheter by tissue debris, irrigate the wound meticulously and connect the external drainage system immediately after placement. Low level suction averts collapse of the tube and causes little tissue damage, while at the same time providing adequate evacuation of fluids. Secure the drain against retracting into the wound tract by use of a sterile safety pin. Drains should be mobilized every 24 to 48 hours to prevent them from adhering to surrounding tissues. Change the dressing as needed, always in an aseptic manner. Dressings saturated by fluid need to be changed frequently to avoid irritation and maceration of the underlying skin. Drainage should be measured and taken into account, if large, in calculating fluid and electrolyte replacement needs (p 22). To assess whether the drainage is from a urinary fistula, if that condition is suspected (p 322), measure the creatinine level in the drained fluid.

E. A drain is removed as soon as it ceases to be useful, that is, when the volume of fluid drained each day has dwindled sufficiently to justify removal or when the drained abscess cavity has been obliterated. To allow adequate closure of a drain tract, withdraw the drain gradually, several centimeters per day. This step-wise sequence encourages the drainage tract to heal from the deepest point outward, rather than risking a situation in which the superficial part closes over, leaving open dead space below for fluid to reaccumulate. After each shortening, advance the safety pin to prevent losing the drain in the wound. A drain from which there has been little or no drainage may be removed entirely in a single operation. After removal, inspect the drain to ensure that it is intact and apply a dry sterile dressing over the drain site.

References

Landers DV, Sweet RL. Current trends in the diagnosis and treatment of tuboovarian abscess. Am J Obstet Gynecol 151:1098, 1985.

Milling MA, Zoltie N. A method of secure fixation of suction drains. J R Coll Surg Edinb 30:195, 1985.

Orr JW Jr, Barter JF, Kilgore LC, et al. Closed suction pelvic drainage after radical pelvic surgical procedures. Am J Obstet Gynecol 155:867, 1986.

Poulsen HK, Borel J, Olsen H. Prophylactic metronidazole or suction drainage in abdominal hysterectomy. Obstet Gynecol 63:291, 1984.

Raves JJ, Slifkin M, Diamond DL. A bacteriologic study comparing closed suction and simple conduit drainage. Am J Surg 148:618, 1984.

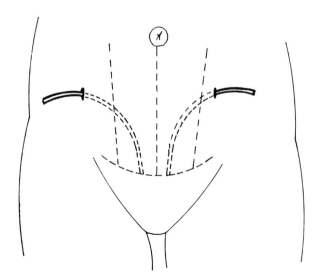

Figure 1 Drains placed into pelvis and led out through abdominal stab wounds separate from the primary operative incision and located laterally to the rectus muscles. Negative pressure applied externally ensures against fluid collections.

INTRAOPERATIVE CONSIDERATION FOR DRAINAGE

(A) Inability to achieve good hemostasis
Abscess cavity or residual wall of abscess
Remaining necrotic tissue bed
Unresectable inflammatory residue
Extensive dissection with denuded
operative site
Probable fluid extravasation

Minimize need for drainage by using
optimal surgical techniques

(A) Evaluate requirement for drainage

(B) Choose drain type according to need:
Prophylactic vs therapeutic
Passive vs active suction drainage
Purulent vs nonpurulent collection
Dependent vs nondependent site

(C) Select drain site appropriately:
Avoid draining through primary operative wound
Use separate stab incisions
Locate drains close to area to be drained
Minimize length of drains
Place drain tip to avert visceral or vascular injury

Purulent material
Dependent location

Collection of blood, serum, lymph
Potential space is involved
Nondependent site to be drained

Passive drainage acceptable

Active drainage necessary

Provide care for
overlying skin to
prevent maceration

(D) Irrigate area thoroughly and
apply negative pressure at once
Secure in place to prevent losing drain

Advance drain slowly
and resecure each time

Assess type and measure amount
of drainage periodically

(E) Remove drain when abscess
resolves or drainage stops

Purulent   Serous   Sanguineous

Administer or
continue antibiotics

Get serial hematocrits
of drainage fluid

Hematocrit   Hematocrit
relatively   reflects
low   active bleeding

Monitor serially
by measuring
amount of drainage

Consider
re-exploring

Moderate output   Large output

Replace fluid loss

Continue drainage

Drainage subsides

(E) Remove drains progressively

LEUKORRHEA

Johanna F. Perlmutter, M.D.

A. Vaginal discharge related to ovulation or sexual stimulation is normal and has to be distinguished from the common discharge of vaginal infection. In a child it may signal a foreign body, infection, or neoplasm (p 8). Probe about exposure to sexually transmitted disease, prior gynecological infection, tampon use, allergies, and concurrent symptoms of itching, burning, dysuria, dyspareunia, and odor. Vaginitis cannot be diagnosed by inspection alone, but a careful pelvic examination is essential to ensure all aspects of the vulva, vagina, and cervix are seen and no lesions are missed. Typically, the discharge of candidiasis is cheesy and that of trichomoniasis is frothy, but one can be easily misled by relying on appearance alone. Objective microscopic study is necessary.

B. Two separate wet mount preparations should be examined microscopically. Use a drop of normal saline on one to look for live, motile trichomonads and clue cells characteristic of leukocytes containing phagocytized *Gardnerella* organisms. Place a drop of potassium hydroxide (KOH) solution on the other to seek the budding hyphae that help identify *Candida*. For completeness, it is prudent to obtain a Papanicolaou smear (p 12), unless one has been done within the past year. Because cervical cytology may be distorted, consider repeating the smear several weeks later after the infection has been treated. Examining a Gram stained smear is helpful for recognizing bacterial infection, especially gonorrhea (p 116). Cultures may be indicated if the diagnosis is unclear, but special culture media are needed for each specific organism. Because cultures are expensive and may give falsely negative results, they cannot always be relied on for accurate early diagnosis.

C. Leukorrhea that is foul smelling suggests either a foreign body (most often a forgotten or lost tampon) necrotic tissue (as from fungating cancer), or poor hygiene. If a foreign body is encountered, removing it and cleansing the vagina should suffice for quickly correcting the problem. If the vaginal mucosa is damaged or infected, a topical preparation containing antibiotics (or estrogen, if the patient is postmenopausal) will help (p 28). Look for specific focal lesions and evaluate them as needed to identify herpes (p 120), chancre (p 114), condyloma (p 118), or neoplasm (p 158). If the inflammation is principally on the vulva, consider the possibility of an allergic reaction (p 40). Inquire about use of new soaps, sprays, cosmetics, and other agents that may be responsible.

D. The diagnosis of *Gardnerella* (previously called *Haemophilus*) vaginitis is made by excluding other causes and observing clue cells on either a wet saline preparation or a Papanicolaou smear. There is as yet no reliably effective form of therapy for this disorder, although systemic metronidazole, ampicillin, or cephalosporins may prove useful, especially if both sexual partners are treated simultaneously. Topical treatment tends to have poor results.

E. Treat vaginal trichomoniasis with oral metronidazole (Flagyl) 250 mg taken three times daily for seven days by both partners, if possible. If compliance is expected to be a problem, consider giving 2 g in divided doses over 30 minutes, although this regimen is not as effective as the seven-day course. Do not use this drug in the first trimester of pregnancy because of possible teratogenic effects, giving symptomatic relief instead with mildly acidic topical agents. Patients on metronidazole should avoid alcohol intake during therapy.

F. Candidal vaginitis requires diligence in treatment to eradicate the organism. Several good topical antifungal drugs are available as gel, cream, or suppository, including miconazole and clotrimazole. It is important for the therapy to be continued for its full prescribed course without interruption, even for menstruation. Resistant or recurrent infections require investigation for diabetes mellitus.

G. If an etiologic organism cannot be identified, the approach to therapy has to be empirical. One can try a topical antibiotic vaginal preparation, but results are inconsistent. Consider the possibility of infection with herpesvirus, *Chlamydia*, and *Actinomyces*; if they can be isolated, management can be directed more appropriately.

H. Persistence of disease should be differentiated from recurrence. Pay particular attention to the patient's partner to help identify a possible source of reinfection. Follow-up evaluation is indicated whenever feasible.

References

Aubert JM, Sesta HJ. Treatment of vaginal trichomoniasis: Single, 2-gram dose of metronidazole as compared with a seven-day course. J Reprod Med 27:743, 1982.

Brown D Jr, Kaufman RH, Gardner HL. Gardnerella vaginalis vaginitis: The current opinion. J Reprod Med 29:300, 1984.

Eschenbach DA. Vaginal infection. Clin Obstet Gynecol 26:186, 1983.

Purdon A, Hanna JH, Morse PL, et al. An evaluation of single-dose metronidazole treatment for Gardnerella vaginalis vaginitis. Obstet Gynecol 64:271, 1984.

PATIENT WITH VAGINAL DISCHARGE

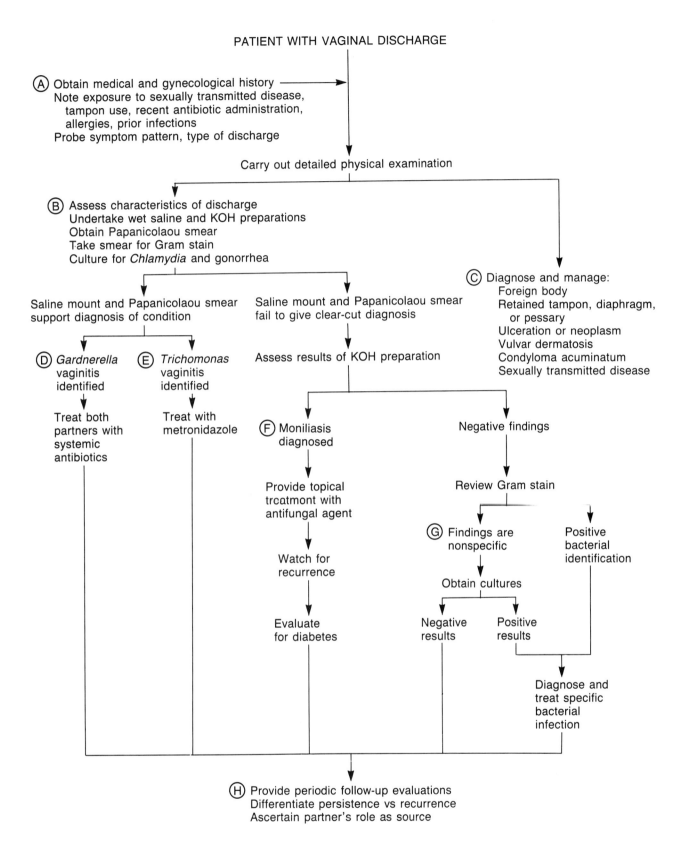

Ⓐ Obtain medical and gynecological history ───────➤
    Note exposure to sexually transmitted disease,
      tampon use, recent antibiotic administration,
      allergies, prior infections
    Probe symptom pattern, type of discharge

Carry out detailed physical examination

Ⓑ Assess characteristics of discharge
    Undertake wet saline and KOH preparations
    Obtain Papanicolaou smear
    Take smear for Gram stain
    Culture for *Chlamydia* and gonorrhea

Saline mount and Papanicolaou smear
support diagnosis of condition

Saline mount and Papanicolaou smear
fail to give clear-cut diagnosis

Ⓒ Diagnose and manage:
    Foreign body
    Retained tampon, diaphragm,
      or pessary
    Ulceration or neoplasm
    Vulvar dermatosis
    Condyloma acuminatum
    Sexually transmitted disease

Ⓓ *Gardnerella*   Ⓔ *Trichomonas*
  vaginitis   vaginitis
  identified   identified

Treat both   Treat with
partners with   metronidazole
systemic
antibiotics

Assess results of KOH preparation

Ⓕ Moniliasis   Negative findings
  diagnosed

Provide topical   Review Gram stain
treatment with
antifungal agent

Watch for   Ⓖ Findings are   Positive
recurrence   nonspecific   bacterial
                                          identification

Evaluate   Obtain cultures
for diabetes
                      Negative   Positive
                      results   results

                              Diagnose and
                              treat specific
                              bacterial
                              infection

Ⓗ Provide periodic follow-up evaluations
    Differentiate persistence vs recurrence
    Ascertain partner's role as source

39

PRURITUS VULVAE

Louis Burke, M.D.

A. Anogenital itching can be a tormenting problem for a patient. It warrants full attention and careful scrutiny. It must not be dismissed summarily, especially since it is usually difficult to find a definitive cause and an effective remedy. Consider and rule out common sources first, such as vulvovaginitis (p 38) and allergic food, drug, or contact dermatosis. Begin with a complete history and general physical examination. Probe for symptoms of physical manifestations of systemic conditions such as diabetes mellitus, anemia, leukemia, lymphoma, hepatitis, cholecystitis, nephritis, cancer, or endocrinopathy. Watch for intertrigo, especially in obese women. Query about recent infections that might have been treated with antibiotics; secondary candidal vaginitis is not an uncommon sequela. Determine when the itching began, what might have started it, and its distribution and periodicity. Look for evidence of skin involvement elsewhere.

B. Confirm the presence of systemic disease or local infection, infestation, or neoplasm by using a range of laboratory investigations as indicated. Determine if the patient has vaginitis and rule out the common causes by wet mount and Gram stained smear microscopy (p 38). In addition, be sure to study smears of exfoliated cells obtained from both vulva and vagina for cytologic evidence of dysplastic cells.

C. Search diligently for a vulvar lesion. If none is found, seek the cause of the pruritus in the vagina. Examining the vagina is important, of course, whether there is a vulvar lesion or not, but the vaginal findings are more likely to be relevant to the presenting complaint if none exists. Inspect the vagina for infection. Test for trichomoniasis, candidiasis, *Gardnerella* vaginitis, and gonococcal disease (p 38). It is common to encounter poorly estrogenized atrophic vaginitis accompanying signs of vulvar atrophy in postmenopausal patients with vulvar pruritus. Urinary incontinence may also cause pruritus from chronic vulvar irritation by urine.

D. The differential diagnosis of vulvar lesions can be extensive. Consider focal infections, parasitic infestations, and dermatoses. Common viral lesions can be distinguished by their typical attributes: herpesvirus lesions appear as grouped vesicles; condyloma acuminatum as pointed, papillary, or flat lesions; and molluscum contagiosum as dome-shaped umbilicated lesions. Among infestations that may be encountered, scabies appears as linear erythematous streaks; pediculosis pubis as nits attached to hair follicles; and threadworm by the organisms found between the labia. Dermatologic lesions include psoriasis, lichen planus, seborrheic dermatitis, and contact dermatitis. Contact sensitivity can arise at any time, although it is more likely to appear in a patient who has an allergic history or has had other dermatoses. It may be related to a wide variety of irritants, ranging from personal soap, bath oil, laundry detergent, deodorant spray, perfume, powder, and douches to spermicidal products and toilet tissue. It may take much probing to uncover the offending agent. Obstruction of the vulvar sweat glands causes intense itching (Fox-Fordyce disease); it is recognized by the presence of dome-shaped papules on the mons pubis.

E. Examination is aided by magnification. Although this approach is better when applied to study of the cervix for dysplasia (p 214), it may prove useful for vulvar lesions as well. Persistent washing with 3 to 5 percent acetic acid may bring out various colposcopic abnormalities. This is especially valuable in the less confined areas of the labia minora, introitus, and perineum. The usual evidence of dysplasia is a white delineated lesion.

F. Vulvar dystrophy may appear in a variety of forms. Diagnosis is generally made by biopsy. They include hyperplastic dystrophy (acanthosis and hyperkeratosis with or without atypia), lichen sclerosis (loss of rete ridges and a homogeneous subepithelial zone), and mixed dystrophy (both of the above features are present with or without atypia). Atypia of varying degrees may occur with cellular crowding and nuclear and cellular abnormalities. Once diagnosis is established, proceed with the specific indicated therapy (p 134).

References

Friedrich EG Jr. The vulvar vestibule. J Reprod Med 28:773, 1983.

Goulamali SK. Pruritus vulvae. Clin Obstet Gynaecol 8:227, 1981.

McKay M. Vulvodynia versus pruritus vulvae. Clin Obstet Gynecol 28:123, 1985.

Young AW. Burning vulva syndrome: Report of the ISSVD task force. J Reprod Med 29:457, 1984.

PATIENT WITH VULVAR ITCHING

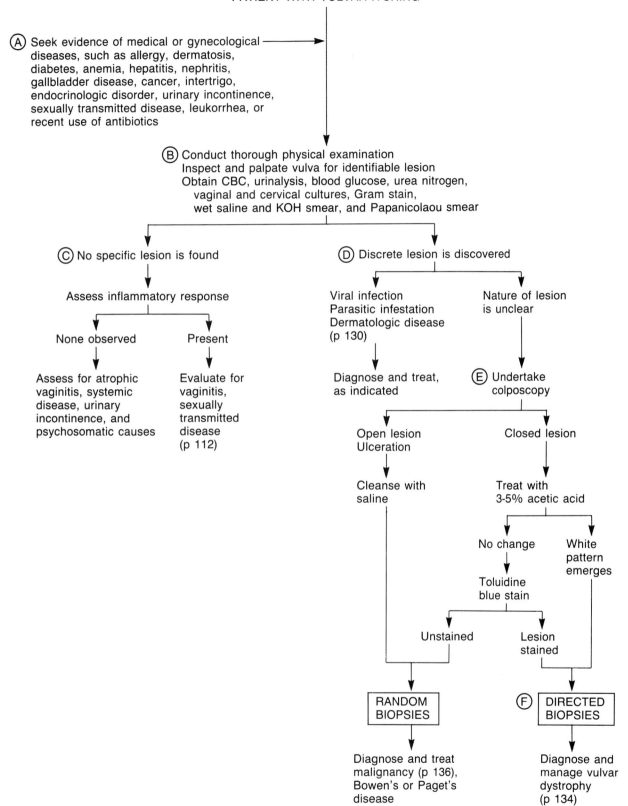

(A) Seek evidence of medical or gynecological diseases, such as allergy, dermatosis, diabetes, anemia, hepatitis, nephritis, gallbladder disease, cancer, intertrigo, endocrinologic disorder, urinary incontinence, sexually transmitted disease, leukorrhea, or recent use of antibiotics

(B) Conduct thorough physical examination
Inspect and palpate vulva for identifiable lesion
Obtain CBC, urinalysis, blood glucose, urea nitrogen,
vaginal and cervical cultures, Gram stain,
wet saline and KOH smear, and Papanicolaou smear

(C) No specific lesion is found

Assess inflammatory response

None observed

Assess for atrophic vaginitis, systemic disease, urinary incontinence, and psychosomatic causes

Present

Evaluate for vaginitis, sexually transmitted disease (p 112)

(D) Discrete lesion is discovered

Viral infection
Parasitic infestation
Dermatologic disease
(p 130)

Diagnose and treat, as indicated

Nature of lesion is unclear

(E) Undertake colposcopy

Open lesion
Ulceration

Cleanse with saline

Closed lesion

Treat with 3-5% acetic acid

No change

Toluidine blue stain

Unstained

White pattern emerges

Lesion stained

RANDOM BIOPSIES

Diagnose and treat malignancy (p 136), Bowen's or Paget's disease

(F) DIRECTED BIOPSIES

Diagnose and manage vulvar dystrophy (p 134)

PREMENSTRUAL SYNDROME

Johanna F. Perlmutter, M.D.

A. Many women experience various symptoms heralding the approach of their menstrual period. They usually include breast engorgement, hypersensitivity, nd tenderness; weight gain associated with fluid retentiu n, sensations of bloatedness, and dependent edema; emotional lability, irritability, depression, or anxiety; fatigue; and headaches. Manifestations may range from negligible to debilitating in nature. Objective signs include breast enlargement with increased thickening and nodularity, appearance or aggravation of acne, and behavioral alterations. It affects upwards of one-third of all women of reproductive age to some degree. There is no consistent agreement about the definition for premenstrual syndrome. There are many authorities who feel that this is not just a single disease entity but probably constitutes a number of different syndromes. Etiology is as yet unclear and management to date has been largely empirical. Among the hypothetical causes considered as most likely are excesses of estrogens, prolactin, and endorphins or deficiency of progesterone, but none of them has been shown to be a reliable diagnostic marker for the syndrome. The syndrome is clearly related to and perhaps a variant of otherwise normal physiologic ovarian cyclic function. This is likely to be the case because its manifestations can be effectively reversed by gonadotropin releasing hormone agonist, which suppresses ovarian function. More than 150 signs and symptoms have been described as part of this syndrome. There is none that is pathognomonic of this condition by itself, nor is any combination reliably diagnostic. It is more the timing of the symptoms concentrated during the week or more prior to the onset of menstruation and their cyclicity that appear to be of some diagnostic significance. However, there is no consensus as to what comprises characteristic cyclicity for affected patients, although most agree that symptoms are worse during ovulatory cycles. Indeed, many women are entirely asymptomatic when anovulatory. The repetitive nature is nonetheless the most typical feature of this syndrome; without it the diagnosis must be doubted. Another very common feature is for symptoms to disappear quite promptly after the onset of menstrual bleeding.

B. It is important to obtain a complete history and thorough physical examination. Laboratory examinations should be performed as needed, looking for such potentially remediable conditions as hyperprolactinemia, estrogen-progesterone imbalance, or impaired aldosterone secretion. It is imperative that a menstrual calendar with annotated diary of symptoms be kept by the patient to document symptoms and their relationship to the cycle. Retrospective analysis and recall are notoriously poor and attempts should be made to collect these data in an ongoing, prospective fashion.

C. If a clear-cut relation to ovarian or menstrual cyclicity cannot be established, the patient's symptoms should not be considered as part of the premenstrual syndrome. Search for related medical disorders and manage accordingly. If none can be found, undertake psychosocial assessment and referral to an appropriate psychiatric resource for more intensive investigation and treatment.

D. Consistently effective therapy for patients with premenstrual syndrome is elusive at best. Numerous treatments have been advocated. About half the patients will respond to any of them, including placebos. Since response rates are so high, carefully controlled pharmacologic studies are needed to demonstrate real effectiveness; few current modalities meet this stringent criterion. In general, simple conservative measures, such as diet, exercise, and vitamins, should be tried before embarking on a program of hormonal therapy. Especially helpful in some cases is dietary modification to reduce sodium intake in the second half of the cycle; women find benefit in avoiding stimulants such as tea, coffee, chocolate, and caffeine-containing soft drinks. Supporting the congested breasts with a brassiere will help relieve discomfort as well.

E. Give low doses of progesterone initially. If the patient does not respond at all, experience has shown she will also be unresponsive to higher doses. Titrate the dosage to achieve maximal benefit without increasing it beyond that which is needed in a given case. If the effect of low-dose progesterone is good, then there is no need to raise the dose further.

References

Dennerstein L, Spencer-Gardner C, Gotts G, et al. Progesterone and the premenstrual syndrome: A double-blind crossover trial. Br J Med 290:1617, 1985.

Keye WR Jr, Hammond DC, Strong T. Medical and psychologic characteristics of women presenting with premenstrual symptoms. Obstet Gynecol 68:634, 1986.

Muse KN, Cetel NS, Futterman LA, Yen SSC. The premenstrual syndrome: Effects of "medical ovariectomy." N Engl J Med 311:1345, 1984.

Reid RL. Premenstrual syndrome: A time for introspection. Am J Obstet Gynecol 155:921, 1986.

PATIENT WITH PREMENSTRUAL MOLIMINA

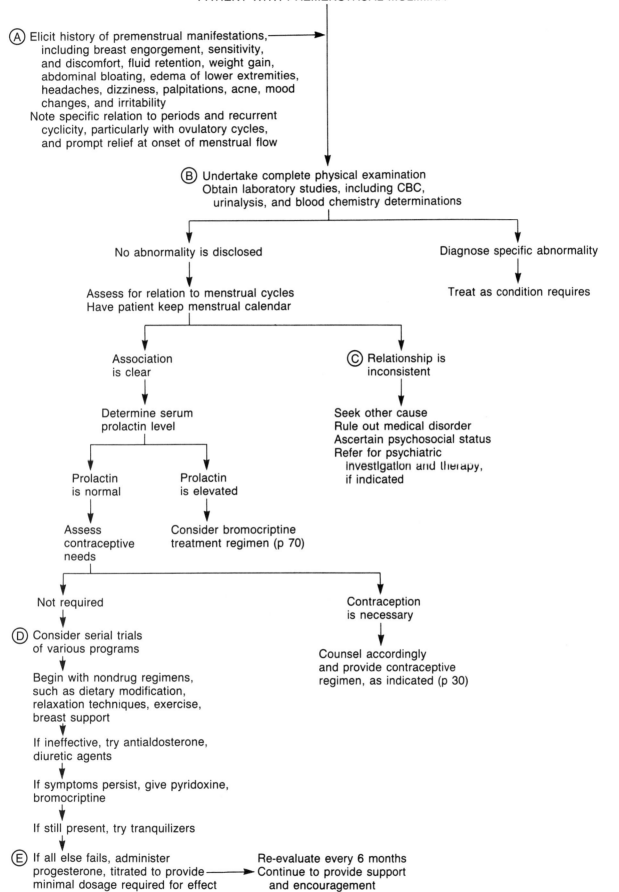

Ⓐ Elicit history of premenstrual manifestations,
    including breast engorgement, sensitivity,
    and discomfort, fluid retention, weight gain,
    abdominal bloating, edema of lower extremities,
    headaches, dizziness, palpitations, acne, mood
    changes, and irritability
Note specific relation to periods and recurrent
    cyclicity, particularly with ovulatory cycles,
    and prompt relief at onset of menstrual flow

Ⓑ Undertake complete physical examination
   Obtain laboratory studies, including CBC,
     urinalysis, and blood chemistry determinations

No abnormality is disclosed

Diagnose specific abnormality

Treat as condition requires

Assess for relation to menstrual cycles
Have patient keep menstrual calendar

Association
is clear

Ⓒ Relationship is
  inconsistent

Determine serum
prolactin level

Seek other cause
Rule out medical disorder
Ascertain psychosocial status
Refer for psychiatric
  investigation and therapy,
  if indicated

Prolactin
is normal

Prolactin
is elevated

Assess
contraceptive
needs

Consider bromocriptine
treatment regimen (p 70)

Not required

Contraception
is necessary

Ⓓ Consider serial trials
  of various programs

Counsel accordingly
and provide contraceptive
regimen, as indicated (p 30)

Begin with nondrug regimens,
such as dietary modification,
relaxation techniques, exercise,
breast support

If ineffective, try antialdosterone,
diuretic agents

If symptoms persist, give pyridoxine,
bromocriptine

If still present, try tranquilizers

Ⓔ If all else fails, administer
  progesterone, titrated to provide ⟶
  minimal dosage required for effect

Re-evaluate every 6 months
Continue to provide support
  and encouragement

SEXUAL DYSFUNCTION

Johanna F. Perlmutter, M.D.

A. Sexual problems are especially pervasive and too often overlooked by gynecologists. They may even be ignored when patients express concerns about them. This reluctance must be addressed and corrected. An inquiry about sexual function should be part of every periodic gynecological examination of an adult female. This gives the patient the opportunity to open the subject at that time or in the future when her inhibitions are overcome. Try to get the presenting complaint characterized in clear and unambiguous terms so as to understand the problem and its causes. Diminished libido may actually represent impotence, premature ejaculation, or loss of sex drive. While it is important to assess both members of the couple, it is equally valuable to interview them separately. This may disclose that the presenting problem is specific to only one of the partners. Careful investigation will help reveal if sexual functioning and satisfaction are adequate under other circumstances and conditions (as with other partners).

B. Bear in mind that libido is a very delicate indicator of general health. While arousability may be somewhat reduced with advancing age, sexual functioning should not be assumed to be of less importance as women get older, even to those of quite advanced age. Libido tends to wane whenever physical or mental well-being diminishes for whatever reason. Diabetes mellitus is quite typically a cause, especially when associated with neuropathy. Recovery from illness does not guarantee that libido will return promptly, however. Thus, resolution of the underlying medical or emotional problem does not always ensure that the sexual symptoms will be corrected. Following convalescence, sexual dysfunction may persist both as a consequence of real difficulty with sexual function and as a result of a sense of anxiety that performance will not be adequate, pleasurable, or even comfortable. A number of medications may also adversely affect sexual desire and response. These include antidepressants, sedatives, antihistamines, and antihypertensives, among many others. Chronic stress, depression, or fatigue may contribute to the problem as well. Of special note, alcohol and drug abusers often have diminished libido. For a patient whose reaction to a needed medication appears to be responsible for her sexual dysfunction, it may be feasible to find an effective substitute and thereby relieve her problem. Alternatively, if the desired result cannot be achieved, the patient may be benefited by counseling or psychiatric referral for more intensive evaluation and care.

C. Counsel the couple troubled by premature ejaculation to help them allay stressful situations in their life and to relieve any anxiety related to sexual performance. The more concern they register the less likely it will be to correct the problem. One utilitarian approach is to encourage them to increase coital frequency. Another is use of the squeeze technique, which consists of digital compression of the penis at the coronal ridge to delay male orgasm and ejaculation.

D. The cause of true male impotence can sometimes be difficult to elucidate. It is important to rule out general medical, neurologic, or endocrinologic illness and to ascertain if there might be a pharmacologic cause (see B). If a drug etiology is found, treatment is facilitated. Inquire about nocturnal erections unassociated with the sex act. They may occur (although less firm and more sporadic) in association with serious medical disorders, neuropathy, or vascular compromise, and even in the presence of low testosterone levels.

E. Explaining the sexual response cycle may serve to help a patient understand the sequence of events leading to orgasm or help her recognize that she is not anorgasmic. Giving reassurances about self-exploration and manipulation helps to relieve inhibitions and facilitates achieving satisfaction. Women who can learn to reach orgasm by autoerotic play or partner activity can be assured of good results from counseling alone. Those who cannot may require more intensive psychotherapy.

F. In a stable relationship, counseling should always involve the couple as a unit. This is true even when the problem appears to be focused in just one member of the pair. Poor sexual functioning clearly affects both parties. Discussions with each partner alone and then with both together may open interesting avenues for further investigation, leading in turn to effective and beneficial solutions.

References

Hammond DC. Screening for sexual dysfunction. Clin Obstet Gynecol 27:732, 1984.

Morrell MJ, Dixen JM, Carter S, Davidson JM. The influence of age and cycling status on sexual arousability in women. Am J Obstet Gynecol 148:66, 1984.

Reamy K. Sexual counseling for the nontherapist. Clin Obstet Gynecol 27:781, 1984.

Weisberg M. Physiology of female sexual function. Clin Obstet Gynecol 27:697, 1984.

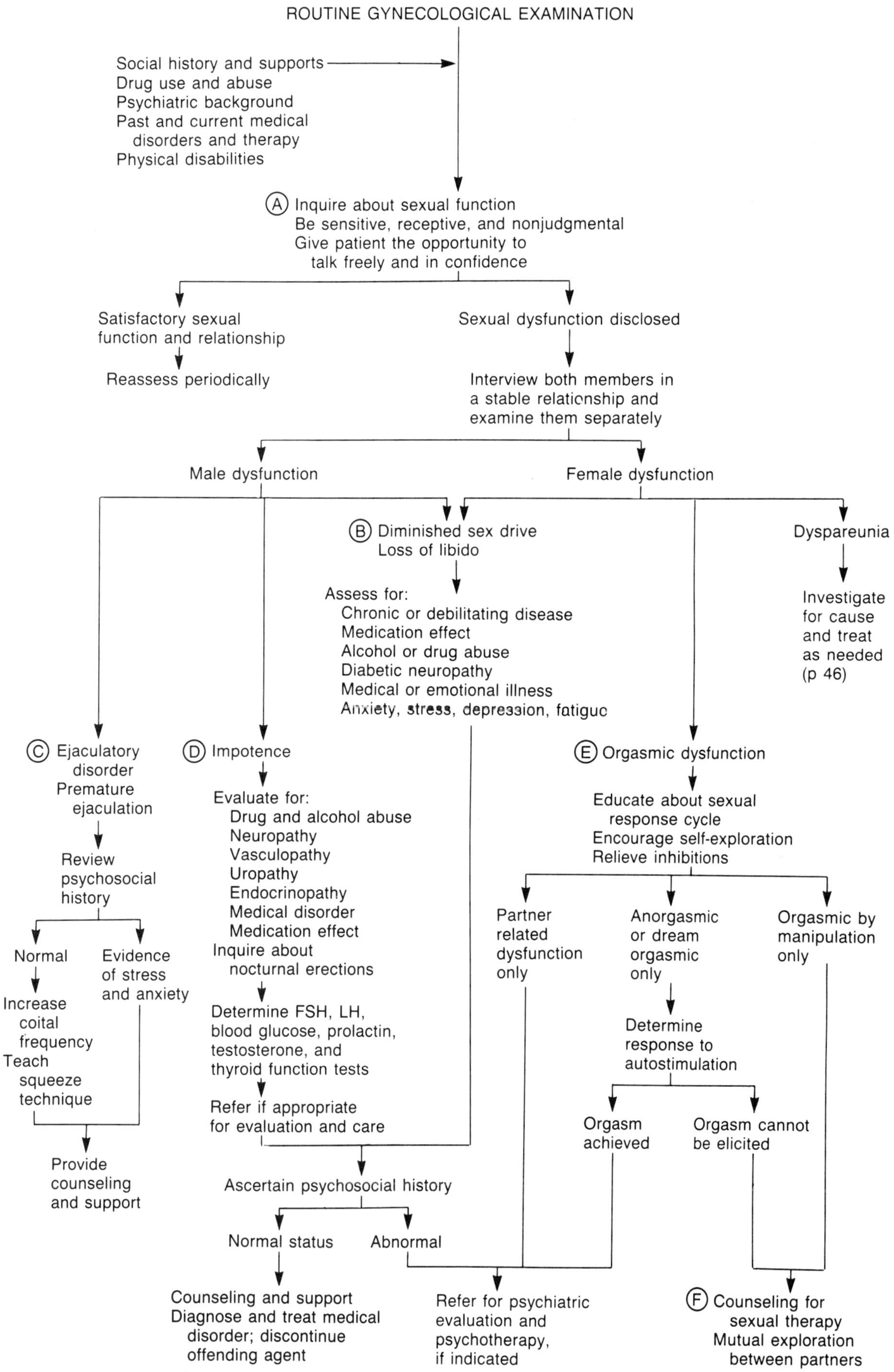

ROUTINE GYNECOLOGICAL EXAMINATION

Social history and supports
Drug use and abuse
Psychiatric background
Past and current medical
  disorders and therapy
Physical disabilities

(A) Inquire about sexual function
    Be sensitive, receptive, and nonjudgmental
    Give patient the opportunity to
       talk freely and in confidence

Satisfactory sexual
function and relationship

Reassess periodically

Sexual dysfunction disclosed

Interview both members in
a stable relationship and
examine them separately

Male dysfunction

Female dysfunction

(B) Diminished sex drive
    Loss of libido

Assess for:
   Chronic or debilitating disease
   Medication effect
   Alcohol or drug abuse
   Diabetic neuropathy
   Medical or emotional illness
   Anxiety, stress, depression, fatigue

Dyspareunia

Investigate
for cause
and treat
as needed
(p 46)

(C) Ejaculatory
    disorder
    Premature
    ejaculation

Review
psychosocial
history

Normal

Evidence
of stress
and anxiety

Increase
coital
frequency
Teach
squeeze
technique

Provide
counseling
and support

(D) Impotence

Evaluate for:
   Drug and alcohol abuse
   Neuropathy
   Vasculopathy
   Uropathy
   Endocrinopathy
   Medical disorder
   Medication effect
Inquire about
nocturnal erections

Determine FSH, LH,
blood glucose, prolactin,
testosterone, and
thyroid function tests

Refer if appropriate
for evaluation and care

Ascertain psychosocial history

Normal status

Abnormal

Counseling and support
Diagnose and treat medical
disorder; discontinue
offending agent

Refer for psychiatric
evaluation and
psychotherapy,
if indicated

(E) Orgasmic dysfunction

Educate about sexual
response cycle
Encourage self-exploration
Relieve inhibitions

Partner
related
dysfunction
only

Anorgasmic
or dream
orgasmic
only

Orgasmic by
manipulation
only

Determine
response to
autostimulation

Orgasm
achieved

Orgasm cannot
be elicited

(F) Counseling for
    sexual therapy
    Mutual exploration
    between partners

45

DYSPAREUNIA

Johanna F. Perlmutter, M.D.

A. Pain during sexual intercourse is a rather common problem and it may arise from a number of different causes. While dyspareunia may be secondary to a psychological problem, it is essential to rule out physical or physiologic factors before ascribing it to the patient's mental status. Gynecological and obstetrical history is important, but a detailed sexual history is even more critical for the evaluation of every woman with dyspareunia. Inquire carefully to determine the specific site of the pain. One should attempt to differentiate pain at the introitus from pain along the barrel of the vagina and from pain that occurs on deep penile penetration. Be alert to psychological problems of potential relevance, including anxiety, phobias, sexual aversions, conversion manifestations, and especially traumatic sexual experiences in the past, such as rape or incest. If possible, probe into past and current orgasmic responses, if any, to provide useful insights into diagnosis and etiology. Recognize that the issue is sensitive and that the patient may not be able to confide in her physician at first. It may take a number of sessions before enough trust can be generated so that sufficient data can be collected to be meaningful. Alternatively, if it is clear that the patient will be unable to confide (or the physician is unable or unwilling to devote the time or attention to the problem), consider referring the refractory patient who has no definable physical cause for psychiatric assessment and care. Such patients may complain of pain with intercourse, but the description of the discomfort tends to be vague and not well localized. Typically, the physical examination will be entirely negative, although one may recognize a reluctance to be examined. Occasionally, involuntary perineal and levator ani muscle spasm, typical of vaginismus, may even preclude inserting a vaginal speculum for the examination. The examination itself may serve a very useful function in reassuring the patient about her anatomy and her ability to accommodate an intravaginal object. It is also an opportunity for the physician to begin teaching the patient about techniques for correcting sexual dysfunction in terms of lubrication, muscle relaxation, and vaginal expansion.

B. A lesion in the lower vagina, introitus, or perineum around the fourchette, especially a focus of infection such as vaginitis, Bartholin duct abscess, urethritis, or chronic vulvitis, can contribute to entrance dyspareunia. If the condition is treated effectively, the dyspareunia generally subsides promptly. Be sure to search carefully with a bright light and perhaps a magnifying lens or colposcope. A tiny laceration or ulcer, particularly if located at the hymenal ring, may cause the discomfort. This type of lesion is generally remediable in the menopausal or postmenopausal woman by topical application of estrogen-containing cream. Minimize use of these preparations because estrogen is readily absorbed through skin and vaginal mucosa. Women athletes or dancers sometimes experience dyspareunia from overdeveloped perineal and levator muscles.

C. Pain or a burning sensation along the barrel of the vagina, either during or following intercourse, may be the presenting complaint. Any discomfort that is related to intercourse, even when it occurs several hours later, may be attributable to such factors as inflammation, obstructive growth, septum, or constriction of the vaginal lumen. Allergic reactions, reported to occur from barrier contraceptives or seminal fluid, may also cause sufficient discomfort to make coitus painful.

D. Deep dyspareunia, usually caused by the penis impacting on the ovary or other structure fixed in the cul-de-sac of Douglas, is seldom due to or associated with any psychological problems. Any tender pelvic structure that the phallus strikes on deep vaginal penetration or thrusting can give rise to deep dyspareunia. Thus, it is often caused by some kind of pathologic condition. If no clear-cut cause can be found, however, it may be difficult to treat adequately. Adjusting coital positions so that deep penetration does not occur may be the only practical solution. Laparoscopy may be needed to determine the true etiology. Unsuspected pelvic inflammatory disease or endometriosis, for example, may be encountered.

References

Friedrich EG. Vulvar vestibulitis syndrome. J Reprod Med 32:110, 1987.

Greiss FC. Equestrian dyspareunia. Am J Obstet Gynecol 150:168, 1984.

Lamont JA. Female dyspareunia. Am J Obstet Gynecol 136:282, 1980.

Sarrel PM, Steege JF, Maltzer M, Bolinsky D. Pain during sex response due to occlusion of the Bartholin gland duct. Obstet Gynecol 62:261, 1983.

Steege JF. Dyspareunia and vaginismus. Clin Obstet Gynecol 27:750, 1984.

PATIENT WITH COITAL PAIN

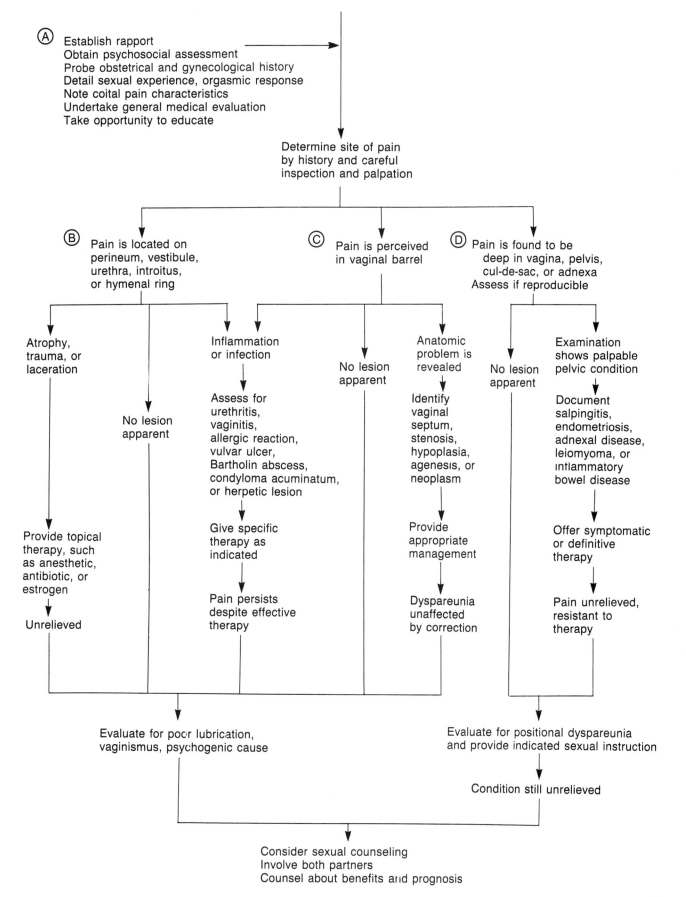

(A) Establish rapport
Obtain psychosocial assessment
Probe obstetrical and gynecological history
Detail sexual experience, orgasmic response
Note coital pain characteristics
Undertake general medical evaluation
Take opportunity to educate

Determine site of pain
by history and careful
inspection and palpation

(B) Pain is located on
perineum, vestibule,
urethra, introitus,
or hymenal ring

(C) Pain is perceived
in vaginal barrel

(D) Pain is found to be
deep in vagina, pelvis,
cul-de-sac, or adnexa
Assess if reproducible

Atrophy,
trauma, or
laceration

No lesion
apparent

Inflammation
or infection

No lesion
apparent

Anatomic
problem is
revealed

No lesion
apparent

Examination
shows palpable
pelvic condition

Assess for
urethritis,
vaginitis,
allergic reaction,
vulvar ulcer,
Bartholin abscess,
condyloma acuminatum,
or herpetic lesion

Identify
vaginal
septum,
stenosis,
hypoplasia,
agenesis, or
neoplasm

Document
salpingitis,
endometriosis,
adnexal disease,
leiomyoma, or
inflammatory
bowel disease

Provide topical
therapy, such
as anesthetic,
antibiotic, or
estrogen

Give specific
therapy as
indicated

Provide
appropriate
management

Offer symptomatic
or definitive
therapy

Unrelieved

Pain persists
despite effective
therapy

Dyspareunia
unaffected
by correction

Pain unrelieved,
resistant to
therapy

Evaluate for poor lubrication,
vaginismus, psychogenic cause

Evaluate for positional dyspareunia
and provide indicated sexual instruction

Condition still unrelieved

Consider sexual counseling
Involve both partners
Counsel about benefits and prognosis

DYSMENORRHEA

David G. Diaz, M.D.

A. Dysmenorrhea ranks with the most common complaints encountered by the gynecologist. Its investigation should be approached systematically. Pelvic discomfort normally occurs in most women to some degree during the menses, although it is not universal in all females and its incidence may vary considerably among populations and cultures. It may be characterized by lower abdominal cramping, backache, and radiating pain to the thighs with associated nausea, vomiting, diarrhea, and headaches. Symptoms range in intensity from mild and readily controlled by analgesics to severe and incapacitating, requiring aggressive medical management and bedrest. Typically, the manifestations recur cyclically in conjunction with menstruation, beginning concurrently with the onset of bleeding or a few hours beforehand and continuing for a variable period of time into the menses itself. They are usually preceded by premenstrual molimina (p 42) and appear almost exclusively in ovulatory cycles only. An important differential diagnostic characteristic is the age of onset.

B. A thorough medical history and physical examination may elicit diagnostic clues related to the origin of dysmenorrhea. A detailed chronology of menstrual events is often helpful as well as a review of general health, sexual function, obstetrical experience, infertility problems, sexually transmitted disease, and use of an intrauterine device. Useful studies include complete blood count, urinalysis, erythrocyte sedimentation rate, and pelvic ultrasonography, searching for evidence of an inflammatory, obstructive, or neoplastic process. If it is felt to be needed, endoscopy (hysteroscopy) and pelvic laparoscopy may also be indicated to diagnose the cause of secondary dysmenorrhea, but these measures are usually held in reserve unless the suspicion of an organic disorder is high or conservative therapeutic measures (see E) have been tried without any success.

C. Primary dysmenorrhea is painful menstruation occurring in the absence of any demonstrable pathologic cause. It is far more common in ovulatory women who have never conceived. An increased circulating level of prostaglandin (PG) is the putative cause of the menstrual pain. Under the influence of progesterone during the luteal phase of the menstrual cycle, there is an outpouring of $PGF_{2\alpha}$ that peaks at the time of menstruation. Uterine hypertonus and contractility at the time of menses presumably stimulate further $PGF_{2\alpha}$ production leading to uterine ischemia and pain, analogous to the angina associated with myocardial ischemia. This conceptual understanding of the mechanism forms the basis for the currently recommended principal program of management (see E).

D. Secondary dysmenorrhea is often related to specific pelvic disease, such as endometriosis, pelvic inflammatory disease, leiomyomas, adenomyosis, uterine polyps, and cervical stenosis. These conditions should be diligently searched for and identified so that they can be treated specifically as needed.

E. It is now possible to direct treatment toward the ostensible cause of primary dysmenorrhea rather than to have to resort to nonspecific and potent drugs. Prostaglandin synthetase inhibitors usually control the most severe symptoms by stopping the production of prostaglandins in the tissues and blocking their action at the receptor level. Reduced myometrial contractility results, averting ischemia of the muscle and preventing or alleviating the resulting pain. Mild cases may be treated using drugs with analgesic, sedative, or antispasmodic properties only. Severe pain is treated with a prostaglandin synthetase inhibitor. Specific contraindications to the use of those drugs include peptic ulcer, inflammatory bowel disease, or sensitivity to aspirin. Preventing ovulation by use of an oral contraceptive regimen is also an effective way to treat this condition and this was the principal method in the past. However, because the primary indication for the use of oral contraceptives is pregnancy prevention and these drugs can cause metabolic derangements, it is no longer necessary to rely upon them for the management of dysmenorrhea. Dilatation and curettage is generally indicated when cervical stenosis is suspected. Presacral neurectomy should be considered only as the last therapeutic resort. Although a major surgical procedure with attendant risks and even the possibility of failure, it can produce almost complete pain relief in up to 70 percent of women with intractable dysmenorrhea.

References

Andersch B, Milsom I. An epidemiologic study of young women with dysmenorrhea. Am J Obstet Gynecol 144:655, 1982.

Dawood MY. Dysmenorrhea. Clin Obstet Gynecol 26:719, 1983.

Kauppila A, Rönnberg L. Naproxen sodium in dysmenorrhea secondary to endometriosis. Obstet Gynecol 65:379, 1985.

Lee RB, Stone K, Magelssen D. Presacral neurectomy for chronic pelvic pain. Obstet Gynecol 68:517, 1986.

Lumsden MA, Kelly RW, Baird DT. Is prostaglandin F_2alpha involved in the increased myometrial contractility of primary dysmenorrhea? Prostaglandins 25:683, 1983.

PATIENT WITH MENSTRUAL PAIN

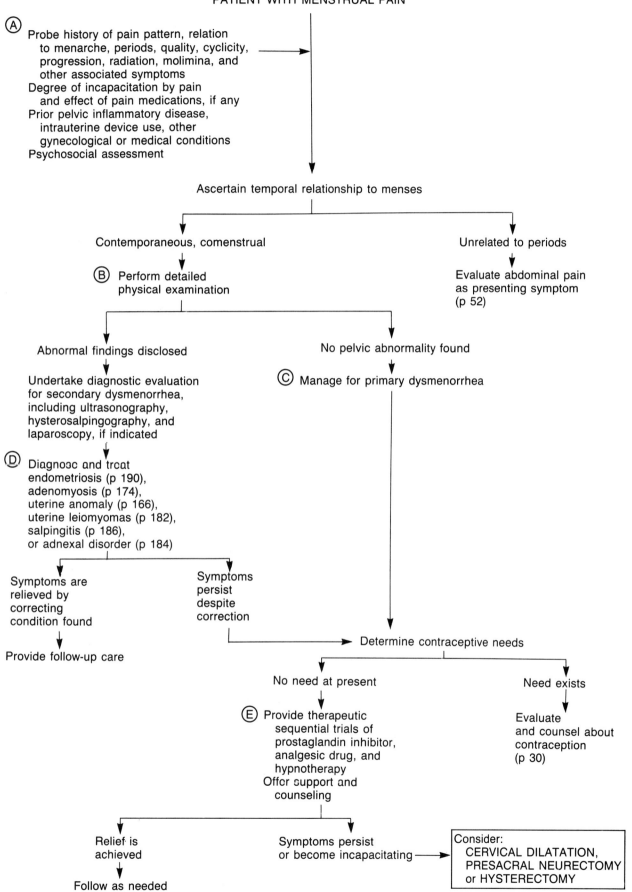

(A) Probe history of pain pattern, relation
to menarche, periods, quality, cyclicity,
progression, radiation, molimina, and
other associated symptoms
Degree of incapacitation by pain
and effect of pain medications, if any
Prior pelvic inflammatory disease,
intrauterine device use, other
gynecological or medical conditions
Psychosocial assessment

Ascertain temporal relationship to menses

Contemporaneous, comenstrual

(B) Perform detailed
physical examination

Unrelated to periods

Evaluate abdominal pain
as presenting symptom
(p 52)

Abnormal findings disclosed

Undertake diagnostic evaluation
for secondary dysmenorrhea,
including ultrasonography,
hysterosalpingography, and
laparoscopy, if indicated

No pelvic abnormality found

(C) Manage for primary dysmenorrhea

(D) Diagnose and treat
endometriosis (p 190),
adenomyosis (p 174),
uterine anomaly (p 166),
uterine leiomyomas (p 182),
salpingitis (p 186),
or adnexal disorder (p 184)

Symptoms are
relieved by
correcting
condition found

Symptoms
persist
despite
correction

Provide follow-up care

Determine contraceptive needs

No need at present

Need exists

(E) Provide therapeutic
sequential trials of
prostaglandin inhibitor,
analgesic drug, and
hypnotherapy
Offer support and
counseling

Evaluate
and counsel about
contraception
(p 30)

Relief is
achieved

Symptoms persist
or become incapacitating

Consider:
CERVICAL DILATATION,
PRESACRAL NEURECTOMY
or HYSTERECTOMY

Follow as needed

PELVIC PAIN

Emanuel A. Friedman, M.D., Sc.D.

A. There are a number of conditions that can cause pelvic pain. Avoid the too common assumption that essentially all pelvic pain represents pelvic inflammatory disease. This very frequent misdiagnosis leads to inappropriate treatment not only for the current episode but for others to come in the future. Once a patient has been labeled with such a diagnosis, she tends to be managed in this light from then on regardless of the fact that the diagnosis may have been made without objective evidence or verification in the first instance. Laparoscopic studies of such cases have shown that diagnostic errors of this kind are made in up to half the cases so designated. Pay attention to the pain pattern in attempting to ascertain the diagnosis. Determine if the pain is acute or chronic and weigh its severity on a scale of mild to incapacitating. Characterize it as crampy, steady, sharp, aching, pulling, stretching, pressure, or burning in nature. Assess its duration, periodicity, location, and radiation. Ask about what initiates or aggravates it, such as menstruation, coitus, or defecation; also learn what relieves or diminishes it, such as medications or position change. The pain pattern and chronology suggest its etiology. Typically, endometriosis is recurrent, progressive, and comenstrual; primary dysmenorrhea is also comenstrual but not progressive and is present in ovulatory cycles only. Intermittent pain reflects obstruction or torsion; constant pain is more likely found with inflammation, infarction, or hemorrhage.

B. Rapid evaluation and management are required for the patient who is in acute distress. Avoid masking changes in the patient's condition by use of sedative-analgesics to provide pain relief. While undoubtedly well intentioned, it may seriously delay recognition of a problem requiring aggressive and timely intervention. Expeditious assessment and appropriate therapy are especially important if the pain-associated condition is progressive or potentially life-threatening. Critically relevant are manifestations of overt or impending shock, peritonitis, intra-abdominal bleeding, or sepsis.

C. Special attention is mandated for evidence of an acute abdominal condition indicating the likelihood that prompt surgical intervention will be needed. Delay under these circumstances is seldom warranted and may jeopardize the patient. Obtain a surgical consultation if a nongynecological disorder, such as acute appendicitis or bowel obstruction, is suspected.

D. Undertake a careful bimanual abdominopelvic examination to help clarify the diagnosis. Evaluate any palpable mass for its location, size, irregularity, mobility, tenderness, fluctuation, and consistency. Try to determine whether it is fixed to or associated with other pelvic organs. A rectal examination and a combined rectovaginal examination are often more useful for assessing the rectovaginal septum, cul-de-sac of Douglas, uterosacral ligaments, and pelvic sidewalls than the vaginal examination.

E. Ultrasonography can be useful for clarifying the cause of the pain. It will help demonstrate the presence of a pelvic mass and provide information as to its nature. It may also diagnose hydroureter secondary to obstruction from a ureteral stone. Radiographic studies tend to be less helpful, but they can also sometimes be of value; they can show bowel obstruction or perforation or disclose teeth in a benign teratoma. Plan the management according to the condition found. Diagnostic laparoscopy is indicated if the diagnosis is still unclear and the patient's symptoms continue.

F. Bear in mind that a nongynecological condition may exist in bowel, urinary tract, or neuromuscular system. Direct the investigation to rule such problems out, if necessary. The patient's pain may be real even if there is no objective laboratory or clinical evidence of any organic cause. A psychosocial evaluation is called for to ascertain an underlying psychosomatic origin. Consultation in related medical disciplines may also be valuable if one suspects other causes. Avoid providing regular analgesics or ataractics because drug dependency can develop. Reserve surgical denervation by presacral neurectomy for use only in patients with incapacitating pain resistant to all conservative efforts and only after all else has failed, but do not expect lasting benefit.

References

Cunanan RG, Courey NG, Lippes J. Laparoscopic findings in patients with pelvic pain. Am J Obstet Gynecol 146:589, 1983.

Lee RB, Stone K, Magelssen D, et al. Presacral neurectomy for chronic pelvic pain. Obstet Gynecol 68:517, 1986.

Slocumb JC. Neurological factors in chronic pelvic pain: Trigger points and the abdominal pelvic pain syndrome. Am J Obstet Gynecol 149:536, 1984.

Spirtos NJ, Bernstine RL, Crawford WL, Fayle J. Sonography in acute pelvic inflammatory disease. J Reprod Med 27:312, 1982.

PATIENT PRESENTING WITH PELVIC PAIN

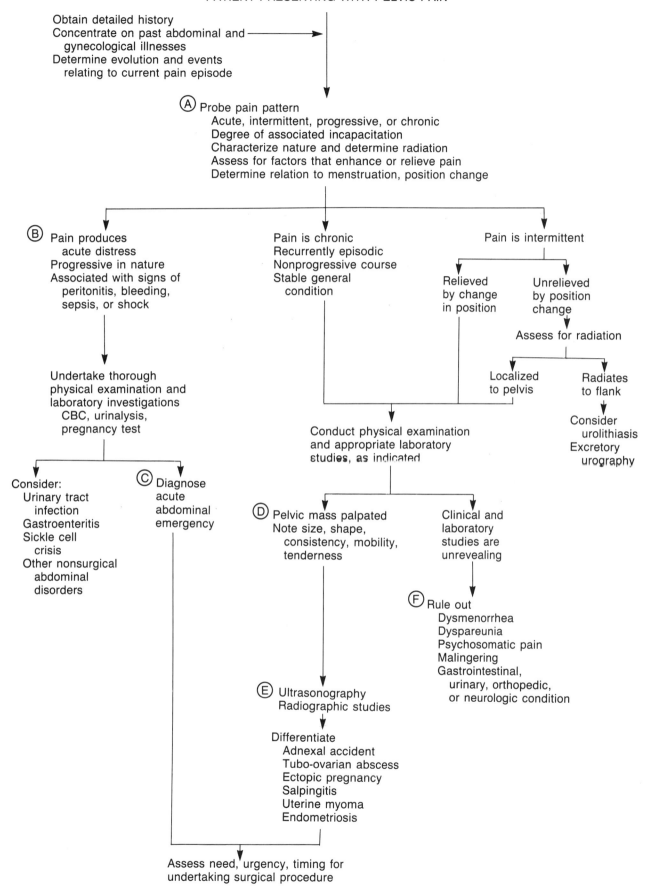

Obtain detailed history
Concentrate on past abdominal and
  gynecological illnesses
Determine evolution and events
  relating to current pain episode

(A) Probe pain pattern
  Acute, intermittent, progressive, or chronic
  Degree of associated incapacitation
  Characterize nature and determine radiation
  Assess for factors that enhance or relieve pain
  Determine relation to menstruation, position change

(B) Pain produces
  acute distress
Progressive in nature
Associated with signs of
  peritonitis, bleeding,
  sepsis, or shock

Pain is chronic
Recurrently episodic
Nonprogressive course
Stable general
  condition

Pain is intermittent

Relieved
by change
in position

Unrelieved
by position
change

Assess for radiation

Localized
to pelvis

Radiates
to flank

Consider
  urolithiasis
Excretory
  urography

Undertake thorough
physical examination and
laboratory investigations
  CBC, urinalysis,
  pregnancy test

Conduct physical examination
and appropriate laboratory
studies, as indicated

Consider:
  Urinary tract
    infection
  Gastroenteritis
  Sickle cell
    crisis
  Other nonsurgical
    abdominal
    disorders

(C) Diagnose
  acute
  abdominal
  emergency

(D) Pelvic mass palpated
Note size, shape,
  consistency, mobility,
  tenderness

Clinical and
laboratory
studies are
unrevealing

(F) Rule out
  Dysmenorrhea
  Dyspareunia
  Psychosomatic pain
  Malingering
  Gastrointestinal,
    urinary, orthopedic,
    or neurologic condition

(E) Ultrasonography
  Radiographic studies

Differentiate
  Adnexal accident
  Tubo-ovarian abscess
  Ectopic pregnancy
  Salpingitis
  Uterine myoma
  Endometriosis

Assess need, urgency, timing for
undertaking surgical procedure

ACUTE ABDOMINAL PAIN

Eric D. Lichter, M.D.

A. A patient who presents with abdominal pain nearly always warrants a comprehensive evaluation to determine the cause and to direct therapy. Persistent or progressive pain demands attention because it may signal an acute intra-abdominal crisis that threatens the patient's life or well-being. Even though delay may contribute discomfort and even enhance the risk somewhat, obtain an accurate and detailed history, if it is at all possible, before undertaking diagnostic tests or beginning any form of treatment. The hazard of such delay, if any, is readily counterbalanced by the risk of proceeding with inappropriate therapeutic measures, thereby allowing a serious disorder to go undiagnosed. In women of reproductive age, the possibility of ectopic pregnancy (p 198) should always be considered and evaluated. The history of contraception, menstrual pattern, and sexual activity is thus essential for the diagnosis. Pay particular attention to a history of prior episodes of similar pain, previous abdominal surgery, and general medical illnesses that might be related or contributory. Do not be deluded by a history of pelvic inflammatory disease, especially if based on nonobjective clinical evidence (p 186), into assuming the current problem merely represents an exacerbation.

B. Extensive laboratory assessment is generally done from the very outset in these cases to establish as quickly as feasible whether one is dealing with an acute surgical problem or a condition that can be effectively and safely treated by a conservative pharmacologic approach. At minimum, complete blood count with differential, urinalysis, erythrocyte sedimentation rate, serum and urine amylase, and blood chemistry and electrolyte determinations will usually be needed. Consider testing for sickle cell disease and porphyrinuria to disclose a possible nonsurgical cause of acute abdominal pain. A pregnancy test is invaluable for diagnosing an ectopic pregnancy. While the radioimmunoassay for beta-subunit human chorionic gonadotropin (hCG) remains the gold standard because of its sensitivity and accuracy, urinary monoclonal antibody tests are faster, more readily available, and have become increasingly more reliable. Ultrasonography is often critical in providing important information to focalize the disease according to the organ system or tissue involved and to identify the nature and extent of the condition. It may be necessary to supplement this information with x-ray studies, as indicated. Upright or lateral decubitus abdominal x-ray exposures, for example, may help identify a ruptured viscus; chest x-ray can show a pleural or pneumonitic process that could be the source of upper abdominal pain; excretory urography will sometimes reveal a renal or ureteral disorder of importance and diagnostic relevance.

C. Study the pain pattern, concentrating on its location, referral, radiation, characteristics, periodicity, progression, changing intensity, duration, and relation to activity, eating, urination, and bowel movement. Probe into other associated symptoms, such as nausea, vomiting, diarrhea, dysuria, and anorexia. Although one may wish to be empathetic, one should generally not give analgesic drugs for pain relief until the diagnosis is reasonably assured. This will avoid masking the clinical findings and thereby delaying definitive therapy.

D. Carry out a complete physical examination. Look for evidence of a systemic disorder and indices of the severity of the presenting problem. Note pallor, cyanosis, tachycardia, tachypnea, fever, chills, and diaphoresis. Examine for bowel sounds, guarding, abdominal distension, and fluid wave, hernia, or mass. Evaluate for direct, referred, and rebound tenderness, noting signs of peritonitis. This will serve to identify a patient with an acute surgical problem and distinguish her from one who can be observed expectantly or treated medically. The vaginal examination helps assess for vaginal bleeding, the status of the pelvic organs, and the presence of any tenderness or mass. Cervical motion tenderness may flag an inflammatory process involving the adnexa. Rectal and rectovaginal examinations aid evaluation of the rectovaginal septum, cul-de-sac of Douglas, and rectum.

References

Cunanan RG Jr, Courey NG, Lippes J. Laparoscopic findings in patients with pelvic pain. Am J Obstet Gynecol 146:589, 1983.

deDombal FT. Analysis of symptoms in the acute abdomen. Clin Gastroenterol 14:531, 1985.

Reiertsen O, Rosseland AR, Hoivik B, Solheim K. Laparoscopy in patients admitted for acute abdominal pain. Acta Chir Scand 151:521, 1985.

Saclarides T, Hopkins W, Doolas A. Abdominal emergencies. Med Clin North Am 70:1093, 1986.

PATIENT WITH SEVERE ABDOMINAL PAIN

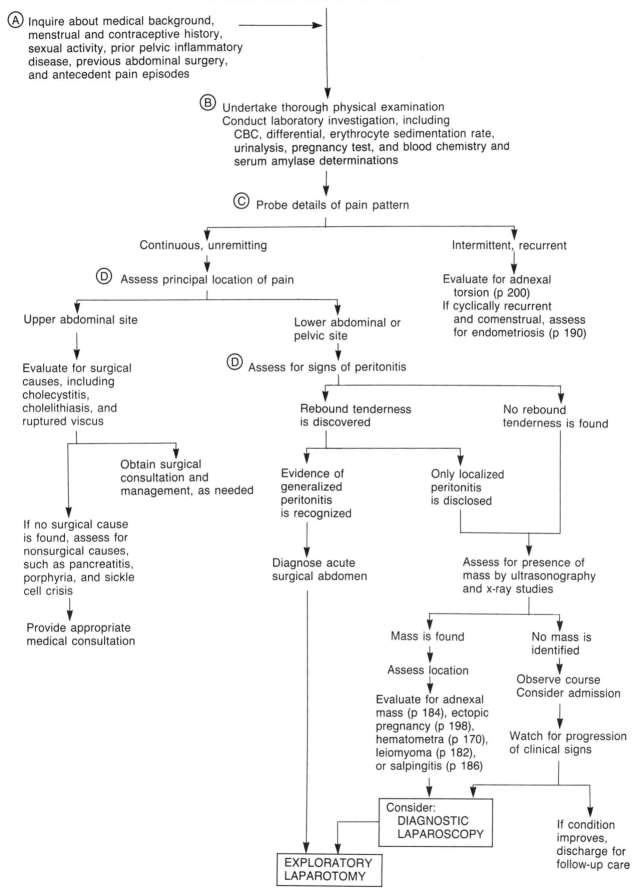

Ⓐ Inquire about medical background, menstrual and contraceptive history, sexual activity, prior pelvic inflammatory disease, previous abdominal surgery, and antecedent pain episodes

Ⓑ Undertake thorough physical examination
Conduct laboratory investigation, including CBC, differential, erythrocyte sedimentation rate, urinalysis, pregnancy test, and blood chemistry and serum amylase determinations

Ⓒ Probe details of pain pattern

Continuous, unremitting

Intermittent, recurrent

Ⓓ Assess principal location of pain

Evaluate for adnexal torsion (p 200)
If cyclically recurrent and comenstrual, assess for endometriosis (p 190)

Upper abdominal site

Lower abdominal or pelvic site

Evaluate for surgical causes, including cholecystitis, cholelithiasis, and ruptured viscus

Ⓓ Assess for signs of peritonitis

Obtain surgical consultation and management, as needed

Rebound tenderness is discovered

No rebound tenderness is found

If no surgical cause is found, assess for nonsurgical causes, such as pancreatitis, porphyria, and sickle cell crisis

Evidence of generalized peritonitis is recognized

Only localized peritonitis is disclosed

Provide appropriate medical consultation

Diagnose acute surgical abdomen

Assess for presence of mass by ultrasonography and x-ray studies

Mass is found

No mass is identified

Assess location

Observe course
Consider admission

Evaluate for adnexal mass (p 184), ectopic pregnancy (p 198), hematometra (p 170), leiomyoma (p 182), or salpingitis (p 186)

Watch for progression of clinical signs

Consider:
DIAGNOSTIC LAPAROSCOPY

If condition improves, discharge for follow-up care

EXPLORATORY LAPAROTOMY

53

INCREASED ABDOMINAL GIRTH

Lenard R. Simon, M.D.

A. There are both physiologic and pathologic causes for a patient's abdominal girth to increase over time. The most common physiologic causes are intrauterine pregnancy and fat deposition due to excess caloric intake. Among the pathologic causes are ascites formation and growth of intra-abdominal benign or malignant tumor. The diagnosis or evaluation of increased abdominal girth by objective criteria is extremely difficult. Even with precise abdominal measurement, there is no accurate way of assessing the degree of increase in abdominal girth. Serial examinations spread over weeks or months would be useful, but they are rarely, if ever, possible to obtain. In practical terms, most patients who present with this complaint will report their clothes, especially fitted skirts or pants, have become tighter around the waist. Characteristically, women with ovarian carcinoma that has disseminated intraperitoneally (p 192) will report wondering why their waistline has increased even though their dietary intake has not changed or has actually decreased somewhat. Because the malignant ascites accompanying carcinoma of the ovary may present in this way, the malignancy having been essentially silent during its early stage of development insofar as any other recognizable signaling symptoms of tumor growth are concerned, it is essential for the physician to be very sensitive to the possible significance of increasing abdominal girth. Obtain historic information about general health and system review, seeking illnesses or symptoms suggestive of cardiac, renal, or hepatic disease. Note weight gain or loss, appetite change, alcohol intake, jaundice, dyspnea and orthopnea, fatigue, and malaise. Menstrual history and associated pregnancy symptoms will flag changing abdominal size due to advancing gestation.

B. Detailed history and physical examination are mandatory first steps in the investigatory process. Note the body distribution of adipose tissue. Look for engorgement of neck veins. Check the breasts carefully. Evaluate the thorax for evidence of pleural effusion or pulmonary congestion. Determine the presence of abdominal distension, fluid wave, hepatomegaly, and palpable or ballotable masses. Examine for palpable lymph nodes in the supraclavicular, axillary, and femoral regions. The pelvic and rectal examinations should be carried out under optimal conditions to ensure detection of an adnexal mass. Remember that even a small ovarian cancer may be the source of malignant ascites. Bulging of the posterior vaginal fornix may indicate the presence of fluid in the cul-de-sac of Douglas. Verify and note any nodularity in this region by rectal or rectovaginal palpation. A Papanicolaou smear may help because cytologic study can detect cancer cells or clusters that have descended from the peritoneal cavity to the vagina by way of the fallopian tubal and uterine lumina. Stool guaiac examination is important as well. Obtain complete blood count, urinalysis, blood chemistry, and electrolyte determinations.

Biochemical and specific organ function profiles, such as liver and renal function tests, may give additional valuable information. Imaging techniques, such as abdominopelvic ultrasonography or computer tomography, aid one to detect and delineate the nature and extent of any masses present or the presence and distribution of fluid within the peritoneal cavity.

C. Invasive procedures, such as paracentesis, must be done under ultrasonographic guidance to avoid injury to adjacent organs. It is essential to prevent perforation of a mass because it will risk spreading infection, tumor, or potentially harmful cyst contents (the very irritating sebaceous material within a dermoid cyst, for example). Take care during paracentesis to drain fluid slowly and thereby avert hypotension and syncope. The fluid obtained should be sent for Gram stained smear, culture, cytologic and cell block evaluation, and biochemical analysis.

D. Even though there is no specific or definitive test to differentiate exudate from transudate, preliminary radionucleide studies have suggested that altered intestinal permeability may be a significant factor in the formation of nonmalignant ascites. Fibronectin concentration in ascitic fluid may also help to differentiate malignant from nonmalignant ascites.

E. Laparoscopy is a safe, simple, and effective tool for obtaining directed biopsies of obvious or suspicious lesions and fluid samples. It is similarly effective for viewing abdominal and pelvic organs in those cases in which a preliminary diagnosis cannot be made by other means or for which there is no clear-cut etiology for the ascites formation. Much information can be obtained in this way pertaining to the presence of tumor, its principal location, and involvement of bowel serosa, omentum, liver surface, or diaphragm. While laparoscopy is unlikely to preclude exploratory laparotomy for ovarian cancer (for staging, extirpation, and debulking), it may facilitate planning and counseling.

References

Aitken RJ, Clifford PC. Girth measurement is not a reliable investigation for the detection of intraabdominal fluid. Ann R Coll Surg 67:241, 1985.

Fairclough JA, Mintowt-Czyz WJ, Mackie I, Nokes L. Abdominal girth: An unreliable measure of intraabdominal bleeding. Injury 16:85, 1984.

Schölmerich J, Volk BA, Köttgen E, et al. Fibronectin concentration in ascites differentiates between malignant and nonmalignant ascites. Gastroenterology 87:1160, 1984.

Souter RG, Wells C, Tarin D, Kettlewell MGW. Surgical and pathologic complications associated with peritoneovenous shunts in the management of malignant ascites. Cancer 55:1973, 1985.

PATIENT WITH RAPID INCREASE OF ABDOMINAL GIRTH

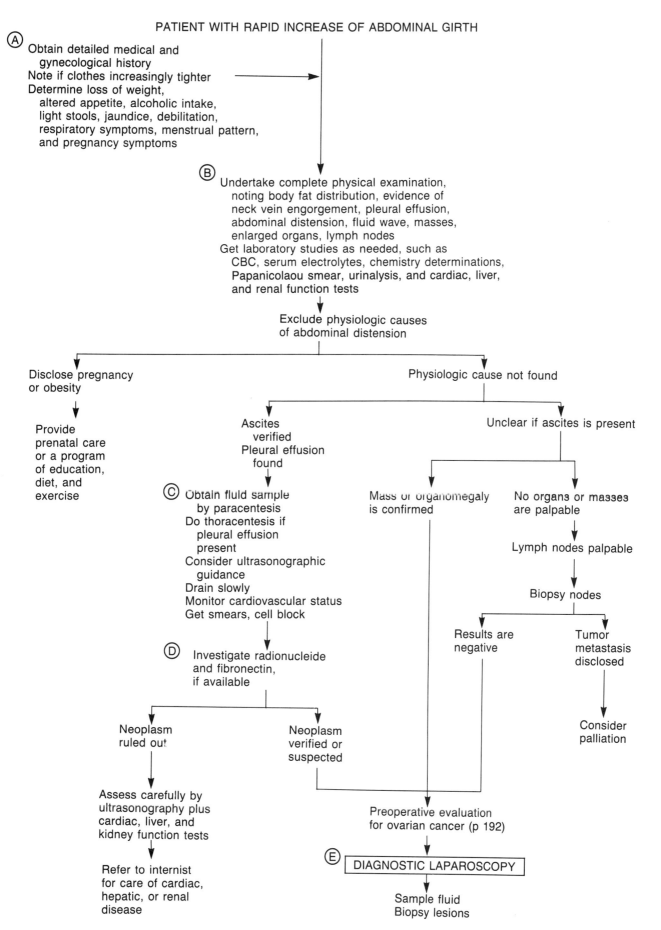

Ⓐ Obtain detailed medical and
   gynecological history
   Note if clothes increasingly tighter
   Determine loss of weight,
     altered appetite, alcoholic intake,
     light stools, jaundice, debilitation,
     respiratory symptoms, menstrual pattern,
     and pregnancy symptoms

Ⓑ Undertake complete physical examination,
   noting body fat distribution, evidence of
   neck vein engorgement, pleural effusion,
   abdominal distension, fluid wave, masses,
   enlarged organs, lymph nodes
   Get laboratory studies as needed, such as
     CBC, serum electrolytes, chemistry determinations,
     Papanicolaou smear, urinalysis, and cardiac, liver,
     and renal function tests

Exclude physiologic causes
of abdominal distension

Disclose pregnancy
or obesity

Provide
prenatal care
or a program
of education,
diet, and
exercise

Physiologic cause not found

Ascites
verified
Pleural effusion
found

Unclear if ascites is present

Ⓒ Obtain fluid sample
   by paracentesis
   Do thoracentesis if
     pleural effusion
     present
   Consider ultrasonographic
     guidance
   Drain slowly
   Monitor cardiovascular status
   Get smears, cell block

Mass or organomegaly
is confirmed

No organs or masses
are palpable

Lymph nodes palpable

Biopsy nodes

Ⓓ Investigate radionucleide
   and fibronectin,
   if available

Results are
negative

Tumor
metastasis
disclosed

Neoplasm
ruled out

Neoplasm
verified or
suspected

Consider
palliation

Assess carefully by
ultrasonography plus
cardiac, liver, and
kidney function tests

Preoperative evaluation
for ovarian cancer (p 192)

Ⓔ DIAGNOSTIC LAPAROSCOPY

Refer to internist
for care of cardiac,
hepatic, or renal
disease

Sample fluid
Biopsy lesions

AMENORRHEA

Machelle M. Seibel, M.D.

A. While the range of normal menarche is great, primary amenorrhea is generally considered to exist if menstruation has not begun by age 16. After puberty, once menstruation has been established, three skipped menstrual periods should be diagnosed as secondary amenorrhea. The most common reason for primary amenorrhea is constitutional. The patient warrants counseling and a full evaluation to rule out some organic or functional disorder. The most frequently encountered cause of secondary amenorrhea is pregnancy, for which one must be alert (see C). Also consider cryptic menstruation in an adolescent who may have an anomaly of the lower genital tract, such as a cervical stenosis (p 160) or imperforate hymen (p 140), preventing outflow and perhaps forming a hematometra (p 170) or hematocolpos. This may be associated with transtubal retrograde peritoneal spillage, potentially leading to inflammatory reaction or even endometriosis. Probe for a history of recurrent periodic pelvic pain with premenstrual molimina (p 42). Inquire about general medical illnesses, drug abuse, weight loss, dietary faddism, and exercise programs. Women who exercise to an extreme or are markedly thin disturb their hormonal homeostasis and become anovulatory and amenorrheic.

B. Undertake a general physical examination to detect evidence of an underlying correctable cause, evaluating for secondary sexual development, nutritional status, endocrinopathy, and debilitating disease. Carefully check the breasts for galactorrhea (p 70). Prolonged amenorrhea, especially in conjunction with hyperprolactinemia, may be associated with osteoporosis. A pelvic examination is essential for disclosing the presence of an anomaly of the lower genital tract. Watch for a bulging perineum or cystic mass indicative of hematocolpos. Note short stature, webbed neck, shield chest, and cubitus valgus of Turner's syndrome. Examine the inguinal region and labia for masses that may represent undescended testes; when present in a feminized patient with little body or pubic hair, consider the androgen insensitivity syndrome of testicular feminization.

C. Because pregnancy is the most common reason for amenorrhea, one must assess for it before proceeding with any other form of evaluation or care. In addition to gathering information from the history and physical examination for this purpose, laboratory assessment is appropriate (p 14).

D. Hyperprolactinemia can cause anovulation and amenorrhea, whether from a pituitary adenoma or not, although it seldom becomes clinically manifest until the serum prolactin level reaches 25 ng per milliliter or more. Referral for neuroendocrine investigation is indicated for patients with prolactin determinations of 100 ng per milliliter or greater because they are likely to have an identifiable pituitary adenoma (see G) requiring suppressive therapy with bromocriptine or even neurosurgery. Because elevated thyrotropin releasing hormone (TRH) or early hypothyroidism also raises prolactin in serum, determine the thyroid stimulating hormone (TSH) level before proceeding.

E. Pituitary x-ray study with a single cone-down view of the sella turcica may suffice for disclosing the presence of an enlarged gland or an adenoma, but it is not very sensitive. Magnetic resonance imaging and computer tomography scanning have now almost entirely replaced sella tomography because of their better resolution and lower exposure to radiation dosage. The relative risk-benefit relationship of surgical versus medical management of a patient with pituitary adenoma is not yet fully settled. Both forms of therapy have their advocates.

F. Progestins are often effective in demonstrating endometrial end-organ responsiveness by yielding a menstrual type flow secondary to progesterone withdrawal. It requires preliminary priming of the endometrial lining by intrinsic estrogens. Give either Provera, 10 mg daily by mouth for five days, or one dose of progesterone in oil, 100 mg intramuscularly. Withdrawal bleeding establishes the diagnosis of anovulation (p 124); the failure to achieve withdrawal bleeding warrants more intensive endocrinologic evaluation.

G. Assess pituitary gonadotropin function by determining luteinizing hormone (LH) and follicle stimulating hormone (FSH) levels. If they are high, ovarian failure exists. If levels are low to normal, hypothalamic amenorrhea (p 124) is probably the problem.

References

Bullen BA, Skrinar GS, Beitins IZ, et al. Induction of menstrual disorders by strenuous exercise in untrained women. N Engl J Med 312:1349, 1985.

Davis PC, Hoffman JC, Tindall GT, Braun IF. CT-surgical correlation in pituitary adenomas: Evaluation in 113 patients. Am J Neuroradiol 6:711, 1985.

Kase NG. The neuroendocrinology of amenorrhea. J Reprod Med 28:251, 1983.

Kilbanski A, Greenspan SL. Increase in bone mass after treatment of hyperprolactinemic amenorrhea. N Engl J Med 315:542, 1986.

Seibel MM, Taymor ML. Emotional aspects of infertility. Fertil Steril 37:137, 1982.

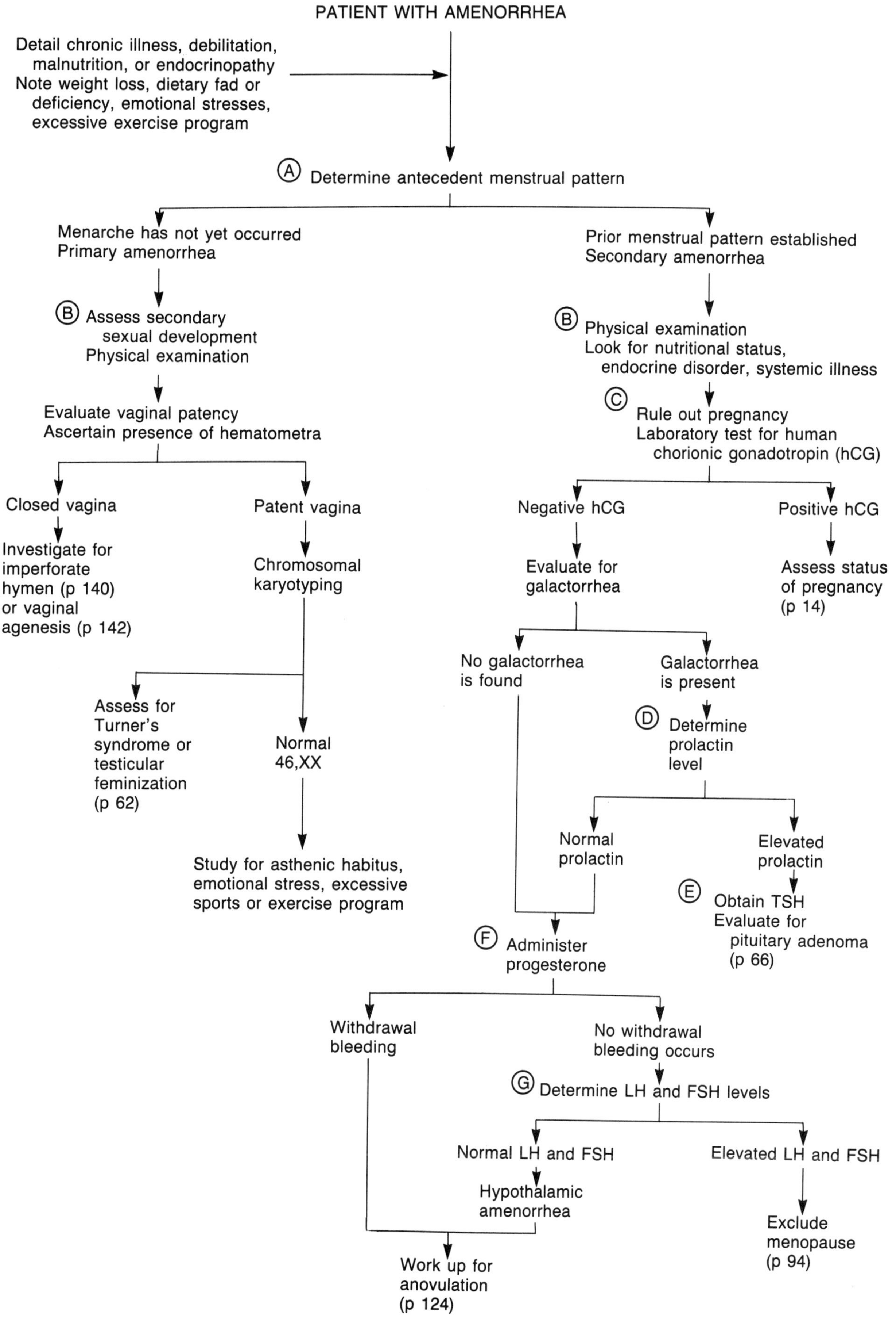

PATIENT WITH AMENORRHEA

Detail chronic illness, debilitation,
malnutrition, or endocrinopathy
Note weight loss, dietary fad or
deficiency, emotional stresses,
excessive exercise program

(A) Determine antecedent menstrual pattern

Menarche has not yet occurred
Primary amenorrhea

Prior menstrual pattern established
Secondary amenorrhea

(B) Assess secondary
sexual development
Physical examination

(B) Physical examination
Look for nutritional status,
endocrine disorder, systemic illness

Evaluate vaginal patency
Ascertain presence of hematometra

(C) Rule out pregnancy
Laboratory test for human
chorionic gonadotropin (hCG)

Closed vagina

Patent vagina

Negative hCG

Positive hCG

Investigate for
imperforate
hymen (p 140)
or vaginal
agenesis (p 142)

Chromosomal
karyotyping

Evaluate for
galactorrhea

Assess status
of pregnancy
(p 14)

No galactorrhea
is found

Galactorrhea
is present

Assess for
Turner's
syndrome or
testicular
feminization
(p 62)

Normal
46,XX

(D) Determine
prolactin
level

Normal
prolactin

Elevated
prolactin

Study for asthenic habitus,
emotional stress, excessive
sports or exercise program

(E) Obtain TSH
Evaluate for
pituitary adenoma
(p 66)

(F) Administer
progesterone

Withdrawal
bleeding

No withdrawal
bleeding occurs

(G) Determine LH and FSH levels

Normal LH and FSH

Elevated LH and FSH

Hypothalamic
amenorrhea

Exclude
menopause
(p 94)

Work up for
anovulation
(p 124)

AMBIGUOUS GENITALIA

Jerold M. Carlson, M.D., M.P.H.

A. Be especially sensitive to the potential emotional impact of ambiguous genitalia. Evaluate in depth, seeking expert consultation to avoid an error that may affect sexual identity and upbringing. Delay the assignment of sex rather than risk such error. Nearly all cases are due to either excessive embryonic exposure of the female fetus to androgens or inadequate androgenic exposure or tissue sensitivity in the male fetus. Obtain a comprehensive medical history of early intrauterine exposure to virilizing drugs or hormones. The risks of virilizing the female fetus by oral contraceptives are generally negligible. Inquire about a family history of endocrinopathy or metabolic disease. In the newborn infant, watch especially for signs of adrenal failure, including dehydration, vomiting, diarrhea, electrolyte imbalance, and shock.

B. Try to diagnose fetal abnormalities early in gravidas who are at special risk. Consider amniocentesis to examine amniotic fluid for human leukocyte antigen and steroid hormone levels. These may help detect congenital adrenal hyperplasia (see C). Following birth, examine every newborn infant carefully to detect any apparent anomalies of the genitalia. Check the internal pelvic organs by rectal palpation and look for abdominal, inguinal, or labial masses.

C. Female pseudohermaphroditism is characterized by virilization of a genetic female with otherwise normal tubes, ovaries, uterus, and upper vagina. The effect may vary from clitoral hypertrophy alone or labial fusion to the formation of a urogenital sinus or even a penile urethra with scrotum. It results from embryonic exposure to excessive androgen. Although the androgen excess may be derived from the mother (as from androgen-secreting tumor or drug intake), it is more often the product of the fetal adrenal glands. A number of enzyme deficiencies can cause congenital adrenal hyperplasia, but deficiency of 21-hydroxylase is the most common. Laboratory studies show increased urinary 17-ketosteroids and reduced 17-hydroxycorticosteroids. These patients can often be managed effectively not only to correct their anatomic defects, but to ensure their ability to reproduce as well. Watch for electrolyte imbalance because some may have an accompanying salt-losing syndrome, which can be quite serious if untreated.

D. Mixed gonadal dysgenesis is a syndrome of ambiguous genitalia in which testicular tissue exists. It is usually associated with chromosomal mosaicism, although this may not always be possible to demonstrate by karyotyping. These patients deserve exploratory surgery to find and remove all testicular tissue. This will facilitate raising the child as a female. Even if assigned a male sex role, however, gonadectomy averts the cancer risk (see F).

E. The patient with both ovarian and testicular tissues is a true hermaphrodite. The structures may be separate as an ovary and a contralateral intra-abdominal testis or combined as an ovotestis. The condition may result from nondisjunction, chimerism, translocation, or mutant genes. Because external virilization is the usual effect, sex assignment is generally male. Karyotyping may show female or mosaic patterns (infrequently male). It is essential to identify and resect the testicular tissue because of the malignant potential.

F. Pure gonadal dysgenesis is associated with sexual infantilism and streak gonads. As distinct from patients with gonadal dysgenesis due to Turner's syndrome, who have characteristic short stature, web neck, and 45,X (or XO) karyotype, these may show male, female, or mosaic patterns. The condition may be transmitted in an X-linked recessive fashion. Neoplastic transformation is very common; because gonadoblastoma or dysgerminoma occurs in half the cases, prophylactic resection is indicated. The reason for this predisposition to malignancy is unclear, but it may be related to poor tissue differentiation or abnormality of receptors.

G. Genetic males (46,XY karyotype) with male gonads, usually undescended testes, but with phenotypic female characteristics (except for diminished or absent body hair) are male pseudohermaphrodites. Consider the possibility in a case with absent uterus and short vagina or in a girl with inguinal hernias. The syndrome of testicular feminization or androgen insensitivity, consistent with failed virilization, may be transmitted in an X-linked recessive fashion. Affected patients are best reared as females, recognizing they are irrevocably sterile but nonetheless female in other respects. The high cancer potential requires surgical extirpation of the testes.

References

Byrne GC, Perry YS, Winter JSD. Kinetic analysis of adrenal 3β-hydroxysteroid dehydrogenase activity during human development. J Clin Endocrinol Metab 60:934, 1985.

Lee PA, Migeon CJ, Bias WB, Jones GS. Familial hypersecretion of adrenal androgens transmitted as a dominant, non-HLA linked trait. Obstet Gynecol 69:259, 1987.

Savage MO. Ambiguous genitalia, small genitalia and undescended testes. Clin Endocrinol Metab 11:127, 1982.

Simpson JL, Golbus MS, Martin AO, Sarto GE. Genetics in Obstetrics and Gynecology. New York: Grune & Stratton, 1982.

NEWBORN INFANT WITH ABNORMAL OR UNCLEAR GENITALIA

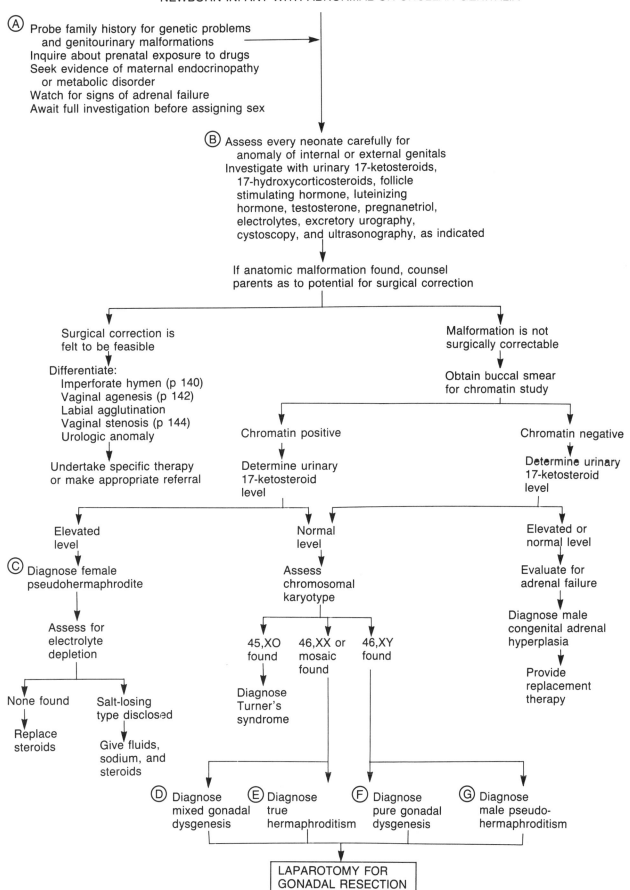

Ⓐ Probe family history for genetic problems
   and genitourinary malformations
Inquire about prenatal exposure to drugs
Seek evidence of maternal endocrinopathy
   or metabolic disorder
Watch for signs of adrenal failure
Await full investigation before assigning sex

Ⓑ Assess every neonate carefully for
   anomaly of internal or external genitals
Investigate with urinary 17-ketosteroids,
   17-hydroxycorticosteroids, follicle
   stimulating hormone, luteinizing
   hormone, testosterone, pregnanetriol,
   electrolytes, excretory urography,
   cystoscopy, and ultrasonography, as indicated

If anatomic malformation found, counsel
parents as to potential for surgical correction

Surgical correction is
felt to be feasible

Differentiate:
   Imperforate hymen (p 140)
   Vaginal agenesis (p 142)
   Labial agglutination
   Vaginal stenosis (p 144)
   Urologic anomaly

Undertake specific therapy
or make appropriate referral

Malformation is not
surgically correctable

Obtain buccal smear
for chromatin study

Chromatin positive

Determine urinary
17-ketosteroid
level

Chromatin negative

Determine urinary
17-ketosteroid
level

Elevated
level

Ⓒ Diagnose female
pseudohermaphrodite

Assess for
electrolyte
depletion

None found

Replace
steroids

Salt-losing
type disclosed

Give fluids,
sodium, and
steroids

Normal
level

Assess
chromosomal
karyotype

45,XO
found

46,XX or
mosaic
found

46,XY
found

Diagnose
Turner's
syndrome

Elevated or
normal level

Evaluate for
adrenal failure

Diagnose male
congenital adrenal
hyperplasia

Provide
replacement
therapy

Ⓓ Diagnose
mixed gonadal
dysgenesis

Ⓔ Diagnose
true
hermaphroditism

Ⓕ Diagnose
pure gonadal
dysgenesis

Ⓖ Diagnose
male pseudo-
hermaphroditism

LAPAROTOMY FOR
GONADAL RESECTION

SEXUAL PRECOCITY

Jerold M. Carlson, M.D., M.P.H.

A. Typically, puberty begins with the appearance of the breast bud (Fig. 1) followed by pubic hair; height spurt takes place later; and development of axillary hair and menarche does not occur until still later between ages 10.5 and 15.5 years. Sexual precocity refers to this process beginning too soon, or by clinical definition before age 8. The sequence is often heralded by growth in stature, although all manifestations may occur simultaneously or, infrequently, menarche may appear first. True sexual precocity results from hormones derived from the patient's own maturing ovary; pseudoprecocious puberty is not associated with normally maturing gonads. Although true or constitutional precocious puberty is by far the more common, it is diagnosed by exclusion. It is necessary to investigate each case in depth to rule out the potentially serious disorders that cause the pseudoprecocious type, such as estrogen-secreting or virilizing ovarian or adrenal lesions, congenital adrenal hyperplasia, chorionepitheliomas, central nervous system tumors, hypothyroidism, and exogenous intake of hormones.

B. Probe thoroughly into the patient's medical and family history, inquiring about drug exposure, head trauma, and encephalitis or other neurologic disease. Undertake a detailed physical examination as well, looking for signs of secondary sexual maturation, accelerated growth, thyroid function disorder, virilization, and neurologic manifestations. Examine especially carefully for any indication of the presence of an ovarian, adrenal, or brain lesion.

C. Search for the source by objective investigation with ultrasonography, intravenous pyelography, computer tomography, and barium enema. If a tumor is identified, laparotomy or neurosurgical exploration may be needed for definitive diagnosis.

D. Evidence of virilization (p 64) requires one to differentiate between congenital adrenal hyperplasia and a virilizing adrenal or ovarian tumor. Assess the adrenal status by ultrasonography and determinations of urinary 17-ketosteroids (17-KS), plasma 17-hydroxyprogesterone, testosterone, and dehydroepiandrosterone sulfate (DHEAS) levels. DHEAS is high with an adrenal tumor. Dexamethasone suppression of 17-KS or DHEAS verifies congenital adrenal hyperplasia.

E. A variety of central nervous system tumors can be responsible for precocious puberty. Examine for them by electroencephalography, skull x-ray studies, and computer tomography scan. Neurosurgical extirpation or radiation is generally done if one is disclosed. Look for other neurologically related causes such as epilepsy, head trauma, intracranial infection, neurofibromatosis, McCune-Albright syndrome (polyostotic fibrous dysplasia), and hydrocephalus.

F. The most common form of precocious puberty, accounting for up to 90 percent of cases, is constitutional. To make this diagnosis, however, all other possible causes must first be ruled out. The goal of treatment is to inhibit sexual and bone maturation. Halting epiphyseal closure will avert short stature. A progestational agent is administered (such as medroxyprogesterone, 400 mg intramuscularly every one to three months) until the time of expected normal puberty. Alternatively, danazol may be used, but its androgenic side effects may prove troublesome.

G. Although not yet widely available, idiopathic precocious puberty may be successfully treated with luteinizing hormone releasing hormone (LHRH) analogues. Future use of these agents may completely alter the treatment of certain endocrinologic and menstrual abnormalities, endometriosis, leiomyomas, breast tumors, and may perhaps affect ovulation induction and contraceptive practices. Both LHRH agonists and antagonists exist, but the agonists have thus far proved clinically more useful due to their potency. The agonists act by production of hypoestrogenic state, thereby ameliorating estrogen dependent disorders. Paradoxically, they decrease the gonadotropin release first. However, with sustained use and high dosage, the agonist causes pituitary desensitization of gonadotropin releasing hormone (GnRH), down-regulation of GnRH receptors, and decreased follicle stimulating hormone (FSH), luteinizing hormone (LH), and plasma estrogen. Long-term studies are still needed to evaluate the safety and efficacy of these medications more fully.

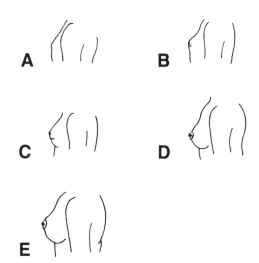

Figure 1 Stages of human breast development during adolescence from preadolescent elevation of papilla (A) to breast bud stage (B), growth of glandular and areolar elements (C), projection of areola and papilla (D), and full maturity with projection of papilla only.

References

Comite F, Cutler GB Jr, Rivier J, et al. Short-term treatment of idiopathic precocious puberty with a long-acting analogue of luteinizing hormone-releasing hormone. N Engl J Med 305:1546, 1981.

CHILD WITH EARLY SEXUAL DEVELOPMENT

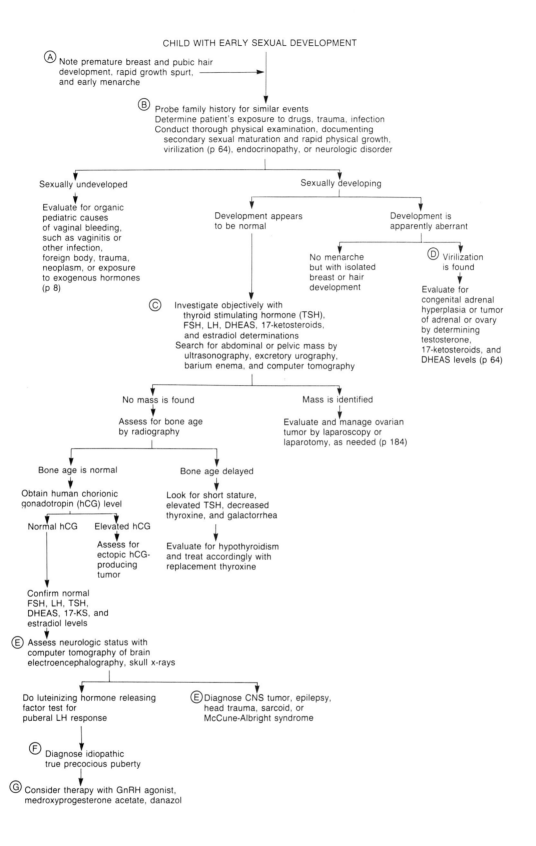

Ⓐ Note premature breast and pubic hair development, rapid growth spurt, and early menarche

Ⓑ Probe family history for similar events
Determine patient's exposure to drugs, trauma, infection
Conduct thorough physical examination, documenting secondary sexual maturation and rapid physical growth, virilization (p 64), endocrinopathy, or neurologic disorder

Sexually undeveloped

Evaluate for organic pediatric causes of vaginal bleeding, such as vaginitis or other infection, foreign body, trauma, neoplasm, or exposure to exogenous hormones (p 8)

Sexually developing

Development appears to be normal

Development is apparently aberrant

No menarche but with isolated breast or hair development

Ⓓ Virilization is found

Evaluate for congenital adrenal hyperplasia or tumor of adrenal or ovary by determining testosterone, 17-ketosteroids, and DHEAS levels (p 64)

Ⓒ Investigate objectively with thyroid stimulating hormone (TSH), FSH, LH, DHEAS, 17-ketosteroids, and estradiol determinations
Search for abdominal or pelvic mass by ultrasonography, excretory urography, barium enema, and computer tomography

No mass is found

Assess for bone age by radiography

Mass is identified

Evaluate and manage ovarian tumor by laparoscopy or laparotomy, as needed (p 184)

Bone age is normal

Obtain human chorionic gonadotropin (hCG) level

Bone age delayed

Look for short stature, elevated TSH, decreased thyroxine, and galactorrhea

Normal hCG

Elevated hCG

Assess for ectopic hCG-producing tumor

Evaluate for hypothyroidism and treat accordingly with replacement thyroxine

Confirm normal FSH, LH, TSH, DHEAS, 17-KS, and estradiol levels

Ⓔ Assess neurologic status with computer tomography of brain electroencephalography, skull x-rays

Do luteinizing hormone releasing factor test for puberal LH response

Ⓔ Diagnose CNS tumor, epilepsy, head trauma, sarcoid, or McCune-Albright syndrome

Ⓕ Diagnose idiopathic true precocious puberty

Ⓖ Consider therapy with GnRH agonist, medroxyprogesterone acetate, danazol

Ducharme JR, Collu R. Pubertal development: Normal, precocious and delayed. Clin Endocrinol Metab 11:57, 1982.

McLachlan RI, Healy DL, Burger HG. Clinical aspects of LHRH analogues in gynecology: A review. Br J Obstet Gynaecol 93:431, 1986.

Pescovitz OH, Comite F, Hench K, et al. The NIH experience with precocious puberty: Diagnosis subgroups and response to short-term luteinizing hormone releasing hormone analogue therapy. J Pediatr 108:47, 1986.

Styne DM, Harris DA, Egli CA, et al. Treatment of true precocious puberty with a potent luteinizing hormone-releasing factor agonist: Effect on growth, sexual maturation, pelvic sonography, and the hypothalamic-pituitary-gonadal axis. J Clin Endocrinol Metab 61:142, 1985.

DELAYED PUBERTY

Jerold M. Carlson, M.D., M.P.H.

A. There is a wide range of biologic variation as to the age puberty normally begins, but the absence of any signs of secondary sexual development by age 14 is generally accepted as abnormal, even though some otherwise normal girls may delay puberty until even later. While menarche is a late manifestation, it is rare for it not to take place by age 18. Maturation usually begins with breast and pubic hair development, followed by the appearance of axillary hair and a growth spurt, and later by menarche. Although the delay in onset may merely be a normal variant, the concern that brought the patient to seek help is sufficient to warrant an evaluation to ascertain if a problem exists. One must consider the possibility of a genetic defect or a disturbance affecting hypothalamic or pituitary function. To pursue it, delve into the family history of congenital anomalies, disorders of puberty, and endocrinopathies, and the patient's nutritional and psychosocial assessment. Perform a thorough physical examination with special attention to neurologic, cardiopulmonary, renal, and gastrointestinal status, and objectively document the lack of sexual development. Rule out apparent endocrinopathy or metabolic disorder.

B. Undertake a detailed pelvic examination to disclose the presence of a genital anomaly, particularly one involving agenesis or obstruction. While delayed sexual maturation does not usually occur in girls with these malformations, it is important to ensure that the genital anatomy is normal. Serious systemic disorders may also be responsible and should be searched for in these cases.

C. Turner's syndrome (45,X karyotype) is one of several variants of gonadal dysgenesis. Failure of gonadal development yields streak gonads without oocytes. The affected patient tends to have underdeveloped sexual characteristics; she is short in stature with a shield type chest, cubitus valgus, and webbed neck. Chromosome analysis is needed to disclose mosaic patterns. These patients may be effectively treated with estrogen replacement to help induce secondary sexual development.

D. Androgen insensitivity with a male (46,XY) chromatin pattern seldom causes delayed puberty. Except for ambiguous genitalia (p 58), these individuals generally mature in a timely manner into typical female phenotypes. Their testicular tissue is at risk of neoplastic degeneration and therefore requires detection and resection.

E. Although most pituitary adenomas do not cause symptoms, large ones may reduce the temporal visual fields and cause headaches. A detailed neurologic examination should be done as well as skull x-rays, brain scan, and computer tomography to detect a craniopharyngioma, germinoma, or chromophobe prolactin-secreting adenoma. Appropriate neurosurgical management will follow.

F. Low follicle stimulating (FSH) and luteinizing hormone (LH) levels with hypogonadism may represent a variety of gonadotropin deficiency syndromes, including those related to central nervous system disorders, panhypopituitarism, and systemic or metabolic conditions. Idiopathic hypopituitarism is often associated with isolated growth hormone deficiency. If the patient is obese and mentally retarded, consider Prader-Willi (carbohydrate intolerance and short stature) or Laurence-Moon-Biedl (retinitis pigmentosa and polydactyly) syndrome as a likely diagnosis. Obesity and diabetes insipidus suggest Hand-Schüller-Christian disease. Use of luteinizing hormone releasing factor (LRF) may differentiate these patients from those with constitutionally delayed puberty. Essentially no response in gonadotropin levels can be expected in patients with gonadotropin deficiency. These cases are best treated with pulsed LRF administered by pump to stimulate gonadotropin release and ultimately induce puberty.

G. Because constitutionally delayed puberty runs in families, be alert to the problem in close relatives. Short stature is common among them, although they are all generally normal in all other respects. Delayed bone age is characteristic. The diagnosis is made by excluding all other possible causes. Affected patients can be reassured and managed expectantly or perhaps given estrogen replacement if they are unduly concerned.

References

Crowley WF Jr, Filicori M, Spratt DI, Santoro NF. The physiology of gonadotropin-releasing hormone (GnRH) secretion in men and women. Recent Prog Horm Res 41:473, 1985.

Ducharme JR, Collu R. Pubertal development: Normal, precocious and delayed. Clin Endocrinol Metab 11:57, 1982.

Stanhope R, Adams J, Brooks CG. Disturbances of puberty. Clin Obstet Gynaecol 12:557, 1985.

Wagner TOF, Brabant G, Warsch F, et al. Pulsatile gonadotropin-releasing hormone treatment in idiopathic delayed puberty. J Clin Endocrinol Metab 62:95, 1986.

PATIENT WITH DELAYED PUBERTY

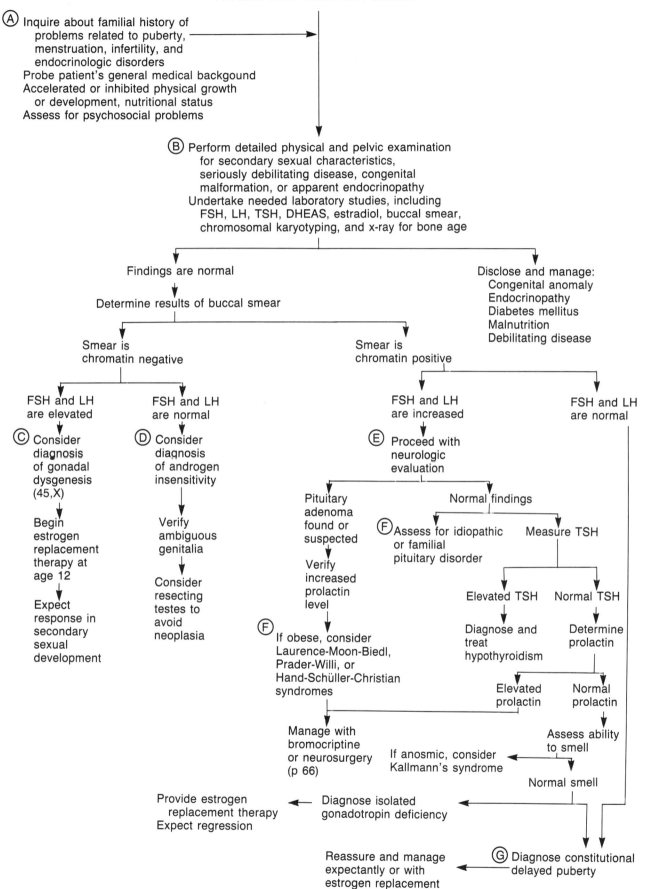

A. Inquire about familial history of problems related to puberty, menstruation, infertility, and endocrinologic disorders
Probe patient's general medical background
Accelerated or inhibited physical growth or development, nutritional status
Assess for psychosocial problems

B. Perform detailed physical and pelvic examination for secondary sexual characteristics, seriously debilitating disease, congenital malformation, or apparent endocrinopathy
Undertake needed laboratory studies, including FSH, LH, TSH, DHEAS, estradiol, buccal smear, chromosomal karyotyping, and x-ray for bone age

Findings are normal

Determine results of buccal smear

Disclose and manage:
Congenital anomaly
Endocrinopathy
Diabetes mellitus
Malnutrition
Debilitating disease

Smear is chromatin negative

Smear is chromatin positive

FSH and LH are elevated

FSH and LH are normal

FSH and LH are increased

FSH and LH are normal

C. Consider diagnosis of gonadal dysgenesis (45,X)

Begin estrogen replacement therapy at age 12

Expect response in secondary sexual development

D. Consider diagnosis of androgen insensitivity

Verify ambiguous genitalia

Consider resecting testes to avoid neoplasia

E. Proceed with neurologic evaluation

Pituitary adenoma found or suspected

Normal findings

F. Assess for idiopathic or familial pituitary disorder

Measure TSH

Verify increased prolactin level

Elevated TSH

Normal TSH

F. If obese, consider Laurence-Moon-Biedl, Prader-Willi, or Hand-Schüller-Christian syndromes

Diagnose and treat hypothyroidism

Determine prolactin

Elevated prolactin

Normal prolactin

Manage with bromocriptine or neurosurgery (p 66)

If anosmic, consider Kallmann's syndrome

Assess ability to smell

Normal smell

Provide estrogen replacement therapy
Expect regression

Diagnose isolated gonadotropin deficiency

Reassure and manage expectantly or with estrogen replacement

G. Diagnose constitutional delayed puberty

VIRILIZATION

Jerold M. Carlson, M.D., M.P.H.

A. Signs of virilization range from relatively common hirsutism to very rare full masculinization. Most affected patients present with minor evidence, but their distress justifies investigation of their complaint. Excessive terminal hair growth reflects an androgenic effect. It may be constitutional or appear during periods of endocrinologic change, such as pregnancy or climacterium. Probe into family history and familial characteristics. Review the personal medical background in detail, noting especially the menstrual pattern (onset and alteration over time), voice change, and dermatologic problems. Note the age of onset, duration, and severity of the presenting symptoms. Inquire about medications as well, especially noting any that might be androgenic. Virilization in a female child or adolescent is indicative of some underlying disease process.

B. Conduct a thorough physical examination to assess the extent and degree of virilization. Assess the distribution of body and facial hair. Look for temporal balding, acne, clitoromegaly, and evidence of Cushing's disease (moon face, malar flush, truncal obesity, buffalo hump, and striae) or other endocrinopathy.

C. Dehydroepiandrosterone sulfate (DHEAS) levels are increased with adrenal hyperplasia or tumor of the adrenal or pituitary. To differentiate between them, administer a low-dose dexamethasone suppression test. This is done by giving dexamethasone 0.5 mg every six hours for five to seven days. Androgen production by adrenal hyperplasia will generally be effectively suppressed, while that from a neoplasm will not. However, interpret the results of this test with caution in patients who are receiving concurrent hormone medications or who have other coexisting medical or psychiatric disorders. A high-dose dexamethasone regimen (2.0 mg every six hours for 48 hours) may be useful for identifying patients with Cushing's syndrome or an adrenocorticotropic hormone (ACTH)-producing tumor.

D. Elevated serum ACTH concentrations signify the presence of a pituitary tumor. Neurosurgical consultation is warranted for evaluation and verification. Craniotomy or transsphenoidal approach is then done for extirpation of the lesion by hypophysectomy.

E. Adrenal tumors are associated with low ACTH levels. Intravenous pyelography (IVP), computer tomography (CT), and arteriography may be needed to show the site. Alternatively, blood samples can be obtained from the adrenal veins by retrograde transfemoral catheterization.

F. A number of enzyme deficiencies can cause adrenal hyperplasia. The one encountered most often involves 21-hydroxylase, the principal enzyme responsible for adrenal synthesis of cortisol; failure of this pathway increases ACTH in compensatory fashion, and this in turn increases 17-hydroxyprogesterone. An 11β-hydroxylase deficiency is encountered less frequently. It affects the last part of the steroidogenesis sequence leading to the synthesis of cortisol and corticosterone. ACTH is increased as a result along with 11-deoxycortisol. Increased 11-deoxycorticosterone production may cause hypertension. These patients need to be treated with enough replacement glucocorticoids to inhibit ACTH secretion and thereby suppress adrenal androgen production. This can usually be accomplished with a regimen of prednisone (5.0 mg nightly plus 2.5 mg every morning) or dexamethasone (0.5 mg nightly).

G. If the ovary proves to be the source of the increased testosterone, try cyclic suppression with oral contraceptives. If the androgen is adrenal in origin, a glucocorticoid is used (see E). Progestational agents or spironolactone may also be effective. Weight reduction programs should be undertaken in appropriate candidates.

H. Consider the probability of an ovarian androgen-producing lesion in cases with very high testosterone levels (but normal DHEAS). Catheterizing the ovarian veins bilaterally (via transfemoral puncture) will help determine which ovary is the site. Ultrasonography and computer tomography may verify the presence of a unilateral mass; laparoscopy can provide additional useful information, if needed. If an ovarian tumor is identified, undertake exploratory laparotomy for definitive resection. Bilateral ovarian sources are improbably tumors; hyperthecosis (ovarian stromal luteinization) is more likely to be the cause. Estrogen suppression (with clomiphene) is usually corrective. Bilateral oophorectomy is generally reserved for the older patient with another concurrent pelvic pathologic condition.

References

Hatch R, Rosenfield RL, Kim MH, Tredway D. Hirsutism: Implications, etiology, and management. Am J Obstet Gynecol 140:815, 1981.

McKenna TJ, Cunningham SK, Loughlin T. The adrenal cortex and virilization. Clin Endocrinol Metab 14:997, 1985.

Wild RA, Umstot ES, Andersen RN, et al. Androgen parameters and their correlation with body weight in one hundred thirty-eight women thought to have hyperandrogenism. Am J Obstet Gynecol 146:602, 1983.

Yen SSC, Jaffe RB. Reproductive Endocrinology. 2nd Ed. Philadelphia: W.B. Saunders, 1986.

PATIENT WITH HIRSUTISM AND OTHER SIGNS OF ANDROGEN EXCESS

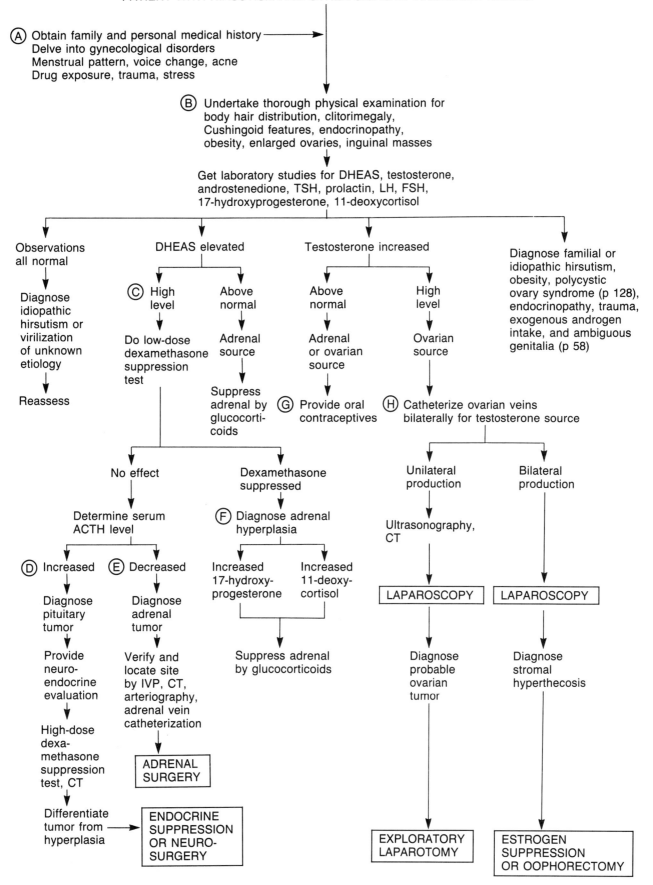

(A) Obtain family and personal medical history
Delve into gynecological disorders
Menstrual pattern, voice change, acne
Drug exposure, trauma, stress

(B) Undertake thorough physical examination for
body hair distribution, clitorimegaly,
Cushingoid features, endocrinopathy,
obesity, enlarged ovaries, inguinal masses

Get laboratory studies for DHEAS, testosterone,
androstenedione, TSH, prolactin, LH, FSH,
17-hydroxyprogesterone, 11-deoxycortisol

Observations all normal

Diagnose idiopathic hirsutism or virilization of unknown etiology

Reassess

DHEAS elevated

(C) High level

Do low-dose dexamethasone suppression test

Above normal

Adrenal source

Suppress adrenal by glucocorticoids

Testosterone increased

Above normal

Adrenal or ovarian source

(G) Provide oral contraceptives

High level

Ovarian source

(H) Catheterize ovarian veins bilaterally for testosterone source

Diagnose familial or idiopathic hirsutism, obesity, polycystic ovary syndrome (p 128), endocrinopathy, trauma, exogenous androgen intake, and ambiguous genitalia (p 58)

No effect

Determine serum ACTH level

(D) Increased

Diagnose pituitary tumor

Provide neuro-endocrine evaluation

High-dose dexamethasone suppression test, CT

Differentiate tumor from hyperplasia

(E) Decreased

Diagnose adrenal tumor

Verify and locate site by IVP, CT, arteriography, adrenal vein catheterization

ADRENAL SURGERY

ENDOCRINE SUPPRESSION OR NEURO-SURGERY

Dexamethasone suppressed

(F) Diagnose adrenal hyperplasia

Increased 17-hydroxy-progesterone

Increased 11-deoxy-cortisol

Suppress adrenal by glucocorticoids

Unilateral production

Ultrasonography, CT

LAPAROSCOPY

Diagnose probable ovarian tumor

EXPLORATORY LAPAROTOMY

Bilateral production

LAPAROSCOPY

Diagnose stromal hyperthecosis

ESTROGEN SUPPRESSION OR OOPHORECTOMY

MASTODYNIA

Max Borten, M.D., J.D.

A. Many women experience some degree of breast discomfort, particularly just prior to menstruation as part of the common, physiologic premenstrual molimina (p 42). If the pain or tenderness is persistent, intensive, focalized, unilateral, noncyclic, unrelated to menses, or associated with a mass (p 72), it must be investigated because it is likely to reflect a pathologic condition. A detailed history will elucidate the character and pattern of pain, its time of onset, duration, relationship to menstruation, radiation, and factors or situations that exacerbate or relieve it. It is of obvious importance to determine the cause of the pain before any therapeutic measure is undertaken so as to avoid delaying definitive diagnosis of a potentially malignant breast lesion. This is the single most critical issue confronting the physician, even though it is unusual for breast cancer to present with pain as the first or only manifestation except late in its natural history.

B. Sudden onset of mastalgia is suggestive of an acute change such as might be associated with bleeding, trauma, thrombosis, or rapid distension of a cyst. Chronic pain or pain with increasing severity is usually related to an underlying inflammatory process. Unilateral pain differs from bilateral mastodynia in its clinical implications. When evaluating unilateral mastalgia, obtain information on handedness preference, occupation, and physical activity. Note periodic recurrences related to the menstrual cycle. Noncyclic unilateral pain may reflect duct ectasia, trauma, sclerosing adenosis, or even cancer.

C. Cyclically recurrent symptoms of bilateral breast enlargement and increased sensitivity can usually be regarded as physiologic (p 42). Spontaneous resolution following menses is reassuring. Persistent bilateral mastodynia, with or without galactorrhea, requires endocrinologic evaluation. Serum prolactin and thyroid stimulating hormone (TSH) measurements are indicated.

D. Pronounced cyclic mastalgia is usually associated with fibroadenosis or cystic breast disease. Nodularity is a common finding, but no distinctive principal nodule should be detectable; any suspicious or changing nodule warrants investigation (p 72). A hormonal basis may exist for this disorder; if so, it may be amenable to treatment with bromocriptine. Lowering the prolactin level reduces symptoms for patients whose pain is cyclic in nature. In more severe cases, use of a low-dose Danocrine regimen, 100 mg daily, has proved effective with minimal side effects.

E. Evaluation of thyroid function is important in women with cyclic mastodynia. Hyperprolactinemia may be seen as a consequence of the hormonal changes occurring with primary hypothyroidism (p 56). A prolonged or exaggerated elevation of TSH following the administration of thyrotropin releasing factor (TRF) in patients with normal or borderline elevations of TSH supports the diagnosis of primary hypothyroidism. A normal TSH response to TRF stimulation eliminates pituitary hypothyroidism. Correcting the hormonal imbalance by giving thyroid hormone, as needed, will usually alleviate the cyclic breast pain in these patients; levothyroxine, 0.1 mg daily, has been shown to soften breast tissues and decrease their nodularity.

F. Care should be taken to evaluate for extramammary causes of mastalgia. Traumatic mastalgia is usually unilateral and limited to the site of injury; it may appear in the scar left by previous surgery. Hematoma formation requires symptomatic relief while awaiting spontaneous resolution. Fat necrosis can usually be identified by x-ray examination. A breast abscess requires incision and drainage supplemented by antibiotics. Chest wall pain may originate in an inflamed costochondral joint (Tietze's syndrome). It is usually medial in location and aggravated by inspiration. Anti-inflammatory treatment (such as ibuprofen 400 mg three times daily) usually affords relief.

References

Doberl A, Tobiassen T, Rasmussen T. Treatment of recurrent cyclical mastodynia in patients with fibrocystic breast disease: A double-blind placebo-controlled study—The Hjorring project. Acta Obstet Gynecol Scand 123:177, 1984.

Estes NC. Mastodynia due to fibrocystic disease of the breast controlled with thyroid hormone. Am J Surg 142:764, 1981.

Gorins A, Cordray JP. Hormonal profile of benign breast disease and premenstrual mastodynia. Eur J Gynaecol Oncol 5:1, 1984.

Peters F, Pickardt CR, Breckwoldt M. Thyroid hormones in benign breast disease: Normalization of exaggerated prolactin responsiveness to thyrotropin-releasing hormone. Cancer 56:1082, 1985.

PATIENT WITH BREAST PAIN

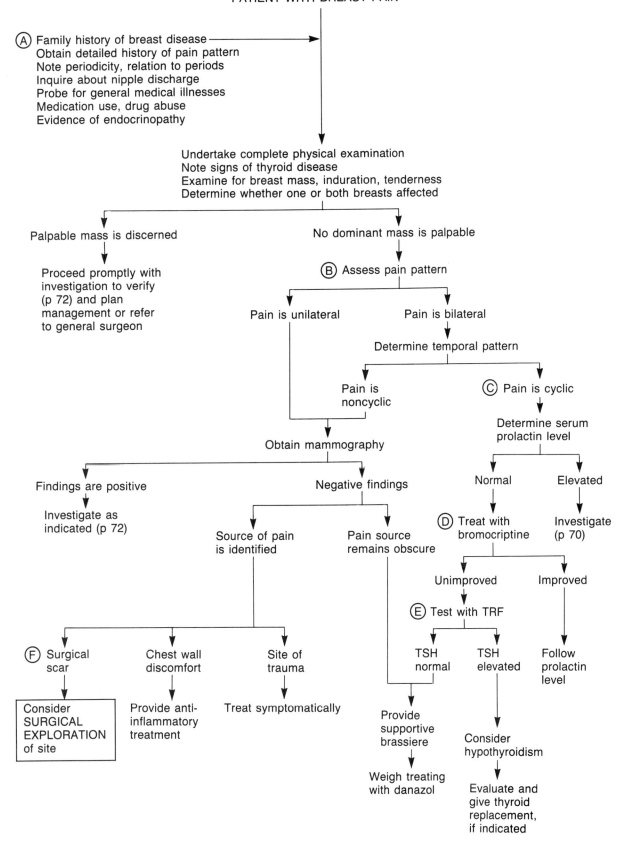

Ⓐ Family history of breast disease ⟶
Obtain detailed history of pain pattern
Note periodicity, relation to periods
Inquire about nipple discharge
Probe for general medical illnesses
Medication use, drug abuse
Evidence of endocrinopathy

Undertake complete physical examination
Note signs of thyroid disease
Examine for breast mass, induration, tenderness
Determine whether one or both breasts affected

Palpable mass is discerned

Proceed promptly with
investigation to verify
(p 72) and plan
management or refer
to general surgeon

No dominant mass is palpable

Ⓑ Assess pain pattern

Pain is unilateral

Pain is bilateral

Determine temporal pattern

Pain is
noncyclic

Ⓒ Pain is cyclic

Determine serum
prolactin level

Obtain mammography

Normal

Elevated

Findings are positive

Investigate as
indicated (p 72)

Negative findings

Ⓓ Treat with
bromocriptine

Investigate
(p 70)

Source of pain
is identified

Pain source
remains obscure

Unimproved

Improved

Ⓔ Test with TRF

Ⓕ Surgical
scar

Chest wall
discomfort

Site of
trauma

TSH
normal

TSH
elevated

Follow
prolactin
level

Consider
SURGICAL
EXPLORATION
of site

Provide anti-
inflammatory
treatment

Treat symptomatically

Provide
supportive
brassiere

Consider
hypothyroidism

Weigh treating
with danazol

Evaluate and
give thyroid
replacement,
if indicated

NIPPLE DISCHARGE

Max Borten, M.D., J.D.

A. Abnormal nipple discharge in a nonlactating woman constitutes less than 5 percent of the reasons women seek consultation for breast examination. Discharge from the nipple, while usually associated with benign conditions, can be a frightening symptom to a woman and it must, therefore, be assessed for its cause. Review the patient's history, concentrating on drug use, especially psychotropic agents and birth control pills, both of which can be responsible for nipple discharge. Also look for signs of pregnancy, the most common and obvious cause of this manifestation. Inquire about breast stimulation, either by a partner or autoerogenously, as another possible etiology. Recognize that disclosing such likely causes does not necessarily mean that other, more serious, conditions could not be present simultaneously. Because any benign lesion causing a nipple discharge may coexist with cancer, a prompt and complete evaluation is indicated. Clinical evaluation limited to physical examination alone is clearly not sufficient to ensure against missing an early, treatable breast carcinoma.

B. Examine carefully to determine whether the discharge is secreted from one or both breasts. This will immediately help differentiate local organic disease from a probable systemic condition, although it is sometimes possible for an intrinsic mammary disorder to affect both breasts at the same time. Unilateral nipple discharge that appears spontaneously is usually clinically significant. However, it may be a physiologic variant. For example, it is often possible to express one or two drops of cloudy fluid by firmly squeezing the nipple or periareolar area in women who have no apparent pathologic condition, especially if it is done premenstrually. Nonetheless, recurrent nipple discharge, even if obtained in this manner, warrants cytologic study to rule out a neoplastic cause.

C. Microscopic evaluation must be done on any secretion discharged from a nonlactating breast. If fat droplets are identified, it means the secretion is lactic, confirming the diagnosis of galactorrhea (p 70). A Wright stained smear will demonstrate the presence of white blood cells or erythrocytes. Documenting a purulent discharge suggests a diagnosis of mastitis or abscess. Systematic cytologic examination should not be limited only to cases with serosanguineous discharge.

D. Nipple discharge, especially if blood-stained, must be regarded as an important symptom of potentially very serious breast disease. Its presence is a justifiable source of anxiety. Although it is not pathognomonic of breast carcinoma, sanguineous nipple discharge mandates a full, expeditious diagnostic work-up. Exfoliative cytology on the smear of the discharge and baseline mammography complement a careful, thorough physical examination. While cancer is the most worrisome condition to be concerned about, fibroadenosis and duct ectasia are most commonly encountered as actual causes of serosanguineous nipple discharge. An intraductal papilloma may also initially manifest itself by this symptom.

E. Papanicolaou cytologic examination should be performed on all nipple discharges, excluding patients with galactorrhea. Pathologic discharge from the nipple may represent the first and only manifestation signaling an early stage of breast carcinoma. The presence of atypical hyperplasia is highly suggestive of cancer; identification of malignant cells is confirmatory. Whenever there is any doubt, evaluation of a fine-needle aspirate is indicated.

F. The absence of atypical cells or papillomatous clusters on cytologic evaluation does not exclude mammary pathology. One must do a careful examination searching for a breast mass and perform mammography. A dominant mass found by palpation or an abnormal radiographic finding in a woman with nipple discharge is highly suspicious for malignancy. If the studies are normal, an expectant attitude with re-evaluation at six-month intervals is acceptable, but further observation and delay are inappropriate if the findings on examination are abnormal.

References

Ciatto S, Bravetti P, Cariaggi P. Significance of nipple discharge clinical patterns in the selection of cases for cytologic examination. Acta Cytol 30:17, 1986.

Knight DC, Lowell DM, Heimann A, Dunn E. Aspiration of the breast and nipple discharge cytology. Surg Gynecol Obstet 163:415, 1986.

Murad TM, Contesso G, Mouriesse H. Nipple discharge from the breast. Ann Surg 195:259, 1982.

Takeda T, Suzuki M, Sato Y, Hase T. Cytologic studies of nipple discharges. Acta Cytol 26:35, 1982.

Teitirick JE. Nipple discharge. Am Fam Physician 22:101, 1980.

PATIENT WITH DISCHARGE FROM NIPPLE

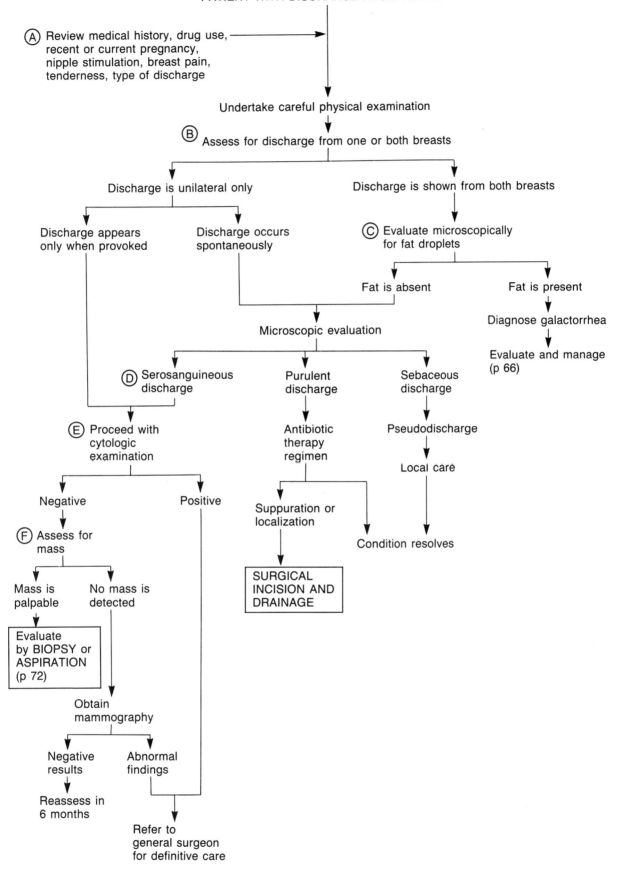

(A) Review medical history, drug use, recent or current pregnancy, nipple stimulation, breast pain, tenderness, type of discharge

Undertake careful physical examination

(B) Assess for discharge from one or both breasts

Discharge is unilateral only

Discharge is shown from both breasts

Discharge appears only when provoked

Discharge occurs spontaneously

(C) Evaluate microscopically for fat droplets

Fat is absent

Fat is present

Microscopic evaluation

Diagnose galactorrhea

Evaluate and manage (p 66)

(D) Serosanguineous discharge

Purulent discharge

Sebaceous discharge

(E) Proceed with cytologic examination

Antibiotic therapy regimen

Pseudodischarge

Local care

Negative

Positive

Suppuration or localization

Condition resolves

(F) Assess for mass

Mass is palpable

No mass is detected

SURGICAL INCISION AND DRAINAGE

Evaluate by BIOPSY or ASPIRATION (p 72)

Obtain mammography

Negative results

Abnormal findings

Reassess in 6 months

Refer to general surgeon for definitive care

69

GALACTORRHEA

Max Borten, M.D., J.D.

A. Galactorrhea is inappropriate lactation in the nonpuerperal woman. It can be unilateral or bilateral. Any stimulus that causes a reduction of prolactin inhibiting factor (PIF) secretion by the hypothalamus enhances the release of pituitary prolactin. Factors associated with hypothalamic PIF suppression include excessive estrogen intake (from oral contraceptives, for example), psychotropic medication (such as diazepam or tricyclic antidepressants), and afferent nerve stimulation (as in scars or herpes zoster lesions). Stress can also inhibit PIF production. Probe for history of breast stimulation and rule out an intrinsic breast disorder (p 68).

B. Primary hypothyroidism with reduced circulating thyroid hormone results in an increased production of thyrotropin releasing hormone by the hypothalamus, which acts in turn as a prolactin releasing factor to raise the circulating prolactin level. Restoration to a euthyroid state by the administration of thyroid hormone corrects the problem. Women with thyrotoxicosis can also develop idiopathic galactorrhea and thus deserve full evaluation. Galactorrhea secondary to hypothyroidism is usually associated with amenorrhea. Menstrual function is usually restored merely by correcting the underlying condition.

C. Hyperprolactinemia can generally be detected by analyzing a single random serum sample for the prolactin level. An increased prolactin concentration may be due to decreased PIF production, increased prolactin elaboration, or secretion from a pituitary tumor. Large extrasellar pituitary adenomas (which are usually nonfunctional tumors) may also mimic the signs and symptoms of a pituitary prolactinoma. Patients affected by such tumors, however, will not respond to bromocriptine therapy with shrinkage of the adenoma. Surgical resection is therefore indicated. Disturbance in dopamine sensitivity to prolactin feedback may also lead to hyperprolactinemia by stimulating the pituitary lactotropes to form an adenoma.

D. Hyperprolactinemia is a major cause of anovulation and infertility. Galactorrhea resulting from a pituitary adenoma is often associated with amenorrhea or oligomenorrhea, although menstrual abnormalities, including anovulation, can be encountered with essentially normal prolactin levels. Some euprolactinemic patients with unexplained infertility and galactorrhea may benefit from low-dose bromocriptine treatment.

E. Hyperprolactinemia may represent the first sign of prolactinoma. Significant elevation of the serum prolactin level is generally regarded as likely to reflect the existence of a pituitary tumor. Radiologic evaluations by computer tomography (CT) scan or coronal x-ray views of the sella turcica are useful for the diagnosis and follow-up of patients with these tumors.

F. A baseline neurologic examination, including visual fields evaluation, is advisable in patients with hyperprolactinemia. Pituitary hormone measurements (growth, luteinizing, follicle stimulating, and adrenocorticotropic hormones) are also useful for initially assessing and serially following these patients. Although inadequate as screening tests, they become most valuable after a tumor has been identified by computer tomography.

G. In most women, hyperprolactinemia has a benign clinical course. There is no strong evidence that small adenomas necessarily progress to grow into large tumors. Bromocriptine in titrated doses is the treatment of choice. During pregnancy, watch for and advise about headaches, blurred vision, and reduced temporal visual fields as warning symptoms of pituitary enlargement. Bromocriptine can also be used for effectively treating a pituitary adenoma during pregnancy. Surgical extirpation or radiation is reserved for cases with extensive tumors that fail to respond to conservative pharmacologic therapy.

H. Galactorrhea unaccompanied by pituitary enlargement or menstrual abnormalities may require nothing more than counseling and reassurance. Bromocriptine therapy may be used to treat patients who have otherwise unexplained infertility or galactorrhea. Close follow-up at three- to six-month intervals is required for visual field, biochemical, and periodic physical examinations.

References

Blackwell RE. Diagnosis and management of prolactinomas. Fertil Steril 43:5, 1985.

Brenner SH, Lessing JB, Quagliarello J, Weiss G. Hyperprolactinemia and associated pituitary prolactinomas. Obstet Gynecol 65:661, 1985.

DeVane GW, Guzick DS. Bromocriptine therapy in normoprolactinemic women with unexplained infertility and galactorrhea. Fertil Steril 46:1026, 1986.

Martin TL, Kim M, Malarkey WB. The natural history of idiopathic hyperprolactinemia. J Clin Endocrinol Metab 60:855, 1985.

Strebel PM, Zacur HA, Gold EB. Headache, hyperprolactinemia, and prolactinomas. Obstet Gynecol 68:195, 1986.

PATIENT WITH GALACTORRHEA

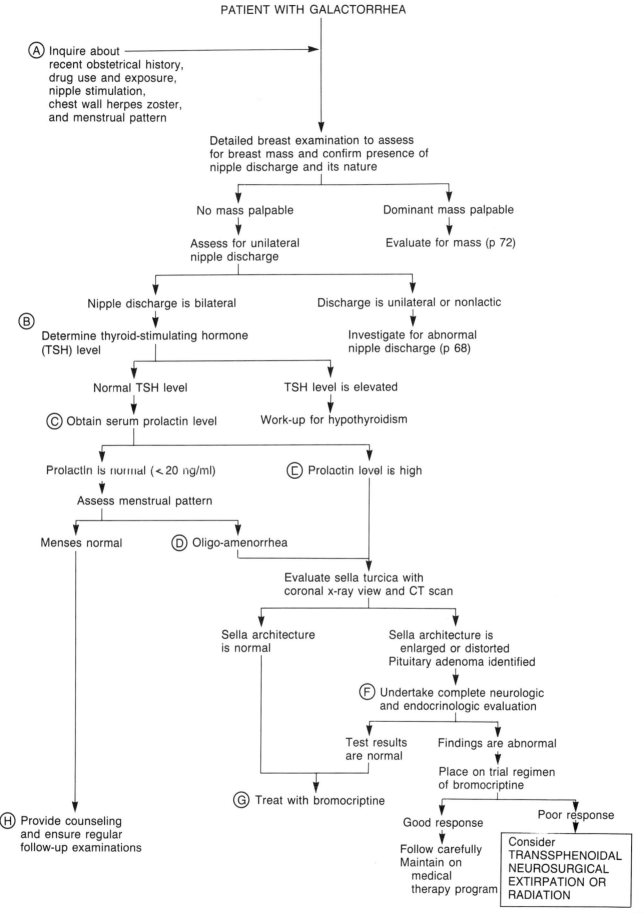

Ⓐ Inquire about
recent obstetrical history,
drug use and exposure,
nipple stimulation,
chest wall herpes zoster,
and menstrual pattern

Detailed breast examination to assess
for breast mass and confirm presence of
nipple discharge and its nature

No mass palpable   Dominant mass palpable

Assess for unilateral   Evaluate for mass (p 72)
nipple discharge

Nipple discharge is bilateral   Discharge is unilateral or nonlactic

Ⓑ Determine thyroid-stimulating hormone   Investigate for abnormal
(TSH) level   nipple discharge (p 68)

Normal TSH level   TSH level is elevated

Ⓒ Obtain serum prolactin level   Work-up for hypothyroidism

Prolactin is normal (<20 ng/ml)   Ⓔ Prolactin level is high

Assess menstrual pattern

Menses normal   Ⓓ Oligo-amenorrhea

Evaluate sella turcica with
coronal x-ray view and CT scan

Sella architecture   Sella architecture is
is normal   enlarged or distorted
Pituitary adenoma identified

Ⓕ Undertake complete neurologic
and endocrinologic evaluation

Test results   Findings are abnormal
are normal

Place on trial regimen
of bromocriptine

Ⓖ Treat with bromocriptine

Good response   Poor response

Ⓗ Provide counseling
and ensure regular
follow-up examinations

Follow carefully
Maintain on
medical
therapy program

Consider
TRANSSPHENOIDAL
NEUROSURGICAL
EXTIRPATION OR
RADIATION

BREAST MASS

Max Borten, M.D., J.D.

A. Breast self-examination is acknowledged to be of limited value principally because it is inconsistently reliable and few women are diligent and attentive. Despite this, the practice can be justified on the basis of the occasional breast cancer it detects. Teaching the needs for and the details of breast self-examination should be reinforced by encouraging the patient to practice it with regularity. The importance of early detection must be repeatedly stressed. Discovery of a mass in the breast will usually prompt a patient to visit her gynecologist, although some exhibit a regrettable reluctance to do so. Notwithstanding that the majority of breast masses are of a benign nature, it is essential to undertake a complete evaluation before one can reassure the patient. Elicit a background of risk factors for breast cancer in her personal and family history (p 10).

B. Inspection of the breasts is the first step in the examination. It should be carried out with the patient sitting, first with her arms at her sides and then overhead. Palpation of the breast is usually performed with the patient supine. Any abnormality noted on inspection or palpation should be further pursued by examination in the sitting and standing positions. Look for significant signs of asymmetry, nipple deviation, retraction, induration, edema, fixation, or tumor bulging. Breast cancer often initially presents as a nontender firm lump with ill-defined, indistinct margins. Identifying this dominant mass is the principal objective of the examination.

C. The absence of an identifiable mass by physical examination is reassuring. Nevertheless, re-evaluation at regular intervals is indicated. In women 30 years of age or more, a baseline mammography should be obtained. It offers objective evidence for the absence of a malignancy and serves for later comparison studies to help in early recognition of any pattern changes that may arise in the future. Foremost, the patient must be made to feel that she has fulfilled an important screening function by self-examining her breasts even though findings are negative at the time of this examination.

D Consistency of the breast mass can be assessed by palpation. When in doubt, ultrasonographic evaluation aids in differentiating between a cystic fluid-filled mass and one with solid components. Cystic masses are amenable to expeditious fine-needle aspiration; the patient should not ordinarily have to return for this simple procedure. Identification of a solid tumor (or cystic mass with residual solid component after aspiration) usually requires surgical exploration. A preoperative baseline mammography is helpful in disclosing unsuspected secondary lesions in either the affected or the contralateral breast.

E. Fine-needle aspiration of a cystic breast mass is usually carried out in the office setting. Fluid aspiration permits cytologic evaluation of any suspicious material. Clear or straw-colored fluid is considered benign and the fluid can be discarded. It is imperative to re-evaluate immediately following aspiration and six weeks thereafter to confirm that the suspicious breast mass is no longer palpable. If one cannot aspirate fluid from a mass that is thought to be cystic, it must be treated as if it were solid. Failure to decompress a cystic breast mass completely by aspiration indicates the tumor probably has some solid component to it. Excisional biopsy is needed even though the aspirated fluid appears to be benign. Bloody or serosanguineous fluid should be viewed as reflecting a potentially neoplastic lesion; because it may contain malignant cells, microscopic cytologic study is essential.

F. A negative mammographic evaluation does not completely rule out the possibility of a breast malignancy. Excisional biopsy of a persistent breast lump is indicated irrespective of the negative results of any diagnostic test. Delayed recognition of an irreducible mass is a common reason breast carcinoma is not diagnosed in its early stages. When in doubt, appropriate referral to a more experienced physician is indicated.

References

Barrows GH, Anderson TJ, Lamb JL, Dixon JM. Fine-needle aspiration of breast cancer: Relationship of clinical factors to cytology results in 689 primary malignancies. Cancer 58:1493, 1986.

Devitt JE. Benign disorders of the breast in older women. Surg Gynecol Obstet 162:340, 1986.

Gonzalez E, Grafton WD, Morris DM, Barr LH. Diagnosing breast cancer using frozen sections from Tru-cut needle biopsies: Six-year experience with 162 biopsies, with emphasis on outpatient diagnosis of breast carcinoma. Ann Surg 202:696, 1985.

Hilton SV, Leopold GR, Olson LK, Willson SA. Real-time breast sonography: Application in 300 consecutive patients. Am J Radiol 147:479, 1986.

Wilkinson S, Forrest APM. Fibro-adenoma of the breast. Br J Surg 72:838, 1985.

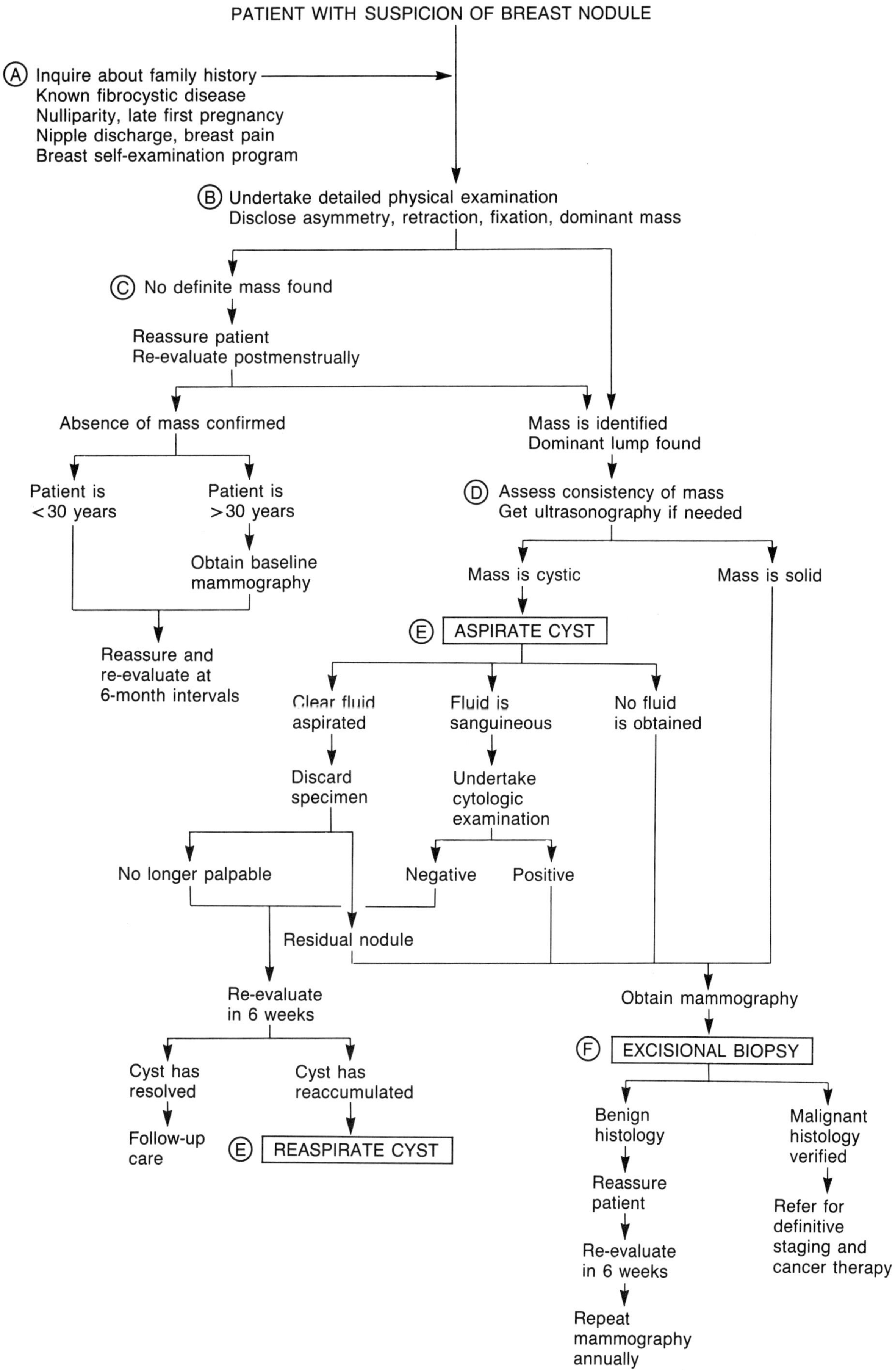

PATIENT WITH SUSPICION OF BREAST NODULE

(A) Inquire about family history
Known fibrocystic disease
Nulliparity, late first pregnancy
Nipple discharge, breast pain
Breast self-examination program

(B) Undertake detailed physical examination
Disclose asymmetry, retraction, fixation, dominant mass

(C) No definite mass found

Reassure patient
Re-evaluate postmenstrually

Absence of mass confirmed

Patient is
<30 years

Patient is
>30 years

Obtain baseline
mammography

Reassure and
re-evaluate at
6-month intervals

Mass is identified
Dominant lump found

(D) Assess consistency of mass
Get ultrasonography if needed

Mass is cystic

Mass is solid

(E) ASPIRATE CYST

Clear fluid
aspirated

Fluid is
sanguineous

No fluid
is obtained

Discard
specimen

Undertake
cytologic
examination

No longer palpable

Negative   Positive

Residual nodule

Re-evaluate
in 6 weeks

Cyst has
resolved

Cyst has
reaccumulated

Follow-up
care

(E) REASPIRATE CYST

Obtain mammography

(F) EXCISIONAL BIOPSY

Benign
histology

Malignant
histology
verified

Reassure
patient

Refer for
definitive
staging and
cancer therapy

Re-evaluate
in 6 weeks

Repeat
mammography
annually

SPONTANEOUS ABORTION

Vicki Heller, M.D.

A. Patients may threaten to abort spontaneously in early pregnancy by developing cramps, low back pain, and vaginal bleeding. Only about half actually abort. Keep pregnancy in mind, including ectopic pregnancy (p 198), as a possible diagnosis when these symptoms arise. Probe about previous pregnancy experience, diethylstilbestrol exposure in utero, general health, and psychosocial background to guide counseling (p 76). Uterine malformations, incompetent cervix, and chromosomal abnormalities constitute some of the known risk factors.

B. Evaluate the hemodynamic status and look for evidence of infection. Determine if uterine size is appropriate for gestational age; if advanced enough, verify the presence of fetal heart tones. Assess the quantity and source of bleeding. Culture for sexually transmitted infections. Watch for expulsion of fetal or placental tissue and examine such tissue both grossly (by floating in saline under good light to see villi clearly) and microscopically.

C. Confirm pregnancy by either beta-subunit human chorionic gonadotropin (hCG) or ultrasonographic fetal heart detection. Ascertain gestational dating accurately. Blood type and screen are mandatory. Give Rh immune globulin in appropriate dosage for unsensitized Rh-negative gravidas. Obtain a complete blood count and differential to evaluate for blood loss and infection. Quantitate the serum beta-subunit hCG level, as an index of trophoplastic function, to determine if the concentration encountered is consistent with that expected for the duration of the pregnancy. If it is considerably lower than expected levels, it is helpful, but the wide variations of normal and dating errors often require serial titers for meaningful interpretation. As a guide, a beta-subunit hCG level over 6,000 mIU per milliliter occurring in a gravida with a singleton gestation of six weeks duration or more means the pregnancy should be sufficiently advanced to be seen by ultrasonography. Failure to identify a gestational sac within the uterus under these circumstances raises the real possibility of ectopic pregnancy.

D. An open internal cervical os indicates the abortion process is irreversible (that is, inevitable) and perhaps already partially or wholly completed (incomplete or complete abortion). The inevitability of the process is even more assured if tissue (not just blood clot) has been passed. Remember, however, that identifiable placental (and even fetal) tissue can be expelled in a twin pregnancy and inexplicably leave the remaining intrauterine twin in situ to continue the pregnancy. While this is a rare event, if there is any doubt, rule out a second gestational sac by ultrasonography. In midtrimester pregnancy, the cervix may efface and dilate without clinical evidence of uterine contractions or bleeding. This condition of cervical incompetence generally leads in due course to spontaneous abortion in the affected pregnancy, as well as in those that follow, unless the anatomic or functional defect is corrected by the use of a cerclage suture to return the integrity of the internal os to normal. Since cerclage can be done in a timely manner to prevent abortion, if dilatation is discovered early enough, this constitutes an exception to the rule that an open cervix signifies an inevitable abortion.

E. If the cervical os is closed, first ascertain if the fetus is alive and the pregnancy is still intact. Imaging techniques are very sensitive for detecting fetal heart activity; if present, there is a reasonably good chance the gestation will continue. Observe closely for continued or increased bleeding and progression of the abortion process nevertheless. If manifestations subside, arrange for long-term prenatal care.

F. If there is no fetal heart or intrauterine gestational sac detected, ectopic pregnancy must be ruled out (p 198). Ultrasonography should be able to detect the gestational sac by six menstrual weeks (and it may sometimes be seen as early as four weeks); at seven weeks, a fetal pole should be visible; at eight weeks, a fetal heart. Serial scans may be needed to document absence of development and thereby rule out the possibility of a miscalculation of gestational age. If no fetal heart can be identified by eight-and-one-half to nine weeks based on crown-rump length (by an experienced ultrasonographer), the fetus must be considered to have died. This constitutes a missed abortion and can be evacuated in much the same way as an induced abortion in an advanced pregnancy (p 232).

G. Few women undergo pregnancy loss without emotional trauma. Counseling should underscore future reproductive potential and relieve the guilt often present in one or both partners (p 76).

References

Huisjes HJ. Spontaneous Abortion. New York: Churchill Livingstone, 1984.

Laferla JJ. Spontaneous abortion. Clin Obstet Gynaecol 13:105, 1986.

Lewis JE, Coulam CB, Moore SB. Immunologic mechanisms in the maternal-fetal relationship. Mayo Clin Proc 61:655, 1986.

Therapel AT, Therapel SA, Bannerman RM. Recurrent pregnancy losses and parental chromosome abnormalities: A review. Br J Obstet Gynaecol 92:899, 1985.

PATIENT WITH UTERINE CRAMPS AND VAGINAL BLEEDING

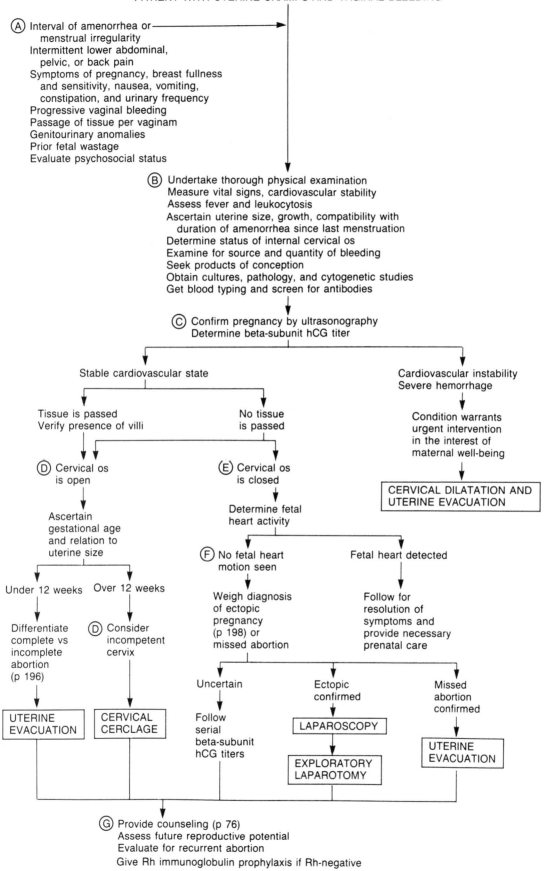

Ⓐ Interval of amenorrhea or
    menstrual irregularity
  Intermittent lower abdominal,
    pelvic, or back pain
  Symptoms of pregnancy, breast fullness
    and sensitivity, nausea, vomiting,
    constipation, and urinary frequency
  Progressive vaginal bleeding
  Passage of tissue per vaginam
  Genitourinary anomalies
  Prior fetal wastage
  Evaluate psychosocial status

Ⓑ Undertake thorough physical examination
  Measure vital signs, cardiovascular stability
  Assess fever and leukocytosis
  Ascertain uterine size, growth, compatibility with
    duration of amenorrhea since last menstruation
  Determine status of internal cervical os
  Examine for source and quantity of bleeding
  Seek products of conception
  Obtain cultures, pathology, and cytogenetic studies
  Get blood typing and screen for antibodies

Ⓒ Confirm pregnancy by ultrasonography
  Determine beta-subunit hCG titer

Stable cardiovascular state

Cardiovascular instability
Severe hemorrhage

Tissue is passed
Verify presence of villi

No tissue
is passed

Condition warrants
urgent intervention
in the interest of
maternal well-being

Ⓓ Cervical os
  is open

Ⓔ Cervical os
  is closed

CERVICAL DILATATION AND
UTERINE EVACUATION

Ascertain
gestational age
and relation to
uterine size

Determine fetal
heart activity

Ⓕ No fetal heart
  motion seen

Fetal heart detected

Under 12 weeks

Over 12 weeks

Weigh diagnosis
of ectopic
pregnancy
(p 198) or
missed abortion

Follow for
resolution of
symptoms and
provide necessary
prenatal care

Differentiate
complete vs
incomplete
abortion
(p 196)

Ⓓ Consider
  incompetent
  cervix

Uncertain

Ectopic
confirmed

Missed
abortion
confirmed

UTERINE
EVACUATION

CERVICAL
CERCLAGE

Follow
serial
beta-subunit
hCG titers

LAPAROSCOPY

UTERINE
EVACUATION

EXPLORATORY
LAPAROTOMY

Ⓖ Provide counseling (p 76)
  Assess future reproductive potential
  Evaluate for recurrent abortion
  Give Rh immunoglobulin prophylaxis if Rh-negative

RECURRENT EARLY PREGNANCY LOSS

Steven R. Bayer, M.D.

A. Spontaneous abortion is associated with chromosomal anomalies incompatible with survival or normal fetal development in more than half the cases. The incidence of such pregnancy wastage, once believed to be about 15 percent, is now known to be very common because sensitive pregnancy tests have made it possible to identify early pregnancies that might not have been recognized clinically. Many of these early losses may be interpreted by the patient as heavy or late menstrual periods and, since the patient does not seek medical evaluation, the pregnancy is never diagnosed. The actual rate of spontaneous abortion may be 40 percent or perhaps considerably more. The patient who has had her first spontaneous abortion can, therefore, be reassured that it is a frequent occurrence and that no specific or detailed evaluation is indicated. It is common for couples to experience a grief reaction following any pregnancy loss. The grieving process may last for a year or more.

B. Habitual abortion is defined as three consecutive pregnancy losses prior to the twentieth week of gestation. While the risk of another spontaneous abortion is somewhat increased in these cases, there is still a high probability of carrying the next pregnancy to viability. Affected patients should be counseled accordingly. If they wish, evaluation can be undertaken to ascertain whether a remediable cause can be found. Since recurrent pregnancy loss may create much patient anxiety, it may be prudent to consider proceeding with the evaluation after only two losses.

C. Luteal phase deficiency should be considered in any woman presenting with a history of recurrent pregnancy loss. The diagnosis is made by endometrial dating based on a biopsy obtained late in the luteal phase (p 126). Suboptimal follicular development or an inadequate surge of luteinizing hormone may compromise progesterone production by the corpus luteum. The resulting deficient corpus luteum is unable to support a newly implanted pregnancy until six to eight weeks of gestation when the placenta takes over as the major source of progesterone.

D. Recurrent pregnancy loss in the second trimester preceded by painless cervical effacement and dilatation suggests the diagnosis of an incompetent cervix. The condition may be due to a congenital defect or it may result from previous surgery or trauma. Evaluate between pregnancies for a concurrent uterine anomaly (see F) and consider placing a McDonald (Fig. 1) or Shirodkar cervical cerclage during the subsequent pregnancy if midtrimester cervical change is detected.

E. Colonization of the genital tract by *Mycoplasma* or *Ureaplasma* is a controversial cause of recurrent abortion. Since it is easily treatable, however, obtain cervical cultures and administer a 10-day course of tetracycline or doxycycline to both partners, if indicated. A follow-up culture should be done to document eradication of the organism.

F. Uterine anomalies may be detected in about one-quarter of patients with recurrent abortion (p 166). Hysterosalpingography allows one to assess the uterine cavity for anatomic defects. Two separate uterine cavities seen by x-ray represent either a septate or a bicornuate uterus; they can be differentiated by laparoscopy. Because the septum in a septate uterus is not well vascularized, it is not a good implantation site, leading to early abortion. A bicornuate uterus, which does not cause early pregnancy loss, may put the patient at risk for premature labor. Asherman's syndrome (intrauterine adhesions) may result from prior curettage, uterine surgery, or pelvic inflammatory disease (p 168). The synechiae can be lysed through a hysteroscope. Hysterosalpingography may show a T-shaped uterus suggesting diethylstilbesterol exposure in utero. The small hypoplastic uterine corpus may be inadequate to accommodate a developing pregnancy. While uterine leiomyomas may distort the uterine cavity and interfere with implantation, they are so common that other causes of recurrent pregnancy loss must be ruled out before considering myomectomy.

G. A cytogenic abnormality may be the etiology of recurrent abortions in 5 percent of couples. Advanced parental age enhances the risk. Karyotyping can be done to seek balanced translocation in both partners. Discuss the

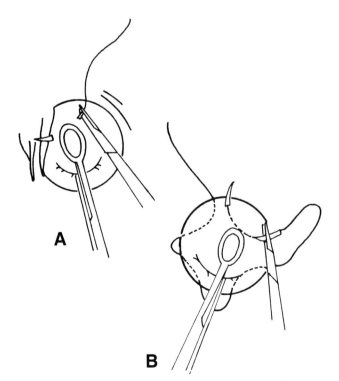

Figure 1 Cervical cerclage for incompetence of cervix, McDonald technique, illustrating anterior lip of cervix held in ring forceps while first mucosal suture is placed in right upper quadrant (A). Suturing is continued circumferentially to form a purse-string (B), which is tied anteriorly and left in place until delivery.

PATIENT WITH RECURRENT PREVIABLE PREGNANCY LOSSES

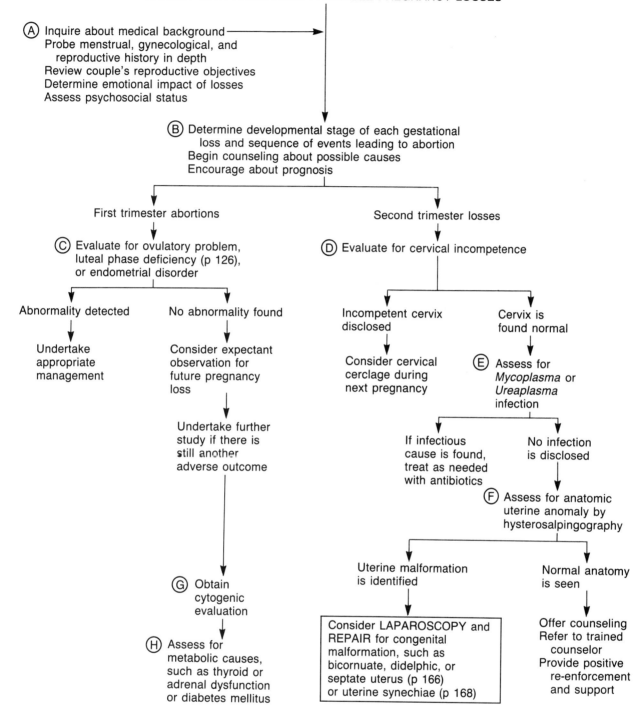

(A) Inquire about medical background
Probe menstrual, gynecological, and
reproductive history in depth
Review couple's reproductive objectives
Determine emotional impact of losses
Assess psychosocial status

(B) Determine developmental stage of each gestational
loss and sequence of events leading to abortion
Begin counseling about possible causes
Encourage about prognosis

First trimester abortions

(C) Evaluate for ovulatory problem,
luteal phase deficiency (p 126),
or endometrial disorder

Abnormality detected

Undertake
appropriate
management

No abnormality found

Consider expectant
observation for
future pregnancy
loss

Undertake further
study if there is
still another
adverse outcome

(G) Obtain
cytogenic
evaluation

(H) Assess for
metabolic causes,
such as thyroid or
adrenal dysfunction
or diabetes mellitus

Second trimester losses

(D) Evaluate for cervical incompetence

Incompetent cervix
disclosed

Consider cervical
cerclage during
next pregnancy

Cervix is
found normal

(E) Assess for
Mycoplasma or
Ureaplasma
infection

If infectious
cause is found,
treat as needed
with antibiotics

No infection
is disclosed

(F) Assess for anatomic
uterine anomaly by
hysterosalpingography

Uterine malformation
is identified

Consider LAPAROSCOPY and
REPAIR for congenital
malformation, such as
bicornuate, didelphic, or
septate uterus (p 166)
or uterine synechiae (p 168)

Normal anatomy
is seen

Offer counseling
Refer to trained
counselor
Provide positive
re-enforcement
and support

benefits of genetic screening and offer counseling services as well, if appropriate.

H. Metabolic causes of recurrent loss include thyroid dysfunction and diabetes mellitus. Other relevant systemic
conditions include debilitating diseases, poor nutrition,
renal disorder, and autoimmune disease.

References

Harger JH, Archer DF, Marchese SG, et al. Etiology of recurrent
pregnancy losses and outcome of subsequent pregnancies.
Obstet Gynecol 62:574, 1983.
McDonough PG. Repeated first-trimester pregnancy loss: Evaluation and management. Am J Obstet Gynecol 153:1, 1985.
McIntyre JA, McConnachie PR, Taylor CG, Faulk WP. Clinical,
immunologic, and genetic definitions of primary and secondary recurrent spontaneous abortions. Fertil Steril 42:849,
1984.
Strobino B, Fox HE, Kline J, et al. Characteristics of women with
recurrent spontaneous abortions and women with favorable
reproductive histories. Am J Public Health 76:986, 1986.

MENORRHAGIA

Jerold M. Carlson, M.D., M.P.H.

A. Patients are seldom able to quantitate their menstrual flow accurately, although they are sensitive to changes in the flow pattern over time. While a woman may subjectively exaggerate the degree of bleeding, the clinician cannot ignore her concerns. Direct observation of the flow during menses is helpful, but rarely possible because of the logistics of scheduling timely office visits. Objectively confirm excess bleeding by determining hemoglobin and hematocrit serially. Pad counts are of limited value because patients vary widely in how compulsive they are in regard to changing pads. Obtain a detailed medical history with special attention to stress, drug use, excessive exercise, marked weight change, and systemic illnesses. Carefully assess for manifestations suggestive of a bleeding disorder. For example, determine if there has ever been any problem associated with prior tooth extraction or other surgery, evidence of petechiae or ecchymoses, a history of liver disease, or exposure to anticoagulants or prostaglandin synthetase inhibitors such as aspirin.

B. A complete physical examination and appropriate laboratory testing are essential to rule out an endocrinopathy, such as thyroid disease or polycystic ovarian syndrome. Pregnancy, gestational trophoblastic disease, or leukemia must also be excluded. The range of blood studies one might consider encompasses a complete blood count (CBC), blood chemistry determinations, beta-subunit human chorionic gonadotropin (hCG), and coagulation profile, including prothrombin time, partial thromboplastin time, platelet count, and bleeding time. Detection of a bleeding or clotting disorder requires full evaluation, with appropriate hematologic consultation, and aggressive management leading to correction. Bear in mind the possibility that such bleeding disorders may coexist with other uterine disorders. If present, they should not be overlooked.

C. Vaginal and rectal examinations are essential in order to determine possible uterine or adnexal causes of the heavy bleeding. Search for leiomyomas, endometriosis, salpingitis, malignancy, foreign body (especially an intrauterine device), and evidence of trauma. Obtain a Papanicolaou smear for cytologic examination unless the bleeding is active; the presence of blood will obscure the microscopic field and make cytologic interpretation difficult. Biopsy any suspicious vaginal or cervical lesion.

D. Evaluate the patient who has an enlarged uterus or adnexal mass with ultrasonography or computer tomography. Consider visualizing the uterine cavity by transcervical hysterography if it is indicated to verify the presence of an endometrial polyp or submucous fibroid.

It is also sometimes possible to treat these conditions by this route. It is important to differentiate other conditions as well, such as cervical cancer, cystic or solid ovarian tumor, and uterine sarcoma.

E. Perhaps the most common cause of menorrhagia is dysfunctional uterine bleeding due to irregular endometrial shedding or anovulation. It can be readily controlled by cyclic hormonal supplementation therapy to mimic the normal cyclic endocrine stimulation of the endometrium that occurs in ovulatory cycles. This can be done with a regimen of birth control pills (see F). However, one should first rule out intrauterine disorders such as submucous leiomyomas and endometrial polyps by curettage. Even if no abnormal endometrial condition is found, the curettage often corrects the menorrhagia, sometimes indefinitely. It is therefore well worth doing.

F. Consider giving several cycles of oral contraceptives, using the lowest effective dosage regimen. Bear in mind and advise the patient that the estrogens contained in these products may sometimes actually cause a leiomyoma to grow, although they are equally likely to cause shrinkage, particularly at low dosage levels. Newer techniques include the use of high-dose progestational agents or gonadotropin releasing hormone agonists (p 60). Acute heavy bleeding may be temporarily controlled by intravenous estrogen administration.

G. If endometrial curettage has been successful in correcting the menorrhagia, even if only transiently, one might consider repeating it if the menorrhagia returns. Weigh the benefits of hysterectomy as a permanent means for alleviating this problem, particularly if the bleeding has been incapacitating or especially distressful to the patient and has not responded to either curettage or a hormonal regimen. Hysterectomy may be warranted if reproductive function is no longer an important consideration.

References

Chamberlain G. Dysfunctional uterine bleeding. Clin Obstet Gynecol 8:93, 1981.

Claessens EA, Cowell CA. Acute adolescent menorrhagia. Am J Obstet Gynecol 139:277, 1981.

Fraser IS, McCarron G, Markham R. A preliminary study of factors influencing perception of menstrual blood loss volume. Am J Obstet Gynecol 149:788, 1984.

Fraser IS, McCarron G, Markham R, et al. Measured menstrual blood loss in women with menorrhagia associated with pelvic disease or coagulation disorder. Obstet Gynecol 68:630, 1986.

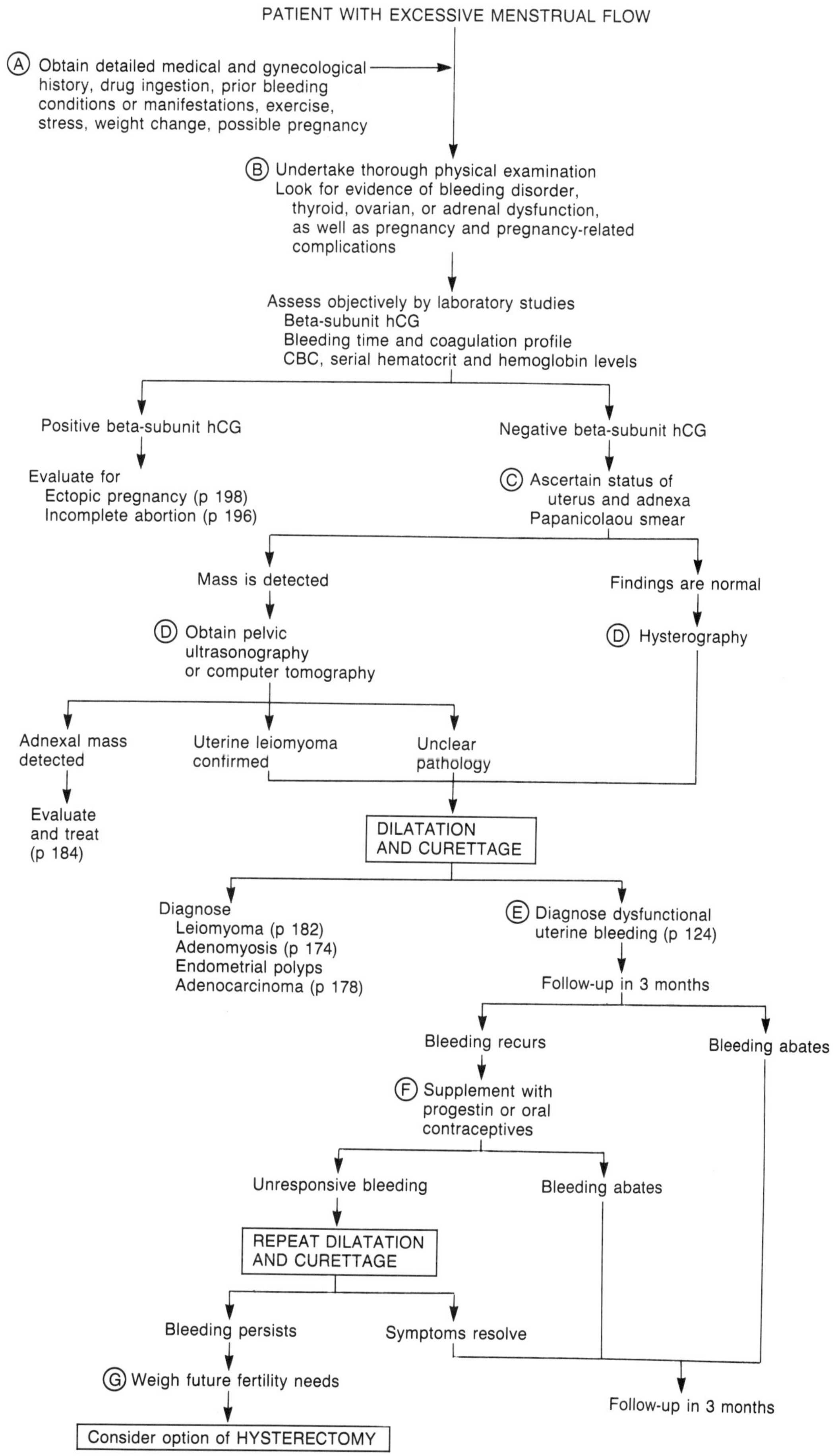

PATIENT WITH EXCESSIVE MENSTRUAL FLOW

(A) Obtain detailed medical and gynecological
history, drug ingestion, prior bleeding
conditions or manifestations, exercise,
stress, weight change, possible pregnancy

(B) Undertake thorough physical examination
Look for evidence of bleeding disorder,
thyroid, ovarian, or adrenal dysfunction,
as well as pregnancy and pregnancy-related
complications

Assess objectively by laboratory studies
Beta-subunit hCG
Bleeding time and coagulation profile
CBC, serial hematocrit and hemoglobin levels

Positive beta-subunit hCG

Negative beta-subunit hCG

Evaluate for
Ectopic pregnancy (p 198)
Incomplete abortion (p 196)

(C) Ascertain status of
uterus and adnexa
Papanicolaou smear

Mass is detected

Findings are normal

(D) Obtain pelvic
ultrasonography
or computer tomography

(D) Hysterography

Adnexal mass
detected

Uterine leiomyoma
confirmed

Unclear
pathology

Evaluate
and treat
(p 184)

DILATATION
AND CURETTAGE

Diagnose
Leiomyoma (p 182)
Adenomyosis (p 174)
Endometrial polyps
Adenocarcinoma (p 178)

(E) Diagnose dysfunctional
uterine bleeding (p 124)

Follow-up in 3 months

Bleeding recurs

Bleeding abates

(F) Supplement with
progestin or oral
contraceptives

Unresponsive bleeding

Bleeding abates

REPEAT DILATATION
AND CURETTAGE

Bleeding persists

Symptoms resolve

(G) Weigh future fertility needs

Follow-up in 3 months

Consider option of HYSTERECTOMY

METRORRHAGIA

Jerold M. Carlson, M.D., M.P.H.

A. Vaginal bleeding independent of and unrelated to periodic menstrual flow is not an uncommon complaint. The major consideration for the patient with metrorrhagia is whether or not she has endometrial or cervical cancer, even though this symptom is much more often due to some other condition of much less serious importance. It may frequently reflect the presence of a benign intrauterine lesion, such as an endometrial polyp or submucous fibroid, or less often a bleeding disorder or other systemic disease. Pregnancy related bleeding is particularly common. Obtain a detailed history to disclose potentially relevant past medical, obstetrical, and gynecological history, including menstrual pattern, sexually transmitted disease, and evidence of a bleeding diathesis. Be especially alert to identify women at high risk for endometrial cancer (p 178), such as those who are obese, hypertensive, diabetic, and perimenopausal.

B. The general physical examination should search for signs of medical illness, especially cardiovascular, endocrinologic, and hematologic illnesses. A careful pelvic examination is essential. The mandatory Papanicolaou cytologic smear (p 12) helps detect cervical cancer, although an ulcerated or fungating friable lesion capable of bleeding should be quite apparent to the naked eye for biopsy purposes. One should appreciate that exfoliative cytology is not very reliable for detecting endometrial cancer. Endometrial sampling (p 210) is clearly preferable, although it is not as good for diagnosis as a full, formal, fractional curettage (see F). For cases in which one suspects pregnancy, get a pregnancy test and pelvic ultrasonography. Undertake other laboratory studies, as indicated, to rule out coagulation defects (p 206), thyroid dysfunction, and diabetes mellitus. Investigate for hematuria by assessing a clean-catch or catheterized specimen of urine, avoiding contamination from vaginal bleeding.

C. It may not always be feasible to identify the site of the bleeding because the patient does not present herself for examination in a timely fashion. If bleeding is present, however, take the opportunity to examine carefully by direct observation under good illumination and with adequate exposure. Cleanse the vagina gently to avoid aggravating bleeding from a cervical or vaginal lesion. Watch for blood escaping from the cervix and look for sources on the cervix, vaginal wall, vestibule, vulva, urethra, or anus. Observe for evidence of neoplasm, vaginitis, foreign object, and trauma.

D. Both normal and abnormal pregnancies can present with isolated or episodic vaginal bleeding indistinguishable from metrorrhagia due to other causes. Such bleeding is especially common in patients with threatened abortion and ectopic pregnancy. Intermenstrual bleeding also occurs in patients who have an intrauterine device in place, perhaps as a reflection of developing endometritis or salpingitis.

E. For definitive diagnosis, proceed with cervical dilatation and fractional curettage under anesthesia (p 230). Take advantage of the anesthetic to perform a pelvic examination to detect any previously undisclosed pathologic condition in the pelvis. Thoroughly sample the entire endometrial cavity and endocervical canal with sharp curettage, keeping each of the specimens separate for detailed histologic study. Curettage alone may prove to be therapeutic for many patients, relieving them of metrorrhagia due to endocervical or endometrial polyps, irregular endometrial shedding, endometritis, or even endometrial hyperplasia. If submucous leiomyomas are identified, further management is dictated by any continuing or recurrent symptoms (p 182) and the patient's desire to retain her reproductive capabilities. If endometrial hyperplasia is discovered, periodic follow-up endometrial biopsies are needed (p 176).

F. If no cause can be found for the metrorrhagia, curettage may inexplicably alleviate uterine bleeding. Only routine follow-up is necessary for such cases. However, if the symptom should later recur, hysteroscopy is worth considering for direct visualization of the endometrial cavity to help reveal the cause. Conditions that can be missed even by careful, competent, and thorough curettage include synechiae (p 168), polyp, submucous leiomyoma, and anatomic anomaly. Normal ovulation may be associated with recurrent midcycle bleeding. It is typically, but not invariably, accompanied by unilateral pelvic or lower quadrant abdominal pain (clinically recognized as mittelschmerz). Because a noncyclic pattern of bleeding is more likely to reflect some disease process, it has to be investigated intensively. The potential impact of ovarian tumors, endometriosis, or functional ovarian cysts must be entertained.

References

Crissman JD, Azoury RS, Barnes AE, Schellhas HF. Endometrial carcinoma in women 40 years of age or younger. Obstet Gynecol 57:699, 1981.

Gal D, Edman CD, Vellios F, Forney JP. Long-term effect of megestrol acetate in the treatment of endometrial hyperplasia. Am J Obstet Gynecol 146:316, 1983.

Iversen OE, Segadal E. The value of endometrial cytology: A comparative study of the Gravlee-Jet washer, Isaac cell sampler and Endoscan versus curettage in 600 patients. Obstet Gynecol Surv 40:14, 1985.

Silverberg DG. New aspects of endometrial carcinoma. Clin Obstet Gynecol 11:189, 1984.

Winkler B, Alvarez S, Richart RM, Crum CP. Pitfalls in the diagnosis of endometrial neoplasia. Obstet Gynecol 64:185, 1984.

PATIENT WITH INTERMENSTRUAL BLEEDING

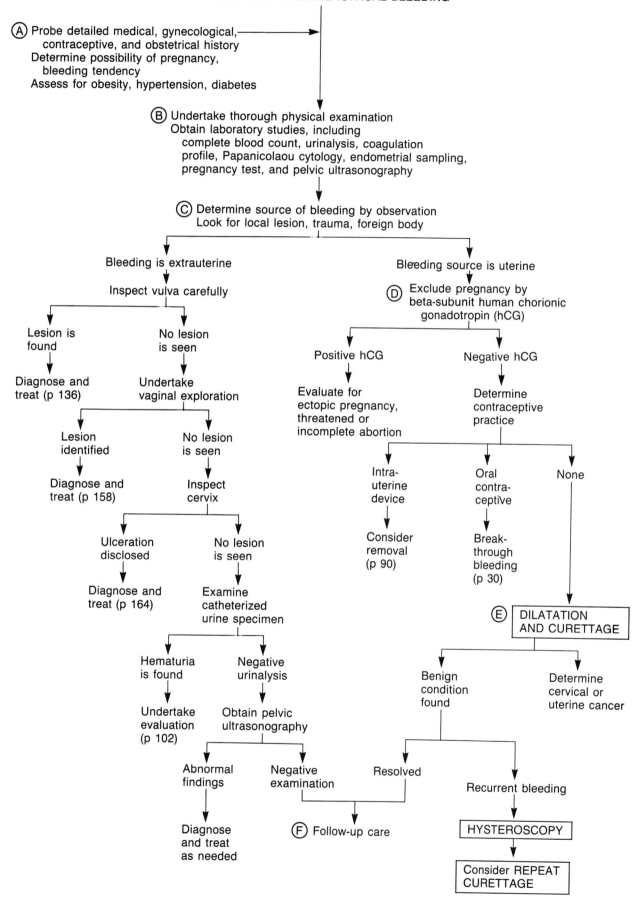

(A) Probe detailed medical, gynecological,
contraceptive, and obstetrical history
Determine possibility of pregnancy,
bleeding tendency
Assess for obesity, hypertension, diabetes

(B) Undertake thorough physical examination
Obtain laboratory studies, including
complete blood count, urinalysis, coagulation
profile, Papanicolaou cytology, endometrial sampling,
pregnancy test, and pelvic ultrasonography

(C) Determine source of bleeding by observation
Look for local lesion, trauma, foreign body

Bleeding is extrauterine

Inspect vulva carefully

Lesion is found → Diagnose and treat (p 136)

No lesion is seen → Undertake vaginal exploration

Lesion identified → Diagnose and treat (p 158)

No lesion is seen → Inspect cervix

Ulceration disclosed → Diagnose and treat (p 164)

No lesion is seen → Examine catheterized urine specimen

Hematuria is found → Undertake evaluation (p 102)

Negative urinalysis → Obtain pelvic ultrasonography

Abnormal findings → Diagnose and treat as needed

Negative examination

Bleeding source is uterine

(D) Exclude pregnancy by beta-subunit human chorionic gonadotropin (hCG)

Positive hCG → Evaluate for ectopic pregnancy, threatened or incomplete abortion

Negative hCG → Determine contraceptive practice

Intra-uterine device → Consider removal (p 90)

Oral contraceptive → Break-through bleeding (p 30)

None

(E) DILATATION AND CURETTAGE

Benign condition found

Determine cervical or uterine cancer

Resolved

Recurrent bleeding

(F) Follow-up care

HYSTEROSCOPY

Consider REPEAT CURETTAGE

FEMALE INFERTILITY

Steven R. Bayer, M.D.

A. Infertility is clinically defined as failure to conceive after one year of unprotected intercourse. The problem, which affects one couple in six, is increasing in prevalence. Both partners should be evaluated. Search for risk factors. In the female, these include sexually transmitted disease, intrauterine device, pelvic inflammatory disease, diethylstilbesterol (DES) exposure in utero, obstetrical history if any, and menstrual pattern. Assess coital frequency and technique. One must also address the emotional impact of infertility, its causes, prognosis, and the frustrations of treatment. Provide supportive discussions and counseling (p 86).

B. The physical examination should be thorough enough to detect malnutrition, debilitating or chronic systemic disease, and an endocrinopathy. Look especially for signs of virilization and thyroid disease. Pelvic examination can often detect genital anomaly, pelvic inflammatory disease, or endometriosis.

C. Ovulation is probably occurring if cyclic vaginal bleeding is preceded by premenstrual molimina (p 42). The basal body temperature chart is a daily record of temperature taken by the patient immediately upon wakening. In an ovulatory cycle, the basal body temperature pattern is biphasic. From the low proliferative phase level, an increase of 0.5 to 1.0° F follows two days after the luteinizing hormone peak that presages ovulation. It parallels circulating progesterone and is maintained throughout the last half of the cycle. If the pattern is inconsistent or unstable, measure serum progesterone or obtain endometrial biopsy during the luteal phase to determine ovulation.

D. Having obtained acceptable results from the semen analysis (p 84), proceed with the postcoital test to assess the quality of the preovulatory mucus and the ability of the sperm to gain access to the mucus. When the mucus has been optimally prepared by the patient's hormonal milieu, it allows the sperm to penetrate and survive. Because optimal cervical mucus production occurs one to two days before ovulation, this is the best time to schedule the postcoital test. Although some advocate performing it within eight hours of intercourse, we instruct the couple to have coitus the night before to relieve their anxiety about the test and to give better information about sperm survival over a longer time period. The quality of the mucus is assessed for its clarity, cellularity, ferning pattern, and spinnbarkeit (elasticity). The most common cause of poor test results is poor cervical mucus due to inappropriate choice of timing. If the timing is good and repeated postcoital tests continue to show substandard quality mucus, then a cervical factor should be considered as probably responsible. If the mucus is of good quality, then the number of motile sperm is counted, although no objective studies have as yet established meaningful criteria for defining normality. If any motile sperm are seen, it demonstrates good coital technique and suggests a normal test. If no sperm are present or all the sperm seen are nonmotile, consider a male factor (p 84) as likely.

E. Luteal phase deficiency (p 126) results in suboptimal progesterone production by the corpus luteum. Progesterone initiates specific changes in the estrogen primed endometrium and a deficiency of this hormone may result in an endometrium that is not conducive to implantation. The endometrial biopsy remains the best test to establish the diagnosis. It should be done just prior to the oncoming menstrual period. A paracervical block decreases the discomfort of the procedure. A small caliber Meigs curette is usually well tolerated by the patient and it provides an adequate specimen. The endometrial specimen is carefully dated by the pathologist according to its histologic characteristics. The chronologic date of the biopsy is determined by counting back to the first day of the prior menstrual period. If the histologic date of the biopsy specimen lags more than two days behind the actual date of the cycle, then luteal phase deficiency must be considered.

F. Hysterosalpingography (HSG) helps rule out uterine causes of infertility and determines tubal patency. The test is done optimally within a few days after menses has ceased during the early proliferative phase. If the x-ray contrast study shows the presence of an intrauterine filling defect, proceed with hysteroscopy to visualize the uterine cavity.

G. If a tubal factor is suspected or the work-up has uncovered no discernible cause of the infertility, the next step is a laparoscopy to rule out peritoneal factors, such as chronic pelvic inflammatory disease or endometriosis.

References

Buttram VC, Reiter RC. Surgical Treatment of the Infertile Female. Baltimore: Williams & Wilkins, 1985.

Grimes EM. Management of the infertile couple. Semin Reprod Endocrinol 3:93, 1985.

Soules MR, Spadoni LR. Oil versus aqueous media for hysterosalpingography: A continuing debate based on many opinions and few facts. Fertil Steril 38:1, 1982.

World Health Organization. Comparative trial of tubal insufflation, hysterosalpingography, and laparoscopy with dye hydrotubation for assessment of tubal patency. Fertil Steril 46:1101, 1986.

COUPLE WITH INFERTILITY PROBLEM

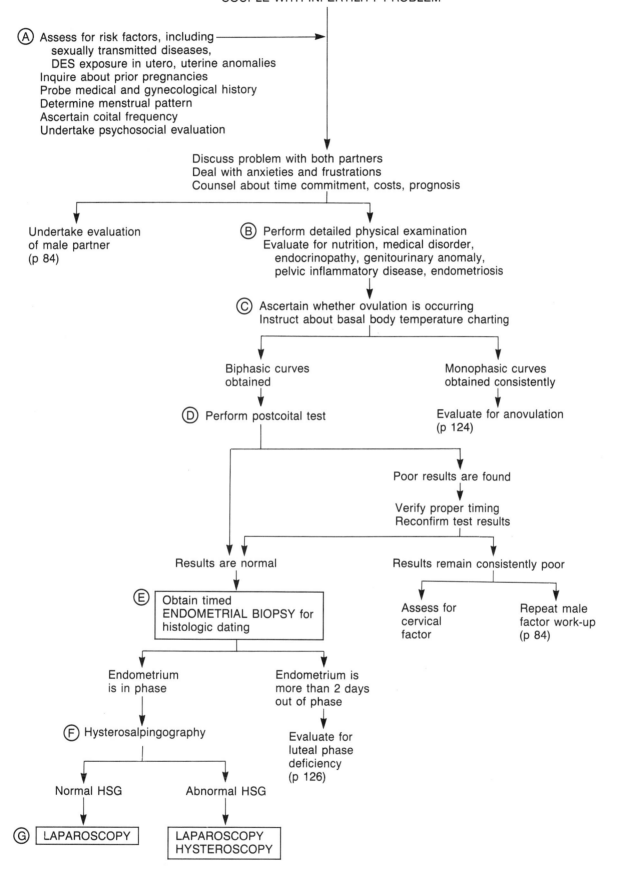

Ⓐ Assess for risk factors, including
    sexually transmitted diseases,
    DES exposure in utero, uterine anomalies
Inquire about prior pregnancies
Probe medical and gynecological history
Determine menstrual pattern
Ascertain coital frequency
Undertake psychosocial evaluation

Discuss problem with both partners
Deal with anxieties and frustrations
Counsel about time commitment, costs, prognosis

Undertake evaluation
of male partner
(p 84)

Ⓑ Perform detailed physical examination
Evaluate for nutrition, medical disorder,
    endocrinopathy, genitourinary anomaly,
    pelvic inflammatory disease, endometriosis

Ⓒ Ascertain whether ovulation is occurring
Instruct about basal body temperature charting

Biphasic curves
obtained

Monophasic curves
obtained consistently

Ⓓ Perform postcoital test

Evaluate for anovulation
(p 124)

Poor results are found

Verify proper timing
Reconfirm test results

Results are normal

Results remain consistently poor

Ⓔ Obtain timed
ENDOMETRIAL BIOPSY for
histologic dating

Assess for
cervical
factor

Repeat male
factor work-up
(p 84)

Endometrium
is in phase

Endometrium is
more than 2 days
out of phase

Ⓕ Hysterosalpingography

Evaluate for
luteal phase
deficiency
(p 126)

Normal HSG

Abnormal HSG

Ⓖ LAPAROSCOPY

LAPAROSCOPY
HYSTEROSCOPY

MALE INFERTILITY

Steven R. Bayer, M.D.

A. To emphasize that infertility assessment should involve both partners actively, a male factor is responsible in 40 percent of cases. Important aspects of the male partner's history include any past testicular injury, sexually transmitted disease, other potentially relevant infections (such as epididymal tuberculosis or mumps orchitis), and delayed puberty; inquire about prior pregnancies he may have sired. Sperm production is a temperature sensitive process. Jockey shorts, hot tubs, and occupations that require long hours of sitting may raise scrotal temperature, theoretically decreasing spermatogenesis. Probe into drug use, especially medications that can interfere with spermatogenesis, such as cimetidine, nitrofurantoin, and sulfasalazine. Alcohol, tobacco, and marijuana, if taken in excess, can also affect sperm production, potency, and libido. General health should be assessed to disclose any chronic or debilitating disease, neuropathy, or endocrinopathy. Specifically look for evidence of thyroid and hepatic disease as well. Determine coital frequency. The physical examination should be thorough. Pay close attention to secondary sexual characteristics, including hair distribution, testicular descent and size, and evidence of gynecomastia or hypospadias. Determine the presence of a varicocele by examining the patient while he is standing and bearing down (Valsalva maneuver).

B. Currently, there is no good test to assess the qualitative aspect of sperm function other than the achievement of pregnancy itself. Despite this, the best laboratory test to evaluate the male factor remains the semen analysis for quantitative assessment only. The specimen should be obtained by masturbation into a clean glass container (not a condom) after 48 hours or more of abstinence from coitus. Normal parameters include a total ejaculatory volume between 1.5 and 5.0 ml with a count greater than 40 million spermatozoa per milliliter, of which at least 60 percent are motile and 60 percent have normal morphology. Because spermatogenesis is sensitive to transient influences, including systemic illnesses and emotional stress, at least two semen analyses should be obtained over a period of one to two months.

C. Normal semen analysis and postcoital test (p 82) probably rule out a male factor. If the postcoital test is suboptimal despite good cervical mucus, then carry out intracervical insemination with the husband's sperm and repeat the postcoital test. Abnormal results mean one should give consideration to an immunologic cause for the infertility. Sperm antibodies can be detected by the immunobead technique. A significantly improved postcoital test following insemination signifies that there may be difficulties in ensuring proper intravaginal deposition of the ejaculate. Artificial insemination may be a logical alternative for such a case.

D. A semen analysis showing either a low count or decreased motility requires additional hormonal assessments, including determination of serum prolactin, testosterone, and follicle stimulating (FSH) and luteinizing (LH) hormone levels. Even though hyperprolactinemia is a rare cause of male infertility, measure the serum prolactin. If it is elevated, rule out a pituitary adenoma (p 70) by computer tomography.

E. In the presence of elevated gonadotropins, consider testicular atrophy secondary to infection or Klinefelter's syndrome (seminiferous tubular dysgenesis, usually with XXY karyotype). The diagnosis can be confirmed by testicular biopsy and karyotyping.

F. Seek other causes when normal gonadotropins are encountered, including varicocele and infection, such as prostatitis. Azoospermia requires a testicular biopsy; if it proves normal, there may be ductal obstruction.

G. Decreased gonadotropins suggest a hypothalamic etiology. Computer tomography helps rule out an intracranial lesion. Kallmann's syndrome, recognized by hypogonadism and anosmia, is treated by Pergonal and gonadotropin releasing hormone (GnRH) to restore gonadal function and spermatogenesis.

H. High semen volume with low sperm counts warrant inseminating a split ejaculate intracervically. Consistently decreased semen volumes justify using the entire ejaculate for the insemination.

I. Immediately after ejaculation, semen coagulates at first and then liquifies again in 20 to 30 minutes. Failure to reliquify may entrap the sperm in the viscous semen so they cannot gain access to the cervical mucus. If hyperviscosity is seen repeatedly, try intracervical insemination with washed sperm or semen agitated by aspiration through a needle.

References

Cockett ATK, Takihara H, Cosentino MJ. The varicocele. Fertil Steril 41:5, 1984.

Lipshultz LI, Howard SS (Editors). Infertility in the Male. New York: Churchill Livingstone, 1983.

McShane PM. Immunologic aspects of male infertility. Semin Urol 2:107, 1984.

Poland ML, Moghissi KS, Giblin PT, et al. Variation of semen measurements within normal men. Fertil Steril 44:396, 1985.

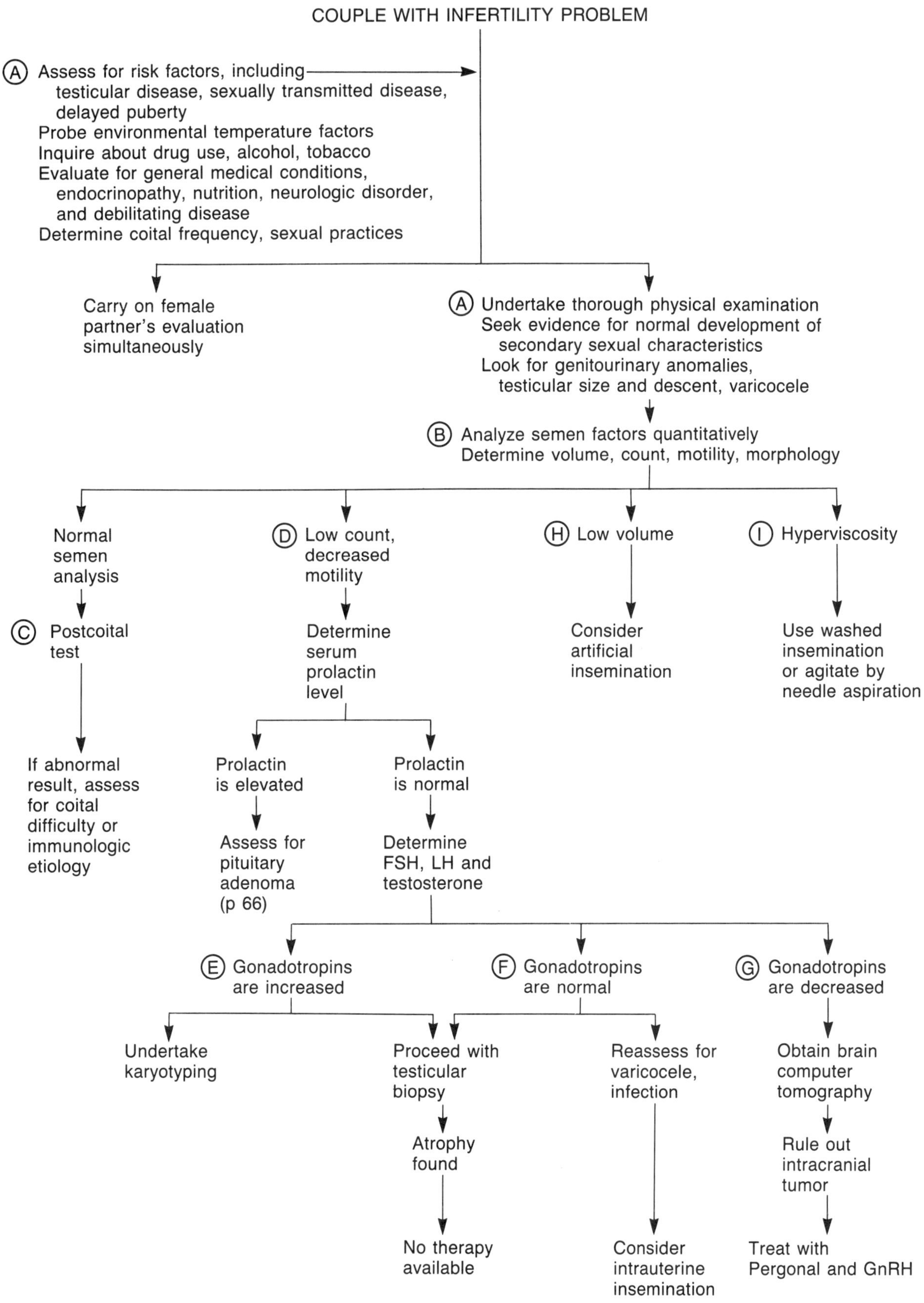

COUPLE WITH INFERTILITY PROBLEM

(A) Assess for risk factors, including————→
    testicular disease, sexually transmitted disease,
    delayed puberty
  Probe environmental temperature factors
  Inquire about drug use, alcohol, tobacco
  Evaluate for general medical conditions,
    endocrinopathy, nutrition, neurologic disorder,
    and debilitating disease
  Determine coital frequency, sexual practices

Carry on female
partner's evaluation
simultaneously

(A) Undertake thorough physical examination
  Seek evidence for normal development of
    secondary sexual characteristics
  Look for genitourinary anomalies,
    testicular size and descent, varicocele

(B) Analyze semen factors quantitatively
  Determine volume, count, motility, morphology

Normal
semen
analysis

(D) Low count,
decreased
motility

(H) Low volume

(I) Hyperviscosity

(C) Postcoital
test

Determine
serum
prolactin
level

Consider
artificial
insemination

Use washed
insemination
or agitate by
needle aspiration

If abnormal
result, assess
for coital
difficulty or
immunologic
etiology

Prolactin
is elevated

Prolactin
is normal

Assess for
pituitary
adenoma
(p 66)

Determine
FSH, LH and
testosterone

(E) Gonadotropins
are increased

(F) Gonadotropins
are normal

(G) Gonadotropins
are decreased

Undertake
karyotyping

Proceed with
testicular
biopsy

Reassess for
varicocele,
infection

Obtain brain
computer
tomography

Atrophy
found

Rule out
intracranial
tumor

No therapy
available

Consider
intrauterine
insemination

Treat with
Pergonal and GnRH

INFERTILITY COUNSELING

Steven R. Bayer, M.D.

A. Infertility is a unique problem in medicine because it is a diagnosis that applies to a couple and not just to an individual. For this reason, the couple should be considered to be a unit for purposes of evaluation, counseling, planning, and treatment program. It is important for both partners to be present at least at the first interview. They should also be involved together whenever major decisions are being made regarding diagnosis or treatment.

B. The purpose of the initial interview is to establish rapport with the couple, to obtain an accurate history, to conduct detailed physical examinations, and to formulate a plan of evaluation. Recognize that infertility is stressful and can generate psychological turmoil. The emotional aspects of infertility cannot be ignored. It is important, therefore, to assess the impact of their barrenness on both individuals as well as its effect on the dynamics of their relationship. Even though a couple may present with the chief complaint of infertility, there may be other subtle and even unrecognized underlying reasons motivating them to seek help and care. Some may be responding to pressure from family members or friends, while others may be experiencing marital discord and be seeking a pregnancy as a potential solution to resolve their conflict and salvage the relationship. This emphasizes that counseling is an important and integral part of the infertility work-up. Those who are involved in the care of infertile couples must be sensitive to and aware of the emotional component of the problem.

C. Although the counseling can be done by the physician, because it is time consuming and demanding, it is beneficial to have the couple assessed by specially trained and interested personnel (perhaps by a knowledgeable social worker or psychologist). In many communities, groups of individuals have been organized to aid in the counseling of infertile couples. If symptoms of depression are noted in either partner or there is a suspicion of more serious psychopathology, be sure to recommend a psychiatric consultation.

D. The medical evaluation can be done concurrently with any counseling that has been undertaken. Be aware that the diagnostic work-up may impose additional stresses on the couple. The private act of coitus had hitherto not come under close examination for them; when it becomes a matter of almost public focus (in their minds), it may no longer prove to be enjoyable. Sexual dysfunction is actually quite common when the male is asked to perform essentially on cue for the postcoital test or to produce a specimen for the semen analysis. It is important for the physician to maintain a flexible attitude insofar as the scheduling of investigative tests is concerned; avoid insisting on adhering to a strict timetable. This helps to minimize the anxiety generated by the sequence of work-up studies.

E. Once the evaluation is complete, the results of the tests should be reviewed and the diagnosis discussed in detail with both partners. Even though they may be more at ease with specific knowledge regarding the etiology of their infertility, be alert to the new anxieties that may arise from their concerns about the disclosed problem. If a male factor is found, the male partner may have feelings of inferiority or inadequacy; he must be reassured that the deficient sperm production, for example, is not related to his virility. The female with chronic pelvic inflammatory disease that developed following elective abortion may have feelings of guilt based on perceived retribution.

F. The physician should formulate a logical long-range treatment plan with the couple. Limitations should be placed on the duration of specific treatments so that if pregnancy is not achieved by a certain time, other treatment options will be undertaken. This avoids overly protracting the course of the management program, a counterproductive factor commonly contributing to frustration and disappointment.

G. If specific treatment designed to correct conditions identified as probably etiologic, such as lysis of adhesions, treatment of endometriosis, and artificial insemination, has been unsuccessful, there are several available alternatives. These should be discussed in detail with the couple. Two options applicable for severe azoospermia are donor insemination and adoption. In vitro fertilization (p 276) is especially valuable for irreversible tubal disease. Gamete intrafallopian tube transfer (p 278) is another technique that can be used for the couple with unexplained infertility. Both are costly and associated with high failure rates. Although they offer hope, they may not be appropriate for all couples.

References

Fagen PJ, Schmidt CW Jr, Rock JA, et al. Sexual functioning and psychological evaluation of in vitro fertilization couples. Fertil Steril 46:668, 1986.

Priest RG. Psychological Disorders in Obstetrics and Gynaecology. London: Butterworth Publishers, 1985.

Rosenfeld DL, Mitchell E. Treating the emotional aspects of infertility: Counseling services in an infertility clinic. Am J Obstet Gynecol 135:177, 1979.

Seibel MM, Taymor ML. Emotional aspects of infertility. Fertil Steril 37:137, 1982.

COUPLE UNABLE TO CONCEIVE

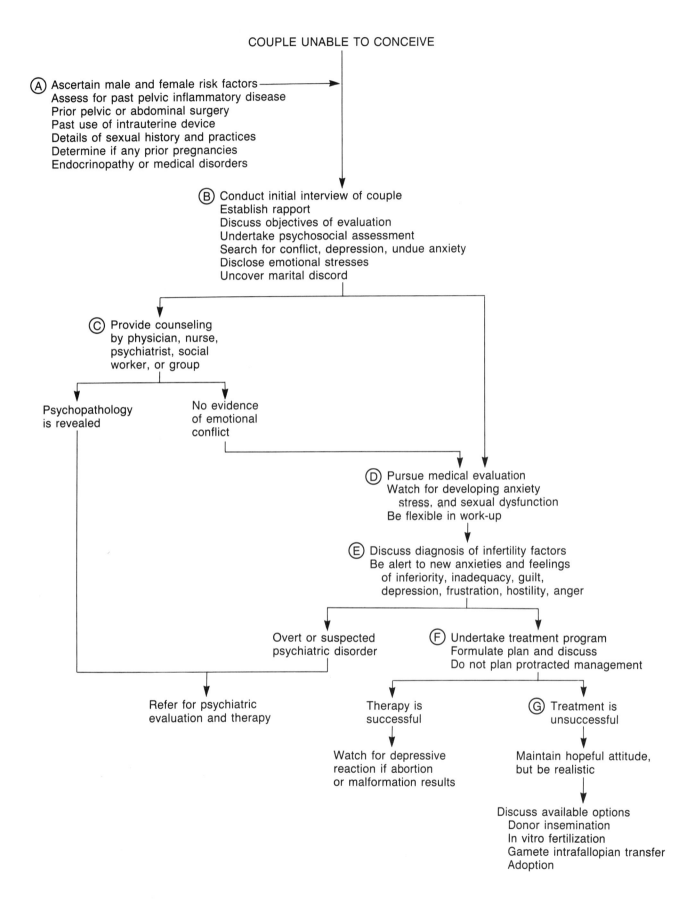

(A) Ascertain male and female risk factors ⟶
Assess for past pelvic inflammatory disease
Prior pelvic or abdominal surgery
Past use of intrauterine device
Details of sexual history and practices
Determine if any prior pregnancies
Endocrinopathy or medical disorders

(B) Conduct initial interview of couple
Establish rapport
Discuss objectives of evaluation
Undertake psychosocial assessment
Search for conflict, depression, undue anxiety
Disclose emotional stresses
Uncover marital discord

(C) Provide counseling
by physician, nurse,
psychiatrist, social
worker, or group

Psychopathology
is revealed

No evidence
of emotional
conflict

(D) Pursue medical evaluation
Watch for developing anxiety
stress, and sexual dysfunction
Be flexible in work-up

(E) Discuss diagnosis of infertility factors
Be alert to new anxieties and feelings
of inferiority, inadequacy, guilt,
depression, frustration, hostility, anger

Overt or suspected
psychiatric disorder

(F) Undertake treatment program
Formulate plan and discuss
Do not plan protracted management

Refer for psychiatric
evaluation and therapy

Therapy is
successful

(G) Treatment is
unsuccessful

Watch for depressive
reaction if abortion
or malformation results

Maintain hopeful attitude,
but be realistic

Discuss available options
Donor insemination
In vitro fertilization
Gamete intrafallopian transfer
Adoption

FAILED CONTRACEPTION

Johanna F. Perlmutter, M.D.

A. It is important to counsel the woman who has become pregnant as a result of a contraceptive failure. Her attitude and feelings toward the new pregnancy should be explored. One must not categorically assume that the pregnancy is necessarily unwanted, although frequently it is. Some women embark on a contraceptive program without full conviction, perhaps succumbing to pressure from partner or peers. Ambivalence is common and manifests in poor contraceptive compliance. Women may be torn between their career objectives and desires to raise a family. Be sensitive to this conflict of values and objectives. Decision making in these cases may be difficult. Much emotional support may be needed. Discuss the options carefully and in depth. Do not press the patient for a decision; give her ample opportunity to weigh her needs and resolve her conflicts.

B. Even though there is now only one intrauterine device still commercially available for insertion in this country (Progestasert), millions of woman have had devices inserted in the past, and some are obtaining them abroad. Thus, the problems associated with their use is a matter of continuing interest and concern. About one in twenty pregnancies conceived with an intrauterine device in place will implant in the fallopian tube. It is unclear whether this reflects an actual increase in the absolute frequency of ectopic pregnancies in these cases or merely the fact that intrauterine implantation is so effectively prevented. Nonetheless, the real risks to health and life posed by an ectopic pregnancy (p 198) demand the closest attention to any conception among them. Whenever pregnancy is suspected, therefore, it is necessary to diagnose it early and to determine its site. At the same time, also try to locate the device, which may have been expelled without the gravida having been aware of it.

C. The urgency for removing an extrauterine device depends on the type of device (p 90). Removal may be done by way of laparoscopy, colpotomy, or laparotomy. The choice depends upon the site, the type of device, and the degree of embedment, surrounding inflammatory reaction, or adhesion formation.

D. The greatest risks of an intrauterine device present within the uterine cavity during pregnancy are sepsis and spontaneous abortion. More than half the affected patients will abort, and many will develop severe infection. The form of septic abortion that occurs can arise with deceptively mild manifestations, often with a flu-like syndrome; it then progresses very rapidly to an over-whelming infection that may be fatal, especially during the second trimester. Because of this very serious hazard, induced abortion is recommended. For the patient who does not wish to terminate the pregnancy, an attempt should be made to remove the device. If the string is protruding from the cervix, gentle traction is often successful in accomplishing removal, usually without disturbing the pregnancy. Once the device is out, a continuing pregnancy can be expected to carry to term uneventfully.

E. If the string is not visible, the device cannot be removed without potentially disturbing the gestation. Induced abortion is preferable to continuing the pregnancy under these conditions. A pregnancy with an intrauterine device in situ is at increased risk for spontaneous abortion, premature rupture of the membranes, bleeding complications, and stillbirths. Moreover, the gravida is at risk for fulminating sepsis, as aforementioned (see D). The patient who chooses to continue pregnancy with a device in place must be carefully counseled and assiduously followed for the earliest sign of infection so that aggressive intervention may be undertaken as needed.

F. The fetal risks of progestins are unclear. Although a wide variety of defects have been reported, only genital malformations (and perhaps heart defects) can be confirmed to be related to in utero exposure to these drugs. Although estrogens (mostly diethylstilbestrol), which were once widely used for pregnancy maintenance, have been documented to be associated with vaginal adenosis and clear cell carcinoma of the vagina, this risk has not been observed with oral contraceptives. Therefore, pregnancies occurring while the gravida is taking birth control pills should not be considered at special risk (except for masculinization effects).

G. There have been sporadic reports of fetal anomalies associated with the use of spermicides. This relationship has not been confirmed in large scale studies. It does not appear that spermicidal agents are teratogenic.

References

Foreman H, Stadel BV, Schlesselman S. Intrauterine device usage and fetal loss. Obstet Gynecol 58:669, 1981.

Gregoire AJ, Blye RT (Editors). Contraceptive Steroids: Pharmacology and Safety. New York: Plenum Press, 1986.

Mills JL, Reed GF, Nugent RP, et al. Are there adverse effects of periconceptional spermicide use? Fertil Steril 43:442, 1985.

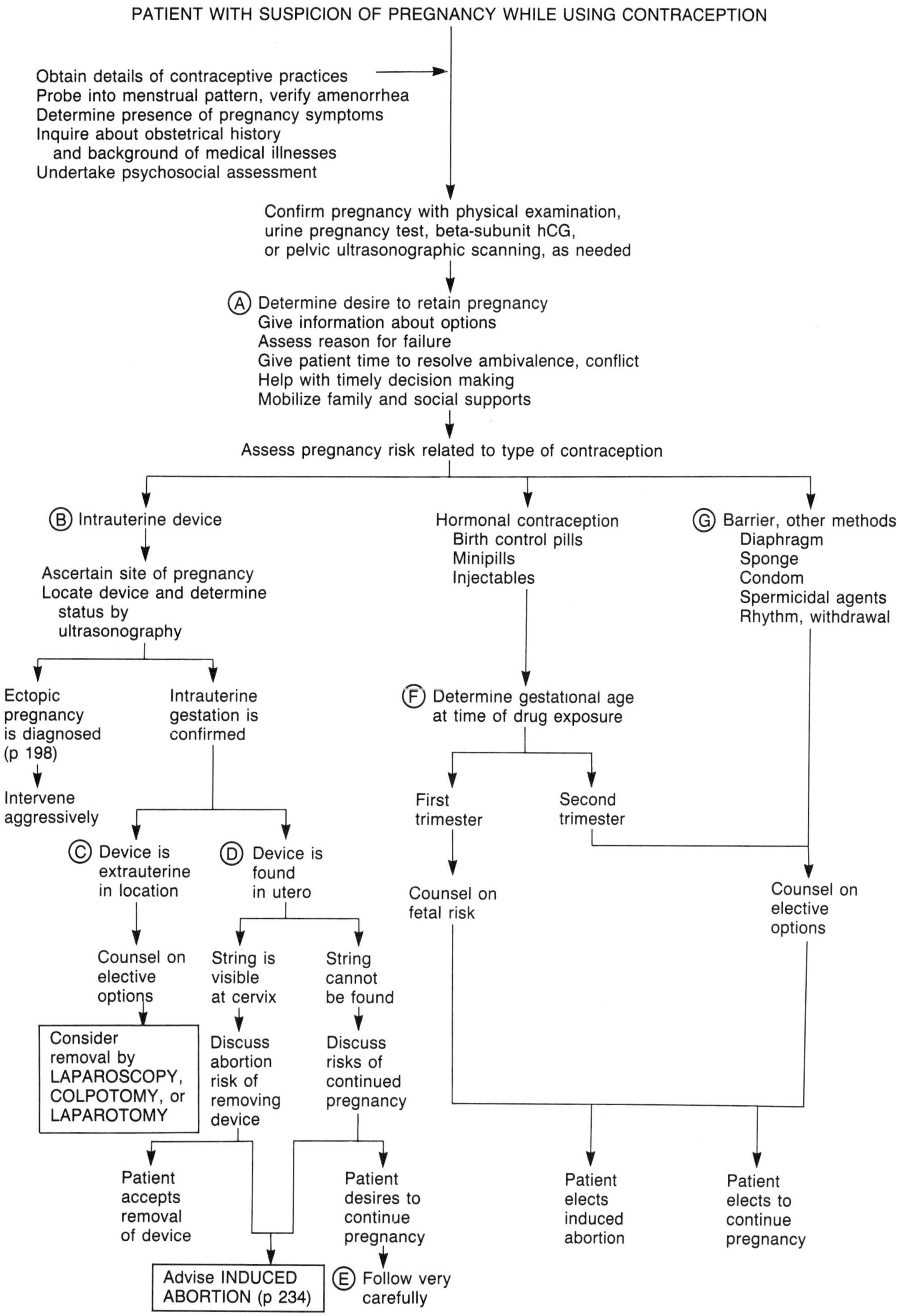

PATIENT WITH SUSPICION OF PREGNANCY WHILE USING CONTRACEPTION

Obtain details of contraceptive practices
Probe into menstrual pattern, verify amenorrhea
Determine presence of pregnancy symptoms
Inquire about obstetrical history
   and background of medical illnesses
Undertake psychosocial assessment

Confirm pregnancy with physical examination,
urine pregnancy test, beta-subunit hCG,
or pelvic ultrasonographic scanning, as needed

(A) Determine desire to retain pregnancy
    Give information about options
    Assess reason for failure
    Give patient time to resolve ambivalence, conflict
    Help with timely decision making
    Mobilize family and social supports

Assess pregnancy risk related to type of contraception

(B) Intrauterine device

Ascertain site of pregnancy
Locate device and determine
   status by
   ultrasonography

Ectopic
pregnancy
is diagnosed
(p 198)

Intervene
aggressively

Intrauterine
gestation is
confirmed

(C) Device is
    extrauterine
    in location

(D) Device is
    found
    in utero

Counsel on
elective
options

String is
visible
at cervix

String
cannot
be found

Consider
removal by
LAPAROSCOPY,
COLPOTOMY, or
LAPAROTOMY

Discuss
abortion
risk of
removing
device

Discuss
risks of
continued
pregnancy

Patient
accepts
removal
of device

Patient
desires to
continue
pregnancy

Advise INDUCED
ABORTION (p 234)

(E) Follow very
    carefully

Hormonal contraception
   Birth control pills
   Minipills
   Injectables

(F) Determine gestational age
    at time of drug exposure

First
trimester

Second
trimester

Counsel on
fetal risk

Patient
elects
induced
abortion

(G) Barrier, other methods
    Diaphragm
    Sponge
    Condom
    Spermicidal agents
    Rhythm, withdrawal

Counsel on
elective
options

Patient
elects to
continue
pregnancy

RETAINED INTRAUTERINE DEVICE

Joseph F. D'Amico, M.D.

A. Despite the current dearth of intrauterine devices available for insertion (only Progestasert remains), so many women still have devices in place that it is important to appreciate the risks to which they are exposed. Probe into the contraceptive history of all gynecological patients to ensure these women are identified and followed for potential problems related to long-term use. In addition to the increased risk of pelvic inflammatory disease and infertility from an intrauterine device, a number of other complications may develop. A device that migrates into the peritoneal cavity (either as a consequence of partial or complete perforation at the time of insertion or the result of progressive embedment) risks certain specific kinds of difficulties according to its design. Closed loop devices, for example, may cause obstruction by herniating a loop of bowel. Those containing copper may cause an intense chemical reaction leading to nonbacterial peritonitis. Removal is indicated whenever there is any sign of intrauterine or tubal infection. Although the patient's desires with regard to continuing use of the device have to be considered, she must be informed of the hazards in clear, unambiguous terms and about the need to have it removed, if removal is indeed indicated. Written informed consent should be mandatory if she chooses to retain her intrauterine device in the face of an overt contraindication.

B. A common problem is one in which the string of the intrauterine device cannot be seen on vaginal examination. This can result from spontaneous expulsion of the device, which may happen without the patient having been aware of it at all, particularly if it takes place during menstruation when the device can be discarded along with a tampon. The string may also have migrated upward into the uterine cavity. If the string cannot be seen, one must consider the possibility that the device is not within the uterine cavity (see C). A number of instruments can be tried in an attempt to retrieve the missing string or to remove the device within the uterus, including special hook, curette, or endometrial biopsy devices. If any of these are used, take care to avoid perforating the uterus. Paracervical block anesthesia is generally recommended for these purposes.

C. Before proceeding to attempt to remove an intrauterine device in a case in which one cannot find the string, try to demonstrate whether or not it is still within the uterus. Ultrasonography can often determine its relationship to the endometrial cavity, if it can be visualized. However, ultrasonography may not always be capable of identifying the device or its location. X-ray studies may sometimes be more helpful in this regard, especially if the device contains radiopaque barium or copper. Hysterography (p 220) is another useful complementary technique for definitively showing an extrauterine location, if it is needed.

D. Direct visualization of the endometrial cavity and its contents can be done by hysteroscopy (p 122). This technique is particularly adapted for locating an intrauterine device, for assessing whether it is feasible to remove it (that is, to determine how deeply it may be embedded in the myometrium), and to guide and facilitate actual removal. Removing an intrauterine device under endoscopic control diminishes the risk of trauma and perforation and averts the need for extensive manipulation. The procedure can ordinarily be done with paracervical block in a minor operating room as an outpatient procedure.

E. Laparoscopy (p 224) is used to locate the intrauterine device that has migrated into the peritoneal cavity. Examine for local reaction in the form of peritonitis, adhesion formation, and incorporation into adjacent tissue, especially the omentum. If the device is found lying free or is readily freeable by gentle translaparoscopic manipulation (p 240), it may be possible to remove it by way of the laparoscope. If it can be done, it will avoid a laparotomy for removal. Using transendoscopic forceps, grasp the device at one end and pull it gently into the laparoscopic sleeve. Since most devices cannot be withdrawn all the way out, it will be necessary to remove both the operating laparoscope and the holding forceps simultaneously along with the device being held. If the device is embedded in the omentum, laparotomy will have to be done unless it is fixed deep in the cul-de-sac of Douglas. This special case warrants an attempt to remove the device by way of a posterior colpotomy incision.

References

Ansari AH, Hoffman D. Retrieval of intrauterine contraceptive device with missing tail by means of a plastic spiral curette (Mi-Mark). Am J Obstet Gynecol 142:1061, 1982.

Daling JR, Weiss NS, Metch BJ, et al. Primary tubal infertility in relation to the use of an intrauterine device. N Engl J Med 312:937, 1985.

Kaufman DW, Watson J, Rosenberg L, et al. The effects of different types of intrauterine devices on the risk of pelvic inflammatory disease. JAMA 250:759, 1983.

McArdle CR. Ultrasonic localization of missing intrauterine contraceptive devices. Obstet Gynecol 51:330, 1978.

PATIENT WITH RETAINED INTRAUTERINE DEVICE

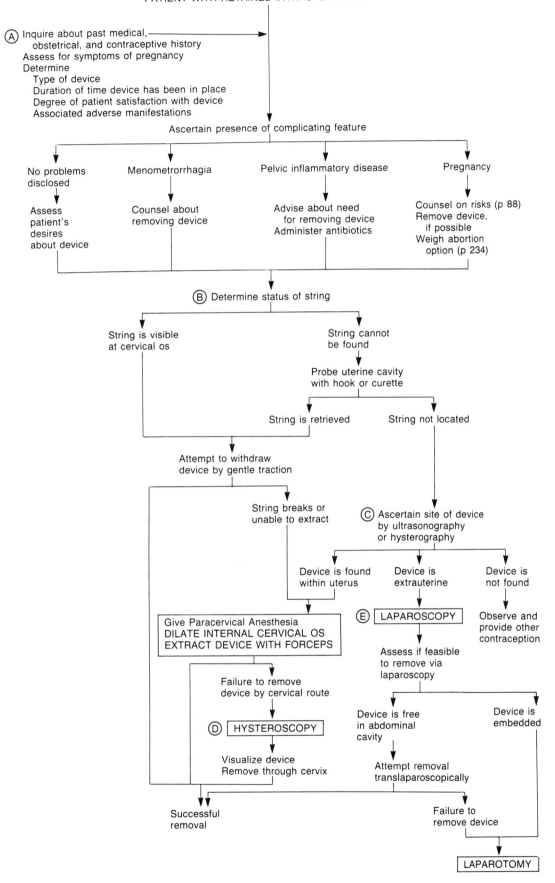

(A) Inquire about past medical,
        obstetrical, and contraceptive history
Assess for symptoms of pregnancy
Determine
    Type of device
    Duration of time device has been in place
    Degree of patient satisfaction with device
    Associated adverse manifestations

Ascertain presence of complicating feature

| No problems disclosed | Menometrorrhagia | Pelvic inflammatory disease | Pregnancy |

Assess patient's desires about device

Counsel about removing device

Advise about need for removing device
Administer antibiotics

Counsel on risks (p 88)
Remove device, if possible
Weigh abortion option (p 234)

(B) Determine status of string

String is visible at cervical os

String cannot be found

Probe uterine cavity with hook or curette

String is retrieved

String not located

Attempt to withdraw device by gentle traction

String breaks or unable to extract

(C) Ascertain site of device by ultrasonography or hysterography

Device is found within uterus

Device is extrauterine

Device is not found

Give Paracervical Anesthesia
DILATE INTERNAL CERVICAL OS
EXTRACT DEVICE WITH FORCEPS

(E) LAPAROSCOPY

Observe and provide other contraception

Failure to remove device by cervical route

Assess if feasible to remove via laparoscopy

(D) HYSTEROSCOPY

Device is free in abdominal cavity

Device is embedded

Visualize device
Remove through cervix

Attempt removal translaparoscopically

Successful removal

Failure to remove device

LAPAROTOMY

CLIMACTERIUM

Jerold M. Carlson, M.D., M.P.H.

A. The climacterium is defined as that phase in the female aging process marking the transition from the reproductive to the nonreproductive era. It may extend over a period of two decades, usually beginning at about age 40 years, in association with diminishing regularity and frequency of ovulation, progressively reduced fertility, and increasingly irregular periods until periods cease completely at the menopause (p 94); it also continues for years beyond menopause with changes affecting pelvic organs and tissues, skeletal system, and vasculature. There is a gradual loss of ovarian function and hence diminution in the amount of estrogens secreted by the ovaries. This is due to attrition and exhaustion of oocytes and follicles within the ovarian cortex until, finally, the only source of estrogen production is peripheral conversion of precursors from the adrenal glands. The manifestations related to this decreased estrogen status may include, but are not limited to, disturbed menstrual pattern (such as menstrual irregularity), vasomotor symptoms (specifically sweats and hot flashes), psychological effects (probably only indirectly related, but nonetheless common, including mood swings, anxiety, insomnia, and altered libido), urogenital atrophy (resulting in dryness, dyspareunia (p 46), and itching), stress incontinence (p 98), pelvic relaxation, osteoporosis (p 96), and atherosclerosis.

B. Each patient should have a complete history recorded with specific attention to her age, race, height, gravidity, parity, weight, menstrual status (including changing pattern or cessation), smoking history, prior breast feeding, and use of medications. Conduct a general physical examination to disclose acute or chronic medical disorders. Examine the pelvis and breasts. Obtain a Papanicolaou smear, urinalysis, and blood chemistry determinations, as well as mammography and any other laboratory or radiographic studies that may be indicated.

C. The patient's estrogen status can be initially assessed as part of the physical examination, looking for signs of atrophy of skin, breasts, and the mucous membranes of vulva, vagina, and urethra. Scrape the lateral vaginal wall at the fornix to make a cytologic smear for maturation or karyopyknotic index. A high proportion of superficial epithelial cells in the smear indicates good estrogen effect. It must be remembered, however, that these indices are nonspecific because other factors, such as infection, medication, prior irradiation, and uterine prolapse, may alter or obscure the results.

D. The hormonal evaluation can be expected to reflect changes due to the decrease in estrogens. One should find increased follicle stimulating (FSH) and luteinizing (LH) hormone levels due to loss of negative feedback by estrogens to the pituitary, along with a slight decrease in prolactin. In addition, the testosterone level is reduced and there is some associated decrease in androstenedione. There is generally no change in dehydroepiandrosterone sulfate since it is derived solely from the adrenal gland. If androgen excess is encountered, investigate for other conditions.

E. If estrogen excess is diagnosed, it is imperative to determine the cause (including endocrine-producing tumor, morbid obesity, or endocrinopathy). It is also essential to rule out significant secondary pathology, such as endometrial hyperplasia and cancer. However, it must also be remembered that other etiologies, such as pregnancy, hypermetabolic states, stress, and medications (such as reserpine and digitalis), should be considered as well.

F. Patients should be followed at six-month intervals or more frequently, if necessary. Special attention should be paid to interim history, physical examination including blood pressure, and indicated laboratory screening. For patients demonstrating decreased estrogen status, hormone replacement may be considered, if it is not contraindicated (p 28).

References

Haney AF. The "physiology" of the climacterium. Clin Obstet Gynecol 29:397, 1986.

Holzman GB, Ravitch MM, Metheny W, et al. Physicians' judgments about estrogen replacement therapy for menopausal women. Obstet Gynecol 63:303, 1984.

Montgomery JC, Appleby L, Brincat M, et al. Effect of oestrogen and testosterone implants on psychological disorders in the climacterium. Lancet 1:297, 1987.

Notelovitz M, Fields C, Caramelli K, et al. Cardiorespiratory fitness evaluation in climacteric women: Comparison of two methods. Am J Obstet Gynecol 154:1009, 1986.

PATIENT WITH SYMPTOMS OF ESTROGEN DEFICIENCY

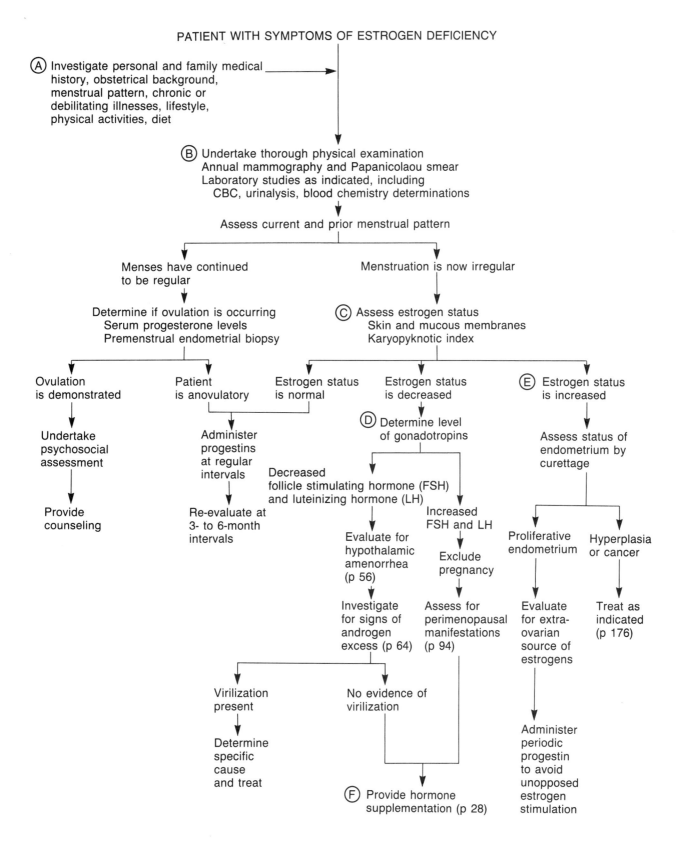

A. Investigate personal and family medical history, obstetrical background, menstrual pattern, chronic or debilitating illnesses, lifestyle, physical activities, diet

B. Undertake thorough physical examination
Annual mammography and Papanicolaou smear
Laboratory studies as indicated, including
CBC, urinalysis, blood chemistry determinations

Assess current and prior menstrual pattern

Menses have continued to be regular

Menstruation is now irregular

Determine if ovulation is occurring
Serum progesterone levels
Premenstrual endometrial biopsy

C. Assess estrogen status
Skin and mucous membranes
Karyopyknotic index

Ovulation is demonstrated

Patient is anovulatory

Estrogen status is normal

Estrogen status is decreased

E. Estrogen status is increased

Undertake psychosocial assessment

Administer progestins at regular intervals

D. Determine level of gonadotropins

Assess status of endometrium by curettage

Provide counseling

Re-evaluate at 3- to 6-month intervals

Decreased follicle stimulating hormone (FSH) and luteinizing hormone (LH)

Increased FSH and LH

Proliferative endometrium

Hyperplasia or cancer

Evaluate for hypothalamic amenorrhea (p 56)

Exclude pregnancy

Evaluate for extra-ovarian source of estrogens

Treat as indicated (p 176)

Investigate for signs of androgen excess (p 64)

Assess for perimenopausal manifestations (p 94)

Virilization present

No evidence of virilization

Administer periodic progestin to avoid unopposed estrogen stimulation

Determine specific cause and treat

F. Provide hormone supplementation (p 28)

MENOPAUSE

Jerold M. Carlson, M.D., M.P.H.

A. As a milestone during the climacterium, menopause is defined as the permanent cessation of the menses. In practical terms, if one year or more passes without a period, menopause is assumed to have occurred. The single event takes place in an endocrinologic milieu characterized by estrogen deficiency, often with clinical symptoms, and associated with increased serum follicle stimulating and luteinizing hormone levels. Early symptoms, usually preceding menopause by several years, include those of vasomotor instability, namely, sweats with hot flushes and flashes; they are found in varying degrees in up to 75 percent of perimenopausal climacteric patients. Later symptoms include urogenital atrophy, genital relaxation, osteoporosis, and atherosclerosis.

B. Estrogens have been shown to be capable of significantly reducing the symptoms of vasomotor instability and urogenital atrophy in most patients. In combination with proper nutrition, calcium supplementation, and exercise, estrogen replacement can probably also prevent loss of bone density over time. It is most beneficial in this regard if it is started as soon after the menopause as possible. It is preferable to begin within four years when the rate of bone loss tends to be fairly rapid. Be alert to risk factors (see C). The full-blown symptoms of osteoporosis often may not become overtly manifest until 10 to 15 years after menopause; at that late date, however, the patient is not likely to derive any benefit from a program of estrogen-progestin therapy begun then.

C. Osteoporosis can result in debilitating symptoms, such as back pain, or expose a woman to serious risk of long bone fracture. Moreover, spinal compression fractures may be seen in up to 25 percent of white and oriental women over 60 years of age. Estrogen replacement may be effective in preventing this problem, especially if complemented by extra calcium intake and an exercise program. Unless contraindicated, therefore, prophylaxis against osteoporosis should be considered in all high-risk individuals. Those at risk include caucasian and oriental women with light bone structure, especially if they are nulliparous, have a family history of osteoporosis, or a personal background that includes early surgical menopause, nutritional deficiency, alcoholism, high caffeine intake, smoking, or a sedentary life style (p 96).

D. Counseling about the risks, benefits, and alternative options of estrogen replacement therapy is an important aspect of care. Estrogens are contraindicated in women with undiagnosed vaginal bleeding, acute or chronic liver disease, acute vascular thrombosis, neuro-ophthalmologic vascular disease, estrogen dependent tumors, breast cancer, or malignant melanoma. They are relatively contraindicated in women with hypertension, migraine, previous thrombophlebitis, gallbladder disease, hyperlipidemia, abnormal glucose tolerance, fibrocystic disease, pancreatitis, cardiac and nephrogenic edema, or allergy to the medication. Patients with psychological complaints, such as fatigue, mood changes, depression, and inability to concentrate, are unlikely to benefit from hormone replacement therapy.

E. Estrogen should be given in a cyclic fashion, such as daily from day 1 to day 25 followed by several days (representing the rest of a calendar month for convenience in recall) without medication. Give a progestin for the last 10 to 14 days of the cycle to help protect against endometrial hyperplasia and cancer. Routine pretreatment sampling of the endometrium is not cost effective, but it should be considered in high-risk individuals, such as obese, hypertensive, or diabetic women, those on estrogens for more than one year, and those who have not been given concomitant progestins. Annual mammograms and Papanicolaou smears are mandatory, as well as endometrial sampling in patients with abnormal vaginal bleeding. The benefit of progestin therapy in patients who have had their uterus previously removed is still controversial. Topical estrogen is useful for relieving mucosal atrophy. Because it is absorbed systemically, it must also be used in combination with progestin therapy unless the amount used is negligible. Give it in the minimal amount needed to relieve the symptoms. Use caution because vaginal absorption is rapid, sometimes yielding estrogen levels in the circulation surpassing those achieved with oral estrogens.

References

Bush TL, Cowan LD, Barrett-Connor E, et al. Estrogen use and all-cause mortality: Preliminary results from the lipid research clinics program follow-up study. JAMA 249:903, 1983.

Chetkowski RJ, Meldrum DR, Steingold KA, et al. Biologic effects of transdermal estradiol. N Engl J Med 314:1615, 1986.

Deutsch S, Ossowski R, Benjamin I. Comparison between degree of systemic absorption of vaginally and orally administrated estrogens at different dose levels in postmenopausal women. Am J Obstet Gynecol 139:967, 1981.

Hammond CB, Ory SJ. Endocrine problems in the menopause. Clin Obstet Gynecol 25:19, 1982.

CESSATION OF MENSTRUATION

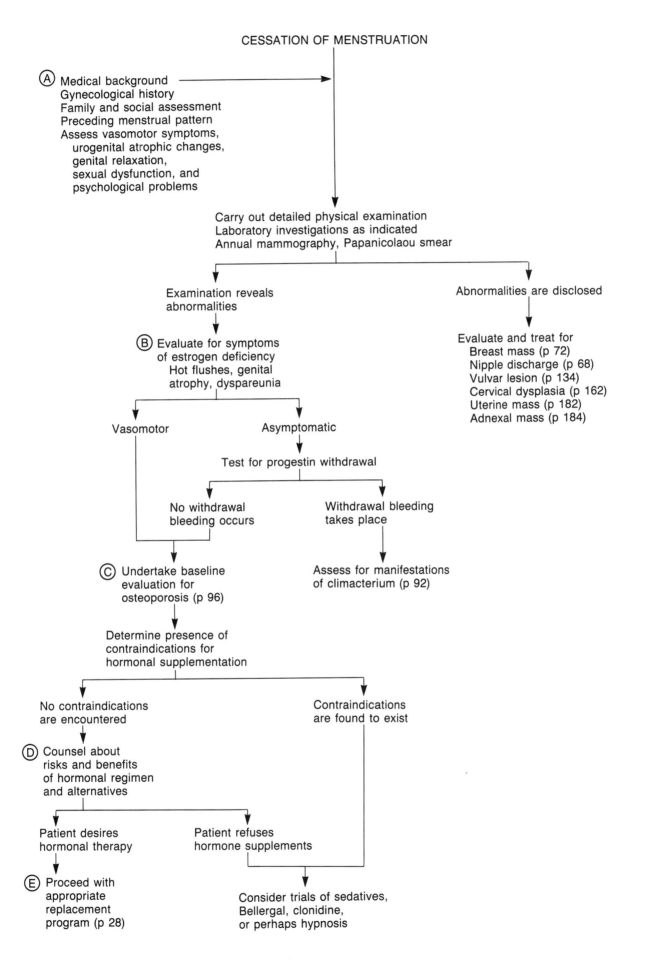

Ⓐ Medical background
Gynecological history
Family and social assessment
Preceding menstrual pattern
Assess vasomotor symptoms,
   urogenital atrophic changes,
   genital relaxation,
   sexual dysfunction, and
   psychological problems

Carry out detailed physical examination
Laboratory investigations as indicated
Annual mammography, Papanicolaou smear

Examination reveals
abnormalities

Abnormalities are disclosed

Ⓑ Evaluate for symptoms
of estrogen deficiency
Hot flushes, genital
atrophy, dyspareunia

Evaluate and treat for
Breast mass (p 72)
Nipple discharge (p 68)
Vulvar lesion (p 134)
Cervical dysplasia (p 162)
Uterine mass (p 182)
Adnexal mass (p 184)

Vasomotor

Asymptomatic

Test for progestin withdrawal

No withdrawal
bleeding occurs

Withdrawal bleeding
takes place

Ⓒ Undertake baseline
evaluation for
osteoporosis (p 96)

Assess for manifestations
of climacterium (p 92)

Determine presence of
contraindications for
hormonal supplementation

No contraindications
are encountered

Contraindications
are found to exist

Ⓓ Counsel about
risks and benefits
of hormonal regimen
and alternatives

Patient desires
hormonal therapy

Patient refuses
hormone supplements

Ⓔ Proceed with
appropriate
replacement
program (p 28)

Consider trials of sedatives,
Bellergal, clonidine,
or perhaps hypnosis

OSTEOPOROSIS

Jerold M. Carlson, M.D., M.P.H.

A. In the United States, the average age at menopause is 51.4 years and longevity of women is now nearly 80 years. With women thus expected to live about one-third of their lives in the postmenopausal period, there should be great concern for their well-being. Although the most common menopausal symptom is related to vasomotor instability, osteoporosis is the most important problem from a public health perspective. It has enormous impact on society because of its associated debilitating morbidity, contributions to mortality, and intensive financial impact. It is incumbent upon all medical providers, especially gynecological personnel, to attempt to prevent osteoporosis and its sequelae by identifying patients who are at risk well in advance so that they can be monitored and treated appropriately. One should be especially attentive for women of slight build, especially if white or oriental, sedentary, and nulliparous. Given the great potential effects of osteoporosis on an aging population, it is perhaps even appropriate to advocate a program of universal prophylaxis for all postmenopausal women regardless of risk status, although care has thus far been individualized because of fears that long-term adverse effects may be uncovered in due course (see D).

B. Osteoporosis may be characterized as a degenerative bone disorder affecting both trabecular and cortical bone. It is associated with an increased risk of fractures of the vertebral body, humerus, radius, and femur. Initially, loss of height and posture changes (dowager's hump) are the result of crush fractures of the vertebral bodies. Low back pain may represent their earliest manifestations. At a later stage, hip and long bone fractures predominate. There is no laboratory test of blood or urine that can accurately diagnose or predict osteoporosis. Nonetheless, associated medical disorders, such as diabetes mellitus and diseases of thyroid, parathyroid, kidney, and liver, must be ruled out since they may compound the problem.

C. Several radiographic techniques are available for assessing bone density. These include single and dual beam photon absorptiometry and computer tomography. Computer tomography offers the greatest precision and accuracy, but none has a predictive value that is completely reliable. It is perhaps most efficacious to consider using a combination of these techniques because the single beam photon absorptiometry measures mainly cortical bone, the dual beam approach assesses both trabecular and cortical bone, and the computer tomography scan evaluates trabecular bone principally.

D. The mechanism of action of estrogen therapy on bone is not yet fully understood. However, well designed studies have demonstrated that a low-dose estrogen regimen (0.625 mg conjugated estrogen daily) is effective in providing protection against bone resorption and fractures. The long-term protective effects of this program are not so well demonstrated and long-term risk, if any, is still undetermined. Unopposed estrogen therapy is known to have some adverse effects, such as an increased incidence of gallbladder disease and endometrial hyperplasia and carcinoma (p 28).

E. Optimum therapy for prevention of osteoporosis currently includes long-term estrogen-progesterone replacement (p 28). It should be initiated at the time of menopause or as soon thereafter as possible. Patients should be instructed and counseled concerning the need for long-term therapy. In addition, instruct the patient about the need for appropriate dietary intake, including 1,500 mg daily calcium supplementation, and weight bearing exercises. Excessive calcium supplementation should be avoided because it may predispose to nephrolithiasis and other stone formation in women who have the propensity to deposit calcium salts. In patients who are unable to take estrogen replacement, progestin supplementation alone may be used. Other agents, such as vitamin D, fluorides, thiazides, and parathormone, have not been found to be helpful in the prevention of osteoporosis; the role of calcitonin in this process is unclear thus far.

References

Aloia JF, Cohn SH, Vaswani A, et al. Risk factors for postmenopausal osteoporosis. Am J Med 78:95, 1985.

Genant HK, Cann CE, Ettinger B, Gordan GS. Quantitative computed tomography of vertebral spongiosa: A sensitive method for detecting early bone loss after oophorectomy. Ann Int Med 97:699, 1982.

Lafferty FW, Helmuth DO. Post-menopausal estrogen replacement: The prevention of osteoporosis and systemic effects. Maturitas 7:147, 1985.

Ott S. Should women get screening bone mass measurements? Ann Int Med 104:874, 1986.

POSTMENOPAUSAL PATIENT WITH ESTROGEN DEFICIENCY

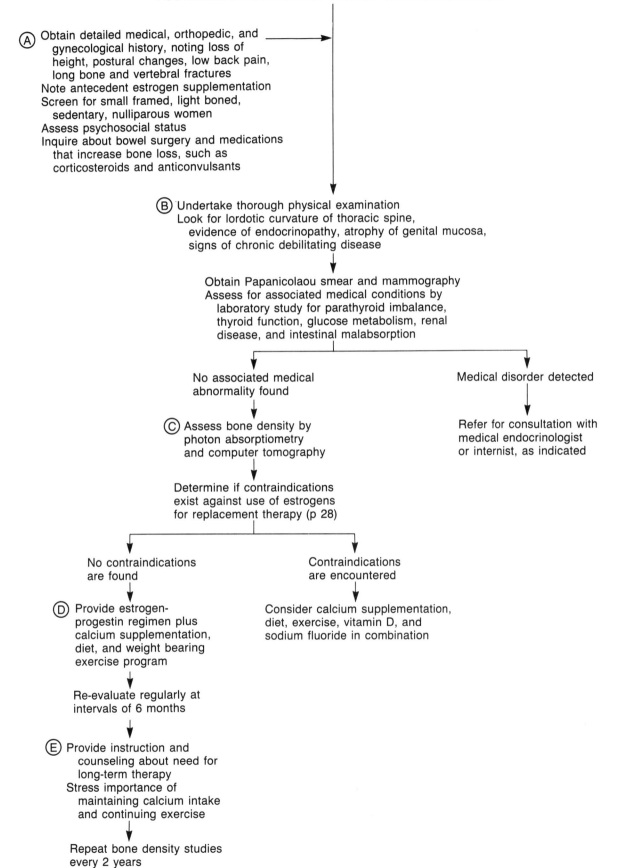

A. Obtain detailed medical, orthopedic, and gynecological history, noting loss of height, postural changes, low back pain, long bone and vertebral fractures
Note antecedent estrogen supplementation
Screen for small framed, light boned, sedentary, nulliparous women
Assess psychosocial status
Inquire about bowel surgery and medications that increase bone loss, such as corticosteroids and anticonvulsants

B. Undertake thorough physical examination
Look for lordotic curvature of thoracic spine, evidence of endocrinopathy, atrophy of genital mucosa, signs of chronic debilitating disease

Obtain Papanicolaou smear and mammography
Assess for associated medical conditions by laboratory study for parathyroid imbalance, thyroid function, glucose metabolism, renal disease, and intestinal malabsorption

No associated medical abnormality found

Medical disorder detected

C. Assess bone density by photon absorptiometry and computer tomography

Refer for consultation with medical endocrinologist or internist, as indicated

Determine if contraindications exist against use of estrogens for replacement therapy (p 28)

No contraindications are found

Contraindications are encountered

D. Provide estrogen-progestin regimen plus calcium supplementation, diet, and weight bearing exercise program

Consider calcium supplementation, diet, exercise, vitamin D, and sodium fluoride in combination

Re-evaluate regularly at intervals of 6 months

E. Provide instruction and counseling about need for long-term therapy
Stress importance of maintaining calcium intake and continuing exercise

Repeat bone density studies every 2 years

URINARY STRESS INCONTINENCE

Balmookoot Balgobin, M.D.

A. For diagnosing true stress incontinence, it is important to take special care to obtain a good history and a thorough physical examination. Seek details about the circumstances in which the patient loses her urine. Note whether it is limited to situations in which intra-abdominal pressure is increased, such as coughing, sneezing or straining. Attempt to determine the severity of the condition, particularly as regards its frequency, progression, and impact on the patient's social relations. This helps one weigh the need for aggressive evaluation and intervention. Urgency incontinence, frequency of urination, nocturia, dysuria, and inability to interrupt the flow suggest unstable detrusor function rather than a stress related problem.

B. The relationship between the degree of anatomic relaxation, especially as reflected in the posterior urethrovesical angle, is not well established. Nonetheless, one should evaluate the posterior urethrovesical angle (Fig. 1) in an effort to differentiate stress incontinence associated with a moderate anatomic defect (Type I) from the more severe kind (Type II). Whether it is really necessary to restore the angle surgically for proper sphincter function is unclear, but there is a general consensus favoring procedures for elevating the urethral sphincter to an intra-abdominal site. Ask the patient to cough; evoking an immediate spurt of urine is probably definitive. Digitally elevating the paraurethral tissue to reform the angle (this is the Bonney-Marshall test) may give misleading results if the urethra is compressed.

C. One should make an effort to treat detrusor instability, whether alone or combined with stress incontinence, with a coordinated program of anticholinergics, anti-depressants, musculotropic relaxants, and peripheral adrenergic stimulants (alpha-adrenergic drugs enhance sphincter activity while beta-adrenergics suppress detrusor activity). Bear in mind that surgery may only aggravate incontinence due to detrusor instability. Surgery may nevertheless be indicated for cases of failed medical management in which intravesical pressure is low and funneling of the proximal urethra can be demonstrated. Urine entering the proximal urethra may thus initiate detrusor activity.

D. Nonsurgical measures are sometimes useful for correcting mild stress incontinence, including perineal exercises. Consider topical estrogen creams for postmenopausal women to help build tissue integrity, substance, and vascularity.

E. Consider undertaking corrective surgery by way of an abdominal approach if the risk of failure is high. This applies, for example, to women with chronic pulmonary disease, bronchial asthma, gross obesity, and chronic or debilitating disorders. It is usually preferable to operate abdominally if the patient has had a previous vaginal plasty procedure or now has need for concomitant abdominal surgery.

F. The prevailing risk factors and the anatomic problem influence the kind of operation one chooses to utilize. The low-risk patients with cystocele and urethrocele may warrant anterior colporrhaphy with placement of paraurethral sutures to elevate the urethrovesical angle, all done vaginally. This approach is simple, safe, and relatively successful. If risk factors are present, however, it is preferable to suspend the urethrovesical angle transabdominally.

G. Abdominal urethral suspension usually entails use of the Marshall-Marchetti-Krantz procedure. Recurrences are infrequent after this type of operation, but it may be complicated by intraoperative hemorrhage, bladder injury, urinary retention, and osteitis pubis. Anatomic dissection, careful placement of sutures, and hemostasis are essential. The Stamey endoscopic technique for elevating the bladder neck is attractive in view of its good cure rate and comparatively less blood loss, pain, and postoperative morbidity.

H. For the patient whose incontinence recurs after surgery, detrusor instability or other causes must be ruled out before another procedure is undertaken. Consider a sling operation for women with chronic cough or congenitally poor tissue supports. If a sling operation is done, take special care to avoid making it too tight, because it may result in urinary retention, infection, and even urethral erosion. Alternatively, a Burch colposuspension can be done to advance the lateral paravaginal fascia to the ileopectineal ligament. Its complications include bladder injury and urinary retention. Palliation for persistent failures involves use of incontinence pants. Ureterostomy, ileal loop, or another urinary diversion technique is rarely indicated.

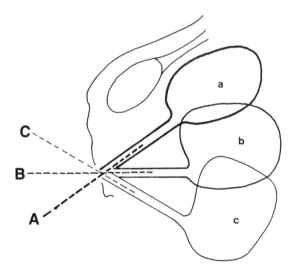

Figure 1 Bladder neck descent from normal (a) to moderate (b) and severe (c) loss of urethral support, shown in exaggerated schematic form. The corresponding angle the urethra makes with reference to the horizontal can be demonstrated by inserting a sterile cotton-tipped applicator and observing the angle change (from A to C) when the patient bears down.

PATIENT WITH URINARY INCONTINENCE

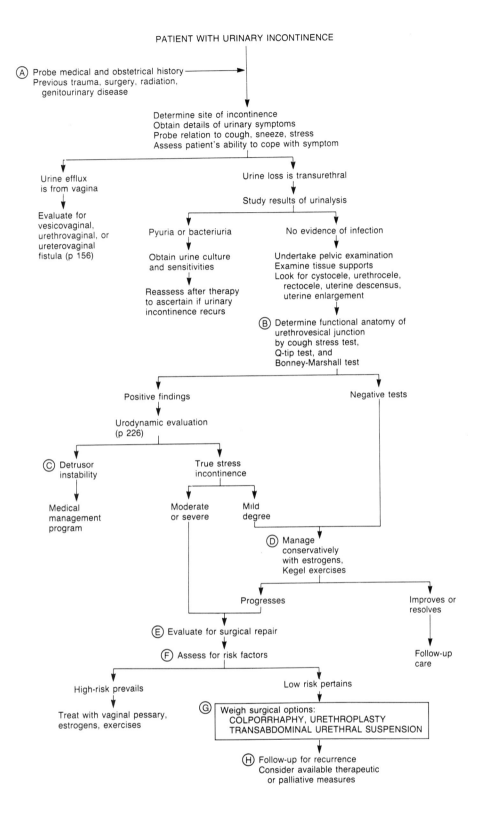

Ⓐ Probe medical and obstetrical history
Previous trauma, surgery, radiation,
genitourinary disease

Determine site of incontinence
Obtain details of urinary symptoms
Probe relation to cough, sneeze, stress
Assess patient's ability to cope with symptom

Urine efflux
is from vagina

Evaluate for
vesicovaginal,
urethrovaginal, or
ureterovaginal
fistula (p 156)

Urine loss is transurethral

Study results of urinalysis

Pyuria or bacteriuria

Obtain urine culture
and sensitivities

Reassess after therapy
to ascertain if urinary
incontinence recurs

No evidence of infection

Undertake pelvic examination
Examine tissue supports
Look for cystocele, urethrocele,
rectocele, uterine descensus,
uterine enlargement

Ⓑ Determine functional anatomy of
urethrovesical junction
by cough stress test,
Q-tip test, and
Bonney-Marshall test

Positive findings

Urodynamic evaluation
(p 226)

Ⓒ Detrusor
instability

Medical
management
program

True stress
incontinence

Moderate
or severe

Mild
degree

Negative tests

Ⓓ Manage
conservatively
with estrogens,
Kegel exercises

Progresses

Ⓔ Evaluate for surgical repair

Ⓕ Assess for risk factors

High-risk prevails

Treat with vaginal pessary,
estrogens, exercises

Low risk pertains

Ⓖ Weigh surgical options:
COLPORRHAPHY, URETHROPLASTY
TRANSABDOMINAL URETHRAL SUSPENSION

Improves or
resolves

Follow-up
care

Ⓗ Follow-up for recurrence
Consider available therapeutic
or palliative measures

References

Bhatia NN, Bergman A. Modified Burch versus Pereyra retropubic urethropexy for stress urinary incontinence. Obstet Gynecol 66:255, 1985.

Gillon G, Stanton SL. Long-term follow-up of surgery for urinary incontinence in elderly women. Br J Urol 56:478, 1984.

Mattingly RF, Davis LE. Primary treatment of anatomic stress urinary incontinence. Clin Obstet Gynecol 27:445, 1984.

Pow-Sang JM, Lockhart JL, Suarez A, et al. Female urinary incontinence: Preoperative selection, surgical complications and results. J Urol 136:831, 1986.

Schaeffer AJ. Treatment of recurrent urinary incontinence. Clin Obstet Gynecol 27:459, 1984.

DYSURIA AND URINARY FREQUENCY

Balmookoot Balgobin, M.D.

A. Almost every woman at some time in her life experiences dysuria and urinary frequency. These are the most common symptoms relating to the female genitourinary system. They usually reflect some disorder affecting the lower urinary tract, but this relationship is not always the case. Urinary tract infection, specifically cystitis, is by far the most frequent disorder associated with urinary frequency and dysuria; its investigation and treatment are obviously the first line of management (p 288). Other causes related to the urinary tract focus primarily on the urethra, which can be affected by a variety of infectious and noninfectious irritative conditions, such as sexually transmitted and nonvenereal urethritis, urethral caruncle, and diverticulum. The bladder may also be involved with nonbacterial cystitis (due to a chronic interstitial process, detrusor spasm from drugs, or radiation effect), foreign body, calculus formation, neoplasm, or detrusor instability. It may also be the site of tuberculous and bilharzial cystitis, although these are rare. Upper urinary tract pathologic disorders, including pyelitis, pyelonephritis, and even ureteral calculus, may present with these symptoms. In addition, they may reflect problems only indirectly related to the urinary tract, such as vaginitis or vulvitis. Even salpingitis can cause them by irritating the ureter where it courses along the posterior leaf of the broad ligament. Perhaps most important because it is so difficult to manage is the so-called "urethral syndrome" (see F), although diagnosed almost entirely by exclusion.

B. The pelvic examination should seek evidence of conditions involving specific pelvic structures to help focus one's investigation on the likely source of the problem. Try to duplicate the symptoms by delicate palpation of each organ in turn. The examination may reveal a specific causative disorder, such as acute vulvar or vestibular inflammation (p 130), vulvar pruritis (p 40), and vaginitis (p 38). Urethral or paraurethral (Skene's gland) disease should be detectable, including urethritis, caruncle, or diverticulitis. Look for inflammation or congestion associated with cystocele or uterine procidentia as well as pelvic mass or pelvic inflammatory disease (p 186). If these conditions exist, they must be appropriately evaluated and treated. If the symptoms persist or recur despite correction, another concurrent disorder is likely to be responsible. Because other conditions may indeed coexist (and commonly do), do not stop the evaluation when a remote condition is discovered. Proceed with corrective measures while continuing to search for other more proximal disorders.

C. At minimum, obtain a complete urinalysis and culture; consider urine cytology, especially with hematuria. Urinary tract infection associated with bacteriuria should receive appropriate therapy depending on culture results and bacterial sensitivity tests (p 288). Pyuria without bacteriuria may indicate tuberculosis or chlamydial infection; these serious disorders should be excluded or, if present, diagnosed and treated. Pay particular attention to the observation of casts in the urinary sediment; because they may reflect kidney disease, evaluation of the renal status is essential. Hematuria or abnormal urinary cytology may indicate the presence of a neoplasm; these findings demand further urologic evaluation, including cystoscopy, and appropriate care.

D. It is important to remember that upper urinary tract abnormalities may sometimes present with urinary frequency and dysuria. If the urine is negative on laboratory examinations, recurrent infections require one to study the urinary tract by means of intravenous pyelography and voiding urethrocystography. Congenital urinary tract abnormalities, vesicoureteral reflex, hydronephrosis, calculi, and neoplasm may be uncovered in this way.

E. Urethrocystoscopy is eminently well suited for investigation of the lower urinary tract. It should help reveal most bladder and urethral conditions that cause urinary frequency and dysuria. Look carefully for irritative foci within the urethral canal and at the bladder trigone. Watch for signs of infection, trauma, anatomic obstruction (constrictive band or fibroelastosis), and spasm.

F. Urodynamic studies (p 226) are indicated whenever the etiology still remains unclear, as in cases without urinary tract infection and negative intravenous pyelography or cystourethroscopy. These patients may have detrusor instability (Fig. 1). Consider the little understood urethral syndrome if everything else is excluded. Affected patients are difficult to treat for this condition, which may be due to estrogen deprivation in postmenopausal women or related to an undiagnosed infection (such as *Chlamydia*) or a psychogenic etiology.

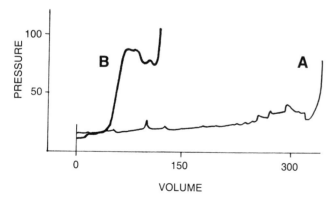

Figure 1 Cystometrogram, intracystic pressure (cm water) versus bladder volume (ml), of a patient with normal detrusor reflex (A) and one with detrusor instability (B), showing involuntary detrusor contractions and voiding associated with frequency and dysuria.

References

Mundy AR. The unstable bladder. Urol Clin North Am 12:317, 1985.

PATIENT WITH DYSURIA AND URINARY FREQUENCY

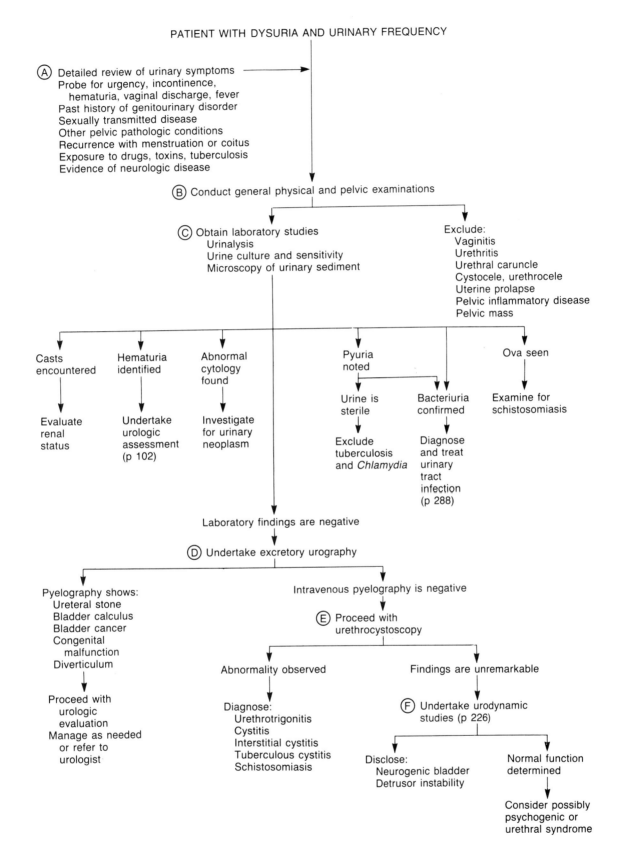

Ⓐ Detailed review of urinary symptoms
  Probe for urgency, incontinence,
    hematuria, vaginal discharge, fever
  Past history of genitourinary disorder
  Sexually transmitted disease
  Other pelvic pathologic conditions
  Recurrence with menstruation or coitus
  Exposure to drugs, toxins, tuberculosis
  Evidence of neurologic disease

Ⓑ Conduct general physical and pelvic examinations

Ⓒ Obtain laboratory studies
  Urinalysis
  Urine culture and sensitivity
  Microscopy of urinary sediment

Exclude:
  Vaginitis
  Urethritis
  Urethral caruncle
  Cystocele, urethrocele
  Uterine prolapse
  Pelvic inflammatory disease
  Pelvic mass

Casts encountered → Evaluate renal status

Hematuria identified → Undertake urologic assessment (p 102)

Abnormal cytology found → Investigate for urinary neoplasm

Pyuria noted
  Urine is sterile → Exclude tuberculosis and *Chlamydia*
  Bacteriuria confirmed → Diagnose and treat urinary tract infection (p 288)

Ova seen → Examine for schistosomiasis

Laboratory findings are negative

Ⓓ Undertake excretory urography

Pyelography shows:
  Ureteral stone
  Bladder calculus
  Bladder cancer
  Congenital
    malfunction
  Diverticulum
→ Proceed with urologic evaluation
  Manage as needed or refer to urologist

Intravenous pyelography is negative

Ⓔ Proceed with urethrocystoscopy

Abnormality observed → Diagnose:
  Urethrotrigonitis
  Cystitis
  Interstitial cystitis
  Tuberculous cystitis
  Schistosomiasis

Findings are unremarkable

Ⓕ Undertake urodynamic studies (p 226)

Disclose:
  Neurogenic bladder
  Detrusor instability

Normal function determined → Consider possibly psychogenic or urethral syndrome

Parsons CL. Urinary tract infections in the female patients. Urol Clin North Am 12:355, 1985.

Scotti RJ, Ostergard DR. The urethral syndrome. Clin Obstet Gynecol 27:515, 1984.

Stamm WE. Measurement of pyuria and its relation to bacteriuria. Am J Med 75(Suppl):53, 1983.

Stamm WE, Counts GW, Running KR, et al. Diagnosis of coliform infection in acutely dysuric women. N Engl J Med 307:463, 1982.

HEMATURIA

Balmookoot Balgobin, M.D.

A. Gross or microscopic hematuria is an important finding that warrants expeditious evaluation. Although often due to a strictly urologic problem, this may reflect a gynecological condition as well. Probe for information about general health, specifically focusing on possible renal disorders or bleeding tendency. Inquire about medications (especially analgesic drugs) and exposure to potential renal toxins. Look for a temporal relation to the menstrual periods and micturition. Hematuria at the onset of urination suggests a urethral condition, such as acute urethritis, caruncle, diverticulum, or cancer. At the end of micturition, it points to involvement of the posterior urethra or bladder neck. If it persists throughout voiding, the bladder, ureter, or kidney is probably the source. Hematuria with menstruation can signal an endometriotic focus (p 190).

B. Verify hematuria objectively. Occult blood is shown by dipstick, which is sensitive to minimal amounts. Confirm by microscopic examination of the centrifuged sediment. Differentiate myoglobinuria or hemoglobinuria by laboratory analysis.

C. Factitious hematuria may result from contamination of the urine by blood from a genital lesion, such as a urethral caruncle or cervical cancer. Similarly, blood coming from the vagina, either during menstruation or exuding from a lesion, can mix with the urine. Even if another source is found, use a tampon or vaginal packing (or catheterize the bladder) to test for hematuria and avoid overlooking a concomitant urologic problem.

D. The presence of casts in the urine should make one suspect glomerulonephritis. This finding warrants a general evaluation for such conditions as poststreptococcal glomerulonephritis, syphilis, bacterial endocarditis, viral hepatitis, and multisystem disease, including lupus erythematosus, polyarteritis nodosa, and other connective tissue disease. Renal evaluation should include determination of 24-hour protein excretion and creatinine clearance.

E. The most common cause of hematuria is a urinary tract infection (p 288). If infection is encountered, effective treatment can be expected to clear the hematuria. If it does not resolve in parallel with the resolution of the urinary tract infection, a coexisting disorder must be considered likely. A complete urologic evaluation is in order.

F. Well conducted gynecological surgery is not ordinarily accompanied by hematuria. However, some traumatic damage is inevitable in some cases even in the best of hands because dissection is difficult or extensive (as in cases with severe infection, endometriosis, or cancer). Bladder (p 320) or ureter (p 322) may be incised, lacerated, clamped, or sutured during surgery. Postoperatively, additional problems can arise from infection, avascular necrosis, kinking, or hematoma formation. Early recognition, preferably at the time of the injury, and appropriate management contribute to a successful outcome.

G. One can expect a small ureteral calculus (up to 4 mm) to pass spontaneously in nearly all cases without the need for surgery or instrumental manipulation, although the pain associated with it is typically very intense. The process can be aided by giving intravenous fluids to increase urine flow. Larger calculi usually require manipulation by way of a cystoscope under anesthesia or by percutaneous nephrolithotomy. Ultrasonic lithotripsy is also available in some areas as a nonsurgical means for management. Open lithotomy may be needed for the removal of very large stones. Intractable pain or colic, concurrent infection, or persistent ureteral obstruction usually warrants surgical intervention regardless of the size or location of the calculus.

H. There are increasing numbers of sophisticated investigative techniques for urologic study today. They include ultrasonography, angiography, venography, computer tomography, and radioisotopic scanning. Renal cysts can be punctured under imaging guidance and the fluid obtained submitted for cytologic assessment. These recent advances in urology enable one to make accurate diagnoses. They assist in planning and counseling about the most appropriate management options.

References

Drach GW. Transurethral ureteral stone manipulation. Urol Clin North Am 10:709, 1983.

Eisenkop SM, Richman R, Platt LD, Paul RH. Urinary tract injury during cesarean section. Obstet Gynecol 60:591, 1982.

Godec CJ, Gleich P. Intractable hematuria and formalin. J Urol 130:688, 1983.

Guerreiro WG. Operative injury to the lower urinary tract. Urol Clin North Am 12:339, 1985.

Lantz EJ, Hattery RR. Diagnostic imaging of urothelial cancer. Urol Clin North Am 11:567, 1984.

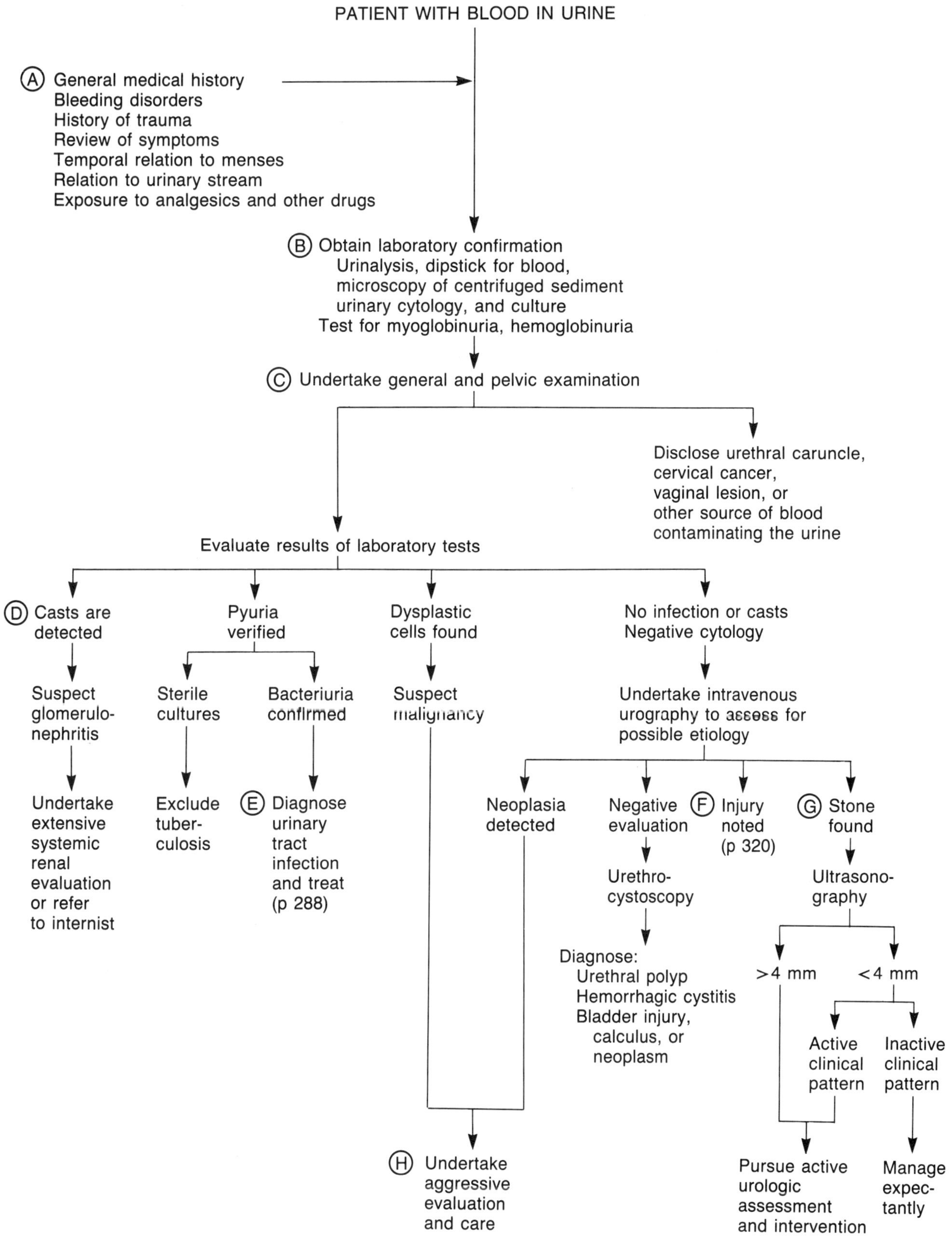

PATIENT WITH BLOOD IN URINE

Ⓐ General medical history
Bleeding disorders
History of trauma
Review of symptoms
Temporal relation to menses
Relation to urinary stream
Exposure to analgesics and other drugs

Ⓑ Obtain laboratory confirmation
Urinalysis, dipstick for blood,
microscopy of centrifuged sediment
urinary cytology, and culture
Test for myoglobinuria, hemoglobinuria

Ⓒ Undertake general and pelvic examination

Disclose urethral caruncle,
cervical cancer,
vaginal lesion, or
other source of blood
contaminating the urine

Evaluate results of laboratory tests

Ⓓ Casts are
detected

Pyuria
verified

Dysplastic
cells found

No infection or casts
Negative cytology

Suspect
glomerulo-
nephritis

Sterile
cultures

Bacteriuria
confirmed

Suspect
malignancy

Undertake intravenous
urography to assess for
possible etiology

Undertake
extensive
systemic
renal
evaluation
or refer
to internist

Exclude
tuber-
culosis

Ⓔ Diagnose
urinary
tract
infection
and treat
(p 288)

Neoplasia
detected

Negative
evaluation

Ⓕ Injury
noted
(p 320)

Ⓖ Stone
found

Urethro-
cystoscopy

Ultrasono-
graphy

Diagnose:
Urethral polyp
Hemorrhagic cystitis
Bladder injury,
calculus, or
neoplasm

>4 mm

<4 mm

Active
clinical
pattern

Inactive
clinical
pattern

Ⓗ Undertake
aggressive
evaluation
and care

Pursue active
urologic
assessment
and intervention

Manage
expec-
tantly

URINARY RETENTION

Balmookoot Balgobin, M.D.

A. Transient urinary retention occurs commonly after gynecological surgery as a result of operative manipulation, pain, anesthesia, and analgesia. This is seldom a problem for very long. It generally subsides in 24 to 48 hours unless there has been extensive dissection to denervate the bladder (as in association with radical hysterectomy). The classic cause of acute urinary retention unrelated to recent surgery in women is extrinsic urethral obstruction due to compression or acute angulation by an impacted pelvic tumor (typically a fundally located leiomyoma) or gross uterine or vaginal prolapse. Attention to the associated symptoms often suggests the diagnosis. Urinary retention associated with primary amenorrhea, for example, should make one suspect hematocolpos; with secondary amenorrhea, consider the possibility of a retroverted gravid uterus; menorrhagia points to leiomyomas. The diagnosis is often quite apparent on pelvic examination. In a case with a retroverted fibroid uterus, the cervix is typically found high in the anterior vaginal fornix, pushed tightly up against the symphysis pubis where it compresses and sharply elevates the urethra and bladder neck (Fig. 1).

B. Bladder dysfunction on a neurologic basis can cause an overdistended, atonic, or hypotonic bladder. Consider such neurologic disorders as multiple sclerosis, cerebrovascular disease, peripheral neuropathy, spinal cord lesions, or prolapsed intervertebral disc. These conditions can produce bladder states characterized variously as hyperreflexic (upper motor neuron bladder), areflexic (lower motor neuron bladder), atonic (sensory denervated bladder), or uninhibited (cerebrovascular disease). Only the uninhibited bladder is not associated with urinary retention. Therefore, when the etiology is not immediately obvious, a full neurologic examination is mandatory.

C. Probe into the type of medications the patient has been taking. Many drugs have adverse effects on bladder function. They may affect detrusor or sphincter tone, sensitivity to stimuli, or reactivity, typically resulting in a large, easily palpable, distended bladder. Be alert especially to exposure to narcotic analgesics, anticholinergics, alpha-adrenergics, ganglionic blockers, phenothiazines, benzodiazepines, and antihypertensives.

D. The patient who cannot void may not be excreting much urine. Therefore, rule out oliguria or anuria by bladder catheterization. If found, proceed to determine the etiology. For the hemodynamically stable patient, ascertain if there is some form of obstructive uropathy. Radiographic contrast studies are indicated for the postoperative patient to assess whether the ureters are occluded by kinking, or extrinsic compression by a hematoma or abscess. Avoid undue delay in diagnosing and correcting the condition to prevent irreversible hydronephrosis and renal damage.

E. Consider renal failure if urinary production remains low and there is no evidence of obstructive uropathy. If it exists, it is most often of the prerenal type rather than the acute parenchymal type. The latter results from acute tubular necrosis or vasomotor nephropathy and carries a much more serious prognosis. Prerenal azotemia is caused instead by poor renal perfusion. It can usually be corrected by improving the patient's cardiovascular status, thereby augmenting blood flow and tissue perfusion. Give adequate intravenous fluids and a diuretic for this purpose. The correct diagnosis is essential before proper and effective treatment can be applied.

F. Less obvious causes of urinary retention can sometimes be found by ultrasonographic imaging. Look for pelvic hematocele, hematoma, or abscess.

G. Intrinsic urethral obstruction is uncommon in the female. Urethral stenosis and valves are rare. Functional spasm due to neurologic disease or anxiety presents with dysuria and urinary frequency (p 100).

H. Uterine prolapse may cause ureteral angulation and obstruction. Intravenous pyelography should, therefore, be done to evaluate for such obstruction and to assess its impact on the kidney in affected patients. This applies for those with chronic urinary retention as well.

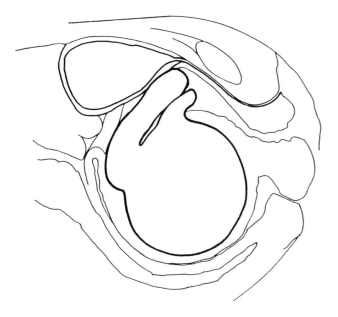

Figure 1 Mechanism of acute urinary retention in patient with large uterine leiomyoma causing uterus to become sharply retroverted, relocating the cervix up behind the symphysis pubis, and angulating and compressing the urethra and bladder base.

References

Cherrie RJ, Leach GE, Raz S. Obstructing urethal valve in a woman: A case report. J Urol 129:1051, 1983.

Diokno AC. Bladder neck obstruction in women. Neurol Urol

PATIENT UNABLE TO VOID

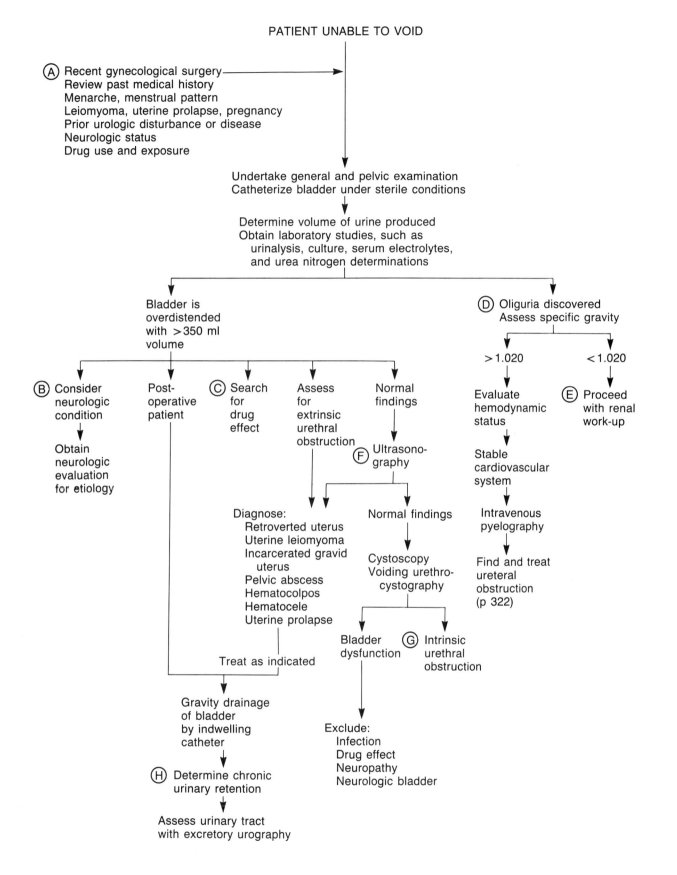

Ⓐ Recent gynecological surgery
Review past medical history
Menarche, menstrual pattern
Leiomyoma, uterine prolapse, pregnancy
Prior urologic disturbance or disease
Neurologic status
Drug use and exposure

Undertake general and pelvic examination
Catheterize bladder under sterile conditions

Determine volume of urine produced
Obtain laboratory studies, such as
  urinalysis, culture, serum electrolytes,
  and urea nitrogen determinations

Bladder is
overdistended
with >350 ml
volume

Ⓓ Oliguria discovered
Assess specific gravity

Ⓑ Consider
neurologic
condition

Post-
operative
patient

Ⓒ Search
for
drug
effect

Assess
for
extrinsic
urethral
obstruction

Normal
findings

>1.020

<1.020

Obtain
neurologic
evaluation
for etiology

Ⓕ Ultrasono-
graphy

Evaluate
hemodynamic
status

Ⓔ Proceed
with renal
work-up

Stable
cardiovascular
system

Diagnose:
  Retroverted uterus
  Uterine leiomyoma
  Incarcerated gravid
    uterus
  Pelvic abscess
  Hematocolpos
  Hematocele
  Uterine prolapse

Normal findings

Cystoscopy
Voiding urethro-
cystography

Intravenous
pyelography

Find and treat
ureteral
obstruction
(p 322)

Treat as indicated

Bladder
dysfunction

Ⓖ Intrinsic
urethral
obstruction

Gravity drainage
of bladder
by indwelling
catheter

Exclude:
  Infection
  Drug effect
  Neuropathy
  Neurologic bladder

Ⓗ Determine chronic
urinary retention

Assess urinary tract
with excretory urography

Urodynam 5:321, 1986.
Fowler CJ, Kirby RS. Electromyography of urethral sphincter in women with urinary retention. Lancet 1:1455, 1986.
Low JA, Mauger GM, Carmichael JA. The effect of Wertheim hys-terectomy upon bladder and urethral function. Am J Obstet Gynecol 139:826, 1981.
Nichols DH. Vaginal prolapse affecting bladder function. Urol Clin North Am 12:329, 1985.

ANAL PAIN

Max Borten, M.D., J.D.

A. A thorough medical history should precede the physical examination. Inquire about the temporal association of the pain because its timing with regard to defecation usually points to the area most likely to be affected. Ascertain whether the pain occurs before, during, or following a bowel movement. Tenesmus, the sphincter spasm preceding evacuation and associated with intense feelings of the desire to defecate, may be related to inflammatory bowel disease or extrinsic irritation of the lower bowel (as from ectopic pregnancy, p 198). Pain during defecation, by contrast, usually reflects a local anal lesion, whereas postdefecation pain is likely to be related to hemorrhoids. Recent change in bowel habits, such as diarrhea or constipation, may also prove to be important clues to etiology. Be particularly alert for the occurrence of perianal itching. Try to quantitate bleeding, if it is reported, and characterize it as fresh or old.

B. Proper preparation before the examination facilitates matters considerably. A disposable enema administered the preceding night is especially valuable. Examining the patient in lithotomy position is unsatisfactory in most cases except for observation of the perianal region and digital palpation of the anal canal. Use either a knee-chest or lateral Sims position instead for better assessment.

C. External hemorrhoids are seldom symptomatic unless prolapsed and thrombosed. Contrastingly, internal hemorrhoids are not uncommonly accompanied by bleeding, itching, anal discharge, and pain. Constipation, prolonged sitting, and straining at stool are factors contributing to their development. Thrombosis, fissure formation, infection, and ulceration generally aggravate symptoms. Conservative therapy includes high roughage diet and use of stool softeners. These measures may suffice for correcting mild hemorrhoids. Keep in mind that overt anal bleeding is a common manifestation of a variety of other colorectal diseases, including carcinoma of the colon or rectum, which may aggravate hemorrhoids. If one is unable to obtain an accurate diagnosis of the source of bleeding, the patient must be referred for full colonic investigation. Thus, treatment of patients whose hemorrhoids present with anal bleeding should generally be preceded by sigmoidoscopy and barium enema. Rubber band ligation has proven effective for the outpatient treatment of hemorrhoids.

D. Small perianal condylomata acuminatum are amenable to ablation by application of a preparation containing 20 percent podophyllum, a topical caustic resin. Be sure to protect the surrounding area with petroleum jelly to avoid skin reaction. Cryocauterization is reserved for persistent disease or extensive lesions that cannot be effectively treated by chemical means.

E. The pain of an anal fissure is typically experienced during and after defecation, often with accompanying pruritus ani and bright red spotting or even heavy bleeding. Treat as for anal cryptitis (see F). Regulation of bowel habits is essential. If symptomatic treatment fails, consider surgical excision.

F. Anal pain and burning during defecation, usually of short duration, are suggestive of cryptitis. Induration can be palpated by rectal examination. Anoscopy demonstrates acutely inflamed crypts. Treatment with stool softeners and warm sitz baths helps relieve symptoms. Inserting a hydrocortisone (HC) rectal suppository after each bowel movement reduces the inflammatory reaction. If the cryptitis is chronic or recurrent, undertake biopsy followed by surgical excision.

G. The presence of an anal abscess should raise the suspicion of inflammatory bowel disease. Use of sitz baths may hasten the process of localization. Incision and drainage are the ultimate treatment of choice, taking special care to open all loculations. The cavity should be packed with iodoform gauze for 24 hours. Consider excising a persistent fistula or recurrent abscess, recognizing that the dissection may have to be extensive.

References

Gartell PC, Sheridan RJ, McGinn FP. Out-patient treatment of haemorrhoids: A randomized clinical trial to compare rubber band ligation with phenol injection. Br J Surg 72:478, 1985.

Goulston KJ, Cook I, Dent OF. How important is rectal bleeding in the diagnosis of bowel cancer and polyps? Lancet 2:261, 1986.

Holland RM, Greiss FC Jr. Perineal Crohn's disease. Obstet Gynecol 62:527, 1983.

Murie JA, Dim AJW, MacKenzie I. The importance of pain, pruritus and soiling as symptoms of haemorrhoids and their response to haemorrhoidectomy or rubber band ligation. Br J Surg 68:247, 1981.

PATIENT WITH ANAL PAIN OR BLEEDING

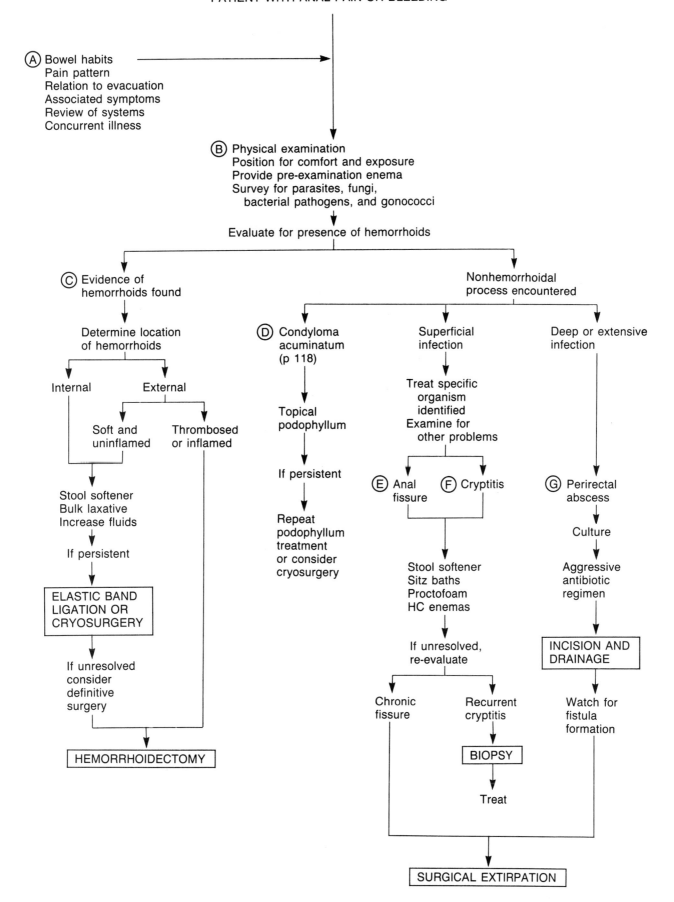

(A) Bowel habits
Pain pattern
Relation to evacuation
Associated symptoms
Review of systems
Concurrent illness

(B) Physical examination
Position for comfort and exposure
Provide pre-examination enema
Survey for parasites, fungi,
    bacterial pathogens, and gonococci

Evaluate for presence of hemorrhoids

(C) Evidence of
hemorrhoids found

Nonhemorrhoidal
process encountered

Determine location
of hemorrhoids

Internal   External

Soft and   Thrombosed
uninflamed   or inflamed

Stool softener
Bulk laxative
Increase fluids

If persistent

ELASTIC BAND
LIGATION OR
CRYOSURGERY

If unresolved
consider
definitive
surgery

HEMORRHOIDECTOMY

(D) Condyloma
acuminatum
(p 118)

Topical
podophyllum

If persistent

Repeat
podophyllum
treatment
or consider
cryosurgery

Superficial
infection

Treat specific
organism
identified
Examine for
other problems

(E) Anal   (F) Cryptitis
fissure

Stool softener
Sitz baths
Proctofoam
HC enemas

If unresolved,
re-evaluate

Chronic   Recurrent
fissure   cryptitis

BIOPSY

Treat

Deep or extensive
infection

(G) Perirectal
abscess

Culture

Aggressive
antibiotic
regimen

INCISION AND
DRAINAGE

Watch for
fistula
formation

SURGICAL EXTIRPATION

RECTAL BLEEDING

Benjamin P. Sachs, M.B., B.S., D.P.H.

A. Assessment of the symptom of rectal bleeding is important to the gynecologist because it may sometimes represent a manifestation of a gynecological problem. It may actually be vaginal or vulvar bleeding misinterpreted as rectal in origin by the patient. It may also be a sign of a gastrointestinal condition that could affect the management of an otherwise unrelated gynecological complication of a gynecological disorder, such as endometriosis, pelvic inflammatory disease (especially tubo-ovarian abscess), or metastatic genital cancer. Moreover, rectal bleeding may flag a concurrent systemic or gastrointestinal condition that could affect the management of an otherwise unrelated gynecological disease; the presence of hemorrhagic disorders or inflammatory bowel disease, for example, would influence and perhaps limit treatment options. The most common causes of rectal bleeding are hemorrhoids and, somewhat less often, anal fissures. Even if these conditions are obvious, however, one must consider the possibility that another, potentially more serious lesion may coexist, such as adenocarcinoma of the rectum or anal canal. Indeed, the earliest manifestation of rectal cancer is generally the appearance of stool streaked or occasionally mixed with bright red blood. Other causes include diverticular, ulcerative, or ischemic colitis. Meckle's diverticulum, regional ileitis, and cancers of the small bowel or ascending colon as well as gastric or duodenal ulcers are more often associated with melena unless the bleeding is very heavy. Angiodysplasia, a microvascular anomaly of the bowel, is another relatively common cause of bleeding. Inquire carefully about prior bleeding, associated pain, changing bowel habits, weight loss, and debilitation.

B. A thorough physical examination is essential to disclose evidence of systemic disease. Undertake vulvovaginal and rectal inspection and palpation to demonstrate the source of the bleeding, if possible, distinguishing vaginal from rectal origin. Digital examination is useful, but it cannot be deemed conclusive by itself. Look for specific sites of tenderness, nodularity, fluctuation, ulceration, fissure, fistula, and thrombosis. Laboratory investigations are needed at minimum to confirm the presence of blood in the stool by guaiac test, unless grossly obvious, and to assess for anemia. Carcinoma of the ascending colon, for example, is characteristically associated with severe anemia.

C. Melena, the passage of dark, tarry stools, is an important sign of significant gastrointestinal bleeding, reflecting a potentially serious lesion mandating aggressive assessment leading to definitive diagnosis. One must not be misled, however, by the black discoloration of the stool from oral iron preparations. True melena is said to reflect an intraluminal bleeding episode of at least 500 ml, whereas as little as 25 ml should be detectable by the stool guaiac test. Guaiac-positive stool also occurs from ingesting rare or raw meat, which can be misleading as well.

D. Proctosigmoidoscopy is indicated for proper evaluation of a patient with rectal bleeding to assess carefully for lower bowel disease. For completeness, barium enema and colonoscopy are also important. Only colonoscopy or angiography demonstrate an arteriovenous malformation or angiodysplasia. Upper gastrointestinal studies, including contrast radiography, are necessary if conditions are suspected in this part of the tract, such as esophageal or gastric varices or ulcer disease. It is prudent to refer the patient to an experienced gastrointestinal disease expert for this purpose. Consider these investigations in women who have ovarian masses and melena, perhaps reflecting their primary gastric or intestinal cancer (Krukenberg) with ovarian metastases (p 192).

E. Therapy is directed by the type of condition encountered and the severity of the symptoms it produces. Most patients with hemorrhoids (p 106) that bleed periodically can be managed conservatively with high roughage diet, stool softeners, and laxatives to avert the constipation that precipitates prolapse and thrombosis. Surgical excision is generally reserved for patients with severe discomfort, with unremitting or heavy bleeding, or with infection and ulceration. Similarly, anal fissures are treated effectively with sitz baths, stool softeners, and enemas; only those failing to respond deserve excision.

References

Dozois RR, Pezim ME, Gunderson LL. Carcinoma of the rectum: Current management. Surg Clin North Am 66:821, 1986.

Goulston KJ, Cook I, Dent OF. How important is rectal bleeding in the diagnosis of bowel cancer and polyps? Lancet 2:261, 1986.

PATIENT WITH APPARENT BLEEDING FROM RECTUM

(A) History of prior rectal bleeding, known
    hemorrhoids, hematochezia, or melena
Inquire about other gastrointestinal
    symptoms, bowel habits, weight loss,
    associated abdominal or anal pain
Probe for comenstrual dysmenorrhea,
    diagnosed endometriosis (p 190),
    recurrent pelvic inflammatory disease
Assess for antecedent systemic disease,
    debilitation, or coagulation disorder

(B) Conduct careful history and physical examination
Document source of bleeding
Pelvic and rectal examination for masses, tenderness
Verify site and degree of bleeding by
    complete blood count and stool guaiac test

Identify vaginal,
vulvar, or urethral
source of bleeding

Evaluate and treat
accordingly

Bleeding confirmed as clearly rectal in origin

(C) Tarry stools are present
    or concurrent with gross
    rectal bleeding

Determine if true melena

Gross blood without melena

Determine degree of bleeding

Appreciable
blood loss

Minimal blood loss

(D) Undertake
    proctoscopy,
    sigmoidoscopy,
    and barium enema
Consider angiography
    for suspicion of
    angiodysplasia
Weigh upper
    gastrointestinal
    series for possible
    esophageal or
    ulcer disease

Ascertain presence of
hemorrhoids, anal fissure,
fistula, or cryptitis

Diagnose and treat
ulcer disease,
inflammatory bowel
disease, diverticulitis,
intestinal polyps,
bowel cancer,
and endometrioma
involving intestines

(E) Manage by stool
    softener, laxative,
    and specific surgery,
    as indicated (p 106)

RAPE MANAGEMENT

Lynn H. Galen, M.D.

A. The victim of a sexual assault needs to feel protected and safe. Approach the patient with a sense of empathy and understanding for her vulnerability. Whenever possible, a person trained in crisis intervention should be present to provide immediate crisis counseling and assist the patient through the medical and legal maze with which she is now confronted. It is not the physician's role to determine whether or not a crime has occurred; rather it is to tend to the patient's medical and emotional needs. Consent is obtained to release specimens and medical records to the legal authorities. Provide the patient with a careful explanation of the physical examination and collection of evidence that will follow. All charting should be objective, descriptive, and nonjudgmental.

B. Obtain a detailed history of the assault, including date, time and circumstances, type of physical abuse, if any, and associated use of drugs and alcohol. Ask about the specifics of sexual contact, including vaginal, oral, or anal penetration. It may be helpful to preface these questions by a statement that these are not uncommon acts occurring in a sexual assault. Ask whether the patient bathed, douched, urinated, defecated, or changed her clothing prior to being examined. Evaluate gynecologically for a history of menstruation, recent vaginal discharge or bleeding, contraceptive practice, sexually transmitted disease, and last voluntary sexual experience. Obtain a pertinent medical history, including allergies and medications being taken.

C. Approach the physical examination in a gentle, unhurried manner. The gathering of evidence proceeds simultaneously with the physical examination. Examine the patient for evidence of trauma and document bruises and wounds with photographs or diagrams. Scrape fingernails and comb pubic hair for foreign material; swab semen stains on the skin with saline moistened applicators. Examine the external genitalia and vagina for abrasions, hematomas, and lacerations. Aspirate vaginal secretions pooled in the posterior fornix and prepare specimens to test for acid phosphatase and blood antigen status. Undertake microscopy of a wet saline preparation. Obtain a cervical Papanicolaou smear and endocervical cultures for *Chlamydia* and gonorrhea. Perform a bimanual examination to determine uterine size and assess the adnexa for tenderness and masses. Collect specimens and cultures from extragenital sites as indicated by the history of the attack.

D. Blood samples are obtained from the patient for blood typing, serology for syphilis, and pregnancy testing. If indicated, obtain a blood alcohol level and urine drug screen. Label all specimens with their source, the patient's name, and date; the label should be signed by the physician. Seal the evidence. If the patient gives her permission, hand it personally to the proper authorities to ensure that the correct "chain of evidence" is maintained.

E. The patient is offered prophylactic treatment against gonorrhea, chlamydial trachomatis, and incubating syphilis according to the Centers for Disease Control guidelines. Tetanus prophylaxis is also given as indicated. If it is determined that the patient is at risk for pregnancy and coitus has occurred within the preceding 72 hours, she should be given verbal and written information as to the effectiveness and safety of postcoital contraception. Explain that the likelihood of pregnancy after a sexual assault is low and a "wait and see" attitude is acceptable. Alternatively, pregnancy prophylaxis may be given in the form of an estrogen-progesterone combination, such as 50 μg ethinyl estradiol and 0.5 mg dl-norgestrel (available as Ovral); give two tablets and repeat in 12 hours.

F. Offer continued supportive counseling after discharge and arrange for it. A return visit after one week is appropriate to treat for positive cultures and evaluate the patient's psychologic adjustment. Make appropriate referrals for more in-depth psychologic counseling at this time, if indicated. The patient should be seen again six weeks later for repeat examination, repeat serologic test for syphilis, and pregnancy testing.

References

Cartwright PS. Reported sexual assault in Nashville-Davidson County, Tennessee, 1980 to 1982. Am J Obstet Gynecol 154:1064, 1986.

Centers for Disease Control. 1985 STD treatment guidelines. MMWR 34:105, 1985.

Glaser JB, Hammerschlag MR, McCormack WM. Sexually transmitted diseases in victims of sexual assault. N Engl J Med 315:625, 1986.

Martin CA, Warfield MC, Braen GR. Physician's management of the psychological aspects of rape. JAMA 249:501, 1983.

Tintinalli J, Hoelzer M. Clinical findings and legal resolutions in sexual assault. Ann Emerg Med 14:447, 1985.

PATIENT REPORTING SEXUAL ASSAULT

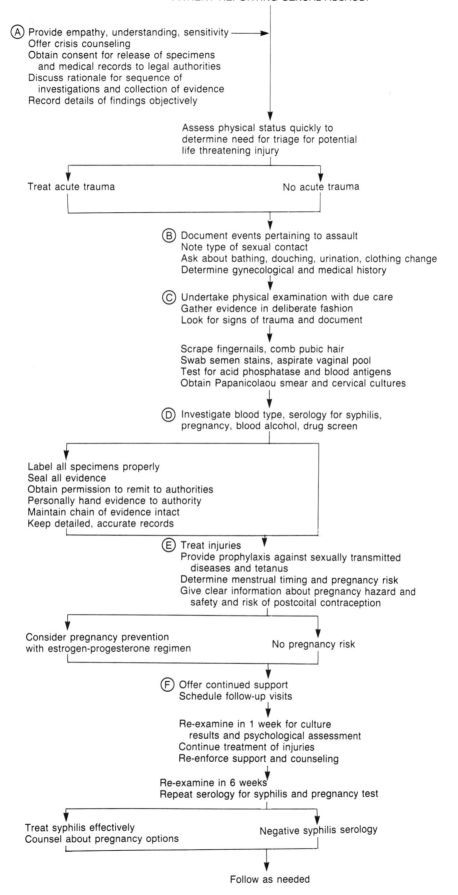

Ⓐ Provide empathy, understanding, sensitivity ──────▶
Offer crisis counseling
Obtain consent for release of specimens
  and medical records to legal authorities
Discuss rationale for sequence of
  investigations and collection of evidence
Record details of findings objectively

Assess physical status quickly to
determine need for triage for potential
life threatening injury

Treat acute trauma   No acute trauma

Ⓑ Document events pertaining to assault
Note type of sexual contact
Ask about bathing, douching, urination, clothing change
Determine gynecological and medical history

Ⓒ Undertake physical examination with due care
Gather evidence in deliberate fashion
Look for signs of trauma and document

Scrape fingernails, comb pubic hair
Swab semen stains, aspirate vaginal pool
Test for acid phosphatase and blood antigens
Obtain Papanicolaou smear and cervical cultures

Ⓓ Investigate blood type, serology for syphilis,
pregnancy, blood alcohol, drug screen

Label all specimens properly
Seal all evidence
Obtain permission to remit to authorities
Personally hand evidence to authority
Maintain chain of evidence intact
Keep detailed, accurate records

Ⓔ Treat injuries
Provide prophylaxis against sexually transmitted
  diseases and tetanus
Determine menstrual timing and pregnancy risk
Give clear information about pregnancy hazard and
  safety and risk of postcoital contraception

Consider pregnancy prevention
with estrogen-progesterone regimen   No pregnancy risk

Ⓕ Offer continued support
Schedule follow-up visits

Re-examine in 1 week for culture
  results and psychological assessment
Continue treatment of injuries
Re-enforce support and counseling

Re-examine in 6 weeks
Repeat serology for syphilis and pregnancy test

Treat syphilis effectively
Counsel about pregnancy options   Negative syphilis serology

Follow as needed

SCREENING FOR SEXUALLY TRANSMITTED DISEASE

Johanna F. Perlmutter, M.D.

A. The classic types of sexually transmitted diseases include gonorrhea, syphilis, chancroid, granuloma inguinale, and lymphogranuloma venereum. To these can be added chlamydial infection as well as condyloma acuminatum, herpesvirus, acquired immune deficiency syndrome (AIDS), cytomegalovirus, and hepatitis, plus a host of others. These infections are not limited to any one sector of the population, but they are likely to appear in those with multiple partners. The current moral climate of sexual permissiveness means that the opportunities for exposure are greater, while at the same time fewer cases can be detected by such measures as premarital testing (given the common practice of cohabitation without marriage). Testing must, therefore, be considered an essential component of the gynecological examination. Routine testing should include culture for gonorrhea and serology for syphilis at minimum. Testing for AIDS is also offered to those at risk (p 122). Other studies are indicated on the basis of presenting complaints, findings, or contacts.

B. There is a latent period before any clinical manifestations develop or can be detected following exposure. Cultures sometimes help to determine infection, particularly for gonorrhea, but they take time and may be falsely negative. It is important, therefore, to examine and follow these patients carefully. The physical examination should be extensive and thorough to disclose any lesions involving the mucous membranes of the mouth, pharynx, vulva, vagina, or rectum. Under good illumination look for evidence of skin rash. Check for enlarged lymph nodes, especially in the femoral regions.

C. It is increasingly likely that a patient diagnosed as having one sexually transmitted disease will have another either concurrently or at a later date. It is logical that the person exposed by sexual contacts to one such infection is at increased risk for acquiring others. Undertake screening by physical and laboratory examinations for the range of relevant diseases whenever one of them is detected. Thus, test for gonorrhea when syphilis is found and vice versa, and test for both in the presence of genital herpesvirus infection (p 120) or condyloma acuminatum (p 118), for example.

D. Painful or tender genital ulcers suggest herpesvirus infection (usually found in clusters) or chancroid. The chancre of syphilis is characteristically pain free (unless secondarily infected by bacteria). It can be recognized by its raised, indurated borders. It arises and subsequently heals spontaneously, giving a false sense of resolution. Careful darkfield examination of secretions from the lesion should reveal *Treponema pallidum* spirochete, but one must distinguish it from other spirochetes present as saprophytes. Because both chancroid and lymphogranuloma venereum are currently being encountered with increasing frequency, consider these diagnoses whenever a painful ulcer is identified. Microscopic examination of a stained smear of exudated material scraped from the soft, shallow chancroid ulcers shows the short, Gram-negative Ducrey bacilli. The ulcerated chlamydial infection of lymphogranuloma venereum is usually painless and heals spontaneously at first, only to reappear after several weeks with acute inguinal lymphadenitis; as the disease becomes more chronic, it may lead to rectal fibrosis, stricture, and fistula formation. Early definitive diagnosis is difficult because the Frei test, which shows skin hypersensitivity reaction to chlamydial antigen, is nonspecific and does not differentiate current from past infection. Cultures are thus probably warranted. The papular nodule of granuloma inguinale breaks down in due course to ulcerate, undermine, and become secondarily infected and purulent with vulvar edema and femoral lymphadenitis. Giemsa stained smears made from biopsied granulation tissue should demonstrate typical Donovan bodies, recognized as vacuoles (containing pleomorphic, blue stained offending organisms), within the cytoplasm of large mononuclear cells.

E. The diagnosis of gonorrhea requires both cultures and Gram stained smears obtained from relevant sites, such as vagina, cervix, urethral meatus, anal canal, and oropharynx, as indicated. Cultures for *Neisseria gonorrhoeae* are placed in an appropriate medium under carbon dioxide. Cultures are more reliable than smears, but still imperfect for definitive diagnosis. Look for paired kidney shaped intracellular Gram-negative diplococci in the stained smear. Always obtain blood for a serologic test for syphilis as well.

References

Corey L. The diagnosis and treatment of genital herpes. JAMA 248:1041, 1982.

Osborne NG, Grubin L, Pratson L. Vaginitis in sexually active women: Relationship to nine sexually transmitted organisms. Am J Obstet Gynecol 142:962, 1982.

Sweet RL, Schachter J, Landers DV. Chlamydial infections in obstetrics and gynecology. Clin Obstet Gynecol 26:143, 1983.

Weinstein AJ. Sexually transmitted diseases and other genital infections during adolescence. J Reprod Med 29:411, 1984.

PATIENT WITH POSSIBLE SEXUALLY TRANSMITTED DISEASE

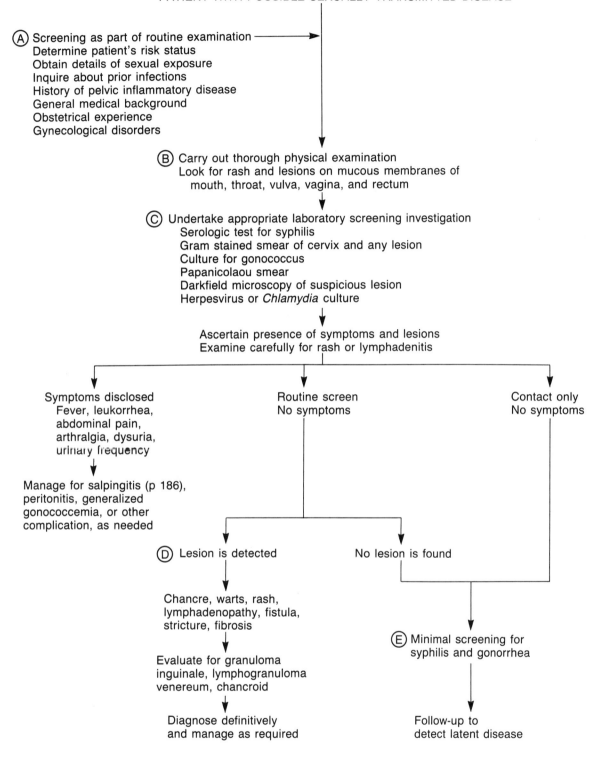

(A) Screening as part of routine examination
Determine patient's risk status
Obtain details of sexual exposure
Inquire about prior infections
History of pelvic inflammatory disease
General medical background
Obstetrical experience
Gynecological disorders

(B) Carry out thorough physical examination
Look for rash and lesions on mucous membranes of
mouth, throat, vulva, vagina, and rectum

(C) Undertake appropriate laboratory screening investigation
Serologic test for syphilis
Gram stained smear of cervix and any lesion
Culture for gonococcus
Papanicolaou smear
Darkfield microscopy of suspicious lesion
Herpesvirus or *Chlamydia* culture

Ascertain presence of symptoms and lesions
Examine carefully for rash or lymphadenitis

Symptoms disclosed
Fever, leukorrhea,
abdominal pain,
arthralgia, dysuria,
urinary frequency

Routine screen
No symptoms

Contact only
No symptoms

Manage for salpingitis (p 186),
peritonitis, generalized
gonococcemia, or other
complication, as needed

(D) Lesion is detected

No lesion is found

Chancre, warts, rash,
lymphadenopathy, fistula,
stricture, fibrosis

Evaluate for granuloma
inguinale, lymphogranuloma
venereum, chancroid

Diagnose definitively
and manage as required

(E) Minimal screening for
syphilis and gonorrhea

Follow-up to
detect latent disease

113

SYPHILIS

Johanna F. Perlmutter, M.D.
Carol London, R.N.

A. Cases of syphilis continue to appear on an endemic basis in all social strata, requiring astute surveillance (p 112) at essentially every opportunity among gynecological patients. Early diagnosis is important to avoid dissemination to other partners and especially to the fetus during an ensuing pregnancy and to prevent the occurrence of long-term irreversible effects. The VDRL (Venereal Disease Research Laboratory) slide test is routinely used in most areas as the standard nontreponemal reagin test to detect nonspecific antibody for screening gynecological patients. It takes between four weeks and three months for the test to become positive following the first infection. False positive results occur in a number of conditions, such as rheumatoid arthritis, collagen disease, atopic eczema, drug abuse, certain viremias, and after immunizations. Even pregnancy can produce false positive results. The RPRC (rapid plasma reagin card) test is easier to perform and somewhat more sensitive than the VDRL test. Treponema tests are used whenever a positive serology test needs confirmation. They include the TPI (*Treponema pallidum* immobilization) test, which is expensive and difficult to conduct, and FTA-ABS (fluorescent treponemal antibody absorption), which is widely used, cost effective, and quite specific.

B. Bear in mind that a chancre can appear before the reagin or treponemal tests turn positive. Thus, a negative test cannot be considered definitive or necessarily reassuring. Repeat the tests to be sure. After the FTA-ABS test becomes positive, it can be expected to remain positive even after effective treatment, although the VDRL test usually becomes negative again (unless therapy was inadequate or the result reflects a false positive status). If a positive serology is encountered but the FTA-ABS done for confirmation proves to be negative, one should repeat the tests in one week to show whether or not there is a new infection. A persistently negative FTA-ABS means a false positive serology test (see E) instead. Negative serology with positive FTA-ABS tests reassures that prior therapy has been successful. If both are positive, diagnose primary syphilis and treat aggressively.

C. For patients who are likely to have had exposure to gonorrhea, such as rape victims, administer 4.8 million units of aqueous procaine penicillin G intramuscularly (half in each buttock) plus 1 g probenecid orally. Incubating syphilis is effectively treated simultaneously by this regimen. Documented contact to syphilis alone should be treated with Bicillin, 2.4 million units, as for a case with known primary disease (see D).

D. The currently recommended treatment for primary syphilis is benzathine penicillin G (Bicillin), 2.4 million units by intramuscular injection, half in each buttock. Give tetracycline, 500 mg four times daily for 12 days, to patients with penicillin allergy. A second course of penicillin may be called for in some areas. Because tetracycline is contraindicated in pregnancy, substitute erythromycin in the same dosage schedule for gravidas who are allergic to penicillin. Carefully inquire about possible past hypersensitivity reaction to penicillin. Testing for penicillin allergy is prudent in pregnant women. Treat sexual partners as well, if possible.

E. If a biologically false positive test result (see B) is encountered, retest in three months. Generally, the reagin test should have become negative. One that is still positive after three months or longer suggests an underlying condition deserving investigation, such as multisystem collagen or hepatic disorder.

F. Patients who are known to have had positive serologic test for syphilis in the past and who continue to have positive tests warrant careful consideration. First ascertain if they have been previously treated for syphilis and if that therapy has been adequate by current standards. A quantitative serologic test should be obtained if prior treatment was deemed to have been acceptable. An increase in titer (of at least two dilutions to account for laboratory variation) signifies inadequate foregoing care or reinfection, requiring another course of antibiotics (see D). If the previous serologic titer cannot be determined, treat again for a positive FTA-ABS.

G. Darkfield examination is useful for diagnosis in cases with chancre or moist secondary luetic lesions (p 112).

H. Serology should be checked every three months until negative or serofast (that is, stable). Follow patients with primary syphilis for at least one year; with secondary syphilis follow for two years; with early latent phase disease (after the secondary stage has subsided) of less than one year's duration, it is necessary to follow for three to five years.

References

Charles D. Syphilis. Clin Obstet Gynecol 26:125, 1983.
Fiumara NJ. Treatment of primary and secondary syphilis: Serologic response. J Am Acad Dermatol 14:487, 1986.
Grimes DA. Deaths due to sexually transmitted diseases: The forgotten component of reproductive mortality. JAMA 255:1727, 1986.
Hart G. Syphilis tests in diagnostic and therapeutic decision making. Ann Intern Med 104:368, 1986.

PATIENT WITH SUSPICION OF SYPHILIS

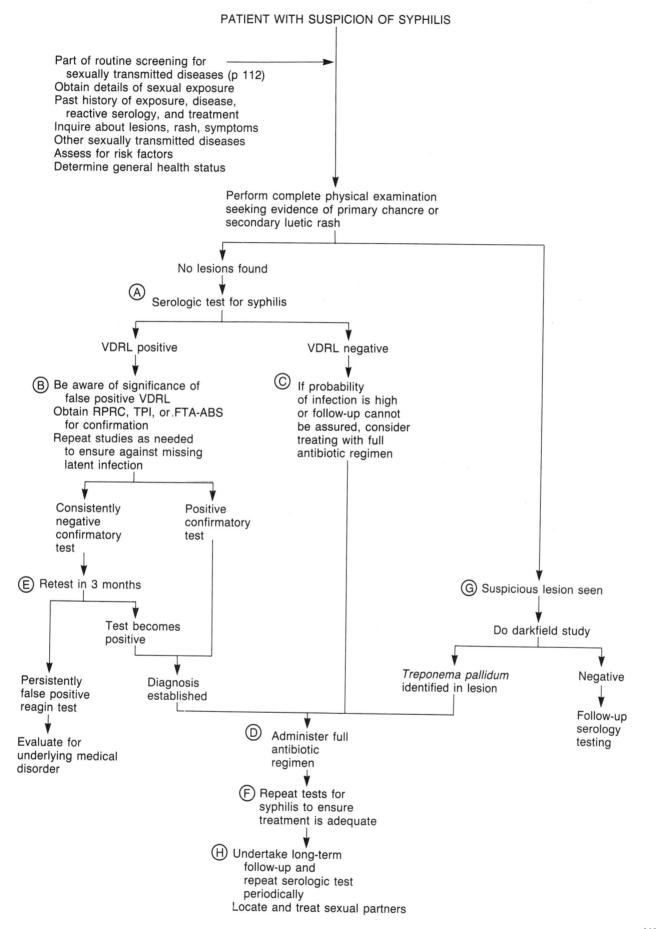

Part of routine screening for
  sexually transmitted diseases (p 112)
Obtain details of sexual exposure
Past history of exposure, disease,
  reactive serology, and treatment
Inquire about lesions, rash, symptoms
Other sexually transmitted diseases
Assess for risk factors
Determine general health status

Perform complete physical examination
seeking evidence of primary chancre or
secondary luetic rash

No lesions found

Ⓐ Serologic test for syphilis

VDRL positive

VDRL negative

Ⓑ Be aware of significance of
  false positive VDRL
  Obtain RPRC, TPI, or FTA-ABS
  for confirmation
  Repeat studies as needed
  to ensure against missing
  latent infection

Ⓒ If probability
  of infection is high
  or follow-up cannot
  be assured, consider
  treating with full
  antibiotic regimen

Consistently
negative
confirmatory
test

Positive
confirmatory
test

Ⓔ Retest in 3 months

Ⓖ Suspicious lesion seen

Test becomes
positive

Do darkfield study

Persistently
false positive
reagin test

Diagnosis
established

Treponema pallidum
identified in lesion

Negative

Evaluate for
underlying medical
disorder

Ⓓ Administer full
  antibiotic
  regimen

Follow-up
serology
testing

Ⓕ Repeat tests for
  syphilis to ensure
  treatment is adequate

Ⓗ Undertake long-term
  follow-up and
  repeat serologic test
  periodically
  Locate and treat sexual partners

GONORRHEA

Janet L. Mitchell, M.D., M.P.H.

A. Gonorrhea is the most frequently reported infectious disease in the United States. Given the current societal attitude about sexual mores, it is likely to continue unchecked. Assiduous screening is, therefore, essential (p 112). The diagnosis of gonorrhea should be suspected in any woman who reports potential exposure or has multiple sexual partners. Although dysuria and vaginal discharge may occur with early infections, most women are entirely asymptomatic at first. The diagnosis is confirmed on the basis of smears and cultures obtained from relevant sites, such as urethra, vagina, cervix, oropharynx, and rectum. Once the infection is confirmed, recommend treatment of both the patient and her sexual partners. They also deserve the benefit of thorough screening for other sexually transmitted diseases as well.

B. The patient with documented uncomplicated localized (genital, rectal, or oropharyngeal) gonorrhea is easily and effectively treated with antibiotics. This applies equally to the patients who have been exposed by contact while they await the results of the cultures. The treatment currently recommended for patients with uncomplicated gonorrhea is aqueous procaine penicillin G, 4.8 million units intramuscularly (half in each buttock) plus 1 g probenecid orally. If the patient has incubating syphilis simultaneously, this treatment should be effective against it. The same cannot be said for alternative regimens used to treat gonorrhea, such as ampicillin (3.5 g orally with 1 g probenecid), erythromycin (1.5 g orally plus 0.5 g four times daily for four days), cefazolin (2 g intramuscularly with probenecid 1 g orally), or tetracycline (500 mg orally four times daily for seven days), because while useful for the gonorrhea, they are inadequate for syphilis. They are also less effective for treating rectal or pharyngeal infection.

C. Two penicillin resistant strains of *Neisseria gonorrhoeae* are becoming increasingly important. Infections with penicillinase-producing organisms, which have been recognized in this country for the past decade, are now joined by those due to gonococci characterized by chromosomally mediated antibiotic resistance. Both strains are sensitive to spectinomycin given as a single 2 g intramuscular dose. Spectinomycin is not effective against pharyngeal infections and its fetal ototoxicity interdicts its use in pregnancy. Consider spectinomycin therapy for cases in which other treatment has failed.

D. *Chlamydia trachomatis* infections coexist with gonorrhea in one-third of symptomatic women. Therefore, tetracy-cline or doxycycline should be added to the treatment regimen.

E. Although gonorrhea may remain clinically silent in women for a variable interval from first contact, it eventually causes acute salpingitis (p 186) if untreated. Typically, spread from the cervical depots to the tubes can be expected to occur at the time of menstruation. Once the infection becomes established in the fallopian tubes, tissue damage facilitates secondary invasion by anaerobic organisms. Broad-spectrum antibiotics are, therefore, generally needed for effective treatment. Suspect Fitz-Hugh-Curtis syndrome (perihepatitis) in a case presenting with abdominal pain in the right upper quadrant. Perihepatic adhesions are characteristically found on laparoscopy.

F. Consider hospitalization for clinical evidence of a tubo-ovarian abscess (p 188), peritonitis, high persistent fever, or failure to respond to therapy administered on an ambulatory basis. Hospitalization facilitates aggressive therapy and ensures close surveillance. If the diagnosis is not clear-cut, undertake laparoscopy to determine the true nature of the patient's condition and its extent. This not only prevents committing her to a long course of unnecessary treatment, but directs the care program more appropriately.

G. Disseminated gonococcemia with joint or cutaneous manifestations, endocarditis, or meningitis can be very serious. Affected patients must be admitted to the hospital for intensive care with appropriate antibiotics given by the intravenous route (such as aqueous procaine penicillin G, 10 million units daily, for at least seven days) and other supportive regimen as indicated.

References

Hook EW, King KK. Gonococcal infections. Ann Int Med 102:229, 1985.

Rice RJ, Thompson SE. Treatment of uncomplicated infections due to *Neisseria Gonorrhoeae*: A review of clinical efficacy and in vitro susceptibility studies from 1982 through 1985. JAMA 255:1739, 1986.

Sanders LL Jr, Harrison HR, Washington AE. Treatment of sexually transmitted chlamydial infections. JAMA 255:1750, 1986.

Washington AE. Preventing complications of sexually transmitted disease. Drugs 28:355, 1984.

PATIENT WITH SUSPICION OF GONORRHEA

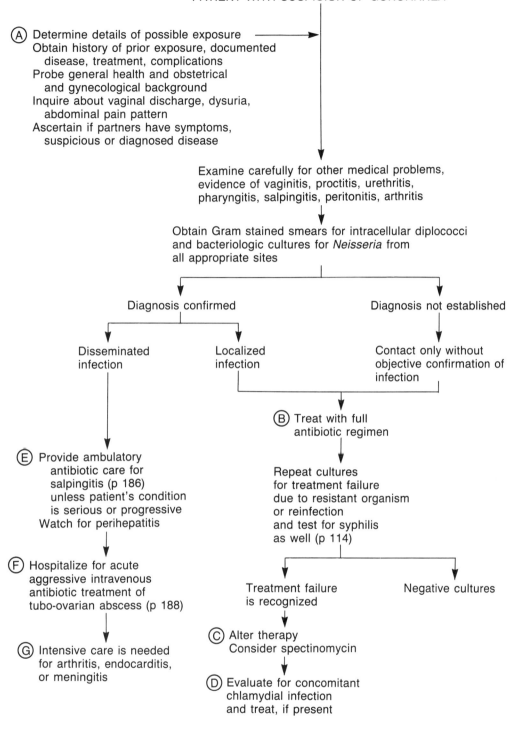

(A) Determine details of possible exposure ⟶
Obtain history of prior exposure, documented
    disease, treatment, complications
Probe general health and obstetrical
    and gynecological background
Inquire about vaginal discharge, dysuria,
    abdominal pain pattern
Ascertain if partners have symptoms,
    suspicious or diagnosed disease

Examine carefully for other medical problems,
    evidence of vaginitis, proctitis, urethritis,
    pharyngitis, salpingitis, peritonitis, arthritis

Obtain Gram stained smears for intracellular diplococci
    and bacteriologic cultures for *Neisseria* from
    all appropriate sites

Diagnosis confirmed   Diagnosis not established

Disseminated   Localized   Contact only without
infection   infection   objective confirmation of
                                             infection

(B) Treat with full
    antibiotic regimen

(E) Provide ambulatory
    antibiotic care for
    salpingitis (p 186)   Repeat cultures
    unless patient's condition   for treatment failure
    is serious or progressive   due to resistant organism
Watch for perihepatitis   or reinfection
                                        and test for syphilis
                                        as well (p 114)

(F) Hospitalize for acute
    aggressive intravenous
    antibiotic treatment of   Treatment failure   Negative cultures
    tubo-ovarian abscess (p 188) is recognized

(G) Intensive care is needed   (C) Alter therapy
    for arthritis, endocarditis,   Consider spectinomycin
    or meningitis

                                  (D) Evaluate for concomitant
                                      chlamydial infection
                                      and treat, if present

CONDYLOMA ACUMINATUM

Louis Burke, M.D.

A. Condyloma acuminatum is a sexually transmitted disease caused by human papillomavirus, a papovavirus. Women of childbearing age are most susceptible to the virus. The growths are rarely seen before puberty or after menopause. They occur frequently in association with other sexually transmitted diseases, including those caused by *Trichomonas, Gardnerella, Monilia,* gonococcus, herpesvirus, and syphilis. They develop more often during pregnancy and in immunosuppressed patients, such as those being treated with corticosteroids, alkylating agents, azathioprine, or cyclosporin A (to prevent organ transplant rejection).

B. The condylomas usually start as small raised warty growths that are soon surrounded by seedling growths. As the individual warts spread and enlarge, they may coalesce to produce a large exophytic mass with a broad sessile base. Lesions may involve the vulva, vagina, cervix, anus, and urethra.

C. Cervical and vaginal condyloma lesions frequently shed cytologically characteristic cells known as koilocytes or balloon cells. These are usually superficial dyskeratotic cells with an enlarged hyperchromatic nucleus surrounded by a distinct, clear cytoplasmic halo. The nuclear membrane may be irregular with a wrinkled, raisin-like appearance.

D. Under colposcopic magnification, exophytic condylomas typically have white finger-like projections, each of which contains within it a regular capillary loop. Early lesions may be recognized as tiny spikes, called asperites, projecting from the surface epithelium. Flat condylomas are common on cervix, vagina, and hair free areas of the vulva, but they can only be visualized by colposcopy after the application of 3 to 5 percent acetic acid. They appear as aceto-white epithelium, frequently with superimposed punctation and mosaicism. They may be difficult to distinguish from intraepithelial neoplasia. Only histologic study of a biopsy specimen determines the precise nature of the lesion.

E. Because they cannot be distinguished from neoplastic lesions visually, it is essential to biopsy flat condylomas, exophytic lesions that are bluish or dark brown in color, and any lesion that does not regress promptly with treatment.

F. There are at least 40 subtypes of the papillomavirus that have thus far been identified by serotyping. Types 6, 11, 16, 18, and 31 are found in genital warts. Among these, types 16, 18, and 31 have been most strongly associated with neoplasia of the lower genital tract. Hybridization, immunofluorescence, and other techniques are becoming available for specific subtyping. The type of virus encountered in a given infection may have some bearing on the method of treatment in the near future.

G. All sexually transmitted diseases should be screened for (p 112) and treated, if encountered, as the first step in managing a patient with condylomas. Any source of leukorrhea should be aggressively addressed (p 38).

H. About two-thirds of the male partners of patients with condylomas have or will develop genital warts. Simple inspection of the penis is usually inadequate for determining the presence of the virus on the genital skin. The examination should be done after soaking the skin surface with 5 percent acetic acid for five minutes, carefully surveying the area under magnification with good illumination. Aceto-white areas can then be seen. Biopsy can be expected to confirm them to represent condylomas.

I. Podophyllin (25 percent in tincture of benzoin) can be used to treat small skin lesions. It is painted on and left on the lesion for six to eight hours and then washed off. It should never be used intravaginally or on the cervix because it is readily absorbed and may lead to severe (even fatal) neurologic toxicity. Do not use it at all during pregnancy, averting fetal effects. Topical trichloracetic acid (50 to 80 percent) is effective for small lesions. Large lesions are best removed by excision. Since the virus has been shown to be present in the epithelium up to 2 cm beyond the visible margin of a condyloma, be sure to ablate or extirpate a collar of normally appearing tissue. Use of the laser technique is especially valuable for eradicating the virus.

J. Treating genital warts is an unrewarding exercise because of the high recurrence rate. Multiple attempts are usually necessary to effect a cure. Persistence and repeated follow-up are essential to accomplish this difficult objective.

References

Butler EB, Stanbridge CM. Condylomatous lesions of the lower female genital tract. Clin Obstet Gynaecol 11:171, 1984.

Carson LF, Twiggs LB, Fukushima M, et al. Human genital papilloma infections: An evaluation of immunologic competence in the genital neoplasia-papilloma syndrome. Am J Obstet Gynecol 155:784, 1986.

Ferenczy A, Mitao M, Nagai N, et al. Latent papillomavirus and recurring genital warts. N Engl J Med 313:784, 1985.

Grundsell H, Larsson G, Bekassy Z. Treatment of condylomata acuminata with the carbon dioxide laser. Br J Obstet Gynaecol 91:193, 1984.

PATIENT WITH SUSPICION OF CONDYLOMA ACUMINATUM

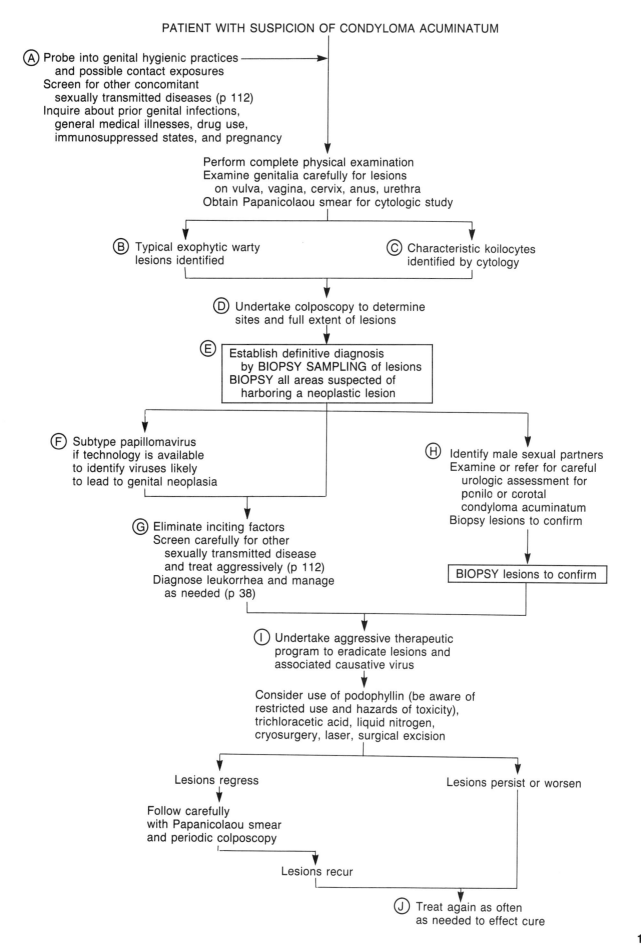

Ⓐ Probe into genital hygienic practices
    and possible contact exposures
  Screen for other concomitant
    sexually transmitted diseases (p 112)
  Inquire about prior genital infections,
    general medical illnesses, drug use,
    immunosuppressed states, and pregnancy

Perform complete physical examination
Examine genitalia carefully for lesions
  on vulva, vagina, cervix, anus, urethra
Obtain Papanicolaou smear for cytologic study

Ⓑ Typical exophytic warty
  lesions identified

Ⓒ Characteristic koilocytes
  identified by cytology

Ⓓ Undertake colposcopy to determine
  sites and full extent of lesions

Ⓔ Establish definitive diagnosis
    by BIOPSY SAMPLING of lesions
  BIOPSY all areas suspected of
    harboring a neoplastic lesion

Ⓕ Subtype papillomavirus
  if technology is available
  to identify viruses likely
  to lead to genital neoplasia

Ⓗ Identify male sexual partners
  Examine or refer for careful
    urologic assessment for
    penile or scrotal
    condyloma acuminatum
  Biopsy lesions to confirm

Ⓖ Eliminate inciting factors
  Screen carefully for other
    sexually transmitted disease
    and treat aggressively (p 112)
  Diagnose leukorrhea and manage
    as needed (p 38)

BIOPSY lesions to confirm

Ⓘ Undertake aggressive therapeutic
  program to eradicate lesions and
  associated causative virus

Consider use of podophyllin (be aware of
restricted use and hazards of toxicity),
trichloracetic acid, liquid nitrogen,
cryosurgery, laser, surgical excision

Lesions regress

Lesions persist or worsen

Follow carefully
with Papanicolaou smear
and periodic colposcopy

Lesions recur

Ⓙ Treat again as often
  as needed to effect cure

GENITAL HERPES

Janet L. Mitchell, M.D., M.P.H.

A. Genital herpesvirus infections are widespread. Of the two antigenic subgroups, all but 15 percent of genital infections are caused by type 2. Primary infection is associated with severe genital pain, inguinal lymphadenopathy, dysuria, fever, and malaise. Recurrent infections are milder, of shorter duration, and without systemic symptoms. Immunosuppression by drugs or disease enhances susceptibility markedly.

B. A reliable clinical diagnosis can usually be made visually. If unclear, take virologic cultures from aspirated vesicular fluid or a swab of the exudate. Cytology of material from the base of the vesicles shows multinucleated cells containing intranuclear inclusions, but results may be falsely negative in many cases. Thus, cytology is helpful only when it is positive. Detection rates are better with immunofluorescence and immunoperoxidase tests, but they are not as good as tissue culture. Serologic tests can detect host immune response; antibodies appear in about one week and rise to a peak in two to three weeks. Because the antibody titer level persists thereafter for life without any further increases apparent from subsequent recurrences, the serologic tests are only of value for documenting a primary infection. Obtain serum specimens during the acute phase and again several weeks later, sending both to the laboratory for testing together.

C. Genital herpesvirus infection in pregnancy warrants special care and counseling because of its fetal risks. The incidence of spontaneous abortion is increased in the first trimester and of premature labor in the third. Congenital malformations, principally affecting the brain and eyes, may occur from early transplacental fetal infection. Exposure to the virus during vaginal delivery can cause a catastrophic infection in the newborn infant. This may be averted by cesarean section.

D. The history of prior episodes and the clinical constellation of manifestations generally make it easy to differentiate between primary and recurrent infections. The duration of a primary infection ranges from three to six weeks on average, whereas recurrent lesions seldom persist for more than two weeks. Primary lesions tend to be severe, extensive, intensely symptomatic, and associated with systemic symptoms. Recurrent lesions are usually confined, much less uncomfortable, and without concurrent fever or malaise. Primary viremia may also be complicated by meningitis, pharyngitis, hepatitis, sacral neuropathy, and secondary infection. Involvement of the cervix is seen in more than 80 percent of women with their first episode. Although the clinical course of primary infections are similar with the two viral types, those due to type 1 appear to have fewer recurrences.

E. Acyclovir is the treatment of choice for both primary and recurrent infections. It may be used topically, orally, or intravenously. For patients experiencing a primary episode, the drug significantly reduces viral shedding and inhibits the formation of new lesions. It hastens the healing of lesions, but has little effect on constitutional symptoms. For those with recurrent infections, it also reduces the duration of viral shedding and suppresses the development of new lesions. However, the drug has no apparent beneficial effect on the rate of recurrence.

F. Symptomatic relief can be offered with analgesic drugs. Minimize use of anesthetic ointments because the potential for allergic reaction is high. To reduce the risk of secondary infection, advise the patient to keep the area clean by simple hygienic measures, such as frequent bathing or douching, supplemented by mild antiseptic or antibacterial applications.

G. The current pandemic of herpesvirus infection coupled with liberal sexual attitudes makes it essential to warn affected patients about the need to ensure against transmitting the disease to their sexual partners. Special precautions, specifically condom use, should be taken even when no lesions are apparent because the virus may continue to shed intravaginally long after the lesion heals. Care is also needed to prevent patients from autoinoculating themselves by contact (genitals to fingers to face, for example). Follow-up should include periodic cytologic smears (p 12) searching for dysplasia, to which women with genital herpes may be especially prone.

References

Baker DA. Herpesvirus. Clin Obstet Gynecol 26:165, 1983.

Corey L. The diagnosis and treatment of genital herpes. JAMA 248:1041, 1982.

Harger JH, Meyer MP, Amortegui AJ. Changes in the frequency of genital herpes recurrences as a function of time. Obstet Gynecol 67:637, 1986.

Monif GRG, Kellner KR, Donnelly WH Jr. Congenital herpes simplex type II infection. Am J Obstet Gynecol 152:1000, 1985.

Nilsen AE, Aasen T, Halsos AM, et al. Efficacy of oral acyclovir in the treatment of initial and recurrent genital herpes. Obstet Gynecol Surv 38:226, 1983.

PATIENT WITH SUSPICION OF GENITAL HERPES INFECTION

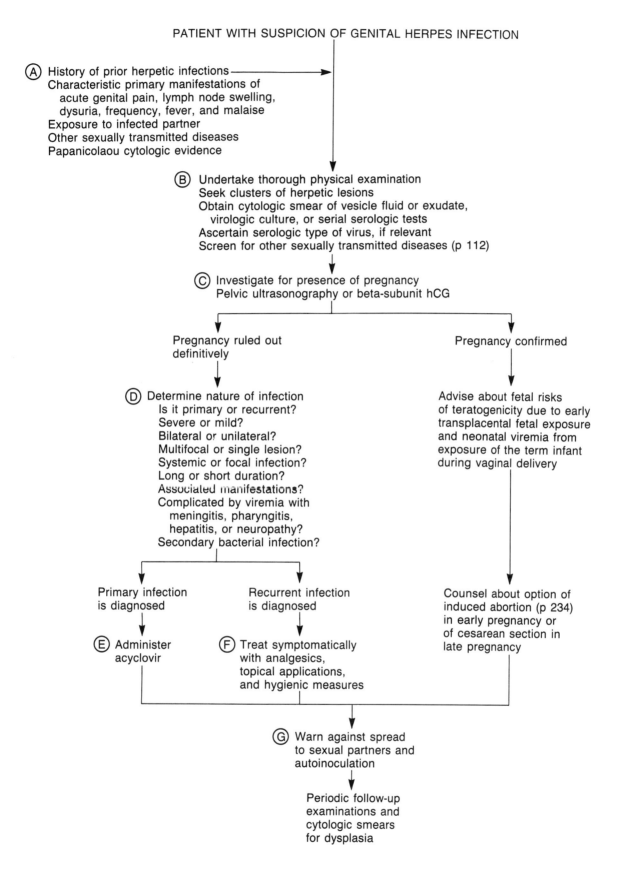

(A) History of prior herpetic infections
Characteristic primary manifestations of
   acute genital pain, lymph node swelling,
   dysuria, frequency, fever, and malaise
Exposure to infected partner
Other sexually transmitted diseases
Papanicolaou cytologic evidence

(B) Undertake thorough physical examination
Seek clusters of herpetic lesions
Obtain cytologic smear of vesicle fluid or exudate,
   virologic culture, or serial serologic tests
Ascertain serologic type of virus, if relevant
Screen for other sexually transmitted diseases (p 112)

(C) Investigate for presence of pregnancy
Pelvic ultrasonography or beta-subunit hCG

Pregnancy ruled out
definitively

Pregnancy confirmed

(D) Determine nature of infection
Is it primary or recurrent?
Severe or mild?
Bilateral or unilateral?
Multifocal or single lesion?
Systemic or focal infection?
Long or short duration?
Associated manifestations?
Complicated by viremia with
   meningitis, pharyngitis,
   hepatitis, or neuropathy?
Secondary bacterial infection?

Advise about fetal risks
of teratogenicity due to early
transplacental fetal exposure
and neonatal viremia from
exposure of the term infant
during vaginal delivery

Primary infection
is diagnosed

Recurrent infection
is diagnosed

Counsel about option of
induced abortion (p 234)
in early pregnancy or
of cesarean section in
late pregnancy

(E) Administer
acyclovir

(F) Treat symptomatically
with analgesics,
topical applications,
and hygienic measures

(G) Warn against spread
to sexual partners and
autoinoculation

Periodic follow-up
examinations and
cytologic smears
for dysplasia

ACQUIRED IMMUNE DEFICIENCY SYNDROME

Miguel Damien, M.D.

A. Acquired immune deficiency syndrome (AIDS) is a rapidly growing, worldwide problem of serious magnitude. As a sexually transmitted disease, it affects both homosexual and, in increasing numbers, heterosexual individuals (see C). The pathogenetic mechanism of the disease can be understood by appreciating that the virus has tropism for the cell surface antigen known as CD4 or T4. This antigen is an essential part of the receptor used by the virus to enter the cell it infects. The virus possesses an enzyme, reverse transcriptase, that enables the virus to make a DNA copy of its RNA; this in turn can be inserted into the host cell genome. Lymphopenia results from depletion of T cells that mediate cellular immunity and regulate immune responses. Specifically depleted is the subset of T cells, known as T helper cells, which have the CD4 antigen on their surface. In addition, the remaining T helper cells function abnormally, as do macrophages and monocytes, cells that collaborate with CD4 lymphocytes in the elimination of facultative intracellular pathogens. The regulation of antibody secretion by B lymphocytes ia also affected.

B. AIDS is the most severe manifestation of a spectrum of diseases associated with human immune deficiency virus (HIV, formerly HTLV-III). Symptoms of acute infection are transient, including fever, rash, arthropathy, headache, and lymphadenopathy. Infection may also lead to an asymptomatic carrier state or to a range of lymphadenopathy-associated syndromes grouped together as AIDS-related complex (ARC). Characteristically, lymphadenopathy persists for three to six months in these cases. Epidemiologic studies suggest that ARC is at least seven-fold more common than AIDS and that many patients who test positive for HIV or have ARC eventually develop full-blown AIDS.

C. Since the virus is transmitted through sexual contact, exposure to infected blood or blood components, and from mother to fetus, certain risk groups can be identified at the initial patient evaluation. These risk categories include past or present intravenous drug abusers and their partners; prostitutes and their partners; women who are or have been sexual partners of bisexual men, hemophiliacs, men with evidence of HIV infection, or men from countries where heterosexual transmission plays a major role; and women from those countries (including Zaire, Zambia, Uganda, and Ruwanda). After consent is obtained, enzyme-linked immunosorbent assay (ELISA) for HIV antibody should be determined for patients who have clinical evidence of infection or who are in an identifiable risk group. This test should be repeated if initially positive because of its high false positive rate. If consistently positive, the more specific Western blot test should then be performed.

D. The clinical problems seen in these patients are largely due to their susceptibility to a particular group of unusual infections and tumors. Their pattern is similar to that seen with other forms of compromised cellular immunity, such as occurs in organ transplant recipients (a drug effect) and children with combined immune deficiency. The tumors that occur in AIDS patients include Kaposi's sarcoma and B cell lymphomas. There is no evidence that HIV is itself oncogenic. It is more likely that these tumors, which have been associated with cytomegalovirus and Epstein-Barr virus, are opportunistic and secondary to the immune deficiency. The infections that are considered at least moderately predictive of underlying cellular immune deficiency and may suggest clinical evidence of HIV infection are as follows: protozoal and helminthic infections, such as cryptosporidiosis (intestinal), *Pneumocystis carinii* pneumonia, *Strongyloides* and *Toxoplasma* pneumonia or central nervous system infection; fungal infections, such as aspergillosis, candidiasis, cryptococcosis; bacterial infections, such as atypical mycobacteriosis causing disseminated infection; and viral infections, such as cytomegalovirus (causing pulmonary, gastrointestinal, or central nervous system infection) and herpes simplex virus (causing chronic mucocutaneous infection with ulcers persisting for more than one month or pulmonary, gastrointestinal, or disseminated infection). Progressive multifocal leukoencephalopathy (presumed to be caused by papovavirus) may also occur.

E. Provide counseling to patients with positive test results and to those in a high-risk group even if their test is negative. Advise about risks to sexual partners and the protection afforded by condoms. Maintain confidentiality. It may take up to six months before antibodies develop to this viral infection. To avoid potential infection, health care workers should, therefore, take appropriate precautions whenever exposed to blood and body fluids of any patient.

References

Jaffe HW, Bregman DJ, Selik RM. Acquired immune deficiency syndrome in the United States: The first 1,000 cases. J Infect Dis 148:339, 1983.

Pinching AJ, Jeffries DJ. AIDS and HTLV-III/LAV infection: Consequences for obstetrics and perinatal medicine. Br J Obstet Gynaecol 92:1211, 1985.

Update: Acquired immunodeficiency syndrome – United States. MMWR 35:17, 1986.

Weber DJ, Redfield RR, Lemon SM. Acquired immunodeficiency syndrome: Epidemiology and significance for the obstetrician and gynecologist. Am J Obstet Gynecol 155:235, 1986.

PATIENT AT RISK FOR AIDS

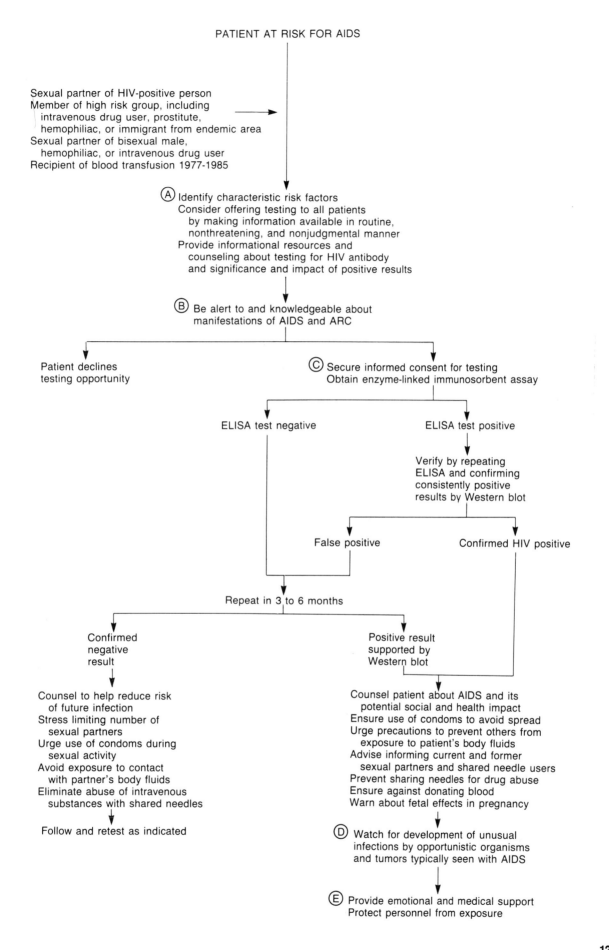

Sexual partner of HIV-positive person
Member of high risk group, including
    intravenous drug user, prostitute,
    hemophiliac, or immigrant from endemic area
Sexual partner of bisexual male,
    hemophiliac, or intravenous drug user
Recipient of blood transfusion 1977-1985

(A) Identify characteristic risk factors
    Consider offering testing to all patients
        by making information available in routine,
        nonthreatening, and nonjudgmental manner
    Provide informational resources and
        counseling about testing for HIV antibody
        and significance and impact of positive results

(B) Be alert to and knowledgeable about
    manifestations of AIDS and ARC

Patient declines
testing opportunity

(C) Secure informed consent for testing
    Obtain enzyme-linked immunosorbent assay

ELISA test negative

ELISA test positive

Verify by repeating
ELISA and confirming
consistently positive
results by Western blot

False positive

Confirmed HIV positive

Repeat in 3 to 6 months

Confirmed
negative
result

Positive result
supported by
Western blot

Counsel to help reduce risk
    of future infection
Stress limiting number of
    sexual partners
Urge use of condoms during
    sexual activity
Avoid exposure to contact
    with partner's body fluids
Eliminate abuse of intravenous
    substances with shared needles

Follow and retest as indicated

Counsel patient about AIDS and its
    potential social and health impact
Ensure use of condoms to avoid spread
Urge precautions to prevent others from
    exposure to patient's body fluids
Advise informing current and former
    sexual partners and shared needle users
Prevent sharing needles for drug abuse
Ensure against donating blood
Warn about fetal effects in pregnancy

(D) Watch for development of unusual
    infections by opportunistic organisms
    and tumors typically seen with AIDS

(E) Provide emotional and medical support
    Protect personnel from exposure

ANOVULATION

Alexander M. Dlugi, M.D.

A. Women can normally experience anovulatory cycles from time to time, particularly after menarche and before menopause. It is seldom a problem unless it is chronic and causes menorrhagia or infertility. Those affected may express concern and deserve the benefit of an evaluation and reassurance. Failure of the hypothalamic-pituitary-ovarian axis to achieve and maintain a regular pattern of cyclicity is the most common cause of anovulation. Aside from ovarian failure and menopause, the problem is nearly always related to a functional defect in the hypothalamus or pituitary; androgens or estrogens (given exogenously or produced endogenously) can cause inappropriate feedback action as can metabolic disorders, such as Cushing's syndrome, prolactin-producing adenoma, or thyroid disease. Anovulation associated with the polycystic ovary syndrome (p 128), virilization (p 64), delayed puberty (p 62), menopause (p 94), and galactorrhea (p 70) needs differentiation. Obtain a thorough personal and family history. Supplement the history with a good review of systems and detailed physical examination. Seek evidence of delayed or abnormal secondary sexual characteristics, androgenic effect, thyroid disease, Cushingoid features, galactorrhea, and malnutrition (especially if the result of dieting or anorexia). Inquire about strenuous exercise, significant weight loss, and intense psychological stresses.

B. Whereas it is seldom necessary to pursue a program of extensive laboratory testing, certain studies are essential in an otherwise healthy and normally developed woman who is chronically anovulatory. To eliminate pregnancy as a cause, obtain a beta-subunit hCG determination. At minimum, serum follicle stimulating hormone (FSH) and luteinizing hormone (LH) and prolactin levels should be measured to offer the best opportunity for rapid and accurate diagnosis. If the clinical features presented by the patient warrant, ascertain the concentrations of serum androgens and undertake the range of thyroid function tests.

C. Ovarian failure is invariably associated with elevated gonadotropins, particularly FSH. The condition may reflect the genetic absence of follicles in the ovaries (gonadal dysgenesis) or, more rarely, inability of the follicles to respond (gonadotropin-resistant ovary). In some women, the supply of ova is prematurely depleted, resulting in premature ovarian failure and unduly early menopause. Ovarian failure before the age of 35 warrants complete investigation to determine whether there is a treatable cause. Be sure to repeat both FSH and LH determinations to ensure against misdiagnosing the condition by having unwittingly tested the patient during a midcycle surge.

D. A LH:FSH ratio greater than 3:1 is typical of polycystic ovary disease (p 128). Serum androgen levels may be somewhat elevated, especially if hirsutism coexists. Elevated prolactin concentrations can also be encountered in some cases. The classic clinical characteristics of oligomenorrhea, hirsutism, obesity, and bilaterally enlarged ovaries, although not consistently present in all cases, make the diagnosis apparent.

E. Patients with hypothalamic anovulation are usually normally developed; they show no pathognomonic physical findings; and most often they have normal laboratory results. More comprehensive surveillance may disclose some alteration of the LH pulse frequency and amplitude. This common problem occurs among young women who experience emotional stresses, many with psychosexual problems. This disturbance in cyclic release of gonadotropin appears to cause the otherwise normally responsive ovaries to fail in their role of sequential maturation of follicles to ovulation. Normal ovulatory and menstrual function generally returns after counseling and reassurance. If pregnancy is desired, ovulation induction is indicated. The use of clomiphene citrate is often beneficial, but it requires careful monitoring of the response because of the high level of ovarian sensitivity to such stimulation. If an adequate regimen of clomiphene citrate fails to effect ovulation, human menopausal gonadotropins may be needed for this purpose.

F. The anovulatory woman who is found to have an elevated serum prolactin level, with or without galactorrhea, should be evaluated first for hypothyroidism by determining the thyroid stimulating hormone (TSH) concentration. This is necessary because the increase in thyroid releasing hormone that is associated with the hypothyroid state increases prolactin. If TSH is normal, consideration must be given to the likelihood that a pituitary adenoma is present. This requires appropriate imaging techniques for detection (p 70).

References

Cumming DE, Strich G, Brunsting L, et al. Acute exercise-related endocrine changes in women runners and non-runners. Fertil Steril 36:421, 1981.

Garcia CR, Freeman EW, Rickels K, et al. Behavioral and emotional factors and treatment responses in study of anovulatory infertile women. Fertil Steril 44:478, 1985.

Reame NE, Sauder SE, Case GD, et al. Pulsatile gonadotropin secretion in women with hypothalamic amenorrhea: Evidence that reduced frequency of gonadotropin-releasing hormone secretion is the mechanism of persistent anovulation. J Clin Endocrinol Metab 61:851, 1985.

Warren MP. Effects of undernutrition on reproduction function in the human. Endoc Rev 4:363, 1983.

PATIENT WITH SUSPICION OF ANOVULATION

(A) Inquire about menstrual pattern,
delayed puberty, infertility,
galactorrhea, hirsutism, voice change,
severe emotional stress, malnutrition,
dietary fads, excessive exercise,
weight changes, symptoms of thyroid disease,
Cushing's syndrome, other endocrinopathy
or metabolic disorder, menopausal changes,
or past or current chronic illness

(A) Evaluate by thorough physical examination
to rule out nonovarian origin

Verify anovulation with basal body temperature
charting and ENDOMETRIAL BIOPSIES (p 56)

Anovulation confirmed
Nonovarian pathologic
condition ruled out

(A) Disclose nonovarian disorder,
such as galactorrhea (p 66),
virilization (p 64),
thyroid dysfunction, or
debilitating disease,
and pregnancy

Manage accordingly

(B) Initiate laboratory investigation
Luteinizing hormone level
Follicle stimulating hormone level
Prolactin concentration
Thyroid function studies
Serum androgens

(C) FSH and LH
are both elevated

Repeat LH and FSH

Levels still
elevated

Diagnose
ovarian failure,
menopause

Manage with
estrogen replacement
as needed (p 94)

(D) LH:FSH ratio
greater than 3:1

Obtain prolactin
level

Prolactin
is normal

Diagnose
polycystic ovary
syndrome

Undertake
necessary
treatment
(p 128)

FSH and LH are normal

Determine prolactin level

(E) Prolactin
is normal

Assess for
immediate
fertility
needs

Pregnancy
is not desired
at this time

Manage
expectantly
or provide
cyclic
hormonal
program

Pregnancy
is desired

Provide
ovulation
induction
regimen with
clomiphene,
monitoring
carefully

(F) Prolactin
is elevated

Repeat
prolactin
determination

Prolactin
remains elevated

Evaluate for
thyroid and
pituitary disorder

LUTEAL PHASE DEFICIENCY

Steven R. Bayer, M.D.

A. The diagnosis of luteal phase deficiency should be considered in any woman presenting with a history of infertility or habitual early abortion. Suboptimal follicular development or inadequate luteinizing hormone surge may compromise progesterone production by the corpus luteum. Progesterone initiates specific changes in the estrogen-primed endometrium. A deficiency of this hormone may result in an endometrium that is not conducive to implantation. If the deficiency is of a lesser degree, implantation may occur; however, the corpus luteum is then unable to produce enough progesterone to support the pregnancy until the placenta takes over that maintenance function.

B. Review the basal body temperature chart to determine the duration of the secretory phase temperature rise. A luteal phase less than 11 days long suggests the possibility of luteal phase inadequacy. Bear in mind that a normal luteal phase length does not preclude the diagnosis. Some advocate measuring several midluteal phase progesterone levels to assess the adequacy of the corpus luteum, but interpretation of the results of these measurements is controversial. Endometrial secretory development (see C) represents the cumulative effect of progesterone on the endometrium. A timed biopsy is the best test to establish the diagnosis of luteal phase deficiency. The endometrial biopsy should be done within a few days prior to the expected menstrual period. Because of its small caliber, the Meigs curette is well tolerated by the patient, while it allows one to collect an adequate specimen for histologic examination. Use a paracervical block with 1 percent lidocaine to reduce the discomfort of the biopsy procedure. If the biopsy should happen to be performed in a pregnancy cycle, there is only a slightly increased risk of pregnancy loss. It is nevertheless prudent to obtain a pregnancy test beforehand or to have the patient avoid unprotected intercourse during the cycle in which the biopsy is taken.

C. Progesterone causes a distinctive sequence of changes in the stroma and glandular structures of the endometrium over time. These changes allow the pathologist to determine the histologic date of the biopsy with an accuracy of one to two days. The onset of the menses is considered to be the fourteenth day after ovulation; counting back from this date permits one to determine the actual date of the cycle on which the biopsy was performed. This chronologic date is then compared with the pathologic dating of the endometrial biopsy.

D. If the endometrial biopsy shows the secretory changes to be less than three days out of phase with the time of the cycle, this rules out a luteal phase defect. Other causes of the infertility (p 82) or habitual abortion must be sought.

E. Biopsy findings that are three days or more out of phase suggest a diagnosis of luteal phase deficiency. Since luteal phase defects may be sporadic events, another biopsy should be taken during the next cycle to confirm the diagnosis. Hyperprolactinemia can directly or indirectly alter corpus luteum function. For this reason, measure the serum prolactin level. If the prolactin is found to be elevated, obtain thyroid function studies including a thyroid stimulating hormone (TSH) determination. Thyroid releasing factor, a potent releaser of prolactin, is elevated in hypothyroidism. If these studies confirm normal thyroid function, then undertake to evaluate the hyperprolactinemia by computer tomography brain scan to rule out a pituitary microadenoma. If this examination is normal, then start bromocriptine treatment (2.5 mg twice daily by mouth).

F. If the prolactin determination is normal, then there is no need to proceed further with diagnostic tests. Treatment can be initiated to induce ovulation. Start clomiphene citrate (50 to 200 mg) on days 5 through 9 of the cycle. Because of its antiestrogen effect, clomiphene causes the follicle stimulating hormone level to increase. This ensures better follicular development and ultimately improves corpus luteum function. Another therapeutic option is to provide luteal supplementation with progesterone vaginal suppositories (25 mg twice daily) starting three days after the basal body temperature rise and continuing until the menses starts or pregnancy occurs. If conception occurs, consider giving 17-hydroxy-progesterone caproate (250 mg intramuscularly weekly) until the tenth week of pregnancy. If these regimens prove ineffective, other options to be weighed include clomiphene citrate plus human chorionic gonadotropin (hCG), pergonal and hCG, or gonadotropin releasing hormone (GnRH). Lack of success with these regimens may mean the patient has a progesterone receptor defect, a rare and untreatable condition.

References

Huang KE. The primary treatment of luteal phase inadequacy: Progesterone versus clomiphene citrate. Am J Obstet Gynecol 155:824, 1986.

Vanrell JA, Balasch J. Prolactin in the evaluation of the luteal phase in infertility. Fertil Steril 39:30, 1983.

Ying YK, Soto-Albors CE, Randolph JF, et al. Luteal phase defect and premenstrual syndrome in an infertile population. Obstet Gynecol 69:96, 1987.

PATIENT WITH SUSPICION OF LUTEAL PHASE DEFICIENCY

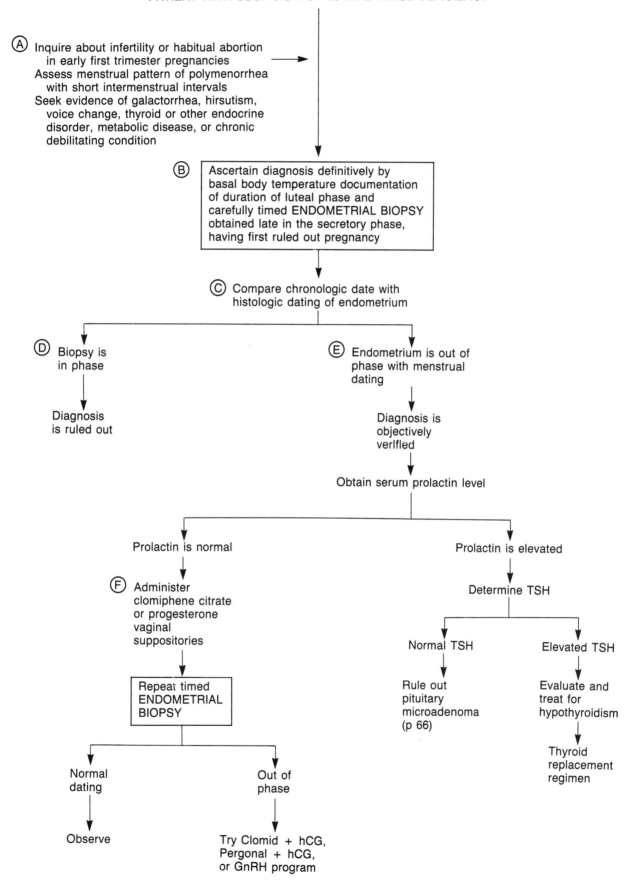

(A) Inquire about infertility or habitual abortion
in early first trimester pregnancies
Assess menstrual pattern of polymenorrhea
with short intermenstrual intervals
Seek evidence of galactorrhea, hirsutism,
voice change, thyroid or other endocrine
disorder, metabolic disease, or chronic
debilitating condition

(B) Ascertain diagnosis definitively by
basal body temperature documentation
of duration of luteal phase and
carefully timed ENDOMETRIAL BIOPSY
obtained late in the secretory phase,
having first ruled out pregnancy

(C) Compare chronologic date with
histologic dating of endometrium

(D) Biopsy is
in phase

Diagnosis
is ruled out

(E) Endometrium is out of
phase with menstrual
dating

Diagnosis is
objectively
verified

Obtain serum prolactin level

Prolactin is normal

(F) Administer
clomiphene citrate
or progesterone
vaginal
suppositories

Repeat timed
ENDOMETRIAL
BIOPSY

Normal
dating

Observe

Out of
phase

Try Clomid + hCG,
Pergonal + hCG,
or GnRH program

Prolactin is elevated

Determine TSH

Normal TSH

Rule out
pituitary
microadenoma
(p 66)

Elevated TSH

Evaluate and
treat for
hypothyroidism

Thyroid
replacement
regimen

POLYCYSTIC OVARY SYNDROME

Steven R. Bayer, M.D.
Machelle M. Seibel, M.D.

A. Although polycystic ovary syndrome (PCO) is a condition characterized by chronic anovulation, it can present clinically in a wide range of patterns. Patients are typically amenorrheic, but others show oligomenorrhea or even menorrhagia recurring irregularly. While advanced virilization (p 64) is unusual, troublesome hirsutism is not uncommon and may actually be the presenting complaint for many patients (or at least it is the symptom that most concerns them). Increased hair growth, when it occurs, often begins during puberty and is slowly progressive. Infertility results from the anovulation. Obesity is also frequently associated with this syndrome, but not invariably. The cause of PCO is unknown, but its pathogenesis has substantive contributions from disturbances of the hypothalamus, pituitary, adrenal glands, and peripheral tissues. These somehow cause luteinizing hormone (LH) secretion to rise in both amplitude and pulsatile frequency, while follicle stimulating hormone (FSH) secretion is somewhat decreased. This perhaps happens in feedback response to estrogens produced peripherally by conversion from adrenal androgens. Additionally, the ovaries themselves produce sustained levels of estrogens because many follicles are undergoing growth (but not to the point of maturation necessary for ovulation) simultaneously. Moreover, hyperplasia of the luteinized theca interna cells surrounding the follicles contributes to the androgen pool. Follicular growth is stimulated in turn by FSH and LH, thereby completing the circle and establishing the chronicity of the condition. The ovaries are generally quite large (although not always) with many follicular cysts and a smooth, thick tunica albuginea (Fig. 1).

B. Patients with PCO can usually be identified by their history (see A) and by findings on physical examination. Secondary sexual characteristics are normally developed and both hirsutism and bilaterally enlarged ovaries should be readily detectable. Consider the diagnosis confirmed if the serum LH level is above 30 mIU per milliliter and the FSH is either normal or decreased

somewhat. Thus, the LH:FSH ratio can be expected to be increased. Determinations of 17-ketosteroids, testosterone, and dehydroepiandrosterone sulfate (DHEAS) are usually in the high normal range; the free testosterone levels may be increased in hirsute patients. Serum prolactin may be increased in some as well. Be alert to the possibility that the condition may result from an androgen producing ovarian tumor or a hyperadrenal state (Cushing's syndrome), although diagnostic differentiation is seldom difficult on the basis of physical and laboratory observations.

C. PCO patients are managed according to their specific objectives, that is, their desire for pregnancy, correction of menstrual dysfunction, or suppression of hirsutism. Oral contraceptives are used to help hirsutism. They effectively suppress ovarian and adrenal production of androgens. Alternatively, one may use a corticosteroid (for example, 5 to 10 mg prednisone daily) for this purpose because of its adrenal suppressive effects. Objectively, monitor the adrenal activity with serial DHEAS determinations.

D. Tailor the treatment of amenorrhea or oligomenorrhea according to the concurrent concern about pregnancy. A regimen of cyclic birth control pills regulates the menstrual periods while simultaneously providing effective contraceptive protection. If contraception is irrelevant, give progestin (in the form of medroxyprogesterone acetate, Provera, 10 mg daily orally for five days) to effect regular endometrial shedding; this can be repeated at intervals of two months. Interrupting the sustained state of unopposed estrogenic stimulation is important because it helps avert development of endometrial hyperplasia leading to adenocarcinoma.

E. Infertility can generally be readily corrected in patients with PCO, but it is essential for them and their partners to have a full infertility evaluation (p 82) before proceeding with ovulation induction. Clomiphene citrate is effective for this purpose. Monitor the response carefully to avoid ovarian hyperstimulation, starting with a low-dosage regimen and limiting both dosage and duration to the least amount necessary by titrating according to the effect achieved. For the occasional patient who fails to respond, consider using purified human FSH (Metrodin) as a useful alternative.

References

Claman PC, Seibel MM. Purified human follicle-stimulating hormone for ovulation induction: A critical review. Semin Reprod Endocrinol 4:3, 1986.

Goldzieher JW. Polycystic ovarian disease. Fertil Steril 35:371, 1981.

Seibel MM. Toward understanding the pathophysiology and treatment of polycystic ovary disease. Semin Reprod Endocrinol 2:297, 1984.

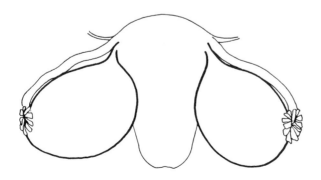

Figure 1 Polycystic ovaries, characteristically recognized by palpation as equivalent in size to (or greater than) the normal uterine corpus and, visually, by their smooth, thickened, white capsule.

PATIENT WITH HIRSUTISM, INFERTILITY, AMENORRHEA

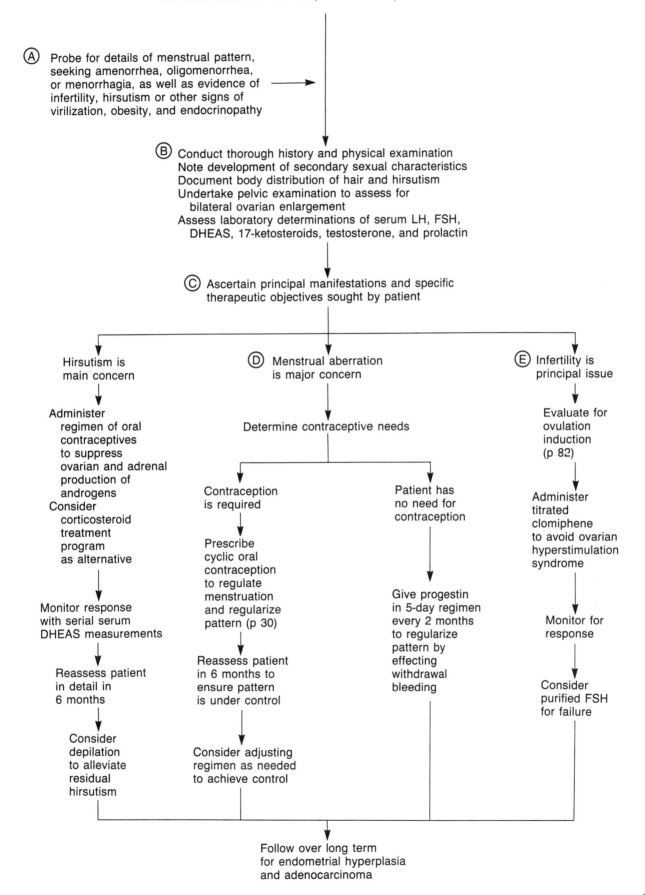

(A) Probe for details of menstrual pattern, seeking amenorrhea, oligomenorrhea, or menorrhagia, as well as evidence of infertility, hirsutism or other signs of virilization, obesity, and endocrinopathy

(B) Conduct thorough history and physical examination
Note development of secondary sexual characteristics
Document body distribution of hair and hirsutism
Undertake pelvic examination to assess for bilateral ovarian enlargement
Assess laboratory determinations of serum LH, FSH, DHEAS, 17-ketosteroids, testosterone, and prolactin

(C) Ascertain principal manifestations and specific therapeutic objectives sought by patient

Hirsutism is main concern

Administer regimen of oral contraceptives to suppress ovarian and adrenal production of androgens
Consider corticosteroid treatment program as alternative

Monitor response with serial serum DHEAS measurements

Reassess patient in detail in 6 months

Consider depilation to alleviate residual hirsutism

(D) **Menstrual aberration is major concern**

Determine contraceptive needs

Contraception is required

Prescribe cyclic oral contraception to regulate menstruation and regularize pattern (p 30)

Reassess patient in 6 months to ensure pattern is under control

Consider adjusting regimen as needed to achieve control

Patient has no need for contraception

Give progestin in 5-day regimen every 2 months to regularize pattern by effecting withdrawal bleeding

(E) **Infertility is principal issue**

Evaluate for ovulation induction (p 82)

Administer titrated clomiphene to avoid ovarian hyperstimulation syndrome

Monitor for response

Consider purified FSH for failure

Follow over long term for endometrial hyperplasia and adenocarcinoma

VULVAR DERMATOSES

Louis Burke, M.D.

A. The vulvar skin may be affected by any of the dermatologic disorders to which epidermis is subject as well as special conditions caused by exposure to irritating stimuli (see C). Tight undergarments and slacks contribute to the problem. Pruritus with scratching may evoke secondary infection (p 40). Vulvar eruptions may also result from a systemic illness or its therapy. Inquire about recent illnesses and medications. Be alert also to history or symptoms suggestive of exposure to or infection by a sexually transmitted disease. Note accompanying symptoms of itching, pain, soreness, and bleeding.

B. A detailed general physical examination may uncover other skin lesions and evidence of systemic disease. Look for seborrhea (see D), atopic eczema, psoriasis (see E), and moniliasis. Examine the vulva and perineum carefully under good light to determine both the nature and extent of the condition. The erythematous characteristics of these dermatologic disorders serve to distinguish them from dysplastic (p 134) or atrophic (p 132) lesions affecting the vulva, but this feature cannot always be relied upon for definitive diagnosis. Consider neoplasia if there are any areas of focal induration or nodularity and pursue histologic diagnosis by biopsy.

C. Intense erythema of the vulva may result from contact dermatitis due to hypersensitivity reaction to one or more of a wide variety of products, including laundry detergents, cosmetics, topical creams, or medications. Beginning as a uniform, delimited red lesion, this form of dermatitis may become edematous and vesicular if untreated. It is sometimes difficult to identify the offending stimulus or irritant, but diligence is often rewarded. In addition to a probing history inquiring about new exposures, patch testing with a variety of possibly relevant allergens may disclose the cause. In practical terms, however, do not wait for such clear-cut identification before trying to correct the problem. The patient who is uncomfortable deserves symptomatic relief as soon as feasible. Therefore, eliminate exposure at once to as many possible factors as feasible, while simultaneously providing a mild astringent solution (such as dilute Burow's solution) and topical anti-inflammatory corticosteroids, if needed. Systemic analgesic drugs may also be necessary until the acute inflammation has subsided.

D. Seborrheic dermatitis is most commonly encountered on the scalp, postauricular area, sternum, and interscapular midback. It is frequently recurrent in sebaceous sites where the typical ill-defined pruritic lesions can be recognized by their red color and greasy scaling. Lesions tend to be symmetric on the vulva, perineum, and inner aspects of the thighs. They respond well to antiseborrheic shampoos. Acute inflammation associated with severe exudative lesions may require preliminary anti-inflammatory treatment with dilute Burow's solution and topical corticosteroids.

E. Psoriasis is recognized by its typical plaques of sharply circumscribed scaling lesions on a reddened base characteristically located on the scalp, behind the ears, and especially on the extensor surfaces of the extremities (elbows and knees). The condition is rather indolent in nature and resistant to most forms of therapy. Occlusive dressings of plastic film applied at night help avoid local trauma and prevent scaling. Topically applied fluorinated corticosteroid cream is also effective, but can result in local atrophic changes if treatment is continued over a long period of time.

F. The severely pruritic lesions of lichen planus are usually seen on the flexor surfaces of the extremities, but they may arise on the trunk and mucous membranes as well. They appear as grouped patches of flattened, red or violaccous, shiny papules. Although they can disappear spontaneously, few affected patients are willing to delay relief of their intense itching. To help them, try prednisone, in a regimen of 20 to 30 mg daily by mouth for two weeks; then slowly taper to withdraw.

G. Acanthosis nigricans is generally encountered in the body skin folds, including axillae, groins, neck, thighs, and submammary areas. It can be recognized by its wart-like, velvety, hyperpigmented lesions. In adults, it is commonly associated with abdominal cancer, but not invariably so (and it is usually benign in children). When diagnosed, it calls for extensive assessment for coexistent malignancy. There is as yet no known form of therapy.

References

Connelly MG, Winkelmann RK. Coexistence of lichen sclerosis, morphea and lichen planus. J Am Acad Dermatol 12:844, 1985.

Dennerstein GJ. Depo-provera in the treatment of recurrent vulvovaginal candidiasis. J Reprod Med 31:801, 1986.

Krueger GG, Bergstrasser PR, Lowe NJ, et al. Psoriasis. J Am Acad Dermatol 11:937, 1984.

PATIENT WITH VULVAR ERUPTION

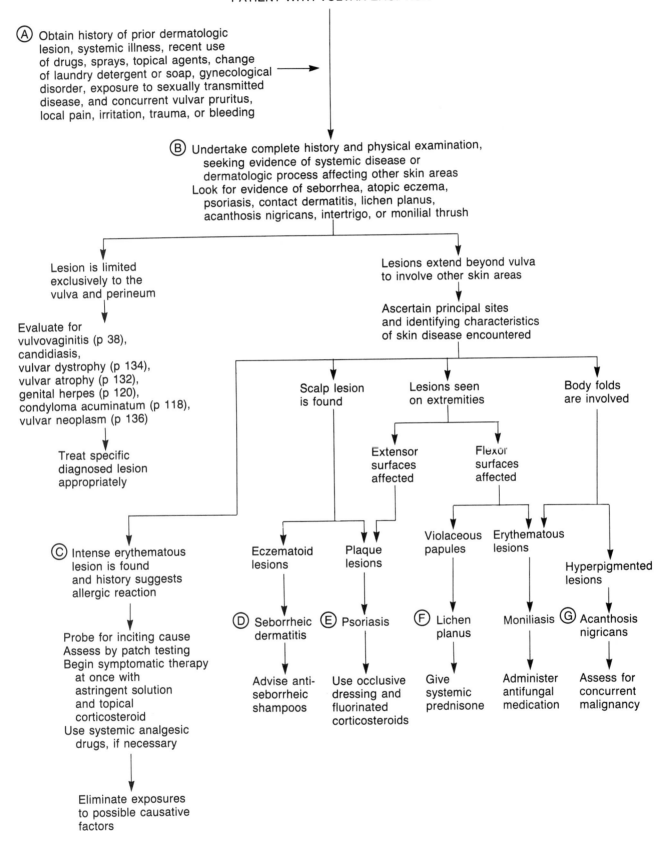

Ⓐ Obtain history of prior dermatologic
lesion, systemic illness, recent use
of drugs, sprays, topical agents, change
of laundry detergent or soap, gynecological
disorder, exposure to sexually transmitted
disease, and concurrent vulvar pruritus,
local pain, irritation, trauma, or bleeding

Ⓑ Undertake complete history and physical examination,
seeking evidence of systemic disease or
dermatologic process affecting other skin areas
Look for evidence of seborrhea, atopic eczema,
psoriasis, contact dermatitis, lichen planus,
acanthosis nigricans, intertrigo, or monilial thrush

Lesion is limited
exclusively to the
vulva and perineum

Lesions extend beyond vulva
to involve other skin areas

Ascertain principal sites
and identifying characteristics
of skin disease encountered

Evaluate for
vulvovaginitis (p 38),
candidiasis,
vulvar dystrophy (p 134),
vulvar atrophy (p 132),
genital herpes (p 120),
condyloma acuminatum (p 118),
vulvar neoplasm (p 136)

Treat specific
diagnosed lesion
appropriately

Scalp lesion
is found

Lesions seen
on extremities

Body folds
are involved

Extensor
surfaces
affected

Flexor
surfaces
affected

Violaceous
papules

Erythematous
lesions

Hyperpigmented
lesions

Ⓒ Intense erythematous
lesion is found
and history suggests
allergic reaction

Eczematoid
lesions

Plaque
lesions

Ⓓ Seborrheic
dermatitis

Ⓔ Psoriasis

Ⓕ Lichen
planus

Moniliasis

Ⓖ Acanthosis
nigricans

Probe for inciting cause
Assess by patch testing
Begin symptomatic therapy
at once with
astringent solution
and topical
corticosteroid
Use systemic analgesic
drugs, if necessary

Advise anti-
seborrheic
shampoos

Use occlusive
dressing and
fluorinated
corticosteroids

Give
systemic
prednisone

Administer
antifungal
medication

Assess for
concurrent
malignancy

Eliminate exposures
to possible causative
factors

ATROPHIC VULVAR LESIONS

Louis Burke, M.D.

A. The vulvar skin in adult women is responsive to estrogenic stimulation for maintenance of its integrity. If ovarian function diminishes spontaneously or as a consequence of surgical castration, the epithelial layer and underlying stroma may slowly undergo atrophic changes. Thus, vulvar atrophy is most often seen in older postmenopausal women who have not had the advantage of long-term estrogen supplementation (p 28). These patients may present with complaints of pruritus, dyspareunia or, more often, recurrent urinary tract infections. A similar form of atrophy with sclerosis may occur in children, but seldom without some inciting factor, such as vulvovaginitis secondary to a foreign body in the vagina, contamination by enteric organisms, or even gonococci. Lichen sclerosus is another form of dystrophic change, rarer in frequency and unrelated to hormonal influence (see F), but similar in clinical appearance and presentation.

B. The physical examination helps to identify the existence of a dermatitis (p 130) or systemic disease to account for the vulvar lesion. Carefully inspect and palpate the vulva to determine the presence of firm, indurated, or nodular lesions that might be neoplastic or dysplastic (p 134, 136). If found, these should be sampled by biopsy for definitive diagnosis. The pallid, thin, parchment-like perineal, labial, and vestibular skin seen with this condition bleeds easily and is readily traumatized. Synechiae may form at the posterior fourchette analogous to those that form in the vaginal fornices.

C. Examine the vulva with good illumination and magnification, using the colposcope (p 214), to differentiate vulvar atrophy, inflammation, dermatitis (p 130), and dysplastic disorders (p 134). Look particularly closely for evidence of neoplasia in the form of neovascularization (p 136).

D. Active cellular division characteristic of dysplastic and neoplastic tissues can be detected by applying a vital stain, such as a solution of toluidine blue dye, for highlighting foci that take up the nuclear stain. For this technique to be effective, be sure to cleanse the vulva beforehand to remove any adherent powder, lubricant, or medication that may interfere with nuclear uptake of the dye. After the dye is applied, it is washed away with dilute acetic acid, which decolorizes all areas except where the dye is bound to the nuclei. Dye sites are thus identified for biopsy sampling.

E. Postmenopausally, estrogen deprivation over a number of years results in benign vulvar atrophy in many women, but inexplicably not all. Patients who do not have problems (see A) require no treatment for this condition, although a prophylactic estrogen replacement program against osteoporosis (p 28) can be expected to prevent vulvar changes from occurring. Similarly, any vulvar atrophy resulting from deprivation should be readily reversible either by topical applications of an estrogen cream or by estrogens administered by mouth. The same reversibility does not apply to osteoporosis when estrogens are first begun after the condition is fully developed.

F. Lichen sclerosus is a dystrophic vulvar lesion of unknown etiology. It is characteristically distributed on the vulva and perineum in a symmetric pattern. The introitus undergoes stenosis and sometimes the labia minora disappear along with the clitoral prepuce. Pruritus is common. Histologically, the epithelium is thinned to a few cell layers; rete ridges are lost; the subepithelial area shows an acellular homogeneous zone with a deeper band of chronic inflammatory cells. If hyperkeratosis is present, the surface appears grossly shiny and wrinkled like parchment. The condition is quite resistant to treatment, but one can try topical creams containing testosterone or progestin. Alternatively, laser ablation may prove useful, but recurrence can be expected. Consider alcohol injection for unremitting pruritus (p 40).

G. Areas of hyperplastic dystrophy may appear concurrently with lichen sclerosus. This combination forms the so-called mixed dystrophy. Thick and thin epithelial regions are intermeshed, showing the shiny wrinkled lichen sclerosus in juxtaposition with the white plaques of hyperplasia. Because dysplastic atypia is more likely to be found in mixed dystrophy than with hyperplastic dystrophy (p 134) alone, careful biopsy surveillance is important.

References

Friedrich EG. Vulvar dystrophy. Clin Obstet Gynecol 28:178, 1985.

Harrington CI, Dunsmore IR. An investigation into the incidence of auto-immune disorders in patients with lichen sclerosus and atrophicus. Br J Dermatol 104:563, 1981.

Lavery HA. Vulval dystrophies: New approaches. Clin Obstet Gynaecol 11:155, 1984.

Soper JT, Creasman WT. Vulvar dystrophies. Clin Obstet Gynecol 29:431, 1986.

PATIENT WITH ATROPHIC VULVAR LESION

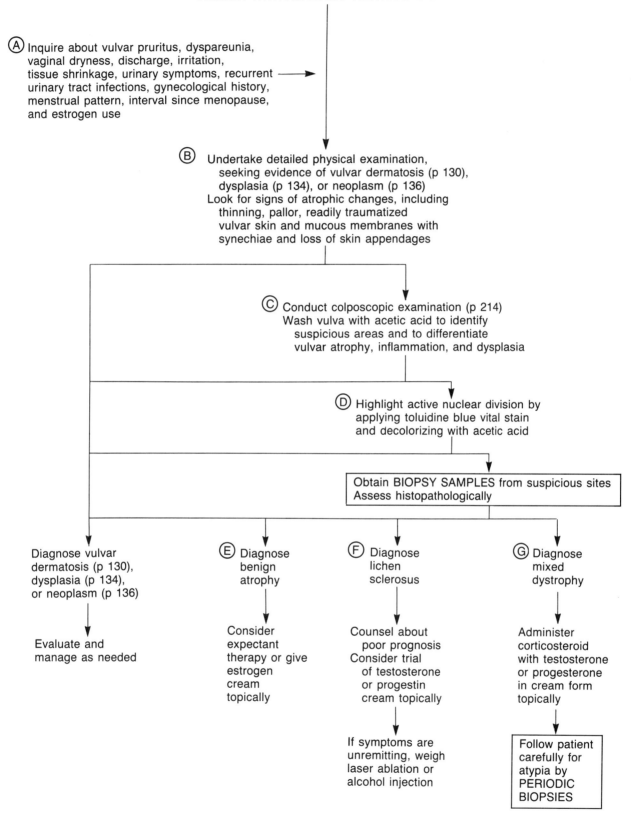

(A) Inquire about vulvar pruritus, dyspareunia,
vaginal dryness, discharge, irritation,
tissue shrinkage, urinary symptoms, recurrent
urinary tract infections, gynecological history,
menstrual pattern, interval since menopause,
and estrogen use

(B) Undertake detailed physical examination,
seeking evidence of vulvar dermatosis (p 130),
dysplasia (p 134), or neoplasm (p 136)
Look for signs of atrophic changes, including
thinning, pallor, readily traumatized
vulvar skin and mucous membranes with
synechiae and loss of skin appendages

(C) Conduct colposcopic examination (p 214)
Wash vulva with acetic acid to identify
suspicious areas and to differentiate
vulvar atrophy, inflammation, and dysplasia

(D) Highlight active nuclear division by
applying toluidine blue vital stain
and decolorizing with acetic acid

Obtain BIOPSY SAMPLES from suspicious sites
Assess histopathologically

Diagnose vulvar
dermatosis (p 130),
dysplasia (p 134),
or neoplasm (p 136)

Evaluate and
manage as needed

(E) Diagnose
benign
atrophy

Consider
expectant
therapy or give
estrogen
cream
topically

(F) Diagnose
lichen
sclerosus

Counsel about
poor prognosis
Consider trial
of testosterone
or progestin
cream topically

If symptoms are
unremitting, weigh
laser ablation or
alcohol injection

(G) Diagnose
mixed
dystrophy

Administer
corticosteroid
with testosterone
or progesterone
in cream form
topically

Follow patient
carefully for
atypia by
PERIODIC
BIOPSIES

DYSPLASTIC VULVAR LESIONS

Louis Burke, M.D.

A. White lesions appearing on the vulva may represent a dysplastic condition and must, therefore, be carefully evaluated. The white appearance derives from the thickened epithelium overlying the superficial vasculature or an actual diminution or constriction of those vessels. Depigmentation, as occurs in vitiligo, also produces pale skin areas, usually well recognized by comparable sites elsewhere. It is important to differentiate between atrophic and hypertrophic dystrophies. While neither has malignant potential unless associated with foci of atypia, they are sometimes clinically indistinguishable from a neoplastic lesion. Worrisome atypia consists of abnormal nuclei, mitotic forms, altered nuclear-cytoplasmic ratio, and keratinized pearls. Confusion in regard to their differences arose in the past because attempts were made to characterize them without histologic confirmation. It is now recognized that one cannot make a diagnosis of vulvar dystrophy by gross examination only. It requires microscopic examination of tissue samples obtained by biopsy. Unlike hyperplastic lesions, atrophic white lesions (p 132) appear principally as lichen sclerosus. Hyperplastic vulvar atrophy appears either as a thick and white lesion or scaly and red one. Both hyperplastic and atrophic forms may be present in a mixed condition on the same vulva. When hyperplastic dystrophic lesions are encountered, they must be distinguished from vulvar dermatoses (p 130), atrophy (p 132), and neoplastic lesions (p 136). Vulvar hyperplastic dystrophy typically presents as a thick pruritic plaque. Histologically, it shows nonspecific hyperkeratosis with chronic inflammatory reaction of the dermis. Acanthosis is seen with the rete pegs deeply elongated and broadly blunted.

B. It is essential to study the vulva extensively to identify those areas most likely to be dysplastic in order to obtain tissue samples for histologic examination. Colposcopic magnification is especially useful in this regard. Wash the vulva several times with dilute 3 to 5 percent acetic acid solution to highlight the white lesions. If colposcopy is unavailable, consider using toluidine blue vital stain (p 132) for delineating the areas with abnormal nuclear activity. Use of acetic acid shows up the suspicious areas for biopsy as white lesions with sharp margins demarcated from the surrounding normal vulvar skin. Once again, it is necessary to stress that diagnosis can only be made by histologic identification, looking especially for atypical dysplastic changes. Pathologic examination should seek evidence of intraepithelial carcinoma or Paget's disease as well. Pagetoid changes include nests of large, pale, clear cells. This lesion may serve as a signal that there is an underlying adenocarcinoma of the sweat glands.

C. As aforementioned, one must be especially attentive to the presence of areas of atypical dysplasia, ranging in intensity from mild to severe, within lesions of hyperplastic dystrophy. Atypia is encountered in about 5 percent of these lesions. The potential for developing a malignancy in these cases appears to be confined to the dysplastic foci. The more severe the atypia, the greater the concern. Inexplicably, the risk seems greater in patients with mixed dystrophy (p 132) than in those with hyperplastic dystrophy unaccompanied by lichen sclerosus.

D. Applications of a topical fluorinated corticosteroid preparation can be effective in alleviating dystrophic vulvar lesions. They usually disappear under this form of treatment in about four to eight weeks. This good prognosis may apply even to lesions containing foci of atypia. Relief of the pruritus may require use of a tranquilizer during the initial phase of treatment. Hyperplastic lesions are very different from atrophic dystrophy in that recurrence is uncommon. Nonetheless, careful follow-up is required to detect any lesions developing subsequently in this area.

E. Recurrence seldom is seen after topical corticosteroid treatment for a hyperplastic vulvar dystrophy. When it is found after a disease-free interval, it should be evaluated and managed as if it were an entirely new entity. Thus, colposcopic surveillance and biopsy are critical. If dysplastic atypia is verified histologically, a premalignant condition is likely to exist, warranting aggressive assessment and therapy. Consider locally ablative techniques to eradicate the lesion under these circumstances. Effective measures include resection by scalpel or laser. Alternatively, one can use 5-fluorouracil cream.

References

DiPaola GR, Rueda-Leverone NG, Belardi MG. Lichen sclerosus of the vulva recurrent after myocutaneous graft. J Reprod Med 27:666, 1982.

Friedrich EG. Vulvar dystrophy. Clin Obstet Gynecol 28:178, 1985.

Friedrich EG, Kalra PS. Serum levels of sex hormone in vulvar lichen sclerosus, and the effect of topical testosterone. N Engl J Med 310:488, 1984.

Lavery HA. Vulvar dystrophies: New approaches. Clin Obstet Gynaecol 11:155, 1984.

PATIENT WITH WHITE OR RED VULVAR LESION

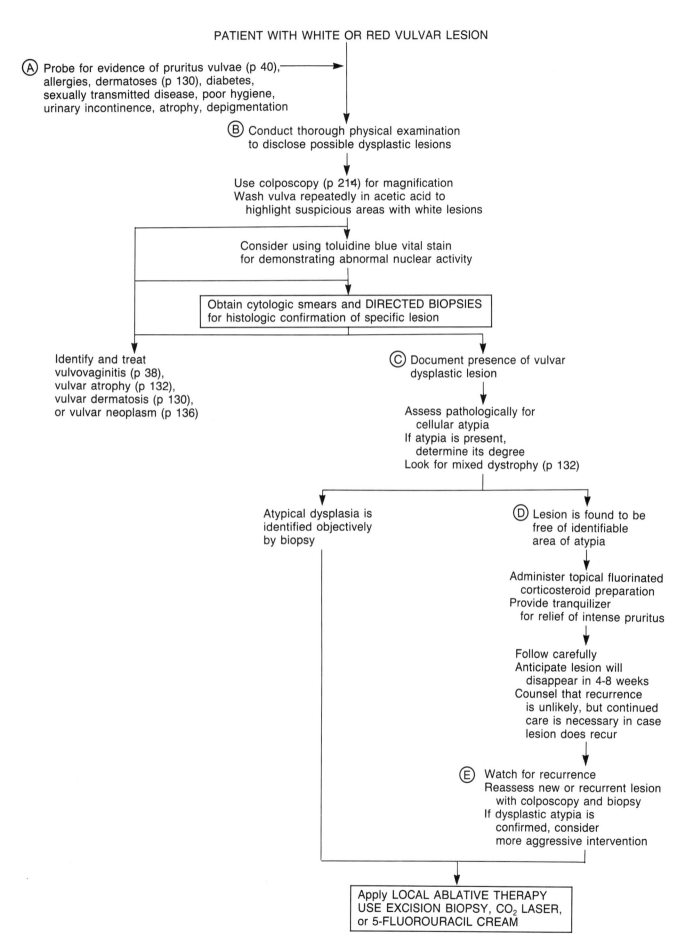

Ⓐ Probe for evidence of pruritus vulvae (p 40),
allergies, dermatoses (p 130), diabetes,
sexually transmitted disease, poor hygiene,
urinary incontinence, atrophy, depigmentation

Ⓑ Conduct thorough physical examination
to disclose possible dysplastic lesions

Use colposcopy (p 214) for magnification
Wash vulva repeatedly in acetic acid to
highlight suspicious areas with white lesions

Consider using toluidine blue vital stain
for demonstrating abnormal nuclear activity

Obtain cytologic smears and DIRECTED BIOPSIES
for histologic confirmation of specific lesion

Identify and treat
vulvovaginitis (p 38),
vulvar atrophy (p 132),
vulvar dermatosis (p 130),
or vulvar neoplasm (p 136)

Ⓒ Document presence of vulvar
dysplastic lesion

Assess pathologically for
cellular atypia
If atypia is present,
determine its degree
Look for mixed dystrophy (p 132)

Atypical dysplasia is
identified objectively
by biopsy

Ⓓ Lesion is found to be
free of identifiable
area of atypia

Administer topical fluorinated
corticosteroid preparation
Provide tranquilizer
for relief of intense pruritus

Follow carefully
Anticipate lesion will
disappear in 4-8 weeks
Counsel that recurrence
is unlikely, but continued
care is necessary in case
lesion does recur

Ⓔ Watch for recurrence
Reassess new or recurrent lesion
with colposcopy and biopsy
If dysplastic atypia is
confirmed, consider
more aggressive intervention

Apply LOCAL ABLATIVE THERAPY
USE EXCISION BIOPSY, CO$_2$ LASER,
or 5-FLUOROURACIL CREAM

VULVAR NEOPLASM

Louis Burke, M.D.

A. Except for simple, uncomplicated vulvar atrophy (p 132), it is not ordinarily possible to rule out neoplastic or dysplastic changes within a vulvar lesion on clinical grounds without histologic study. Thus, if one encounters a vulvar lesion that cannot clearly be identified as benign, it must be investigated objectively and definitively to ensure it does not contain foci of dysplasia or neoplasia. Although this applies especially to indolent, longstanding, and recurrent lesions, it does not relieve the clinician of the responsibility to evaluate every freshly discovered vulvar lesion if its nature is not completely evident. Too often, women neglect to seek care for a small lesion they find on their vulva, assuming it to be a minor skin disorder. It is quite inappropriate for the physician to contribute to the delay in diagnosis and treatment, perhaps missing the opportunity to undertake therapy while the condition is still curable.

B. Carcinoma in situ of the vulva may present as a diffuse or discrete raised maculopapular area or lesion; it may be associated with pigmentary changes or be whitened from hyperkeratosis. Basal cell carcinoma is typically an ulcer with rolled edges, whereas invasive squamous cell carcinoma often presents as a diffusely infiltrating and ulcerating nodular mass with surrounding edema. The form these lesions take may vary considerably, however. They may have to be differentiated from a vulvar dermatosis (p 130) or a sexually transmitted disease (p 112) by appropriate laboratory investigations.

C. Even though the colposcope can be useful for examining the vulva, it is not as valuable as for studying cervix and vagina (p 214). The skin of the labia minora is comparable to the vaginal mucous membrane in regard to its ability to reflect dysplastic changes, but the cornified skin of the labia majora is not as translucent, so that the vascular changes in the stroma may not be readily visible. Characteristic punctation and mosaic patterns are thus not apparent on the labia majora. Try persistent washing with 5 percent acetic acid for this purpose. The most frequent colposcopic patterns encountered on the vulva are leukoplakia or aceto-white epithelium. The abnormal blood vessels of an invasive lesion should be identifiable.

D. A woman with vulvar intraepithelial carcinoma is a candidate for other genital, bowel, or breast neoplasms. It is mandatory, therefore, for her to have a thorough evaluation for a concurrent tumor and to be followed periodically for any new lesion that may develop in the future. Treatment for vulvar carcinoma in situ is local ablation. This can be done by wide excision, skinning vulvectomy with scalpel or laser, or by topical 5-fluorouracil destruction.

E. Paget's disease (p 134) is frequently a marker for an underlying cancer, such as squamous cell carcinoma or adenocarcinoma of sweat glands. It may also reflect a more distant cancer of the cervix, breast, or gastrointestinal tract. Investigate affected patients comprehensively to uncover concurrent malignancy. The vulvar Pagetoid lesion can be treated effectively by simple vulvectomy. Resection of deep tissues well below the lesion is important for detecting a hidden lesion in the vicinity.

F. Invasive squamous cell cancer of the vulva is best treated in a center where intensive investigation and radical surgery can be carried out and full resources are available to manage any complications that may arise. Radical vulvectomy is an effective means for treating a patient with a potentially curable lesion. Dissection of the superficial femoral nodes is done to determine whether tumor has metastasized to these primary regional drainage sites. Deep femoral lymphadenectomy is indicated if the superficial nodes are involved. An effective alternative to node dissection is radiotherapy to help eradicate locally metastatic tumor. Microinvasive cancer to a depth of more than 5 mm can be treated by radical vulvectomy alone, without the necessity of node dissection. A single focus of a more superficially invasive lesion needs only wide surgical resection.

G. Malignant melanoma can be expected to spread rapidly by lymphogenous and hematogenous routes if it invades the stroma deeply. Although the prognosis for affected patients is grave, radical surgery must be carried out expediently and aggressively unless distant metastases are already present.

References

Buckley CH, Butler EB, Fox H. Vulvar intraepithelial neoplasia and microinvasive carcinoma of the vulva. J Clin Pathol 37:1201, 1984.

Dorsey JH. Understanding CO_2 laser surgery of the vulva. Colp Gynecol Laser Surg 1:205, 1984.

Ferenczy A. Using the laser to treat vulvar condyloma acuminata and intraepithelial neoplasia. Can Med Assoc J 128:135, 1983.

Rettenmaier MA, Berman ML, DiSaia PJ. Skinning vulvectomy for the treatment of multifocal vulvar intraepithelial neoplasia. Obstet Gynecol 69:247, 1987.

PATIENT WITH VULVAR LESION SUSPICIOUS FOR CANCER

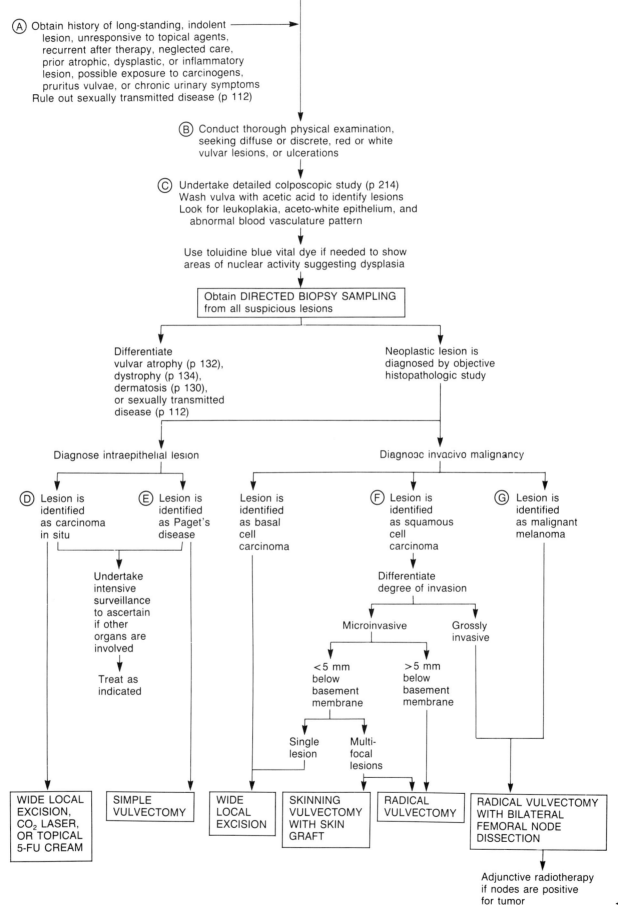

Ⓐ Obtain history of long-standing, indolent
   lesion, unresponsive to topical agents,
   recurrent after therapy, neglected care,
   prior atrophic, dysplastic, or inflammatory
   lesion, possible exposure to carcinogens,
   pruritus vulvae, or chronic urinary symptoms
   Rule out sexually transmitted disease (p 112)

Ⓑ Conduct thorough physical examination,
   seeking diffuse or discrete, red or white
   vulvar lesions, or ulcerations

Ⓒ Undertake detailed colposcopic study (p 214)
   Wash vulva with acetic acid to identify lesions
   Look for leukoplakia, aceto-white epithelium, and
   abnormal blood vasculature pattern

Use toluidine blue vital dye if needed to show
areas of nuclear activity suggesting dysplasia

Obtain DIRECTED BIOPSY SAMPLING
from all suspicious lesions

Differentiate
vulvar atrophy (p 132),
dystrophy (p 134),
dermatosis (p 130),
or sexually transmitted
disease (p 112)

Neoplastic lesion is
diagnosed by objective
histopathologic study

Diagnose intraepithelial lesion

Diagnose invasive malignancy

Ⓓ Lesion is
   identified
   as carcinoma
   in situ

Ⓔ Lesion is
   identified
   as Paget's
   disease

Lesion is
identified
as basal
cell
carcinoma

Ⓕ Lesion is
   identified
   as squamous
   cell
   carcinoma

Ⓖ Lesion is
   identified
   as malignant
   melanoma

Undertake
intensive
surveillance
to ascertain
if other
organs are
involved

Treat as
indicated

Differentiate
degree of invasion

Microinvasive

Grossly
invasive

<5 mm
below
basement
membrane

>5 mm
below
basement
membrane

Single
lesion

Multi-
focal
lesions

WIDE LOCAL
EXCISION,
CO_2 LASER,
OR TOPICAL
5-FU CREAM

SIMPLE
VULVECTOMY

WIDE
LOCAL
EXCISION

SKINNING
VULVECTOMY
WITH SKIN
GRAFT

RADICAL
VULVECTOMY

RADICAL VULVECTOMY
WITH BILATERAL
FEMORAL NODE
DISSECTION

Adjunctive radiotherapy
if nodes are positive
for tumor

BARTHOLIN DUCT MASS

David S. Chapin, M.D.

A. Bartholin glands are compound, racemose, posterolateral vestibular structures that can be the site of acute infection, thereby leading to ductal obstruction and abscess formation. Much more rarely, transitional cell cancer may arise in the gland (see G). Ductal obstruction can also occur from other causes, such as traumatic or congenital stenosis or lining hyperplasia. Typically, one can palpate the enlarged gland in the posterior third of the labium majus where it usually protrudes medially toward the vaginal introitus. Nontender fluctuance signifies that the gland has been converted to an uninfected cyst. A cyst located anteriorly to the horizontal midpoint of the introitus is not a Bartholin mass. This does not mean that a Bartholin abscess cannot extend anteriorly as it enlarges progressively in the vulvar tissues, although it is more likely to point outwardly toward the perineum or the vestibule, where it can be readily incised for effective drainage (see D). When present, but causing no symptoms, Bartholin cysts require no treatment.

B. Intense pain signals infection in a Bartholin duct cyst, often to the point of incapacitation. The mass is exquisitely tender with evident erythema, heat, edema, and induration. The edema may extend widely to involve the entire labium on the affected side. Femoral and inguinal nodes may be enlarged, matted, and tender from regional lymphadenitis. Observe for fluctuance and pointing as signs that the abscess is ripe for effective surgical drainage.

C. While awaiting its resolution or evolution to the point at which drainage can be safely accomplished, a number of conservative measures can be used to effect temporary relief of the intense pain associated with Bartholin duct or gland infection. Have the patient soak her vulva in warm water several times daily, for example. Provide analgesic drugs as needed. After obtaining cultures, consider giving broad-spectrum antibiotics effective against the organisms commonly found in these infections, such as coliform, chlamydial, and gonococcal bacteria. Bartholin adenitis, even when accompanied by vulvar cellulitis, may be effectively treated by this approach. When resolved, weigh future options for preventing recurrence, including marsupialization (see F) to ensure good drainage.

D. If the abscess persists or worsens, it becomes necessary to incise and drain it completely (Fig. 1A). This is not necessarily the simple procedure it appears to be; because one must be sure to open the many separate loculations of pus within the abscessed gland. Despite the common practice of attempting it with local anesthesia, for which there is no adequate technique, this procedure is best accomplished under general anesthesia. Choose the site for incision overlying the cavity where the abscess is pointing, preferably within the vestibule. Digitally open all loculations and insert a gauze drain. Unless efforts are made to establish a new tract for drainage (see F), recurrence can be expected.

E. A simple stab incision can be made under local anesthesia for the purpose of forming a new duct for a sterile Bartholin cyst. Following this, insert a short Word catheter and leave it in place for up to 30 days to permit complete epithelization of the stoma to occur (Fig. 1B, 1C). Alternatively, a small Foley catheter can be used, but it

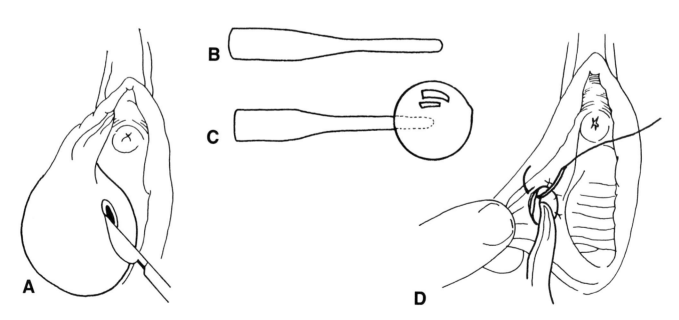

Figure 1 Bartholin abscess is best incised at the vestibule (A) for drainage. Re-epithelization can be facilitated by use of a Word catheter (B), which is left indwelling when inflated (C). Alternatively, the cyst wall can be sutured to the skin (D) for marsupialization.

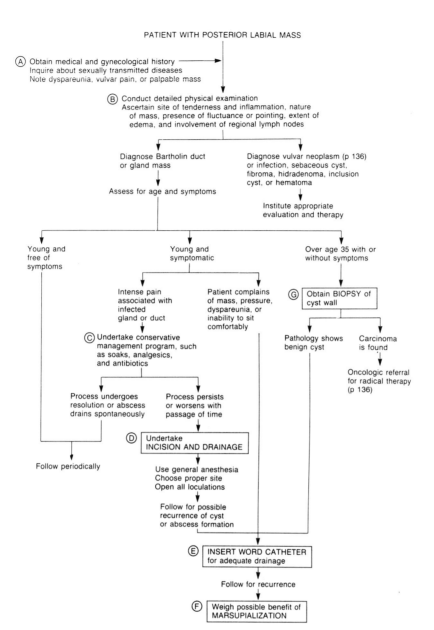

PATIENT WITH POSTERIOR LABIAL MASS

Ⓐ Obtain medical and gynecological history
Inquire about sexually transmitted diseases
Note dyspareunia, vulvar pain, or palpable mass

Ⓑ Conduct detailed physical examination
Ascertain site of tenderness and inflammation, nature
of mass, presence of fluctuance or pointing, extent of
edema, and involvement of regional lymph nodes

Diagnose Bartholin duct
or gland mass

Diagnose vulvar neoplasm (p 136)
or infection, sebaceous cyst,
fibroma, hidradenoma, inclusion
cyst, or hematoma

Assess for age and symptoms

Institute appropriate
evaluation and therapy

Young and
free of
symptoms

Young and
symptomatic

Over age 35 with or
without symptoms

Intense pain
associated with
infected
gland or duct

Patient complains
of mass, pressure,
dyspareunia, or
inability to sit
comfortably

Ⓖ Obtain BIOPSY of
cyst wall

Ⓒ Undertake conservative
management program, such
as soaks, analgesics,
and antibiotics

Pathology shows
benign cyst

Carcinoma
is found

Oncologic referral
for radical therapy
(p 136)

Process undergoes
resolution or abscess
drains spontaneously

Process persists
or worsens with
passage of time

Follow periodically

Ⓓ Undertake
INCISION AND DRAINAGE

Use general anesthesia
Choose proper site
Open all loculations

Follow for possible
recurrence of cyst
or abscess formation

Ⓔ INSERT WORD CATHETER
for adequate drainage

Follow for recurrence

Ⓕ Weigh possible benefit of
MARSUPIALIZATION

is somewhat less satisfactory. This approach not only avoids anesthesia and hospitalization, but also results in good drainage and fewer recurrences.

F. It is seldom necessary to resort to marsupialization, but it may have to be done if the condition recurs after the catheter technique has failed. It can be achieved under local or regional block anesthesia. This simple and effective procedure is best undertaken when the area is free of infection. Make a vertical or cruciate incision within the vestibule outside of the hymenal ring. Excise any suspicious areas on the gland wall for histologic study (see G). Form a permanent opening by suturing the edges of the cyst wall to the overlying skin edges (Fig 1D). Total resection of the gland is difficult, cosmetically poor, and may be associated with hemorrhage; therefore, it is rarely, if ever, done.

G. Although Bartholin gland carcinoma is rare, it must be considered in elderly patients who present with a mass in the posterolateral fourchette or who develop a Bartholin

cyst or abscess late in life. Diagnosis is made by biopsy. If the lesion is small and localized, it can be readily excised in its entirety. If invasive, but still limited to its primary site and regional lymph nodes, it can be managed aggressively by radical vulvectomy, lymphadenectomy, and adjunctive radiation therapy.

References

Cheetham DR. Bartholin's cyst: Marsupialization or aspiration? Am J Obstet Gynecol 152:569, 1985.

Copeland LJ, Smeige N, Gershenson DM, et al. Bartholin gland carcinoma. Obstet Gynecol 67:794, 1986.

Sarrel PM, Steege JF, Maltzer M, Bolinsky D. Pain during sex response due to occlusion of the Bartholin gland duct. Obstet Gynecol 62:621, 1983.

Wheelock JB, Goplerud DR, Dunn LJ, Oates JF. Primary carcinoma of the Bartholin gland: A report of ten cases. Obstet Gynecol 63:820, 1984.

IMPERFORATE HYMEN

Louis Burke, M.D.

A. Imperforate hymen is a rare condition due to a defect in embryologic development in which the vaginal bud arising from the urogenital sinus fails to canalize fully. It has to be differentiated from labial agglutination, vaginal agenesis (p 142), and vaginal stenosis (p 144). Labial agglutination is the end result of acute vulvitis during infancy or childhood, the inflamed and denuded labia becoming adherent and partially or even completely fused together in the midline. Careful inspection makes this minor problem apparent. By contrast, imperforate hymen may not be readily detectable until it becomes symptomatic during puberty. Sometimes it can be recognized in the newborn girl by a bulging of the hymenal membrane due to accumulation of mucus and desquamated epithelium in the blind vagina. In an older child, a thorough pediatric examination (p 8) can reveal this condition if an effort is made to visualize the vaginal opening or probe the canal. In adolescence, the patient begins menstruation with premenstrual molimina during ovulatory cycles (p 42), but there is no externalized menstrual flow. While some affected teenagers are brought to the gynecologist for care of their amenorrhea, most present with cyclically recurrent abdominal or pelvic pain. The pain is generally caused by retrograde menstruation with spillage of menstrual detritus into the fallopian tubes and adjacent peritoneal cavity. Occasionally, urinary retention may occur due to urethral obstruction from the growing hematocolpos.

B. It is essential to perform a detailed physical examination to search for evidence of genitourinary anomalies, genetic disorders, or endocrinopathy. Evaluate for development of secondary sexual characteristics, usually quite normal in association with imperforate hymen, and look for signs of virilization (p 64). Obtain chromosomal karyotyping and consider ultrasonography or excretory urography to assess for any concomitant upper urinary tract malformation. Ultrasonography is also useful for showing the presence of the uterus and ovaries and to demonstrate hematometra, hematosalpinges, or hematoperitoneum. A tender suprapubic mass felt suprapubically may represent a large hematocolpos. Pelvic examination typically shows perineal midline bulging from the distended hematocolpos. The blood seen through the membranes may impart a blue color. Verify the fluctuant mass by rectal palpation and simultaneously ascertain the presence of the uterus and adnexa and their status.

C. A bulging hymenal membrane with inspissated blood behind it makes the diagnosis of imperforate hymen clear. If it is not so clear-cut, gently explore the vaginal introitus and canal with a cotton-tipped applicator or fine probe to distinguish it from vaginal stenosis or septum. Intravaginal digital palpation should help supply additional confirmatory information.

D. Unless one can be sure there is a uterus present on the basis of the findings on rectal examination, undertake ultrasonography for objective assessment. Agenesis of the lower vagina may or may not be associated with failure of the uterus to develop, but an absent uterus is very likely to coexist with an absent upper vagina. Bear in mind that urinary tract anomalies are common in these cases, thereby warranting urologic evaluation (see B).

E. Imperforate hymen is managed surgically with appropriate anesthesia in an operating room facility under sterile conditions. The hymen is incised by a cruciate incision (Fig. 1). If there is redundant mucosa, it is excised, taking care to avoid future stenosis. Then suture the edges together for hemostasis with fine, interrupted, absorbable suture material. The vaginal contents are evacuated. Watch for infection and re-examine the patient in several weeks to ensure that the introitus has not coapted and that no residual masses are palpable. It may be necessary to consider dilating the cervix to effect adequate drainage of hematometra (p 170).

References

MacLachlan AK, Stuart-Houston C, Chudley AE. Hydrometrocolpos in Kaufman's syndrome. J Can Assoc Radiol 31:193, 1980.

Pinsonneault O, Goldstein DP. Obstructing malformations of the uterus and vagina. Fertil Steril 44:241, 1985.

Rock JA, Zacur HA, Dlugi AM, et al. Pregnancy success following surgical correction of imperforate hymen and complete transverse vaginal septum. Obstet Gynecol 59:448, 1982.

Shaw LM, Jones WA, Brereton RJ. Imperforate hymen and vaginal atresia and their associated anomalies. J R Soc Med 76:560, 1983.

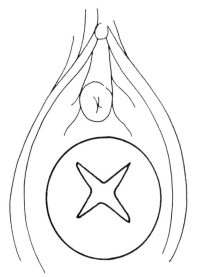

Figure 1 Cruciate incision to drain hematocolpos and correct imperforate hymen. Bleeding sites at cut edges are suture ligated for hemostasis.

PATIENT WITH SUSPICION OF IMPERFORATE HYMEN

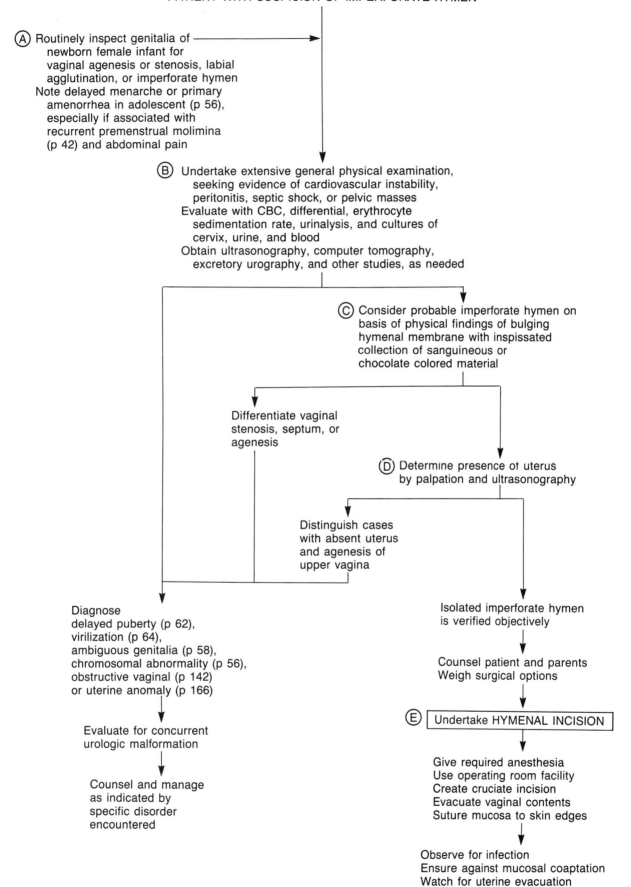

Ⓐ Routinely inspect genitalia of
   newborn female infant for
   vaginal agenesis or stenosis, labial
   agglutination, or imperforate hymen
   Note delayed menarche or primary
   amenorrhea in adolescent (p 56),
   especially if associated with
   recurrent premenstrual molimina
   (p 42) and abdominal pain

Ⓑ Undertake extensive general physical examination,
   seeking evidence of cardiovascular instability,
   peritonitis, septic shock, or pelvic masses
   Evaluate with CBC, differential, erythrocyte
   sedimentation rate, urinalysis, and cultures of
   cervix, urine, and blood
   Obtain ultrasonography, computer tomography,
   excretory urography, and other studies, as needed

Ⓒ Consider probable imperforate hymen on
   basis of physical findings of bulging
   hymenal membrane with inspissated
   collection of sanguineous or
   chocolate colored material

Differentiate vaginal
stenosis, septum, or
agenesis

Ⓓ Determine presence of uterus
   by palpation and ultrasonography

Distinguish cases
with absent uterus
and agenesis of
upper vagina

Diagnose
delayed puberty (p 62),
virilization (p 64),
ambiguous genitalia (p 58),
chromosomal abnormality (p 56),
obstructive vaginal (p 142)
or uterine anomaly (p 166)

Isolated imperforate hymen
is verified objectively

Evaluate for concurrent
urologic malformation

Counsel patient and parents
Weigh surgical options

Ⓔ Undertake HYMENAL INCISION

Counsel and manage
as indicated by
specific disorder
encountered

Give required anesthesia
Use operating room facility
Create cruciate incision
Evacuate vaginal contents
Suture mucosa to skin edges

Observe for infection
Ensure against mucosal coaptation
Watch for uterine evacuation

VAGINAL AGENESIS

Louis Burke, M.D.

A. Two separate types of vaginal agenesis occur. They can be understood and differentiated on the basis of knowledge about embryologic development. The lower two-thirds of the vagina derive from the urogenital sinus and the rest is of müllerian derivation. Incomplete fusion and canalization may result in formation of a stricture or septum (p 146) where they join. Failure of the urogenital sinus to evolve properly leads to lower vaginal atresia or agenesis (Fig. 1). Affected patients usually have normal secondary sexual characteristics and internal genitalia. When the upper vagina is involved, the müllerian involvement is reflected in either a rudimentary or an absent uterus. In these cases, one often finds normal ovaries. Some müllerian remnants may persist, such as intact or vestigial fallopian tubes and even a fibromuscular uterus. Urinary anomalies are frequently associated, having developed concurrently during intrauterine life. This combination of anomalies involves partial or complete müllerian aplasia; the incomplete form is the Mayer-Rokitansky-Küster-Hauser syndrome. It can be distinguished from complete testicular feminization by chromosomal karyotyping (see D). Counsel carefully (see F) because the condition has lifelong impact in regard to sterility and sexual function.

B. A woman with vaginal agenesis usually develops normally at puberty and does not come to the gynecologist's attention except for primary amenorrhea (p 56) or inability to achieve coital penetration. Alternatively, if only the lower vagina is atretic and functional endometrium is present, menstrual blood begins to accumulate after menarche, although it is seldom recognized as such because external evidence does not appear. This causes hematocolpos (if the upper vagina is canalized), hematometra, and hematosalpinges to develop. Careful inquiry ordinarily reveals periodic abdominal pain and urinary symptoms, often preceded by characteristic premenstrual molimina (p 42). Even if there is no uterus, molimina may occur because the ovaries function normally.

C. Agenesis limited to the upper vagina leaves a normally developed blind and shortened lower vagina with normal hymen. Contrastingly, absence of the lower vagina is associated with absence of the hymen. In both conditions, the external genitalia and secondary sexual characteristics are normal. Rectal examination shows whether there is a uterus and reveals the presence of ovaries. Careful investigation with a cotton-tipped applicator or fine probe is necessary to assess the extent of vaginal development.

D. Cytogenic study by chromosomal karyotyping is useful for differentiating complete testicular feminization. This condition of androgen insensitivity has to be considered in the differential diagnosis of patients who have no vagina or one that has developed minimally as a blind pouch. Both müllerian and wolffian duct derivatives are absent in these cases; the gonads are testicles. Affected patients have a 46,XY karyotype. Pubic and axillary hair growth is absent or meager. These pseudohermaphrodites are genetically male with failure of virilization, but unambiguously female in gender identity and phenotype. The undescended testes, located intra-abdominally or within the inguinal canals, are at neoplastic risk and should therefore be removed. If orchidectomy is delayed until after puberty, adolescent development of female secondary sexual characteristics takes place normally (in response to testicular estrogen production). Estrogen replacement is needed in these cases. Vaginal reconstruction is appropriate (p 272).

E. Intravenous pyelography is important because up to half of the cases with upper vaginal agenesis have major urinary tract anomalies, including renal agenesis, pelvic kidney, and various ureteral malformations. About one in ten also have skeletal defects involving the vertebrae, which warrant radiographic study. Ultrasonography can be helpful for demonstrating a uterus and ovaries. Laparoscopy is seldom needed for confirmation.

F. Management begins with a thorough discussion of the condition with the patient and her parents, if appropriate. Counseling and support are important to minimize the psychological impact of the problem. In cases without a functional uterus, reconstruction of the vagina (p 272) is generally deferred until sexual activity is contemplated. For those in whom hematometra develops, it may be necessary to undertake such surgery earlier in order to effect adequate menstrual drainage.

References

Bates GW, Wiser WL. A technique for uterine conservation in adolescents with vaginal agenesis and a functional uterus. Obstet Gynecol 66:290, 1985.

Rock JA, Reeves LA, Retto H, et al. Success following vaginal creation for müllerian agenesis. Fertil Steril 39:809, 1983.

Smith MR. Vaginal aplasia: Therapeutic options. Am J Obstet Gynecol 146:488, 1983.

Williams JK, Ingram JM, Welden SW. Management of noncongenital vaginal stenosis and distortion by the bicycle seat pressure method. Am J Obstet Gynecol 150:166, 1984.

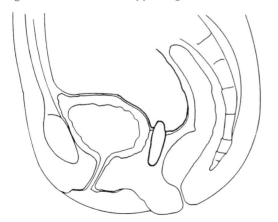

Figure 1 Vaginal agenesis, due to failure of canalization of the vagina, is shown here with vestigial uterus.

PATIENT WITH SUSPICION OF ABSENT VAGINA

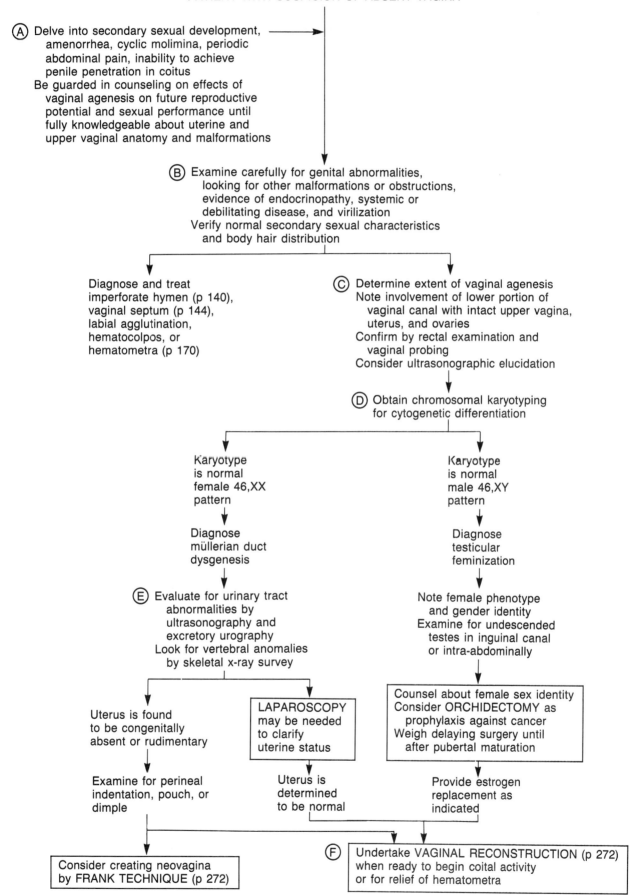

Ⓐ Delve into secondary sexual development,
amenorrhea, cyclic molimina, periodic
abdominal pain, inability to achieve
penile penetration in coitus
Be guarded in counseling on effects of
vaginal agenesis on future reproductive
potential and sexual performance until
fully knowledgeable about uterine and
upper vaginal anatomy and malformations

Ⓑ Examine carefully for genital abnormalities,
looking for other malformations or obstructions,
evidence of endocrinopathy, systemic or
debilitating disease, and virilization
Verify normal secondary sexual characteristics
and body hair distribution

Diagnose and treat
imperforate hymen (p 140),
vaginal septum (p 144),
labial agglutination,
hematocolpos, or
hematometra (p 170)

Ⓒ Determine extent of vaginal agenesis
Note involvement of lower portion of
vaginal canal with intact upper vagina,
uterus, and ovaries
Confirm by rectal examination and
vaginal probing
Consider ultrasonographic elucidation

Ⓓ Obtain chromosomal karyotyping
for cytogenetic differentiation

Karyotype
is normal
female 46,XX
pattern

Diagnose
müllerian duct
dysgenesis

Ⓔ Evaluate for urinary tract
abnormalities by
ultrasonography and
excretory urography
Look for vertebral anomalies
by skeletal x-ray survey

Karyotype
is normal
male 46,XY
pattern

Diagnose
testicular
feminization

Note female phenotype
and gender identity
Examine for undescended
testes in inguinal canal
or intra-abdominally

Uterus is found
to be congenitally
absent or rudimentary

LAPAROSCOPY
may be needed
to clarify
uterine status

Counsel about female sex identity
Consider ORCHIDECTOMY as
prophylaxis against cancer
Weigh delaying surgery until
after pubertal maturation

Examine for perineal
indentation, pouch, or
dimple

Uterus is
determined
to be normal

Provide estrogen
replacement as
indicated

Consider creating neovagina
by FRANK TECHNIQUE (p 272)

Ⓕ Undertake VAGINAL RECONSTRUCTION (p 272)
when ready to begin coital activity
or for relief of hematometra

VAGINAL STENOSIS

Emanuel A. Friedman, M.D., Sc.D.

A. Stenosis of the vagina not only has an emotional impact on the patient, but it can prove difficult to correct. It may be congenital or acquired. Embryologic failure of müllerian development produces congenital absence of the vagina (p 142), cervix, and uterus, although the ovaries and external genitalia are usually normal. Partial failure may leave no upper vagina and cervix or merely an anatomic encircling fibromuscular constriction or transverse septum. Distal occlusion by a transverse septum can result if full embryologic development takes place except for persistence of the membrane separating the vagina from the urogenital sinus. This differs from the condition of imperforate hymen. Acquired vaginal stenosis can result from a destructive agent, such as radiation or chemical burn, from extensive surgery or surgical complications, or from a dystrophic or neoplastic vulvar or vaginal lesion. Because the external genitalia are usually normally developed, congenital atresia is seldom detected until puberty. In the presence of a functioning uterus, hematometra may occur. Inability to achieve penile penetration may be the first manifestation.

B. Diagnosis of vaginal stenosis or septum requires a careful vaginal examination. The full extent of the problem may not be completely revealed, however, because the upper canal may be neither accessible to direct vision nor readily palpable to the examining hand. Palpation by way of a rectal examination may prove helpful. If the lower vaginal lumen is patent and there appears to be extension of the canal beyond a partially occluding septum or band, injecting radiopaque dye for contrast x-ray study may show how far the constriction extends and whether more cephalad vagina, cervix and uterus are intact.

C. It is important to differentiate true vaginal stenosis from other hymenal and vaginal conditions. Take special care to consider them in the diagnosis because their management can be quite different. Functional vaginismus (p 44), which is a much more common problem, may mimic anatomic stenosis in regard to presenting complaints and physical findings. To institute surgical correction or a long course of dilatational measures would be quite inappropriate for these cases. These methods would be unlikely to correct the problem; surgery would probably aggravate it considerably.

D. Urinary tract anomalies are frequently encountered in patients with vaginal atresia (or other genital disorders) secondary to disturbed embryologic development. Therefore, thorough evaluation of the urinary tract must be undertaken whenever a genital malformation is diagnosed. Intravenous pyelography is useful in such cases.

E. The etiology can generally be ascertained from the history and physical examination. If there has been no prior destructive procedure, agent, or lesion, the congenital form can be assumed. A stenosis resulting from tissue destruction tends to be much more resistant to treatment than a congenital stenosis. Nonsurgical conservative measures are, therefore, preferable for patients with severe tissue destruction.

F. Active means are needed to prevent vaginal stenosis after radiotherapy for cervical, vaginal, or vulvar cancer. The dense fibrosis resulting from radiation or chemical burn resists all forms of treatment. Moreover, surgical management in these cases may cause further damage, including fistula formation (p 156), which is an especially difficult complication to manage. It often proves intractable because the tissue will not heal well and surgical fistula repair is so likely to fail. Repetitive dilatation, applied diligently over a prolonged period of time with progressively larger diameter dilators, is worth trying instead. Success has been reported with use of a bicycle seat stool equipped with plastic dilators when applied to such cases of noncongenital vaginal stenosis.

G. Incise a simple septum or band longitudinally along its full thickness. Take care to avoid encroaching on bladder or rectum and ensure hemostasis. To enlarge the vaginal lumen, reapproximate the vaginal walls and underlying fascia transversely with absorbable interrupted sutures. Guard against postoperative recurrence by advising regular coitus as soon as feasible. Dilator use is not usually needed unless the patient has no sexual partner, coitus is unsuccessful, or the procedure fails to accomplish adequate dilatation.

References

Bates GW, Wiser WL. A technique for uterine conservation in adolescents with vaginal agenesis and a functional uterus. Obstet Gynecol 66:290, 1985.

Berek JS, Hacker NF, Lagasse LD, Smith ML. Delayed vaginal reconstruction in the fibrotic pelvis following radiation or previous reconstruction. Obstet Gynecol 61:743, 1983.

Lees DH, Singer A. Vaginal surgery for congenital abnormalities and acquired constrictions. Clin Obstet Gynecol 25:883, 1982.

Smith MR. Vaginal aplasia: Therapeutic options. Am J Obstet Gynecol 146:488, 1983.

Williams JK, Ingram JM, Welden SW. Management of noncongenital vaginal stenosis and distortion by the bicycle seat stool pressure technique. Am J Obstet Gynecol 150:166, 1984.

PATIENT WITH SUSPICION OF VAGINAL STENOSIS

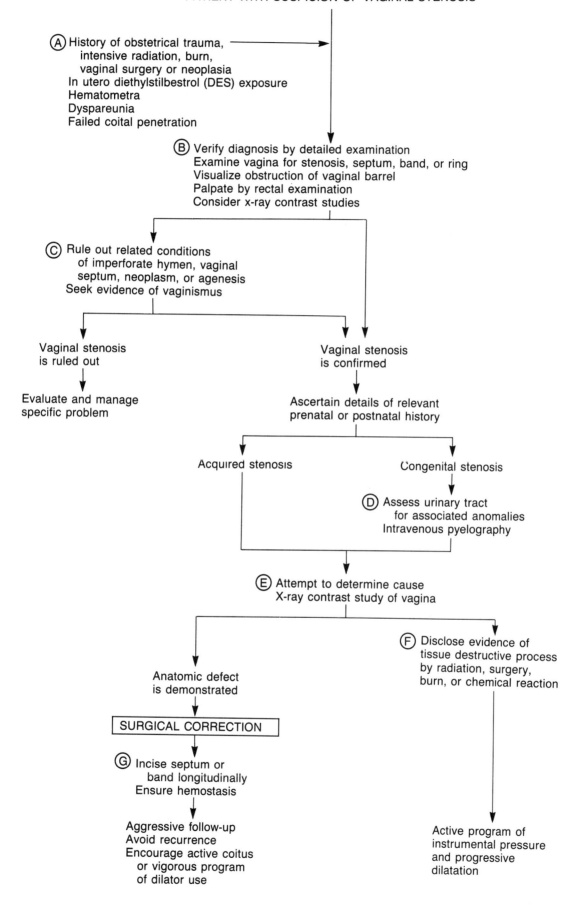

A. History of obstetrical trauma,
intensive radiation, burn,
vaginal surgery or neoplasia
In utero diethylstilbestrol (DES) exposure
Hematometra
Dyspareunia
Failed coital penetration

B. Verify diagnosis by detailed examination
Examine vagina for stenosis, septum, band, or ring
Visualize obstruction of vaginal barrel
Palpate by rectal examination
Consider x-ray contrast studies

C. Rule out related conditions
of imperforate hymen, vaginal
septum, neoplasm, or agenesis
Seek evidence of vaginismus

Vaginal stenosis
is ruled out

Evaluate and manage
specific problem

Vaginal stenosis
is confirmed

Ascertain details of relevant
prenatal or postnatal history

Acquired stenosis

Congenital stenosis

D. Assess urinary tract
for associated anomalies
Intravenous pyelography

E. Attempt to determine cause
X-ray contrast study of vagina

Anatomic defect
is demonstrated

SURGICAL CORRECTION

G. Incise septum or
band longitudinally
Ensure hemostasis

Aggressive follow-up
Avoid recurrence
Encourage active coitus
or vigorous program
of dilator use

F. Disclose evidence of
tissue destructive process
by radiation, surgery,
burn, or chemical reaction

Active program of
instrumental pressure
and progressive
dilatation

VAGINAL SEPTUM

Louis Burke, M.D.

A. Total or partial embryonic development of the müllerian system and urogenital sinus derivatives can result in a range of vaginal malformations from complete agenesis (p 142), at one extreme, to imperforate hymen p 140), at the other. The former is generally associated with müllerian aplasia, the latter with failure of urogenital sinus canalization. Formation of transverse vaginal septa, which falls between these extremes, results from incomplete fusion and canalization at the junction between the müllerian ducts or, rarely, from müllerian duplication. In most patients, the septum is an incidental finding encountered on physical examination. If the septum is transverse and complete so that menstrual outflow is obstructed, hematocolpos, hematometra, and hematosalpinges develops over time after menarche. This is manifest by periodic abdominal pain and urinary symptoms identical to those seen with imperforate hymen. The ovaries usually function normally and yield characteristic premenstrual molimina (p 42). A common presenting complaint is dyspareunia or failure to achieve adequate coital penetration. Septa may also cause insurmountable soft tissue dystocia in labor.

B. Longitudinal vaginal septa are twice as common as transverse septa. They result from incomplete embryologic müllerian fusion, usually in association with some degree of uterine malformation, ranging from arcuate deformation to completely duplicated hemiuteri. Such septa can extend the entire length of the vagina or be incomplete, principally affecting the uppermost portion. The external genitalia and secondary sexual characteristics are normally developed in these cases. Uterine and vaginal development can be very asymmetric so that one uterine horn may exit by way of a cervix entering a blind vaginal pouch (Fig. 1). Obstruction of outflow causes accumulation of menstrual flow with formation of hematocolpos on the occluded side, while normal menstrual flow occurs from the patent side. The growing upper vaginal cystic mass and cyclic pain should suggest the diagnosis.

C. Most transverse septa are found at the junction of the middle and upper thirds of the vagina, although they can also be encountered more caudally as well. They vary in degree from a mild circumferential constriction to total occlusion. A small central opening commonly exists, thereby allowing menstrual flow. Pubertal and genital development is otherwise normal in these patients. They may present with periodic pain or urinary symptoms (from hematocolpos), dyspareunia, incomplete coital penetration, or obstructed labor.

D. Asymptomatic adults with either transverse or longitudinal septum require no special care. The prepubertal child with an occlusive septum can be expected to develop hematocolpos at menarche; the septum can be opened electively or the corrective procedure can be delayed until necessary.

E. Intravenous pyelography helps to detect urinary tract anomalies, although such malformations occur less often than with vaginal agenesis (p 142). They can be expected to be associated with failure of müllerian fusion, but are seldom encountered with a transverse septum. If the status of the adnexa and uterus is of interest (because of infertility or recurrent midtrimester abortions, for example) and cannot be determined by palpation, ultrasonography may help. If it is still unclear, the patient with a longitudinal septum may be well served by laparoscopy in order to determine the presence of one of the commonly concurrent uterine anomalies. Hysterosalpingography can also provide valuable information, if feasible.

F. Undertake incision of the septum with due care and thought. A longitudinal septum is best incised, taking care to ensure hemostasis and avoid damage to bladder and rectum. Minimize the risks of fistula formation or stenosis by limiting the extent of the surgery only to that which is required. Use a cruciate incision for a transverse septum and apply sutures longitudinally to enlarge the lumen. To prevent circumferential stenosis by the fibrosis of healing, avoid actual excision of the septum.

References

Eisenberg E, Farber M, Mitchell GW Jr, et al. Complete duplication of the uterus and cervix with a unilaterally imperforate vagina. Obstet Gynecol 60:259, 1982.

Lees DH, Singer A. Vaginal surgery for congenital abnormalities and acquired constrictions. Clin Obstet Gynecol 25:883, 1982.

Rock JA, Zacur JA, Dlugi AM, et al. Pregnancy success following surgical correction of imperforate hymen and complete transverse vaginal septum. Obstet Gynecol 59:448, 1982.

Sueldo CE, Rotman CA, Cooperman WR, Rana N. Transverse vaginal septum. J Reprod Med 30:127, 1985.

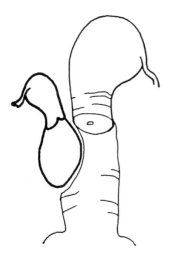

Figure 1 Congenital duplication of uterus, cervix, and vagina. The right uterine horn is rudimentary; it opens into a blind vagina that does not communicate externally by virtue of the occluding vaginal septum. If the rudimentary hemiuterus contains functional endometrium, menstrual detritus collects to form a lateral cyst.

PATIENT SUSPECTED OF HAVING VAGINAL SEPTUM

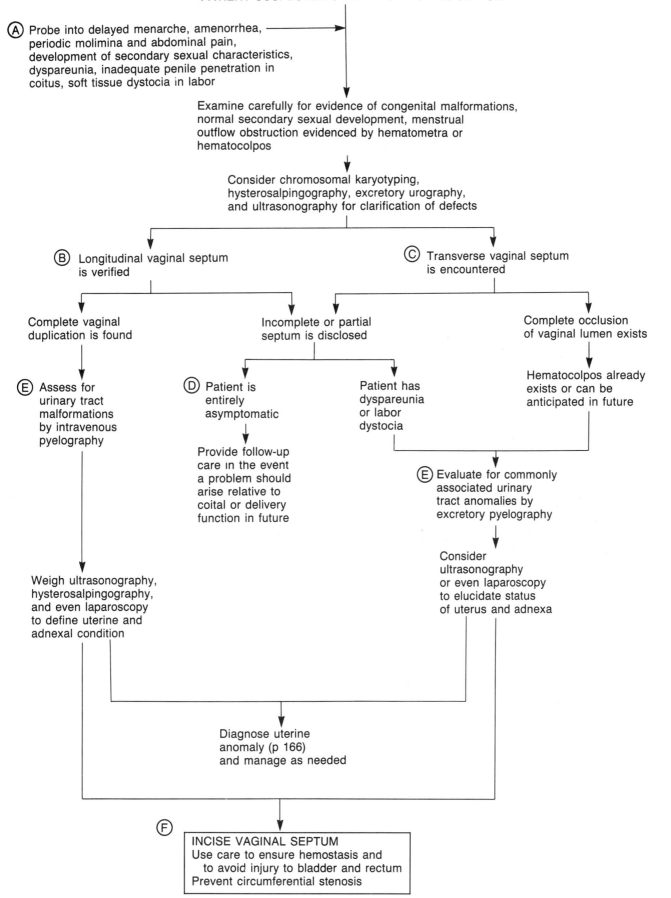

(A) Probe into delayed menarche, amenorrhea, periodic molimina and abdominal pain, development of secondary sexual characteristics, dyspareunia, inadequate penile penetration in coitus, soft tissue dystocia in labor

Examine carefully for evidence of congenital malformations, normal secondary sexual development, menstrual outflow obstruction evidenced by hematometra or hematocolpos

Consider chromosomal karyotyping, hysterosalpingography, excretory urography, and ultrasonography for clarification of defects

(B) Longitudinal vaginal septum is verified

(C) Transverse vaginal septum is encountered

Complete vaginal duplication is found

Incomplete or partial septum is disclosed

Complete occlusion of vaginal lumen exists

(E) Assess for urinary tract malformations by intravenous pyelography

(D) Patient is entirely asymptomatic

Patient has dyspareunia or labor dystocia

Hematocolpos already exists or can be anticipated in future

Provide follow-up care in the event a problem should arise relative to coital or delivery function in future

(E) Evaluate for commonly associated urinary tract anomalies by excretory pyelography

Weigh ultrasonography, hysterosalpingography, and even laparoscopy to define uterine and adnexal condition

Consider ultrasonography or even laparoscopy to elucidate status of uterus and adnexa

Diagnose uterine anomaly (p 166) and manage as needed

(F) INCISE VAGINAL SEPTUM
Use care to ensure hemostasis and to avoid injury to bladder and rectum
Prevent circumferential stenosis

147

VAGINAL ADENOSIS

Louis Burke, M.D.

A. Vaginal adenosis is a condition characterized by the presence of benign glands (singly or in clusters) in the vaginal epithelium, which is ordinarily composed entirely of well differentiated squamous cell layers. The glandular tissue of vaginal adenosis is derived from the vestigial embryologic müllerian anlage. It may be submucosal in location or at the surface. Infrequently, it can appear spontaneously, but most cases identified today are the result of intrauterine exposure to diethylstilbestrol. This drug is now interdicted in pregnancy because it is implicated as a cause of clear cell adenocarcinoma (see C). Typically, its effect is recognized by the appearance of ectopy (columnar epithelium on the exocervix) and an easily recognized cervicovaginal hood of exocervical mucosa. The relationship between vaginal adenosis and clear cell adenocarcinoma is unclear. It is doubtful that the adenosis undergoes malignant degeneration to adenocarcinoma, although rare, isolated cases have suggested the possibility of such a transition. For practical purposes, therefore, vaginal adenosis can be considered a marker for intrauterine exposure to diethylstilbestrol, which in turn is a known risk factor for clear cell adenocarcinoma. Intraepithelial carcinoma is not so rare, however, in these cases (see E). Affected patients, therefore, deserve close assessment and frequent follow-up surveillance examinations.

B. While it is important to obtain routine Papanicolaou smears (p 12) on general principles of good gynecological care, the dysplasia sometimes seen with adenosis cannot be reliably disclosed by this means. A concerted effort should nonetheless be made to scrape exfoliated cells directly from the actual sites of the adenosis, such as the common foci in the lateral vaginal fornices. This enhances the value of the smear, but it is still imperfect.

C. Carefully palpate the entire length of the vaginal wall to detect any nodularity. Nodules detected in this way must be biopsied. Clear cell adenocarcinoma, if present, can thus be diagnosed. Only biopsy can identify this very serious neoplasm early enough to make cure possible. These cancers can be very small or extensive. Because most of them are covered by normal vaginal mucosa, they do not desquamate cells that can be detected by cytologic smear. The surgery indicated for contained operable lesions consists of radical hysterectomy, colpectomy, and pelvic lymphadenectomy. Vaginal reconstruction can also be done for affected patients (p 272).

D. The best prognosis applies for patients with the smallest lesions. It is essential, therefore, to try to identify small lesions while they are still amenable to effective treatment. Use colposcopy to provide the magnification needed. Search diligently, looking for submucosal foci of adenosis or adenocarcinoma. Lesions that have advanced to involve the surface epithelium can be highlighted by staining the vaginal mucosa with Lugol's iodine solution. The superficial nonglycogenated tissues will appear unstained in the normally dark brown stained vagina. Unfortunately, the more common subsurface lesions cannot be flagged by this method.

E. A prominent histologic feature of vaginal adenosis is metaplasia. This is similar in appearance to the analogous process that occurs on the endocervix. The metaplastic process appears to be an evolutionary one in which there are progressive changes in the adenosis, the cervical ectopy, and even the cervicovaginal hood over the course of many years, leading to complete resolution of these lesions in some patients. This does not apply to all patients, however, because women with adenosis have a four-fold increased likelihood of developing intraepithelial neoplasia of the cervix and vagina. Whether or not invasive cancer can also eventuate in these cases is yet to be determined. Thus, it is imperative for all patients with known vaginal adenosis to be followed annually to check for any changes suggestive of neoplasia. This is especially important because of concern over the possibility that clear cell carcinoma will occur. Patients and their mothers, who may feel considerable guilt about having exposed their fetus in this way, deserve intensive counseling and support.

References

Burke L. Diethylstilbestrol: Effect of in utero exposure. Curr Probl Obstet Gynecol 5:7, 1981.

Kaufman RH, Noller K, Adam E, et al. Upper genital abnormalities and pregnancy outcome in diethylstilbestrol-exposed progeny. Am J Obstet Gynecol 148:973, 1984.

Melnick S, Cole P, Anderson D, Herbst A. Rates and risks of diethylstilbestrol-related clear-cell adenocarcinoma of the vagina and cervix. An update. N Engl J Med 316:514, 1987.

Richart RM. The incidence of cervical and vaginal dysplasia after exposure to DES. JAMA 255:36, 1986.

Robboy SJ, Young RH, Welch WR, et al. Atypical vaginal adenosis and cervical ectropion: Association with clear cell adenocarcinoma in diethylstilbestrol-exposed offspring. Cancer 54:869, 1984.

PATIENT SUSPECTED OF HAVING VAGINAL ADENOSIS

(A) Inquire about known or
suspected intrauterine exposure to
diethylstilbestrol, incidental finding
of characteristic ectopy or cervical
hood during vaginal examination

(B) Undertake thorough physical examination,
searching for evidence of vaginal adenosis
and gross changes typically associated with
diethylstilbestrol effect, namely ectopy and hood
Obtain Papanicolaou cytologic smears from
vaginal fornices, scraping vigorously

(C) Palpate carefully for nodularity along entire
vaginal barrel, looking for possible neoplasm

Nodules are identified

Secure BIOPSY samplings
from suspicious nodules
under direct visualization

Nodules are not disclosed

Inspect diligently under good
light and with magnification

(D) Undertake colposcopic study of vagina
Stain with Lugol's solution to
highlight nonglycogenated mucosa

Obtain DIRECTED BIOPSIES of
suspicious areas of vaginal mucosa

Diagnose
clear cell
adenocarcinoma
of vagina

(E) Diagnose
vaginal adenosis

Provide support and annual
follow-up examinations
for observation of
progression or regression,
for palpation, and for
repeating cytology
and colposcopy with
biopsies as indicated

Refer to gynecological
oncologist for evaluation
and definitive care

Undertake
RADICAL HYSTERECTOMY AND
RADICAL VAGINECTOMY WITH
VAGINAL RECONSTRUCTION BY
SPLIT THICKNESS GRAFT
Preserve ovarian function

Intensive counseling and
follow-up for persistence
or recurrence of disease

PELVIC RELAXATION

David S. Chapin, M.D.

A. Women who are most likely to develop pelvic relaxation are those who have constitutionally poor tissue or who have experienced some form of injury to the endopelvic fascial supports investing the genital structures, perhaps related to obstetrical delivery trauma. Inciting or aggravating factors include massive obesity and chronic pulmonary obstructive disease. Patients may present with no symptoms other than a protruding introital mass. More often, they complain of urinary stress incontinence, pelvic pressure, or a bearing down sensation. Coital difficulty is a rare symptom. Urinary retention or fecal impaction may result from outpouching of the bladder and rectum. It is essential to look for other possible causes of these symptoms, such as neurogenic bladder, before considering any form of surgical repair. Evaluate for urinary tract infection, diabetes mellitus, and cardiovascular or renal disorder. Look for debilitating diseases and genital atrophy.

B. The physical assessment should search for signs of systemic disorders. The pelvic examination should assess for cystocele, urethrocele, rectocele, and uterine prolapse. Examining the patient while she is standing helps to evaluate the real extent of relaxation. The use of a standard Graves vaginal speculum may obscure the anterior and posterior wall defects. Use one blade as a right angle retractor to depress the posterior wall and demonstrate the cystocele and urethrocele by having the patient bear down. With the retractor supporting the anterior wall, then demonstrate the rectocele. Simultaneous rectal palpation helps to define the extent of the rectocele and show the presence of an enterocele that contains small bowel (Fig. 1). If unrecognized and left uncorrected, an enterocele recurs following surgical repair. Look closely for a dividing transverse posterior wall indentation separating the upper end of the rectocele from the lower end of the enterocele. To help evaluate urinary incontinence, place the end of a sterile cotton-tipped applicator into the urethra and assess the exit angle before and during bearing down. Additionally, if the bladder is full, gently elevate the paraurethral tissues (the Bonney-Marshall test) to show whether urinary stress incontinence might be correctable surgically (p 258). However, false results occur from urethral compression. These tests are helpful, but they cannot replace urodynamic testing.

C. Urodynamic measurement techniques (p 226) have become very sophisticated and are essential for identifying those patients whose incontinence is due to detrusor instability rather than any anatomic defect. These patients are unlikely to be improved by surgery and may actually have more severe problems afterwards. The studies should include assessment of urinary voiding flow rate and urethral pressure profile with supplemental urethroscopy and cystometrography.

D. Women with severe uterine descensus of long duration show evidence of cervical edema, hypertrophy, inflammation, and even ulcerative degeneration of the most dependent tissues. The same changes can happen to the mucous membranes of a large cystocele or rectocele. Before any surgery is done, this must be corrected by a regimen of topical antibiotics and estrogens. Be sure to biopsy any suspicious lesions, especially if ulcerated or eroded.

E. Perineal (Kegel) exercises involve repetitively contracting the levator ani muscles to build them and the associated perineal structures over time. Patients have to be instructed carefully and must be strongly motivated for them to be of any real value. At least six months may be necessary for the patient to notice an effect, and she often becomes bored and lax in the performance. Use of a pessary, especially of the Smith-Hodge or Gellhorn type, should be considered for the patient who is a poor operative risk or who requires temporizing management (for correction of an ulcer, for example). It can achieve anatomic correction, but long-term use requires frequent changes and often leads to mucosal ulceration and bleeding.

F. The patient's general health and desire for fertility and sexual activity play a role in surgical decision making. Vaginal plasty (p 258), with or without hysterectomy, is the basic procedure needed for correcting the anatomy. Urinary stress incontinence with minimal anatomic defect is better managed by one of the transabdominal needle methods. Transvaginal suspension of the vaginal apex to the sacrospinous ligament is preferable to colpocleisis, even in very elderly women. The safety and effectiveness of the LeFort colpocleisis has been overestimated.

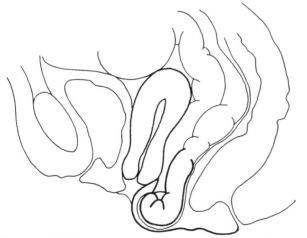

Figure 1 Pelvic relaxation showing cystocele, partial uterine descensus, rectocele, and fully developed enterocele containing loop of intestine descended to the introitus within the hernial sac of peritoneum and posterior vaginal wall.

References

Bhatia NN, Ostergard DR. Urodynamics in women with stress urinary incontinence. Obstet Gynecol 60:552, 1982.

PATIENT WITH SUSPICION OF PELVIC RELAXATION

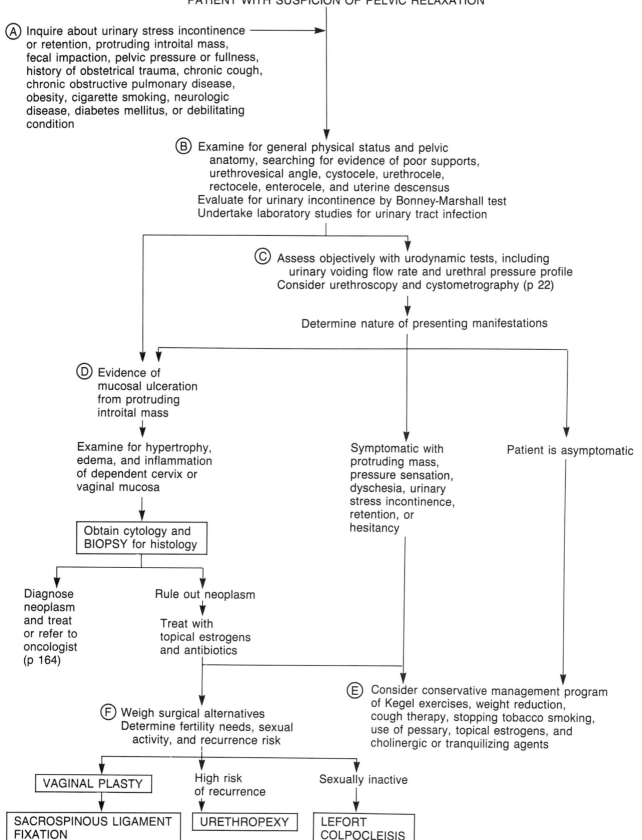

Ⓐ Inquire about urinary stress incontinence
or retention, protruding introital mass,
fecal impaction, pelvic pressure or fullness,
history of obstetrical trauma, chronic cough,
chronic obstructive pulmonary disease,
obesity, cigarette smoking, neurologic
disease, diabetes mellitus, or debilitating
condition

Ⓑ Examine for general physical status and pelvic
anatomy, searching for evidence of poor supports,
urethrovesical angle, cystocele, urethrocele,
rectocele, enterocele, and uterine descensus
Evaluate for urinary incontinence by Bonney-Marshall test
Undertake laboratory studies for urinary tract infection

Ⓒ Assess objectively with urodynamic tests, including
urinary voiding flow rate and urethral pressure profile
Consider urethroscopy and cystometrography (p 22)

Determine nature of presenting manifestations

Ⓓ Evidence of
mucosal ulceration
from protruding
introital mass

Examine for hypertrophy,
edema, and inflammation
of dependent cervix or
vaginal mucosa

Obtain cytology and
BIOPSY for histology

Diagnose
neoplasm
and treat
or refer to
oncologist
(p 164)

Rule out neoplasm

Treat with
topical estrogens
and antibiotics

Symptomatic with
protruding mass,
pressure sensation,
dyschesia, urinary
stress incontinence,
retention, or
hesitancy

Patient is asymptomatic

Ⓕ Weigh surgical alternatives
Determine fertility needs, sexual
activity, and recurrence risk

Ⓔ Consider conservative management program
of Kegel exercises, weight reduction,
cough therapy, stopping tobacco smoking,
use of pessary, topical estrogens, and
cholinergic or tranquilizing agents

VAGINAL PLASTY

High risk
of recurrence

Sexually inactive

SACROSPINOUS LIGAMENT
FIXATION

URETHROPEXY

LEFORT
COLPOCLEISIS

Mattingly RF, Davis LE. Primary treatment of anatomic stress uri-
nary incontinence. Clin Obstet Gynecol 27:445, 1984.
Montez FJ, Stanton SL. Q-tip test in female urinary incontinence.
Obstet Gynecol 67:258, 1986.
Nichols DH. Sacrospinous fixation for massive eversion of the
vagina. Am J Obstet Gynecol 142:901, 1982.

UTERINE DESCENSUS

David S. Chapin, M.D.

A. Prolapse of the uterus seldom occurs without concurrent (usually antecedent) cystocele and rectocele as part of the complex of anatomic defects associated with pelvic relaxation (p 150) (Fig. 1). The risk factors are the same. If the cervix appears to have descended, be alert to the possibility of cervical elongation by hypertrophy. Patients with descensus are generally asymptomatic or just have pelvic pressure, generally relieved when recumbent. A vaginal mass may represent a benign or malignant growth, including vaginal cyst or cervical polyp, leiomyoma, or cancer. These conditions need to be ruled out by careful pelvic examination and biopsy, if indicated. The differential diagnosis is compounded by infection and ulceration affecting the most dependent tissues. Ulceration makes it essential to rule out cancer by histologic study of biopsy samples.

B. To determine the full extent of a uterine descensus, examine the patient while she is standing and bearing down. The degree of descensus has been classified in various ways, but in the absence of a uniformly acceptable consensus, it is preferable merely to record the descriptive details of each case; include an accurate measure of the level to which the cervix descends, the length of the cervix, its condition, and the status of the uterine corpus. Examine for concomitant cystocele, urethrocele, rectocele, and enterocele (p 150). Note the condition of the rectal sphincter and the levator ani muscles. A much better functional assessment is obtained at this examination than can be done when the patient is under anesthesia.

C. Some patients are too ill or debilitated to have anesthesia or surgical correction of their uterine descensus. Others need to have the repair delayed so that an ulceration can be healed. It would risk potentially serious postoperative morbidity to undertake surgery in the presence of an infection. Therefore, reposit the prolapsed organ (see D) and treat with topical antibiotics. Estrogenic preparations, administered either locally or systemically, are also beneficial in improving the vascularity and integrity of the genital tissues. Estrogens prove especially beneficial in elderly postmenopausal women who have not had the benefit of estrogen maintenance. Preoperative treatment enhances healing after surgery.

D. Use a Smith-Hodge pessary to support the reposited uterus in place. It is designed somewhat like the coil in a contraceptive diaphragm, permitting satisfactory coital function. It is especially valuable, therefore, for young women with uterine prolapse in whom surgery is to be delayed. This includes those who are pregnant and those who wish to preserve their reproductive potential as well as those who need some form of treatment for a systemic or genital problem. The large, space-occupying Gellhorn type pessary is used only in women who do not engage in sexual intercourse and whose uterine descensus is so great (and supports so poor) that it cannot be effectively managed in any other way.

E. LeFort colpocleisis, in which the anterior and posterior vaginal walls are coapted surgically, has only a negligible place in gynecology today because it is not very successful and its effect in supporting the uterus is transient at best. It can be used only in women who will never again be expected to have coitus and who are poor operative risks.

F. The Manchester-Fothergill operation consists of cervical amputation, plication of the cardinal ligaments anterior to the neocervix, plus anterior and posterior colporrhaphy. It is effective in repositing the uterus into the midpelvis and anteverting it out of the vaginal axis, thereby relieving symptoms and correcting the anatomy. It is most useful in cases with elongated cervix and a corpus in about normal position or only moderately descended. Because one can expect any future pregnancy and delivery to disrupt this repair, it is recommended only for use in patients who have completed their childbearing.

G. Vaginal hysterectomy is the principal approach for treating uterine descensus. Except for the unusual case with isolated uterine descensus, other procedures are usually necessary, especially anterior and posterior colpoperineorrhaphy (p 258). For a patient with complete uterine prolapse, consider sacrospinous fixation of the vaginal apex as a prophylactic measure against vault prolapse (p 154) following the hysterectomy.

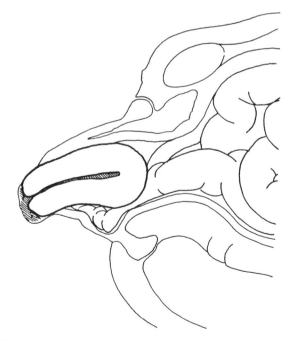

Figure 1 Complete uterine procidentia or prolapse with exteriorization of the uterus and eversion of the vaginal walls containing cystocele and rectocele.

References

Kuhn RJP, Hollyock VE. Observations on the anatomy of the rec-

PATIENT WITH SUSPICION OF UTERINE DESCENSUS

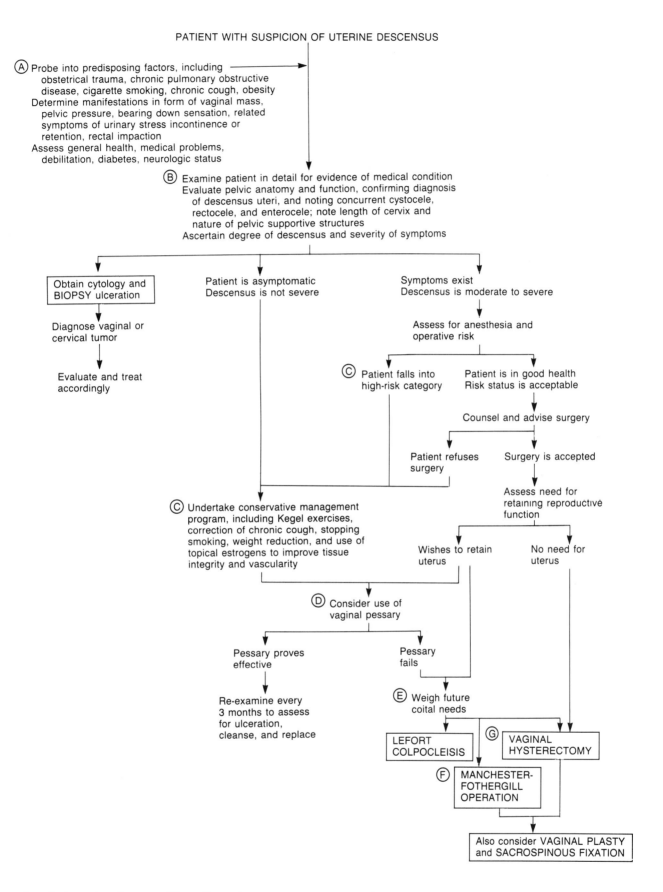

Ⓐ Probe into predisposing factors, including
   obstetrical trauma, chronic pulmonary obstructive
   disease, cigarette smoking, chronic cough, obesity
Determine manifestations in form of vaginal mass,
   pelvic pressure, bearing down sensation, related
   symptoms of urinary stress incontinence or
   retention, rectal impaction
Assess general health, medical problems,
   debilitation, diabetes, neurologic status

Ⓑ Examine patient in detail for evidence of medical condition
Evaluate pelvic anatomy and function, confirming diagnosis
   of descensus uteri, and noting concurrent cystocele,
   rectocele, and enterocele; note length of cervix and
   nature of pelvic supportive structures
Ascertain degree of descensus and severity of symptoms

Obtain cytology and
BIOPSY ulceration

Diagnose vaginal or
cervical tumor

Evaluate and treat
accordingly

Patient is asymptomatic
Descensus is not severe

Symptoms exist
Descensus is moderate to severe

Assess for anesthesia and
operative risk

Ⓒ Patient falls into
high-risk category

Patient is in good health
Risk status is acceptable

Counsel and advise surgery

Patient refuses
surgery

Surgery is accepted

Assess need for
retaining reproductive
function

Ⓒ Undertake conservative management
program, including Kegel exercises,
correction of chronic cough, stopping
smoking, weight reduction, and use of
topical estrogens to improve tissue
integrity and vascularity

Wishes to retain
uterus

No need for
uterus

Ⓓ Consider use of
vaginal pessary

Pessary proves
effective

Pessary
fails

Re-examine every
3 months to assess
for ulceration,
cleanse, and replace

Ⓔ Weigh future
coital needs

Ⓖ

LEFORT
COLPOCLEISIS

VAGINAL
HYSTERECTOMY

Ⓕ MANCHESTER-
FOTHERGILL
OPERATION

Also consider VAGINAL PLASTY
and SACROSPINOUS FIXATION

tovaginal pouch and septum. Obstet Gynecol 59:445, 1982.
Mäkinen J, Söderström KO, Kiilholma P, Hirvonen T. Histologi-
cal changes in the vaginal connective tissue of patients with
and without uterine prolapse. Arch Gynecol 239:17, 1986.
Nichols DH, Randall CL. Vaginal Surgery. 2nd ed. Baltimore:
Williams & Wilkins, 1983.

VAGINAL VAULT PROLAPSE

David S. Chapin, M.D.

A. It is not uncommon to encounter some minimal degree of prolapse of the vaginal vault following hysterectomy, regardless of the method used to suspend the vaginal cuff intraoperatively (if any), generally involving only the apex and perhaps the upper third. This degree of vault prolapse is of no significance and is generally asymptomatic. Much less often, vault prolapse involves more of the vaginal sleeve so that the vault inverts and becomes exteriorized. This condition is usually the result of a previously undetected enterocele, which reflects serious defects in the endopelvic investing fascia and the levator ani supports. In relative terms, failure to identify an enterocele is more common in the course of an abdominal hysterectomy (although the repair is easier by this route) than during a vaginal hysterectomy. This is because the vaginal operation is so often done for correcting uterine descensus (p 152) and the evaluations before and during surgery are aimed at detecting this condition. Because correction of vault prolapse is difficult and success cannot be guaranteed, it is well worth taking extra time and effort to discover an occult enterocele and to ensure good tissue approximation, suspension, and re-enforcement intraoperatively. The presenting symptom is generally the appearance of the mass at the introitus.

B. Evaluate the patient in depth, searching for relevant risk factors that may have contributed to the vault prolapse following the original hysterectomy and that may still be acting to cause any contemplated reparative procedure to fail. Seek evidence of a chronic systemic or debilitating disorder possibly interfering with the healing process. Watch for chronic cough, obstructive pulmonary disease, such as bronchial asthma, and heavy cigarette smoking. Assess cardiopulmonary and renal status in anticipation of anesthesia and surgery. During the pelvic examination ascertain the condition of the vaginal mucosa, es-pecially noting atrophy and any areas of infection, ulceration, or nodularity. Biopsy suspicious sites for histologic study. Carefully study the vaginal anatomy, differentiating vault prolapse from cystocele, rectocele, or new growth. The presence of loops of small intestine within the prolapsed sac is a clear-cut sign that it represents an enterocele.

C. Nonsurgical measures may be called for in a patient who is too ill to have anesthesia or surgery safely. They are appropriate for temporizing to enable the woman who would clearly benefit from some form of preoperative special care, for example, to correct mucosal atrophy with estrogens or to clear infection with antibiotics. The vault can be gently elevated digitally in these cases, taking care to avoid any trauma to the bowel contained therein. Positioning the patient in Trendelenburg position, if feasible, is helpful in facilitating this process. Once back in proper place, the vault can be supported by inserting a properly fitted Smith-Hodge pessary. Close fit is important with the distal end comfortably lodged under the urethrovesical angle behind the symphysis pubis. If too large, it causes pain, urinary obstruction, and erosion; if too small, it can be readily dislodged and ejected. Sexual intercourse is entirely feasible with this type of pessary in place. The doughnut type pessaries (solid or inflatable) tend to be less effective, more uncomfortable, and interdict coitus entirely. Neither may prove useful in women with poor perineal supports and gaping introitus because they cannot retain the pessary.

D. The procedure most likely to benefit a patient with a large enterocele and vaginal vault prolapse and offer her the best chance of permanent correction is transabdominal sacropexy, although even this technique can fail in some cases. This procedure involves placing a graft of autologous rectus fascia or of synthetic (Marlex) mesh to suspend the vaginal vault to the sacral periosteum after the enterocele sac and cul-de-sac have been closed by concentric pursestring sutures.

E. The LeFort colpocleisis procedure should be considered only when it is clear that any other procedure would be too hazardous and coital function is not a consideration. Modern techniques of anesthesia and vaginal surgery permit one to undertake alternative methods that allow preservation of vaginal function in nearly all cases.

F. Sacrospinous fixation (Fig. 1) is best for providing low-risk, secure support of the vaginal apex and restoring the horizontal axis and depth of the vagina. This applies especially if perineorrhaphy proves to be necessary and is properly performed. The operation attaches the vaginal apex directly to the sacrospinous ligament.

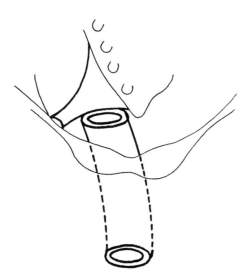

Figure 1 Sacrospinous fixation, shown schematically, with freshly dissected vaginal vault mucosa sutured to midportion of the right sacrospinous ligament.

References

Kauppila O, Punnonen R, Teisala K. Prolapse of the vagina after hysterectomy. Surg Gynecol Obstet 161:9, 1985.

Nichols DH. Sacrospinous fixation for massive eversion of the vagina. Am J Obstet Gynecol 142:901, 1982.

PATIENT WITH SUSPICION OF VAGINAL VAULT PROLAPSE

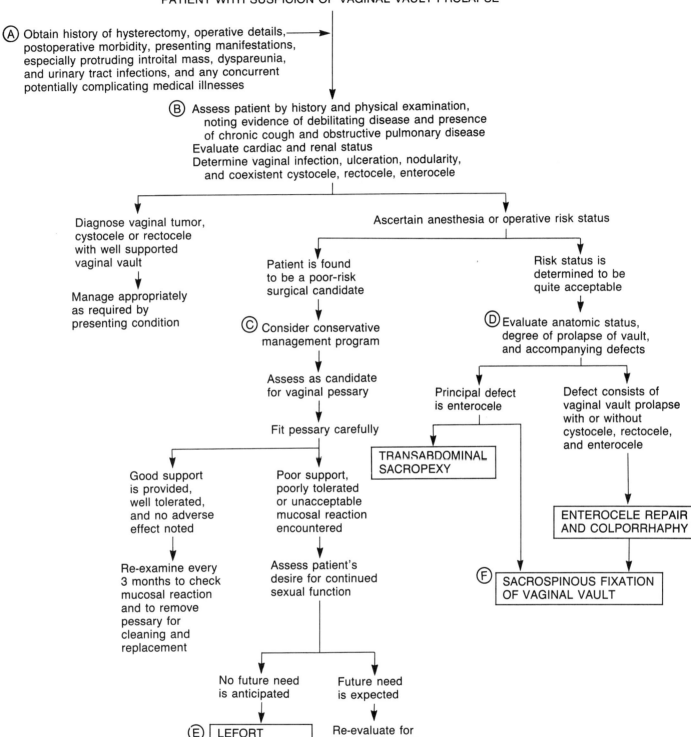

(A) Obtain history of hysterectomy, operative details, postoperative morbidity, presenting manifestations, especially protruding introital mass, dyspareunia, and urinary tract infections, and any concurrent potentially complicating medical illnesses

(B) Assess patient by history and physical examination, noting evidence of debilitating disease and presence of chronic cough and obstructive pulmonary disease
Evaluate cardiac and renal status
Determine vaginal infection, ulceration, nodularity, and coexistent cystocele, rectocele, enterocele

Diagnose vaginal tumor, cystocele or rectocele with well supported vaginal vault

Manage appropriately as required by presenting condition

Ascertain anesthesia or operative risk status

Patient is found to be a poor-risk surgical candidate

Risk status is determined to be quite acceptable

(C) Consider conservative management program

(D) Evaluate anatomic status, degree of prolapse of vault, and accompanying defects

Assess as candidate for vaginal pessary

Principal defect is enterocele

Defect consists of vaginal vault prolapse with or without cystocele, rectocele, and enterocele

Fit pessary carefully

TRANSABDOMINAL SACROPEXY

Good support is provided, well tolerated, and no adverse effect noted

Poor support, poorly tolerated or unacceptable mucosal reaction encountered

ENTEROCELE REPAIR AND COLPORRHAPHY

Re-examine every 3 months to check mucosal reaction and to remove pessary for cleaning and replacement

Assess patient's desire for continued sexual function

(F) SACROSPINOUS FIXATION OF VAGINAL VAULT

No future need is anticipated

Future need is expected

(E) LEFORT COLPOCLEISIS

Re-evaluate for surgical correction

Nichols DH, Randall CL. Vaginal Surgery. 2nd ed. Baltimore: Williams & Wilkins, 1983.

Thornton WN Jr, Peters WA. Repair of vaginal prolapse following hysterectomy. Am J Obstet Gynecol 147:140, 1983.

VAGINAL FISTULA

Lenard R. Simon, M.D.

A. The postoperative gynecological patient who complains of drainage of fluid by way of the vagina must be evaluated for vesicovaginal or ureterovaginal fistula, especially following hysterectomy or extensive pelvic dissection for cancer, endometriosis, or pelvic inflammatory disease. Consider the possibility of a rectovaginal fistula if passage of feces or flatus occurs vaginally. Most surgery done in the vicinity of the bladder, ureters, or rectum does not ordinarily cause any significant damage, especially if it is carried out in a technically optimal manner with attention to dissecting in properly defined tissue planes, handling tissues gently, avoiding trauma, ensuring good hemostasis, and reapproximating tissue layers accurately. However, even well conducted surgery can sometimes be associated with fistula formation, notably when done in a previously irradiated field or one with severe inflammation, fibrosis, or anatomic distortion caused by disease or previous surgery. Fistulas can also arise following obstetrical delivery. A long, difficult labor with the fetal head impacted against the maternal bony pelvis can cause avascular necrosis of the interposed tissue, principally at the urethra and bladder trigone; this type of injury is seldom seen any longer as the rates of cesarean section have increased and long trials of labor have essentially vanished. Despite these trends, fistulas are still seen occasionally in obstetrical cases, related more to bladder and ureteral trauma during cesarean section than to the trauma of vaginal delivery. Spontaneous fistula formation occurs with severe inflammatory bowel disease and malignancy.

B. Carry out a fully detailed physical examination and try to confirm the presence of a fistula, as well as its site and extent. A number of different tests can be used for this purpose. Pack the vagina lightly with a series of rolled sponges and instill a solution of methylene blue in the bladder; the dye stains one or more of the sponges to demonstrate a vesicovaginal fistula (Fig. 1A) and its location in the vagina (p 320). Use cystoscopic observation to find the site of the intravesical opening, noting its proximity to the ureteral ostia. Intravenous and retrograde pyelographic studies are needed to demonstrate a ureterovaginal fistula (p 322) and any associated ureteral injury or obstruction. A rectovaginal fistula (Fig. 1B) can sometimes be clearly recognized by combined rectal and vaginal inspection and palpation, particularly if it opens into the lower half of the vagina or introitus. Proctoscopy may reveal a fistula that cannot be readily seen. Sinography is a useful technique for demonstrating a long sinus tract between bowel and vagina; radiopaque dye is injected to delineate the pathway of this type of fistula.

C. Management of fistulas that occur in radiated, infected, or neoplastic tissues is particularly difficult and any surgical repair procedure done while the inciting process is still active is likely to fail. Prognosis is obviously related to the existence of these factors. The only fistulas that can be expected to heal spontaneously are those relatively small ones occurring in otherwise healthy individuals with healthy tissues. If the damage is discovered intraoperatively or early in the postoperative course, immediate repair is appropriate. If discovered later, the inflammatory reaction in the vicinity warrants delaying the repair until a more optimal time (see D). Conservative measures to enhance the chances of spontaneous healing include administration of antibiotics and use of vaginal douches to help cleanse the affected tissues. Postmenopausal women may benefit from topical or systemic estrogens, which improve the integrity of atrophic mucous membranes and thereby enhance the healing process.

D. Large fistulas require temporary diversion procedures to ensure the fistulous site and the surrounding damaged tissues will not be bathed in urine or feces. This may require ureterostomy or nephrostomy for ureterovaginal fistulas or colostomy for rectovaginal fistulas. As long as six months may have to elapse before one can be sure that healing has been adequate and inflammation has subsided enough to permit proceeding with the definitive operation necessary to excise the fistulous tract, to dissect the tissue planes widely, to reapproximate each tissue layer meticulously, and thereby to return anatomic continuity to the structures affected (p 274).

E. Fistulas occurring in previously irradiated areas cannot be expected to be successfully repaired because the ischemia and resulting poor tissue nutrition make healing unlikely and failure of any surgical repair procedure very probable. Therefore, the best (and perhaps only) treatment plan is to recommend permanent urinary or fecal diversion (p 256) as an effective means for returning the patient to a useful life.

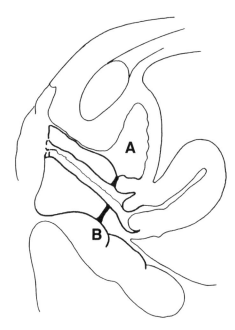

Figure 1 Sites of vesicovaginal (A) and rectovaginal fistula (B), shown in lateral cross-sectional view.

PATIENT WITH SUSPICION OF VAGINAL FISTULA

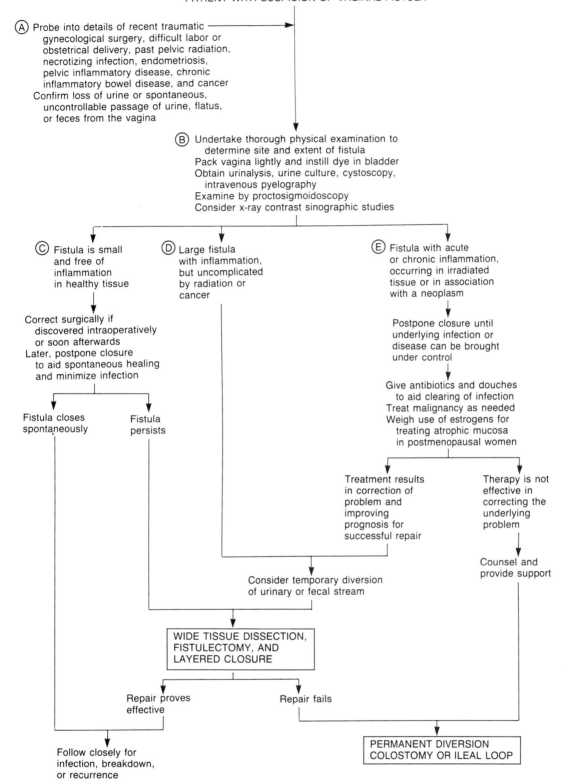

Ⓐ Probe into details of recent traumatic
gynecological surgery, difficult labor or
obstetrical delivery, past pelvic radiation,
necrotizing infection, endometriosis,
pelvic inflammatory disease, chronic
inflammatory bowel disease, and cancer
Confirm loss of urine or spontaneous,
uncontrollable passage of urine, flatus,
or feces from the vagina

Ⓑ Undertake thorough physical examination to
determine site and extent of fistula
Pack vagina lightly and instill dye in bladder
Obtain urinalysis, urine culture, cystoscopy,
intravenous pyelography
Examine by proctosigmoidoscopy
Consider x-ray contrast sinographic studies

Ⓒ Fistula is small
and free of
inflammation
in healthy tissue

Ⓓ Large fistula
with inflammation,
but uncomplicated
by radiation or
cancer

Ⓔ Fistula with acute
or chronic inflammation,
occurring in irradiated
tissue or in association
with a neoplasm

Correct surgically if
discovered intraoperatively
or soon afterwards
Later, postpone closure
to aid spontaneous healing
and minimize infection

Postpone closure until
underlying infection or
disease can be brought
under control

Give antibiotics and douches
to aid clearing of infection
Treat malignancy as needed
Weigh use of estrogens for
treating atrophic mucosa
in postmenopausal women

Fistula closes
spontaneously

Fistula
persists

Treatment results
in correction of
problem and
improving
prognosis for
successful repair

Therapy is not
effective in
correcting the
underlying
problem

Counsel and
provide support

Consider temporary diversion
of urinary or fecal stream

WIDE TISSUE DISSECTION,
FISTULECTOMY, AND
LAYERED CLOSURE

Repair proves
effective

Repair fails

PERMANENT DIVERSION
COLOSTOMY OR ILEAL LOOP

Follow closely for
infection, breakdown,
or recurrence

References

Aitken RJ, Elliot MS. Sigmoid exclusion: A new technique in the
management of radiation-induced fistula. Br J Surg 72:731,
1985.

Henriksson C, Kihl B, Pettersson S. Ureterovaginal and vesicovaginal fistula: A review of 29 patients. Acta Obstet Gynecol
Scand 61:143, 1982.

Murphy DM, Grace PA, O'Flynn JD. Ureterovaginal fistula: A
report of 12 cases and review of the literature. J Urol 128:924,
1982.

Webster GD, Sihelnik SA, Stone AR. Urethrovaginal fistula: A
review of the surgical management. J Urol 132:460, 1984.

VAGINAL CANCER

Jonathan M. Niloff, M.D.

A. Most patients with vaginal cancer present with bleeding and a visible lesion readily identified at the time of vaginal examination. Vaginal lesions must also be suspected if a Papanicolaou smear (p 12) is reported to show abnormal cytology in a woman who has no apparent lesion on the cervix or who has already undergone total hysterectomy. Be especially alert in cases with cancer or dysplasia elsewhere in the genital tract (concurrently or in the past), because the risk is greatly increased in them. A history of diethylstilbestrol exposure in utero places a woman at risk for clear cell adenocarcinoma of the vagina (p 148), although the magnitude of risk is small.

B. Conduct a thorough physical examination, concentrating on ensuring optimal visualization of the entire vagina. Avoid overlooking lesions obscured on the anterior and posterior walls by the Graves speculum. Undertake colposcopy (p 124) with directed biopsies and evaluate the entire vaginal tube, as these lesions are so often multifocal. Schiller's solution (Lugol's) highlights otherwise invisible sites. Selective differential cytology may also help locate an obscure lesion. To accomplish this, obtain separate smears from each suspicious area and label them carefully. Every evaluation for vaginal neoplasia should also include close attention to the cervix and vulva to rule out concurrent lesions.

C. The management of vaginal intraepithelial neoplasia is guided by the size and location of the lesion as well as by its multifocal nature. Histologic sampling is essential in order to exclude invasion and must be done before any nonsurgical therapy is instituted. A patient with isolated focal lesions can be managed with local excision, laser ablation, or intravaginal topical 5-fluorouracil (5 percent cream). This last is also particularly valuable in the treatment of multifocal disease, although its inflammatory effects can be unpleasant to the patient (and at times unacceptable). Another option for the case with widespread involvement is vaginectomy plus placement of a split-thickness skin graft. Careful post-treatment follow-up is mandatory.

D. Preoperative evaluation for patients with invasive vaginal cancer should include a complete blood count (CBC), urinalysis, blood chemistry determinations, chest radiography, and intravenous pyelography or computer tomography.

E. Formal clinical staging of the cancer is performed under anesthesia. It should include careful palpation of the vagina, paracolpos, and parametrium by both vaginal and rectal examination, as well as cystoscopy and proctoscopy. If the tumor involves the cervix or the vulva, it is staged by convention as a primary cervical (p 164) or vulvar carcinoma (p 136), and evaluated and managed accordingly.

F. Uniform criteria have not as yet been established for diagnosis and treatment of microinvasive carcinoma of the vagina. However, it appears reasonable to treat young women who have a minimally invasive lesion with a modality that preserves fertility and sexual function, such as partial vaginectomy (with skin graft, if necessary) or interstitial radiation therapy. This therapy should only be undertaken by an experienced specialist to optimize outcome results. Rigorous follow-up is mandatory.

G. Small Stage I tumors (2 cm or less) limited to the upper third of the vagina may be treated with either radiation therapy or radical surgery. The surgical procedure consists of a radical hysterectomy, radical vaginectomy, and pelvic lymphadenectomy to remove the tumor and a wide margin of normal surrounding tissue along with efferent lymphatic drainage channels and primary regional lymph nodes.

H. Large Stage I lesions, those involving the lower two-thirds of the vagina, and all Stage II and III carcinomas are best treated with radiation therapy. The anatomic proximity of the bladder and rectum precludes treating these lesions surgically with any real prospects of cure. External beam therapy is usually delivered first to reduce the size of the lesion; this is followed after an interval of time by interstitial or intracavitary implants. Because the lymphatic drainage of the distal vagina is primarily to the femoral nodes, this area must be included in the radiation field when treating tumors of the lower vagina.

References

Benedet JL, Murphy KJ, Fairey RN, Boyes DA. Primary invasive carcinoma of the vagina. Obstet Gynecol 62:715, 1983.

Benedet JL, Sanders BH. Carcinoma in situ of the vagina. Am J Obstet Gynecol 148:695, 1984.

Curtin JP, Twiggs LB, Julian TM. Treatment of vaginal intraepithelial neoplasia with the CO_2 laser. J Reprod Med 30:940, 1985.

Peters WA, Kumar NB, Morley G. Microinvasive carcinoma of the vagina: A distinct clinical entity? Am J Obstet Gynecol 153:505, 1985.

Puthawala A, Syed AMN, Nalick R, et al. Integrated external and interstitial radiation therapy for primary carcinoma of the vagina. Obstet Gynecol 62:367, 1983.

PATIENT WITH SUSPICION OF VAGINAL CANCER

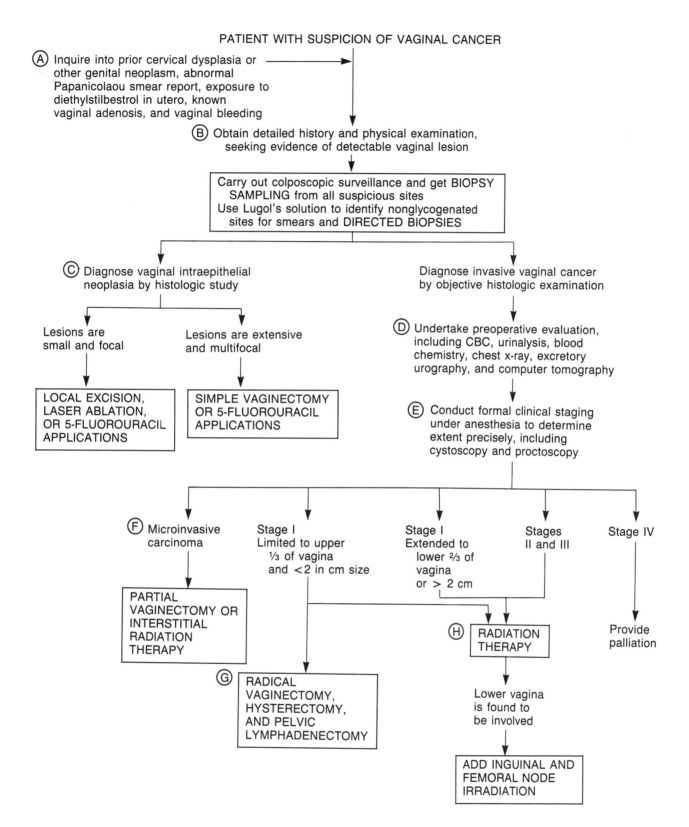

Ⓐ Inquire into prior cervical dysplasia or other genital neoplasm, abnormal Papanicolaou smear report, exposure to diethylstilbestrol in utero, known vaginal adenosis, and vaginal bleeding

Ⓑ Obtain detailed history and physical examination, seeking evidence of detectable vaginal lesion

Carry out colposcopic surveillance and get BIOPSY SAMPLING from all suspicious sites
Use Lugol's solution to identify nonglycogenated sites for smears and DIRECTED BIOPSIES

Ⓒ Diagnose vaginal intraepithelial neoplasia by histologic study

Diagnose invasive vaginal cancer by objective histologic examination

Lesions are small and focal

Lesions are extensive and multifocal

LOCAL EXCISION, LASER ABLATION, OR 5-FLUOROURACIL APPLICATIONS

SIMPLE VAGINECTOMY OR 5-FLUOROURACIL APPLICATIONS

Ⓓ Undertake preoperative evaluation, including CBC, urinalysis, blood chemistry, chest x-ray, excretory urography, and computer tomography

Ⓔ Conduct formal clinical staging under anesthesia to determine extent precisely, including cystoscopy and proctoscopy

Ⓕ Microinvasive carcinoma

Stage I Limited to upper ⅓ of vagina and <2 in cm size

Stage I Extended to lower ⅔ of vagina or > 2 cm

Stages II and III

Stage IV

PARTIAL VAGINECTOMY OR INTERSTITIAL RADIATION THERAPY

Ⓖ RADICAL VAGINECTOMY, HYSTERECTOMY, AND PELVIC LYMPHADENECTOMY

Ⓗ RADIATION THERAPY

Provide palliation

Lower vagina is found to be involved

ADD INGUINAL AND FEMORAL NODE IRRADIATION

CERVICAL STENOSIS

Emanuel A. Friedman, M.D., Sc.D.

A. Congenital atresia of the cervix, which may be associated with a partially stenotic or even completely obstructed canal, is often accompanied by other genitourinary anomalies. It develops as an embryologic consequence of defective canalization. While cervical stenosis may be congenital in origin, it is more likely to be secondary to fibrosis from cervical trauma or neoplasm. Cervical conization or extensive cauterization is especially likely to cause stenosis (Fig. 1), whereas laser ablation of dysplastic cervical lesions generally is not. Dysmenorrhea is suggestive of partial stenosis, especially if this symptom arises following cervical surgery, instrumentation, cautery, or radiation. Cessation of menstrual flow altogether may occur from complete stenosis. This can result in hematometra (p 170) from the continued cyclic menstrual sloughing and bleeding collecting within the uterine cavity because it is incapable of being spontaneously discharged. Retrograde flow via the fallopian tubes may be associated with pelvic pain, pelvic inflammatory disease, and endometriosis. Secondary infection of the collected blood and debris within the uterine cavity yields a pyometra (p 172). Cervical stenosis can develop from atrophic changes occurring in elderly women; it tends to be asymptomatic unless also associated with cervical or endometrial cancer. In the presence of a neoplasm, the uterus slowly enlarges as it fills with tissue detritus and fluid, thereby becoming a cystic structure that may not be distinguishable from an adnexal cyst. Cervical stenosis appears to be a special risk in women who were exposed to diethylstilbestrol (DES) during intrauterine development and who are subjected to ablative cervical treatment for cervical dysplasia; such treatment should be minimized in these women to avoid serious damage that may have an irreparably adverse impact on their reproductive function.

B. Probing the cervix yields a definitive diagnosis only if it can demonstrate an impatent cervical canal or opens into an intrauterine collection of pus or blood. The partially stenosed endocervical canal admits only a fine probe. Graduated vascular dilators, if available, may prove useful and are much safer than the metal sounds generally used in gynecology. Larger sounds cannot usually be passed through the stenosed segment without applying pressure. Care must be taken to guard against a sudden thrust into the endometrial cavity and through the uterine wall at the fundus. False passages into the substance of the cervix are easy to create under these circumstances. Uterine perforation occurring by way of a false passage at the level of the internal cervical os may enter the parametrium laterally and disrupt uterine vasculature, leading to hematoma formation and hypovolemic shock while endangering the integrity of the ureter hat courses in this site.

C. Cervical stenosis that is neither congenital nor acquired on the basis of an iatrogenic factor may arise from a cervical or endometrial neoplasm, especially one located just at or close to the internal os. Therefore, it is important at the onset to rule out cervical cancer (p 164). This generally requires cervical cytology (p 12), colposcopy (p 214), and directed biopsies. The relationship must be kept in mind because a malignant focus is easy to miss when it is located out of sight and well within the endocervical canal.

D. Undertake careful cervical dilatation and avoid perforation (see B), if possible. Then proceed with a thorough fractional endometrial curettage. This helps provide the diagnosis and may be therapeutic as well. Adequate sampling is essential in order to detect endometrial adenocarcinoma (p 178). In the absence of any malignancy, the dilatation of the stenotic site alone may prove sufficient to keep the canal open permanently.

E. Although recurrence of stenosis is seldom seen, resistant cases occur. Patients with congenital atresia and those with very severe anatomic destruction fall into this group. They are especially difficult to treat. Cervical dilatation may be attempted again, but the fact that it failed to achieve a good result the first time makes it unlikely to be successful without some additional effort. Cervical pessaries are no longer available, but use of an indwelling catheter has proved beneficial for keeping the canal open and for maintaining drainage. Surgical reconstruction is sometimes possible in especially resistant cases, but only isolated reports attest to its value.

References

Baker ER, Horger EO, Williamson HO. Congenital atresia of the uterine cervix: Two cases. J Reprod Med 27:39, 1982.

Jefferies JA, Robboy SJ, O'Brien PC, et al. Structural anomalies of the cervix and vagina in women enrolled in the diethylstilbestrol adenosis (DESAD) project. Am J Obstet Gynecol 148:59, 1984.

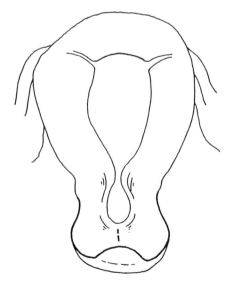

Figure 1 Cervical stenosis, involving the lower half of the endocervical canal, may result from cauterization, surgical conization, or radiation.

PATIENT WITH POSSIBLE CERVICAL STENOSIS

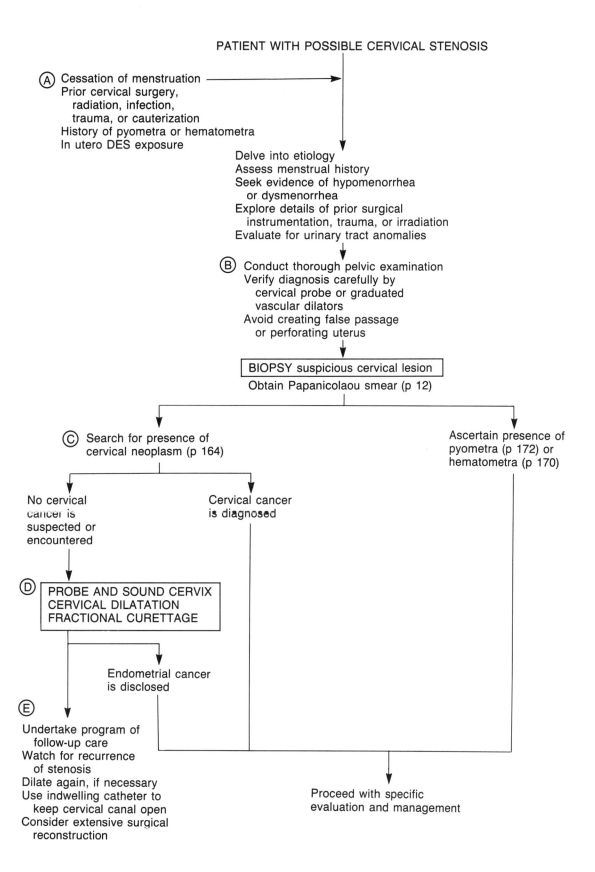

Ⓐ Cessation of menstruation ─────────────▶
Prior cervical surgery,
  radiation, infection,
  trauma, or cauterization
History of pyometra or hematometra
In utero DES exposure

Delve into etiology
Assess menstrual history
Seek evidence of hypomenorrhea
  or dysmenorrhea
Explore details of prior surgical
  instrumentation, trauma, or irradiation
Evaluate for urinary tract anomalies

Ⓑ Conduct thorough pelvic examination
Verify diagnosis carefully by
  cervical probe or graduated
  vascular dilators
Avoid creating false passage
  or perforating uterus

BIOPSY suspicious cervical lesion
Obtain Papanicolaou smear (p 12)

Ⓒ Search for presence of
cervical neoplasm (p 164)

Ascertain presence of
pyometra (p 172) or
hematometra (p 170)

No cervical
cancer is
suspected or
encountered

Cervical cancer
is diagnosed

Ⓓ PROBE AND SOUND CERVIX
CERVICAL DILATATION
FRACTIONAL CURETTAGE

Endometrial cancer
is disclosed

Ⓔ
Undertake program of
  follow-up care
Watch for recurrence
  of stenosis
Dilate again, if necessary
Use indwelling catheter to
  keep cervical canal open
Consider extensive surgical
  reconstruction

Proceed with specific
evaluation and management

Pittaway DE, Daniell J, Maxson W, et al. Reconstruction of the cervical canal after complete postconization obstruction: A case report. J Reprod Med 29:339, 1984.

Schmidt G, Fowler WC. Cervical stenosis following minor gynecologic procedures on DES-exposed women. Obstet Gynecol 56:333, 1980.

CERVICAL DYSPLASIA

Louis Burke, M.D.

A. There is a continuum of disease encompassing the spectrum from the mildest form of cervical dysplasia to invasive carcinoma of the cervix. It is generally agreed that the condition is probably reversible in its earliest phases, but as it progresses to involve more and more of the epidermal layers, at some point it becomes irreversible. It is essential, therefore, to study every case in depth to ascertain extent (along the exocervix and up the endocervical canal), depth of involvement (proportion of squamous cell layers affected), and intensity (degree of atypia associated). Most patients are identified on the basis of routine Papanicolaou smears (p 12), although some few present with postcoital staining or vaginal discharge. Those at greatest risk warrant special attention, especially women who have been exposed to multiple sexual partners, sexually transmitted disease, genital herpes, and perhaps most importantly, papillomavirus infections as manifested by condyloma acuminatum (p 118). To reduce confusion, terminology has been simplified to include three subgroups of cervical intraepithelial neoplasia: CIN 1, mild dysplasia; CIN 2, moderate; CIN 3, severe. Extension below the basement membrane signifies invasive carcinoma (p 164), which must be assessed and managed more aggressively.

B. Carry out a full physical examination, concentrating the pelvic component on a thorough search for cervical and vaginal lesions. Use good illumination to expose the field well. Without preliminary preparation of the area, look for white patches, friable sites that bleed easily, and any eroded or ulcerated lesions. If colposcopy is unavailable, the patient is best served by referral to an expert consultant for this purpose. A less reliable, but nonetheless useful, alternative is use of dilute acetic acid or iodine solution to flag potentially important sites for biopsy sampling. Recognize that this approach cannot be considered definitive for diagnostic purposes, however. Schiller's iodine stain discolors the glycogenated cells of normal cervical and vaginal epithelium so that it appears deep brown, but nonglycogenated dysplastic epithelium is left unstained. Other nonglycogenated areas also fail to take up the stain, however, including any denuded, debrided, atrophic, or traumatized sites. Some dysplastic areas may not be detectable because they are covered on the surface by a layer or layers of glycogenated cells that stain normally. Acetic acid solution highlights lesions of interest, just as for colposcopy, but they may not be readily visible without the benefit of the magnification provided by the colposcope.

C. Colposcopy (p 214) has made it possible to survey the cervical and vaginal epithelium with exquisite sensitivity, thereby identifying mucosal patterns representing probable sites of dysplasia or neoplasia for focused biopsy sampling. The specific pattern often provides a strong indication of the kind of lesion one is likely to find by histologic study, but tissue histology is nonetheless mandatory for definitive diagnosis. Study the subepithelial vascular architecture and search diligently for acetowhite lesions with punctation or mosaic features. Identify flat condylomas as well. Note any lesion that extends up the endocervical canal and attempt to examine such lesions in their entirety by means of exposure by endocervical speculum. Carefully document sites, extent, and patterns by a detailed note in the patient's record. Colpophotographic documentation is also beneficial for follow-up comparisons.

D. Obtain samples for histologic examination under colposcopic guidance. Sample sites with patterns designated as likely to represent dysplasia, concentrating on those with the most severe changes. For large lesions, choose a site near the margin with normal mucosa. Use a sharp biopsy instrument to avoid distorting the tissue; this can diminish the value of microscopic assessment somewhat. Place the sample in fixative solution before it has a chance to dry. For a lesion that extends into the endocervical canal, it may be possible to obtain a suitable biopsy if the cervix is patulous or can be distended by a small speculum. If the lesion continues up the canal and out of sight, endocervical curettage is called for; take special care to avoid scraping the area of the external os or any exocervical sites. Including tissue scrapings from these distal sites in the endocervical curettings makes interpretation of the findings difficult. Since conization of the cervix (p 238) may become necessary if the status of the endocervical mucosa is unclear, any confusion must be prevented, if possible, by careful pursuit of an accurate diagnosis. This applies especially in these cases, because cervical conization is not an innocuous procedure and most patients with cervical dysplasia, including many with minor degrees of endocervical involvement, can be managed well without it.

References

Clarke EA, Hatcher J, McKeown-Eyssen GE, Lickrish GM. Cervical dysplasia: Association with sexual behavior, smoking, and oral contraceptives? Am J Obstet Gynecol 151:612, 1985.

Fu YS, Reagan JW, Richart RM. Definition of precursors of dysplasia. Gynecol Oncol 12:280, 1981.

Jones RW. Malignant progression of carcinoma in situ of the cervix. Colp Gynecol Laser Surg 1:237, 1985.

McIndoe WA, McLean M, Jones RW, Mullins PR. The invasive potential of carcinoma in situ of the cervix. Obstet Gynecol 64:451, 1984.

PATIENT WITH SUSPICION OF CERVICAL DYSPLASIA

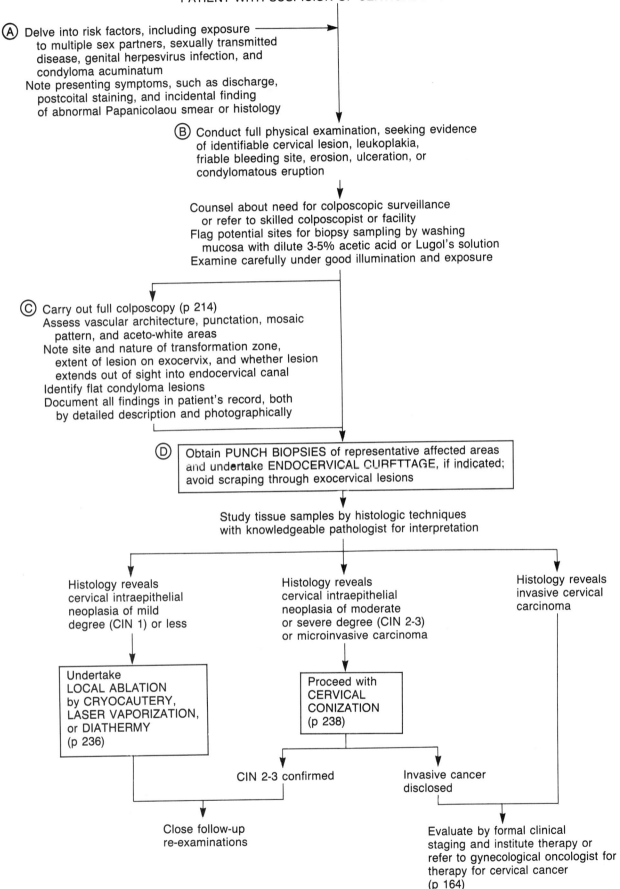

(A) Delve into risk factors, including exposure
    to multiple sex partners, sexually transmitted
    disease, genital herpesvirus infection, and
    condyloma acuminatum
Note presenting symptoms, such as discharge,
    postcoital staining, and incidental finding
    of abnormal Papanicolaou smear or histology

(B) Conduct full physical examination, seeking evidence
    of identifiable cervical lesion, leukoplakia,
    friable bleeding site, erosion, ulceration, or
    condylomatous eruption

Counsel about need for colposcopic surveillance
    or refer to skilled colposcopist or facility
Flag potential sites for biopsy sampling by washing
    mucosa with dilute 3-5% acetic acid or Lugol's solution
Examine carefully under good illumination and exposure

(C) Carry out full colposcopy (p 214)
    Assess vascular architecture, punctation, mosaic
        pattern, and aceto-white areas
    Note site and nature of transformation zone,
        extent of lesion on exocervix, and whether lesion
        extends out of sight into endocervical canal
    Identify flat condyloma lesions
    Document all findings in patient's record, both
        by detailed description and photographically

(D) Obtain PUNCH BIOPSIES of representative affected areas
    and undertake ENDOCERVICAL CURETTAGE, if indicated;
    avoid scraping through exocervical lesions

Study tissue samples by histologic techniques
    with knowledgeable pathologist for interpretation

Histology reveals
cervical intraepithelial
neoplasia of mild
degree (CIN 1) or less

Histology reveals
cervical intraepithelial
neoplasia of moderate
or severe degree (CIN 2-3)
or microinvasive carcinoma

Histology reveals
invasive cervical
carcinoma

Undertake
LOCAL ABLATION
by CRYOCAUTERY,
LASER VAPORIZATION,
or DIATHERMY
(p 236)

Proceed with
CERVICAL
CONIZATION
(p 238)

CIN 2-3 confirmed

Invasive cancer
disclosed

Close follow-up
re-examinations

Evaluate by formal clinical
staging and institute therapy or
refer to gynecological oncologist for
therapy for cervical cancer
(p 164)

CARCINOMA OF THE CERVIX

Jonathan M. Niloff, M.D.

A. The diagnosis of cervical cancer is made by histologic confirmation of biopsy specimens. Patients are generally identified by Papanicolaou smear (p 12) or symptoms of postcoital staining or irregular vaginal bleeding. Patients with invasive carcinoma are best managed by experienced oncologists in centers with special facilities for providing radical therapy and dealing with the complications of treatment. Before one can begin to plan the proper therapeutic program, it is necessary to determine the extent of the lesion and its depth of invasion. This is done preliminarily by colposcopy (p 214) and definitively for grossly invasive lesions by examination under anesthesia (see E).

B. A cervical cone biopsy is performed prior to therapy in patients with a biopsy diagnosis of microinvasive carcinoma of the cervix. Conization is unnecessary and contraindicated if the cervical biopsy has already demonstrated deep invasion. In this situation, one should instead proceed directly to the preoperative evaluation and staging under anesthesia.

C. Patients should be considered to have Stage IB carcinoma if the cone biopsy reveals invasion deeper than 3 mm, confluence, capillary or lymphatic space invasion, or invasive tumor at the surgical margin of the specimen, and treated accordingly.

D. Preoperative evaluation for a patient with invasive cancer of the cervix consists of a complete blood count (CBC), urinalysis, blood chemistry determinations, chest radiography, and intravenous pyelography. Computer tomography scanning may be performed in patients with larger lesions in order to look for node involvement; if done, pyelography is not needed. Other studies are undertaken as indicated by the patient's condition.

E. The formal clinical staging examination is done with the patient under anesthesia, preferably jointly by the gynecologist and the radiation therapist. It includes a detailed pelvic examination, cystoscopy, and proctoscopy. Particular attention should be directed to the rectal and rectovaginal examinations to evaluate the parametrium and detect lateral tumor extension.

F. Treatment of small Stage I and IIA carcinoma with either radical hysterectomy and pelvic lymphadenectomy or radiation therapy yields comparable cure rates. Larger tumors are best treated with radiation therapy. Radical hysterectomy permits one to preserve the ovaries and results in better vaginal function than is possible with radiation therapy. At laparotomy, carefully evaluate the aortic and pelvic lymph nodes before proceeding with the radical procedure. Because obesity makes radical hysterectomy technically difficult, it constitutes a relative contraindication.

G. Barrel shaped Stage I cervical lesions are poorly treated with intracavitary radioactive sources because of their anatomic configuration (Fig. 1). These tumors have high local failure rates and are preferably managed with radiation therapy followed by extrafascial hysterectomy.

H. Aortic lymph node metastases, which occur frequently with Stage II and III carcinomas of the cervix (15 and 33 percent, respectively), may be detected by computer tomography scan and confirmed cytologically by percutaneous aspiration. If the scan is negative, consider surgical aortic node sampling, which is best done by an extraperitoneal approach to minimize complications. Treatment with extended field irradiation may benefit one-fourth of affected patients, using a radiation port that includes the aortic lymph node chain up to the diaphragm. Although promising, this is not yet considered standard therapy. It should only be undertaken after a thoughtful review of the risks and benefits for the individual patient.

I. Postoperative pelvic radiation is generally prescribed for patients whose surgical margins are involved with tumor. Although commonly administered, its value in cases with positive lymph nodes is not established.

References

Bandy LC, Clarke-Pearson DL, Silverman PM, Creasman WT. Computed tomography in evaluation of extrapelvic lymphadenopathy in carcinoma of the cervix. Obstet Gynecol 65:73, 1985.

Gallion HH, Van Nagell JR Jr, Donaldson ES, et al. Combined radiation therapy and extrafascial hysterectomy in the treatment of Stage IB barrel-shaped cervical cancer. Cancer 56:262, 1985.

Hogan WM, Littman P, Griner L, et al. Results of radiation therapy given after radical hysterectomy. Cancer 49:1278, 1982.

Twiggs LB, Potish RA, George RJ, Adcock LL. Pretreatment extraperitoneal surgical staging in primary carcinoma of the cervix uteri. Surg Gynecol Obstet 158:243, 1984.

Van Nagell JR Jr, Greenwell N, Powell DF, et al. Microinvasive carcinoma of the cervix. Am J Obstet Gynecol 145:981, 1983.

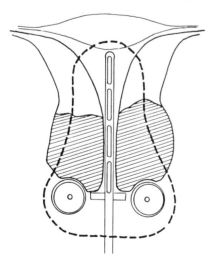

Figure 1 Intracavitary radium applicator with lateral ovoids to supply radiation field (broken line) for cervical cancer (shaded area). Note limitation of this form of radiation therapy for large cervical lesions.

PATIENT WITH SUSPICION OF CERVICAL
CARCINOMA

(A) Delve into risk factors and suggestive clinical
symptoms or postcoital staining or metrorrhagia
Note Papanicolaou smear cytology report and
nature of current findings as to type of lesion
and degree of dysplasia or neoplasia (p 12)
Probe antecedent gynecological disorders with
special attention to cervical, vaginal, and
vulvar lesions and their therapy

Undertake thorough physical examination
Ascertain presence of identifiable cervical lesion
Search for other lesions in lower genital tract
Determine and document extent of observed lesions
Biopsy any apparent lesions for histologic study

Survey by colposcopy for type of lesion and its extent
Determine whether lesion extends up endocervical canal,
out of sight for acceptable coloposcopic assessment

Histology shows
invasive carcinoma

Obtain colposcopically DIRECTED BIOPSIES

Histology reveals
microinvasive carcinoma

(B) CERVICAL CONIZATION (p 238)

Microinvasion
is verified

(C) Invasive carcinoma with
vascular involvement,
confluence, or more
than 3 mm invasion is found

TOTAL ABDOMINAL
EXTRAFASCIAL
HYSTERECTOMY

(D) Evaluate patient preparatory to
definitive cancer therapy
Obtain CBC, urinalysis, blood chemistry,
chest x-ray, and excretory urography or
computer tomography

(E) FORMAL CLINICAL STAGING
UNDER ANESTHESIA WITH
CYSTOSCOPY AND PROCTOSCOPY

Stage IB or IIA

Stage IIB, III, or IVA

Stage IVB

Size 3 cm
or less

Size over
3 cm

Barrel shaped
tumor or
adenocarcinoma

(H) Evaluate for
aortic node
metastases

Palliation

RADICAL
HYSTERECTOMY
AND PELVIC
LYMPHADENECTOMY

PELVIC
RADIATION
THERAPY

(G) RADIATION
THERAPY PLUS
EXTRAFASCIAL
HYSTERECTOMY

RADIATION
THERAPY

If surgical margins
or lymph nodes contain
tumor, consider giving
radiation therapy as well

UTERINE ANOMALY

Joseph F. D'Amico, M.D.

A. Malformations of the uterus range from complete agenesis to complete duplication. The true incidence is unknown because many otherwise normal women with normally functioning reproductive tracts have uterine anomalies that are never discovered (or only incidentally uncovered) because they cause no identifiable problems. They are brought to light most often in the course of evaluations for infertility, habitual midtrimester abortion, or premature labor. These are conditions that may be associated with uterine malformations. In addition, outflow obstruction from a rudimentary horn can cause hematometra, with resulting dysmenorrhea and perhaps endometriosis. Cervical incompetence is frequently associated as well. Women with uterine anomalies are also likely to have concomitant urologic anomalies. During embryologic development, the parallel müllerian ducts normally fuse in the midline to form the uterus and the upper vagina. Failure of fusion in part or entirely results in varying degrees of duplications, from a single arcuate uterus to a fully developed uterus didelphys with two hemiuteri (Fig. 1). The uterine corpus can be completely divided to form two corpora with a single cervix (uterus bicornis unicollis) or partially divided by a septum to form two cavities within a unified corpus (uterus septus or subseptus). Inexplicably, the more severe the anomaly, the less likely it is to be associated with pregnancy problems.

B. Suspect a uterine anomaly in a patient who has experienced prior midtrimester spontaneous abortion or premature labor, especially if there was evidence of silent cervical dilatation preceding the event. Look for evidence on physical examination of an asymmetric uterus or one that is broadened in the lateral dimension or has an indentation at the top. Physical findings are seldom clear enough for definitive diagnosis. Supplemental studies are needed for this purpose. Hysterosalpingography is very useful for demonstrating the shape of the uterine cavity, provided it is (or both are) accessible by way of the vagina for instilling contrast dye. Even when well visualized radiographically, however, the uterine shape may be misleading. Observing two horns does not necessarily distinguish between a septate and a bicornuate uterus. This requires additional differentiation by ultrasonography and especially by laparoscopy. While attempting to determine the precise nature of the uterine anomaly, assess the urinary tract for malformations that are likely to coexist, including ureteral duplication, unilateral agenesis, and pelvic kidney, by excretory urography.

C. Carefully designate the type of anomaly by gathering all relevant information together. This step should be done with due deliberation because counseling and recommendations about therapy and prognosis rest heavily on this information. At one extreme, patients with a single residual unicornuate uterus, for example, in which one müllerian duct has failed to descend and develop, leaving just a hemiuterus and its associated ipsilateral fallopian tube, cannot be benefited by any form of therapy. At the other, those with a rudimentary horn, whether or not it is connected to the fully developed contralateral hemiuterus, should be counseled about surgery for extirpation of the vestigial horn. This recommendation is based on the probability of hematometra and hematosalpinx if menstrual outflow is obstructed, or rupture with hemorrhage if pregnancy implantation should occur in it. If the uterine malformation is amenable to surgical correction and the patient's presenting manifestations warrant it, corrective surgery should be weighed. Since few have large experience, it is in the patient's best interest to refer her to an infertility expert who can advise her about the options available, review their risks and possible benefits, and recommend whether it is appropriate for her to undertake this course of action.

D. Metroplasty (p 262) is done to reunite the horns of a uterus. The major types of procedures, which involve incising the uterus and resecting or dividing the intervening walls or septum before reapposing the remodeled walls, are intended to create a single unified cavity from two. They are still useful for limited numbers of cases in which the two horns are truly separated and the anomaly interferes directly with fecundity. For most cases in which pregnancy problems are encountered, however, the problem is related to a septum that divides a single corpus into two cavities. These cases are being managed increasingly by a simpler approach, specifically by transhysteroscopic resection (p 222), which has much to recommend it as a preferred approach.

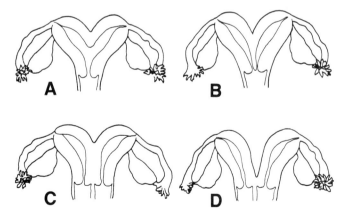

Figure 1 Spectrum of müllerian anomalies resulting in duplication of the uterus, from arcuate (A) and bicornuate (B) to duplex bicornis (C) and didelphys (D) forms.

References

DeCherney AH, Russell JB, Graebe RA, Polan ML. Resectoscopic management of müllerian fusion defects. Fertil Steril 45:726, 1986.

Kessler I, Lancet M, Appelman Z, Borenstein R. Indications and results of metroplasty in uterine malformations. Int J Gy-

PATIENT SUSPECTED OF HAVING A UTERINE MALFORMATION

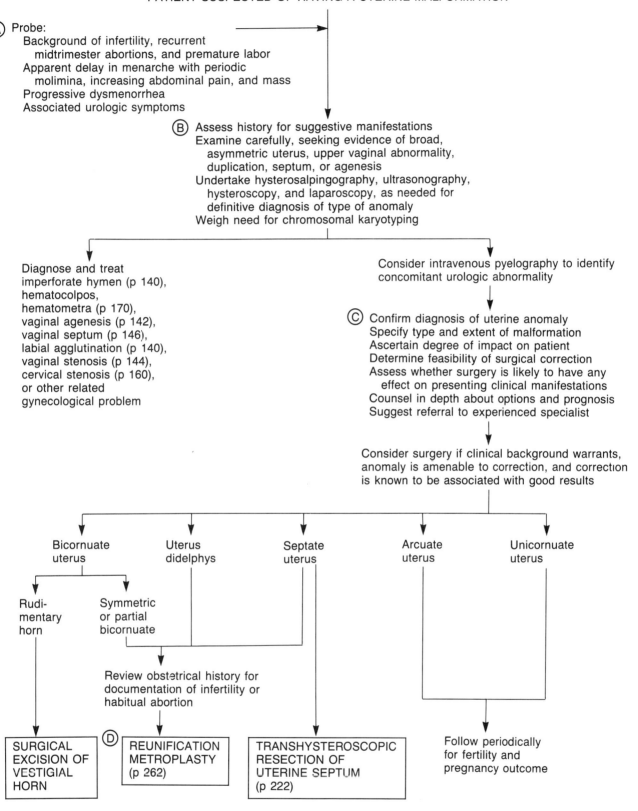

Ⓐ Probe:
    Background of infertility, recurrent
        midtrimester abortions, and premature labor
    Apparent delay in menarche with periodic
        molimina, increasing abdominal pain, and mass
    Progressive dysmenorrhea
    Associated urologic symptoms

Ⓑ Assess history for suggestive manifestations
    Examine carefully, seeking evidence of broad,
        asymmetric uterus, upper vaginal abnormality,
        duplication, septum, or agenesis
    Undertake hysterosalpingography, ultrasonography,
        hysteroscopy, and laparoscopy, as needed for
        definitive diagnosis of type of anomaly
    Weigh need for chromosomal karyotyping

Diagnose and treat
imperforate hymen (p 140),
hematocolpos,
hematometra (p 170),
vaginal agenesis (p 142),
vaginal septum (p 146),
labial agglutination (p 140),
vaginal stenosis (p 144),
cervical stenosis (p 160),
or other related
gynecological problem

Consider intravenous pyelography to identify
concomitant urologic abnormality

Ⓒ Confirm diagnosis of uterine anomaly
    Specify type and extent of malformation
    Ascertain degree of impact on patient
    Determine feasibility of surgical correction
    Assess whether surgery is likely to have any
        effect on presenting clinical manifestations
    Counsel in depth about options and prognosis
    Suggest referral to experienced specialist

Consider surgery if clinical background warrants,
anomaly is amenable to correction, and correction
is known to be associated with good results

Bicornuate uterus | Uterus didelphys | Septate uterus | Arcuate uterus | Unicornuate uterus

Rudi-mentary horn

Symmetric or partial bicornuate

Review obstetrical history for
documentation of infertility or
habitual abortion

SURGICAL
EXCISION OF
VESTIGIAL
HORN

Ⓓ REUNIFICATION
METROPLASTY
(p 262)

TRANSHYSTEROSCOPIC
RESECTION OF
UTERINE SEPTUM
(p 222)

Follow periodically
for fertility and
pregnancy outcome

naecol Obstet 24:137, 1986.
Perino A, Cittadini E, Hamou J, Mencaglia L. Hysteroscopic treat-
    ment of uterine septa. Acta Eur Fertil 16:331, 1985.

Portuondo JA, Camara MM, Echanojauregui AD, Calonge J.
    Müllerian abnormalities in fertile women and recurrent
    aborters. J Reprod Med 31:616, 1986.

ASHERMAN'S SYNDROME

Joseph F. D'Amico, M.D.

A. Partial or complete obliteration of the uterine cavity can result from intrauterine adhesions forming between the normally apposed walls as a consequence of destruction of the endometrial lining. This condition, called Asherman's syndrome, causes problems with menstrual and reproductive functions. The synechiae that occlude the cavity derive from a variety of precipitating factors, mostly related to trauma and infection. Patients frequently have had one or more curettages following delivery or, more often, after abortion when the endometrium appears to be especially susceptible to this type of severe damage. Although less common, the condition can follow cesarean section, myomectomy, and even simple endometrial biopsy. Cases may also be associated with both pelvic inflammatory disease and pelvic tuberculosis. Characteristic manifestations include menstrual disorder, especially hypomenorrhea, severe secondary dysmenorrhea, and infertility. The menstrual pattern may actually vary from menometrorrhagia to amenorrhea. Amenorrhea accompanied by regular, periodically recurrent molimina is highly suggestive of this condition, reflecting normal ovulatory function and endometrial endorgan failure on an anatomic rather than a physiologic basis.

B. Diagnostic evaluation should include a complete history and physical examination to determine the presence of other possible causes of the presenting menstrual aberration or infertility; seek evidence of systemic disease, debilitating condition, or endocrinopathy. Look especially for signs of congenital malformations; anomalies that affect the configuration of the uterine cavity (p 166) may make the differential diagnosis difficult. Unless Asherman's syndrome is considered, it will not be readily diagnosed because it is unlikely the specific tests will be done to detect it. Among these, hysterosalpingography is perhaps most helpful. It demonstrates the irregular filling defect or defects produced by the intrauterine adhesions; the defects must be distinguished from those produced by artifacts (particularly gas bubbles or blood clots) or other conditions, such as a septum, endometrial polyp, or submucous leiomyoma. This contrast dye study is doubly useful in these patients because it will also provide information about the status of the fallopian tubes, which may have been adversely affected by the same infection that caused the synechiae to form. Sounding the uterus carefully is sometimes helpful for diagnosis, but much less reliable than hysterosalpingography or hysteroscopy (see D). Hysteroscopy not only provides direct visualization and confirmation of the synechiae, but it also facilitates correction. For the patient who presents with amenorrhea, one can attempt to effect withdrawal bleeding by administering estrogen and progesterone in sequence. Failed response is strong evidence for the diagnosis.

C. If the surface area involved is small and the adhesions are few in number, one can try to correct the problem by dilating the cervix and sweeping the endometrial cavity gently with a sound. This sometimes restores function and obviates the need for more aggressive intervention. However, it is important not to persist in this conservative approach because trauma and infection may only aggravate the problem.

D. The best results are obtained with hysteroscopic lysis of the intrauterine adhesions. Under hysteroscopic observation, the adhesions are readily demonstrated and their site and extent are noted. Applying force carefully with the end of the hysteroscope against them often divides them. If this fails, surgical incision transhysteroscopically will be necessary. This technique risks myometrial injury and perforation of the subjacent uterine wall. Avoid this complication by visualizing the uterus simultaneously through a laparoscope. Laparoscopy is a valuable adjunct in these cases because it provides information on the condition of the adnexa and, in infertility cases, permits lysis of peritubal and ovarian adhesions as well.

E. After the anatomic integrity of the uterine cavity has been re-established, it is essential to prevent adhesions from reforming. This can be done by keeping the uterine walls apart mechanically with an intrauterine contraceptive device or a small indwelling catheter. Administer estrogens daily for two months to stimulate endometrial proliferation, and then produce withdrawal bleeding by adding progesterone for several days. Follow-up is important in order to reassess for recurrence by hysteroscopy. Recurrence requires reconsideration about undertaking another attempt to correct the problem by surgical lysis.

References

Friedman A, DeFazio J, DeCherney A. Severe obstetric complications after aggressive treatment of Asherman's syndrome. Obstet Gynecol 67:864, 1986.

Hamou J, Salat-Baroux J, Siegler AM. Diagnosis and treatment of intrauterine adhesions by microhysteroscopy. Fertil Steril 39:321, 1983.

Sanfilippo JS, Fitzgerald MR, Badawy SZA, et al. Asherman's syndrome: A comparison of therapeutic methods. J Reprod Med 27:328, 1982.

Stillman RJ, Asarkof N. Association between müllerian duct malformations and Asherman's syndrome in infertile women. Obstet Gynecol 65:673, 1985.

PATIENT SUSPECTED OF HAVING ASHERMAN'S SYNDROME

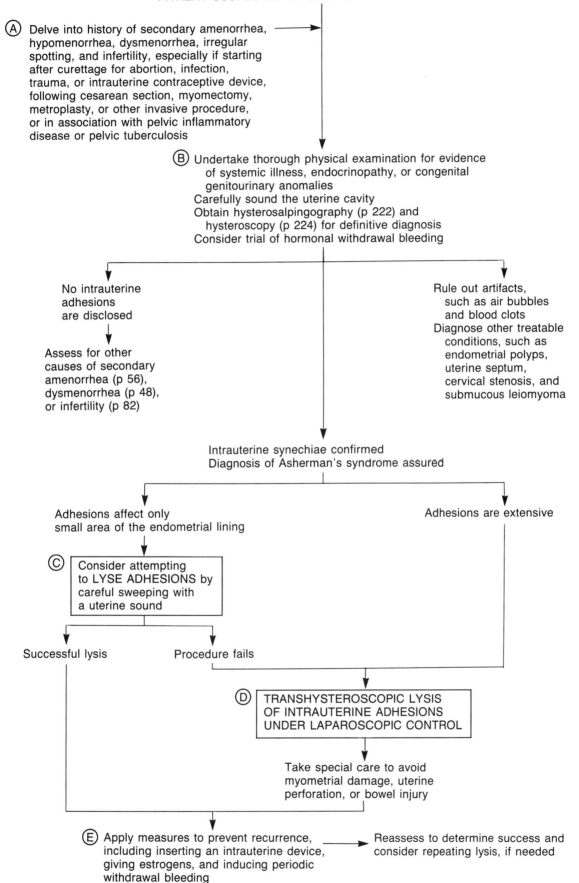

(A) Delve into history of secondary amenorrhea, hypomenorrhea, dysmenorrhea, irregular spotting, and infertility, especially if starting after curettage for abortion, infection, trauma, or intrauterine contraceptive device, following cesarean section, myomectomy, metroplasty, or other invasive procedure, or in association with pelvic inflammatory disease or pelvic tuberculosis

(B) Undertake thorough physical examination for evidence of systemic illness, endocrinopathy, or congenital genitourinary anomalies
Carefully sound the uterine cavity
Obtain hysterosalpingography (p 222) and hysteroscopy (p 224) for definitive diagnosis
Consider trial of hormonal withdrawal bleeding

No intrauterine adhesions are disclosed

Assess for other causes of secondary amenorrhea (p 56), dysmenorrhea (p 48), or infertility (p 82)

Rule out artifacts, such as air bubbles and blood clots
Diagnose other treatable conditions, such as endometrial polyps, uterine septum, cervical stenosis, and submucous leiomyoma

Intrauterine synechiae confirmed
Diagnosis of Asherman's syndrome assured

Adhesions affect only small area of the endometrial lining

Adhesions are extensive

(C) Consider attempting to LYSE ADHESIONS by careful sweeping with a uterine sound

Successful lysis

Procedure fails

(D) TRANSHYSTEROSCOPIC LYSIS OF INTRAUTERINE ADHESIONS UNDER LAPAROSCOPIC CONTROL

Take special care to avoid myometrial damage, uterine perforation, or bowel injury

(E) Apply measures to prevent recurrence, including inserting an intrauterine device, giving estrogens, and inducing periodic withdrawal bleeding

Reassess to determine success and consider repeating lysis, if needed

HEMATOMETRA

Lynn H. Galen, M.D.

A. The etiology of hematometra may be congenital or acquired. Hematometra may accompany hematocolpos secondary to an imperforate hymen (p 140). Other causes include transverse vaginal septum (p 146) and vaginal atresia (p 142) when associated with a functioning uterus. With the onset of menstruation, patients with obstructed fusion defects of the müllerian system accumulate menstrual blood and detritus on the obstructed side. In adults, occluded outflow may result secondarily from infection, obstetrical trauma, instrumentation, cervical cauterization, amputation, or conization, neoplasm, and radiation causing atrophy, scarring, or stenosis. Postmenopausal women who are started on hormonal replacement may develop hematometra if vaginal or cervical stenosis has occurred earlier to obstruct the egress of blood.

B. In adolescence, a young woman with hematometra may be asymptomatic except for apparently delayed menarche or perhaps a complaint of monthly lower abdominal pain. If the patient has an obstructed lateral fusion anomaly of the müllerian duct (p 166), the possibility of hematometra formation in the blind uterine horn may not be considered, since the patient will experience cyclic menstruation from the unobstructed side. On physical examination, a lower abdominal tender cystic mass may be palpated; the lower pole of the mass may terminate in a purpuric bulge within the vagina. Alternatively, the vagina may be absent (p 142). With increasing intrauterine pressure, retrograde passage of blood can cause the development of hematosalpinx or hemoperitoneum. Free blood in the abdomen may produce signs and symptoms of peritonitis. Urinary retention may occur from bladder outlet obstruction due to the growing mass.

C. In order to preserve reproductive potential and avoid partial or complete destruction of the genital organs due to chronic cryptomenorrhea, it is important to make a diagnosis as soon as possible. Hematometra should, therefore, be included in the differential diagnosis of a pelvic mass. Exclude the possibility of pregnancy first in a woman with amenorrhea (p 56) and an enlarging midline mass. Accurate assessment of patients with suspected anomalies of the urogenital tract is imperative if inappropriate surgery is to be avoided. If adequate examination is difficult, consider performing a combined pelvic and rectal examination under anesthesia, both to ensure correct diagnosis and to initiate drainage (see D). Ultrasonography, computerized tomography, or magnetic resonance imaging is used additionally to help define the mass and attempt to characterize the complex of anomalies. Laparoscopy may prove to be necessary to define the anatomy of the internal genitalia. The diagnosis of any genital tract malformation mandates thorough work-up of the urinary system for commonly associated defects as well.

D. Treatment consists of the most appropriate surgical procedure that will adequately relieve the obstruction. The procedure chosen will depend on the abnormality found. Intrauterine instrumentation of a uterus with an attenuated wall should be avoided, if possible, or minimized; if done, use great care and gentleness because of the risk of perforation and infection. Adequate drainage of the uterine contents should be established and time allowed to elapse for complete involution to occur before proceeding to definitive corrective intrauterine or intravaginal surgery.

E. Hematometra may develop acutely with characteristic clinical manifestations immediately following pregnancy termination by suction curettage. Uterine atony allows for rapid uterine distension with accumulated blood from the placental site as clotted blood impedes normal drainage from the cervical os. The patient complains of constant and intensely severe suprapubic pain. She is often weak and exhibits diaphoresis and tachycardia. The uterus is tense and frequently found to be larger than it was before the evacuation. Treatment involves re-evacuation, usually by suction curettage, and administration of uterotonic agents. Cervical dilatation is rarely necessary. Alternatively, uterine drainage may be effected by inserting a large bore Foley catheter (20 F) through the cervix into the uterine cavity and mechanically draining the uterus by evacuating it with an attached 60 cc syringe. Concomitant administration of either methylergonovine maleate or oxytocin helps prevent recurrence. Routine administration of an oxytocic agent during and following pregnancy termination may decrease the incidence of postabortal hematometra.

References

Bates GW, Wiser WL. A technique for uterine conservation in adolescents with vaginal agenesis and a functional uterus. Obstet Gynecol 66:290, 1985.

Borten M, Friedman EA. Drainage of postabortion hematometra by Foley catheter. Am J Obstet Gynecol 149:908, 1984.

Eisenberg E, Farber M, Mitchell GW Jr, et al. Complete duplication of the uterus and cervix with a unilaterally imperforate vagina. Obstet Gynecol 60:259, 1982.

Hamlin DJ, Pettersson H, Ramey SL, Moazam F. Magnetic resonance imaging of bicornuate uterus with unilateral hematometrosalpinx and ipsilateral renal agenesis. Urol Radiol 8:52, 1986.

PATIENT WITH SUSPICION OF HEMATOMETRA

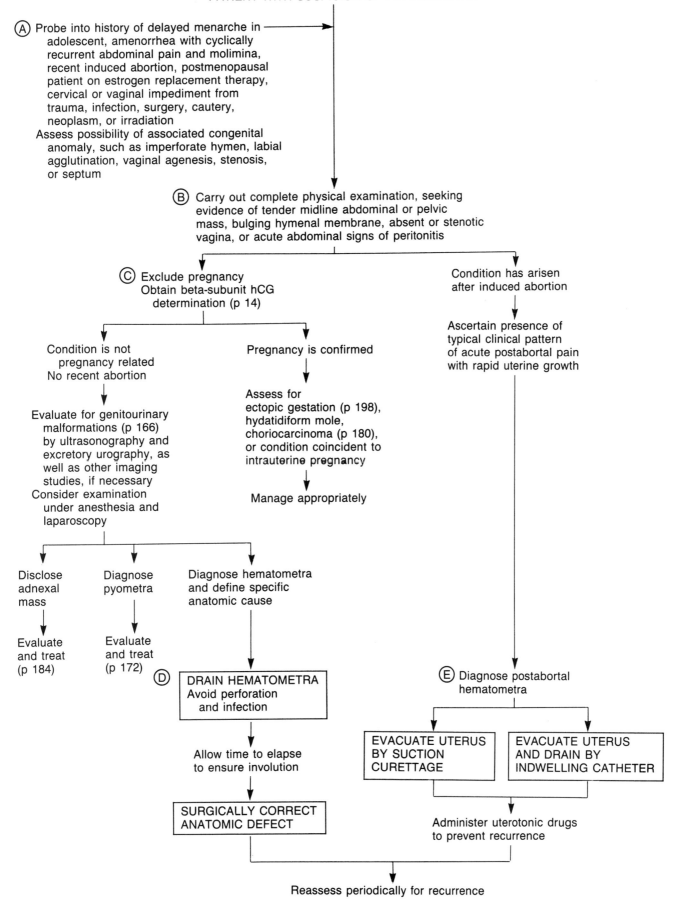

(A) Probe into history of delayed menarche in adolescent, amenorrhea with cyclically recurrent abdominal pain and molimina, recent induced abortion, postmenopausal patient on estrogen replacement therapy, cervical or vaginal impediment from trauma, infection, surgery, cautery, neoplasm, or irradiation
Assess possibility of associated congenital anomaly, such as imperforate hymen, labial agglutination, vaginal agenesis, stenosis, or septum

(B) Carry out complete physical examination, seeking evidence of tender midline abdominal or pelvic mass, bulging hymenal membrane, absent or stenotic vagina, or acute abdominal signs of peritonitis

(C) Exclude pregnancy
Obtain beta-subunit hCG determination (p 14)

Condition is not pregnancy related
No recent abortion

Pregnancy is confirmed

Condition has arisen after induced abortion

Ascertain presence of typical clinical pattern of acute postabortal pain with rapid uterine growth

Evaluate for genitourinary malformations (p 166) by ultrasonography and excretory urography, as well as other imaging studies, if necessary
Consider examination under anesthesia and laparoscopy

Assess for ectopic gestation (p 198), hydatidiform mole, choriocarcinoma (p 180), or condition coincident to intrauterine pregnancy

Manage appropriately

Disclose adnexal mass

Diagnose pyometra

Diagnose hematometra and define specific anatomic cause

Evaluate and treat (p 184)

Evaluate and treat (p 172)

(D) DRAIN HEMATOMETRA
Avoid perforation and infection

(E) Diagnose postabortal hematometra

EVACUATE UTERUS BY SUCTION CURETTAGE

EVACUATE UTERUS AND DRAIN BY INDWELLING CATHETER

Allow time to elapse to ensure involution

SURGICALLY CORRECT ANATOMIC DEFECT

Administer uterotonic drugs to prevent recurrence

Reassess periodically for recurrence

171

PYOMETRA

Lynn H. Galen, M.D.

A. Pyometra results from accumulation of purulent material within the uterine cavity. Two conditions have to be met for this condition to develop, namely obstruction of outflow and infection. Any condition that prevents the normal drainage of endometrial secretions from the uterus may cause the problem. Most commonly, pyometra arises as a result of obstruction of the cervical canal at the internal os by a malignant disease of either the cervix or the endometrium. Thus, it is essential to seek evidence of cancer whenever confronted by a case of pyometra. The procedure for effecting drainage by re-establishing patency of the outflow tract by dilatation (see C) is also useful for determining the cause by curettage. Pyometra can also be associated with benign tumors (such as endometrial polyps or leiomyomas), traumatic or destructive operations on the cervix (including conization, amputation, cauterization, and repair of cervical lacerations), radiation fibrosis, congenital cervical anomalies, tuberculous endometritis, or cervical stenosis due to senile changes. It may even occur in the absence of any recognizable predisposing conditions.

B. Although about half the women found to have a pyometra are entirely free of symptoms, the clinical presentation is frequently that of an elderly woman complaining of lower abdominal pain, vaginal bleeding, and discharge. The condition is usually indolent with few clear-cut signs pointing to a pelvic disease or systemic infection. Low grade fever is sometimes seen, but even this is an inconsistent finding. Because its manifestations are so nonspecific, one has to be especially alert to suspect pyometra; it requires a high index of suspicion. A tense, often nontender, cystic, midline mass may be palpable on bimanual pelvic examination. Rarely, a patient will present with manifestations of acute peritonitis due to spontaneous intraperitoneal rupture of a pyometra. If uterine perforation has occurred, the patient may present with signs of an acute surgical abdomen and septic shock (p 202). Ultrasonography, used as a diagnostic adjunct, may show a symmetrically enlarged uterus with an enlarged, homogeneous, fluid filled, cystic uterine cavity; the uterine wall may appear to be thinned from the distension. The diagnosis of pyometra is confirmed by passing a sound or probe through the internal cervical os into the uterine cavity and demonstrating the escape of pus through the os. Take special care to be very gentle when probing the stenosed cervix so as not to create a false passage.

C. On initial evaluation, obtain cervical smears for cytologic evaluation as well as Gram staining for bacteria and polymorphonuclear leukocytes. A pyometra is an abscess and should be managed as such. The basic surgical principle applicable here is that the nidus of infection must be drained. Cervical dilatation and endometrial curettage (p 230) are the mainstays of management for providing a drainage route, for debriding necrotic tissue within the uterine cavity, and for diagnosing associated malignant disease. To repeat, be gentle in dilating a stenotic cervix and curetting a friable and necrotic uterine cavity in order to avoid perforation. All curettings should be subject to histologic examination for evidence of malignancy. Both aerobic and anaerobic cultures should be taken at the time of dilatation and curettage. If evidence of systemic infection (such as fever, tachycardia, and leukocytosis) or peritonitis is present, antibiotic therapy is indicated. Start them only after appropriate cultures have been taken. Most appropriate for patients with pyometra are broad-spectrum antibiotics that are effective against both anaerobic and aerobic bacteria. Ensure that there is adequate drainage of the uterine cavity. An indwelling catheter is seldom necessary, although it may prove effective for long-term drainage. If the patient presents in septic shock, stabilize her cardiovascular system and begin broad-spectrum antibiotic therapy. Delay definitive surgical intervention until after she has been stabilized, if possible under these circumstances.

D. Most women with pyometra respond well to effective drainage, all systemic signs of inflammatory disease subsiding rapidly. The uterus usually regresses to normal size over the course of a few weeks. Hysterectomy should be reserved for patients who show persistent infection despite appropriate antibiotic therapy. Still more aggressive management may become necessary if a cervical (p 164) or endometrial cancer (p 178) is diagnosed. The optimal therapy for these conditions depends on the patient's general condition and one's ability to control or eradicate the infection. If the cervical stenosis is related to senile atrophy, consider estrogen therapy to prevent recurrence. Close periodic follow-up is indicated.

References

Barber HRK. Cancer of the endometrium. In: Van Nagell JR Jr, Barber HRK (Editors). Modern Concepts of Gynecologic Oncology. Boston: John Wright–PSG, 1982.

Cove H. Surgical Pathology of the Endometrium: Practical Aspects in the Interpretation of Endometrial Curettings. Philadelphia: J.B. Lippincott, 1981.

Jones VA, Elkins TE, Wood SA, Buxton BH. Spontaneous rupture of pyometra due to leiomyomata: A case report. J Reprod Med 31:637, 1986.

PATIENT WITH MIDLINE PELVIC MASS AND FEVER

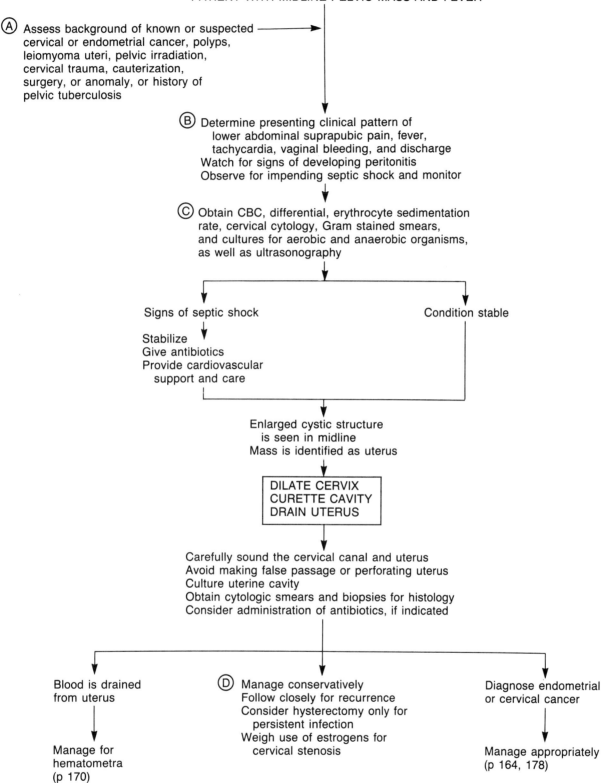

Ⓐ Assess background of known or suspected ——————⟶
cervical or endometrial cancer, polyps,
leiomyoma uteri, pelvic irradiation,
cervical trauma, cauterization,
surgery, or anomaly, or history of
pelvic tuberculosis

Ⓑ Determine presenting clinical pattern of
lower abdominal suprapubic pain, fever,
tachycardia, vaginal bleeding, and discharge
Watch for signs of developing peritonitis
Observe for impending septic shock and monitor

Ⓒ Obtain CBC, differential, erythrocyte sedimentation
rate, cervical cytology, Gram stained smears,
and cultures for aerobic and anaerobic organisms,
as well as ultrasonography

Signs of septic shock   Condition stable

Stabilize
Give antibiotics
Provide cardiovascular
support and care

Enlarged cystic structure
is seen in midline
Mass is identified as uterus

DILATE CERVIX
CURETTE CAVITY
DRAIN UTERUS

Carefully sound the cervical canal and uterus
Avoid making false passage or perforating uterus
Culture uterine cavity
Obtain cytologic smears and biopsies for histology
Consider administration of antibiotics, if indicated

Blood is drained   Ⓓ Manage conservatively   Diagnose endometrial
from uterus   Follow closely for recurrence   or cervical cancer
                                 Consider hysterectomy only for
                                   persistent infection
                                 Weigh use of estrogens for
Manage for   cervical stenosis   Manage appropriately
hematometra   (p 164, 178)
(p 170)

173

ADENOMYOSIS

Lynn H. Galen, M.D.

A. Uterine adenomyosis is a condition characterized by the invasion of ectopic, but otherwise normally functioning, endometrial tissue into the uterine musculature. It is often an incidental pathologic finding disclosed in a uterus removed for some other reason. The etiology of adenomyosis is obscure. Previous uterine surgery, particularly cesarean section, in which the endometrium may have been inadvertently included within the myometrium during closure, does not appear to be a risk factor for the development of symptomatic adenomyosis.

B. Adenomyosis is three to four times more common in multiparous women, usually occurring in the fourth to fifth decade. This parity and age preponderance distinguishes cases with adenomyosis from those with endometriosis (p 190), who tend to be younger, nulliparous, and often infertile. Most women with adenomyosis have no identifiable symptoms referable to this condition. However, some affected patients complain of progressively severe dysmenorrhea, slowly increasing in intensity over a span of years. The pain is frequently cramping in nature and persists through the entire menstrual flow. During the remainder of the cycle, patients are usually quite asymptomatic. Occasionally, there may be menorrhagia or intermenstrual spotting. For those who have had symptoms for a long time, the history will often reveal unsuccessful attempts previously made to treat the dysmenorrhea or menometrorrhagia by curettage or cyclic hormonal therapy. Postmenopausal symptoms cannot be ascribed to adenomyosis, because the condition generally subsides after the cyclic ovarian hormone stimulation stops. On physical examination, the uterus may be found to be diffusely enlarged (rarely to as large as twice normal size) and somewhat softened. Tenderness can be elicited, particularly during menses.

C. The triad of uterine enlargement, dysmenorrhea, and menorrhagia may suggest a diagnosis of adenomyosis, but the symptoms have to be considered nonspecific. Patients with these manifestations should be investigated for more obvious pelvic disease, such as endometrial hyperplasia, polyps, or malignancy, and dysfunctional uterine bleeding. The correct diagnosis of adenomyosis is made preoperatively in only about one-fifth of affected patients. Not only is it common to fail to make the diagnosis, but the diagnosis, when made, is often wrong. Testing is modified according to the patient's complaints. Examine the patient thoroughly. Obtain a complete blood count (CBC) with differential and erythrocyte sedimentation rate. If the history is suggestive of hormonal dysfunction, also pursue endocrinologic studies. Uterine sampling by curettage is indicated in all patients giving a history of abnormal uterine bleeding in order to exclude hyperplastic changes and carcinoma of the endometrium. Adenomyosis will not be diagnosed by curettage unless a polypoid submucous adenomyoma is found or the myometrium is entered by excessive (and unacceptable) force on the curette. Adenocarcinoma rarely arises in an isolated focus of adenomyosis; usually, neoplastic changes are found in the surface endometrium and may also affect underlying adenomyosis. Ultrasonography is of little use in diagnosing adenomyosis; rarely, it can demonstrate the presence of cystic spaces within the myometrium. Hysterography may show unusual trabeculations at the endometrial-myometrial junction. By differentiating the uterine wall into distinct layers, magnetic resonance imaging may prove to be capable of detecting adenomyosis within the myometrium. Laparoscopy is done if the diagnosis of endometriosis is being considered.

D. Dilatation and curettage is not effective for treating the abnormal bleeding and dysmenorrhea caused by adenomyosis. Similarly, the bleeding does not respond to cyclic exogenous progesterone therapy. If anemia is present, treat with hematinic agents as needed. Prostaglandin synthetase inhibitors may substantially decrease the blood loss and pain associated with menstruation. Start these drugs at the beginning of the menstrual flow in a dosage regimen of four times daily until the flow abates. Consider definitive extirpative surgery only for unremitting menorrhagia or dysmenorrhea. Simple total hysterectomy is most effective. It is preferably carried out by the vaginal route if the uterus is not too large. In a young woman who wishes to preserve her fertility, it is possible to shell out an encapsulated adenomyoma, but this is rarely done.

References

Fraser IS, McCarron G, Markham R, et al. Measured menstrual blood loss in women with menorrhagia associated with pelvic disease or coagulation disorder. Obstet Gynecol 68:630, 1986.

Harris WJ, James FD, Baxter JW. Prior cesarean section: A risk factor for adenomyosis. J Reprod Med 30:173, 1985.

Kilkku P, Erkkola R, Gronroos M. Non-specificity of symptoms related to adenomyosis. Acta Obstet Gynecol Scand 63:229, 1984.

Lee JKT, Gersell DJ, Balfe DM, et al. The uterus: In vitro magnetic resonance-anatomic correlation of normal and abnormal specimens. Radiology 157:175, 1985.

Woodruff JD, Erozan YS, Genadry R. Adenocarcinoma arising in adenomyosis detected by atypical cytology. Obstet Gynecol 67:145, 1986.

PATIENT WITH SUSPICION OF ADENOMYOSIS

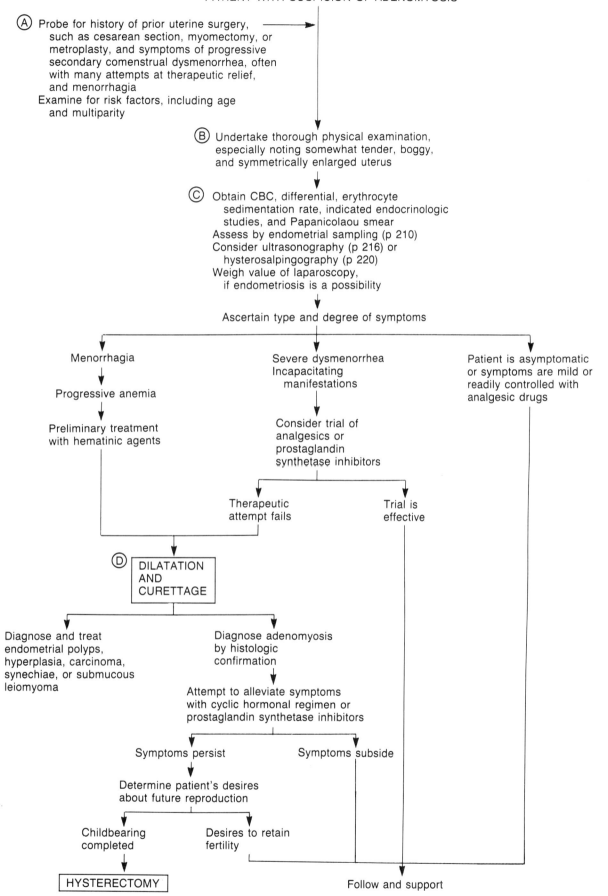

(A) Probe for history of prior uterine surgery, such as cesarean section, myomectomy, or metroplasty, and symptoms of progressive secondary comenstrual dysmenorrhea, often with many attempts at therapeutic relief, and menorrhagia
Examine for risk factors, including age and multiparity

(B) Undertake thorough physical examination, especially noting somewhat tender, boggy, and symmetrically enlarged uterus

(C) Obtain CBC, differential, erythrocyte sedimentation rate, indicated endocrinologic studies, and Papanicolaou smear
Assess by endometrial sampling (p 210)
Consider ultrasonography (p 216) or hysterosalpingography (p 220)
Weigh value of laparoscopy, if endometriosis is a possibility

Ascertain type and degree of symptoms

Menorrhagia

Progressive anemia

Preliminary treatment with hematinic agents

Severe dysmenorrhea Incapacitating manifestations

Consider trial of analgesics or prostaglandin synthetase inhibitors

Patient is asymptomatic or symptoms are mild or readily controlled with analgesic drugs

Therapeutic attempt fails

Trial is effective

(D) DILATATION AND CURETTAGE

Diagnose and treat endometrial polyps, hyperplasia, carcinoma, synechiae, or submucous leiomyoma

Diagnose adenomyosis by histologic confirmation

Attempt to alleviate symptoms with cyclic hormonal regimen or prostaglandin synthetase inhibitors

Symptoms persist

Symptoms subside

Determine patient's desires about future reproduction

Childbearing completed

Desires to retain fertility

HYSTERECTOMY

Follow and support

ENDOMETRIAL HYPERPLASIA

Lenard R. Simon, M.D.

A. Endometrial hyperplasia is a histopathologic entity that may itself be a forerunner in the developmental sequence leading to full-blown adenocarcinoma of the endometrium or just serve as a marker for concurrent or future development of endometrial cancer. The diagnosis of endometrial hyperplasia, once established on the basis of endometrial biopsy or preferably by curettage, raises concern about its proclivity to progress to endometrial carcinoma. Some studies have shown endometrial adenocarcinoma already present in up to one-fourth of patients with documented endometrial hyperplasia, while others fail to confirm this high frequency of association.

B. The histologic features of endometrial hyperplasia include focal or more generalized patterns of glandular proliferation with intraluminal budding and papillary formation; nuclear size is increased and chromatin clumping is seen as the process becomes more advanced. There are as yet no uniform criteria for defining this process or uniform terminology for describing it. Indeed, it is difficult at times to distinguish some forms of endometrial hyperplasia from adenocarcinoma itself. There is growing agreement that special importance can be placed on the appearance of cellular atypia. The greater the degree of atypia, the more likely the lesion represents a premalignant state or neoplastic marker. Recent investigations have cogently shown the prognostic value of a finding of cellular atypia; nearly one-third of cases are associated with or progress to cancer, whereas few if any of those without atypia do so.

C. While one can suspect this condition in any given patient on the basis of risk factors (such as obesity, diabetes, hypertension, and long-term unopposed estrogen exposure) or symptoms (including menorrhagia, anovulation, or postmenopausal bleeding), the diagnosis must rest on endometrial sampling and histologic examination. This is accomplished preliminarily by endometrial biopsy (p 210) or, more definitively, by thorough curettage (p 230). The latter is essential for ensuring that one has not inadvertently overlooked a small focus of hyperplasia or of carcinoma. While performing a full, formal curettage under anesthesia, it is prudent (and strongly recommended) to carry out a systematic fractional curettage in the event the patient proves to have adenocarcinoma. The sampling procedure shows the extent of the lesion and documents whether there is concurrent endocervical involvement, which may modify management.

D. If adenocarcinoma is actually encountered or the hyperplastic lesion is essentially indistinguishable from an early cancer, the patient should be treated with appropriate aggressiveness (p 178), according to the clinical stage it falls into, that is, extrafascial hysterectomy and adnexectomy with or without aortic and pelvic lymphadenectomy and pelvic irradiation.

E. The patient whose endometrial hyperplasia shows cellular atypia, but lacks clear evidence of progression to adenocarcinoma, warrants somewhat less aggressive intervention than one with cancer, but the condition cannot be ignored because of the future risk to which it exposes her. Two options are available, namely simple total hysterectomy or a program of hormonal therapy. In general, postmenopausal women and patients who have fulfilled their childbearing needs are best served by hysterectomy. Those who have medical conditions that make them poor operative or anesthetic risks and those who wish to retain their reproductive function can be treated hormonally. Young women in the reproductive age group can be given cyclic progesterone in a dosage schedule of 10 mg per day for the last 11 to 14 days of each menstrual cycle for three to six months. Older postmenopausal women are given an uninterrupted progesterone regimen of 10 mg per day for three to six months. Recurrence after therapy warrants reconsideration for hysterectomy.

F. In the absence of any objective demonstration of cellular atypia, conservative management is appropriate. Expectancy with annual re-examination and endometrial sampling should suffice for postmenopausal patients. Younger women can be given cyclic progesterone (see E) for three to six months. If curettage repeated afterwards shows no hyperplasia, only annual reassessments are needed. If the hyperplasia persists, give continuous daily progesterone for six months and then consider hysterectomy for persistent hyperplasia.

References

Fox H, Buckley CH. The endometrial hyperplasias and their relationship to endometrial neoplasia. Histopathology 6:493, 1982.

Kurman RJ, Kaminski PF, Norris HJ. The behavior of endometrial hyperplasia: A long-term study of "untreated" hyperplasia in 170 patients. Cancer 56:403, 1985.

Norris HJ, Tavassoli FA, Kurman RJ. Endometrial hyperplasia and carcinoma: Diagnostic considerations. Am J Surg Pathol 7:839, 1983.

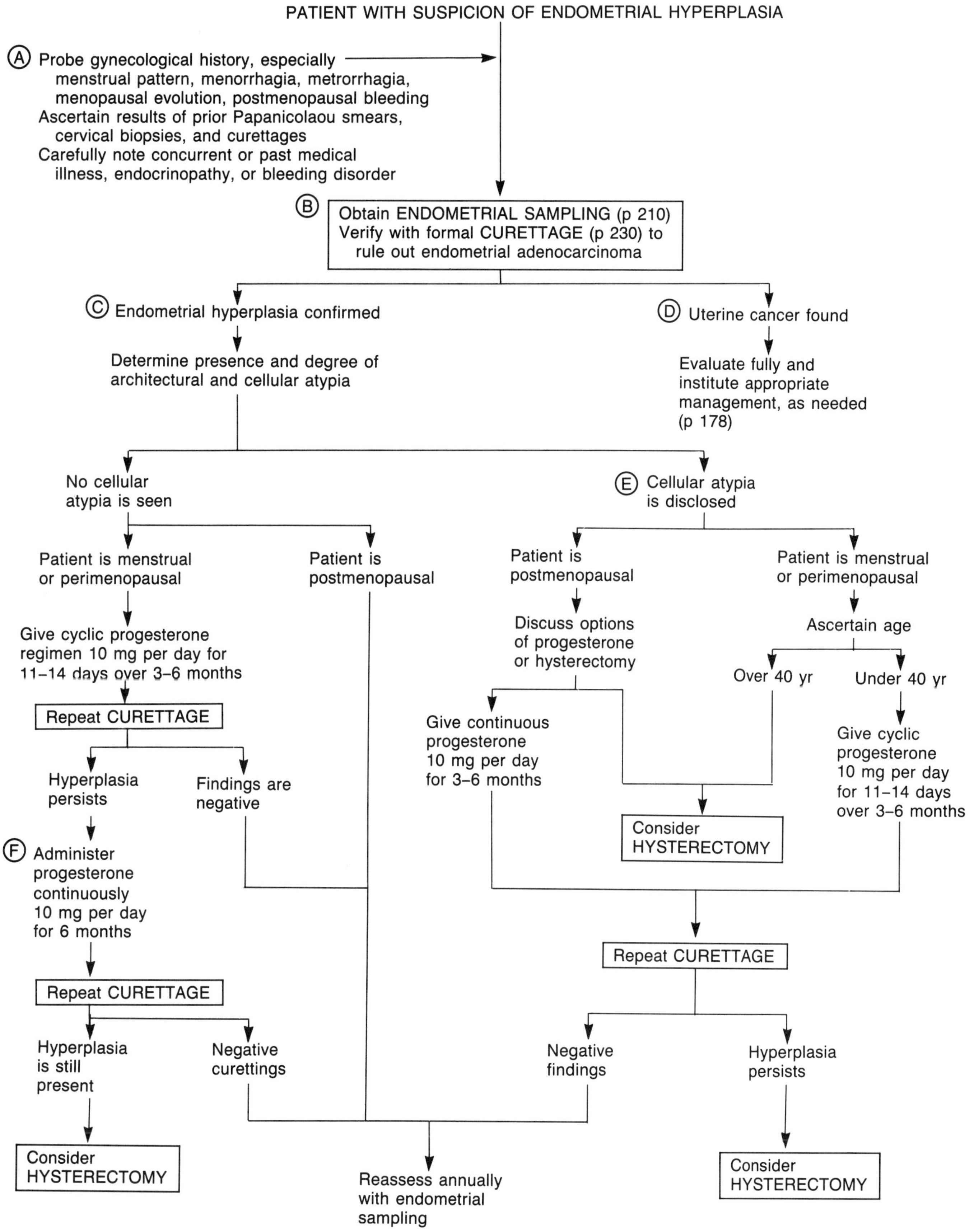

PATIENT WITH SUSPICION OF ENDOMETRIAL HYPERPLASIA

(A) Probe gynecological history, especially
menstrual pattern, menorrhagia, metrorrhagia,
menopausal evolution, postmenopausal bleeding
Ascertain results of prior Papanicolaou smears,
cervical biopsies, and curettages
Carefully note concurrent or past medical
illness, endocrinopathy, or bleeding disorder

(B) Obtain ENDOMETRIAL SAMPLING (p 210)
Verify with formal CURETTAGE (p 230) to
rule out endometrial adenocarcinoma

(C) Endometrial hyperplasia confirmed

Determine presence and degree of
architectural and cellular atypia

(D) Uterine cancer found

Evaluate fully and
institute appropriate
management, as needed
(p 178)

No cellular
atypia is seen

Patient is menstrual
or perimenopausal

Give cyclic progesterone
regimen 10 mg per day for
11–14 days over 3–6 months

Repeat CURETTAGE

Hyperplasia
persists

Findings are
negative

(F) Administer
progesterone
continuously
10 mg per day
for 6 months

Repeat CURETTAGE

Hyperplasia
is still
present

Negative
curettings

Consider
HYSTERECTOMY

Patient is
postmenopausal

Reassess annually
with endometrial
sampling

(E) Cellular atypia
is disclosed

Patient is
postmenopausal

Discuss options
of progesterone
or hysterectomy

Give continuous
progesterone
10 mg per day
for 3–6 months

Consider
HYSTERECTOMY

Patient is menstrual
or perimenopausal

Ascertain age

Over 40 yr   Under 40 yr

Give cyclic
progesterone
10 mg per day
for 11–14 days
over 3–6 months

Repeat CURETTAGE

Negative
findings

Hyperplasia
persists

Consider
HYSTERECTOMY

ENDOMETRIAL CANCER

Jonathan M. Niloff, M.D.

A. The symptom of postmenopausal bleeding demands evaluation for endometrial adenocarcinoma. This applies even if the bleeding is not excessive and does not persist. It should not be ignored even if it is transient. Be especially alert in cases presenting with relevant risk factors, typically including obesity, diabetes, and hypertension as well as prolonged unopposed exposure to estrogens, such as occurs in women with polycystic ovary syndrome (p 128). All patients with postmenopausal bleeding must have histologic evaluation of the endometrium by an appropriate biopsy (p 210) or curettage technique (p 230).

B. Cytologic assessment of a smear obtained from the cervix or vaginal pool (p 12) is an inadequate screening technique for endometrial cancer. Nonetheless, the presence of endometrial cells in a smear obtained from a postmenopausal woman, even if they are normal in appearance, may be significant. This finding requires thorough histologic evaluation of the endometrium.

C. Office endometrial biopsy sampling may establish the diagnosis and thus obviate the need for an anesthesia for this purpose. The staging fractional curettage (see D) can then be performed at the same time as the hysterectomy (see E). A negative office sampling result in a woman with postmenopausal bleeding, however, cannot be relied upon to rule out cancer; it should be followed by a diagnostic curettage under anesthesia.

D. Fractional curettage is necessary for proper clinical staging of endometrial cancer. With the patient under anesthesia, carefully palpate the pelvic structures to exclude pelvic metastases. Endocervical curettage should then be performed. This is followed by uterine sounding and then by systematic endometrial curettage. Cystoscopy and proctoscopy are indicated only if there is some suspicion of contiguous spread of tumor to the bladder or the bowel based on symptoms or palpable extension or fixation of the lesion to these organs. Consider excretory urography and barium enema contrast study if they appear to be indicated on the same basis. Before one proceeds to definitive surgical therapy, objective evaluation should include complete blood count (CBC), urinalysis, blood chemistry determinations, and chest radiography at minimum.

E. A surgical attack is generally preferred in cases with endometrial cancer because it facilitates staging and individualization of adjuvant therapy. Undertake laparotomy and obtain peritoneal washings at once. Then palpate all peritoneal surfaces, including the undersurface of the diaphragm. Omental biopsy is performed. Extrafascial hysterectomy and bilateral salpingo-oophorectomy are the definitive therapeutic procedures of choice for operable cases.

F. Aortic lymph node biopsy is indicated if the endometrial tumor is poorly differentiated. The extirpated uterus should be opened by the pathologist in the operating room to demonstrate the depth of myometrial invasion and to determine if tumor involves the cervix. Assess intraoperatively for extrauterine pelvic extension. In the presence of upper abdominal serosal metastases, the information provided by these observations is superfluous.

G. Postoperative therapy is guided by the surgical and pathologic findings, particularly histologic grade, depth of myometrial invasion, lymph node status, and surgical staging. Pelvic radiation therapy prevents pelvic recurrences and should be given to patients who have poorly differentiated tumors, deep myometrial invasion, or Stage II or III disease. Patients with positive aortic nodes can be spared the morbidity of pelvic irradiation unless they are candidates for extended field irradiation (see H). The implications of positive peritoneal washings remain controversial. Additional treatment is not given here for positive washings alone. Whole abdominal irradiation for patients with positive washings, Stage III disease, or papillary serous type of endometrial carcinoma may be promising, but it is still under investigation. Adjuvant progestational therapy has not been demonstrated to be efficacious in early stages of this disease, but it may be useful for palliation.

H. Extended field irradiation to treat lateral pelvic and aortic regional node groups has been associated with five-year survival rates approaching 50 percent. However, it is not innocuous and cannot, therefore, be considered standard therapy as yet.

References

Boronow RC, Morrow CP, Creasman WT, et al. Surgical staging in endometrial cancer: Clinical-pathologic findings of a prospective study. Obstet Gynecol 63:825, 1984.

Cowles TA, Magrina JF, Masterson BJ, Capen CV. Comparison of clinical and surgical staging in patients with endometrial carcinoma. Obstet Gynecol 66:413, 1985.

Eifel PJ, Ross J, Hendrickson M, et al. Adenocarcinoma of the endometrium: Analysis of 256 cases with disease limited to the uterine corpus: Treatment comparisons. Cancer 52:1026, 1983.

Henrickson M, Ross J, Eifel PJ, et al. Uterine papillary serous carcinoma. Am J Surg Pathol 6:93, 1982.

Potish RA, Twiggs LB, Adcock LL, et al. Paraaortic lymph node radiotherapy in cancer of the uterine corpus. Obstet Gynecol 65:251, 1985.

PATIENT WITH SUSPICION OF ADENOCARCINOMA OF ENDOMETRIUM

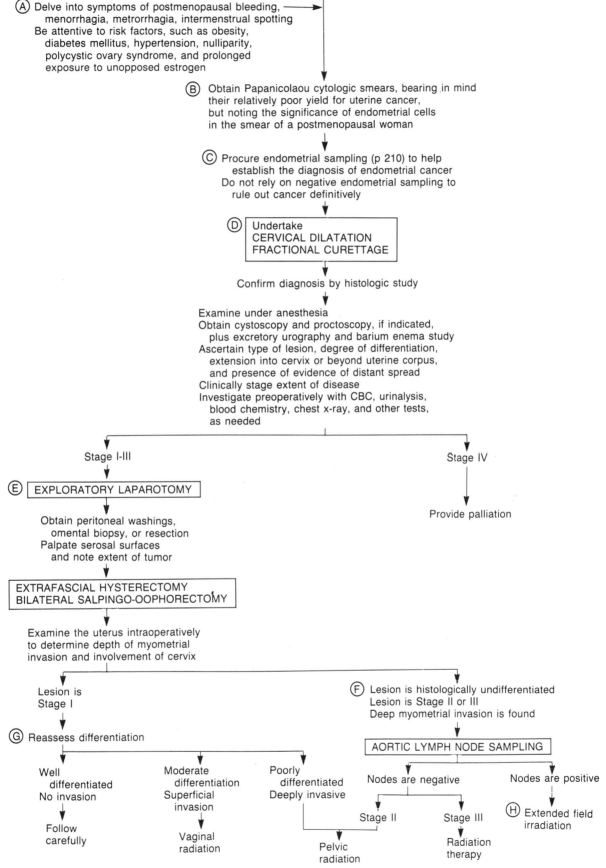

Ⓐ Delve into symptoms of postmenopausal bleeding,
menorrhagia, metrorrhagia, intermenstrual spotting
Be attentive to risk factors, such as obesity,
diabetes mellitus, hypertension, nulliparity,
polycystic ovary syndrome, and prolonged
exposure to unopposed estrogen

Ⓑ Obtain Papanicolaou cytologic smears, bearing in mind
their relatively poor yield for uterine cancer,
but noting the significance of endometrial cells
in the smear of a postmenopausal woman

Ⓒ Procure endometrial sampling (p 210) to help
establish the diagnosis of endometrial cancer
Do not rely on negative endometrial sampling to
rule out cancer definitively

Ⓓ Undertake
CERVICAL DILATATION
FRACTIONAL CURETTAGE

Confirm diagnosis by histologic study

Examine under anesthesia
Obtain cystoscopy and proctoscopy, if indicated,
plus excretory urography and barium enema study
Ascertain type of lesion, degree of differentiation,
extension into cervix or beyond uterine corpus,
and presence of evidence of distant spread
Clinically stage extent of disease
Investigate preoperatively with CBC, urinalysis,
blood chemistry, chest x-ray, and other tests,
as needed

Stage I-III

Stage IV

Ⓔ EXPLORATORY LAPAROTOMY

Obtain peritoneal washings,
omental biopsy, or resection
Palpate serosal surfaces
and note extent of tumor

Provide palliation

EXTRAFASCIAL HYSTERECTOMY
BILATERAL SALPINGO-OOPHORECTOMY

Examine the uterus intraoperatively
to determine depth of myometrial
invasion and involvement of cervix

Lesion is
Stage I

Ⓕ Lesion is histologically undifferentiated
Lesion is Stage II or III
Deep myometrial invasion is found

Ⓖ Reassess differentiation

AORTIC LYMPH NODE SAMPLING

Well
differentiated
No invasion

Moderate
differentiation
Superficial
invasion

Poorly
differentiated
Deeply invasive

Nodes are negative

Nodes are positive

Follow
carefully

Vaginal
radiation

Pelvic
radiation

Stage II

Stage III

Ⓗ Extended field
irradiation

Radiation
therapy

179

CHORIOCARCINOMA

Lenard R. Simon, M.D.

A. Gestational trophoblastic disease encompasses a spectrum from essentially benign hydatidiform mole to highly malignant, hematogenously metastasizing choriocarcinoma. The terminology has been formalized to distinguish nonmetastatic low-risk forms from high-risk metastatic or poor prognosis gestational trophoblastic disease. The latter are those trophoblastic lesions that are histopathologically undifferentiated, generally unresponsive to therapy, and have increased propensity to metastasize. Be alert to the possibility of this potentially serious condition in a woman who has had a molar pregnancy in the past, who develops vaginal bleeding following delivery or abortion, or who experiences hemoptysis, an ominous signal of lung metastases. Cough, chest pain, and dyspnea are commonly associated in this latter circumstance. In pregnancy, consider the diagnosis of gestational trophoblastic disease if the uterine size grows too rapidly or is greater than expected for the time elapsed since the last menstrual period, if no fetal heart sounds can be heard electronically by eight weeks' gestational age, or if signs of hyperemesis, hypertension, or hyperthyroidism develop in the early months.

B. Evaluate the patient carefully by history and physical examination. For purposes of designating the patient's risk category, probe the medical and gynecological history and delve into details of the obstetrical experience with dates of pregnancies and their outcomes. Look for evidence of metastasis, especially in the lung fields, and stigmata of hyperthyroidism. Obtain quantitative beta-subunit human chorionic gonadotropin (hCG) levels from both serum and urine and determine results of prior tests, if any were done. Get a chest x-ray examination and metabolic profile, including liver, kidney, and thyroid function tests. Ultrasonography is especially useful for diagnosis in pregnancy. Computer tomography and radionucleide scanning may be indicated to search for distant metastases, if findings warrant.

C. Assign the patient to a prognostic category according to the presence or absence of factors recognized to affect outcome. Adverse results can be expected, for example, if the hCG levels prior to therapy are above 100,000 IU per 24 hours in urine or 40,000 mIU per milliliter in serum; if there has been a prior treatment failure; if more than three months have elapsed since prior pregnancy or treatment failure (and the greater the interval beyond that, the greater the risk); if the antecedent pregnancy was a term gestation; and if there is evidence of cerebral, hepatic, renal, splenic, or bowel metastases. Other risk factors of somewhat less prognostic significance include a prior hydatidiform mole and the presence of metastases to the pelvis, vagina, and lung.

D. In the low- and moderate-risk groups, virtually 100 percent remission can be achieved with initial single agent or multiagent chemotherapy. It should be noted that the toxicity of single agent chemotherapy is much lower than multiagent chemotherapy. Choices of single drugs for this purpose include methotrexate and actinomycin D. A valuable triple agent combination is methotrexate, actinomycin D, and cyclophosphamide.

E. For patients who fall into the high-risk group, there is virtually no place for single agent chemotherapy, and the aforementioned multiagent programs (see D) have generally been disappointing. This has led to the development of newer, more potent, and much more toxic regimens. Combinations of VP 16 (etoposide), methotrexate, actinomycin D, cyclophosphamide, and vincristine are somewhat promising in this regard, but remain to be evaluated in depth for otherwise drug resistant cases. To optimize outcome results and to ensure proper follow-up, early recognition, and treatment of complications of both the chemotherapy and the disease, these patients are best managed by individuals with considerable expertise and experience in centers that are fully equipped to deal with them.

F. Close follow-up is essential for patients with gestational trophoblastic disease. Serial beta-subunit hCG titers are especially valuable as a tumor marker in these cases; they will serve to register effectiveness of chemotherapy (or lack thereof) and help guide the subsequent management program. Treatment is individualized and limited use of surgical extirpation and radiation therapy for isolated metastatic lesions, if feasible, may be appropriate in high-risk patients unless hCG titers show continued, progressive fall.

References

Bagshawe KD. Treatment of high risk choriocarcinoma. J Reprod Med 29:813, 1984.

Driscoll SG. Placental site chorioma. J Reprod Med 29:821, 1984.

DuBeshter B, Berkowitz R, Goldstein DB, et al. Metastatic gestational trophoblastic disease: Experience at the New England Trophoblastic Disease Center 1965–1985. Obstet Gynecol 69:390, 1987.

Gordon AN, Gershenson DM, Copeland LJ, et al. High-risk metastatic gestational trophoblastic disease. Obstet Gynecol 65:550, 1985.

World Health Organization Scientific Group. Gestational trophoblastic disease. Technical Report No. 692. Geneva: World Health Organization, 1983.

PATIENT WITH SUSPICION OF GESTATIONAL TROPHOBLASTIC DISEASE

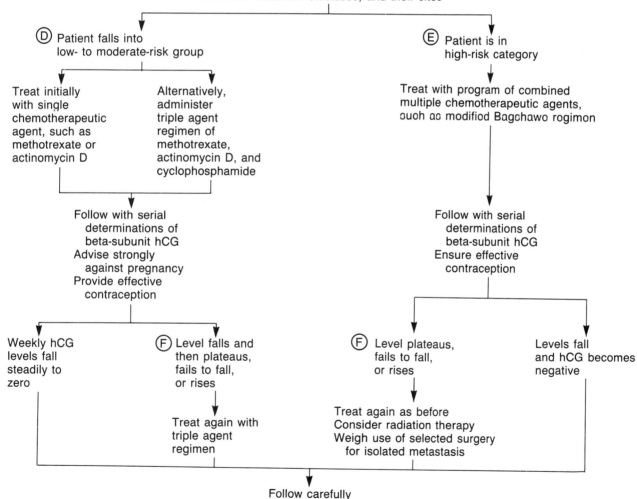

(A) Probe history of prior or current pregnancy,
noting abnormal bleeding, rapid uterine growth,
absent fetal heart tones, hypertension, severe
nausea and vomiting, hemoptysis, chest pain,
and thyrotoxic manifestations

(B) Conduct history and physical examination in detail
Seek evidence of lung metastases
Obtain quantitative beta-subunit hCG determination
Investigate chest x-ray, pelvic ultrasonography,
computer tomography of head, abdomen, and pelvis,
and liver, thyroid, and renal function studies

Diagnose gestational trophoblastic disease

EVACUATE UTERUS BY SUCTION CURETTAGE
Avoid uterine trauma or perforation

(C) Assign prognostic risk category status on basis of
beta-subunit hCG level, duration of disease, failure
of antecedent therapy, nature of preceding pregnancy,
evidence of distant metastases, and their sites

(D) Patient falls into
low- to moderate-risk group

Treat initially
with single
chemotherapeutic
agent, such as
methotrexate or
actinomycin D

Alternatively,
administer
triple agent
regimen of
methotrexate,
actinomycin D, and
cyclophosphamide

Follow with serial
determinations of
beta-subunit hCG
Advise strongly
against pregnancy
Provide effective
contraception

Weekly hCG
levels fall
steadily to
zero

(F) Level falls and
then plateaus,
fails to fall,
or rises

Treat again with
triple agent
regimen

(E) Patient is in
high-risk category

Treat with program of combined
multiple chemotherapeutic agents,
such as modified Bagshawe regimen

Follow with serial
determinations of
beta-subunit hCG
Ensure effective
contraception

(F) Level plateaus,
fails to fall,
or rises

Levels fall
and hCG becomes
negative

Treat again as before
Consider radiation therapy
Weigh use of selected surgery
for isolated metastasis

Follow carefully
with monthly
hCG levels until
negative for at
least 1 year

LEIOMYOMA UTERI

Alexander M. Dlugi, M.D.

A. Uterine fibroids are relatively common and generally asymptomatic (Fig. 1). Some affected women have meno-metrorrhagia, dysmenorrhea, and even pressure or pain. Submucous leiomyomas may cause habitual abortion (p 76). Fibroids rarely, if ever, cause sterility (p 82). Acute complications may include urinary retention, torsion (in association with a pedunculated fibroid only), infection, carneous degeneration (usually in the course of pregnancy), or obstetrical complications, specifically as related to obstructed labor. Acute urinary retention is a consequence of urethral obstruction caused by sharp angulation resulting from cervical pressure as the uterus, which contains a fundal myoma, retroflexes; in these cases, the cervix is high up behind the symphysis where it cannot be readily seen on speculum examination. Growth is ordinarily quite slow, taking place and being detectable by physician and patient over a period of years; however, fibroids can sometimes enlarge quite rapidly, usually in association with edema, infection, or carneous degeneration with bleeding.

B. In most cases, it is relatively easy to make the diagnosis on physical examination. Bimanual palpation of the pelvic structures reveals the typically enlarged uterus with smooth globular irregularities. These are generally uniformly firm or rubbery and nontender. They are also usually mobile in contiguity with or indistinguishable from the uterus, unless one or more are attached by a stalk. Leiomyomas may also coexist with or be indistinguishable from a pregnancy. A pregnancy test is, therefore, mandatory in most cases before proceeding with further evaluation. Subserous or intraligamentous fibroids are easily confused with ovarian masses, and vice versa. Ultrasonography often confirms the diagnosis, but it cannot always exclude an ovarian neoplasm. Intravenous pyelography should be performed whenever the mass encroaches upon the pelvic sidewalls or occupies the pelvis fully. Consider hysterosalpingography for the patient with a uterus under 12 weeks' gestational size

who presents with irregular bleeding or recurrent pregnancy wastage.

C. Management is guided by the presence or absence of symptoms and the intensity of manifestations related to the leiomyomas. The majority of women who have small or moderate size fibroids (under 12 weeks' size collectively) have no relevant symptoms and, therefore, need no special care. They can be followed periodically at intervals of six months to one year, watching for growth or the development of any symptoms that might warrant intervention. Any change in menstrual pattern, especially irregular or heavy vaginal bleeding, requires investigation by dilatation and curettage (p 80).

D. It is essential to determine the patient's desire to maintain her reproductive potential. For the patient with large or symptomatic leiomyomas, the choice between myomectomy (if feasible) and hysterectomy depends principally on this factor. Before the patient decides in favor of myomectomy, she should be fully informed about the increased morbidity relative to hysterectomy, the likelihood of future recurrence of fibroids, the possibility that the procedure cannot be accomplished (risking hysterectomy anyway) or might actually enhance infertility, and the need for cesarean section in ensuing pregnancies.

E. Gonadotropin releasing hormone (GnRH) agonists act by down-regulating the pituitary release of gonadotropins. Consequently, ovarian function ceases and a reversible "menopausal" state is created. As much as a 70 percent reduction in uterine size has recently been reported by this approach, suggesting it may benefit patients who are perimenopausal by retarding or reversing fibroid growth until natural menopause takes place. Information is lacking about the risks of long-term GnRH agonist use and possible recurrence of fibroids after the medication is discontinued, but it should soon be forthcoming from ongoing clinical studies.

F. Transhysteroscopic resection of a submucous myoma should only be performed by an appropriately trained endoscopist. Stringent selection criteria apply to ensure safety. The fibroid must be discrete and clearly seen in its entirety to qualify for this procedure. Simultaneous laparoscopic visualization of the uterus is essential during the operation for guidance. Marked distortion of the uterine cavity precludes hysteroscopic resection.

References

Boyd ME. Myomectomy. Can J Surg 29:161, 1986.

Coddington CC, Collins RC, Shawker TH, et al. Long-acting gonadotropin hormone-releasing hormone analog used to treat uteri. Fertil Steril 45:624, 1986.

DeCherney AH, Polan ML. Hysteroscopic management of intrauterine lesions and intractable uterine bleeding. Obstet Gynecol 61:392, 1983.

Hricak H, Tscholakoff D, Heinrichs S, et al. Uterine leiomyomas: Correlation of magnetic resonance, histopathologic findings, and symptoms. Radiology 158:385, 1986.

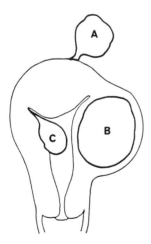

Figure 1 Leiomyomas are classified according to location into subserous (A), intramural (B), or submucosal (C) varieties.

PATIENT WITH SUSPICION OF LEIOMYOMA UTERI

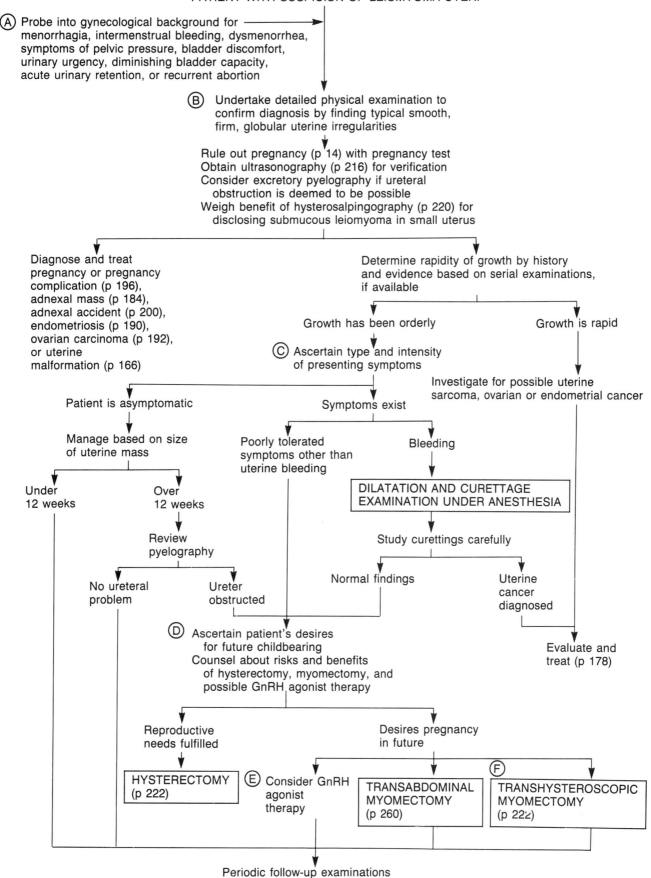

(A) Probe into gynecological background for menorrhagia, intermenstrual bleeding, dysmenorrhea, symptoms of pelvic pressure, bladder discomfort, urinary urgency, diminishing bladder capacity, acute urinary retention, or recurrent abortion

(B) Undertake detailed physical examination to confirm diagnosis by finding typical smooth, firm, globular uterine irregularities

Rule out pregnancy (p 14) with pregnancy test
Obtain ultrasonography (p 216) for verification
Consider excretory pyelography if ureteral obstruction is deemed to be possible
Weigh benefit of hysterosalpingography (p 220) for disclosing submucous leiomyoma in small uterus

Diagnose and treat pregnancy or pregnancy complication (p 196), adnexal mass (p 184), adnexal accident (p 200), endometriosis (p 190), ovarian carcinoma (p 192), or uterine malformation (p 166)

Determine rapidity of growth by history and evidence based on serial examinations, if available

Growth has been orderly

Growth is rapid

(C) Ascertain type and intensity of presenting symptoms

Investigate for possible uterine sarcoma, ovarian or endometrial cancer

Patient is asymptomatic

Symptoms exist

Manage based on size of uterine mass

Poorly tolerated symptoms other than uterine bleeding

Bleeding

Under 12 weeks

Over 12 weeks

DILATATION AND CURETTAGE EXAMINATION UNDER ANESTHESIA

Review pyelography

Study curettings carefully

No ureteral problem

Ureter obstructed

Normal findings

Uterine cancer diagnosed

(D) Ascertain patient's desires for future childbearing
Counsel about risks and benefits of hysterectomy, myomectomy, and possible GnRH agonist therapy

Evaluate and treat (p 178)

Reproductive needs fulfilled

Desires pregnancy in future

HYSTERECTOMY (p 222)

(E) Consider GnRH agonist therapy

TRANSABDOMINAL MYOMECTOMY (p 260)

(F) TRANSHYSTEROSCOPIC MYOMECTOMY (p 222)

Periodic follow-up examinations for further growth or recurrence

ADNEXAL MASS

Emanuel A. Friedman, M.D., Sc.D.

A. Most women with an adnexal mass have no symptoms to signal its presence. The mass is generally detected on routine physical examination in these cases. Because ovarian malignancy (p 192) is always a possibility, the need for such periodic examinations should be stressed for purposes of detecting the disease while it is still amenable to cure. Pelvic pain is an important flag pointing to the existence of a pathologic condition in the adnexa. Its pattern can be helpful diagnostically. Pain that recurs periodically may be related to an adnexal accident, such as torsion with intermittent occlusion of arterial blood supply and/or venous drainage, which leads eventually to infarction with necrosis and hemorrhage. Contrastingly, actual infarction, hemorrhage, and infection are more often associated with continuous and progressively worsening pain. Peritoneal signs may also be present in these cases. Comenstrual dysmenorrhea suggests endometriosis. Acute pain of short duration arising suddenly, particularly after exertion or intercourse, may reflect rupture of a cyst. If such an episode is followed by a course of progressive symptoms, intraperitoneal bleeding or peritoneal inflammatory reaction should be considered. If preceded by amenorrhea or pregnancy symptoms, consider ectopic pregnancy (p 198).

B. There are epochal intervals during the life of the female when any adnexal mass has dire significance. Before menarche and after menopause, finding an adnexal mass should set into motion a train of events leading to rapid diagnosis and definitive treatment. A mass of this nature must be regarded as abnormal because it may be neoplastic. Thus, the age of the patient is important in determining the need for subsequent evaluation. Postmenopausally, even a palpable ovary, which would otherwise be considered normal in a woman of reproductive age, should be viewed with suspicion. Appropriate investigation must be pursued in such a case. In the menstruating woman, one is generally less aggressive about investigating an adnexal mass because the ovary varies in size according to the cyclic physiologic changes that result in ovulation with its accompanying corpus hemorrhagicum and corpus luteum. Seldom do such normally cystic structures attain a size greater than 5 cm, however (see D).

C. If ultrasonography demonstrates that an adnexal mass is solid or has both solid and cystic components, it must be deemed to be potentially neoplastic, regardless of its size. Thorough evaluation must be undertaken under these circumstances.

D. A cystic adnexal mass may present a functional physiologic process in the ovary associated with the preovulation development of a graafian follicle or a postovulation corpus luteum cyst. If one encounters an asymptomatic adnexal cyst that is less than 5 cm in diameter, the patient may be safely observed expectantly through the next menstrual cycle, re-examining her during the first 10 days after her menstrual flow begins. This is an optimal time in the proliferative phase of the cycle when functional cysts should not normally be palpable. If the mass is still present or has enlarged in the interim, it must be investigated further. If the cyst is smaller or has vanished, only follow-up examinations are needed to ensure against recurrence or later growth.

E. A complete history and a physical examination are essential, plus pelvic ultrasonography to distinguish between an adnexal mass and a nongynecological condition involving bowel or retroperitoneal structures. Although x-ray examination is preferably avoided, especially before puberty, it may nonetheless help differentiate a benign teratoma by demonstrating the presence of a tooth or the telltale radiolucency of the mass. The characteristic anterior location and sebaceous contents of a dermoid cyst often make it possible to identify its nature ultrasonographically. Intravenous pyelography is reserved for cases in which it is necessary to exclude congenital anomalies of the urologic system, especially a pelvic kidney. A barium enema is important in order to rule out large bowel neoplasms in older women. Laparoscopy helps make a definitive diagnosis as to the nature of the mass. The information obtained and the associated symptoms determine whether a laparotomy is required.

References

Ehren IM, Mahour GH, Isaacs H. Benign and malignant ovarian tumors in children and adolescents: A review of 63 cases. Am J Surg 147:339, 1984.

El-Minawi MF, El-Halafawy AA, Abdel HM, et al. Laparoscopic, gynecographic and ultrasonographic vs. clinical evaluation of a pelvic mass. J Reprod Med 29:197, 1984.

Rome RM, Fortune DW, Quinn MA, Brown JA. Functioning ovarian tumors in postmenopausal women. Obstet Gynecol 57:705, 1981.

Voss SC, Lacey CG, Pupkin M, et al. Ultrasound and the pelvic mass. J Reprod Med 28:833, 1983.

Wade RV, Smythe AR, Watt GW, et al. Reliability of gynecologic sonographic diagnosis, 1978-1984. Am J Obstet Gynecol 153:186, 1985.

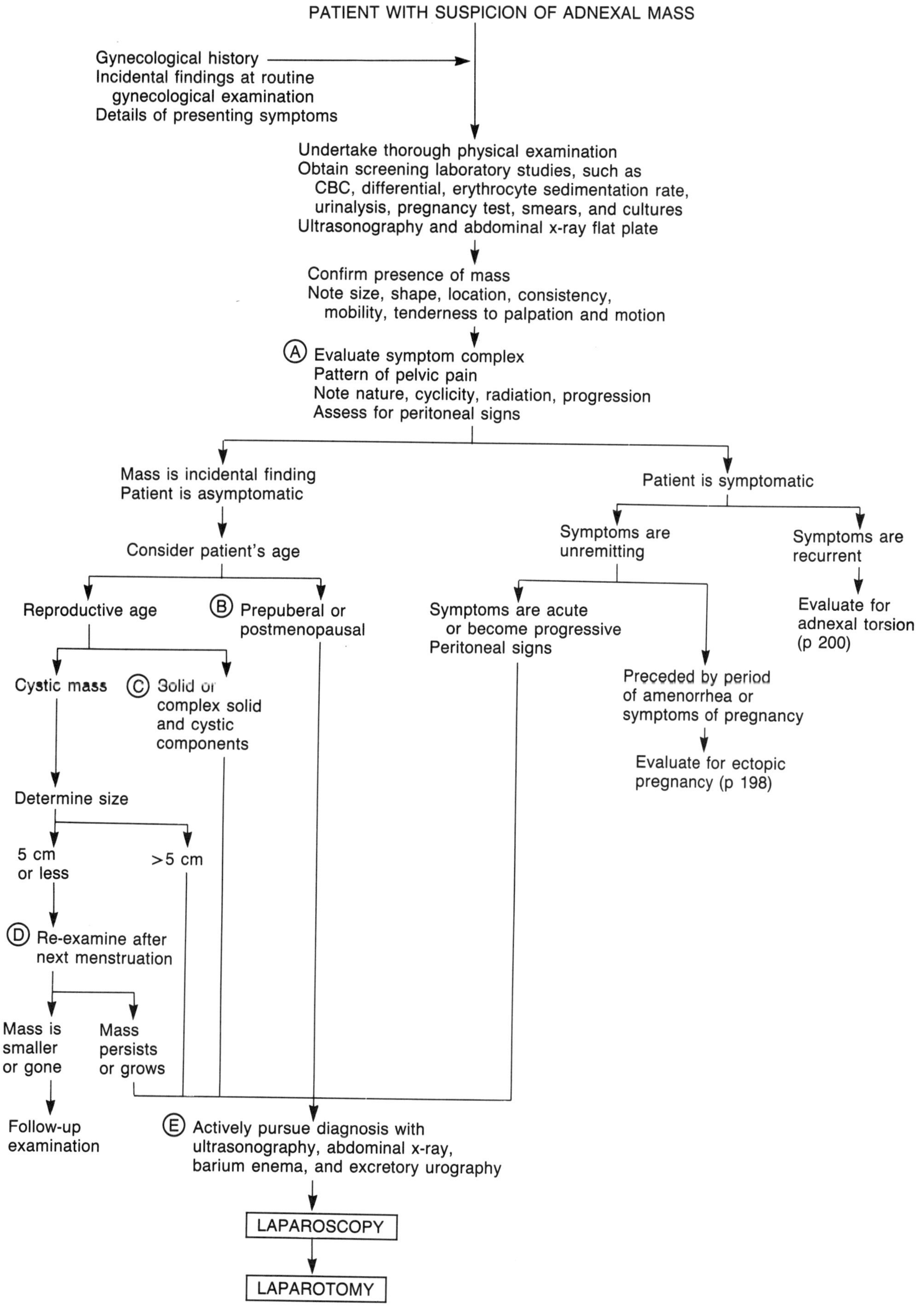

PATIENT WITH SUSPICION OF ADNEXAL MASS

Gynecological history
Incidental findings at routine
  gynecological examination
Details of presenting symptoms

Undertake thorough physical examination
Obtain screening laboratory studies, such as
  CBC, differential, erythrocyte sedimentation rate,
  urinalysis, pregnancy test, smears, and cultures
Ultrasonography and abdominal x-ray flat plate

Confirm presence of mass
Note size, shape, location, consistency,
  mobility, tenderness to palpation and motion

(A) Evaluate symptom complex
Pattern of pelvic pain
Note nature, cyclicity, radiation, progression
Assess for peritoneal signs

Mass is incidental finding
Patient is asymptomatic

Consider patient's age

Reproductive age   (B) Prepuberal or
                              postmenopausal

Cystic mass   (C) Solid or
                   complex solid
                   and cystic
                   components

Determine size

5 cm   >5 cm
or less

(D) Re-examine after
    next menstruation

Mass is   Mass
smaller   persists
or gone   or grows

Follow-up   (E) Actively pursue diagnosis with
examination   ultrasonography, abdominal x-ray,
                   barium enema, and excretory urography

Patient is symptomatic

Symptoms are   Symptoms are
unremitting   recurrent

Symptoms are acute   Evaluate for
or become progressive   adnexal torsion
Peritoneal signs   (p 200)

                  Preceded by period
                  of amenorrhea or
                  symptoms of pregnancy

                  Evaluate for ectopic
                  pregnancy (p 198)

LAPAROSCOPY

LAPAROTOMY

SALPINGITIS

Eric D. Lichter, M.D.

A. Acute salpingitis can be readily diagnosed if all objective signs and symptoms are present and consistent. However, a number of other conditions can mimic all or part of the spectrum of manifestations commonly encountered. It is a serious error to diagnose salpingitis in a woman who does not actually have it. This not only subjects her to a long regimen of antibiotic therapy with its attendant costs and risks, but it delays disclosure of the real diagnosis and its management. Moreover, health care providers tend to attribute every future pelvic problem to this infection. Probe for recent or past exposure to sexually transmitted diseases (p 112), especially gonococcal and chlamydial infections, well documented pelvic inflammatory disease, use of an intrauterine device, or postabortal or postpartum infection.

B. The physical examination must be carried out meticulously to help distinguish among the several different conditions that the clinical picture may represent. Determine by abdominal examination whether there is evidence of peritonitis, including involuntary guarding, direct, referred, and rebound tenderness, a positive psoas sign, and costovertebral angle tenderness. Undertake a careful and gentle pelvic examination, including both vaginal and rectal palpation bimanually, seeking to elicit information about the precise location and nature of the process, noting tenderness by palpation as well as by moving the cervix to one side or the other. Determine the presence of adnexal thickening or masses. If a mass is found and confirmed by ultrasonography, the patient must be assessed for tubo-ovarian abscess (p 188) and managed accordingly.

C. Make a concerted effort to demonstrate causes of pelvic pain (p 50). Determine if the pattern has been recurrent, progressive over time, and related to menstruation, for example, as possible evidence of endometriosis (p 190), or acute, intermittent, and associated with flank pain and dysuria, reflecting pyelitis or urolithiasis (p 288). It may be difficult to differentiate pyelonephritis from salpingitis because ureteral irritation may occur when the inflamed tube rests (or is fixed) against the posterior leaf of the broad ligament under which the ureter crosses. Seek laboratory verification by obtaining at least a complete blood count (CBC), differential, sedimentation rate, and urinalysis. Recall that some noninfectious inflammatory processes, such as avascular tissue necrosis associated with adnexal torsion or infarction, can induce systemic effects recognized by leukocytosis, differential shift, and elevated sedimentation rate. Also note that the laboratory markers of infection may be delayed in appearance in cases of salpingitis; they can lag behind the clinical signs by hours (rarely, even days), thereby giving rise to much confusion. Acute phase serum C-reactive protein concentration can sometimes be very helpful in this regard. Menstrual aberrations, suggestive signs of pregnancy, shoulder pain, or tenesmus warrant serious consideration of ectopic pregnancy (p 198). Pregnancy testing, preferably the beta-subunit human chorionic gonadotropin (hCG) assay, and ultrasonographic scanning are clearly needed under these circumstances.

D. To minimize permanent damage to the delicate tubal anatomy and function, patients with acute salpingitis must be treated early and aggressively with an appropriate antibiotic regimen. Obtain cultures first, but recognize that there is at best a poor correlation between the organisms found by cervical culture and those present and active in the tubes. Salpingitis is often found to be associated with polymicrobial aerobic and anaerobic organisms, possibly as secondary invaders. Antibiotic choices must take this into account. Discuss the possibilities of future problems, including infertility, ectopic pregnancy, chronic pelvic pain, recurrence potential, and abscess formation in order to ensure the patient is fully apprised of her condition and its prognosis. In this way, she can take measures to avoid reinfection and be knowledgeable about and alert to potential complications.

E. Patients whose salpingitis recurs periodically ultimately develop irreparable tubal damage with distal and proximal occlusion, resulting in hydrosalpinx, pyosalpinx, or tubo-ovarian abscess. They can be counseled about the benefits of sexual abstinence as a means for helping to optimize healing or the use of barrier contraception (p 30) to minimize risk of reinfection. Chronic pelvic pain, especially if associated with recurrent pyosalpinx (Fig. 1), warrants surgical intervention to remove the damaged organs. The best time for surgery is when the inflammatory process has subsided maximally between recurrences.

References

Jones RB, Mammel JB, Shepard MK, Fisher RR. Recovery of *Chlamydia trachomatis* from the endometrium of women at risk for chlamydial infection. Am J Obstet Gynecol 155:35, 1986.

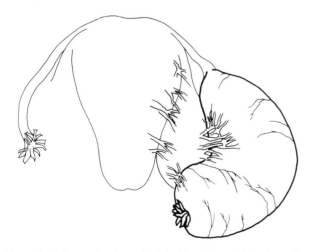

Figure 1 Advanced unilateral salpingitis with pyosalpinx formation, showing retort shaped distension, distorted residual fimbria, and dense adhesions.

PATIENT WITH SUSPICION OF SALPINGITIS

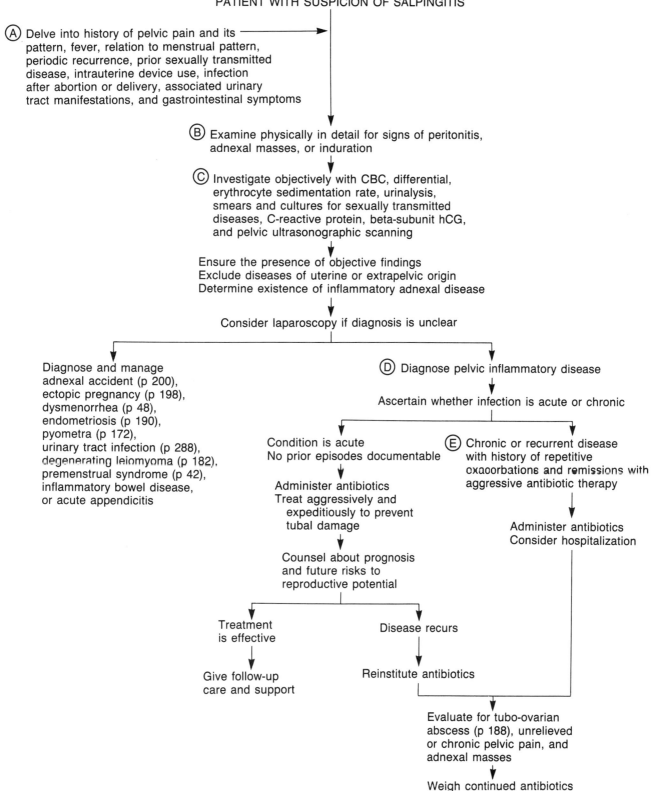

A. Delve into history of pelvic pain and its pattern, fever, relation to menstrual pattern, periodic recurrence, prior sexually transmitted disease, intrauterine device use, infection after abortion or delivery, associated urinary tract manifestations, and gastrointestinal symptoms

B. Examine physically in detail for signs of peritonitis, adnexal masses, or induration

C. Investigate objectively with CBC, differential, erythrocyte sedimentation rate, urinalysis, smears and cultures for sexually transmitted diseases, C-reactive protein, beta-subunit hCG, and pelvic ultrasonographic scanning

Ensure the presence of objective findings
Exclude diseases of uterine or extrapelvic origin
Determine existence of inflammatory adnexal disease

Consider laparoscopy if diagnosis is unclear

Diagnose and manage
adnexal accident (p 200),
ectopic pregnancy (p 198),
dysmenorrhea (p 48),
endometriosis (p 190),
pyometra (p 172),
urinary tract infection (p 288),
degenerating leiomyoma (p 182),
premenstrual syndrome (p 42),
inflammatory bowel disease,
or acute appendicitis

D. Diagnose pelvic inflammatory disease

Ascertain whether infection is acute or chronic

Condition is acute
No prior episodes documentable

E. Chronic or recurrent disease with history of repetitive exacerbations and remissions with aggressive antibiotic therapy

Administer antibiotics
Treat aggressively and expeditiously to prevent tubal damage

Administer antibiotics
Consider hospitalization

Counsel about prognosis and future risks to reproductive potential

Treatment is effective

Disease recurs

Give follow-up care and support

Reinstitute antibiotics

Evaluate for tubo-ovarian abscess (p 188), unrelieved or chronic pelvic pain, and adnexal masses

Weigh continued antibiotics vs extirpative surgery

Lehtinen M, Laine S, Heinonen PK, et al. Serum C-reactive protein determination in acute pelvic inflammatory disease. Am J Obstet Gynecol 154:158, 1986.

Phillips AJ, d'Ablaing G. Acute salpingitis subsequent to tubal ligation. Obstet Gynecol 67:55S, 1986.

Sweet RL, Blankfort-Doyle M, Robbie MO, Schacter J. The oc-currence of chlamydial and gonococcal salpingitis during the menstrual cycle. JAMA 255:2062, 1986.

Wølner-Hanssen P. Oral contraceptive use modifies the manifestations of pelvic inflammatory disease. Br J Obstet Gynaecol 93:619, 1986.

TUBO-OVARIAN ABSCESS

Eric D. Lichter, M.D.

A. Formation of a tubo-ovarian abscess is the end stage of unchecked salpingitis. It is usually the result of repetitive bouts of infection, with increasing lower abdominal pain, fever, and enlarging pelvic mass. Menstrual disorders, urinary symptoms, dyspareunia, and infertility are also prominent. Relevant risk factors include sexually transmitted disease and use of an intrauterine device.

B. Examine for unstable cardiovascular status and evidence of peritonitis or palpable pelvic mass. Undertake laboratory studies to clarify the diagnosis, such as complete blood count (CBC), differential, urinalysis, and cultures. Ultrasonography generally proves quite useful for diagnostic purposes, but it may be necessary to consider computer tomography or magnetic resonance imaging, if available. Intravenous urography may also be needed, especially if surgical intervention is contemplated. Oblique x-ray contrast views may prove especially valuable for determining whether the ureters have been displaced anteriorly or medially by the growing masses; this information may enable one to avert serious intraoperative ureteral injury.

C. Minimize the number of pelvic examinations to prevent bacteremia or intraperitoneal spillage. Treat the patient in stable condition by nonsurgical means at first, giving broad-spectrum antibiotics. Choose a combination of those capable of achieving therapeutic levels rapidly, able to penetrate into the abscess cavity, and effective against both anaerobic and aerobic organisms. Ascertain the effect by close observation over the ensuing 48 to 72 hours. If there is some response with no evidence of collapse, peritonitis, or sepsis, the regimen should be continued longer; periodically reassess for decreasing white blood count, sedimentation rate, and mass size. Surgical intervention is called for if there is no objective evidence of response or if the patient's condition worsens under this conservative program.

D. The most ominous event in the course of a tubo-ovarian abscess is rupture with gross intraperitoneal spillage of its contents. The resulting generalized peritonitis can be devastating. Spontaneous leakage preceding overt rupture can be recognized by progressively developing signs of pelvic peritonitis for which one must be especially attentive. Early diagnosis and operative intervention for drainage or extirpation are essential to avoid serious and even fatal consequences. A patient whose abscess ruptures requires intensive care, monitoring, and support as for septic shock (p 202).

E. Tubo-ovarian abscesses walled off in the cul-de-sac of Douglas occasionally point into the rectovaginal septum or posterior vaginal fornix. Under these circumstances, transvaginal colpotomy can prove to be a very utilitarian means for effecting drainage and allowing time to improve the patient's condition before having to proceed to a more elaborate and hazardous surgical operation (Fig. 1). When carrying out the colpotomy, be sure to open all loculations of the abscess, but try to avoid injuring the bowel in the vicinity. The time gained can be

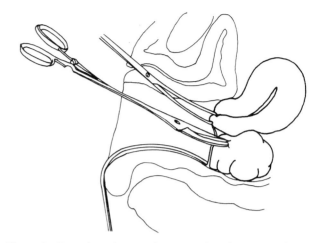

Figure 1 Posterior colpotomy for evacuation of a tubo-ovarian abscess occupying the cul-de-sac of Douglas and pointing into the posterior vaginal fornix. With the posterior vaginal wall well exposed and on tension, the abscess cavity is entered sharply for drainage.

used profitably to bring the infection under full control. Drainage is sometimes, but not often, so effective that a more definitive procedure may be obviated entirely.

F. The patient whose pelvic organs are so damaged by the chronic inflammatory process and tubo-ovarian abscesses is best served by bilateral salpingo-oophorectomy. If this is undertaken, it is usually done in conjunction with total hysterectomy as a standard and acceptable practice. However, if the patient is young, desirous of future pregnancy, and understands and accepts the risks and costs involved, one might consider leaving the uterus as a receptacle for a future donor oocyte or embryo procedure (p 276). Limited surgery might also be considered for women with a unilateral abscess in whom the opposite adnexa may be safely salvaged. For patients in precarious condition because of age, debilitation, sepsis, or shock, draining the abscesses transabdominally may suffice (p 36). Definitive surgery can be considered in the future, if needed, when the patient is better able to withstand the anesthesia and operation. Drainage should also be kept in mind as an option when it is found that surgical extirpation is technically too difficult because the patient's tissues are too inflamed to be dealt with safely.

References

Burnakis TG, Hildebrandt NB. Pelvic inflammatory disease: A review with emphasis on antimicrobial therapy. Rev Infect Dis 8:86, 1986.

Landers DV, Sweet RL. Current trends in the diagnosis and treatment of tuboovarian abscess. Am J Obstet Gynecol 151:1098, 1985.

Mahboubi S, Caro PA. Computed tomography in the evaluation of tubo-ovarian abscesses in children. J Comput Tomogr 10:67, 1986.

Stubbs RE, Monif GR. Ruptured tubo-ovarian abscess in pregnancy: Recovery of a penicillinase-producing strain of *Neisseria gonorrhoeae*. Sex Transm Dis 12:235, 1986.

PATIENT WITH SUSPICION OF PELVIC ABSCESS

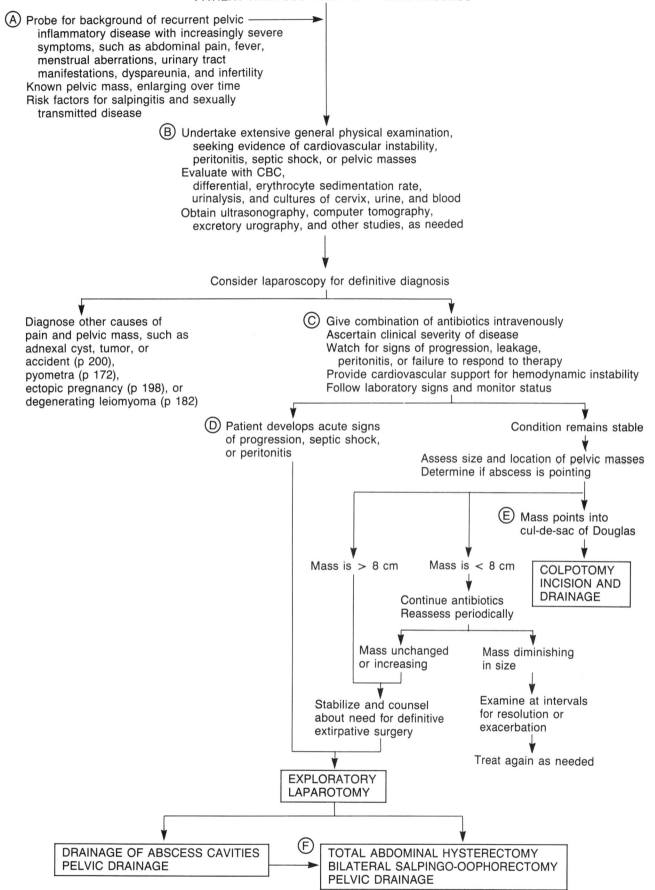

Ⓐ Probe for background of recurrent pelvic
inflammatory disease with increasingly severe
symptoms, such as abdominal pain, fever,
menstrual aberrations, urinary tract
manifestations, dyspareunia, and infertility
Known pelvic mass, enlarging over time
Risk factors for salpingitis and sexually
transmitted disease

Ⓑ Undertake extensive general physical examination,
seeking evidence of cardiovascular instability,
peritonitis, septic shock, or pelvic masses
Evaluate with CBC,
differential, erythrocyte sedimentation rate,
urinalysis, and cultures of cervix, urine, and blood
Obtain ultrasonography, computer tomography,
excretory urography, and other studies, as needed

Consider laparoscopy for definitive diagnosis

Diagnose other causes of
pain and pelvic mass, such as
adnexal cyst, tumor, or
accident (p 200),
pyometra (p 172),
ectopic pregnancy (p 198), or
degenerating leiomyoma (p 182)

Ⓒ Give combination of antibiotics intravenously
Ascertain clinical severity of disease
Watch for signs of progression, leakage,
peritonitis, or failure to respond to therapy
Provide cardiovascular support for hemodynamic instability
Follow laboratory signs and monitor status

Ⓓ Patient develops acute signs
of progression, septic shock,
or peritonitis

Condition remains stable

Assess size and location of pelvic masses
Determine if abscess is pointing

Ⓔ Mass points into
cul-de-sac of Douglas

Mass is > 8 cm

Mass is < 8 cm

COLPOTOMY
INCISION AND
DRAINAGE

Continue antibiotics
Reassess periodically

Mass unchanged
or increasing

Mass diminishing
in size

Stabilize and counsel
about need for definitive
extirpative surgery

Examine at intervals
for resolution or
exacerbation

Treat again as needed

EXPLORATORY
LAPAROTOMY

DRAINAGE OF ABSCESS CAVITIES
PELVIC DRAINAGE

Ⓕ TOTAL ABDOMINAL HYSTERECTOMY
BILATERAL SALPINGO-OOPHORECTOMY
PELVIC DRAINAGE

ENDOMETRIOSIS

David G. Diaz, M.D.
Machelle M. Seibel, M.D.

A. The ectopic foci of endometrial glands and stroma of endometriosis generally involve the tubes, ovaries, and pelvic peritoneum, but they can appear in many other sites. The classic presenting complaint is progressive comenstrual dysmenorrhea. Endometriosis is commonly associated with and a probable cause of infertility (p 82), even with minimal disease. Other symptoms may also be referable to distant sites, such as lung (hemoptysis), bladder (hematuria), or bowel (melena or hematochezia). Be especially alert to the cyclic relationship of the patient's symptoms to her menstruation.

B. Examine the patient carefully, during menstruation if possible, for typical signs of endometriosis, including focal or diffuse tenderness, discrete adnexal masses, and utero-sacral and cul-de-sac nodularity. An endometrioma that leaks its contents into the peritoneal cavity can be expected to produce abdominal signs indistinguishable from those of acute peritonitis. It is inappropriate to consider a diagnosis of endometriosis based solely on symptoms or physical findings to be definitive.

C. The woman with a large adnexal mass generally requires exploratory surgery for both diagnosis and extirpation (p 184). For those with less pressing manifestations, before undertaking a management program involving a long and costly course of drug therapy, it is essential to verify the diagnosis. This is accomplished by direct visualization under laparoscopy. Lesions vary from superficial powder burns to huge endometriomas, usually with considerable dense reactive adhesion formation. Biopsy sampling of representative foci, if feasible, is especially valuable for making a definitive histologic diagnosis. Take the opportunity of the laparoscopy to stage the extent of the disease: Stages I and II, superficial lesions only; Stage III, associated scarring or mild adhesions; Stage IV, endometriomas, dense adhesions, and bowel, bladder, or distant lesions.

D. Patients with endometriosis who desire to become pregnant can be observed expectantly or, if symptoms warrant, managed just with analgesic drugs. In others, pharmacologic suppression of ovulatory function, while not always completely effective, may prove beneficial. Danazol inhibits pituitary gonadotropin release to induce pseudomenopause, yielding anovulation, amenorrhea, and, most importantly, endometrial atrophy. Aside from its cost, danazol has androgenic effects, including acne, hair growth, and voice changes as well as hot flashes and mucosal atrophy. It is contraindicated in pregnancy and in women with liver, heart, or renal disorders. A regimen of up to 800 mg daily for three to 12 months is generally most effective. Alternatively, pseudopregnancy with continuous use of combined estrogen and progestin (in the form of oral contraceptives) over a period of six to 12 months may also be beneficial, although side effects occur frequently, especially nausea, mastodynia, and fluid retention.

E. More advanced endometriosis may respond somewhat to danazol, but it is unlikely to respond completely. Surgery is generally needed in due course. Preliminary danazol therapy for three or more months may make the lesions more amenable to surgery, thereby facilitating the procedure and perhaps even making a conservative operation feasible in cases in which it would not otherwise be technically possible. The objective here is to eradicate disease foci and restore the normal spatial relations of tubes and ovaries. This is done by lysing adhesions carefully, ablating endometriotic foci, and suspending the uterus. Presacral neurectomy is sometimes also done for pain relief, recognizing its limitations. Avoid suppressive hormonal medication postoperatively to give the patient the opportunity to conceive during a time when her chances are optimal.

F. Patients with extensive or debilitating endometriosis are best served by bilateral adnexectomy, usually done in conjunction with hysterectomy. This is particularly so for women in whom antecedent medical suppression trials have failed. Preoperative danazol makes the operation technically easier and is well worth trying if time permits.

References

American Fertility Society. Classification of endometriosis. Fertil Steril 32:633, 1979.

Barbieri R, Evans S, Kistner RW. Danazol in the treatment of endometriosis: Analysis of 100 cases with a 4-year follow-up. Fertil Steril 37:737, 1982.

Management of Endometriosis. Technical Bulletin No. 85. Washington: American College of Obstetricians and Gynecologists, 1985.

Seibel MM. Minimal pelvic endometriosis and infertility. Semin Reprod Endocrinol 3:4, 1985.

Seibel MM, Berger MJ, Weinstein F, Taymor ML. The effectiveness of danazol on subsequent fertility in minimal endometriosis. Fertil Steril 37:310, 1982.

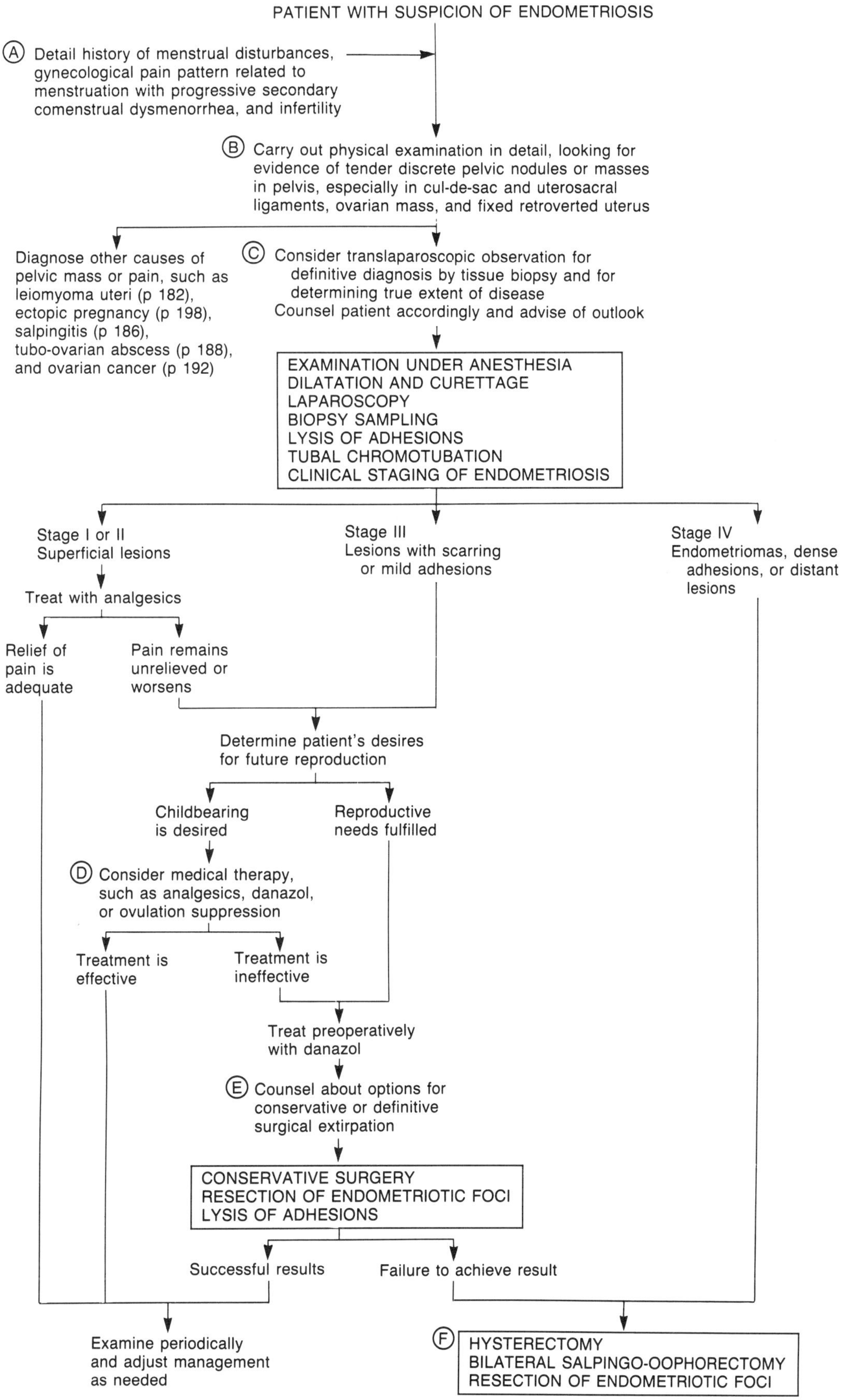

PATIENT WITH SUSPICION OF ENDOMETRIOSIS

Ⓐ Detail history of menstrual disturbances, gynecological pain pattern related to menstruation with progressive secondary comenstrual dysmenorrhea, and infertility

Ⓑ Carry out physical examination in detail, looking for evidence of tender discrete pelvic nodules or masses in pelvis, especially in cul-de-sac and uterosacral ligaments, ovarian mass, and fixed retroverted uterus

Diagnose other causes of pelvic mass or pain, such as leiomyoma uteri (p 182), ectopic pregnancy (p 198), salpingitis (p 186), tubo-ovarian abscess (p 188), and ovarian cancer (p 192)

Ⓒ Consider translaparoscopic observation for definitive diagnosis by tissue biopsy and for determining true extent of disease
Counsel patient accordingly and advise of outlook

EXAMINATION UNDER ANESTHESIA
DILATATION AND CURETTAGE
LAPAROSCOPY
BIOPSY SAMPLING
LYSIS OF ADHESIONS
TUBAL CHROMOTUBATION
CLINICAL STAGING OF ENDOMETRIOSIS

Stage I or II
Superficial lesions

Stage III
Lesions with scarring or mild adhesions

Stage IV
Endometriomas, dense adhesions, or distant lesions

Treat with analgesics

Relief of pain is adequate

Pain remains unrelieved or worsens

Determine patient's desires for future reproduction

Childbearing is desired

Reproductive needs fulfilled

Ⓓ Consider medical therapy, such as analgesics, danazol, or ovulation suppression

Treatment is effective

Treatment is ineffective

Treat preoperatively with danazol

Ⓔ Counsel about options for conservative or definitive surgical extirpation

CONSERVATIVE SURGERY
RESECTION OF ENDOMETRIOTIC FOCI
LYSIS OF ADHESIONS

Successful results

Failure to achieve result

Examine periodically and adjust management as needed

Ⓕ HYSTERECTOMY
BILATERAL SALPINGO-OOPHORECTOMY
RESECTION OF ENDOMETRIOTIC FOCI

OVARIAN CANCER

Jonathan M. Niloff, M.D.

A. Although ovarian cancer is not the most frequent cancer among women, it is the most devastating because it tends to be clinically silent, that is, free of symptoms, until it has already disseminated intra-abdominally. The best prognosis applies to lesions disclosed incidentally at routine annual gynecological examinations. Be alert to increasing abdominal girth (p 54). Finding a pelvic mass or ascites should raise suspicion for ovarian cancer. Palpating an ovary in a postmenopausal woman is an important observation; it demands surgical exploration.

B. Conduct a thorough examination, seeking evidence of ascites, masses, lymphadenopathy, and distant metastases. Preoperative evaluation should include complete blood count (CBC), blood chemistry determinations, and chest radiography. If a pleural effusion is observed, perform a thoracentesis and send the fluid for cytologic evaluation. Ultrasonography is often helpful in determining the origin of a pelvic mass. A barium enema contrast study will rule out a primary colon neoplasm.

C. The diagnosis is made by laparotomy in all cases. Laparoscopy may precede the laparotomy in young women when the diagnosis is in question, but care must be taken to avoid spilling the neoplastic contents of an intact tumor into the peritoneal cavity. Before any manipulations, obtain a sample of ascitic fluid; in the absence of ascites, instill saline and reaspirate for peritoneal washings. These are necessary for proper assessment. Then explore the abdominal cavity systematically, documenting the extent of disease in detail. Note especially the omentum, mesenteric root, serosal surfaces, and undersurfaces of the diaphragm for metastatic seedings, and palpate the aortic lymph nodes up to the renal axis.

D. Conservation of fertility is possible in young women with Stage IA borderline or well differentiated tumor confined entirely to one ovary. Obtain frozen section histology during surgery. If the histologic diagnosis is uncertain and the patient desires to retain her fertility, perform the conservative procedure while realizing that another laparotomy may be necessary when the permanent microscopic sections are fully evaluated. This must be discussed with the patient beforehand. The conservative operation consists of a unilateral salpingo-oophorectomy and biopsy of the contralateral ovary and the omentum. Adjuvant therapy is not required for patients with well differentiated Stage IA tumors or with borderline tumors of any stage.

E. Sample the aortic lymph nodes in cases with Stage I ovarian carcinoma that proves to be poorly differentiated. Finding metastatic cancer in the lymph nodes reclassifies a disease as Stage IIIB.

F. The standard operation for Stage I ovarian cancer entails total abdominal hysterectomy, bilateral salpingo-oophorectomy, and omental biopsy. With Stage I or IIA tumors, any area of adhesion to adjacent structures should be biopsied to disclose a site of contiguous tumor spread.

G. Response to chemotherapy and survival is improved if it is possible to accomplish leaving minimal residual tumor after surgery. Whenever feasible, therefore, every effort should be made to leave no single tumor mass greater than 2 cm in the peritoneal cavity. It is even more preferable to have no visible residual disease at all. If there is a large mass that is technically not possible to resect, however, do not persist with an aggressive surgical effort because the prognosis is related to the single largest residual mass. Bear in mind that the pelvic dissection may be facilitated by a retroperitoneal approach.

H. Response rates with combination chemotherapy are superior to those achievable with single agents. However, improvements in survival with combination regimens are almost exclusively limited to individuals with minimal residual tumor remaining after cytoreductive surgery. Combinations including cisplatinum are given to such patients. Symptomatic patients with large residual disease may also be effectively palliated by these chemotherapeutic combinations. Asymptomatic patients with large residual disease may be treated with a single oral alkylating agent and thus be spared the morbidity of the combination regimens.

I. Consider whole abdominal radiation therapy (Fig. 1) for patients with advanced disease who have no gross residual tumor after surgery. Patients with poorly differentiated tumors are better treated with combination chemotherapy.

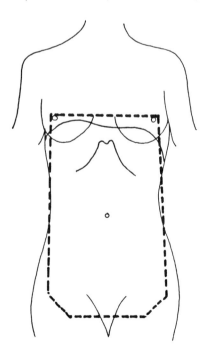

Figure 1 Radiation therapy field for providing total abdominal irradiation for advanced (Stage III) ovarian carcinoma.

PATIENT WITH SUSPICION OF OVARIAN CANCER

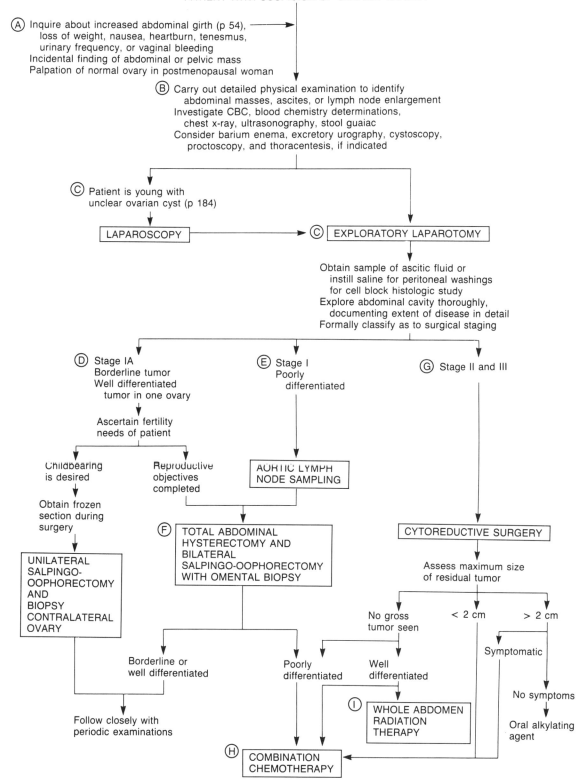

Ⓐ Inquire about increased abdominal girth (p 54),
    loss of weight, nausea, heartburn, tenesmus,
    urinary frequency, or vaginal bleeding
  Incidental finding of abdominal or pelvic mass
  Palpation of normal ovary in postmenopausal woman

Ⓑ Carry out detailed physical examination to identify
    abdominal masses, ascites, or lymph node enlargement
  Investigate CBC, blood chemistry determinations,
    chest x-ray, ultrasonography, stool guaiac
  Consider barium enema, excretory urography, cystoscopy,
    proctoscopy, and thoracentesis, if indicated

Ⓒ Patient is young with
    unclear ovarian cyst (p 184)

LAPAROSCOPY

Ⓒ EXPLORATORY LAPAROTOMY

Obtain sample of ascitic fluid or
  instill saline for peritoneal washings
  for cell block histologic study
Explore abdominal cavity thoroughly,
  documenting extent of disease in detail
Formally classify as to surgical staging

Ⓓ Stage IA
  Borderline tumor
  Well differentiated
    tumor in one ovary

Ⓔ Stage I
  Poorly
  differentiated

Ⓖ Stage II and III

Ascertain fertility
  needs of patient

Childbearing
is desired

Reproductive
objectives
completed

AORTIC LYMPH
NODE SAMPLING

Obtain frozen
section during
surgery

Ⓕ TOTAL ABDOMINAL
  HYSTERECTOMY AND
  BILATERAL
  SALPINGO-OOPHORECTOMY
  WITH OMENTAL BIOPSY

CYTOREDUCTIVE SURGERY

UNILATERAL
SALPINGO-
OOPHORECTOMY
AND
BIOPSY
CONTRALATERAL
OVARY

Assess maximum size
of residual tumor

No gross
tumor seen

< 2 cm

> 2 cm

Borderline or
well differentiated

Poorly
differentiated

Well
differentiated

Symptomatic

No symptoms

Follow closely with
periodic examinations

Ⓘ WHOLE ABDOMEN
  RADIATION
  THERAPY

Oral alkylating
agent

Ⓗ COMBINATION
  CHEMOTHERAPY

References

Barber HRK. Ovarian cancer: Diagnosis and management. Am J Obstet Gynecol 150:910, 1984.

Heintz APM, Hacker NF, Berek JS, et al. Cytoreductive surgery in ovarian carcinoma: Feasibility and morbidity. Obstet Gynecol 67:783, 1986.

Piver MS. Ovarian carcinoma: A decade of progress. Cancer 54:2706, 1984.

Richardson GS, Scully RE, Nikrui N, Nelson JH Jr. Common epithelial cancer of the ovary. N Engl J Med 312:415, 1985.

Schray M, Martinez A, Cox R, Ballon S. Radiotherapy in epithelial ovarian cancer: Analysis of prognostic factors based on long-term experience. Obstet Gynecol 62:373, 1983.

TUBAL CARCINOMA

Jonathan M. Niloff, M.D.

A. Seldom is the diagnosis of fallopian tube carcinoma made or even suspected before it is encountered intraoperatively. This is so because the condition is rare, seldom considered, easily mistaken for a number of other more common conditions, and its presenting manifestations tend to be nonspecific. The most common presenting symptoms are pelvic pain and abnormal vaginal bleeding; its only differentiating feature is a watery vaginal discharge often admixed with blood, appearing early in its course. The tubal distension accompanying the watery discharge yields a palpable structure similar to a hydrosalpinx, for which it can be readily mistaken. The most common physical finding is a palpable adnexal mass usually encountered unexpectedly during a gynecological examination. Ascites may be the first presenting symptom, analogous to the clinical pattern of ovarian cancer (p 192). While primary tubal carcinoma is usually papillary in nature, other forms do occur, including mixed mesodermal, sarcomatous, and gestational trophoblastic varieties. Most tubal malignancies are metastatic lesions from other abdominal primary sites. Tubal cancer tends to be particularly malignant, perhaps related more to its late diagnosis than any inherently aggressive trait.

B. Examine the patient carefully, looking for evidence of intraperitoneal or distal spread. The preoperative evaluation includes a complete blood count (CBC), blood chemistries, urinalysis, stool guaiac, and a chest radiograph. Ultrasonographic scanning may clarify the origin of a pelvic mass, perhaps distinguishing it from an ovarian tumor, and a barium enema excludes a primary neoplasm of the colon. Cervical cytology (p 12) may suggest a tubal carcinoma, but it is unsatisfactory as a screening or diagnostic technique for this tumor.

C. The diagnosis is usually first made during or following surgery. Because of its rarity, there is as yet no official staging system for tubal carcinoma. However, since fallopian tube carcinoma spreads in a transperitoneal fashion similar to ovarian cancer, it is reasonable to perform a comparable surgical staging procedure (p 192). This includes obtaining peritoneal washings immediately on opening the abdomen and doing an omental biopsy. Carefully explore the abdomen for tumor spread, including palpation of the diaphragm, colonic gutters, the root of the mesentery, and the splenic hilum, and biopsy any

suspicious lesions. Undertake a total abdominal hysterectomy and bilateral salpingo-oophorectomy, if feasible. Consider aortic lymph node sampling for patients with tumor limited to one or both adnexa. Carcinoma in situ of the fallopian tube is a diagnosis usually made by histologic examination of specimens of tubal segments removed at the time of a sterilization procedure. It is also best treated by total abdominal hysterectomy and bilateral salpingo-oophorectomy.

D. Primary carcinoma of the fallopian tube is so rare that large series are not available for review. However, the natural history of this tumor appears to be similar to that of ovarian cancer. The limited experience suggests a beneficial role for cytoreductive surgery. Long-term survival is influenced inversely by the size of the largest residual tumor remaining in the peritoneal cavity after surgery. Best results are achievable if no gross tumor is left, but one should strive, if possible, to leave no single tumor mass greater than 2 cm.

E. All patients with invasive tubal carcinoma (except those with extraperitoneal metastases) should receive adjuvant therapy, including those with tumors limited to the adnexa. Give chemotherapy to patients who have any grossly visible residual tumor remaining after primary cytoreductive surgery. If no gross residual tumor is present, one can administer either chemotherapy or radiation therapy. It remains to be determined whether one of these modalities is superior to the other. The transcoelomic spread of tubal carcinomas means that whole abdomen radiation is needed if this modality is chosen.

References

Amendola BE, LaRouere J, Amendola MA, et al. Adenocarcinoma of the fallopian tube. Surg Gynecol Obstet 157:223, 1983.

Denham JW, Maclennan KA. The management of primary carcinoma of the fallopian tube: Experience of 40 cases. Cancer 53:166, 1984.

Eddy GL, Copeland LJ, Gershenson DM, et al. Fallopian tube carcinoma. Obstet Gynecol 64:546, 1984.

Podratz KC, Podczaski ES, Gaffey TA, et al. Primary carcinoma of the fallopian tube. Am J Obstet Gynecol 154:1319, 1986.

PATIENT WITH SUSPICION OF TUBAL CANCER

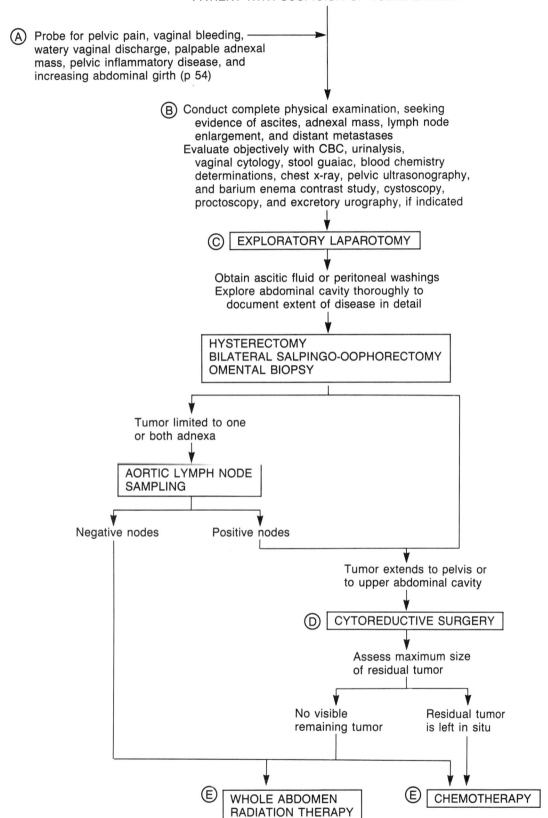

Ⓐ Probe for pelvic pain, vaginal bleeding,
watery vaginal discharge, palpable adnexal
mass, pelvic inflammatory disease, and
increasing abdominal girth (p 54)

Ⓑ Conduct complete physical examination, seeking
evidence of ascites, adnexal mass, lymph node
enlargement, and distant metastases
Evaluate objectively with CBC, urinalysis,
vaginal cytology, stool guaiac, blood chemistry
determinations, chest x-ray, pelvic ultrasonography,
and barium enema contrast study, cystoscopy,
proctoscopy, and excretory urography, if indicated

Ⓒ EXPLORATORY LAPAROTOMY

Obtain ascitic fluid or peritoneal washings
Explore abdominal cavity thoroughly to
document extent of disease in detail

HYSTERECTOMY
BILATERAL SALPINGO-OOPHORECTOMY
OMENTAL BIOPSY

Tumor limited to one
or both adnexa

AORTIC LYMPH NODE
SAMPLING

Negative nodes   Positive nodes

Tumor extends to pelvis or
to upper abdominal cavity

Ⓓ CYTOREDUCTIVE SURGERY

Assess maximum size
of residual tumor

No visible   Residual tumor
remaining tumor   is left in situ

Ⓔ WHOLE ABDOMEN   Ⓔ CHEMOTHERAPY
RADIATION THERAPY

INCOMPLETE ABORTION

David G. Diaz, M.D.

A. Incomplete abortion refers to the spontaneous loss of pregnancy (p 74) prior to 20 weeks' gestational age in which a portion of the products of conception has been expelled while additional tissue still remains in the uterus. The event is heralded clinically by vaginal bleeding and crampy pain due to uterine contractions. Typically, the evacuation process is preceded by cervical dilatation and tissue is passed in due course. The important conditions to be differentiated are continuing pregnancy (the bleeding and cramping merely representing those of a threatened abortion) and ectopic pregnancy (the tissue being a decidual cast rather than fetal or placental fragments). To intervene aggressively in the former case will inadvertently interrupt an otherwise intact and potentially salvageable conception; to fail to do so in the latter risks intra-abdominal hemorrhage and imperils health and life. Up to half the pregnancies among patients with first trimester vaginal bleeding may progress to viability. Bear this in mind as a guide to management. Be alert to a history of amenorrhea, perhaps with accompanying manifestations of pregnancy, such as breast fullness and tenderness, abdominal bloating, altered appetite, nausea, vomiting, constipation, and urinary frequency.

B. Perform a complete physical examination, including a detailed pelvic survey. Note especially cervical congestion and softening as well as uterine enlargement and softening. A uterine size incompatible with the growth of gestation over the period of time that has elapsed since the last menstrual period makes incomplete abortion a likely diagnosis, especially if the uterus was previously found to be larger (and compatible with dates) and is now smaller. For more confirmation, search for any tissue that may have been passed. Examine it under good illumination after floatation in saline to visualize villi using magnification. The histologic finding of chorionic villi or a gestational sac in the tissue establishes the diagnosis definitively. A possible dilemma arises in differentiating between incomplete and complete abortion (in the latter, the uterus evacuates itself completely). Whereas evacuation of the uterus by curettage is essential following an incomplete abortion, it is not after a complete abortion, although it is common practice to assume all spontaneous abortions to be incomplete, and therefore warranting curettage, in order to avoid late bleeding or infection from retained material (see E).

C. A diligent search should be made by ultrasonography to discern whether the uterine cavity is empty. A gestational sac should be detectable at six weeks' gestation and fetal cardiac activity by seven to eight weeks. Decidual reaction can be confused with a gestational sac. Look for the "double ring" sign, which can be visualized as early as eight weeks. The outer concentric ring represents the decidual lining and the inner ring, the accompanying gestational sac.

D. Serial determinations of beta-subunit human chorionic gonadotropin (hCG) levels are useful when it is necessary to ascertain clinically whether a given gestation is salvageable. This applies especially to a gravida with threatened abortion who desires to retain her pregnancy. A normal level (consistent with gestational duration) that rises as expected facilitates favorable prognostication. Missed abortion (fetal death unaccompanied by spontaneous abortion) or complete abortion is typically associated with falling hCG levels. The hCG titer ordinarily doubles about every 2.2 days on average in early pregnancy; serial titers that fail to show a rate of rise of at least two-thirds every 48 hours signal a poor outcome.

E. Following spontaneous abortion, many clinicians prefer to subject all patients to uterine evacuation by suction curettage. This practice has the advantage of decreasing the incidence of further bleeding and averting the possibility of endometritis for both cases of incomplete abortion and those assumed to be complete but in fact are not. Alternatively, the sensitive beta-subunit hCG assay may be substituted as a more conservative approach for managing these women. A baseline assay is obtained and repeated every 48 hours. Those with falling titers can be observed expectantly, while curettage is reserved for those with unchanged levels.

F. Spontaneous abortion may potentially sensitize an Rh-negative woman to the fetal Rh factor, risking erythroblastosis fetalis in subsequent pregnancies. Rh immunoglobulin should, therefore, be administered following abortion. Give a dose of 50 μg to unsensitized Rh-negative patients who abort prior to 12 weeks; a 300 μg dose is needed after 12 weeks' gestation.

References

Bernard KG, Cooperberg PL. Sonographic differentiation between blighted ovum and early viable pregnancy. Am J Roentgenol 144:597, 1985.

Farrell RG, Stonington DT, et al. Incomplete and inevitable abortion: Treatment by suction curettage in the emergency department. Ann Emerg Med 11:652, 1982.

Laferla JJ. Spontaneous abortion. Clin Obstet Gynaecol 13:105, 1986.

Lindahl B, Ahlgrem M. Identification of chorionic villi in abortion specimens. Obstet Gynecol 67:79, 1986.

PATIENT WITH VAGINAL BLEEDING AND PAIN

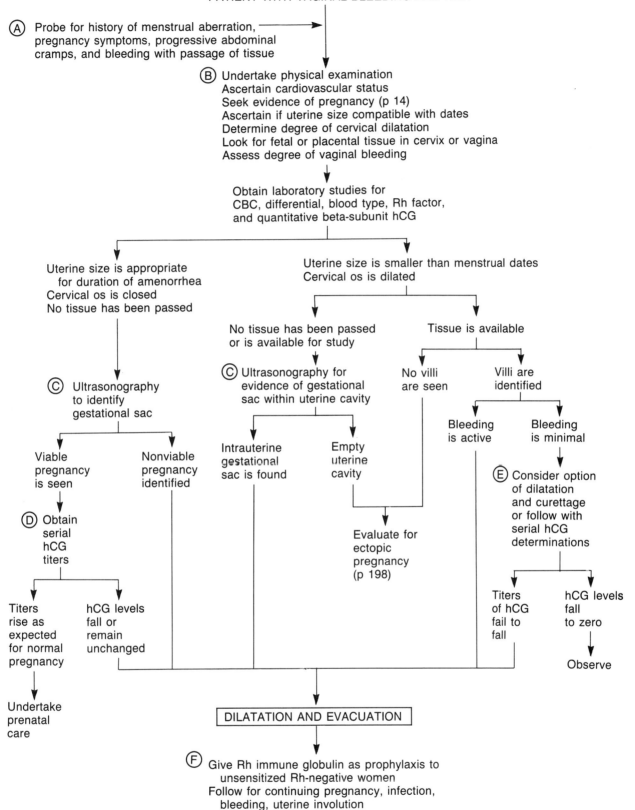

Ⓐ Probe for history of menstrual aberration, pregnancy symptoms, progressive abdominal cramps, and bleeding with passage of tissue

Ⓑ Undertake physical examination
Ascertain cardiovascular status
Seek evidence of pregnancy (p 14)
Ascertain if uterine size compatible with dates
Determine degree of cervical dilatation
Look for fetal or placental tissue in cervix or vagina
Assess degree of vaginal bleeding

Obtain laboratory studies for
CBC, differential, blood type, Rh factor,
and quantitative beta-subunit hCG

Uterine size is appropriate
for duration of amenorrhea
Cervical os is closed
No tissue has been passed

Uterine size is smaller than menstrual dates
Cervical os is dilated

No tissue has been passed
or is available for study

Tissue is available

Ⓒ Ultrasonography
to identify
gestational sac

Ⓒ Ultrasonography for
evidence of gestational
sac within uterine cavity

No villi
are seen

Villi are
identified

Viable
pregnancy
is seen

Nonviable
pregnancy
identified

Intrauterine
gestational
sac is found

Empty
uterine
cavity

Bleeding
is active

Bleeding
is minimal

Ⓓ Obtain
serial
hCG
titers

Ⓔ Consider option
of dilatation
and curettage
or follow with
serial hCG
determinations

Evaluate for
ectopic
pregnancy
(p 198)

Titers
rise as
expected
for normal
pregnancy

hCG levels
fall or
remain
unchanged

Titers
of hCG
fail to
fall

hCG levels
fall
to zero

Observe

Undertake
prenatal
care

DILATATION AND EVACUATION

Ⓕ Give Rh immune globulin as prophylaxis to
unsensitized Rh-negative women
Follow for continuing pregnancy, infection,
bleeding, uterine involution

TUBAL PREGNANCY

Alexander M. Dlugi, M.D.

A. The classic triad of lower abdominal pain, menstrual aberration, and adnexal mass occurs frequently in patients with ectopic pregnancy, but in its earlier stages the symptoms and findings may be very subtle and misleading. Patients with tubal damage are at risk, including those with a history of tubal surgery, endometriosis, pelvic inflammatory disease, or use of an intrauterine contraceptive device. Symptoms of dizziness, orthostatic changes, shoulder pain, and tenesmus are encountered and serve as warning flags.

B. The physical examination is essential for diagnosis. Examine for cardiovascular instability and evidence of intra-abdominal bleeding or peritonitis. Look for cervical motion tenderness, a tender adnexal mass, or bulging in the posterior vaginal fornix. Obtain a complete blood count (CBC), serial hematocrit levels, and a quantitative

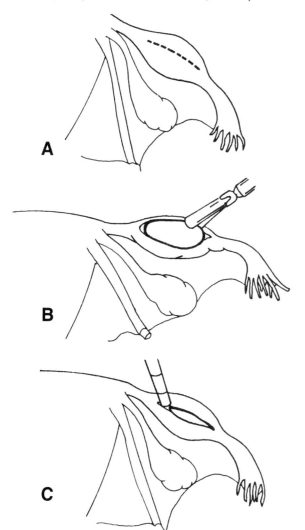

Figure 1 Translaparoscopic salpingostomy for unruptured ectopic pregnancy. Incision (broken line) is made over gestational sac (A); sac and surrounding clots are extracted (B); and bleeding points coagulated for hemostasis (C).

beta-subunit human chorionic gonadotropin (hCG) assay. A negative serum beta-subunit hCG excludes the diagnosis. Ultrasonography is very useful for differentiating a complication of intrauterine pregnancy. It is critical for each laboratory to determine is own discriminatory zone of serum beta-subunit hCG level (usually 6,000 mIU per milliliter), above which an intrauterine pregnancy should be detectable by ultrasonography.

C. Visualizing an intrauterine fetal heart beat is diagnostic of intrauterine pregnancy; a gestational sac, particularly with a double ring sign, is also presumptive evidence, although an intrauterine blood clot or even thickened decidual tissue can be misleading. Follow-up ultrasonography is indicated if the findings are equivocal or inconsistent with the course.

D. When the index of suspicion is high, a positive culdocentesis may expedite surgical intervention. A negative culdocentesis does not rule out ectopic pregnancy and a positive result does not guarantee the diagnosis. Any intraperitoneal bleeding process can yield a collection of nonclotting blood (previously clotted and now lysed) in the cul-de-sac. It does not necessarily mean that laparotomy is indicated at once, particularly in the stable patient. Diagnostic laparoscopy is the appropriate next step in order to exclude the possibility of a ruptured hemorrhagic ovarian cyst (or other transient bleeding process) and to afford one the opportunity to consider translaparoscopic surgery.

E. Because the beta-subunit hCG titer is expected to double approximately every 48 to 72 hours under normal circumstances, it is reasonable to obtain serial levels every two to three days in the clinically stable patient. When the hCG level rises above the discriminatory level, obtain ultrasonography to document the presence or absence of an intrauterine pregnancy.

F. Falling serial beta-subunit hCG levels may signify that a tubal abortion has occurred. If the patient remains stable and the hCG continues to fall to undetectable levels, these patients can be managed expectantly. This conservative approach can avert surgery in some patients.

G. Beta-subunit hCG levels that fail to double or that plateau over a 72-hour period raise concern. It would be unusual to base a decision to proceed with surgical intervention in the clinically stable patient on just two hCG values; it ordinarily requires at least three (and as many as five) to be confident about interpreting clinical significance and translating it into action.

H. An intact ampullary ectopic pregnancy that is less than 3 cm in diameter may sometimes be safely removable via translaparoscopic linear salpingostomy (Fig. 1) by an experienced operative laparoscopist (p 240). Larger gestations and those located in the isthmic segment of the tube are best treated by partial salpingectomy. This is usually accomplished by laparotomy. Translaparoscopic salpingectomy techniques have been developed for par-

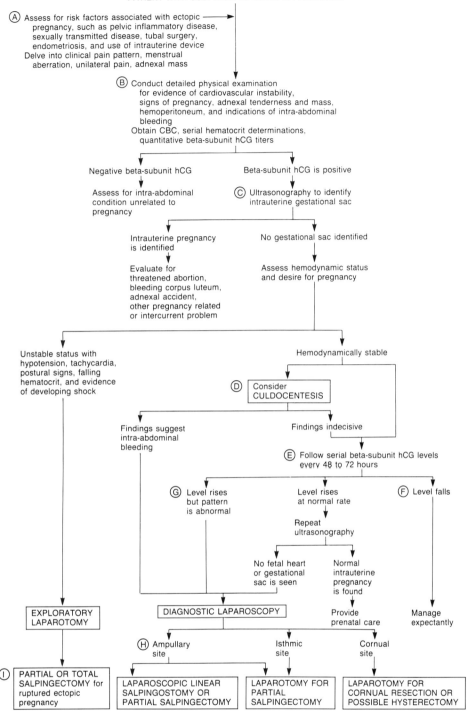

PATIENT WITH SUSPICION OF ECTOPIC PREGNANCY

Ⓐ Assess for risk factors associated with ectopic
   pregnancy, such as pelvic inflammatory disease,
   sexually transmitted disease, tubal surgery,
   endometriosis, and use of intrauterine device
   Delve into clinical pain pattern, menstrual
   aberration, unilateral pain, adnexal mass

Ⓑ Conduct detailed physical examination
   for evidence of cardiovascular instability,
   signs of pregnancy, adnexal tenderness and mass,
   hemoperitoneum, and indications of intra-abdominal
   bleeding
   Obtain CBC, serial hematocrit determinations,
   quantitative beta-subunit hCG titers

Negative beta-subunit hCG   Beta-subunit hCG is positive

Assess for intra-abdominal   Ⓒ Ultrasonography to identify
condition unrelated to   intrauterine gestational sac
pregnancy

Intrauterine pregnancy   No gestational sac identified
is identified

Evaluate for   Assess hemodynamic status
threatened abortion,   and desire for pregnancy
bleeding corpus luteum,
adnexal accident,
other pregnancy related
or intercurrent problem

Unstable status with   Hemodynamically stable
hypotension, tachycardia,
postural signs, falling   Ⓓ Consider
hematocrit, and evidence   CULDOCENTESIS
of developing shock

Findings suggest   Findings indecisive
intra-abdominal
bleeding   Ⓔ Follow serial beta-subunit hCG levels
                         every 48 to 72 hours

Ⓖ Level rises   Level rises   Ⓕ Level falls
but pattern   at normal rate
is abnormal
                   Repeat
                   ultrasonography

              No fetal heart   Normal
              or gestational   intrauterine
              sac is seen   pregnancy
                                is found

EXPLORATORY   DIAGNOSTIC LAPAROSCOPY   Provide   Manage
LAPAROTOMY   prenatal   expectantly
                                          care

                 Ⓗ Ampullary   Isthmic   Cornual
                   site   site   site

Ⓘ PARTIAL OR TOTAL   LAPAROSCOPIC LINEAR   LAPAROTOMY FOR   LAPAROTOMY FOR
SALPINGECTOMY for   SALPINGOSTOMY OR   PARTIAL   CORNUAL RESECTION OR
ruptured ectopic   PARTIAL SALPINGECTOMY SALPINGECTOMY   POSSIBLE HYSTERECTOMY
pregnancy

tial salpingectomy, but they require special skills, training, and equipment.

I. Conservation of the fallopian tube is possible even in the face of a grossly ruptured ectopic pregnancy. Hemostasis must be secured first in the interest of the patient's well-being. If feasible, use soft clamps to avoid irreversible damage that would interdict any attempt to salvage the tube. The damaged portion of tube can then be carefully inspected and excised. Postpone corrective surgery if the patient's condition is unstable. Complete destruction of the tube obviously warrants total salpingectomy.

References

Batzer FR, Corson SL. Diagnostic techniques used for ectopic pregnancy. J Reprod Med 31:86, 1986.

DeCherney AH, Maheaux R. Modern management of tubal pregnancy. Curr Probl Obstet Gynecol 9:15, 1983.

Murphy AA. Operative laparoscopy. Fertil Steril 47:1, 1987.

Peterson HB. Extratubal ectopic pregnancies. J Reprod Med 31:108, 1986.

Romero R, Kadar N, Copel JA, et al. The value of serial human chorionic gonadotropin testing as a diagnostic tool in ectopic pregnancy. Am J Obstet Gynecol 155:392, 1986.

ADNEXAL TORSION

Eric D. Lichter, M.D.

A. Torsion of the adnexal structures is an uncommon, but important, gynecological problem encountered both in children and in adults during their reproductive years. It is one of the causes of acute abdominal pain that must be considered in the differential diagnosis (p 52). Torsion usually involves the entire adnexa, but it may affect just the tube, the ovary, or a paraovarian cyst. Ordinarily, the inciting factor is a cyst or tumor, although otherwise normal adnexa may also be inexplicably affected. An essential component in the mechanism of twisting is the free mobility of the tissues; if fixed by inflammatory reaction or adhesions, torsion should not be possible, yet hydrosalpinx and even pyosalpinx may twist, albeit very rarely. Adnexal torsion occurs more frequently on the right side than the left; this is explained perhaps by the protective support afforded by the adjacent sigmoid colon and the relatively shorter and more fixed infundibulopelvic ligament on the left. The patient who is known to have an adnexal mass (p 184) is clearly at risk, but the condition nearly always arises in patients in whom there is no such prior knowledge. The pattern of the unilateral (rarely bilateral) pain is characteristic with irregularly intermittent, recurrent, acute episodes, which are often (but not always) progressive. Periodicity may vary from hours to days (and even weeks or months), contrasting with the more rapidly recurrent and regular peristaltic time sequence of obstructed bowel, ureter, or gall duct. Onset is generally sudden without any apparent precipitating factor, such as trauma or exertion. Nausea and vomiting are common, limited almost exclusively to the intervals when the pain is most intense

Figure 1 Characteristic finding of an adnexal cyst undergoing axial torsion of its stalk, usually with thrombosis of the draining vessels. Untwisting the pedicle prior to clamping it proximally risks dislodging a clot and causing serious embolization.

(probably on a peritoneal reflex basis). With infarction, the pain becomes more intense and constant, and signs of an acute surgical abdomen develop. Early diagnosis is essential to minimize tissue damage (thereby optimizing the possibility for salvaging the adnexa) and avoid gangrene and the resulting shock state.

B. Astute physical examination is critical for diagnosis. Palpate carefully for an abdominal mass arising from the pelvis. Its lower pole is more readily discernible by bimanual pelvic examination. Note its size, consistency, tenderness, and mobility. Investigate with laboratory studies to differentiate ectopic pregnancy (p 198), pelvic inflammatory disease (p 186), acute appendicitis, urolithiasis, and ruptured diverticulum or ovarian cyst; include complete blood count (CBC), differential, erythrocyte sedimentation rate, urinalysis, pregnancy test, ultrasonography, and abdominal x-ray examinations. Adnexal torsion yields few objective systemic manifestations before actual infarction occurs; the absence of fever, leukocytosis, or high sedimentation rate in a patient with peritonitic signs should suggest the diagnosis, whereas their presence does not rule it out entirely.

C. Laparoscopy is indicated for definitive diagnosis whenever there is doubt about the nature of the condition or the need for interventive surgery. Usually, it is clear that a surgical emergency exists, although its nature may be uncertain. If the patient's condition permits and there are no contraindications present, preliminary laparoscopy gives useful information for planning the definitive procedure, such as helping to choose the optimal type of incision and to solicit appropriate consultants for preoperative and intraoperative aid.

D. At laparotomy, examine the affected structures carefully to determine whether they are potentially salvageable. Note the condition of the contralateral organs; if normal, there may be less concern about the need to try to save infarcted tissues. Determine if the vessels are thrombosed and the tube and ovary have undergone gangrenous degeneration. Do not untwist the pedicle if there is any possibility of venous thrombosis, because doing so risks major pulmonary embolization (Fig. 1). Ordinarily, one finds the entire adnexa involved, including tube, ovary, round ligament, utero-ovarian ligament, and infundibulopelvic ligament. The tissues are congested, hemorrhagic, cyanotic, and edematous. Salpingo-oophorectomy is usually required under these circumstances. If the torsion is incomplete, the tissues are not compromised, and there is no venous thrombosis, consider conservative surgery. This entails resecting the ovarian cyst, correcting the torsion, and stabilizing the adnexa, if necessary.

References

Farrell TP, Boal DK, Teale RL, Ballantine TV. Acute torsion of normal uterine adnexa in children: Sonographic demonstration. Am J Roentgenol 139:1223, 1982.

PATIENT WITH SUSPICION OF ADNEXAL TORSION

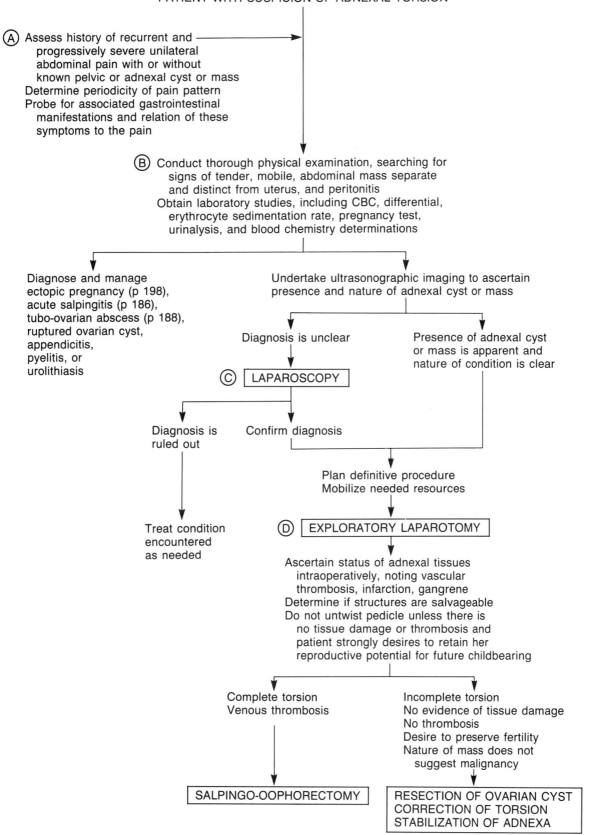

Ⓐ Assess history of recurrent and
   progressively severe unilateral
   abdominal pain with or without
   known pelvic or adnexal cyst or mass
Determine periodicity of pain pattern
Probe for associated gastrointestinal
   manifestations and relation of these
   symptoms to the pain

Ⓑ Conduct thorough physical examination, searching for
   signs of tender, mobile, abdominal mass separate
   and distinct from uterus, and peritonitis
Obtain laboratory studies, including CBC, differential,
   erythrocyte sedimentation rate, pregnancy test,
   urinalysis, and blood chemistry determinations

Diagnose and manage
ectopic pregnancy (p 198),
acute salpingitis (p 186),
tubo-ovarian abscess (p 188),
ruptured ovarian cyst,
appendicitis,
pyelitis, or
urolithiasis

Undertake ultrasonographic imaging to ascertain
presence and nature of adnexal cyst or mass

Diagnosis is unclear

Presence of adnexal cyst
or mass is apparent and
nature of condition is clear

Ⓒ LAPAROSCOPY

Diagnosis is
ruled out

Confirm diagnosis

Plan definitive procedure
Mobilize needed resources

Treat condition
encountered
as needed

Ⓓ EXPLORATORY LAPAROTOMY

Ascertain status of adnexal tissues
   intraoperatively, noting vascular
   thrombosis, infarction, gangrene
Determine if structures are salvageable
Do not untwist pedicle unless there is
   no tissue damage or thrombosis and
   patient strongly desires to retain her
   reproductive potential for future childbearing

Complete torsion
Venous thrombosis

Incomplete torsion
No evidence of tissue damage
No thrombosis
Desire to preserve fertility
Nature of mass does not
   suggest malignancy

SALPINGO-OOPHORECTOMY

RESECTION OF OVARIAN CYST
CORRECTION OF TORSION
STABILIZATION OF ADNEXA

Nichols DH, Julian PJ. Torsion of the adnexa. Clin Obstet Gynecol 28:375, 1985.
Russin LD. Hydrosalpinx and tubal torsion: A late complication of tubal ligation. Radiology 159:115, 1986.
Tollefson JE. Obstetric and gynecologic emergencies in the emergency department. Curr Probl Obstet Gynecol 7:4, 1984.

SEPTIC SHOCK

Eric D. Lichter, M.D.

A. Shock occurs when the intravascular blood volume is less than the capacity of the vascular bed (even when maximally contracted) and, as a consequence, the tissues are inadequately perfused. Septic shock is a special case because it is particularly difficult to treat and may be fatal if unchecked. The associated infection is commonly caused by a Gram-negative endotoxin-producing bacillus. Patients at risk include those with tubo-ovarian abscess (p 188), infected abortion (p 306), septic pelvic thrombophlebitis (p 298), intraoperative bowel injury (p 318) or surgery, and toxic shock syndrome (p 204), as well as those on immunosuppressive therapy.

B. Rapid but thorough physical assessment is critical for guiding evaluation and care. Differentiate those in the early phase of primary shock by their peripheral vasodilation and increased cardiac output from those in more advanced primary shock characterized by vasoconstriction, increased capillary permeability, and decreased

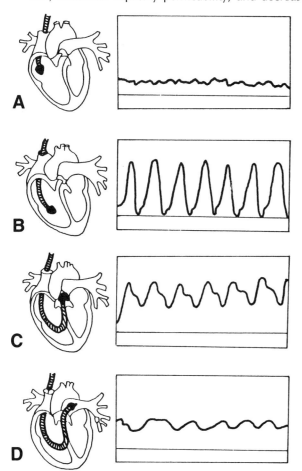

Figure 1 Pulmonary capillary wedge pressure determination. The Swan-Ganz catheter tip is advanced through the right atrium (A) and the right ventricle (B) to the pulmonary artery (C). Pressure recordings show zero or negative baseline in right ventricle and high diastolic baseline in pulmonary artery. When balloon occludes pulmonary arterial flow, the capillary wedge pressure is shown (D).

cardiac output. Also distinguish secondary or irreversible shock, which so often proves fatal, with severe acidosis, anuria, and coma. Assess the patient's condition with complete blood count (CBC), differential, erythrocyte sedimentation rate, urinalysis, serum electrolyte and chemistry determinations, arterial blood gas analyses, requisite smears and cultures, and coagulation studies. Ultrasonography or computer tomography may be needed to find the source of the infection. Monitor by central venous or pulmonary artery wedge pressure catheters (see E).

C. Primary shock is managed aggressively by volume replacement and an antibiotic regimen, with vasopressors if indicated. Second only to hemodynamic maintenance is the need to find the source of the infection, identify the offending organisms, and correct the problem. This usually involves finding the abscess and surgically draining or excising it; for septic abortion, it requires uterine evacuation and possibly hysterectomy; for pelvic thrombophlebitis, consider heparin and perhaps inferior vena cava plication (p 294).

D. Although it is best to choose the antibiotic program based on the specific organisms identified in a given case by smears and microbiologic cultures, it is inappropriate to delay instituting treatment for a patient in septic shock. Therefore, assume endotoxic shock is generally caused by Gram-negative coliform organisms and that infections of the reproductive organs usually involve anaerobic organisms and clostridia. While awaiting specific identification, administer a suitable combination of antibiotics intravenously to deal with these organisms, such as penicillin (10 million units every four hours) and chloramphenicol (1 g every six hours).

E. Re-establishing hemodynamic homeostasis is an imperative objective that is not easily accomplished in a patient in septic shock. It requires intensive effort under expert guidance and close monitoring. One can use central venous pressure observations and urinary output measurements to provide information about fluid overload, but they are not as valuable as pulmonary capillary wedge pressure measurements (Fig. 1) obtained by way of a Swan-Ganz catheter (advanced through the right heart into the pulmonary artery where balloon occlusion of arterial flow gives the capillary wedge pressure reading). The latter type of measurement provides a sensitive means for following the cardiovascular dynamics to prevent overload and pulmonary edema while rapidly administering colloidal fluids.

F. The use of corticosteroids in septic shock is controversial, but if they are to have any benefit at all, there is agreement that they must be given early and in large amounts. For example, administer dexamethasone in a 20 mg intravenous loading dose followed by 6 mg per kilogram daily or methylprednisolone, 125 mg followed by 30 mg per kilogram daily. The regimen should be tapered gradually to avoid adverse withdrawal effects.

PATIENT WITH FEVER AND HYPOTENSION

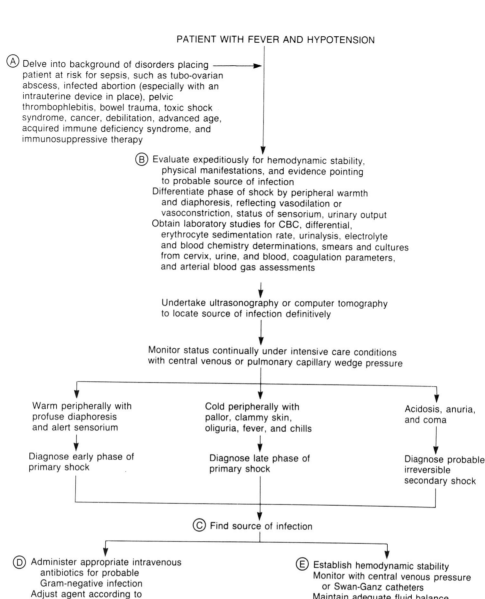

Ⓐ Delve into background of disorders placing
patient at risk for sepsis, such as tubo-ovarian
abscess, infected abortion (especially with an
intrauterine device in place), pelvic
thrombophlebitis, bowel trauma, toxic shock
syndrome, cancer, debilitation, advanced age,
acquired immune deficiency syndrome, and
immunosuppressive therapy

Ⓑ Evaluate expeditiously for hemodynamic stability,
physical manifestations, and evidence pointing
to probable source of infection
Differentiate phase of shock by peripheral warmth
and diaphoresis, reflecting vasodilation or
vasoconstriction, status of sensorium, urinary output
Obtain laboratory studies for CBC, differential,
erythrocyte sedimentation rate, urinalysis, electrolyte
and blood chemistry determinations, smears and cultures
from cervix, urine, and blood, coagulation parameters,
and arterial blood gas assessments

Undertake ultrasonography or computer tomography
to locate source of infection definitively

Monitor status continually under intensive care conditions
with central venous or pulmonary capillary wedge pressure

Warm peripherally with
profuse diaphoresis
and alert sensorium

Cold peripherally with
pallor, clammy skin,
oliguria, fever, and chills

Acidosis, anuria,
and coma

Diagnose early phase of
primary shock

Diagnose late phase of
primary shock

Diagnose probable
irreversible
secondary shock

Ⓒ Find source of infection

Ⓓ Administer appropriate intravenous
antibiotics for probable
Gram-negative infection
Adjust agent according to
culture results and response

INCISION AND
DRAINAGE OF
ABSCESS CAVITY

EXCISION OF
ABSCESSED OR
INFECTED ORGAN

Ⓔ Establish hemodynamic stability
Monitor with central venous pressure
or Swan-Ganz catheters
Maintain adequate fluid balance

Ⓕ Provide measures to combat
vasoconstriction, support
cardiac function, protect against
congestive heart failure, and
avoid hyperthermia, hypothermia,
or hypoxemia
Consider dopamine, glucocorticoids,
and digitalis

Ⓖ Evaluate for and correct disseminated
intravascular coagulation
Administer blood transfusions

G. Disseminated intravascular coagulation (p 208), which
may occur as a serious complicating factor in conjunction with septic shock, must be managed expeditiously
and with great care. It requires assiduous evaluation and
correction. Blood transfusion is generally needed to
replace blood loss and to prevent compounding the
problem with hypovolemia.

References

Berringer R, Harwood-Nuss AL. Septic shock. J Emerg Med 3:475,
1985; 4:49, 1986.

Cavanagh D, Rao P, Roberts WS. Septic shock in the gynecologic patient. Clin Obstet Gynecol 28:355, 1985.

Clark SL, Horenstein JM, Phelan JP, et al. Experience with the
pulmonary artery catheter in obstetrics and gynecology. Am
J Obstet Gynecol 152:374, 1985.

Karakusis PH. Considerations in the therapy of septic shock. Med
Clin North Am 70:933, 1986.

TOXIC SHOCK SYNDROME

Miguel Damien, M.D.

A. Toxic shock syndrome is a potentially very serious disorder principally affecting menstruating women. It should be considered as a possible diagnosis in a woman who presents with sudden onset of high fever (at least 38.9° C or 102° F), hypotension (below 90 mm Hg systolic blood pressure), and a variety of associated symptoms, such as vomiting, watery diarrhea, myalgia, headache, and abdominal pain. Some report a burning sensation in the vagina with a watery discharge at the onset of menstruation. Most characteristic is the appearance of a rash. It is a diffuse maculopapular erythroderma at first, progressing over the course of five days to two weeks to desquamation of the skin of the palms and the soles. Multisystem involvement is typical, affecting gastrointestinal, hepatic, muscular, renal, cardiovascular, and central nervous systems variously. Whereas it appears most often to be related to tampon use, it does occur in children and even in adult men. It has been reported in association with prolonged use of the contraceptive diaphragm or sponge and after laser therapy for condyloma acuminatum or nongynecological surgery. The syndrome is caused by absorption of a toxin produced by colonized *Staphylococcus aureus* of phage type 1, a penicillinase-producing bacterium. The presence of a highly absorbent vaginal tampon, especially if left in place for long, in combination with the nutrient media of the menstrual efflux, enhances the multiplication of this noninvasive organism. Tampon use may also damage the cervical and vaginal mucous membrane, thereby encouraging absorption of the exotoxin.

B. Detailed history, physical examination, and laboratory evaluation are needed for definitive diagnosis of the toxic shock syndrome. Patients are quite ill and the clinical picture may have to be differentiated from a wide variety of conditions. To this end, consider soliciting support for evaluation and care from an infectious disease specialist. One has to be sure to rule out meningococcal meningitis, mumps, Rocky Mountain spotted fever, and leptospirosis, among other esoteric infections. Obtain complete blood count, differential, peripheral smear, platelet count, serum electrolyte and chemistry determinations, serology for syphilis, skin biopsy, wound, vaginal, cervical and blood cultures, and cerebrospinal fluid culture and analysis.

C. The treatment program must be instituted expeditiously and pursued aggressively. Hemodynamic instability, a prominent feature of this condition, must be corrected and stabilized. To this end, give large amounts of colloidal solutions, taking care to avoid fluid overload with cardiac decompensation and pulmonary edema by monitoring the central venous or pulmonary capillary wedge pressure. If necessary, administer vasopressor agents to correct sudden hypotension transiently. In the event oxygenation becomes problematic, it may be necessary to provide mechanical ventilatory assistance. Monitor arterial blood gases serially to guide the ventilation parameters.

D. Antibiotics are given to combat the penicillin-resistant organisms, choosing either cephalosporins or beta-lactamase-resistant penicillin. Recognize that the syndrome results from the exotoxin produced by the organism; therefore, this treatment is not directly effective, but it will reduce the number of organisms and ultimately prevent further toxin formation. Give vancomycin or rifampicin to the patient who is allergic to penicillin. Advise vaginal douching with antibacterial iodine solution to reduce the number of intravaginal organisms still further. The value of corticosteroids in this condition is unclear.

E. Hypocalcemia occurs in about half the affected patients, apparently resulting from a direct effect on the calcium-parathormone mechanism. Treat this with intravenous calcium chloride to prevent seizures. Electrolyte imbalances have to be corrected, such as hyponatremia, hypokalemia, and mild metabolic acidosis. The large fluid volumes that these patients need aggravate the situation. Myocarditis can develop in the advanced stages, manifested by cardiac dilatation, electrocardiographic changes, pulmonary congestion, and bradycardia. Hemorrhage due to thrombocytopenia and coagulation disorder, while rare, should be treated with fresh frozen plasma and platelets.

F. Watch for recurrence at the time of the next several menstruations. These tend to be somewhat less severe, but they can be fatal. Myopathy and mildly diminished mental functioning may persist for years.

References

Bowen LW, Sand PK, Ostergard DR. Toxic shock syndrome following carbon dioxide laser treatment of genital tract condyloma acuminatum. Am J Obstet Gynecol 154:145, 1986.

Faich G, Pearson K, Fleming D, et al. Toxic shock syndrome and the vaginal contraceptive sponge. JAMA 255:216, 1986.

Kreiswirth BN, Kravitz GR, Schlievert PM, Novick RP. Nosocomial transmission of a strain of *Staphylococcus aureus* causing toxic shock syndrome. Ann Int Med 105:704, 1986.

Lanes SF, Poole C, Dreyer NA, Lanza LL. Toxic shock syndrome, contraceptive methods, and vaginitis. Am J Obstet Gynecol 154:989, 1986.

Thomas D, Withington PS. Toxic shock syndrome: A review of the literature. Ann Coll Surg Engl 67:156, 1985.

PATIENT WITH FEVER AND RASH

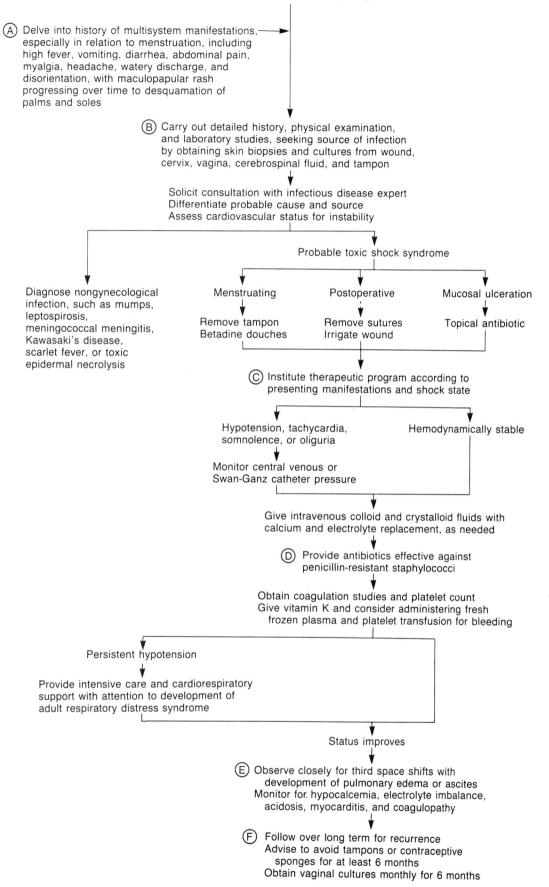

Ⓐ Delve into history of multisystem manifestations, →
especially in relation to menstruation, including
high fever, vomiting, diarrhea, abdominal pain,
myalgia, headache, watery discharge, and
disorientation, with maculopapular rash
progressing over time to desquamation of
palms and soles

Ⓑ Carry out detailed history, physical examination,
and laboratory studies, seeking source of infection
by obtaining skin biopsies and cultures from wound,
cervix, vagina, cerebrospinal fluid, and tampon

Solicit consultation with infectious disease expert
Differentiate probable cause and source
Assess cardiovascular status for instability

Probable toxic shock syndrome

Diagnose nongynecological
infection, such as mumps,
leptospirosis,
meningococcal meningitis,
Kawasaki's disease,
scarlet fever, or toxic
epidermal necrolysis

Menstruating   Postoperative   Mucosal ulceration

Remove tampon   Remove sutures   Topical antibiotic
Betadine douches   Irrigate wound

Ⓒ Institute therapeutic program according to
presenting manifestations and shock state

Hypotension, tachycardia,   Hemodynamically stable
somnolence, or oliguria

Monitor central venous or
Swan-Ganz catheter pressure

Give intravenous colloid and crystalloid fluids with
calcium and electrolyte replacement, as needed

Ⓓ Provide antibiotics effective against
penicillin-resistant staphylococci

Obtain coagulation studies and platelet count
Give vitamin K and consider administering fresh
frozen plasma and platelet transfusion for bleeding

Persistent hypotension

Provide intensive care and cardiorespiratory
support with attention to development of
adult respiratory distress syndrome

Status improves

Ⓔ Observe closely for third space shifts with
development of pulmonary edema or ascites
Monitor for hypocalcemia, electrolyte imbalance,
acidosis, myocarditis, and coagulopathy

Ⓕ Follow over long term for recurrence
Advise to avoid tampons or contraceptive
sponges for at least 6 months
Obtain vaginal cultures monthly for 6 months

CHRONIC COAGULATION DISORDER

Miguel Damien, M.D.

A. Some chronic coagulation factor deficiencies are inherited, such as hemophilia A, hemophilia B, and von Willebrand's disease. Acquired deficiencies include those caused by vitamin K deficiency, liver disease, disseminated intravascular coagulation, anticoagulant therapy, and rare disorders of platelet function.

B. Most significant hemorrhagic disorders can be detected by careful history and physical examination, paying attention to familial episodes of hemorrhagic symptoms. An X-linked recessive inheritance pattern is characteristic of hemophilia (see E). Note use of medications known to influence hemostasis adversely, such as aspirin, oral anticoagulants, phenylbutazone, and indomethacin.

C. Deficiency of plasma clotting factors can affect secondary hemostasis. Bleeding stops at first by vasoconstriction and platelet aggregation, but the platelet plug that forms is not reinforced by fibrin so that it yields to the force of arteriolar pressure. Tests of primary hemostasis, such as the bleeding time, are normal unless there is also a defect in platelet function, as in von Willebrand's disease.

D. Some rare inherited disorders involve impairment of platelet clumping. In thrombasthenia (Glanzmann's disease), the platelets fail to aggregate with adenosine diphosphate, epinephrine, or other agents. Portsmouth syndrome shows impaired "release reaction" of platelets to yield deficient platelet aggregation. Plasma coagulation is normal in these disorders, but the bleeding time is prolonged. Both can be treated effectively with platelet transfusions.

E. Hemophilia A is a congenital deficiency of factor VIII; hemophilia B lacks factor IX (Christmas disease). Both are X-linked recessive disorders. The A variety is five times more frequent than B. The clinical presentation of both types is similar, varying by degree of factor deficiency. Those with less than 1 percent of normal factor levels are severely affected. Activity levels up to 5 percent yield lesser manifestations. Bleeding is not usually a problem above 5 percent unless there is trauma or surgery.

F. Before undertaking major surgery in a type A hemophiliac, one should administer factor VIII by infusion to achieve 100 percent activity level; follow with half the initial dose every eight hours for one to two days and every 12 hours for three to five days. Titrate replacement needs by assaying factor VIII activity daily. Because factor VIII has a short half-life, 2 to 3 liters of plasma may be required per day to maintain a high concentration.

This risks circulatory overload, which is avoidable by use of concentrated preparations of the deficient factor instead. Some patients with severe hemophilia develop a natural anticoagulatory inhibiting factor that neutralizes circulating factor VIII and thus frustrates attempts at replacement therapy. Other acquired anticoagulants may also arise, but infrequently. The half-life of factor IX in vivo is about twice that of factor VIII. Therefore, factor IX replacement needs to be repeated at intervals of 16 to 24 hours. Treat minor bleeding with fresh frozen plasma and severe bleeding with prothrombin-complex concentrates containing factors X and IX.

G. Von Willebrand's disease is an inherited autosomal dominant disorder. Prolonged bleeding time is due to a defect in platelet adhesiveness and a factor VIII deficiency. Failure of platelet aggregation by ristocin aids its diagnosis. Bleeding episodes are readily controllable in most cases with cryoprecipitate, which contains factor VIII and von Willebrand factor and raises factor VIII coagulant activity to 30 to 50 percent. A single dose controls most minor bleeding episodes; repeat every 12 hours if bleeding continues.

H. Vitamin K is a necessary cofactor for hepatic gamma-carboxylation of certain glutamate residues in coagulation factors VII, IX, X, prothrombin, and proteins C and S. Prothrombin time is prolonged in acquired vitamin K deficiency, which is associated with biliary obstruction, malabsorption syndromes, antibiotic therapy, and nutritional deficiency. Patients on antibiotics who ingest nothing by mouth can become vitamin K deficient in one to two weeks. Serious hemorrhage requires fresh frozen plasma plus vitamin K supplementation. Correct mild deficiencies with parenteral vitamin K (10 to 15 mg) daily for one to three days.

References

Giddings JC, Peake IR. Laboratory support in the diagnosis of coagulation disorders. Clin Haematol 14:571, 1985.

Holmberg L, Nilsson IM. Von Willebrand disease. Clin Haematol 14:461, 1985.

Salzman E. Hemorrhagic disorders. In: Dudrick SJ (Editor). Manual of Preoperative and Postoperative Care. Philadelphia: W.B. Saunders, 1983.

Weinstein D, Rabinowitz R, Malach R, et al. Ovarian hemorrhage in women with von Willebrand's disease: A report of two cases. J Reprod Med 28:500, 1983.

PREOPERATIVE PATIENT WITH HISTORY OF BLEEDING DIATHESIS

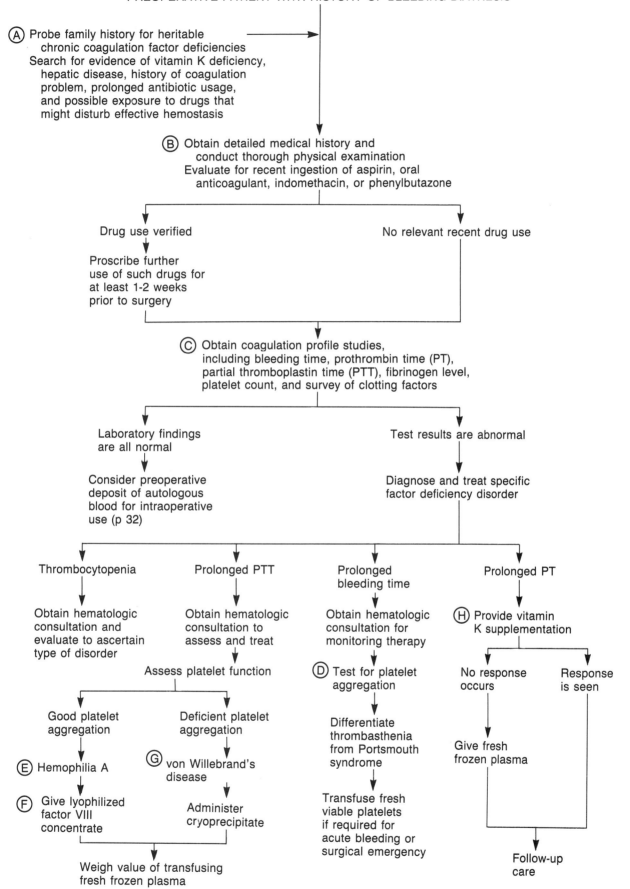

(A) Probe family history for heritable
    chronic coagulation factor deficiencies
    Search for evidence of vitamin K deficiency,
    hepatic disease, history of coagulation
    problem, prolonged antibiotic usage,
    and possible exposure to drugs that
    might disturb effective hemostasis

(B) Obtain detailed medical history and
    conduct thorough physical examination
    Evaluate for recent ingestion of aspirin, oral
    anticoagulant, indomethacin, or phenylbutazone

Drug use verified

No relevant recent drug use

Proscribe further
use of such drugs for
at least 1-2 weeks
prior to surgery

(C) Obtain coagulation profile studies,
    including bleeding time, prothrombin time (PT),
    partial thromboplastin time (PTT), fibrinogen level,
    platelet count, and survey of clotting factors

Laboratory findings
are all normal

Test results are abnormal

Consider preoperative
deposit of autologous
blood for intraoperative
use (p 32)

Diagnose and treat specific
factor deficiency disorder

Thrombocytopenia

Prolonged PTT

Prolonged
bleeding time

Prolonged PT

Obtain hematologic
consultation and
evaluate to ascertain
type of disorder

Obtain hematologic
consultation to
assess and treat

Obtain hematologic
consultation for
monitoring therapy

(H) Provide vitamin
    K supplementation

Assess platelet function

(D) Test for platelet
    aggregation

No response
occurs

Response
is seen

Good platelet
aggregation

Deficient platelet
aggregation

Differentiate
thrombasthenia
from Portsmouth
syndrome

Give fresh
frozen plasma

(E) Hemophilia A

(G) von Willebrand's
    disease

(F) Give lyophilized
    factor VIII
    concentrate

Administer
cryoprecipitate

Transfuse fresh
viable platelets
if required for
acute bleeding or
surgical emergency

Follow-up
care

Weigh value of transfusing
fresh frozen plasma

207

ACUTE COAGULATION DISORDER

Miguel Damien, M.D.

A. Probe into the past medical history of patients for whom surgery is contemplated to determine if there has been any prior prolonged bleeding episode, easy bruisability, or other evidence of a clotting problem. Determine any use of medications that are known to affect hemostasis adversely, such as aspirin, indomethacin, or phenylbutazone. These individuals should have a thorough investigation, preferably under the guidance of an expert in the field. It is essential to avoid undertaking any surgical procedure without completing the necessary work-up, except in a dire emergency. If it is determined that a chronic bleeding disorder exists, evaluate and manage appropriately (p 206).

B. Coagulopathy associated with missed or septic incomplete abortion or septic shock can lead to the development of disseminated intravascular coagulation (DIC). Substances released in the circulation by tumors and traumatized or necrotic tissues and endotoxin derived from Gram-negative bacteria activate the coagulation cascade. These thrombogenic stimuli cause the deposition of small thrombi throughout the microvasculature in the early phase of DIC. The secondary phase involves fibrinolysis, which depletes the coagulation proteins and platelets, thereby leading to hemorrhage.

C. The clinical presentation varies with the stage and severity of the syndrome. Hemorrhage may arise from multiple sites. There can be extensive skin and mucous membrane bleeding. Patients sometimes present with peripheral acrocyanosis and even pregangrenous changes of digits, genitalia, and nose. Prompt recognition of the signs of impending shock is necessary. Monitor the coagulation parameters and expedite an aggressive program of care.

D. Thrombocytopenia appears early along with schistocytes or fragmented red blood cells in the peripheral blood. As the process develops, bleeding correlates best with the plasma fibrinogen level. Follow the course of the disorder with serial determinations of fibrinogen level, fibrin degradation products, partial thromboplastin time, prothrombin time, platelet count, and peripheral blood smear. Because a consumption coagulopathy can progress very rapidly to uncontrollable hemorrhage and irreversible shock, it must be diagnosed early, followed carefully, and managed effectively. Pay attention to the quality of clot formation and retraction, and note the time it takes for the clot to lyse. These simple bedside observations are valuable for assessing the circulating levels of fibrinogen, platelets, and fibrin degradation products,

often more quickly than laboratory determinations. Control the major manifestations first, as needed. Bleeding and shock must be aggressively managed, for example, with rapid blood volume expansion by colloidal solutions and blood replacement in suitable quantities (p 32). Since large volumes of fluid and blood may have to be given under these circumstances, take care to avoid volume overload, which leads to cardiac decompensation. It is especially important, therefore, to undertake continuous monitoring of the cardiovascular status by central venous pressure or Swan-Ganz catheter pressure recordings (p 24).

E. The patient with acute bleeding from DIC must be carefully followed by periodic re-evaluations of her clotting factors. She should be given fresh frozen plasma and cryoprecipitate to replace specifically depleted clotting factors. Platelet concentrates can be effective in correcting thrombocytopenia. Antifibrinolytic agents are seldom warranted. Their use should be limited to the rare case of acute, unremitting hemorrhage in a patient who can be demonstrated to have increased fibrinolytic activity.

F. After the etiologic condition for the coagulopathy is corrected and the patient is stabilized in regard to cardiovascular status and acid-base balance, the accelerated intravascular coagulation process stops and the body begins to regenerate the depleted clotting factors. If the patient's liver function is intact, coagulation factors are rapidly resynthesized and replaced to normal levels. In due course, often less than six hours, the clotting mechanism returns to normal function. Surgical intervention for correcting the underlying cause may have to be done to save the patient's life if preliminary conservative measures fail, but it is much preferable to delay operating, if possible, until after the coagulation disorder is controlled.

References

Fruchtman S, Aledort LM. Disseminated intravascular coagulation. J Am Coll Cardiol 8(Suppl):159B, 1986.

Watkins J. The early diagnosis of impending coagulopathies following surgery and multiple trauma. Klin Wochenschr 63:1019, 1985.

Weekes LR. Disseminated intravascular coagulation. J Nat Med Assoc 77:830, 1985.

White PF, Coe V, Dworsky WA, Margolis A. Disseminated intravascular coagulation following midtrimester abortions. Anesthesiology 58:99, 1983.

PATIENT WITH ACUTE BLEEDING EPISODE

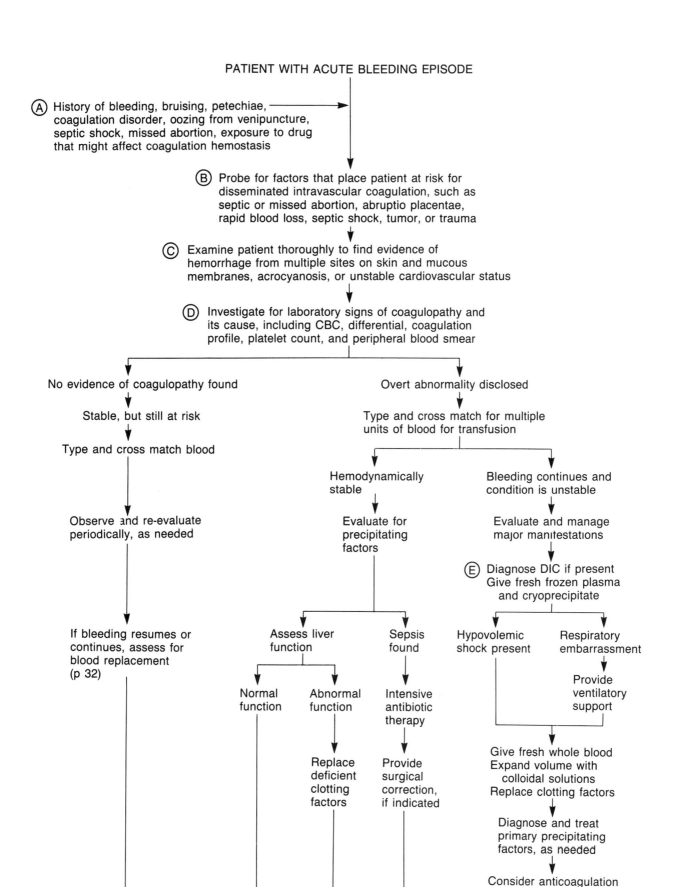

Ⓐ History of bleeding, bruising, petechiae,
coagulation disorder, oozing from venipuncture,
septic shock, missed abortion, exposure to drug
that might affect coagulation hemostasis

Ⓑ Probe for factors that place patient at risk for
disseminated intravascular coagulation, such as
septic or missed abortion, abruptio placentae,
rapid blood loss, septic shock, tumor, or trauma

Ⓒ Examine patient thoroughly to find evidence of
hemorrhage from multiple sites on skin and mucous
membranes, acrocyanosis, or unstable cardiovascular status

Ⓓ Investigate for laboratory signs of coagulopathy and
its cause, including CBC, differential, coagulation
profile, platelet count, and peripheral blood smear

No evidence of coagulopathy found

Stable, but still at risk

Type and cross match blood

Observe and re-evaluate
periodically, as needed

If bleeding resumes or
continues, assess for
blood replacement
(p 32)

Overt abnormality disclosed

Type and cross match for multiple
units of blood for transfusion

Hemodynamically
stable

Evaluate for
precipitating
factors

Assess liver
function

Normal
function

Abnormal
function

Replace
deficient
clotting
factors

Sepsis
found

Intensive
antibiotic
therapy

Provide
surgical
correction,
if indicated

Bleeding continues and
condition is unstable

Evaluate and manage
major manifestations

Ⓔ Diagnose DIC if present
Give fresh frozen plasma
and cryoprecipitate

Hypovolemic
shock present

Respiratory
embarrassment

Provide
ventilatory
support

Give fresh whole blood
Expand volume with
colloidal solutions
Replace clotting factors

Diagnose and treat
primary precipitating
factors, as needed

Consider anticoagulation
with heparin

Ⓕ Periodically re-evaluate coagulation profile
and give blood replacement, if indicated

ENDOMETRIAL SAMPLING

David G. Diaz, M.D.

A. Information about the endometrial lining is useful for diagnosis and treatment of infertility (p 82), menstrual dysfunction (p 78), menopause, infection, and neoplasia. Tissue sampling can usually be effectively achieved in an ambulatory office setting with minimal discomfort to the patient, but it may not always be sufficient to ensure optimal care. One has to recognize when it is more appropriate to proceed to a full formal curettage (p 230) under anesthesia.

B. A variety of small devices are available for endometrial sampling. Most commonly used is the Novak endometrial curette. Aspiration techniques are also used principally for cytologic assessment (see D). A recently introduced flexible suction cannula (Pipelle) has been shown to be excellent for gathering adequate quantities of tissue for effective histologic study. It requires only hand held suction and can be used in most cases without either anesthesia or cervical dilatation. By contrast, the Novak curette, which yields substantial strips of intact endometrium for optimal study, generally does require paracervical block anesthesia and some cervical dilatation.

C. While the technique is simple, it should be carried out with care to avoid complications (perforation, bleeding, and infection) and to ensure success. First, determine the size and position of the uterus by bimanual examination. Administer the paracervical anesthesia by infiltrating bilaterally with no more than 10 ml of 0.5 percent lidocaine (Xylocaine). Some additional anesthetic agent can be injected into the anterior lip of the cervix to permit a tenaculum to be applied painlessly. Traction on the tenaculum can be expected to straighten the uterus, thereby helping to avert perforation. Sound the uterus and dilate the cervix next, if needed, with graduated metal dilators, using gentleness and control. Then insert the curette or cannula and sample the anterior fundal region of the uterine cavity. Quickly fix the obtained specimen in 10 percent formalin solution to prevent architectural distortion by drying and transport it in fixative to the pathology laboratory for examination.

D. Cytologic screening by the Papanicolaou cervical technique (p 12) is recognized to be particularly poor for detecting endometrial carcinoma. Its yield can be considerably improved, although still well below that for cervical cancer, by intrauterine washing, brushing, or aspiration. It has fallen in and out of favor over the years due to inconsistent success rates. To be at all effective, it requires expert cytologic interpretaton by experienced cytologists; such expertise is not widely available. The combination of brush cytology and endometrial biopsy in ideal circumstances (skilled hands and excellent cytologic facility) is highly accurate (90 percent or more). For diagnosing endometrial cancer (p 178), clearly positive findings are reliable; for ruling it out, negative or equivocal results are not.

E. Menopausal patients (p 94) who fall into the high-risk category in regard to possible endometrial adenocarcinoma must have endometrial sampling preliminary to hormonal replacement. Disclosing evidence of hyperplasia, especially with cellular atypia (p 176), warrants further investigation for cancer (p 178) while withholding estrogens. Others can be treated, but they may require repeat endometrial biopsy studies periodically (or when bleeding occurs) to help guide management.

F. All infertile patients (p 82) need one or more endometrial biopsies as part of their evaluation. It is done to rule out endometritis, to confirm that ovulation has occurred (p 124), to verify effective secretory response to luteal stimulation (p 126), and to date the endometrium (relative to the chronologic date from ovulation). It is best performed as close to the onset of menstruation as possible or, if necessary, up to 12 hours after its onset.

G. Acute postoperative, postabortal, or postpartum endometritis can be readily diagnosed by endometrial biopsy. In addition to histologic examination, some of the material obtained should be cultured. Information about the causative organisms helps to tailor antibiotic treatment for febrile morbidity. Chronic endometritis, such as might result from tuberculous, mycoplasma, or ureaplasma infections, can be elucidated in this way as well. It should be considered in patients with chronic pelvic pain or vaginal bleeding.

References

Anderson B. Diagnosis of endometrial cancer. Clin Obstet Gynaecol 13:739, 1986.

Cornier E. The Pipelle: A disposable device for endometrial biopsy. Am J Obstet Gynecol 148:109, 1984.

Estrogen Replacement Therapy. ACOG Technical Bulletin No. 93. Washington, DC: American College of Obstetricians and Gynecologists, 1986.

Huang KE. The primary treatment of luteal phase human endometrium. Fertil Steril 47:76, 1987.

Polson DW, Morse A, Beard RW. An alternative to the diagnostic dilatation and curettage: Endometrial cytology. Br Med J 288:981, 1984.

PATIENT WITH INDICATION FOR ENDOMETRIAL SAMPLING

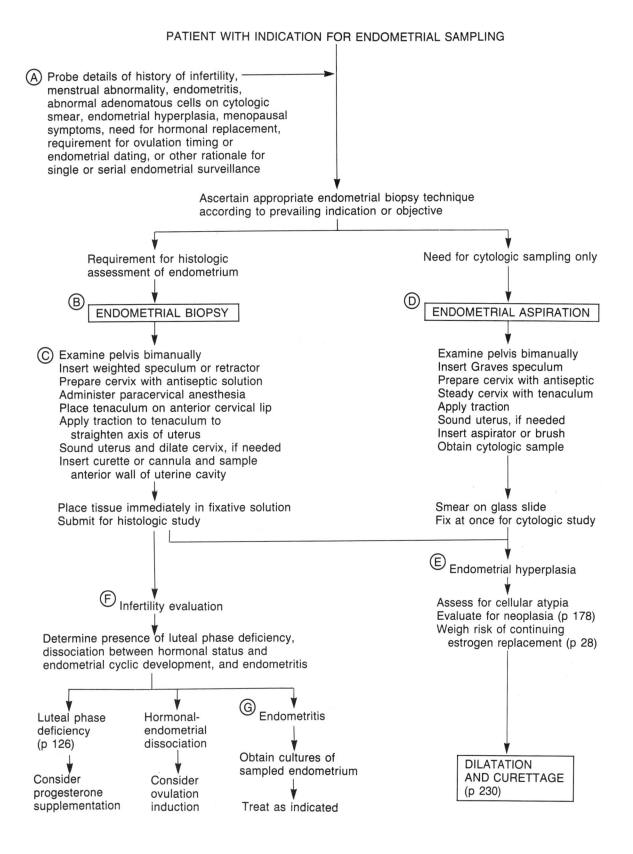

(A) Probe details of history of infertility, menstrual abnormality, endometritis, abnormal adenomatous cells on cytologic smear, endometrial hyperplasia, menopausal symptoms, need for hormonal replacement, requirement for ovulation timing or endometrial dating, or other rationale for single or serial endometrial surveillance

Ascertain appropriate endometrial biopsy technique according to prevailing indication or objective

Requirement for histologic assessment of endometrium

Need for cytologic sampling only

(B) | ENDOMETRIAL BIOPSY |

(D) | ENDOMETRIAL ASPIRATION |

(C) Examine pelvis bimanually
Insert weighted speculum or retractor
Prepare cervix with antiseptic solution
Administer paracervical anesthesia
Place tenaculum on anterior cervical lip
Apply traction to tenaculum to
    straighten axis of uterus
Sound uterus and dilate cervix, if needed
Insert curette or cannula and sample
    anterior wall of uterine cavity

Examine pelvis bimanually
Insert Graves speculum
Prepare cervix with antiseptic
Steady cervix with tenaculum
Apply traction
Sound uterus, if needed
Insert aspirator or brush
Obtain cytologic sample

Place tissue immediately in fixative solution
Submit for histologic study

Smear on glass slide
Fix at once for cytologic study

(E) Endometrial hyperplasia

Assess for cellular atypia
Evaluate for neoplasia (p 178)
Weigh risk of continuing
    estrogen replacement (p 28)

(F) Infertility evaluation

Determine presence of luteal phase deficiency, dissociation between hormonal status and endometrial cyclic development, and endometritis

Luteal phase deficiency (p 126)

Hormonal-endometrial dissociation

(G) Endometritis

Obtain cultures of sampled endometrium

Consider progesterone supplementation

Consider ovulation induction

Treat as indicated

| DILATATION AND CURETTAGE (p 230) |

CULDOCENTESIS

Eric D. Lichter, M.D.

A. With the widespread availability of ultrasonographic imaging, the clinical value of culdocentesis has waned considerably. Its principal value today is the information it can provide about the nature of the fluid that has accumulated in the cul-de-sac of Douglas secondary to some intraperitoneal pathologic process. It was also used in the past to determine the presence of fluid, but ultrasonography has proved much more sensitive, accurate, and universally applicable than culdocentesis for this purpose. Culdocentesis falls short in this regard because fluid may be sequestered out of reach or there may be bowel, ovary, or retroverted uterus in the cul-de-sac obstructing access. Moreover, culdocentesis cannot distinguish between free intra-abdominal fluid and encapsulated fluid in an abscess or cyst as ultrasonography can. Nonetheless, despite these limitations, the needling procedure can sometimes serve to elucidate the diagnosis of ectopic pregnancy, ruptured ovarian cyst, or acute salpingitis, thereby helping to differentiate these conditions and guide therapy in a rational way. Culdocentesis is also of value as a preliminary step in assessing whether a pointing tubo-ovarian abscess should be drained by way of the posterior vaginal fornix (p 188). Be especially attentive to a history of recurrent salpingitis (p 186), acute appendicitis, inflammatory bowel disease, or pelvic surgery, because these conditions are likely to have formed adhesions to fix the bowel and adnexa in the cul-de-sac.

B. Thorough pelvic examination is mandatory before considering a culdocentesis. Ascertain the status of the pelvic organs and especially note the structures located within the cul-de-sac. Determine whether it contains fixed adnexal mass, retroverted uterine corpus, or loops of intestine. If encountered, their presence makes the procedure both likely to fail and unacceptably hazardous. Optimal conditions include clear foreknowledge that an intraperitoneal fluid collection exists and extends into the cul-de-sac, as determined objectively by ultrasonography, that the cul-de-sac is free of mass or organ, and that the posterior fornix is bulging. In addition to the need for preliminary ultrasonographic surveillance (see A), consider upright abdominal x-ray studies before proceeding in cases in which there is suspicion of free air in the abdominal cavity from a perforated viscus.

C. The procedure should be preceded by an interval of no less than 20 minutes during which the patient lies prone in reverse Trendelenburg position to allow the intraperitoneal fluid to gravitate caudally to the cul-de-sac. With the patient then placed in lithotomy position (still with her pelvis lower than her head), use a Graves speculum or weighted right-angle retractor to expose the upper vagina. Grasp the posterior lip of the cervix with a tenaculum and elevate it to put tension on the posterior fornix (Fig. 1). This may require readjusting the posterior retractor. Unless the forniceal regional is put on vertical stretch, the needle insertion will not be optimal. Swab the area with antiseptic solution and infiltrate anesthesia (1 percent lidocaine) locally at the site chosen for puncture. Under sterile conditions, thrust a long, sharp, large bore (at least 18-gauge) needle perpendicularly through the vaginal mucosa and peritoneal lining, advancing no more than 2 cm into the cul-de-sac space. Aspirate the contents by means of a syringe attached distally.

D. Grossly examine the specimen of fluid aspirated from the cul-de-sac. Straw-colored or cloudy serous fluid should be sent for aerobic and anaerobic cultures and a smear made for Gram staining. If possible, try to get a second specimen using a fresh sterile syringe; this will reduce contamination by vaginal flora and provide more meaningful microbiologic information from the cultures. A bloody specimen is observed briefly for clotting. If it clots, it is likely to represent fresh blood obtained by inadvertent venipuncture; failure to clot is strong evidence of prior clotting and subsequent intraperitoneal lysis. Verify the latter by placing a small amount on a gauze sponge to visualize the tiny residual clots commonly found in this material. Finding nonclotting blood verifies an antecedent intra-abdominal bleeding episode. This information has to be weighed in conjunction with the rest of the clinical picture to assess its source and to determine whether the bleeding is still ongoing and in need of intervention.

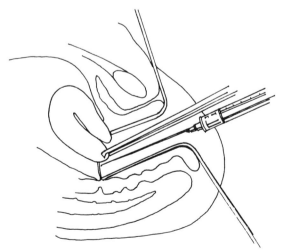

Figure 1 Culdocentesis accomplished by placing the posterior vaginal fornix on stretch with anterior cervical pressure and posterior vaginal wall retraction.

References

Cartwright PS, Vaughn B, Tuttle D. Culdocentesis and ectopic pregnancy. J Reprod Med 29:88, 1984.

Monif GRG, Baer H. Impact of diverging anaerobic technology on cul-de-sac isolates from patients with endometritis-salpingitis-peritonitis. Am J Obstet Gynecol 142:896, 1982.

Romero R, Copel JA, Kadar N, et al. Value of culdocentesis in the diagnosis of ectopic pregnancy. Obstet Gynecol 65:519, 1985.

PATIENT WITH SYMPTOMS SUGGESTING NEED FOR CULDOCENTESIS

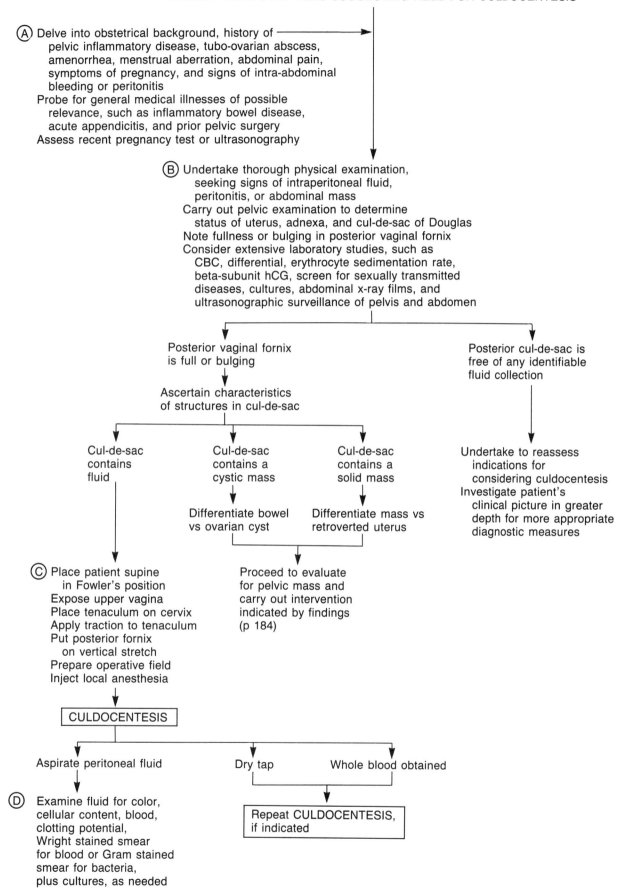

(A) Delve into obstetrical background, history of
        pelvic inflammatory disease, tubo-ovarian abscess,
        amenorrhea, menstrual aberration, abdominal pain,
        symptoms of pregnancy, and signs of intra-abdominal
        bleeding or peritonitis
    Probe for general medical illnesses of possible
        relevance, such as inflammatory bowel disease,
        acute appendicitis, and prior pelvic surgery
    Assess recent pregnancy test or ultrasonography

(B) Undertake thorough physical examination,
        seeking signs of intraperitoneal fluid,
        peritonitis, or abdominal mass
    Carry out pelvic examination to determine
        status of uterus, adnexa, and cul-de-sac of Douglas
    Note fullness or bulging in posterior vaginal fornix
    Consider extensive laboratory studies, such as
        CBC, differential, erythrocyte sedimentation rate,
        beta-subunit hCG, screen for sexually transmitted
        diseases, cultures, abdominal x-ray films, and
        ultrasonographic surveillance of pelvis and abdomen

Posterior vaginal fornix
is full or bulging

Posterior cul-de-sac is
free of any identifiable
fluid collection

Ascertain characteristics
of structures in cul-de-sac

Cul-de-sac
contains
fluid

Cul-de-sac
contains a
cystic mass

Cul-de-sac
contains a
solid mass

Undertake to reassess
    indications for
    considering culdocentesis
Investigate patient's
    clinical picture in greater
    depth for more appropriate
    diagnostic measures

Differentiate bowel
vs ovarian cyst

Differentiate mass vs
retroverted uterus

(C) Place patient supine
        in Fowler's position
    Expose upper vagina
    Place tenaculum on cervix
    Apply traction to tenaculum
    Put posterior fornix
        on vertical stretch
    Prepare operative field
    Inject local anesthesia

Proceed to evaluate
for pelvic mass and
carry out intervention
indicated by findings
(p 184)

CULDOCENTESIS

Aspirate peritoneal fluid

Dry tap   Whole blood obtained

(D) Examine fluid for color,
    cellular content, blood,
    clotting potential,
    Wright stained smear
    for blood or Gram stained
    smear for bacteria,
    plus cultures, as needed

Repeat CULDOCENTESIS,
if indicated

COLPOSCOPY

Louis Burke, M.D.

A. Colposcopy is especially valuable for assessing patients with abnormal Papanicolaou smears (p 12). It provides an objective means for careful surveillance of the entire lower genital tract, including vulva, vagina, exocervix, and lower endocervix. It locates suspicious lesions, helps identify probable dysplastic or neoplastic disorders, and designates sites for biopsy sampling. Colposcopy can also serve as a practical way to follow patients who have been treated for cervical or vaginal lesions, determine efficacy of therapy, and detect failure or recurrence early. It has also proved useful for examining and following women who were exposed in utero to diethylstilbestrol (p 148). Counsel the patient about the procedure, detailing why it is being used and what she can expect at each step.

B. A detailed pelvic examination should precede the colposcopy. If one expects to obtain a cytologic smear (a good practice for verifying the findings previously reported), do not use a lubricant that will distort cellular morphology. While it is likely that attention will be directed to one area based on the reason the colposcopy is being done, it is imperative to assess the entire lower genital tract so as not to overlook a lesion in an area left uninspected. This is especially good advice because a woman with one gynecological dysplastic lesion is very likely to have another concurrently or to develop others in the future.

C. Inspect the vulvar skin and vaginal and cervical mucosa carefully under good light with the magnification afforded by the colposcope. Begin without wiping or washing the surface epithelium. Look for white patches, red lesions, and raised areas, watching especially for abnormal arrangements of the blood vessels visible through the epithelium. Vascular patterns, best studied prior to applying acetic acid, are valuable indicators of malignancy if they show aberrant distribution with irregular dilatation, stenosis, and corkscrew or hairpin shapes.

D. Gently swab the surface being studied with dilute acetic acid solution (3 to 5 percent) to dissolve overlying mucus that might be obscuring the field. The acetic acid causes areas in which there is cellular proliferation to become whitened transiently. It may be necessary to repeat acetic acid applications periodically to highlight these aceto-white areas as needed. Multiple washings are generally required to demonstrate vulvar lesions (see G).

E. Colposcopic surveillance of the cervix is generally concentrated in the area of the transformation zone between the squamous epithelium of the exocervix and the columnar epithelium of the endocervix. While this is ordinarily located on the portio vaginalis in adult women of reproductive age, it may be found well up (and out of view) in the cervical canal in postmenopausal patients and those who have had a prior operative procedure for ablation of this area (p 236). The colposcopic image reflects the histologic pattern as regards the thickness of the epithelium and its cellular organization, morphology, architecture, and vascular arrangement. Be alert for characteristic punctation, mosaic pattern, aceto-white lesions, and atypical blood vessels (see C). Having identified the lesion sites, biopsy those deemed to be most suspicious and representative under direct visualization, guided by the patterns they demonstrate. If the lesion extends up the canal, attempt to expose its upper margins by an endocervical speculum. Inability to visualize the lesion in its entirety requires endocervical curettage; take care to avoid scraping through the exocervical part of the lesion because this will only confuse interpretation of the findings.

F. Vaginal lesions can be identified using the same criteria for defining potentially abnormal sites for directed biopsy. If no lesions are found with acetic acid applications, consider use of Lugol's iodine staining. The normally glycogenated vaginal mucosa stains deep brown, flagging nonstaining areas for investigation.

G. Colposcopy tends to be less valuable for detecting and evaluating vulvar lesions than for disclosing cervical or vaginal pathologic conditions, because overlying keratinization makes visualization difficult at best. Prolonged and repeated acetic acid washings are needed to reveal relevant patterns under colposcopic magnification. If lesions are suspected, but cannot be demonstrated with acetic acid, try toluidine blue vital stain to highlight dysplastic areas with nuclear hyperactivity. These sites are biopsied with a dermatologic punch and studied histologically.

References

Moseley KR, Tung VD, Hannigan EV, et al. Necessity for endocervical curettage in colposcopy. Am J Obstet Gynecol 154:992, 1986.

Oliveira A, Keppler M, Luisi A, et al. Comparative evaluation of abnormal cytology, colposcopy and histopathology in preclinical cervical malignancy during pregnancy. Acta Cytol 26:636, 1982.

Sakuma T, Hasegawa T, Tsutsui F, Kurihara S. Quantitative analysis of the whiteness of the atypical cervical transformation zone. J Reprod Med 30:773, 1985.

Toplis PJ, Casemore V, Hallam M, Charnock M. Evaluation of colposcopy in the postmenopausal woman. Br J Obstet Gynaecol 93:843, 1986.

Wetrich D. An analysis of the factors involved in the colposcopic evaluation of 2194 patients with abnormal Papanicolaou smears. Am J Obstet Gynecol 154:1339, 1986.

PATIENT WITH ABNORMAL PAPANICOLAOU CYTOLOGIC SMEAR

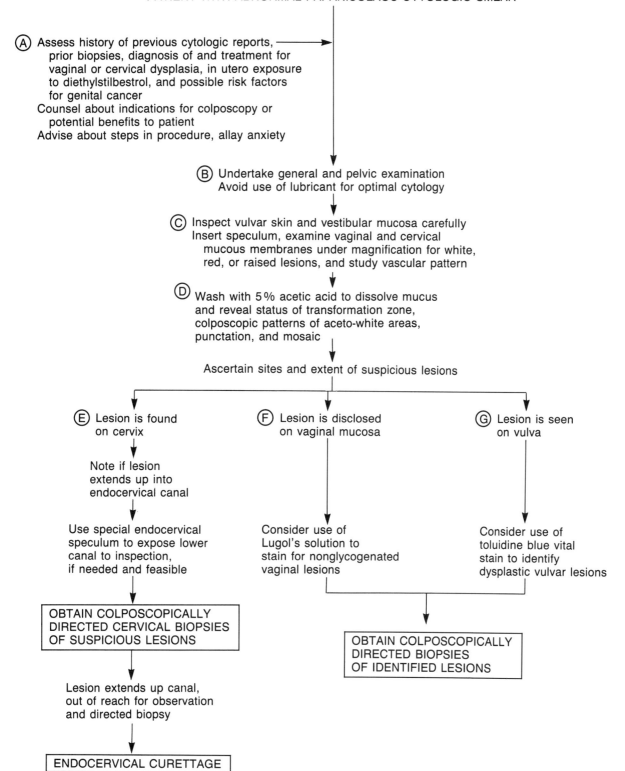

Ⓐ Assess history of previous cytologic reports,
     prior biopsies, diagnosis of and treatment for
     vaginal or cervical dysplasia, in utero exposure
     to diethylstilbestrol, and possible risk factors
     for genital cancer
Counsel about indications for colposcopy or
     potential benefits to patient
Advise about steps in procedure, allay anxiety

Ⓑ Undertake general and pelvic examination
     Avoid use of lubricant for optimal cytology

Ⓒ Inspect vulvar skin and vestibular mucosa carefully
Insert speculum, examine vaginal and cervical
     mucous membranes under magnification for white,
     red, or raised lesions, and study vascular pattern

Ⓓ Wash with 5% acetic acid to dissolve mucus
     and reveal status of transformation zone,
     colposcopic patterns of aceto-white areas,
     punctation, and mosaic

Ascertain sites and extent of suspicious lesions

Ⓔ Lesion is found
     on cervix

Note if lesion
extends up into
endocervical canal

Use special endocervical
speculum to expose lower
canal to inspection,
if needed and feasible

OBTAIN COLPOSCOPICALLY
DIRECTED CERVICAL BIOPSIES
OF SUSPICIOUS LESIONS

Lesion extends up canal,
out of reach for observation
and directed biopsy

ENDOCERVICAL CURETTAGE

Ⓕ Lesion is disclosed
     on vaginal mucosa

Consider use of
Lugol's solution to
stain for nonglycogenated
vaginal lesions

Ⓖ Lesion is seen
     on vulva

Consider use of
toluidine blue vital
stain to identify
dysplastic vulvar lesions

OBTAIN COLPOSCOPICALLY
DIRECTED BIOPSIES
OF IDENTIFIED LESIONS

PELVIC ULTRASONOGRAPHY

Henry Klapholz, M.D.

A. Ultrasonographic imaging is a virtually risk free modality with a large number of applications for surveying abdominal organs and for diagnosing pelvic and intra-abdominal pathologic conditions. It also serves as an invaluable aid for guiding invasive gynecological procedures. The range of gynecological uses extends from differentiating intrauterine and ectopic pregnancy (p 198) to identifying free fluid in the abdominal cavity (p 212), distinguishing solid versus cystic ovarian tumors (p 192), diagnosing tubo-ovarian abscess (p 188), and measuring graafian follicles preparatory to ovum harvest for in vitro fertilization (IVF) (p 276), among many others. Introduction and wide use of this utilitarian technique has had numerous beneficial effects, facilitating and expanding diagnostic capabilities, expediting intervention when indicated, and often averting major surgery. Ultrasonographic study is best carried out by a skilled, experienced ultrasonographer for optimally reliable results. Growing availability of sophisticated ultrasonographic equipment in well equipped gynecological offices means that the preliminary examinations are increasingly likely to be done by others. Interpretation of the findings under these circumstances should be done cautiously to guard against incorrect diagnoses.

B. Before proceeding with an ultrasonographic examination, ensure that the patient's bladder is completely filled so as to provide a good sonic window through which to visualize the pelvic organs. This is generally achieved by having the patient drink a plentiful amount of fluid beforehand and instructing her not to void prior to the test. An excessive amount of intraluminal gas within loops of bowel may interfere with a good examination by obscuring the image of structures located behind the gas collections. With the patient in a comfortable supine position on the examining table, expose the abdomen and create a good sonic interface between the ultrasound transducer (which both emits the sound signals and receives the reflected return sound waves) and the skin surface with a suitable lubricant. Real-time imaging technology has made it possible to obtain two-dimensional patterns outlining pelvic and abdominal organs. Conduct a full survey to ensure against missing some unexpected condition and concentrate detailed study in the area of greatest interest as dictated by the presenting complaint or the findings on foregoing physical examination and laboratory investigations.

C. Ultrasonography can effectively facilitate a number of invasive procedures. Abscesses (p 188), for example, can be drained under such guidance, perhaps with complementary assistance of computer tomography, markedly reducing the need for laparotomy for this purpose. Fine-needle (Surecut) biopsies of liver, pancreas, pelvic organs, and retroperitoneal lymph nodes can be accomplished by this means as well, with a very high degree of accuracy. Amniocentesis for assessment of fetal genetic status or lung maturity in pregnancy is almost always done under ultrasonographic control to avoid fetal and placental injury. Ovum harvest for in vitro fertilization (p 276) can be done by aspiration of mature follicles using ultrasonographic visualization in patients who have been examined serially by ultrasound imaging both to ensure proper follicular maturation and to time the egg retrieval procedure. Aspiration averts laparoscopy for this purpose.

D. Extrapelvic surveillance should be able to visualize the liver and biliary tree, demonstrating obstruction if present. A cystic hepatic lesion can be differentiated from a solid metastatic tumor. Implants on the liver surface may reflect dissemination from ovarian cancer (p 192). Always study the kidneys to ensure both are present and normally located. Look for ureteral dilatation and extrinsic compression or intrinsic distortion of the bladder. Assess the retroperitoneal region for enlarged pelvic and aortic lymph nodes or masses. Large amounts of intraperitoneal fluid can be seen collected along the lumbar gutters. Detecting more than 30 ml of free fluid in the cul-de-sac of Douglas suggests an abnormality, such as ruptured cyst, abscess, or ectopic pregnancy. The uterus should be readily identifiable; its cavity is ordinarily empty. The presence of a double bubble sign (Fig. 1), consisting of two concentric rings, is diagnostic of intrauterine pregnancy (the gestational sac within a ring of thickened decidua). Be wary of mistaking a pseudosac for a pregnancy. An active fetal heart is confirmatory. Infection often produces an indistinct uterine contour sign. Adenomyosis (p 174) is also distinguishable by its characteristic uterine wall pattern.

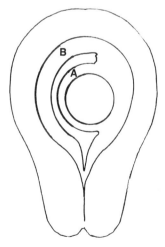

Figure 1 Double ring sign of early intrauterine gestation as seen on ultrasonography appears to be related to separate concentric layers of condensated tissue, an inner decidua capsularis (A) surrounding the gestational sac, and an outer decidua parietalis (B).

References

Chinn DH, Callen PW. Ultrasound of the acutely ill obstetrics and gynecology patient. Radiol Clin North Am 21:585, 1983.

Grant EG, Richardson JD, Smirniotopoulos JG, Jacobs NM. Fine-

PATIENT WITH POSSIBLE NEED FOR ULTRASONOGRAPHIC EXAMINATION

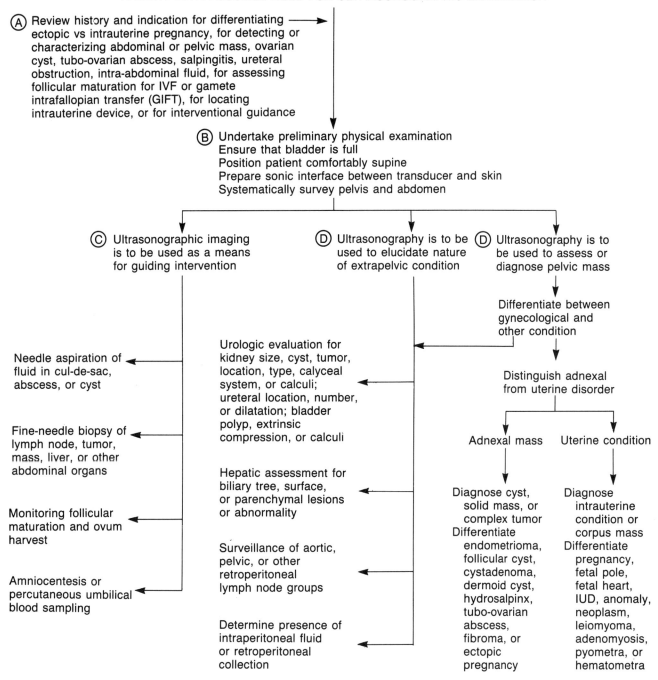

(A) Review history and indication for differentiating ectopic vs intrauterine pregnancy, for detecting or characterizing abdominal or pelvic mass, ovarian cyst, tubo-ovarian abscess, salpingitis, ureteral obstruction, intra-abdominal fluid, for assessing follicular maturation for IVF or gamete intrafallopian transfer (GIFT), for locating intrauterine device, or for interventional guidance

(B) Undertake preliminary physical examination
Ensure that bladder is full
Position patient comfortably supine
Prepare sonic interface between transducer and skin
Systematically survey pelvis and abdomen

(C) Ultrasonographic imaging is to be used as a means for guiding intervention

(D) Ultrasonography is to be used to elucidate nature of extrapelvic condition

(D) Ultrasonography is to be used to assess or diagnose pelvic mass

Differentiate between gynecological and other condition

Distinguish adnexal from uterine disorder

Adnexal mass

Uterine condition

Needle aspiration of fluid in cul-de-sac, abscess, or cyst

Fine-needle biopsy of lymph node, tumor, mass, liver, or other abdominal organs

Monitoring follicular maturation and ovum harvest

Amniocentesis or percutaneous umbilical blood sampling

Urologic evaluation for kidney size, cyst, tumor, location, type, calyceal system, or calculi; ureteral location, number, or dilatation; bladder polyp, extrinsic compression, or calculi

Hepatic assessment for biliary tree, surface, or parenchymal lesions or abnormality

Surveillance of aortic, pelvic, or other retroperitoneal lymph node groups

Determine presence of intraperitoneal fluid or retroperitoneal collection

Diagnose cyst, solid mass, or complex tumor
Differentiate endometrioma, follicular cyst, cystadenoma, dermoid cyst, hydrosalpinx, tubo-ovarian abscess, fibroma, or ectopic pregnancy

Diagnose intrauterine condition or corpus mass
Differentiate pregnancy, fetal pole, fetal heart, IUD, anomaly, neoplasm, leiomyoma, adenomyosis, pyometra, or hematometra

needle biopsy directed by real-time sonography: Technique and accuracy. Am J Roentgenol 141:29, 1983.

Moyle JW, Rochester D, Sider L, et al. Sonography of ovarian tumors: Predictability of tumor type. Am J Roentgenol 141:985, 1983.

O'Brien WF, Buck DR, Nash JD. Evaluation of sonography in the initial assessment of the gynecologic patient. Am J Obstet Gynecol 149:598, 1984.

Rifkin MD, Needleman L, Kurtz AB, et al. Sonography of non-gynecologic cystic masses of the pelvis. Am J Roentgenol 142:1169, 1984.

NEWER IMAGING TECHNIQUES

Benjamin P. Sachs, M.B., B.S., D.P.H.

A. Potential carcinogenic and teratogenic effects have been clearly demonstrated for high-dose therapeutic radiation. Extrapolation has suggested possible effects from diagnostic x-ray as well. As a guiding principle, therefore, one should avoid any unnecessary x-ray examinations. Limit studies to those in which benefits justify risks. Carry them out in the proliferative phase of the menstrual cycle to ensure against inadvertent radiation of a zygote.

B. There is a wide range of available diagnostic techniques in current wide use, such as x-ray studies of the abdomen (flat plate, upright), chest, pelvis (hysterosalpingography [p 220], sinography, gynecography), urinary system (excretory urography), bowel (upper and lower gastrointestinal series, barium enema), and vasculature (angiography). Ultrasonography (p 216) also has broad application. More definitive procedures carry greater risk, including laparoscopy (p 224), hysteroscopy (p 222), cystoscopy, cystourethrography, retrograde pyelography, colonoscopy, culdocentesis (p 212), and fine-needle biopsy (under ultrasonographic guidance). Newer imaging techniques should also be considered where available, particularly if it is likely that their use may clarify an otherwise obscure condition and improve management.

C. Nuclear magnetic resonance imaging delivers no ionizing radiation. It also requires no use of contrast medium or invasive catheterization of the patient. Three magnetic fields are used: a static uniform field, a pulsed or radio frequency field, and a static nonuniform field. These fields excite tissues so that they produce a weak radio frequency signal that is detected and stored by computer for construction into an image. The signal thus generated is not related to physical or radiographic density of the tissue, but reflects the proton density instead. The protons currently being examined derive from the hydrogen atom, but more powerful magnets may be able to generate images from the protons of other chemical elements in the future, such as sodium and phosphorus. Very precise vascular definition is possible by this method because circulating blood leaves the field as the radio frequency pulse is terminated and newly arrived blood volume emits no signal.

D. The specific advantages of magnetic resonance imaging are the total absence of exposure to ionizing radiation and the very good soft tissue contrast it provides. Bowel gas, which can interfere with ultrasonographic and computer tomographic visualization, does not cause similar problems with this technique. Moreover, the subtle tissue changes that occur over time as a result of cyclic hormonal stimulation can be displayed by this approach.

Growths can be identified, although the type of tumor and its malignant nature cannot be distinguished. It has proved useful for staging both endometrial and cervical carcinoma because invasion into adjacent soft tissue is readily seen. The extent of ovarian cancers is less well defined because of confusion between ovaries and nearby loops of bowel. Ureters are poorly visualized. Cardiac pacemakers and cerebral aneurysm clips disturb the magnetic fields. Because movement obscures the images, which take minutes to create, fetal activity limits obstetrical applications.

E. Computer tomography employs low-dose x-ray exposure with sensitive radiation detectors to register electrical impulses that can be digitized and stored on computer. The image is generated by x-ray beams fired from many different angles. Computer technology manipulates the data to provide enhanced sectional images without any superimposition of organs on each other. Very small variations in tissue density are thus detectable, yielding superior contrast; anatomic resolution to show detailed structure is poor, however. Use of contrast materials enhances imaging, analogous to standard urographic or bowel x-ray studies.

F. An especially valuable clinical application for computer tomography is the detection of pituitary prolactinomas (p 70). It is also useful in the evaluation of patients with cervical, uterine, or ovarian malignancy, especially in assessing for lymphadenopathy. A high rate of false negative results means that a negative computer tomographic scan cannot substitute for retroperitoneal exploration at laparotomy where indicated. The method is also useful for diagnosis and sequential evaluation of tubo-ovarian abscesses (p 188).

References

Brenner DE, Shaff MI, Jones HW, et al. Abdominopelvic computed tomography: Evaluation in patients undergoing second-look laparotomy for ovarian carcinoma. Obstet Gynecol 65:715, 1985.

Clarke-Pearson DL, Bandy LC, Dudzinski M, et al. Computed tomography in evaluation of patients with ovarian carcinoma in complete clinical remission: Correlation with surgical-pathologic findings. JAMA 255:627, 1986.

Hricak H. Magnetic resonance imaging of the female pelvis: A review. Am J Roentgenol 146:1115, 1986.

Thickman D, Kressel H, Gussman D, et al. Nuclear magnetic resonance imaging in gynecology. Am J Obstet Gynecol 149:835, 1984.

PATIENT WITH POSSIBLE NEED FOR NEWER IMAGING EXAMINATION

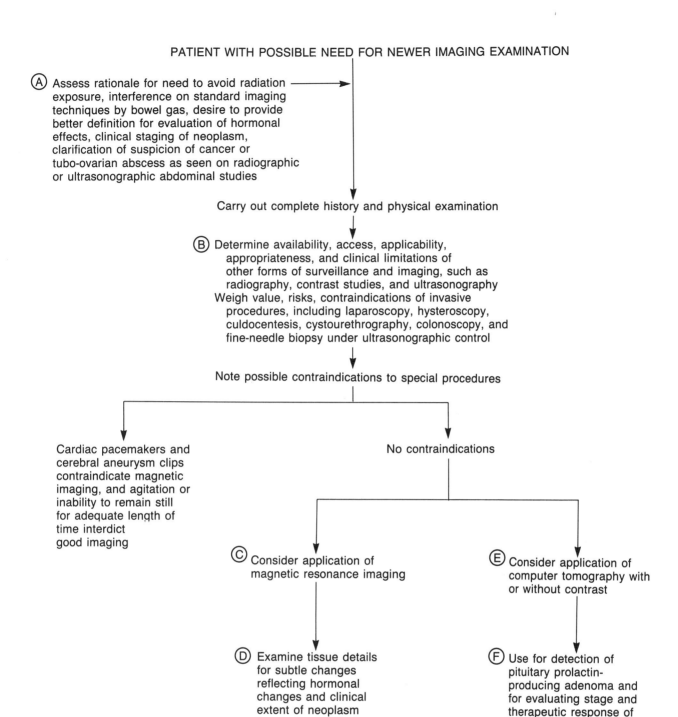

Ⓐ Assess rationale for need to avoid radiation exposure, interference on standard imaging techniques by bowel gas, desire to provide better definition for evaluation of hormonal effects, clinical staging of neoplasm, clarification of suspicion of cancer or tubo-ovarian abscess as seen on radiographic or ultrasonographic abdominal studies

Carry out complete history and physical examination

Ⓑ Determine availability, access, applicability, appropriateness, and clinical limitations of other forms of surveillance and imaging, such as radiography, contrast studies, and ultrasonography Weigh value, risks, contraindications of invasive procedures, including laparoscopy, hysteroscopy, culdocentesis, cystourethrography, colonoscopy, and fine-needle biopsy under ultrasonographic control

Note possible contraindications to special procedures

Cardiac pacemakers and cerebral aneurysm clips contraindicate magnetic imaging, and agitation or inability to remain still for adequate length of time interdict good imaging

No contraindications

Ⓒ Consider application of magnetic resonance imaging

Ⓔ Consider application of computer tomography with or without contrast

Ⓓ Examine tissue details for subtle changes reflecting hormonal changes and clinical extent of neoplasm for staging or for follow-up surveillance

Ⓕ Use for detection of pituitary prolactin-producing adenoma and for evaluating stage and therapeutic response of cervical, uterine, or ovarian cancer, and tubo-ovarian abscess

HYSTEROSALPINGOGRAPHY

Joseph F. D'Amico, M.D.

A. Testing for tubal patency is an essential component of infertility investigation (p 82). Carbon dioxide insufflation (Rubin's test) is more convenient than hysterosalpingography and avoids radiation, but is uncomfortable and not reliable because tubal spasm cannot be distinguished from occlusion by disease. Gas insufflation provides neither visual verification of patency nor any of the additional information needed for assessing tubal anatomy, function, and spatial relation to the ovaries. Hysterosalpingography offers such information and can elucidate vaginal septum (p 146), uterine malformation (p 166), Asherman's syndrome (p 168), cervical incompetence (p 76), submucous leiomyoma (p 182), or endometrial polyps, thus largely replacing gas insufflation as an investigative tool.

B. Before proceeding, determine sensitivity to the iodine-containing contrast material. Patients with prior adverse reactions to dye warrant careful assessment. Skin testing can be done. Consider substituting gas insufflation (see A) instead. If hysterosalpingography must be done, give antihistaminic drugs in advance and be ready to treat an allergic reaction.

C. For patients with a history of salpingitis (p 186), test for residual inflammation with erythrocyte sedimentation rate. If it is elevated, postpone the examination and institute antibiotic therapy. Alternatively, consider laparoscopy instead.

D. Optimally, hysterosalpingography should be performed in the first half of the menstrual cycle, after menstruation has ceased but before ovulation. This avoids exposing a zygote to radiation. In practical terms, on the first day of menstrual bleeding, have the patient schedule her appointment within the next 10 days. Test patients with irregular or infrequent cycles or amenorrhea for pregnancy just before the x-ray study.

E. Essentially all hysterosalpingographic studies can be performed in an ambulatory radiology setting without anesthesia. Patients with a background of severe dysmenorrhea (p 48) or pelvic pain (p 50) may benefit from pretreatment with an antispasmodic agent. Such therapy should be considered for women shown to have proximal tubal obstruction as a means for attempting to alleviate possible tubal spasm in this region. Bowel preparation with enemas is not ordinarily necessary.

F. The choice of oil-soluble versus water-soluble contrast dye is a matter of continuing debate. Oil medium may cause granuloma formation and it risks rare embolic complications if extravasated into veins or lymphatics. However, it produces better studies with less discomfort than watery medium. It is also better for assessment of postinjection peritoneal spread.

G. The technique involves preliminary preparation of the cervix to reduce bacterial contamination and placement of an intracervical cannula for delivering the dye. A Jarcho type cannula is effective for this purpose because it provides an olive to assure a watertight fit and can be held in place by countertraction applied to an attached tenaculum. A suction device is also available for attachment to the cervix; it has the advantage of averting the discomfort of the tenaculum. The cannula and dye-containing syringe should be entirely freed of air bubbles before beginning the instillation. Bubbles within the uterine cavity cannot be easily distinguished from filling defects due to leiomyomas or polyps. Dye is injected slowly while observing the uterus and tubes fill under image intensification fluoroscopy. Obtain a preliminary x-ray scout film and another to document spillage from the tubal fimbria or to show obstruction; a follow-up radiograph is done later (after 24 hours if an oil-soluble dye was used) to confirm peritoneal dissemination or loculation.

H. The value of hysterosalpingography for enhancing fertility is unclear, but reports suggest fertility may indeed be improved somewhat for at least the next six months. If so, it might be the result of mechanically flushing or straightening the tubes or perhaps the bacteriostatic or stimulatory effect of the iodinated dye on the tubal cilia.

References

Alper MM, Garner PR, Bchir MB, et al. Pregnancy rates after hysterosalpingography with oil- and water-soluble contrast media. Obstet Gynecol 68:6, 1986.

Randolph JR Jr, Ying YK, Maier DB, et al. Comparison of real-time ultrasonography, hysterosalpingography, and laparoscopy/laparotomy in the evaluation of uterine abnormalities and tubal patency. Fertil Steril 46:828, 1986.

Soules MR, Spadoni LR. Oil versus aqueous media for hysterosalpingography: A continuing debate based on many opinions and few facts. Fertil Steril 38:1, 1982.

World Health Organization. Comparative trial of tubal insufflation, hysterosalpingography, and laparoscopy with dye hydrotubation for assessment of tubal patency. Fertil Steril 46:1101, 1986.

PATIENT WITH POSSIBLE NEED FOR HYSTEROSALPINGOGRAPHY

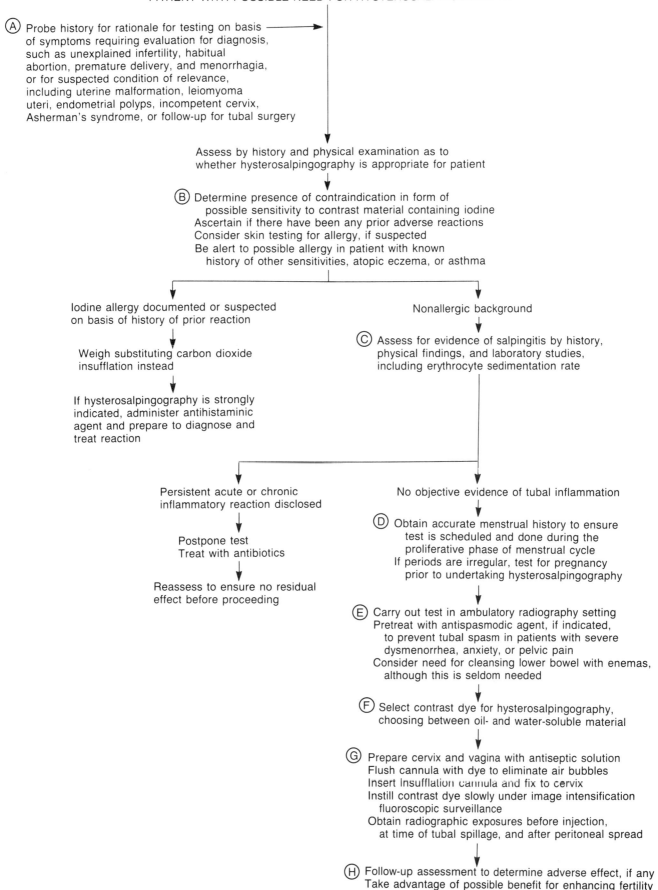

(A) Probe history for rationale for testing on basis of symptoms requiring evaluation for diagnosis, such as unexplained infertility, habitual abortion, premature delivery, and menorrhagia, or for suspected condition of relevance, including uterine malformation, leiomyoma uteri, endometrial polyps, incompetent cervix, Asherman's syndrome, or follow-up for tubal surgery

Assess by history and physical examination as to whether hysterosalpingography is appropriate for patient

(B) Determine presence of contraindication in form of possible sensitivity to contrast material containing iodine
Ascertain if there have been any prior adverse reactions
Consider skin testing for allergy, if suspected
Be alert to possible allergy in patient with known history of other sensitivities, atopic eczema, or asthma

Iodine allergy documented or suspected on basis of history of prior reaction

Weigh substituting carbon dioxide insufflation instead

If hysterosalpingography is strongly indicated, administer antihistaminic agent and prepare to diagnose and treat reaction

Nonallergic background

(C) Assess for evidence of salpingitis by history, physical findings, and laboratory studies, including erythrocyte sedimentation rate

Persistent acute or chronic inflammatory reaction disclosed

Postpone test
Treat with antibiotics

Reassess to ensure no residual effect before proceeding

No objective evidence of tubal inflammation

(D) Obtain accurate menstrual history to ensure test is scheduled and done during the proliferative phase of menstrual cycle
If periods are irregular, test for pregnancy prior to undertaking hysterosalpingography

(E) Carry out test in ambulatory radiography setting
Pretreat with antispasmodic agent, if indicated, to prevent tubal spasm in patients with severe dysmenorrhea, anxiety, or pelvic pain
Consider need for cleansing lower bowel with enemas, although this is seldom needed

(F) Select contrast dye for hysterosalpingography, choosing between oil- and water-soluble material

(G) Prepare cervix and vagina with antiseptic solution
Flush cannula with dye to eliminate air bubbles
Insert insufflation cannula and fix to cervix
Instill contrast dye slowly under image intensification fluoroscopic surveillance
Obtain radiographic exposures before injection, at time of tubal spillage, and after peritoneal spread

(H) Follow-up assessment to determine adverse effect, if any
Take advantage of possible benefit for enhancing fertility by encouraging conception attempts in infertility cases

HYSTEROSCOPY

Joseph F. D'Amico, M.D.

A. The application of endoscopic techniques to examination of the internal surface structure of the endometrial cavity has been limited by the very poor distensibility of the uterus, its friable lining membrane, rigid walls, and peritoneal communication. Improved instrumentation has not only now made it possible to visualize the uterine cavity, its contents, lining, and anatomic architecture, but it is also feasible to consider undertaking a number of operative procedures under direct visualization by transcervical manipulation, analogous to operations capable of being done translaparoscopically (p 240). Thus, hysteroscopy has proved to be a useful clinical tool in the armamentarium for both diagnosis and therapy. The principal and most compelling advantage of hysteroscopy over the inherently blind procedure of curettage (p 230) is its ability to provide direct visualization.

B. Evaluate carefully to detect or rule out possible contraindications. Patients with active uterine bleeding or pelvic infection are inappropriate candidates as are those who are or may be pregnant. Recent uterine perforation will make distension of the cavity impossible; distension adequate for good visualization is not usually possible if the uterine cavity is enlarged to or beyond 10 cm depth as determined by sounding. There is understandable concern about using hysteroscopy to study the location and extent of a uterine cancer because of possible transtubal dissemination, but this concern does not appear to be justified.

C. Counsel the patient about both benefits, in improved diagnostic data and possible therapeutic options, and risks. The latter include anesthesia complications, uterine perforation, cervical laceration, bleeding, infection, or embolization; transhysteroscopic surgery may also damage uterus or bowel as well.

D. Place the patient in lithotomy position and prepare the field with antiseptic solution. Intracervical anesthetic injection or paracervical block is generally adequate, but general anesthesia may be needed. Use of a narrow hysteroscope may only require intravenous narcotic analgesia. Grasp the cervix with a tenaculum, sound the uterus, and insert the hysteroscope. A suction cap is fixed in place if carbon dioxide is to be used as the distension medium; no cap is needed for dextran or dextrose solutions. The safest and most effective distension medium appears to be high molecular weight dextran, but the others are also widely used and acceptable. The medium is insufflated to separate the apposed uterine walls and permit adequate visualization. The procedure should be carried out expeditiously to minimize the amount of medium flowing into the peritoneal cavity by way of the tubes. At the conclusion of the procedure, remove the instruments and check the patient carefully.

E. Contact hysteroscopy requires neither cervical dilatation nor anesthesia in many cases. It provides magnified views of the surface structure of the endocervix and endometrium without distension of the cavity. The instrument is self-contained and independent of external connections. It can be used even in the presence of uterine bleeding and, because it requires no distension, in pregnancy or post partum. It does not offer the opportunity for any interventive procedure and it does not provide an overview of the cavity. It should be considered an adjunct for examining the vagina and cervix of infants and children. Microhysterography is a still more recent development that offers up to X150 magnification using carbon dioxide distension and both contact and panoramic capabilities. It affords a means for detailed study of the endocervical and endometrial lining at the cellular level.

F. Under direct visualization, it is possible to obtain endometrial biopsies from precisely selected sites, remove polyps and small submucous fibroids, locate and remove lost or imbedded intrauterine devices or radium capsules, occlude the tubes for sterilization, and correct some anatomic defects by lysing adhesions or dividing a septum. In addition to direct pressure, one can use cautery electrode, grasping or biopsy forceps, and scissors for these procedures by way of the operating channel in the hysteroscope. Skill gained by experience under supervision is essential.

References

Daly DC, Walters CA, Soto-Albors CE, Riddick DH. Hysteroscopic metroplasty: Surgical technique and obstetric outcome. Fertil Steril 39:623, 1983.

Devore GR, Schwartz PE, Morris JM. Hysterography: A 5-year follow-up in patients with endometrial carcinoma. Obstet Gynecol 60:369, 1982.

Israel R, March CM. Hysteroscopic incision of the septate uterus. Am J Obstet Gynecol 149:66, 1984.

Neuwirth RS. Hysteroscopic management of symptomatic submucous fibroids. Obstet Gynecol 62:509, 1983.

Reed TP, Erb R. Hysteroscopic tubal occlusion with silicone rubber. Obstet Gynecol 61:388, 1983.

Valle RF, Sciarra JJ. Hysteroscopic treatment of the septate uterus. Obstet Gynecol 67:253, 1986.

PATIENT WITH POSSIBLE NEED FOR HYSTEROSCOPY

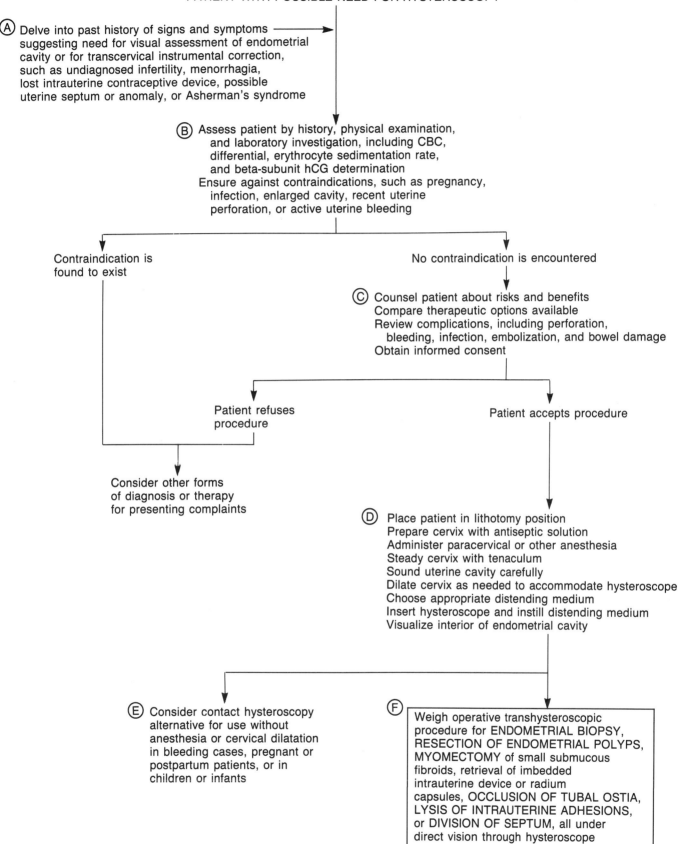

A Delve into past history of signs and symptoms suggesting need for visual assessment of endometrial cavity or for transcervical instrumental correction, such as undiagnosed infertility, menorrhagia, lost intrauterine contraceptive device, possible uterine septum or anomaly, or Asherman's syndrome

B Assess patient by history, physical examination, and laboratory investigation, including CBC, differential, erythrocyte sedimentation rate, and beta-subunit hCG determination
Ensure against contraindications, such as pregnancy, infection, enlarged cavity, recent uterine perforation, or active uterine bleeding

Contraindication is found to exist

No contraindication is encountered

C Counsel patient about risks and benefits
Compare therapeutic options available
Review complications, including perforation, bleeding, infection, embolization, and bowel damage
Obtain informed consent

Patient refuses procedure

Patient accepts procedure

Consider other forms of diagnosis or therapy for presenting complaints

D Place patient in lithotomy position
Prepare cervix with antiseptic solution
Administer paracervical or other anesthesia
Steady cervix with tenaculum
Sound uterine cavity carefully
Dilate cervix as needed to accommodate hysteroscope
Choose appropriate distending medium
Insert hysteroscope and instill distending medium
Visualize interior of endometrial cavity

E Consider contact hysteroscopy alternative for use without anesthesia or cervical dilatation in bleeding cases, pregnant or postpartum patients, or in children or infants

F Weigh operative transhysteroscopic procedure for ENDOMETRIAL BIOPSY, RESECTION OF ENDOMETRIAL POLYPS, MYOMECTOMY of small submucous fibroids, retrieval of imbedded intrauterine device or radium capsules, OCCLUSION OF TUBAL OSTIA, LYSIS OF INTRAUTERINE ADHESIONS, or DIVISION OF SEPTUM, all under direct vision through hysteroscope

LAPAROSCOPY

Max Borten, M.D., J.D.

A. The indications for laparoscopy in gynecology have multiplied as experience with this useful technique has accumulated. At present, a wide variety of gynecological conditions can be effectively evaluated by laparoscopy. The most common applications include evaluation for pelvic pain (p 50), pelvic mass (p 184), ectopic pregnancy (p 198), and infertility (p 86) and for undertaking sterilization procedures (p 266). Laparoscopy is also proving to be a valuable tool for determining progression of or response to adjunctive therapy in ovarian cancer (p 192). A number of translaparoscopic operative procedures (p 240) are being developed and utilized with increasing frequency by experienced endoscopists.

B. Analogous to the principle applicable to other surgical procedures, assessment of the risk factors that may contraindicate laparoscopy must be undertaken before laparoscopy can be recommended. Circumstances in which a laparoscopic procedure is likely to expose the patient to a serious complication include cardiopulmonary instability or compromise, disseminated peritonitis, intestinal obstruction, or the presence of a periumbilical mass; these should be considered absolute contraindications. Relative contraindications make the operation somewhat more hazardous than ordinarily, but their range of risk-to-benefit relationships means that each case must be evaluated on its own merits. Relative contraindications to laparoscopy include previous abdominal or pelvic surgery, antecedent peritonitis, and chronic pulmonary or cardiac disease.

C. A good doctor-patient relationship is a basic ingredient in the therapeutic armamentarium of a physician. Rapport is accomplished in part by educating the patient well in order to enable her to participate in the decision making process. Explain the need for laparoscopy, the technical aspects of the procedure itself, and its risks and alternatives. These are essential elements of information to help the patient make an intelligent choice. The discussion should be a dialogue in which the patient participates actively. Informed consent should be obtained as a by-product of this process rather than its sole motivation.

D. Open laparoscopy has gained wide acceptance as an alternative means for entering the peritoneal cavity. Its main advantage is that it is carried out under continuous visual surveillance. Sharp dissection exposes the peritoneum, which is then opened by blunt perforation or by sharp incision. Take care to dissect perpendicularly to the plane of the abdominal wall. Use the open laparoscopic technique whenever adhesions to the anterior parietal peritoneum are likely to be present, thereby adding to the safety of the procedure.

E. Choosing the most appropriate type of anesthesia for laparoscopy has to take into account the patient's condition, the indication for the procedure, and the goals of the operation. The decision to utilize one anesthetic technique over another should be made in collaboration with the anesthesiologist. Minimizing the anesthetic risk for a given patient is more important than adhering to a single standardized endoscopic method. The experienced laparoscopist should be able to perform the operation under diverse conditions and utilize different anesthetic modalities.

F. Following insertion of the Verres needle, it is essential to assess the position of the needle tip. Instill 5 ml normal saline solution and attempt to reaspirate by syringe to establish whether the needle tip is within the peritoneal cavity; this is known as the syringe test. If the fluid cannot be recovered, the tip is probably placed properly. One can readily recognize the complication represented by aspiration of blood, urine, or feces (p 310).

G. Diagnostic laparoscopy should not be limited to the visual inspection of the pelvis only. Just as every laparotomy should generally include a thorough assessment of the entire abdominal cavity, one can usually explore visually by way of laparoscopy irrespective of the primary indication for the procedure. In this way, the location, configuration, and interorgan relationship of the appendix can often be seen and the hepatic surface, gallbladder, and right hemidiaphragm examined.

References

Borten M. Laparoscopic Complications: Prevention and Management. Toronto: B.C. Decker, 1986.

Borten M, Friedman EA. Visual field obstruction in single-puncture operative laparoscopy. J Reprod Med 31:1102, 1986.

Cunnanan RG, Courey NG, Lippes J. Laparoscopic findings in patients with pelvic pain. Am J Obstet Gynecol 146:389, 1983.

Penfield AJ. How to prevent complications of open laparoscopy. J Reprod Med 30:660, 1985.

Rosenfeld DL, Seidman SM, Bronson RA, Scholl GM. Unsuspected chronic pelvic inflammatory disease in the infertile female. Fertil Steril 39:44, 1983.

PATIENT BEING CONSIDERED FOR LAPAROSCOPY

Ⓐ Assess by prior history, physical examination,
   and laboratory findings for indication for
   laparoscopic evaluation of pelvic pain, mass,
   infertility, ectopic pregnancy, or salpingitis
   Determine applicability for translaparoscopic
   operative procedure (p 240)

Ⓑ Determine presence of risk factors contraindicating
   anesthesia or laparoscopic procedure
   Examine for cardiopulmonary problems, peritonitis,
   bowel distension, parietal peritoneal adhesions,
   periumbilical mass, prior abdominal or pelvic
   surgery, or inflammatory bowel or pelvic disease

Absolute
contraindication
is encountered

Relative
contraindication
is disclosed

No contraindication is found

Ⓒ Explain procedure in detail
   Review relative risks (p 310) and benefits
   of laparoscopy and alternatives
   Obtain informed consent

Ⓓ Weigh resorting
   to use of open
   laparoscopic
   technique

Discuss relative
risks and benefits

Patient does
not accept
option

Patient accepts
open laparoscopy

Consider alternative
management options

Ⓔ Undertake preoperative evaluation
   Seek anesthesia consultation, if indicated

   Provide appropriate anesthesia
   Place patient in semilithotomy position
   Insert intrauterine cannula
   Prepare abdomen as sterile field
   Apply Verres needle intraperitoneally

Ⓕ Determine location of needle tip with
   saline instillation-aspiration test

Improper placement verified

Needle properly placed intraperitoneally

Evaluate aspirated fluid for
blood, urine, gastrointestinal
fluid to diagnose possible
trauma and manage as needed

Proceed to create pneumoperitoneum with carbon
   dioxide insufflation under adequate
   surveillance of flow and pressure
Insert laparoscopic trocar
Verify intraperitoneal position of laparoscope

Evaluate merit of considering
another attempt to insert
Verres needle vs abandoning
technique in favor of other
exploratory options

Ⓖ Inspect entire abdominal cavity and pelvis
   Collect fluid sample, if indicated,
   for culture, cytology, histology

Weigh need for additional punctures for
insertion of probes and operative instruments

Consider TRANSLAPAROSCOPIC SURGERY (p 240)

URODYNAMIC EVALUATION

Balmookoot Balgobin, M.D.

A. Urodynamic evaluation of the lower urinary tract involves study of the flow of urine from the bladder through the urethra. The assessment is advantageous for differentiating between true stress urinary incontinence and urgency incontinence. It is also of value for studying patients whose lower urinary tract symptoms are of unclear etiology. Moreover, it can be used to monitor the effect of drugs in the management of patients with unstable bladder and to study those with neurogenic bladder with a view to optimizing management.

B. Determination of the voiding flow rate (Fig. 1) is useful for assessing incipient lower urinary tract obstruction in the absence of bladder hypotonia. The rate is measured with a full bladder. Peak flow rates above 20 ml per second are considered normal; below 10 ml per second, they are abnormal. Rates between 10 and 20 ml per second need to be interpreted in the context of the prevailing clinical conditions. In women over the age of 50 years, for example, a peak flow rate over 15 ml per second is generally within normal limits. Peak flow rates above 40 ml per second, often termed "superflow," are most commonly seen in women with severe true stress urinary incontinence. A rapid rise to a high peak flow rate of 30 to 35 ml per second and an equally rapid cessation of flow is fairly typical of detrusor instability.

C. The urethral pressure profile measures the maximum urethral closing pressure and the functional urethral length. Although both tend to be small in patients with true stress incontinence, there is so much overlap in the range of recordings among otherwise functionally normal patients that they can only be regarded as data supportive of the diagnosis of true stress incontinence, but not actually diagnostic.

D. Urethroscopy may identify normal or poor sphincter closure during a cough or Valsalva maneuver. Observing poor urethral sphincter closure favors the diagnosis of true stress incontinence, although it too is not sufficiently diagnostic to be of value by itself.

E. A cystometrogram done in the supine position tends to miss some involuntary detrusor activity that can be more readily elicited by the test being done with the patient upright. The greater accuracy and sensitivity of standing cystometrography makes it preferable. More sophisticated, but more costly, is synchronous videourethrocystography, which provides simultaneous independent recordings of intravesical, intraurethral, and intraabdominal pressures. It utilizes a dual microtip transducer in the bladder and the urethra plus a single transducer in the rectum.

F. In patients with a mixed syndrome of detrusor instability and stress incontinence, medical management should be tried first. If pharmacologic treatment with anticholinergic and other drugs (p 98) fails and urinary incontinence persists, surgery should be considered. This applies especially if the detrusor instability is controlled. It is also appropriate if the incontinence is associated with lower intravesical pressure and an anatomic defect characterized by funneling of the proximal urethra. This defect allows urine to enter the upper urethra and reflexively stimulate detrusor activity.

G. A diminished voiding flow rate may reflect detrusor hypotonia caused by drugs, extensive gynecological surgery, or neuropathy (see H). It may also result from bladder outlet obstruction due to urethral stenosis, bladder neck hypertrophy, or distortion of the urethra from cystourethrocele or previous surgery. Functional obstruction is sometimes seen in patients with psychogenic voiding disorders. Irregular micturition occurs with fluctuating detrusor contraction or detrusor-sphincter dyssynergia. The latter abnormalities often appear in association with neurologic disorders.

H. Patients with a neurogenic bladder include those with sensory denervated, atonic bladder; others with hyporeflexic, lower motor neuron bladder; some with hyperreflexic upper motor neuron bladder; and a few with uninhibited bladder associated with cerebral lesions such as Parkinson's disease. Each type has its own characteristic abnormal cystometrographic pattern.

References

Awad SA, McGinnis RH. Factors that influence the incidence of detrusor instability in women. J Urol 130:114, 1983.

Fantl JA. Urinary incontinence due to detrusor instability. Clin Obstet Gynecol 27:474, 1984.

Hilton P, Stanton SL. Urethral pressure measurement by microtransducer: The results in symptom-free women and those with genuine stress incontinence. Br J Obstet Gynaecol 90:919, 1983.

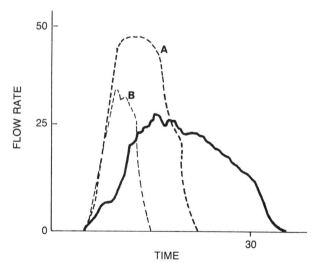

Figure 1 Voiding flow rate study, flow rate in ml per second versus time in seconds, in normal patient (solid line) as compared with pattern of "superflow" rate of a patient with urinary stress incontinence (A) and that of one with an unstable bladder (B).

PATIENT WITH URINARY INCONTINENCE

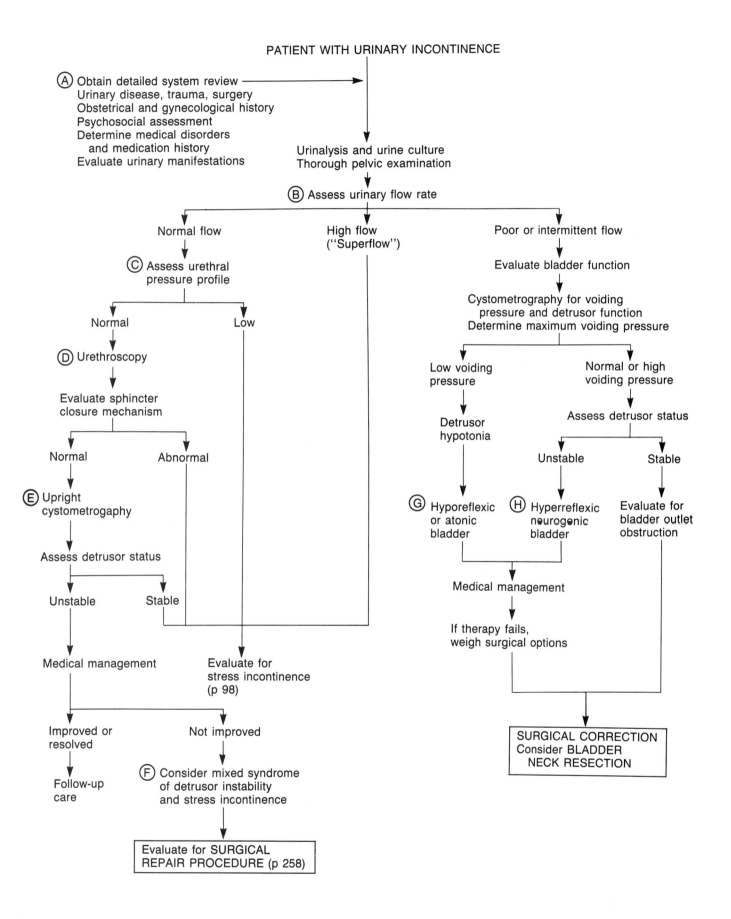

Massey A, Abrams P. Urodynamics of the female lower urinary tract. Urol Clin North Am 12:231, 1985.

Mundy, AR. The unstable bladder. Urol Clin North Am 12:317, 1985.

PREOPERATIVE COUNSELING

David S. Chapin, M.D.

A. All patients confronted with the need to have a surgical operation have some degree of fear, apprehension, and anxiety. Patients who have had prior unpleasant surgical or anesthetic experiences are especially frightened of the prospect. The physician must be sensitive to these feelings and offer maximum support and understanding. Bear in mind the conflicting requirements to provide fully informed consent (p 326) and, simultaneously, to offer solace and reassurance. Giving information leading to truly informed consent is a practice that cannot avoid generating real concerns in the patient about her personal well-being and the risks to which she is exposing herself. It runs counter to the role the physician must also play as counselor to help her cope with both the problem for which she is seeking help and the potentially hazardous procedure that is being recommended for therapy. Resolving these paradoxical objectives is inherently difficult. It requires the clinician to spend an appropriate amount of time talking to the patient and others who will serve to help her through this trying time; while involving others requires the patient's permission, mobilizing such additional supports is important for her and warrants the time and trouble it takes. This process cannot be rushed. Even the most stable patient must be given ample opportunities to verbalize her concerns and to have her questions answered in a forthright, detailed, and temperate manner and in language that she can understand.

B. Consider the patient's psychosocial background, psychiatric history, emotional stability, basic intellectual level, education, and professional achievements in order to learn the proper level at which to conduct the discussion. One has to communicate clearly and exchange information with the patient so that she will comprehend, being careful not to appear to be condescending or patronizing. This is often a problem because even patients who are health care providers, such as nurses or physicians in other specialties, may not be sufficiently knowledgeable about gynecological matters to understand technical terminology and relevant pathophysiologic mechanisms and relationships. Addressing them in lay terms and assuming no medical knowledge can be demeaning, but to do otherwise risks failure to communicate. The best approach is to outline the dilemma beforehand so the patient can guide the discussion actively.

If other consultants are involved in the patient's care, be sure to coordinate their input as well, avoiding conflicting messages if at all possible.

C. Delve into the specific issues about which the patient is most concerned, if expressed, or from which she is likely to have the most serious adverse impact. Be alert not only to worries pertaining to survival and functional recovery, but to fears about the effects of the operation on aging, femininity, attractiveness, body image, libido, sexual satisfaction (as well as ability to satisfy her sexual partner), and reproductive potential. If the surgery is specifically intended to sterilize (p 266), discussion must probe for ambivalence and cover the possibility of failure; it is inappropriate to hold out hope or reassurances of future surgical reversal or in vitro fertilization in order to resolve a patient's uncertainty about proceeding. Contrariwise, it is essential to disabuse patients about mistaken impressions that even otherwise knowledgeable, intelligent, and educated women often have about the effect of a procedure on their future hormonal or sexual function. They deserve full reassurances with suitable supportive explanations. This may require clarification of details of anatomy and physiology in lucid terms, preferably with simple illustrations to ensure full grasp and comprehension. Similarly, the proposed procedure should be spelled out in unambiguous particulars. Bear in mind that some gynecological terms have acquired unexpected meaning to the layman; for example, total hysterectomy signifies removal of uterus and ovaries to some, whereas subtotal hysterectomy is often interpreted as an operation in which the ovaries are left in place. These widely held errors must be addressed in the course of preoperative counseling.

References

Gonzalez BL. Counselling for sterilization. J Reprod Med 26:538, 1981.

Ridgeway B, Mathews A. Psychological preparation for surgery: A comparison of methods. Br J Clin Psychol 21:271, 1982.

Rozovsky FA. Consent to Treatment: A Practical Guide. Boston: Little, Brown and Co., 1984.

Tsoi MM, Ho PC, Poon RS. Pre-operative indicators and posthysterectomy outcome. Br J Clin Psychol 23:151, 1984.

PATIENT BEING CONSIDERED FOR GYNECOLOGICAL SURGERY

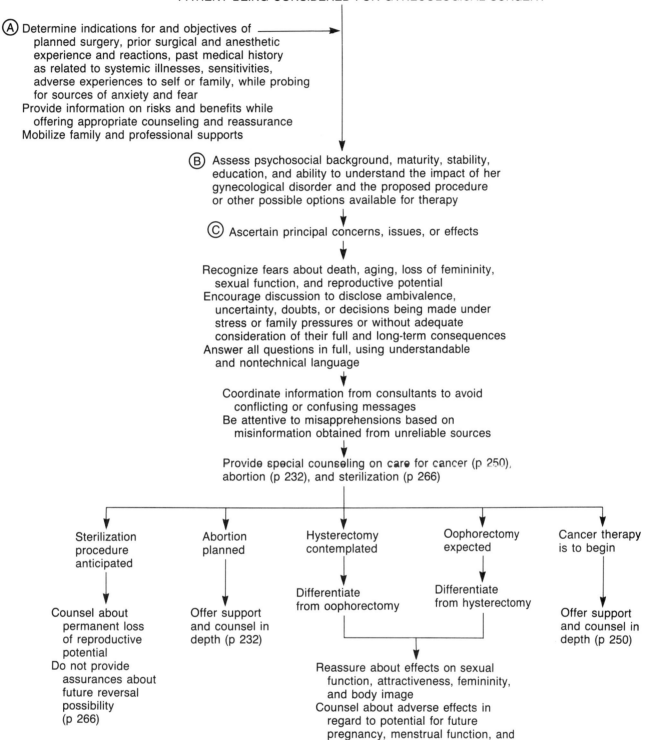

Ⓐ Determine indications for and objectives of
    planned surgery, prior surgical and anesthetic
    experience and reactions, past medical history
    as related to systemic illnesses, sensitivities,
    adverse experiences to self or family, while probing
    for sources of anxiety and fear
  Provide information on risks and benefits while
    offering appropriate counseling and reassurance
  Mobilize family and professional supports

Ⓑ Assess psychosocial background, maturity, stability,
    education, and ability to understand the impact of her
    gynecological disorder and the proposed procedure
    or other possible options available for therapy

Ⓒ Ascertain principal concerns, issues, or effects

Recognize fears about death, aging, loss of femininity,
  sexual function, and reproductive potential
Encourage discussion to disclose ambivalence,
  uncertainty, doubts, or decisions being made under
  stress or family pressures or without adequate
  consideration of their full and long-term consequences
Answer all questions in full, using understandable
  and nontechnical language

Coordinate information from consultants to avoid
  conflicting or confusing messages
Be attentive to misapprehensions based on
  misinformation obtained from unreliable sources

Provide special counseling on care for cancer (p 250),
  abortion (p 232), and sterilization (p 266)

Sterilization procedure anticipated | Abortion planned | Hysterectomy contemplated | Oophorectomy expected | Cancer therapy is to begin

Differentiate from oophorectomy

Differentiate from hysterectomy

Counsel about
  permanent loss
  of reproductive
  potential
Do not provide
  assurances about
  future reversal
  possibility
  (p 266)

Offer support
and counsel in
depth (p 232)

Offer support
and counsel in
depth (p 250)

Reassure about effects on sexual
  function, attractiveness, femininity,
  and body image
Counsel about adverse effects in
  regard to potential for future
  pregnancy, menstrual function, and
  hormonal deprivation
Advise about hormonal replacement

229

ENDOMETRIAL CURETTAGE

David S. Chapin, M.D.

A. As the most common operative procedure performed in the United States, endometrial curettage has both diagnostic and therapeutic objectives. Suction curettage in an office setting generally suffices for all purely diagnostic procedures. More thorough scraping of the endometrial lining is possible, however, if the procedure is done under effective anesthesia; this usually requires a hospital operating room facility. Curettage is done as a preparatory procedure prior to hysterectomy to rule out conditions, such as pregnancy, pregnancy complications, or cancer, that would make alternative therapy more appropriate or for uterine bleeding, thereby seeking the cause, directing evaluation, and guiding management.

B. How extensive the curettage and whether to fractionate it (that is, to curette the endocervix and the endometrium separately) depend on the goals of the procedure. For diagnostic curettage in cases in which cancer is not at issue, a few scrapings may suffice, yielding representative samples from several endometrial sites. For therapeutic purposes, more extensive curettage is needed to debride more of the lining, bearing in mind that even vigorous curettage affects only a relatively small proportion of the lining. For cancer diagnosis, thorough curettage is important, separately sampling endometrium and endocervix to provide valuable information for clinical staging (see D). Aside from simple endometrial sampling for biopsy purposes (p 210), there are two basic methods from which to choose, namely suction and sharp curettage techniques. Suction or vacuum aspiration is applicable principally to pregnancy termination and the management of pregnancy related complications, such as incomplete abortion or retained products of conception following abortion or delivery (see F). The sharp curette is used in all other cases.

C. Paracervical block is an effective anesthesia for induced abortion, office aspiration, or completion of spontaneous incomplete abortion, but it may prove to be inadequate for an extensive procedure, especially if it involves fractional curettage or dilatation of the stenotic postmenopausal cervix. General anesthesia is usually needed under these circumstances. Patients who require an examination under anesthesia for diagnosis or cancer staging or who have associated pelvic pain also need general anesthesia. If local block is being used, consider concurrent intravenous sedation to allay anxiety and apprehension.

D. Fractional curettage should always be done if malignancy is suspected; in fact, it should perhaps be considered for every curettage being done for conditions that are not pregnancy related, especially if the patient is over age 35 years. Submit the specimens of endocervix and endometrium separately for histologic study. Therapy depends on the extent of the disease as determined in this way, because it helps distinguish a cancer limited to the endometrial cavity from one that has extended to the cervix (p 178). Curettage at the time of cervical conization, if undertaken at all, should be done after the resection is completed to ensure against distorting the histologic architecture.

E. Curettage sometimes effects removal of polyps and correction of chronic endometritis. It also helps diagnose submucous leiomyomas. However, consistent long-term benefit cannot be expected from curettage, particularly if it is done for dysfunctional uterine bleeding (p 56), because it does not influence the underlying ovarian cause. The traditional belief that dilatation and curettage has any therapeutic value at all is being challenged increasingly.

F. Curettage for pregnancy related conditions is almost always done by suction rather than sharp method to avoid damage to the vulnerable uterine wall. The most common indications are induced abortion (p 232), incomplete abortion, and postpartum hemorrhage. It is often unnecessary to dilate the cervix, but if it is, consider prior use of laminaria.

G. Although it is unusual to encounter any serious complications with dilatation and curettage, they can occur even in well conducted procedures. Watch for hemorrhage, infection, uterine perforation, cervical laceration, and bowel injury. Perforations occurring at the uterine fundus or midline cervix can be managed expectantly. Observe for signs of bleeding or peritonitis before intervening. Lateral perforation tends to be more hazardous and often requires a more aggressive approach (p 302).

References

Goldrath MH, Sherman AI. Office hysteroscopy and suction curettage: Can we eliminate the hospital diagnostic dilatation and curettage? Am J Obstet Gynecol 152:220, 1985.

Grimes DA. Diagnostic dilatation and curettage: A reappraisal. Am J Obstet Gynecol 142:1, 1982.

Lichter ED, Laff SP, Friedman EA. Value of routine dilation and curettage at time of interval sterilization. Obstet Gynecol 67:763, 1986.

Rubin SC, Battistini M. Endometrial curettage at the time of conization. Obstet Gynecol 67:663, 1986.

Smith JJ, Schulman H. Current dilatation and curettage practice: A need for revision. Obstet Gynecol 65:516, 1985.

PATIENT WITH PROBABLE NEED FOR CURETTAGE

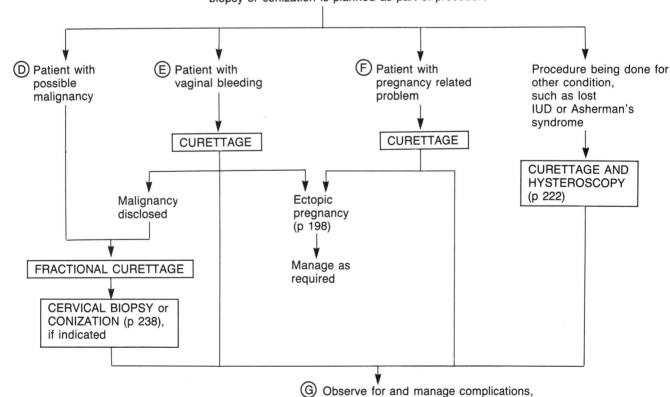

A Delve into medical and gynecological history
for manifestations warranting evaluation or
treatment by curettage, such as vaginal bleeding,
menstrual aberration, incomplete abortion,
possible cancer, postmenopausal bleeding, and
pregnancy interruption and for preoperative examination
prior to hysterectomy or other procedure

Conduct thorough preoperative physical examination and
laboratory investigation, including CBC, cervical
cytology, pregnancy test, urinalysis, and blood
chemistries, to ensure that indications are
appropriate and that no contraindications
exist to interdict the anesthesia or procedure

B Discuss risks and benefits
Define objectives to determine proper choices
of anesthetic and operative technique, weighing
diagnostic vs therapeutic requirement,
malignant condition vs benign disorder,
pregnancy related vs not pregnancy related,
isolated procedure vs concurrent with other surgery

C Choose anesthesia according to patient's subjective
needs and requirements for anticipated procedure
Consider paracervical block for simple curettage
or general anesthesia for more extensive procedure

Prepare operative field with antiseptic solution
Examine pelvis under anesthesia
Sound uterus and dilate cervix first unless cervical
biopsy or conization is planned as part of procedure

D Patient with
possible
malignancy

E Patient with
vaginal bleeding

F Patient with
pregnancy related
problem

Procedure being done for
other condition,
such as lost
IUD or Asherman's
syndrome

CURETTAGE

CURETTAGE

CURETTAGE AND
HYSTEROSCOPY
(p 222)

Malignancy
disclosed

Ectopic
pregnancy
(p 198)

FRACTIONAL CURETTAGE

Manage as
required

CERVICAL BIOPSY or
CONIZATION (p 238),
if indicated

G Observe for and manage complications,
such as uterine perforation, bleeding,
and infection, as needed (p 302)

PREABORTION COUNSELING

Vicki L. Heller, M.D.

A. Women seeking abortion for nonmedical indications deserve nonjudgmental counseling. Women who are denied termination of pregnancy often seek illegal abortion and thus expose themselves to considerable risk. Regardless of the indication for the abortion, the gravida can be expected to have feelings of ambivalence, guilt, shame, grief, loss, and occasionally even desperation. Compassionate and unbiased discussion of all available options and thorough consideration of her particular needs and circumstances best serve her.

B. Careful psychosocial evaluation is mandatory. Most women suffer temporary emotional disruption. Each patient should be encouraged to express her feelings and anticipate feelings. In the case of a woman who is intellectually or psychiatrically impaired, it is necessary to involve a parent or guardian. Consider psychiatric or social work consultation if there is a suggestion of emotional instability, a background of psychiatric illness, evidence of serious social problems, unstable home environment, chaotic life style, or inadequate or inappropriate social support.

C. Probing the reasons for which a woman seeks abortion indicates the most appropriate form and direction of counseling. Some who have no apparent medical indications are found to be under social pressure by family or partner to terminate the pregnancy. They require support and guidance in making a decision in their own best interest. They need to know that an abortion cannot be performed against their will. Review their legal rights with them along with information for options on adoption or foster care and financial resources that might be available. Contraceptive education is important as well. Specialized counseling should be given to rape victims (p 110). While individual counseling is of benefit in creating alliance and trust, group counseling that includes the partner or other family supports may serve a useful purpose as well. Counseling should be continued after the procedure for as long as necessary.

D. The gravida should be given every opportunity to change her mind at any point prior to the abortion. This entails allowing enough time to elapse for her to weigh her decision carefully between initial counseling and the procedure itself. If she chooses to continue the pregnancy, begin rigorous prenatal care. If adoption or foster care placement for the child is desired, refer her to a licensed agency. Evaluation of the adequacy of social support, financial resources, ability to continue education or work, and emotional maturity is important to ensure appropriate guidance and early intervention.

E. When medical assessment is complete, the patient needs to understand the specific risks of the procedure. Discuss the discomforts to be expected and the analgesia that can be given if needed. Address the potential effect on her future fertility. Discuss a medically appropriate plan of contraception. The gravida should be informed about what to expect during the recovery period, including bleeding, psychological reactions, and return of menses. Advise her about signs and symptoms of complications, such as fever, bleeding, and abdominal or pelvic pain. Give her detailed information about the procedure and its risks (p 322) as well as long-term sequelae. Competent informed consent must be obtained.

F. At the procedure, continue anticipatory teaching regarding the emotional impact the patient can expect to feel. Also review contraceptive information. A discussion of postabortal physiology is prudent so that the patient is better able to discern normal from troublesome symptoms. Provide the necessary contact for her as a source for answering questions and dealing with any problems that may arise.

G. At the time of the return visit for examination, reinforce contraceptive planning and routine health maintenance issues. Discuss availability of current and future counseling once again. Good counseling has been shown to improve teen compliance with birth control, enhance decision making skills, and augment personal sense of responsibility for health care.

References

Beeman PB. Peers, parents and partners: Determining the needs of the support person in an abortion clinic. J Obstet Gynecol Neonatal Nurs 14:54, 1985.

Handy JA. Psychological and social aspects of induced abortion. Br J Clin Psychol 21:29, 1982.

Landy U. Abortion counselling: A new component of medical care. Clin Obstet Gynaecol 13:33, 1986.

Lazarus A, Stern R. Psychiatric aspects of pregnancy termination. Clin Obstet Gynaecol 13:125, 1986.

PATIENT REQUESTING PREGNANCY TERMINATION

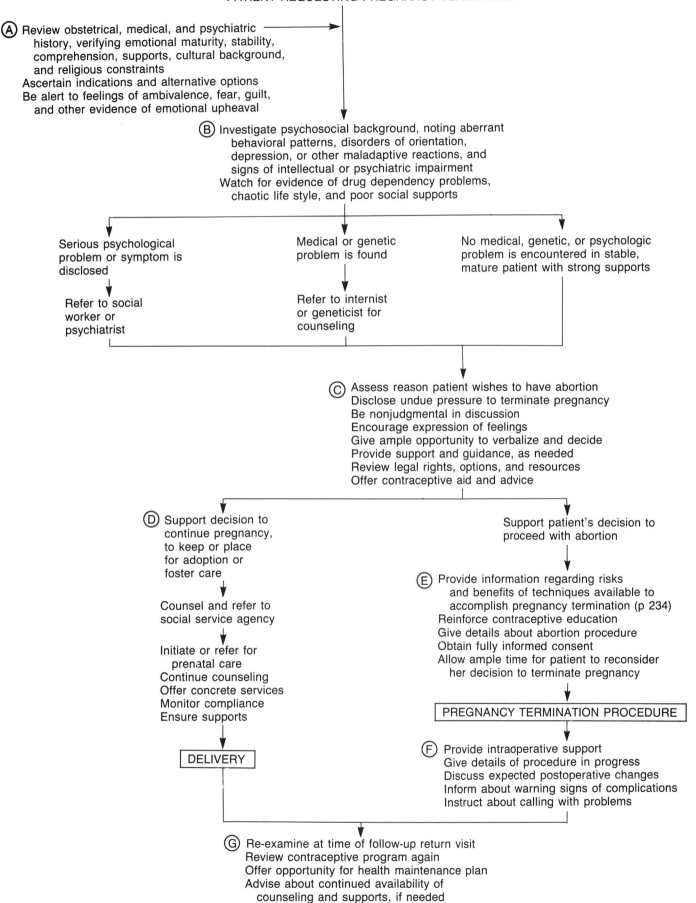

(A) Review obstetrical, medical, and psychiatric
history, verifying emotional maturity, stability,
comprehension, supports, cultural background,
and religious constraints
Ascertain indications and alternative options
Be alert to feelings of ambivalence, fear, guilt,
and other evidence of emotional upheaval

(B) Investigate psychosocial background, noting aberrant
behavioral patterns, disorders of orientation,
depression, or other maladaptive reactions, and
signs of intellectual or psychiatric impairment
Watch for evidence of drug dependency problems,
chaotic life style, and poor social supports

Serious psychological
problem or symptom is
disclosed

Medical or genetic
problem is found

No medical, genetic, or psychologic
problem is encountered in stable,
mature patient with strong supports

Refer to social
worker or
psychiatrist

Refer to internist
or geneticist for
counseling

(C) Assess reason patient wishes to have abortion
Disclose undue pressure to terminate pregnancy
Be nonjudgmental in discussion
Encourage expression of feelings
Give ample opportunity to verbalize and decide
Provide support and guidance, as needed
Review legal rights, options, and resources
Offer contraceptive aid and advice

(D) Support decision to
continue pregnancy,
to keep or place
for adoption or
foster care

Support patient's decision to
proceed with abortion

Counsel and refer to
social service agency

(E) Provide information regarding risks
and benefits of techniques available to
accomplish pregnancy termination (p 234)
Reinforce contraceptive education
Give details about abortion procedure
Obtain fully informed consent
Allow ample time for patient to reconsider
her decision to terminate pregnancy

Initiate or refer for
prenatal care
Continue counseling
Offer concrete services
Monitor compliance
Ensure supports

PREGNANCY TERMINATION PROCEDURE

DELIVERY

(F) Provide intraoperative support
Give details of procedure in progress
Discuss expected postoperative changes
Inform about warning signs of complications
Instruct about calling with problems

(G) Re-examine at time of follow-up return visit
Review contraceptive program again
Offer opportunity for health maintenance plan
Advise about continued availability of
counseling and supports, if needed

233

INDUCED ABORTION

Vicki L. Heller, M.D.

A. Psychosocial evaluation and counseling must precede induced abortion (p 232). Confirm pregnancy and determine the gestational age. Assess medical risks and refer gravidas with significant disease to regional hospital centers for the special care they may need. Most other patients can be managed effectively in free-standing surgical units, provided these facilities are suitably staffed and equipped to detect and handle all complications.

B. Laminaria tents, hygroscopic cervical dilators, or prostaglandins prepare the cervix in advance. They reduce complications and may increase uterine sensitivity to uterotonic agents, thereby making the procedure safer and easier for the patient. However, they require an extra visit for administration and can sometimes cause problems themselves.

C. Menstrual extraction is a relatively safe office procedure for terminating an early gestation (up to seven weeks' gestation based on menstrual dating). No cervical dilatation is necessary. Its drawback is its high rate of failure. Villi are difficult to recognize; therefore, ectopic pregnancy cannot be differentiated. Similarly, patients who are not pregnant or who have a continuing pregnancy cannot be identified easily. Follow-up is, therefore, essential for all patients subjected to this procedure.

D. Suction evacuation is a reliable method for pregnancy termination in skilled hands until the middle of the second trimester. Paracervical block anesthesia is usually used along with short-acting narcotics and benzodiazepines. General anesthesia is seldom given unless clearly indicated. Because halogenated anesthetics relax uterine muscle and cause hemorrhage from atony, they should be avoided. Under sterile conditions, dilate the cervix sufficiently to accommodate the suction cannula needed to accomplish the evacuation. As a guide, the size needed is the same as the gestational age (for example, 10 mm for a 10-week gestation). Take care to avoid perforation, especially with a sound or sharp curette.

E. In late second trimester (beyond 17 weeks), intra-amniotic infusion of prostaglandin $F_{2\alpha}$ (40 mg) may be used in patients with intact membranes. Intravascular injection can cause intense bronchospasm, vomiting, and diarrhea. Avoid this drug in patients with asthma or seizure disorder. It can be combined with hypertonic saline (up to 50 ml) to avert a live birth. Do not give oxytocin in addition because of the risk of cervical laceration or uter-ine rupture. Prostaglandin E_2 vaginal suppository can be used if the membranes are ruptured. Consider prophylaxis against headache, hyperpyrexia, and gastrointestinal hypermotility to reduce side effects.

F. Carefully inspect to be sure that fetal tissue is present and complete. If fetal parts cannot be seen grossly, chorionic villi must be confirmed objectively. If no villi are found, it is imperative to rule out ectopic pregnancy (p 198). Consider re-evacuation if the reassembled fetal parts suggest missing components (especially the head). Be sure to give an appropriate volume of Rh immune globulin (RhoGam) to unsensitized Rh-negative patients. Administer dilute oxytocin infusion (20 IU in 1,000 ml at a rate of 20 to 40 mIU per minute) after the fetus has been expelled to aid uterine contractility and effect spontaneous evacuation of the placenta. More than 40 mIU per minute can lead to water intoxication; if this rate of flow is needed, reduce the fluid given by increasing the oxytocin concentration. If the placenta is retained for more than two hours or if bleeding is excessive, undertake suction evacuation or careful curettage. Watch for hemorrhage, disseminated intravascular coagulation, and sepsis; treat aggressively, if encountered. Uterine perforation is managed expectantly or by intervention as required by its location and manifestations (p 230).

G. At the postoperative examination, review the procedure and the patient's course with her. Continue counseling and offer contraceptive education. Take the opportunity to institute or modify any additional medical care the patient may require.

References

Castadot RG. Pregnancy termination: Techniques, risks, and complications and their management. Fertil Steril 45:5, 1986.

Bygdeman M. The use of prostaglandins and their analogues for abortion. Clin Obstet Gynaecol 11:573, 1984.

Frank PI, Kay CR, Lewis TLT, Parish S: Outcome of pregnancy following induced abortion. Br J Obstet Gynaecol 92:308, 1985.

Rayburn WF, Laferla JJ. Mid-gestational abortion for medical or genetic indications. Clin Obstet Gynaecol 13:71, 1986.

VanLith DA, Wittman R, Keith LG. Early and late abortion methods. Clin Obstet Gynaecol 11:585, 1984.

PATIENT REQUESTING TERMINATION OF PREGNANCY

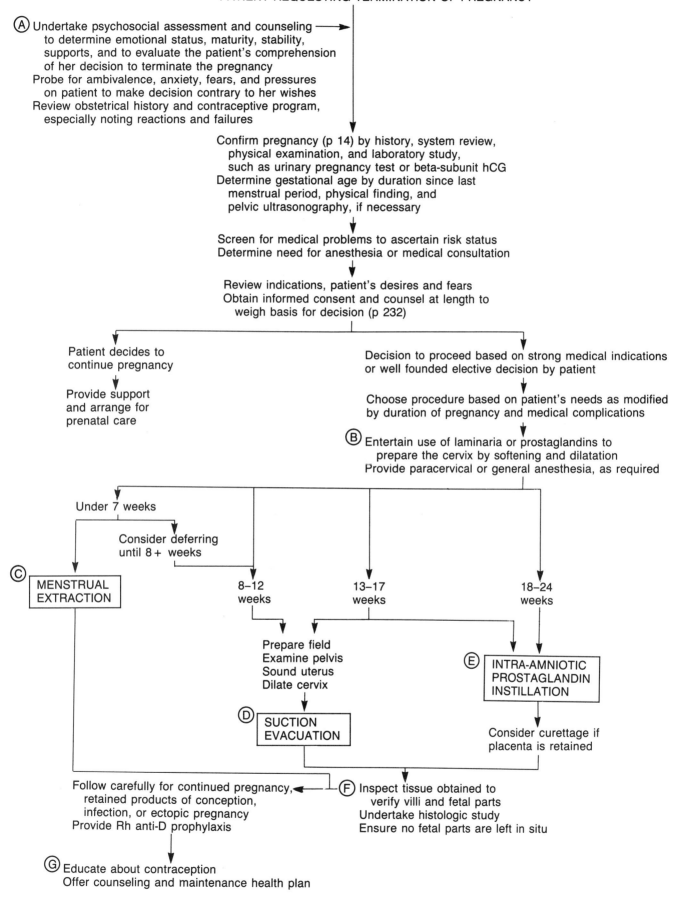

Ⓐ Undertake psychosocial assessment and counseling
        to determine emotional status, maturity, stability,
        supports, and to evaluate the patient's comprehension
        of her decision to terminate the pregnancy
    Probe for ambivalence, anxiety, fears, and pressures
        on patient to make decision contrary to her wishes
    Review obstetrical history and contraceptive program,
        especially noting reactions and failures

Confirm pregnancy (p 14) by history, system review,
        physical examination, and laboratory study,
        such as urinary pregnancy test or beta-subunit hCG
    Determine gestational age by duration since last
        menstrual period, physical finding, and
        pelvic ultrasonography, if necessary

Screen for medical problems to ascertain risk status
    Determine need for anesthesia or medical consultation

Review indications, patient's desires and fears
    Obtain informed consent and counsel at length to
        weigh basis for decision (p 232)

Patient decides to
continue pregnancy

Provide support
and arrange for
prenatal care

Decision to proceed based on strong medical indications
    or well founded elective decision by patient

Choose procedure based on patient's needs as modified
    by duration of pregnancy and medical complications

Ⓑ Entertain use of laminaria or prostaglandins to
        prepare the cervix by softening and dilatation
    Provide paracervical or general anesthesia, as required

Under 7 weeks

Consider deferring
until 8 + weeks

Ⓒ MENSTRUAL
   EXTRACTION

8–12
weeks

13–17
weeks

18–24
weeks

Prepare field
Examine pelvis
Sound uterus
Dilate cervix

Ⓔ INTRA-AMNIOTIC
   PROSTAGLANDIN
   INSTILLATION

Ⓓ SUCTION
   EVACUATION

Consider curettage if
placenta is retained

Follow carefully for continued pregnancy,
    retained products of conception,
    infection, or ectopic pregnancy
Provide Rh anti-D prophylaxis

Ⓕ Inspect tissue obtained to
        verify villi and fetal parts
    Undertake histologic study
    Ensure no fetal parts are left in situ

Ⓖ Educate about contraception
    Offer counseling and maintenance health plan

ABLATION OF CERVICAL LESIONS

Louis Burke, M.D.

A. No ablative procedure should ever be undertaken for cervical intraepithelial dysplasia (p 162) until an evaluation has been completed to ensure there is no hidden focus of invasive carcinoma. To destroy surface epithelium by cryocautery, electrocautery, laser vaporization, or surgical excision by conization (p 238) risks subjecting the patient to an inadequate procedure, delaying diagnosis and institution of essential definitive therapy, and reducing the chances of curing her. Examine by colposcopy (p 214) to identify suspicious sites and sample them for precise histologic verification. Be especially alert if the cytology suggests more advanced dysplasia than can be detected by tissue study. Re-examine with renewed intensity, particularly concentrating on the vaginal wall and the endocervical canal.

B. It is ordinarily easy to see the entire squamocolumnar junction and transformation zone on the portio vaginalis of the cervix of women of reproductive age. Even when there is some slight extension above the anatomic external os into the cervical canal, it is generally possible to visualize these tongues of extension by exposing them with a small endocervical speculum. However, in postmenopausal women or those previously subjected to ablation of the cervical mucosa, the squamocolumnar junction may have advanced cephalad into the cervical canal where the presence or nature of a dysplastic lesion cannot be determined. In these cases, proceed with endocervical curettage, taking care to avoid scraping through an identified lesion in the distal canal or on the exocervix; tissue from these lower sites contaminates the specimen and confuses interpretation. This suffices if it shows invasive cancer, which is unlikely because the pathologic diagnosis requires intact stroma to demonstrate progression of disease below the basement membrane. Therefore, unless the endocervical curettings show mild to moderate dysplasia (cervical intraepithelial neoplasia [CIN] 1–2) compatible with the cytologic findings, conization of the cervix (p 238) is generally mandated even though it requires operating room facilities and anesthesia and carries immediate and long-term risks.

C. Be guided in the choice of ablative method by the depth of tissue destruction that must be accomplished. This is determined by the pathologic observations as to whether cervical glands are involved in the dysplastic process. If they are unaffected, any superficial ablative technique is satisfactory. If the dysplasia extends into the gland crypts, it is essential to recognize the limitations of some techniques for therapy. These constraints apply especially to cryocautery, which is recognized to be capable of destroying only lesions involving surface layers of the epidermis, such as small exocervical lesions of mild to moderate dysplasia (CIN 1–2) that do not extend at all into the glands. Severe dysplasia (CIN 3), which is often found to affect gland crypts to a depth in excess of 5 mm, requires an ablative technique sufficiently destructive at this depth to avert persistence of disease and thus help prevent recurrence at the treated site. Most effective in this regard, with least anatomic distortion, is carbon dioxide laser beam vaporization. It can be carefully controlled under colposcopic guidance to limit its effect with precision to the confines of the lesions and it can be enhanced to provide the depth of tissue destruction desired. If laser is unavailable, consider diathermy or cervical excision conization as a conservative approach for patients with severe dysplasia who wish to retain their reproductive potential.

D. Seldom is hysterectomy done any longer for cervical intraepithelial neoplasia, although it is still considered appropriate in some areas for cases with advanced lesions of severe dysplasia or even superficially invasive disease (less than 1 mm below the basement membrane). Invasion of greater depth should be managed as for grossly invasive cancer with appropriate evaluation and aggressive care (p 164). Most patients with dysplastic cervical lesions can be managed conservatively if they wish (see C); their decision should be made with full knowledge of the potential risks and the need for long-term, rigorous follow-up reassessments. If hysterectomy is chosen instead, simple total hysterectomy either by the abdominal or vaginal route is acceptable. Follow-up care is important for them as well, because their potential for developing similar lesions elsewhere in the genital tract is high.

References

Baggish MS. Laser management of cervical intraepithelial neoplasia. Clin Obstet Gynecol 26:980, 1983.

Burke L. The use of carbon dioxide laser in the treatment of cervical intraepithelial neoplasia. Colp Gynecol Laser Surg 2:77, 1986.

Chanen W, Rome RM. Electrocoagulation diathermy for cervical dysplasia and carcinoma in situ: A 15-year survey. Obstet Gynecol 61:673, 1983.

Creasman WT, Hinshaw WM, Clark-Pearson DL. Cryosurgery in the management of cervical intraepithelial neoplasia. Obstet Gynecol 63:145, 1984.

Townsend DE, Richart RM. Cryotherapy and carbon dioxide laser management of cervical intraepithelial neoplasia: A controlled comparison. Obstet Gynecol 61:75, 1983.

PATIENT WITH CERVICAL LESION BEING CONSIDERED FOR ABLATIVE PROCEDURE

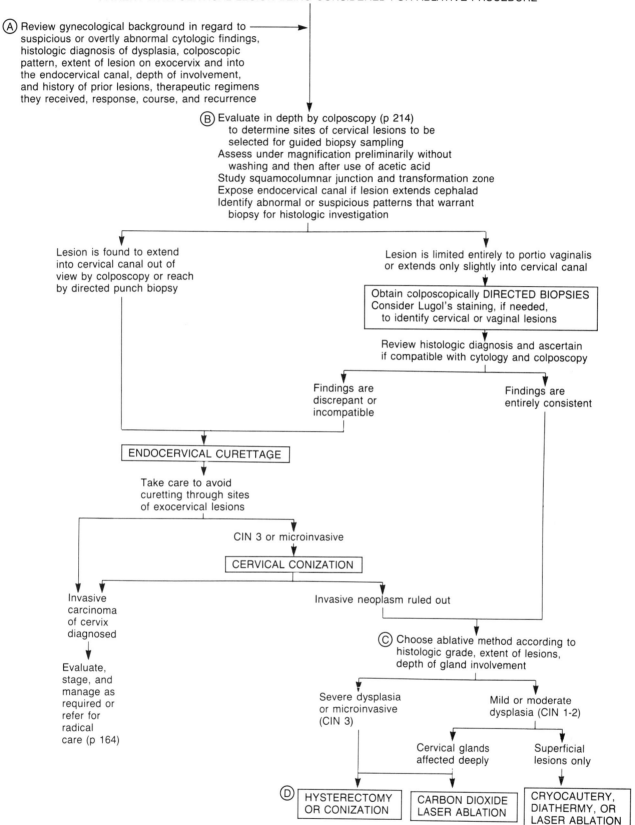

Ⓐ Review gynecological background in regard to
suspicious or overtly abnormal cytologic findings,
histologic diagnosis of dysplasia, colposcopic
pattern, extent of lesion on exocervix and into
the endocervical canal, depth of involvement,
and history of prior lesions, therapeutic regimens
they received, response, course, and recurrence

Ⓑ Evaluate in depth by colposcopy (p 214)
to determine sites of cervical lesions to be
selected for guided biopsy sampling
Assess under magnification preliminarily without
washing and then after use of acetic acid
Study squamocolumnar junction and transformation zone
Expose endocervical canal if lesion extends cephalad
Identify abnormal or suspicious patterns that warrant
biopsy for histologic investigation

Lesion is found to extend
into cervical canal out of
view by colposcopy or reach
by directed punch biopsy

Lesion is limited entirely to portio vaginalis
or extends only slightly into cervical canal

Obtain colposcopically DIRECTED BIOPSIES
Consider Lugol's staining, if needed,
to identify cervical or vaginal lesions

Review histologic diagnosis and ascertain
if compatible with cytology and colposcopy

Findings are
discrepant or
incompatible

Findings are
entirely consistent

ENDOCERVICAL CURETTAGE

Take care to avoid
curetting through sites
of exocervical lesions

CIN 3 or microinvasive

CERVICAL CONIZATION

Invasive
carcinoma
of cervix
diagnosed

Invasive neoplasm ruled out

Evaluate,
stage, and
manage as
required or
refer for
radical
care (p 164)

Ⓒ Choose ablative method according to
histologic grade, extent of lesions,
depth of gland involvement

Severe dysplasia
or microinvasive
(CIN 3)

Mild or moderate
dysplasia (CIN 1-2)

Cervical glands
affected deeply

Superficial
lesions only

Ⓓ HYSTERECTOMY
OR CONIZATION

CARBON DIOXIDE
LASER ABLATION

CRYOCAUTERY,
DIATHERMY, OR
LASER ABLATION

237

CERVICAL CONIZATION

Louis Burke, M.D.

A. The operation of cervical conization should not be undertaken lightly and without strong indication to counterbalance its risks. Intraoperatively, it can be associated with considerable bleeding, sometimes difficult to control, and infrequently even requiring hysterectomy. This applies especially for conization undertaken during pregnancy, which may also cause abortion or premature labor. Other complications include infection, cervical stenosis (p 160) or incompetence, and infertility, plus the risks of the anesthesia it requires. Patients must be fully informed about the risks and counseled accordingly.

B. Indications include situations in which it is necessary to determine the presence of invasive cervical cancer (p 164) and this information cannot be obtained by biopsy. In patients with cervical dysplasia (p 162), for example, conization is indicated if the lesion extends up

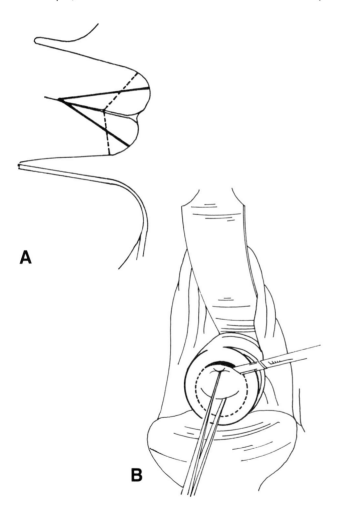

A

B

Figure 1 Conization of cervix (A) may be done superficially to encompass the entire endocervical canal and relatively little exocervix (solid line) or broadly to extend over more of the portio vaginalis, but excise less canal (broken line). The anterior lip is held in a tenaculum (B) while the cervix is circumcised by scalpel (as shown) or by laser beam.

the canal out of sight and the Papanicolaou smear or endocervical curettage suggests moderate or severe cervical intraepithelial neoplasia (CIN 2 or CIN 3). Similarly, if the cytologic report is abnormal and no lesion is found by colposcopy on the exocervix, conization should be done to identify the lesion in the cervical canal; before proceeding, however, look carefully for a hidden vaginal lesion to explain the cytologic finding. The same applies for cytologic observation of a more advanced dysplasia than can be found by colposcopically directed biopsies. A principal indication for conization is a diagnosis of microinvasive carcinoma to look for a focus of deep stromal invasion. Conization may also have therapeutic value, as for the patient with moderate or severe dysplasia who is unreliable as a candidate for the close follow-up surveillance. Excising a cervical cone may also prove useful if laser beam modality is not available or if the lesion recurs after ablation.

C. Prepare the field with care and gentleness to preserve the surface epithelium for histologic study. Disturbing the mucosal lining by vigorous rubbing or cleansing or by use of tenaculum, clamp, or forceps adversely affects its integrity and thereby makes it difficult to interpret the nature of the lesion for which the operation is being done. Be sure to undertake the conization before doing any instrumentation of the endocervix by sound, dilator, or curette.

D. Because the objective of a therapeutic conization operation is to excise a cervical lesion, rather than merely to sample it for diagnosis, it is usually more extensive. This refers especially insofar as its cephalad extent is concerned, because the apex of the cone is intended to encompass the entire endocervical lesion (Fig. 1). Anything less leaves dysplastic tissue behind; the situation can be recognized by histologic examination of the surgical excision margins of the tissue for dysplasia. The exocervical extent of the excision can usually be designated with precision by careful inspection under colposcopy to ensure the conization encompasses the entire lesion. Endocervical curettage should follow the conization as a means for assessing whether any dysplasia may still remain above the apex of the excised cone.

E. Some cervical lesions may be so large that they involve much or all the portio vaginalis or even reach out onto the vaginal mucosa. They cannot be readily encompassed in a conization procedure without defeating its objective of preserving reproductive potential. Consider using a combined approach, namely excising the central component as for a conization and then applying laser ablation (p 236) for the peripheral exocervical portion.

F. It is essential to ensure hemostasis during and following cervical conization. Intraoperatively, one can inject dilute vasopressin along the anticipated excision line. Discuss this with the anesthetist beforehand so that monitoring can be done to detect systemic effects and preparations

PATIENT WITH CERVICAL LESION BEING CONSIDERED FOR CONIZATION

(A) Review patient's needs with regard to future
childbearing, stressing risks of infertility,
abortion, cervical incompetence, and premature
labor as well as those of bleeding, infection,
and cervical stenosis
Counsel about benefits and risks relative to
other forms of treatment, such as hysterectomy
and less definitive ablative procedures (p 236)

(B) Assess indications for therapy of cervical
lesion on basis of its histologic type, degree
of severity, depth, extension on exocervix
and up endocervical canal, or incompatibility
between histologic and cytologic findings

Examine by history, physical examination, and
laboratory studies to ensure against presence of
systemic disorders that might serve to
contraindicate anesthesia or surgery

Obtain fully informed consent

Patient is poor operative
risk or chooses not to
undergo procedure

Consider other options
for eradicating lesions

Patient is suitable candidate and
agrees to accept procedure

(C) Place patient in lithotomy position
Choose anesthetic, as appropriate
Prepare sterile operative field carefully
Avoid tissue trauma prior to conization
Defer uterine sounding and cervical dilatation
until after cervical cone has been resected
Reduce intraoperative blood loss by means of
vasopressin infiltration beforehand

(D) Plan extent of tissue cone to be removed
according to need and based on expected margins
of dysplasia to be sampled or eradicated
Conduct conization under colposcopic control
or with iodine staining to map exocervix

Undertake wide therapeutic conization,
encompassing entire lesion,
if possible

Carry out shallow cone dissection
for diagnostic purposes

(E) Consider combining shallow conization
with laser ablation of portio vaginalis
in cases with extensive exocervical and
vaginal forniceal lesions

(F) Ensure hemostasis at conclusion of procedure
by applying paracervical sutures, but avoid
ureteral damage by close placement to cervix

(G) Follow with endocervical curettage
and fractional endometrial curettage
Mark tissue cone for pathologist
Open specimen and pin in fresh state

made in advance to deal with them if they should arise. Laterally placed sutures to ligate the descending branches of the uterine arteries may be a satisfactory alternative, but take care to avert ureteral injury by ensuring they are not placed too far out in the vaginal fornices or too deeply. If vasopressin is used, ensure good hemostasis with sutures as needed to prevent bleeding when the effect of the agent abates.

G. Tag the cone specimen with a marker suture at the 12 o'clock position to help the pathologist map the lesion. It is good practice to have the cone of tissue opened and pinned in its fresh state before it is placed in fixative.

References

Baggish MS. A comparison between laser excisional conization and laser vaporization for the treatment of cervical intraepithelial neoplasia. Am J Obstet Gynecol 155:39, 1986.

Killackey MA. Diagnostic conization of the cervix: Review of 460 consecutive cases. Obstet Gynecol 67:766, 1986.

Larsson G. Conization of preinvasive and early invasive carcinoma of the uterine cervix. Acta Obstet Gynecol Scand 114 (Suppl):1, 1983.

Luesley DM, McCrum A, Terry PB, et al. Complications of cone biopsy related to the dimensions of the cone and the influence of prior colposcopic assessment. Br J Obstet Gynaecol 92:158, 1985.

OPERATIVE LAPAROSCOPY

Max Borten, M.D., J.D.

A. Diagnostic laparoscopy is an integral component of the basic infertility work-up. It is also useful for the evaluation of acute and chronic pelvic pain. Not infrequently, findings at the time of laparoscopy are amenable to translaparoscopic correction at the same sitting, thus saving the patient the need for laparotomy. Experienced laparoscopists have found that some procedures that previously required laparotomy can now be safely performed transendoscopically without jeopardizing success or safety. To ensure appropriate and satisfactory outcome with minimal risk, careful assessment of each patient is in order before and during surgery. The criteria for undertaking diagnostic laparoscopy in the first instance (p 224), including necessary informed consent, must be fulfilled in any case in which operative intervention is planned or potentially possible.

B. Before one considers performing translaparoscopic surgery, it is important to determine the extent of informed consent (p 330) given by the patient. It is imperative for the surgeon to have disclosed the benefits and risks involved in attempting to substitute innovative translaparoscopic surgery for a standard surgical procedure carried out through a full-scale laparotomy incision. The patient must be informed of the expected limitations, the possibility that the attempted procedure will not be possible to achieve, and, in the event the transendoscopic surgical approach is unsuccessful or complications arise as a result of it, a laparotomy will have to be performed.

C. An increasing number of translaparoscopic surgical procedures are being performed. These are done principally in an attempt to avoid laparotomy whenever it is feasible to do so within the constraints of technical capabilities and safety. Weigh the decision to undertake a procedure by this route prudently. Careful selection of appropriate candidates is paramount. Even more essential is a realistic self-assessment of one's experience, skill, and capability. Not unlike all other surgical procedures, a period of training followed by another period during which procedures are done under careful supervision is required before one should feel confident in replacing standard surgical techniques by translaparoscopic surgery.

D. Translaparoscopic lysis of pelvic adhesions may be feasible to do in many cases. One must possess knowledge about the equipment to be used for the procedure. Bipolar electrocoagulation and sharp division with scissors are commonly utilized. Care must be exercised not to sever vascularized adhesions before hemostasis is se-

cured; otherwise, bleeding occurs. The advent of transendoscopic laser technology has facilitated the performance of the lysis procedure and increased its safety.

E. Before any transendoscopic surgery (for example, biopsy or puncture) is done on an enlarged ovary, one must be sure of its benign nature. When in doubt, laparotomy is still considered the standard acceptable technique needed for adequate exploration. If a benign ovarian cyst has been punctured and drained, one might prevent closure and reaccumulation of its contents by fenestrating the capsule. Biopsy of a solid ovarian mass may lead to local hemorrhage. Hemostasis can be achieved translaparoscopically by local application of microfibrillar collagen.

F. Translaparoscopic resection of an ectopic pregnancy can be carried out by salpingotomy or salpingectomy. The need to preserve adequate tubal function is the deciding factor. Patients with eccyesis located in the isthmic and ampullary segments of the tube are the most suitable candidates for this procedure. The presence of massive hemoperitoneum or brisk active bleeding in the region contraindicates this approach. Knowledge of the vasculature of the fallopian tubes is essential before undertaking this operation. Careful selection of patients enhances the chance of success.

G. Translaparoscopic surgical excision or destruction of foci of endometriotic implants by electrocoagulation can be performed in selected cases. Care must be exercised not to injure underlying organs. The use of transendoscopic laser beam makes it possible to extend this approach to more widely disseminated stages of endometriosis than previously with improved safety.

References

Borten M. Laparoscopic Complications: Prevention and Management. Toronto: B.C. Decker, 1986.

Borten M, Friedman EA. Translaparoscopic hemostasis with microfibrillar collagen. J Reprod Med 28:804, 1983.

Dubuisson JB, Aubriot FX, Cardone V. Laparoscopic salpingectomy for tubal pregnancy. Fertil Steril 47:225, 1987.

Fayez JA. An assessment of the role of operative laparoscopy in tuboplasty. Fertil Steril 39:476, 1983.

Gomel V. Salpingo-ovariolysis by laparoscopy in infertility. Fertil Steril 40:607, 1983.

Keye WR, Dixon J. Photocoagulation of endometriosis by the argon laser through the laparoscope. Obstet Gynecol 62:383, 1983.

PATIENT BEING CONSIDERED FOR TRANSLAPAROSCOPIC SURGICAL PROCEDURE

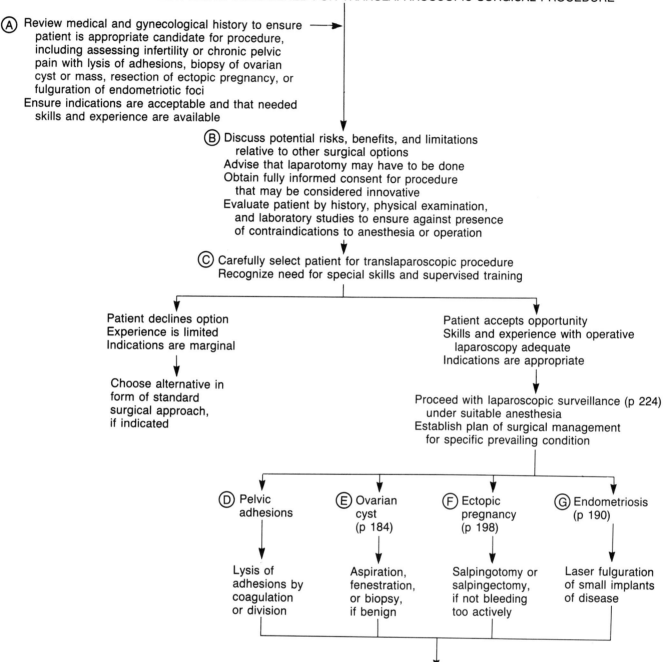

(A) Review medical and gynecological history to ensure
     patient is appropriate candidate for procedure,
     including assessing infertility or chronic pelvic
     pain with lysis of adhesions, biopsy of ovarian
     cyst or mass, resection of ectopic pregnancy, or
     fulguration of endometriotic foci
Ensure indications are acceptable and that needed
     skills and experience are available

(B) Discuss potential risks, benefits, and limitations
     relative to other surgical options
Advise that laparotomy may have to be done
Obtain fully informed consent for procedure
     that may be considered innovative
Evaluate patient by history, physical examination,
     and laboratory studies to ensure against presence
     of contraindications to anesthesia or operation

(C) Carefully select patient for translaparoscopic procedure
Recognize need for special skills and supervised training

Patient declines option
Experience is limited
Indications are marginal

Choose alternative in
form of standard
surgical approach,
if indicated

Patient accepts opportunity
Skills and experience with operative
     laparoscopy adequate
Indications are appropriate

Proceed with laparoscopic surveillance (p 224)
     under suitable anesthesia
Establish plan of surgical management
     for specific prevailing condition

(D) Pelvic
    adhesions

(E) Ovarian
    cyst
    (p 184)

(F) Ectopic
    pregnancy
    (p 198)

(G) Endometriosis
    (p 190)

Lysis of
adhesions by
coagulation
or division

Aspiration,
fenestration,
or biopsy,
if benign

Salpingotomy or
salpingectomy,
if not bleeding
too actively

Laser fulguration
of small implants
of disease

Consider translaparoscopic use of
microfibrillar collagen for hemostasis

241

LAPAROTOMY INCISION OPTIONS

David B. Acker, M.D.

A. Choose the type of incision for laparotomy according to what one expects to encounter and what exposure one anticipates will be required. Speed may be a consideration if there is active bleeding or some concurrent medical problem. Cosmetic objectives can only be considered if all medical and surgical demands have first been met.

B. A vertical midline incision can be extended to provide the greatest access to the abdominal contents. This incision is especially necessary if it is likely that the upper abdomen will have to be explored or operated on. This applies for patients whose diagnosis is unclear or who may have intra-abdominal spread of cancer. If infection is suspected, use a vertical incision to reduce risk of wound breakdown. If bowel or urinary diversion is anticipated, a vertical incision leaves ample room laterally for stoma placement. A vertical incision can be made quickly and is thus preferred whenever it is important to expedite surgery. Seldom is a paramedian incision needed, although it may sometimes offer better exposure for the case in which unilateral disease exists. Do not limit the length of the incision at the expense of adequate exposure. Intraoperative difficulties and postoperative complications may be increased as a consequence of an improperly chosen type, site, or size of incision.

C. In most patients with benign gynecological conditions, a transversely placed lower abdominal incision is quite satisfactory. It takes somewhat longer and is a bit more difficult to perform than a vertical incision, but it is stronger, less painful, and more cosmetic. Dehiscence is rare, but hematomas and seromas can occur, sometimes with secondary infection, if hemostasis is not meticulous.

D. A Pfannenstiel incision is useful for a benign pelvic condition accessible by way of a limited operative field. It is a slightly curved lower abdominal transverse incision (Fig. 1) that can be extended to reach from one anterior superior iliac spine to the other, if necessary. The incision is carried down transversely through the abdominal fascial layers and then the abdominal cavity is entered vertically between the rectus muscles. Take special care to identify and ligate the perforating branches of the inferior epigastric vessels while dissecting under the rectus sheath, thereby averting the risk of hematoma formation. Also avoid damage to the iliohypogastric and ilioinguinal nerves, both of which course between internal oblique and transversalis muscles, to prevent persistent hypesthesia or numbness in the lower abdomen.

E. Exposure can be increased in a transverse incision by cutting the rectus muscles entirely or partially across to create a Maylard incision. The rectus muscles can alternatively be detached from their insertion at the anterior pubic rami; this reduces bleeding and facilitates closure. The incision may prove adequate even for radical pelvic surgery, but upper abdominal visualization or aortic node dissection cannot be easily achieved.

F. Self-retaining retractors are not necessarily innocuous. Avoid pressure damage to the femoral nerve within the psoas muscle. Both motor and sensory neuropathies may result with impaired leg extension or flexion and anteromedial thigh numbness. Take precautions to ensure the blades do not press on the psoas muscle. Pad the ends with gauze and relax the retractor pressure periodically during the surgery.

G. Use a McBurney incision only if the diagnosis of appendicitis is very likely, because visualization and access to pelvic structures is limited. This incision is seldom employed by the gynecologist unless the diagnosis has been confirmed by prior laparoscopy.

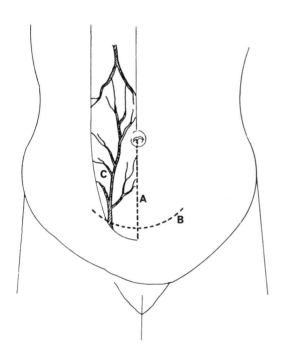

Figure 1 Principal types of abdominal incision for gynecological procedures include either vertical midline (A) or transverse suprapubic (B). Pfannenstiel incision is transverse in skin and fascia and vertical in deeper layers. Maylard incision is transverse in all layers, dividing the rectus muscles and the inferior epigastric vessels (C) coursing in it.

References

Guillou PJ, Hall TJ, Donaldson DR, et al. Vertical abdominal incisions: A choice? Br J Surg 67:395, 1980.

Hudson AR, Hunter GA, Waddell JP. Iatrogenic femoral nerve injuries. Can J Surg 22:62, 1979.

Mattingly RF, Thompson JD. TeLinde's Operative Gynecology. 6th Ed. Philadelphia: J.B. Lippincott, 1985.

Tovell HMM, Dank LD. Gynecologic Operations. Hagerstown: Harper & Row, 1978.

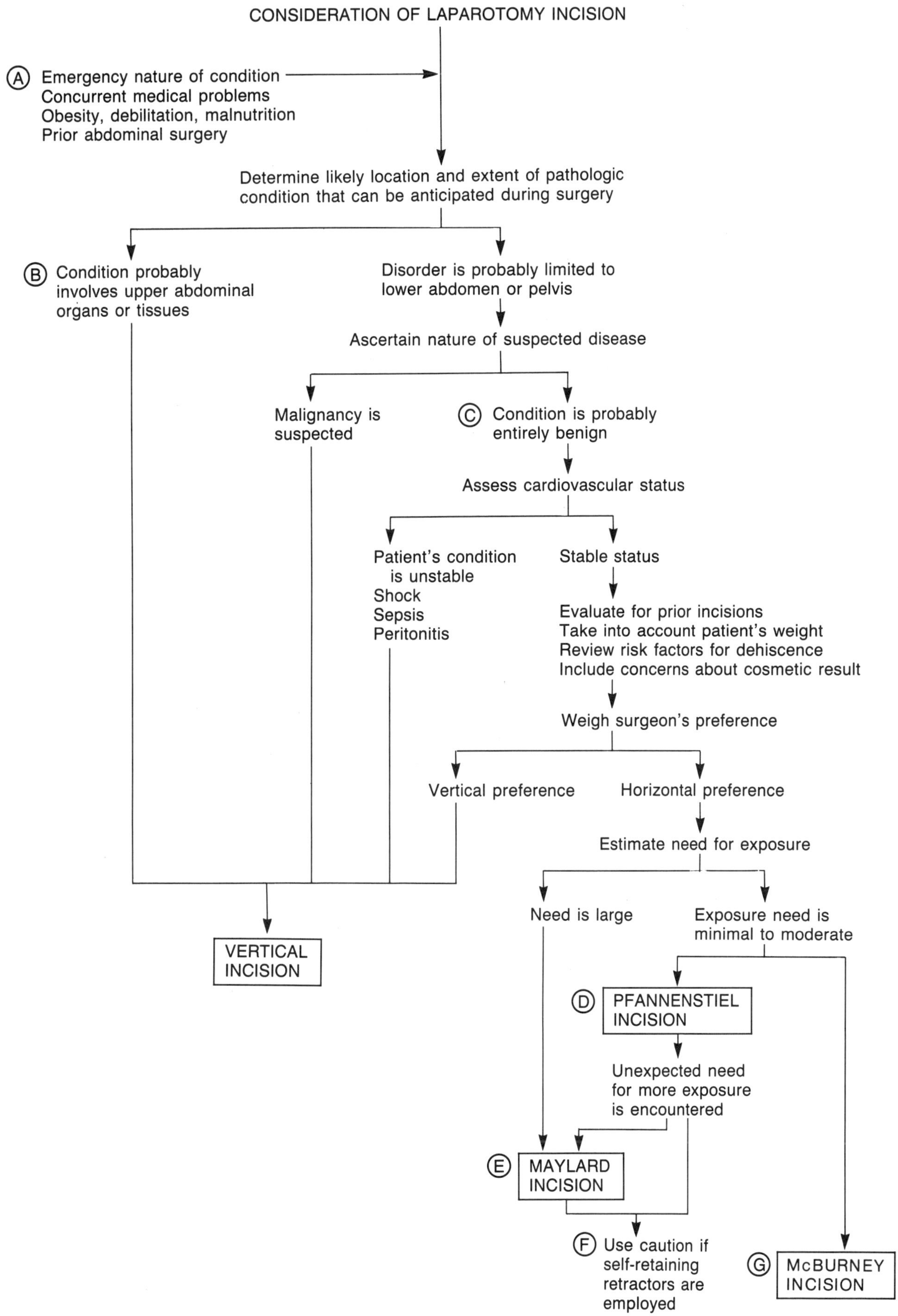

CONSIDERATION OF LAPAROTOMY INCISION

(A) Emergency nature of condition
Concurrent medical problems
Obesity, debilitation, malnutrition
Prior abdominal surgery

Determine likely location and extent of pathologic
condition that can be anticipated during surgery

(B) Condition probably
involves upper abdominal
organs or tissues

Disorder is probably limited to
lower abdomen or pelvis

Ascertain nature of suspected disease

Malignancy is
suspected

(C) Condition is probably
entirely benign

Assess cardiovascular status

Patient's condition
is unstable
Shock
Sepsis
Peritonitis

Stable status

Evaluate for prior incisions
Take into account patient's weight
Review risk factors for dehiscence
Include concerns about cosmetic result

Weigh surgeon's preference

Vertical preference

Horizontal preference

Estimate need for exposure

Need is large

Exposure need is
minimal to moderate

VERTICAL
INCISION

(D) PFANNENSTIEL
INCISION

Unexpected need
for more exposure
is encountered

(E) MAYLARD
INCISION

(F) Use caution if
self-retaining
retractors are
employed

(G) McBURNEY
INCISION

243

WOUND CLOSURE

David S. Chapin, M.D.

A. In choosing closure method and materials, consider problems with healing or inordinate physical forces on the wound that threaten dehiscence (p 292). Adverse conditions include obesity, advanced age, debilitating disease, cancer, severe anemia, hypoproteinemia, malnutrition, or prolonged immobilization, as well as prior radiation, infection, and poor hemostasis. Patients with chronic cough and obstructive pulmonary disease are also at special risk. Give serious consideration to use of retention sutures. The location and length of incision are lesser considerations, rarely dictating the type of closure. Drains should be led out through separate stab incisions away from the primary operative wound, unless the wound itself requires drainage.

B. Choice of suture material depends on a number of factors, including strength desired, duration of holding power needed, probable tissue reaction expected, and resistance to bacterial contamination, if present. Aside from considerations of tensile strength, absorbability, and wicking are those of surface characteristics and elasticity. The more rapidly a suture is absorbed by enzymatic action (catgut) or hydrolysis (polyglycolic acid), the sooner it loses strength. Wicking of braided fibers enhances bacterial growth and migration. Tissue reactivity evoked by material such as catgut may adversely affect healing. The smoother the suture surface, the greater the likelihood that the knot will slip; counterbalancing this, suture with a coarse surface tends to cut through tissues. Elastic sutures stretch under tension and may thereby loosen ligatures. Given the distinct advantages of slowly absorbable polyglycolic acid sutures, and the relative disadvantages of catgut, there seems little justification for using catgut any longer. While surgical habit patterns usually determine which suture is selected (and it is seldom critical), there may be special circumstances warranting a more thoughtful choice. Under such circumstances, the surgeon must be sufficiently informed to choose properly.

C. Weigh the benefits of retention sutures in preventing dehiscence against their adverse attributes, namely greater discomfort and poorer cosmetic result. If retention sutures are deemed to be necessary, apply them through-and-through all layers of the abdominal wall, sheathing the externalized suture ends to prevent them from cutting into the tissues. An effective alternative method is the Smead-Jones technique, which provides placement of subsurface nonabsorbable retention sutures to hold the abdominal fascial layers securely. It has the added advantages of better appearance, less discomfort, and surer approximation than the mass retention technique; since the sutures remain in place permanently, however, the discomfort they cause cannot be relieved and, if infection occurs, they serve as foci of foreign bodies. Allowing a wound to heal by secondary intent, while seldom necessary, is an appropriate option in a grossly contaminated or overtly infected wound (p 290). Periodic debridement and frequent irrigations augment granulation formation. Ventral hernia, expected in such cases, can be repaired later.

D. Closure is ideally done by re-establishing all tissue layers in continuity in the same anatomic relation they were before the surgery. If circumstances permit, careful re-approximation should be done in all cases. Closing the peritoneum, while commonly practiced by gynecological surgeons, is of no proven value. Indeed, placement of sutures in the peritoneal serosa causes local tissue reaction that enhances adhesion formation. This defeats the very purpose of this step in the closure procedure. Fascial closure, by contrast, is a critical component of the closure. Place sutures back far enough from the cut fascial edge (at least 1.5 cm to ensure they will not pull through) and closely enough to prevent a gap through which a loop of bowel may extrude. Make them tight enough to appose cut edges, but not so tight as to cause avascular necrosis. If continuous suture is used for fascial closure, the tension is evenly distributed along the entire incision, but a great deal of reliance is placed in a single knot. If problems are anticipated, therefore, it is preferable to use interrupted sutures for the added security they provide. Suturing the subcutaneous fat and fascial layers is generally unnecessary and may actually serve to increase the wound infection rate. Choice of skin closure is a cosmetic decision among sutures, staples, or adhesive strips with little advantage of one over another. The skin and subcutaneous layers can be left open if infected; consider closure with tape after the infection is controlled.

References

Fagniez PL, Hay JM, Lacaine F, Thomsen C. Abdominal midline incision closure: A multicenter randomized prospective trial of 3,135 patients, comparing continuous vs interrupted polyglycolic acid sutures. Arch Surg 120:1351, 1985.

McNeill PM, Sugerman HJ. Continuous absorbable vs interrupted nonabsorbable fascial closure: A prospective, randomized comparison. Arch Surg 121:821, 1986.

Poole GV Jr. Mechanical factors in abdominal wound closure: The prevention of fascial dehiscence. Surgery 97:631, 1985.

INTRAOPERATIVE GYNECOLOGICAL PATIENT

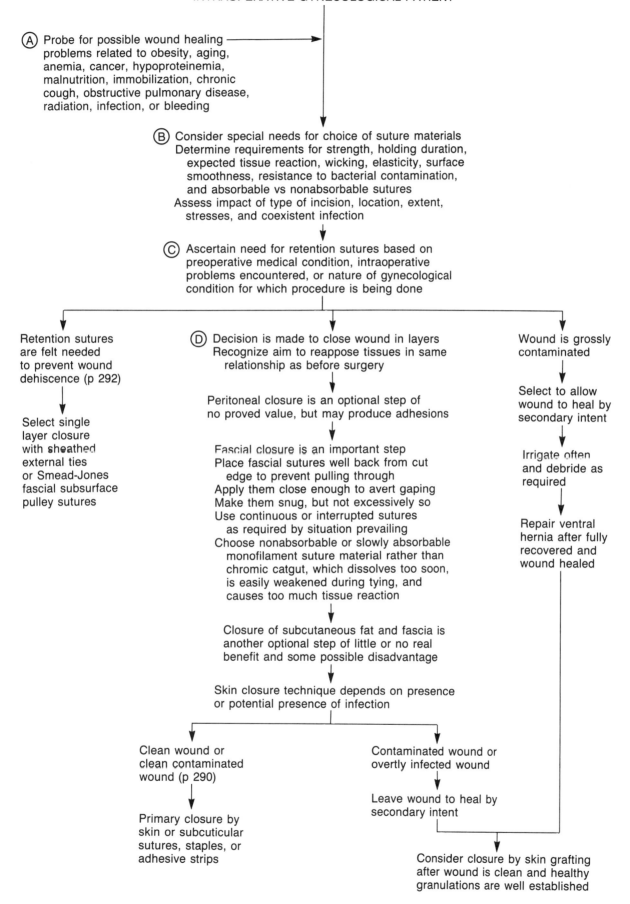

(A) Probe for possible wound healing problems related to obesity, aging, anemia, cancer, hypoproteinemia, malnutrition, immobilization, chronic cough, obstructive pulmonary disease, radiation, infection, or bleeding

(B) Consider special needs for choice of suture materials
Determine requirements for strength, holding duration, expected tissue reaction, wicking, elasticity, surface smoothness, resistance to bacterial contamination, and absorbable vs nonabsorbable sutures
Assess impact of type of incision, location, extent, stresses, and coexistent infection

(C) Ascertain need for retention sutures based on preoperative medical condition, intraoperative problems encountered, or nature of gynecological condition for which procedure is being done

Retention sutures are felt needed to prevent wound dehiscence (p 292)

Select single layer closure with sheathed external ties or Smead-Jones fascial subsurface pulley sutures

(D) Decision is made to close wound in layers
Recognize aim to reappose tissues in same relationship as before surgery

Peritoneal closure is an optional step of no proved value, but may produce adhesions

Fascial closure is an important step
Place fascial sutures well back from cut edge to prevent pulling through
Apply them close enough to avert gaping
Make them snug, but not excessively so
Use continuous or interrupted sutures as required by situation prevailing
Choose nonabsorbable or slowly absorbable monofilament suture material rather than chromic catgut, which dissolves too soon, is easily weakened during tying, and causes too much tissue reaction

Closure of subcutaneous fat and fascia is another optional step of little or no real benefit and some possible disadvantage

Skin closure technique depends on presence or potential presence of infection

Clean wound or clean contaminated wound (p 290)

Primary closure by skin or subcuticular sutures, staples, or adhesive strips

Contaminated wound or overtly infected wound

Leave wound to heal by secondary intent

Wound is grossly contaminated

Select to allow wound to heal by secondary intent

Irrigate often and debride as required

Repair ventral hernia after fully recovered and wound healed

Consider closure by skin grafting after wound is clean and healthy granulations are well established

ABDOMINAL HYSTERECTOMY

David S. Chapin, M.D.

A. Although hysterectomy is commonly performed, it must never be undertaken without clear-cut specific indications to counterbalance its risks. Acceptable indications include uterine cancer (p 178), large or symptomatic leiomyoma (p 182), and descensus (p 152); it is done incidental to management of endometriosis (p 190), tubo-ovarian abscess (p 188), chronic pelvic inflammatory disease (p 186), and ovarian carcinoma (p 192). Even women who have a normal uterus, but have persistent menorrhagia (p 78) unresponsive to curettage and cyclic hormones, can benefit. However, one must be sure there are no serious contraindications.

B. Carry out a detailed history and physical examination to assess medical risk. Obtain preoperative laboratory studies, such as complete blood count (CBC), urinalysis, blood chemistry determinations, and pulmonary, renal, and cardiac function tests, as indicated by the patient's history, symptoms, and physical findings. Assess the urgency of the procedure against prevailing risks. It will be apparent that the urgency depends on the nature of the condition and its presenting symptoms. Cancer or an unresponsive abscess demands action, whereas leiomyoma or descensus seldom does unless associated with intense manifestations. Troublesome symptoms that press for action include severe or unremitting pain, urinary retention, and hemorrhage resulting in progressive anemia despite hematinic therapy.

C. Determine the patient's desires with regard to future childbearing. Discuss her condition and the various options available for care, along with their relative risks and benefits (p 332) so that she is fully informed and thereby better able to make an intelligent choice in her own best interests. Counsel her at length about the physical and emotional sequelae of hysterectomy. If oophorectomy is also being contemplated, review the effects of surgical castration as well as the measures that can be used to alleviate them (p 28). Ensure that the patient understands and concurs in the planned procedure and gives permission for alternatives based on possible unexpected findings.

D. Deciding between abdominal and vaginal approaches to hysterectomy depends on issues of feasibility and access. Whenever possible, vaginal hysterectomy (p 248) is preferable because if antibiotics are given prophylactically, the frequency of complications is decidedly lower, recovery is accelerated, and patients feel subjectively better during their postoperative rehabilitation period. However, vaginal hysterectomy is not always technically possible, as in cases in which the uterus is very large or fixed; moreover, it is inappropriate if the hysterectomy is being done incidental to adnexal surgery or requires access to the upper abdomen.

E. Supracervical hysterectomy is seldom done because it is a widely held standard of practice to remove the cervix at the time of hysterectomy and thereby avert any future problems with dysplasia or neoplasm. However, it is also recognized as imprudent to pursue this objective when it is technically so difficult that it subjects the patient to unacceptable perils of excessive blood loss, unduly prolonged operative time, and damage to the bladder or ureters. This applies in cases with obliteration of the cul-de-sac of Douglas and distortion of the anatomy in this region by endometriosis or pelvic inflammatory disease.

F. A number of intraoperative decisions have to be made of a technical nature pertaining to choice of incision (p 242); suture materials for vascular pedicles, ligaments, and closure (p 244); use of clamps versus clampless method; type of exposure and retraction; packing the bowel; preserving or extirpating the adnexa (see C); concomitant appendectomy; and pelvic drainage (p 36). These decisions are generally made on the basis of prevailing conditions and the patient's stated needs or imposed constraints, often modified by the physician's experience, training, and surgical preferences. As a general guideline, removing the adnexa is justified in postmenopausal women but not in younger women unless they are diseased or require extirpation for technical reasons. It is also good practice to drain the pelvis in contaminated or infected cases either through the vagina or transabdominally (but not through the operative wound). If there is any concern about possible hematoma or seroma formation in the retroperitoneal space above the vaginal cuff, suction drainage through the vault is beneficial.

References

Dicker RC, Scally MJ, Greenspan JR, et al. Hysterectomy among women of reproductive age: Trends in the United States. JAMA 248:323, 1982.

Ledger WJ. Current problems in antibiotic treatment in obstetrics and gynecology. Rev Infect Dis 4:5679, 1985.

Senior CC, Steigard SJ. Are preoperative antibiotics helpful in abdominal hysterectomy? Am J Obstet Gynecol 154:1004, 1986.

PATIENT BEING CONSIDERED FOR ABDOMINAL HYSTERECTOMY

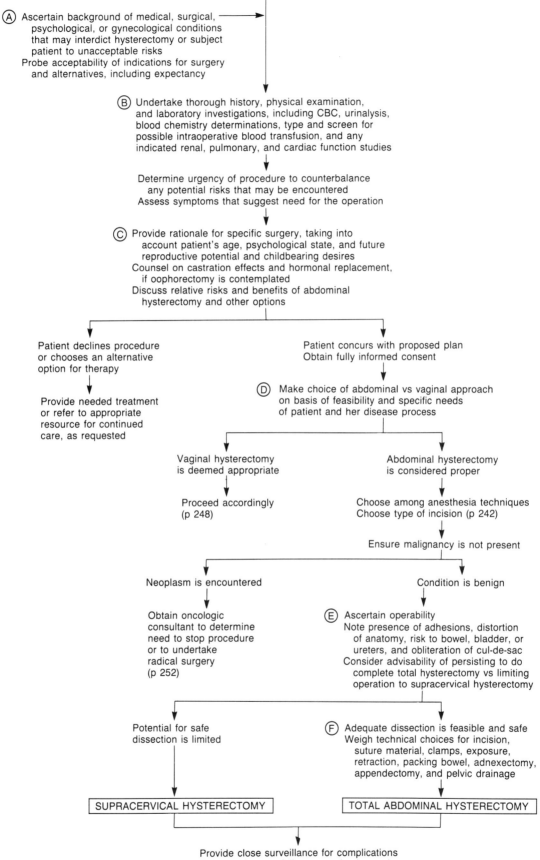

Ⓐ Ascertain background of medical, surgical,
psychological, or gynecological conditions
that may interdict hysterectomy or subject
patient to unacceptable risks
Probe acceptability of indications for surgery
and alternatives, including expectancy

Ⓑ Undertake thorough history, physical examination,
and laboratory investigations, including CBC, urinalysis,
blood chemistry determinations, type and screen for
possible intraoperative blood transfusion, and any
indicated renal, pulmonary, and cardiac function studies

Determine urgency of procedure to counterbalance
any potential risks that may be encountered
Assess symptoms that suggest need for the operation

Ⓒ Provide rationale for specific surgery, taking into
account patient's age, psychological state, and future
reproductive potential and childbearing desires
Counsel on castration effects and hormonal replacement,
if oophorectomy is contemplated
Discuss relative risks and benefits of abdominal
hysterectomy and other options

Patient declines procedure
or chooses an alternative
option for therapy

Patient concurs with proposed plan
Obtain fully informed consent

Provide needed treatment
or refer to appropriate
resource for continued
care, as requested

Ⓓ Make choice of abdominal vs vaginal approach
on basis of feasibility and specific needs
of patient and her disease process

Vaginal hysterectomy
is deemed appropriate

Abdominal hysterectomy
is considered proper

Proceed accordingly
(p 248)

Choose among anesthesia techniques
Choose type of incision (p 242)

Ensure malignancy is not present

Neoplasm is encountered

Condition is benign

Obtain oncologic
consultant to determine
need to stop procedure
or to undertake
radical surgery
(p 252)

Ⓔ Ascertain operability
Note presence of adhesions, distortion
of anatomy, risk to bowel, bladder, or
ureters, and obliteration of cul-de-sac
Consider advisability of persisting to do
complete total hysterectomy vs limiting
operation to supracervical hysterectomy

Potential for safe
dissection is limited

Ⓕ Adequate dissection is feasible and safe
Weigh technical choices for incision,
suture material, clamps, exposure,
retraction, packing bowel, adnexectomy,
appendectomy, and pelvic drainage

| SUPRACERVICAL HYSTERECTOMY | TOTAL ABDOMINAL HYSTERECTOMY |

Provide close surveillance for complications
Ensure adequate follow-up evaluation and care

VAGINAL HYSTERECTOMY

David S. Chapin, M.D.

A. Whenever feasible, vaginal hysterectomy is preferable to abdominal hysterectomy (p 246) because of its more favorable impact on the patient. Relative to the postopera-

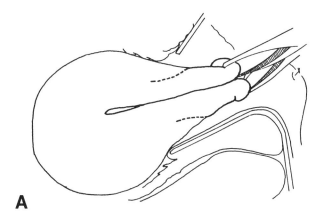

A

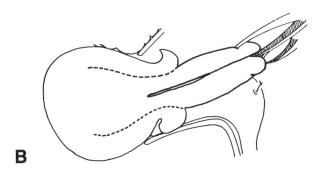

B

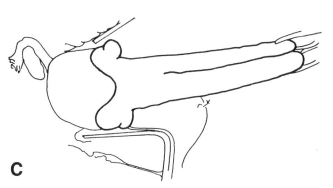

C

Figure 1 Technique for reducing mass of a bulky uterus by serial coring to facilitate vaginal hysterectomy. After the cardinal and uterosacral ligaments and uterine vessels have been ligated and divided, a circumferential cephalad myometrial incision (A, broken line) permits the uterus to descend somewhat with cervical traction. Another similar incision (B, broken line) should reduce the uterine mass sufficiently to expose the adnexal pedicles at the cornua for clamping (C).

tive course after abdominal hysterectomy, patients who have had a vaginal hysterectomy need less narcotic analgesics for shorter periods of time, have fewer complications (since the advent of prophylactic antibiotics), and have to stay in the hospital fewer days. These benefits appear to accrue principally from the absence of an abdominal wound. Indications for vaginal hysterectomy are the same as for those done by abdominal route, except for situations requiring access to the upper abdomen or when the hysterectomy is being done incidentally to adnexal surgery, as in cases of uterine cancer, pelvic inflammatory disease, or endometriosis. Similarly, the operation may not be appropriate to undertake if the uterus is fixed to the adnexa or bowel by adhesions or is too large to permit the procedure to be done safely, even with morcellation techniques (p 260). Vaginal hysterectomy is done most often for uterine descensus (p 152) or pelvic relaxation (p 150); other common applications are menorrhagia unresponsive to curettage and cyclic hormonal therapy (p 78), cervical intraepithelial neoplasia (p 162), and small to moderate size leiomyomas (p 182). It is not essential for the uterus to descend well into the vagina for the patient to be a suitable candidate for vaginal hysterectomy.

B. After a detailed history and physical examination plus appropriate preoperative laboratory studies, counsel the patient as to her condition, the several possible options for therapy, and their relative risks and benefits (p 332). Rule out contraindications, especially as regards conditions that tend to obliterate the cul-de-sac, cause adhesions to the uterus, or require upper abdominal exploration. However, prior pelvic surgery need not necessarily contraindicate the procedure; it may even be done after one or more cesarean sections in some cases. Ensure there are no medical problems making anesthesia or surgery unacceptably hazardous.

C. Administer a brief regimen of antibiotics prophylactically, beginning one to four hours before surgery and continuing for one or two doses thereafter. Use of a first or second generation cephalosporin has been clearly shown to reduce morbidity greatly. Preoperative preparation of the vagina with antiseptic solution is also beneficial. Position the patient well down on the operating table for optimal exposure. Elevating her legs high up flexes her pelvis and facilitates the surgery, improving access to the field and reducing stress on the assistants. If perineal or vaginal narrowing impedes the procedure, make a deep mediolateral episiotomy incision to enlarge the field.

D. Intraoperatively, maintain hemostasis at all times. Take care to dissect in the correct planes, especially at the outset when separating the bladder from the anterior aspect of the cervix. Failure to find the space causes bleeding and risks damage to the bladder wall. Dissect with good control under full visualization of tissues and structures. Inspect the cul-de-sac and rectovaginal septum to detect a previously unrecognized enterocele (p 150) and take precautions to occlude this space to prevent future

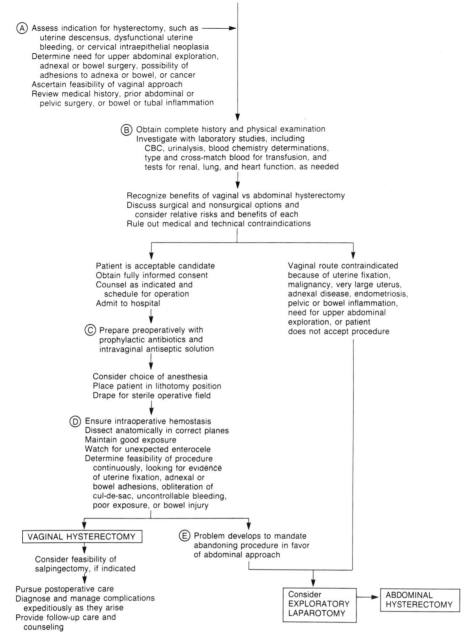

Ⓐ Assess indication for hysterectomy, such as
uterine descensus, dysfunctional uterine
bleeding, or cervical intraepithelial neoplasia
Determine need for upper abdominal exploration,
adnexal or bowel surgery, possibility of
adhesions to adnexa or bowel, or cancer
Ascertain feasibility of vaginal approach
Review medical history, prior abdominal or
pelvic surgery, or bowel or tubal inflammation

Ⓑ Obtain complete history and physical examination
Investigate with laboratory studies, including
CBC, urinalysis, blood chemistry determinations,
type and cross-match blood for transfusion, and
tests for renal, lung, and heart function, as needed

Recognize benefits of vaginal vs abdominal hysterectomy
Discuss surgical and nonsurgical options and
consider relative risks and benefits of each
Rule out medical and technical contraindications

Patient is acceptable candidate
Obtain fully informed consent
Counsel as indicated and
schedule for operation
Admit to hospital

Vaginal route contraindicated
because of uterine fixation,
malignancy, very large uterus,
adnexal disease, endometriosis,
pelvic or bowel inflammation,
need for upper abdominal
exploration, or patient
does not accept procedure

Ⓒ Prepare preoperatively with
prophylactic antibiotics and
intravaginal antiseptic solution

Consider choice of anesthesia
Place patient in lithotomy position
Drape for sterile operative field

Ⓓ Ensure intraoperative hemostasis
Dissect anatomically in correct planes
Maintain good exposure
Watch for unexpected enterocele
Determine feasibility of procedure
continuously, looking for evidence
of uterine fixation, adnexal or
bowel adhesions, obliteration of
cul-de-sac, uncontrollable bleeding,
poor exposure, or bowel injury

VAGINAL HYSTERECTOMY

Ⓔ Problem develops to mandate
abandoning procedure in favor
of abdominal approach

Consider feasibility of
salpingectomy, if indicated

Pursue postoperative care
Diagnose and manage complications
expeditiously as they arise
Provide follow-up care and
counseling

Consider
EXPLORATORY
LAPAROTOMY

ABDOMINAL
HYSTERECTOMY

problems with vault prolapse (p 154). If the uterus is large, consider morcellation, bisection, and coring techniques, which have been refined for relatively safe application in skilled hands (Fig. 1). Access to the adnexal structures is limited somewhat by the vaginal route, but it is generally possible with good exposure to examine them carefully and, if necessary, to extirpate them safely.

E. One must not persist to the detriment of the patient's well-being. While it is seldom necessary to abandon a planned vaginal hysterectomy and proceed with abdominal surgery to complete the operation, it is sometimes necessary to do so. Because this change of plans may arise unexpectedly, it should be dealt with in preoperative counseling (see B). The procedure may prove to be impossible to accomplish because of technical constraints, such as finding an obliterated cul-de-sac or a uterus too fixed to descend even after the uterosacral ligaments and uterine vascular pedicles have been ligated

and divided. Similarly, abdominal operation is required if bleeding vessels cannot be visualized and controlled or if the bowel or bladder is injured.

References

Benigno BB, Evrard J, Faro S, et al. A comparison of piperacillin, cephalothin and cefoxitin in the prevention of postoperative infections in patients undergoing vaginal hysterectomy. Surg Gynecol Obstet 163:421, 1986.

Cruikshank SH. Preventing posthysterectomy vaginal vault prolapse and enterocele during vaginal hysterectomy. Am J Obstet Gynecol 156:1433, 1987.

Hirsch HA. Prophylactic antibiotics in obstetrics and gynecology. Am J Med 78(Suppl):170, 1985.

Kovac SR. Intramyometrial coring as an adjunct to vaginal hysterectomy. Obstet Gynecol 67:131, 1986.

CANCER COUNSELING

Lenard R. Simon, M.D.

A. The need for the physician to provide sensitive support for the gynecological patient is magnified for cancer cases. In addition to those emotional reactions to anticipated surgery seen in nearly all preoperative patients, namely anxiety, regression, and grief sequence, patients who have or are suspected of having cancer commonly exhibit fears relating to death, the treatment, abandonment, loss of independence, and self-worth. They are frightened and expect the worst. Sympathetic concern is essential with an unhurried, comforting attitude; give ample time for talking, listening, and explaining. Honesty is undoubtedly the best approach, balanced and softened by compassionate reassurance. Provide information and begin counseling at the time of the initial evaluation if cancer is suspected. To do otherwise would support the patient's denial mechanisms and tend to make later acceptance of the diagnosis more difficult and emotional response to it more intense. Bear in mind that while the possibility of cancer is frightening, the certainty of the diagnosis can, but need not, be devastating. The more time the patient is given to work through her emotional reaction and its stages of denial, guilt, depression, and anger, the sooner her resolution and integration occur.

B. Once the diagnosis of cancer is objectively established, the patient and her family have to be advised about the specific details of the disorder and the several therapeutic options available, along with their relative risks and benefits. Special care should be taken to give information in easily understood language, verifying periodically that the patient understands what is being conveyed. The news can be so anxiety provoking that she fails to grasp any details beyond the diagnosis. Nonetheless, clear, repeated, and consistent communication is essential. Given the great biologic variations in the natural history of cancers and the variability of their response to therapy, it is inappropriate to be too specific about prognostic outlook. Acknowledge these limitations and, if pressed, provide known data on survival probabilities. This generally offers sufficient hope to motivate the patient to accept one or another meaningful treatment option and to carry on through a particularly trying time.

C. Begin to assess and mobilize the patient's family supports and resources. Consider invoking social service consultation, especially if the patient can be anticipated to experience a severe or aberrant reaction. Such individuals include those with a history of psychological or behavioral problems, psychiatric illness, or a background of abuse, neglect, drug dependency, poor social supports, or chaotic lifestyle. All available resources, including family, hospital, and community based agencies, should be viewed as potentially valuable in caring for the cancer patient. In addition to medical personnel, involve specially trained oncology nurses and social workers as well as community lay self-help support groups, as needed. Only through a well coordinated team approach can there be reasonable assurance of meeting all the needs of the cancer patient and her family.

D. At different times in the course of therapy, the stresses on the patient vary in terms of specific physical demands and emotional responses. Be sensitive to these changing stresses and provide needed supports. Do not react adversely to expressions of anger and hostility, recognizing instead that they constitute a phase in the natural progression of grief; they may actually be a harbinger of good psychological acceptance and resolution. If the disease goes into remission, formulate plans for long-term follow-up care with periodic reassessments.

E. If the disease continues to progress despite treatment, the patient and her family must be prepared for death. Intensification of fear, anger, and depression may severely tax the capabilities of even the most comprehensive program and challenge the structure of stable family relationships. However, the needs for such services and supports are never more important than at this time. If contacts and rapport have been properly established beforehand, matters will be greatly facilitated now. The decision for home care versus hospital or hospice depends on medical needs, but it should be heavily weighted by social and emotional considerations. Take great pain to avoid the appearance of abandoning the patient or losing interest in her as a patient or person. Continuing sympathetic concern for the dying patient is essential. Death with dignity should be our goal. Also remember that the need for support services for family and friends does not end with the death of the patient.

References

Blumberg B. Adult Patient Education in Cancer. United States Department of Health and Human Services. Bethesda: National Institutes of Health, 1982.

Fredette SL, Beattie HM. Living with cancer. Cancer Nurs 9:308, 1986.

Kaplan M. Viewpoint: The cancer patient. Cancer Nurs 6:103, 1983.

Stark DE, Johnson EM. Implications of hospice concepts for social work practice with oncology patients and their families in an acute care teaching hospital. Soc Work Health Care 9:63, 1983.

PATIENT WITH SUSPICION OR DIAGNOSIS OF CANCER

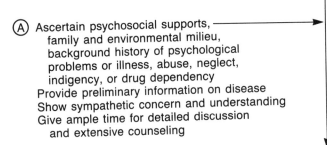

Ⓐ Ascertain psychosocial supports,
    family and environmental milieu,
    background history of psychological
    problems or illness, abuse, neglect,
    indigency, or drug dependency
  Provide preliminary information on disease
  Show sympathetic concern and understanding
  Give ample time for detailed discussion
    and extensive counseling

Ⓑ Confirm diagnosis as required by
    specific organ affected by the cancer
  Advise patient and significant others about
    disease, therapeutic options, and their
    relative risks and benefits
  Use understandable language
  Be consistent and clear
  Stress limited ability to prognosticate
  Solicit cooperation in evaluation

Ⓒ Assess patient fully for extent of disease,
    emotional supports, and social resources
  Seek social service consultation, if required
  Provide information and contacts for any
    future agency or professional care that will
    probably be needed

Select optimal treatment program mandated by
  condition and acceptable to patient
Support patient's decision
Institute primary therapeutic regimen

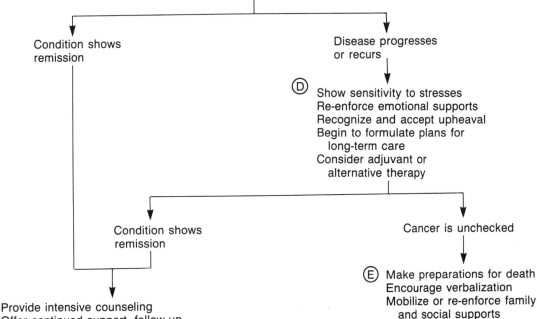

Condition shows
remission

Disease progresses
or recurs

Ⓓ Show sensitivity to stresses
  Re-enforce emotional supports
  Recognize and accept upheaval
  Begin to formulate plans for
    long-term care
  Consider adjuvant or
    alternative therapy

Condition shows
remission

Cancer is unchecked

Provide intensive counseling
Offer continued support, follow-up
  care, surveillance, and information
Observe for evidence of recurrence
Discuss details of plans for
  sequence of visits and examinations

Ⓔ Make preparations for death
  Encourage verbalization
  Mobilize or re-enforce family
    and social supports
  Open discussion of home,
    hospice, or hospital care
  Avoid abandoning patient
  Maintain personal concern
    for comfort and welfare of
    patient, family, and friends

RADICAL HYSTERECTOMY

Jonathan M. Niloff, M.D.

A. Radical hysterectomy is an effective treatment for selected cases of early stage invasive carcinoma of the cervix (p 164) and the vagina (p 158). Microinvasive carcinoma of the cervix diagnosed by conization biopsy (p 238) is managed with an extrafascial hysterectomy. The preoperative evaluation consists at minimum of a complete blood count (CBC), blood chemistry determinations, urinalysis, intravenous pyelogram or computer tomography, and a chest radiograph. Blood should be typed and cross-matched for use in transfusion replacement. Distant metastases make a radical surgical procedure inappropriate; the affected patient becomes a candidate for palliative therapy instead. Evaluate for conditions that may expose the patient to serious operative or anesthesia risk.

B. Staging is performed under anesthesia, preferably in conjunction with the radiation therapist. Cystoscopy and proctoscopy are done at this time. The lesion is measured and a careful rectovaginal examination is undertaken to assess the parametria and uterosacral ligaments for tumor extension (Fig. 1). Candidates for radical hysterectomy are limited to patients with Stage IB and IIA cervical carcinomas up to 3 cm in size and those with small Stage I vaginal cancers limited to the upper vagina. Patients with larger or more advanced lesions are better treated with radiation therapy.

C. It is important to consider the patient's age, menopausal status, general medical condition, and body habitus when choosing the optimal mode of therapy for a given woman. Obesity is a relative contraindication to radical hysterectomy. Significant cardiovascular, pulmonary, or other medical problems make radiation therapy a preferred choice. Relative to radiation therapy, the advantages of radical surgery include preservation of ovarian steroidogenesis, better coital function, and avoidance of the long-term gastrointestinal complications of radiation. Its disadvantages are its greater immediate morbidity, especially bladder and ureteral injury, and the special skills and facilities it demands. It is not a procedure that should be done by the inexperienced surgeon or at institutions not equipped or staffed to deal with the complications that can arise.

D. Anticipate cure rates equivalent for patients with early stage carcinomas of the cervix or the vagina who are treated with either radiation therapy or radical hysterectomy. This must be discussed with the patient along with the advantages, risks, and potential complications of both therapies. Radical hysterectomy is generally recommended and selected by younger patients to preserve ovarian and vaginal function.

E. Thorough intraoperative evaluation must be performed before proceeding with the radical hysterectomy. Palpate the liver and aortic lymph nodes to exclude metastases; if either is involved, do not continue. Explore retroperitoneally for parametrial tumor extension and metastases to lymph nodes. Some surgeons do not undertake radical hysterectomy in the presence of involved pelvic nodes because of the significant morbidity that occurs when radical surgery is combined with radical radiotherapy. Consider relocating the ovaries out of the anticipated radiation field and mark them with radiopaque clips. The abdomen is then closed and radical radiation therapy is given.

F. The procedure of radical hysterectomy consists of resection of uterus and parametrium en bloc plus bilateral pelvic lymphadenectomy. The upper third of the vagina is routinely removed; a more extensive vaginectomy is done in cases of vaginal cancer. The dissection is facilitated by creating the paravesical and pararectal spaces (see Fig. 1). Careful ureteral dissection below the uterine vasculature permits wide resection of the parametria. We do not use ureteral catheters. Prophylactic antibiotics and suction drainage are employed. An indwelling suprapubic or transurethral catheter is left in the bladder for a minimum of one week, and longer if the return of bladder function is delayed. With these maneuvers, urinary fistulas occur in fewer than 2 percent of these cases.

G. Pelvic radiation therapy is administered if postoperative histologic evaluation of the surgical specimen reveals the margins to be involved with tumor. Irradiation is also commonly given when tumor is found in the excised pelvic lymph nodes, but it has not been shown to improve survival and does give rise to considerable morbidity.

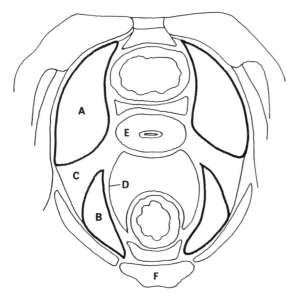

Figure 1 Coronal view of pelvis showing anatomic relationships of paravesical (A) and pararectal spaces (B) with intervening web of parametrial tissue and uterine vasculature (C). Uterosacral ligaments (D) course between cervix (E) and sacrum (F).

References

Bleker OP, Ketting BW, Wayjen-Eecen BV, Kloosterman GJ. The

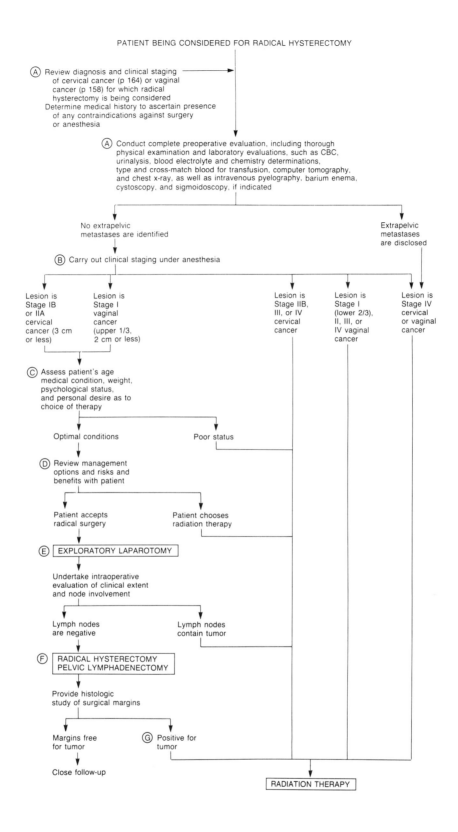

PATIENT BEING CONSIDERED FOR RADICAL HYSTERECTOMY

(A) Review diagnosis and clinical staging
of cervical cancer (p 164) or vaginal
cancer (p 158) for which radical
hysterectomy is being considered
Determine medical history to ascertain presence
of any contraindications against surgery
or anesthesia

(A) Conduct complete preoperative evaluation, including thorough
physical examination and laboratory evaluations, such as CBC,
urinalysis, blood electrolyte and chemistry determinations,
type and cross-match blood for transfusion, computer tomography,
and chest x-ray, as well as intravenous pyelography, barium enema,
cystoscopy, and sigmoidoscopy, if indicated

No extrapelvic
metastases are identified

Extrapelvic
metastases
are disclosed

(B) Carry out clinical staging under anesthesia

Lesion is
Stage IB
or IIA
cervical
cancer (3 cm
or less)

Lesion is
Stage I
vaginal
cancer
(upper 1/3,
2 cm or less)

Lesion is
Stage IIB,
III, or IV
cervical
cancer

Lesion is
Stage I
(lower 2/3),
II, III, or
IV vaginal
cancer

Lesion is
Stage IV
cervical
or vaginal
cancer

(C) Assess patient's age
medical condition, weight,
psychological status,
and personal desire as to
choice of therapy

Optimal conditions

Poor status

(D) Review management
options and risks and
benefits with patient

Patient accepts
radical surgery

Patient chooses
radiation therapy

(E) EXPLORATORY LAPAROTOMY

Undertake intraoperative
evaluation of clinical extent
and node involvement

Lymph nodes
are negative

Lymph nodes
contain tumor

(F) RADICAL HYSTERECTOMY
PELVIC LYMPHADENECTOMY

Provide histologic
study of surgical margins

Margins free
for tumor

(G) Positive for
tumor

Close follow-up

RADIATION THERAPY

significance of microscopic involvement of the parametrium and/or pelvic lymph nodes in cervical cancer stages Ib
and IIa. Gynecol Oncol 16:56, 1983.

Creasman WT, Soper JT, Clarke-Pearson D. Radical hysterectomy for early carcinoma of the cervix. Am J Obstet Gynecol
155:964, 1986.

Goodman HM, Bowling MC, Nelson JH Jr. Cervical Malignan-

cies. In: Knapp RC, Berkowitz RS (Editors). Gynecologic Oncology. New York: Macmillan, 1986.

Morgan LS, Nelson JH Jr. Surgical treatment of early cervical
cancer. Semin Oncol 9:312, 1982.

Patanaphan V, Poussin-Rosillo H, Santa UV, Salazar OM. Cancer
of uterine cervix stage IB: Treatment results and prognostic
factors. Cancer 57:866, 1986.

LYMPHADENECTOMY

Lenard R. Simon, M.D.

A. In the management of gynecological oncology patients, information about the status of the regional lymph nodes draining sites of those primary cancer that spread lymphogenously is very important for determining the prognosis and for guiding the treatment regimen. It is well established that the outlook for cure is considerably diminished if the primary regional nodes are found to contain metastatic tumor, regardless of the extent of the disease as determined by preoperative clinical staging. Lymphadenectomy is done as a sampling procedure to obtain suspiciously enlarged lymph nodes for histologic examination. Alternatively, it can be done in a more thorough fashion to dissect out and extirpate all potentially cancer bearing tissues, usually *en bloc*. The latter is intended to influence the prognosis by surgically removing a likely site of persistent malignant disease or source of future recurrence and dissemination. Whether prognosis can actually be affected by such extensive lymphadenectomy has not been clearly demonstrated, although the procedure is widely practiced. Introduction of sophisticated imaging techniques (p 218) may make it possible to obtain information about the condition of the regional lymph nodes, especially if serially done or the nodes are enlarged by metastatic tumor, without having to resort to surgical exploration. However, microscopic foci cannot be detected. Lymphangiographic contrast dye techniques have not been shown to be of value for assessing lymph nodes in gynecological cancer cases. Fine-needle biopsy technique under ultrasonographic guidance is an interesting development that may supercede node sampling by way of laparotomy. The lymph node groups of greatest relevance in cases of cervical carcinoma (p 164) are the interiliac and external iliac node chains; important inferior and superior gluteal nodes are surgically inaccessible. Ovarian cancer (p 192), which commonly disseminates intraperitoneally, may also metastasize to the aortic nodes, especially at the level of the renal vessels, as well as the aforementioned lateral pelvic nodes. Endometrial adenocarcinoma (p 178) also spreads to both pelvic and aortic nodes. Vulvar carcinomas (p 136) metastasize primarily to the superficial and deep femoral nodes and, in special circumstances, to the iliac nodes as well.

B. Preoperative evaluation is essential by physical examination and laboratory studies to ensure satisfactory general health and to detect the presence of illness or distant metastases that would make the proposed surgery unacceptably inappropriate or superfluous. Extensive assessments pertaining to the primary disease, its clinical extent, histologic type, and degree of differentiation are mandatory. Because the lymph nodes of interest are all located in the vicinity of large blood vessels, lymphadenectomy exposes the patient to the hazard of intense blood loss. Blood must, therefore, be made ready for transfusion and facilities and skilled personnel should be available to deal with the complications of hemorrhage and vascular injury.

C. While the choice of incision (p 242) is dictated principally by the procedure planned for the primary cancer site, it may have to be modified if lymphadenectomy is also contemplated. It is difficult, for example, to gain adequate access to the aortic node region through a lower abdominal transverse incision. A Pfannenstiel incision is seldom appropriate for a pelvic cancer operation, but it can be effectively converted to a Maylard incision by cutting across the rectus abdominis muscles to provide adequate lower abdominal exposure for pelvic lymphadenectomy, but not ordinarily for a satisfactory aortic node dissection. For this latter purpose, a vertical incision is clearly preferable with cephalad extension around the umbilicus as high as deemed necessary to accomplish the operative procedure. If intra-abdominal exploration is not required, consider approaching the lateral pelvic nodes extraperitoneally by way of bilateral inguinal incisions, reflecting the intact peritoneum and underlying bowel medially to expose the pelvic vessels and associated nodes. Femoral lymphadenectomy can be done through separate vertical groin incisions or oblique inguinal extensions (up to the anterior superior spine of the ilium) of the concurrent vulvectomy incision.

D. It is imperative for the gynecologist who undertakes a lymphadenectomy to be thoroughly familiar with all details of the anatomic relationships of the lymph nodes and blood vessels in the areas of interest. Knowledge about the node groups likely to be affected, the adjacent structures at risk, and technical measures needed to carry out surgical extirpation safely is essential. The dissection must be done with great care, under full visualization, with meticulous attention to hemostasis and anatomical dissection.

References

Gallup DG, Jordan GH, Talledo OE. Extraperitoneal lymph node dissections with use of a midline incision in patients with female genital cancer. Am J Obstet Gynecol 155:559, 1986.

Kjorstad KE, Kolbenstvedt A, Strickert T. The value of complete lymphadenectomy in radical treatment of cancer of the cervix, Stage IB. Cancer 54:2215, 1984.

Orr JW Jr, Barter JF, Kilgore LC, et al. Closed suction pelvic drainage after radical pelvic surgical procedures. Am J Obstet Gynecol 155:867, 1986.

Powell JL, Burrell MO, Franklin EW. Radical hysterectomy and pelvic lymphadenectomy. South Med J 77:596, 1984.

PATIENT BEING CONSIDERED FOR LYMPHADENECTOMY

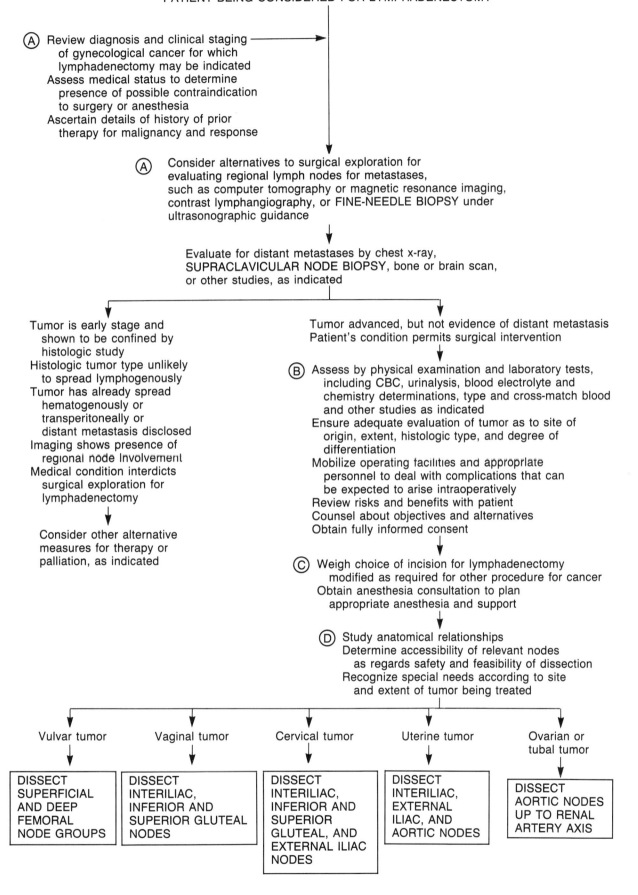

(A) Review diagnosis and clinical staging
of gynecological cancer for which
lymphadenectomy may be indicated
Assess medical status to determine
presence of possible contraindication
to surgery or anesthesia
Ascertain details of history of prior
therapy for malignancy and response

(A) Consider alternatives to surgical exploration for
evaluating regional lymph nodes for metastases,
such as computer tomography or magnetic resonance imaging,
contrast lymphangiography, or FINE-NEEDLE BIOPSY under
ultrasonographic guidance

Evaluate for distant metastases by chest x-ray,
SUPRACLAVICULAR NODE BIOPSY, bone or brain scan,
or other studies, as indicated

Tumor is early stage and
shown to be confined by
histologic study
Histologic tumor type unlikely
to spread lymphogenously
Tumor has already spread
hematogenously or
transperitoneally or
distant metastasis disclosed
Imaging shows presence of
regional node involvement
Medical condition interdicts
surgical exploration for
lymphadenectomy

Consider other alternative
measures for therapy or
palliation, as indicated

Tumor advanced, but not evidence of distant metastasis
Patient's condition permits surgical intervention

(B) Assess by physical examination and laboratory tests,
including CBC, urinalysis, blood electrolyte and
chemistry determinations, type and cross-match blood
and other studies as indicated
Ensure adequate evaluation of tumor as to site of
origin, extent, histologic type, and degree of
differentiation
Mobilize operating facilities and appropriate
personnel to deal with complications that can
be expected to arise intraoperatively
Review risks and benefits with patient
Counsel about objectives and alternatives
Obtain fully informed consent

(C) Weigh choice of incision for lymphadenectomy
modified as required for other procedure for cancer
Obtain anesthesia consultation to plan
appropriate anesthesia and support

(D) Study anatomical relationships
Determine accessibility of relevant nodes
as regards safety and feasibility of dissection
Recognize special needs according to site
and extent of tumor being treated

Vulvar tumor

Vaginal tumor

Cervical tumor

Uterine tumor

Ovarian or
tubal tumor

DISSECT
SUPERFICIAL
AND DEEP
FEMORAL
NODE GROUPS

DISSECT
INTERILIAC,
INFERIOR AND
SUPERIOR GLUTEAL
NODES

DISSECT
INTERILIAC,
INFERIOR AND
SUPERIOR
GLUTEAL, AND
EXTERNAL ILIAC
NODES

DISSECT
INTERILIAC,
EXTERNAL
ILIAC, AND
AORTIC NODES

DISSECT
AORTIC NODES
UP TO RENAL
ARTERY AXIS

EXENTERATION

Lenard R. Simon, M.D.

A. Pelvic exenteration is rarely done any longer because its complications and emotional impact are so intense that it must not be undertaken unless there is a reasonable chance of cure. It is not done for palliative purposes. Exenteration is indicated for cervical carcinoma Stage IV extending anteriorly to invade the bladder or posteriorly to the rectum without concomitant lateral extension. Since the usual natural history of cancer of the cervix (p 164) is extension laterally to the pelvic wall, most advanced cases do not qualify. Patients with cancer recurrent locally after radiation therapy may also prove suitable candidates. It cannot be undertaken without an experienced and skilled surgical team in an institution fully equipped and staffed to deal with the many serious problems that can arise during and following the operation.

B. Before embarking on this type of surgery, be sure to assess the patient's general medical status by detailed history, physical examination, and laboratory study. Intensive search must be made to disclose distant metastases; their presence interdicts exenteration. This search should include radiography and computer tomography investigations to detect hidden foci of tumor, especially in retroperitoneal lymph nodes. Suspicious nodes can be biopsied by fine-needle technique under ultrasonographic guidance. Moreover, the patient's emotional status must be evaluated to determine if she is stable and mature enough to tolerate the expected emotional trauma. Counseling has to be done in depth to ensure the patient is properly prepared for the disfigurement, urinary and/or fecal diversion, colostomy care, complications, and prolonged recovery. Unless she fully understands and accepts this information, she cannot be said to be adequately informed in regard to giving her operative consent.

C. Given the large blood loss that can be expected, blood must be readied in large amounts for transfusion. As aforementioned, exenteration should not be done if the tumor has already extended beyond the operative field. Therefore, even though preoperative evaluations may not have revealed any metastases, it is still necessary to conduct an intraoperative search to ascertain whether it is feasible to resect adequately. To accomplish this, undertake sampling of any suspicious lymph nodes, indurated areas, adhesions, or nodules in the pelvis and abdomen outside of the surgical borders of the tissue one expects to resect. If frozen section histologic examination demonstrates tumor present in these biopsy samples, exenteration is contraindicated.

D. For cases in which there is only anterior spread to the bladder, anterior exenteration is done. It encompasses radical hysterectomy (p 252), pelvic lymphadenectomy

(p 254), total cystectomy, and diversion of the urinary tract. The diversion usually requires creating an ileal loop by isolating a segment of terminal ileum into which the divided distal ends of the ureters are implanted. A loop of sigmoid or transverse colon, although less preferable, may be substituted instead, if the ileum cannot be used because of prior irradiation. If the cancer has extended to the lateral pelvic nodes, the chances of cure by anterior exenteration becomes so remote that the operation should not be done.

E. Rarely will cervical cancer extend posteriorly to the rectum alone. If it does, posterior exenteration may be indicated. In addition to radical hysterectomy and pelvic node dissection, extirpation of rectum and sigmoid is required plus sigmoid colostomy. The procedure is not appropriate for cases of radiation failure because the radiated field does not heal well and enterocutaneous fistula formation can be expected.

F. If the cervical cancer has grown both anteriorly and posteriorly to invade bladder and rectum, consider total exenteration. The extremely extensive surgical attack involves all the features of both anterior and posterior exenterations with double diversion conduits for the urinary and intestinal tracts, respectively. It is reserved for those very limited numbers of cases for whom no other modality of care is available. Consider using omental grafts or peritoneal flaps to help reconstruct the extensively denuded raw surfaces of the pelvic floor, thereby perhaps averting adhesions, infection, bowel obstruction, and fistulas.

G. Intensive postoperative care is essential to manage the great fluid shifts, severe electrolyte balance problems, blood loss, and numerous complications likely to develop following exenteration.

References

Averette HE, Lichtinger M, Sevin BU, Girtanner RE. Pelvic exenteration: A 15-year experience in a general metropolitan hospital. Am J Obstet Gynecol 150:179, 1984.

Jakowatz JG, Porudominsky D, Riihimaki DU, et al. Complications of pelvic exenteration. Arch Surg 120:1261, 1985.

Lichtinger M, Averette HE, Girtanner R, et al. Small bowel complications after supravesical urinary diversion in pelvic exenteration. Gynecol Oncol 24:137, 1986.

Monaghan JM. Surgical management of advanced and recurrent cervical carcinoma: The place of pelvic exenteration. Clin Obstet Gynaecol 12:169, 1985.

Stanhope CR, Symmonds RE. Palliative exenteration: What, when, and why? Am J Obstet Gynecol 152:12, 1985.

PATIENT BEING CONSIDERED FOR EXENTERATION

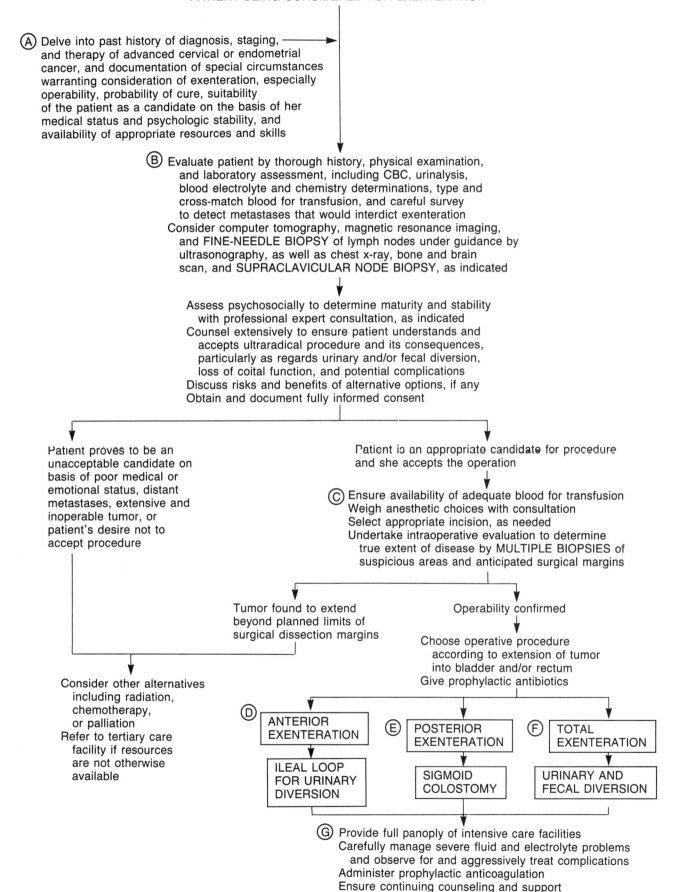

(A) Delve into past history of diagnosis, staging, and therapy of advanced cervical or endometrial cancer, and documentation of special circumstances warranting consideration of exenteration, especially operability, probability of cure, suitability of the patient as a candidate on the basis of her medical status and psychologic stability, and availability of appropriate resources and skills

(B) Evaluate patient by thorough history, physical examination, and laboratory assessment, including CBC, urinalysis, blood electrolyte and chemistry determinations, type and cross-match blood for transfusion, and careful survey to detect metastases that would interdict exenteration
Consider computer tomography, magnetic resonance imaging, and FINE-NEEDLE BIOPSY of lymph nodes under guidance by ultrasonography, as well as chest x-ray, bone and brain scan, and SUPRACLAVICULAR NODE BIOPSY, as indicated

Assess psychosocially to determine maturity and stability with professional expert consultation, as indicated
Counsel extensively to ensure patient understands and accepts ultraradical procedure and its consequences, particularly as regards urinary and/or fecal diversion, loss of coital function, and potential complications
Discuss risks and benefits of alternative options, if any
Obtain and document fully informed consent

Patient proves to be an unacceptable candidate on basis of poor medical or emotional status, distant metastases, extensive and inoperable tumor, or patient's desire not to accept procedure

Patient is an appropriate candidate for procedure and she accepts the operation

(C) Ensure availability of adequate blood for transfusion
Weigh anesthetic choices with consultation
Select appropriate incision, as needed
Undertake intraoperative evaluation to determine true extent of disease by MULTIPLE BIOPSIES of suspicious areas and anticipated surgical margins

Consider other alternatives including radiation, chemotherapy, or palliation
Refer to tertiary care facility if resources are not otherwise available

Tumor found to extend beyond planned limits of surgical dissection margins

Operability confirmed

Choose operative procedure according to extension of tumor into bladder and/or rectum
Give prophylactic antibiotics

(D) ANTERIOR EXENTERATION

(E) POSTERIOR EXENTERATION

(F) TOTAL EXENTERATION

ILEAL LOOP FOR URINARY DIVERSION

SIGMOID COLOSTOMY

URINARY AND FECAL DIVERSION

(G) Provide full panoply of intensive care facilities
Carefully manage severe fluid and electrolyte problems and observe for and aggressively treat complications
Administer prophylactic anticoagulation
Ensure continuing counseling and support

VAGINAL PLASTY

David S. Chapin, M.D.

A. Surgical intervention for pelvic relaxation (p 150) or urinary stress incontinence (p 98) should only be considered if it is clear the patient for whom it is being done has an anatomical defect that is likely to be correctable and that defect is severe enough or is causing sufficiently intense symptoms to warrant the operation. Moreover, there must not be any serious medical contraindication against surgery or anesthesia to make the procedure unsafe. Obtain a detailed history and review of systems to uncover potential illnesses. Probe for risk factors in the form of limited cardiac, pulmonary, or renal function, particularly since most of the women presenting with complaints relating to pelvic relaxation, such as protruding introital mass, pelvic pressure, and bearing down sensation, are elderly. Look for evidence of debilitating disease, diabetes mellitus, or genital atrophy. Concurrent chronic obstructive pulmonary disease, chronic cough, or massive obesity are factors that aggravate the condition in the first place, and they may also enhance the risk of recurrence after surgery. Recognizing their existence helps plan the most appropriate procedure to minimize this problem (see C).

B. Conduct a thorough physical examination, not only attempting to find indicators of poor health and disease, but seeking to assess the type and degree of anatomic defect and functional deficiency. Identify cystocele, rectocele, enterocele, uterine descensus (p 152), and posthysterectomy vault prolapse (p 154). Recall the value of examining the patient while she is in a standing position. Assess urinary function by observing the changing exit angle formed by a sterile cotton-tipped applicator inserted into the urethra before and after bearing down. This helps differentiate anatomic stress incontinence from detrusor instability or a neurogenic bladder. More objective evidence is available by urodynamic testing (p 226), including measurement of voiding flow rate and urethral pressure profile plus urethroscopy and cystometrography.

C. Counsel the patient on the various options for managing her condition, providing clear information on the failure rates and the relative benefits and risks of each. Patients with medical contraindications to surgery or anesthesia and those with intense risk factors should be advised about the available nonsurgical conservative measures (p 150), including perineal exercises and pessary use. The choice of surgical procedure depends on the presence of adverse factors, the patient's desire for future pregnancy (if she is still in the reproductive age and has an intact uterus), the presence of adequate uterine support tissues, and her need to retain coital function. Isolated urinary stress incontinence with no contributory pelvic relaxation can be treated by urethropexy alone without vaginal plasty.

D. Patients with high risk of failure due to chronic cough, poor tissue integrity, or prior failure may benefit from a transabdominal Marshall-Marchetti-Krantz (Fig. 1A) or Burch type procedure or a combined abdominal urethral suspension plus vaginal plasty, with or without hysterectomy. Those who fail after this type of "failsafe" method may be offered a sling procedure, but they are probably better served by conservative nonsurgical measures.

E. Those who have no prevailing risk factors can often be treated successfully with anterior colporrhaphy (Fig. 1B) and posterior colpoperineorrhaphy as a first line option procedure to correct the anatomical problem and relieve symptoms. If cervical hyperplasia exists, consider a Manchester-Fothergill operation (Fig. 1C) consisting of a cervical amputation, anterior plication of the cardinal ligaments, and anterior and posterior vaginal plasty. This procedure can also be used if reproductive potential must be preserved. However, because a subsequent pregnancy may undo any benefit derived from the surgery, it is perhaps better to recommend that the operation be delayed until childbearing needs have been fulfilled. At that time, a definitive procedure can be done. In the

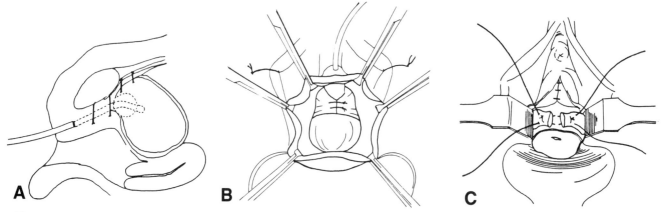

Figure 1 Vaginal plasty procedures. Sagittal view (A) illustrates suprapubic urethral suspension with paraurethral and paravesical fixation sutures in place. Frontal view (B) demonstrates critical plication of endopelvic fascia of urogenital diaphragm beneath the bladder neck to elevate the urethrovesical angle. Manchester-Fothergill operation (C) involves trachelectomy for cervical hypertrophy and advancing the divided cardinal ligaments anteriorly to the midline.

PATIENT BEING CONSIDERED FOR VAGINAL PLASTY PROCEDURE

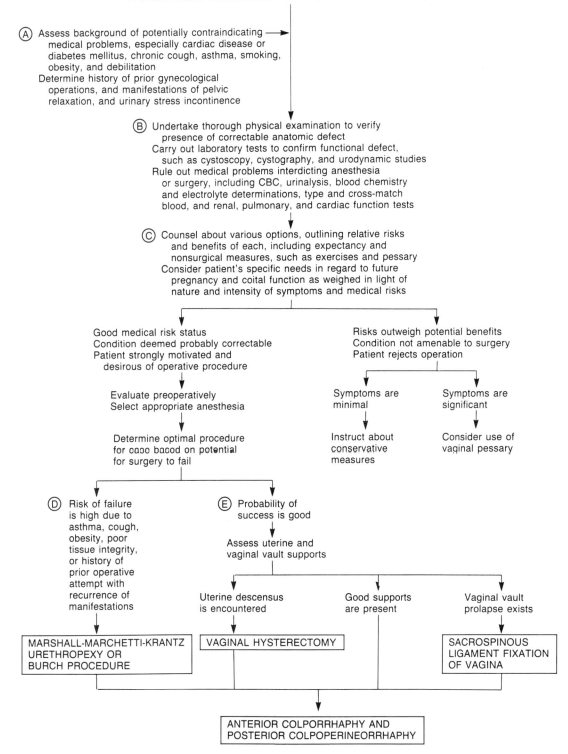

Ⓐ Assess background of potentially contraindicating ⟶
medical problems, especially cardiac disease or
diabetes mellitus, chronic cough, asthma, smoking,
obesity, and debilitation
Determine history of prior gynecological
operations, and manifestations of pelvic
relaxation, and urinary stress incontinence

Ⓑ Undertake thorough physical examination to verify
presence of correctable anatomic defect
Carry out laboratory tests to confirm functional defect,
such as cystoscopy, cystography, and urodynamic studies
Rule out medical problems interdicting anesthesia
or surgery, including CBC, urinalysis, blood chemistry
and electrolyte determinations, type and cross-match
blood, and renal, pulmonary, and cardiac function tests

Ⓒ Counsel about various options, outlining relative risks
and benefits of each, including expectancy and
nonsurgical measures, such as exercises and pessary
Consider patient's specific needs in regard to future
pregnancy and coital function as weighed in light of
nature and intensity of symptoms and medical risks

Good medical risk status
Condition deemed probably correctable
Patient strongly motivated and
desirous of operative procedure

Risks outweigh potential benefits
Condition not amenable to surgery
Patient rejects operation

Evaluate preoperatively
Select appropriate anesthesia

Symptoms are
minimal

Symptoms are
significant

Determine optimal procedure
for case based on potential
for surgery to fail

Instruct about
conservative
measures

Consider use of
vaginal pessary

Ⓓ Risk of failure
is high due to
asthma, cough,
obesity, poor
tissue integrity,
or history of
prior operative
attempt with
recurrence of
manifestations

Ⓔ Probability of
success is good

Assess uterine and
vaginal vault supports

Uterine descensus
is encountered

Good supports
are present

Vaginal vault
prolapse exists

| MARSHALL-MARCHETTI-KRANTZ URETHROPEXY OR BURCH PROCEDURE | VAGINAL HYSTERECTOMY | SACROSPINOUS LIGAMENT FIXATION OF VAGINA |

ANTERIOR COLPORRHAPHY AND
POSTERIOR COLPOPERINEORRHAPHY

presence of overt uterine descensus, the vaginal plasty procedure should be combined with vaginal hysterectomy. Hysterectomy alone without the plasty is seldom appropriate and risks vault prolapse.

References

Bhatia NN, Ostergard DR. Urodynamics in women with stress urinary incontinence. Obstet Gynecol 60:552, 1982.

Boyd SD, Raz S. Needle bladder neck suspension for female stress incontinence. Urol Clin North Am 11:357, 1984.

Mintz FJ, Stanton SL. Q-tip test in female urinary incontinence. Obstet Gynecol 67:258, 1986.

Nichols DH, Randall CL. Vaginal Surgery, 2nd ed. Baltimore: Williams & Wilkins, 1983.

MYOMECTOMY

Alexander M. Dlugi, M.D.

A. Uterine leiomyomas (p 182) are common among adult women, but seldom cause problems or warrant surgical intervention. When symptomatic, a number of therapeutic options are available, namely expectancy, hysterectomy, myomectomy, and the recently introduced regimen of gonadotropin releasing hormone agonist. In practical terms, the patient with severe symptoms and large fibroids can only choose between hysterectomy and myomectomy. Ascertain the nature and intensity of the manifestations, probing into bleeding problems, pelvic pressure and pain, urinary symptoms, and pregnancy losses. Determine the need for future childbearing.

B. Evaluate by history, physical examination, and laboratory investigations to provide detailed information pertaining to operative risk and suitable indication for surgery. In addition to complete blood count (CBC), urinalysis, and blood chemistry determinations, it is necessary to type and cross-match blood for intraoperative use since hemorrhage is common. Rule out pregnancy objectively, unless the procedure is being undertaken during a known pregnancy because of unremitting pain from carneous degeneration (see D). Obtain ultrasonography (p 216) for verification of the presence and status of the leiomyomas, if needed. Consider hysterosalpingography (p 220) to identify submucous leiomyomas, especially when weighing the option of transhysteroscopic myomectomy (see E).

C. Counsel the patient in depth about the relative benefits and risks of the several options, concentrating on issues of relevance to her in regard to preservation of reproductive function and amelioration of habitual abortion, for example. Stress counterbalancing risks as related to morbidity due to excessive blood loss, infection, adhesion formation which may actually impair future fertility, and the potential for recurrence of the leiomyomas. Aside from medical disorders that might make any operation unsafe, there are no absolute contraindications against myomectomy except uterine or cervical malignancy. In the past, any concurrent condition that was likely to prevent conception, such as tubal occlusion, precluded myomectomy. Since the advent of in vitro fertilization (p 276), however, this is no longer the case because the objective of reconstructing an essentially normal uterus, anatomically and functionally, can be achieved for this purpose.

D. Pregnancy may lead to a marked enlargement of preexistent leiomyomas with resultant abdominal discomfort, pulmonary compromise, premature labor, or obstructed labor. Carneous degeneration may also occur to cause prolonged pain, fever, leukocytosis, and even signs of peritonitis. An acute episode can generally be managed with bedrest and analgesic drugs. If symptoms worsen, it is valid to consider myomectomy, although it risks abortion or premature labor. Be prepared for excessive blood loss due to the increased uterine vascularity.

Hysteroscopic resection (p 222) is applicable only for the removal of a small submucous leiomyoma when clinically indicated. Appropriate experience in operative hysteroscopy is mandatory before undertaking this procedure.

Myomectomy is difficult, and sometimes impossible, to perform safely if leiomyomas occupy the cervix and lower uterine segment. If extirpation irreparably distorts the anatomy of the uterine cavity, consider hysterectomy instead. Intraoperative hemostasis is essential. Rapid deployment of well placed hemostatic sutures is of primary importance. In addition, one can inject a dilute solution of vasopressin around the leiomyoma prior to incision (with prior knowledge and consent of the anesthetist), manually elevate the uterus and digitally compress the uterine vessels, or apply an occlusive rubber tourniquet around the lower uterine segment through the broad ligaments (Fig. 1). Use of a tourniquet may enhance adhesion formation unless the peritoneal defects are meticulously closed.

G. Multiple myomectomies should ideally be done through a single small incision. Where possible, a vertical midline anterior or (less preferably) posterior incision is made to minimize blood loss. Take care to avoid entering the endometrial cavity, if possible. Instill indigo carmine transcervically preoperatively to stain the uterine cavity for identification. If the cavity is entered, avoid suturing the anterior wall to the posterior wall. Close the surgical defect in layers. Approximate the serosal surfaces by imbricating the edges (using baseball stitches) with fine nonreactive suture (such as 6-0 Vicryl) in order to minimize subsequent adhesion formation.

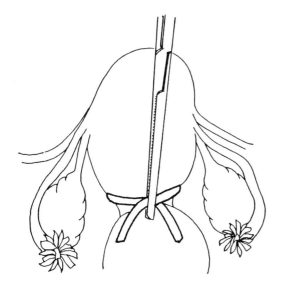

Figure 1 Use of tourniquet for hemostasis during myomectomy. The broad ligament is perforated just superiorly to the uterine vascular pedicle and laterally to the ascending uterine vessels to ensure against vascular and ureteral damage.

References

Berkeley AS, DeCherney AH, Polan ML. Abdominal myomectomy and subsequent fertility. Surg Gynecol Obstet 156:319, 1983.

PATIENT BEING CONSIDERED FOR MYOMECTOMY

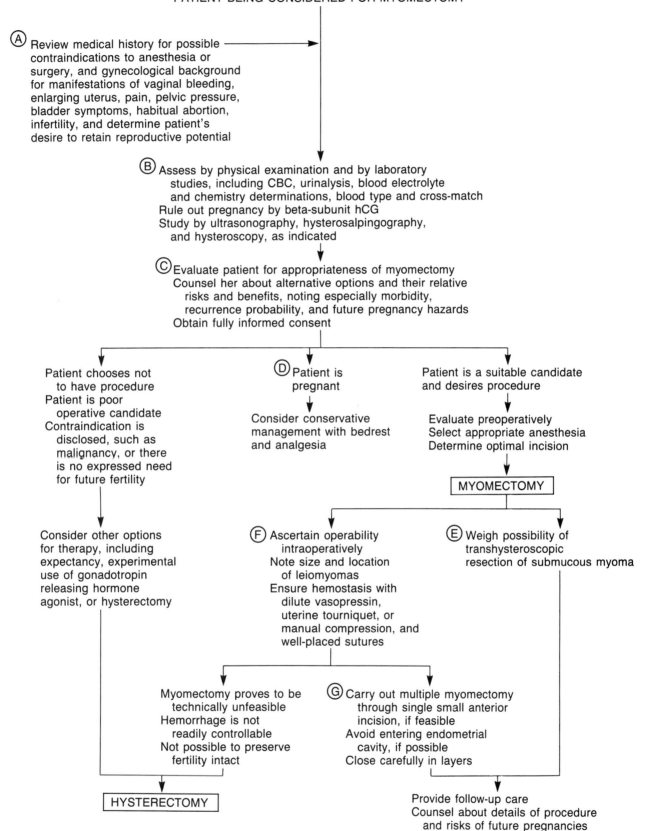

Ⓐ Review medical history for possible contraindications to anesthesia or surgery, and gynecological background for manifestations of vaginal bleeding, enlarging uterus, pain, pelvic pressure, bladder symptoms, habitual abortion, infertility, and determine patient's desire to retain reproductive potential

Ⓑ Assess by physical examination and by laboratory studies, including CBC, urinalysis, blood electrolyte and chemistry determinations, blood type and cross-match
Rule out pregnancy by beta-subunit hCG
Study by ultrasonography, hysterosalpingography, and hysteroscopy, as indicated

Ⓒ Evaluate patient for appropriateness of myomectomy
Counsel her about alternative options and their relative risks and benefits, noting especially morbidity, recurrence probability, and future pregnancy hazards
Obtain fully informed consent

Patient chooses not to have procedure
Patient is poor operative candidate
Contraindication is disclosed, such as malignancy, or there is no expressed need for future fertility

Ⓓ Patient is pregnant

Patient is a suitable candidate and desires procedure

Consider conservative management with bedrest and analgesia

Evaluate preoperatively
Select appropriate anesthesia
Determine optimal incision

MYOMECTOMY

Consider other options for therapy, including expectancy, experimental use of gonadotropin releasing hormone agonist, or hysterectomy

Ⓕ Ascertain operability intraoperatively
Note size and location of leiomyomas
Ensure hemostasis with dilute vasopressin, uterine tourniquet, or manual compression, and well-placed sutures

Ⓔ Weigh possibility of transhysteroscopic resection of submucous myoma

Myomectomy proves to be technically unfeasible
Hemorrhage is not readily controllable
Not possible to preserve fertility intact

Ⓖ Carry out multiple myomectomy through single small anterior incision, if feasible
Avoid entering endometrial cavity, if possible
Close carefully in layers

HYSTERECTOMY

Provide follow-up care
Counsel about details of procedure and risks of future pregnancies

Dlugi AM. Uterine surgery. In: DeCherney AH, Polan ML (Editors). Reproductive Surgery. Chicago: Year Book, 1987.
Neuwirth RS. Hysteroscopic management of symptomatic sub-mucous fibroids. Obstet Gynecol 62:509, 1983.
Rosenfield DL. Abdominal myomectomy for otherwise unexplained infertility. Fertil Steril 46:328, 1986.

METROPLASTY

Alexander M. Dlugi, M.D.

A. At least 80 percent of patients with a uterine anomaly (p 166) have no reproductive problems at all; for these women, surgical correction is clearly not indicated. Repeated pregnancy wastage, usually in midtrimester, is an indication for evaluation and possible surgery. The proportion of those who develop such problems is probably smaller than reported because many women who have uterine anomalies have no overt manifestations and, therefore, their malformation is never disclosed. Probe the obstetrical history carefully to identify other causes, such as chromosomal abnormalities or debilitating diseases. Infertility (p 82) is rarely benefited by metroplasty.

B. A complete work-up for habitual abortion (p 76) must first be done. Confirm the presence of a uterine malformation and define its nature (p 166). Ascertain if the con-

dition is amenable to surgical correction and if symptoms warrant such intervention. Because urinary tract anomalies may be associated in up to 20 percent of cases, obtain intravenous pyelography. Hysterosalpingography (p 22) will show a defect, but it cannot distinguish between septate and bicornuate uterus. Only assessment of the external architecture by direct visualization under laparoscopy can make this important distinction. Hysteroscopy (p 222) is confirmatory and offers an opportunity for repair (see E).

C. Although pregnancy wastage is increased somewhat in the presence of a unicornuate uterus, viable pregnancy rates approach 50 to 60 percent. Since the malformation is not amenable to correction by any surgical procedure and affected patients generally do well, they can be managed expectantly.

D. A rudimentary horn may or may not communicate with the larger contralateral horn. The noncommunicating horn with functional endometrium often presents as a pelvic mass, representing a hematometra (p 170). If a patent fallopian tube is present on the side of a functioning noncommunicating rudimentary horn, endometriosis may develop. This type of rudimentary horn should be excised. A communicating horn, while usually posing no problems to the nonpregnant patient, is commonly the site of uterine rupture if a gestation should implant in it. For this reason, some advocate excision of any rudimentary horn with a functional fallopian tube.

E. The septate uterus is often amenable to resection or division by the hysteroscopic approach. To perform this procedure safely, a panoramic view of the uterine cavity must be obtained and the septum should be clearly visualized. The operation may be accomplished with either an electrical cautery loop or with hysteroscopic scissors. Simultaneous laparoscopic surveillance of the uterus must be maintained constantly to lessen the chance of perforation. Retraction of the septum occurs as the incision is carried to its base. Bleeding is rarely a problem due to the relatively poor vascularization of the septum. Hysteroscopic metroplasty is associated with a high rate of successful term pregnancies (70 to 80 percent). It does not require a cesarean section for delivery in a subsequent pregnancy.

F. A variety of techniques have been described for transabdominal metroplasty (Fig. 1). The two most commonly employed are Tompkins metroplasty (in which a vertical midline fundal incision is made through the septum) and Jones metroplasty (which excises a wedge of tissue containing the septum). Both procedures yield comparable term pregnancy rates. The choice is generally based on the surgeon's experience and training. Careful multilayer closure is essential with either procedure. Unlike hysteroscopic resection, transabdominal metroplasty is associated with formation of pelvic adhesions and it does necessitate delivery by cesarean section in subsequent pregnancy.

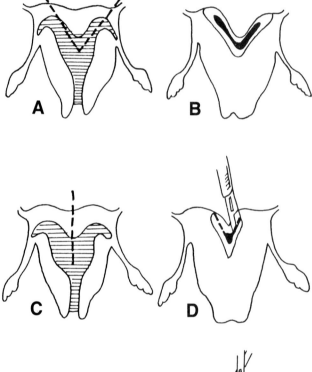
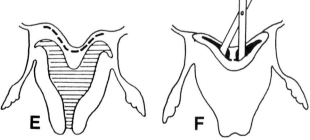

Figure 1 Types of metroplasty procedures. Method of Jones and Jones (A,B) involves a wedge incision to remove the uterine septum. Tompkins procedure (C,D) utilizes a midline incision followed by bilateral division of the septum. Strassman operation (E,F) opens the uterus with a transverse fundal incision, avoiding the tubal ostia, and incises the septum.

PATIENT BEING CONSIDERED FOR METROPLASTY

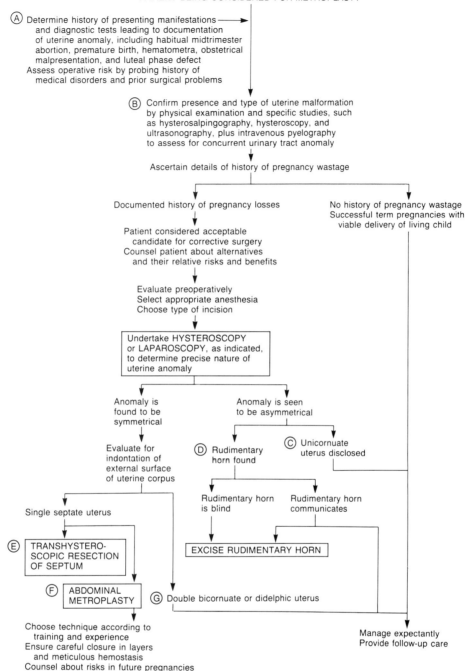

Ⓐ Determine history of presenting manifestations
and diagnostic tests leading to documentation
of uterine anomaly, including habitual midtrimester
abortion, premature birth, hematometra, obstetrical
malpresentation, and luteal phase defect
Assess operative risk by probing history of
medical disorders and prior surgical problems

Ⓑ Confirm presence and type of uterine malformation
by physical examination and specific studies, such
as hysterosalpingography, hysteroscopy, and
ultrasonography, plus intravenous pyelography
to assess for concurrent urinary tract anomaly

Ascertain details of history of pregnancy wastage

Documented history of pregnancy losses

No history of pregnancy wastage
Successful term pregnancies with
viable delivery of living child

Patient considered acceptable
candidate for corrective surgery
Counsel patient about alternatives
and their relative risks and benefits

Evaluate preoperatively
Select appropriate anesthesia
Choose type of incision

Undertake HYSTEROSCOPY
or LAPAROSCOPY, as indicated,
to determine precise nature of
uterine anomaly

Anomaly is
found to be
symmetrical

Anomaly is seen
to be asymmetrical

Ⓓ Rudimentary
horn found

Ⓒ Unicornuate
uterus disclosed

Evaluate for
indontation of
external surface
of uterine corpus

Rudimentary horn
is blind

Rudimentary horn
communicates

Single septate uterus

Ⓔ TRANSHYSTERO-
SCOPIC RESECTION
OF SEPTUM

EXCISE RUDIMENTARY HORN

Ⓕ ABDOMINAL
METROPLASTY

Ⓖ Double bicornuate or didelphic uterus

Choose technique according to
training and experience
Ensure careful closure in layers
and meticulous hemostasis
Counsel about risks in future pregnancies

Manage expectantly
Provide follow-up care

G. Both bicornuate and didelphic uterine malformations are associated with acceptable term pregnancy rates, approaching 50 to 60 percent. Rarely is a unification procedure appropriate, but it may be considered for the patient with repetitive pregnancy losses who is otherwise completely normal based on an extensive evaluation. The Strassman procedure is the procedure of choice for her. This technique involves a transverse incision across the uterine fundus from cornu to cornu. The tubal ostia may be seriously compromised. Be especially careful with hemostasis and layered closure. The risk of uterine rupture in a future pregnancy means that cesarean section will have to be done.

References

Chervenak FA, Neuwirth RS. Hysteroscopic resection of the uterine septum. Am J Obstet Gynecol 141:351, 1981.

DeCherney AH, Russell JB, Graebe RA, Polan ML. Resectoscopic management of müllerian fusion defects. Fertil Steril 45:726, 1986.

Dlugi AM. Uterine surgery. In: DeCherney AH, Polan ML (Editors). Reproductive Surgery. Chicago: Year Book, 1987.

Kessler I, Lancet M, Appelman Z, Borenstein R. Indications and results of metroplasty in uterine malformations. Int J Gynaecol Obstet 24:137, 1986.

TUBOPLASTY

Machelle M. Seibel, M.D.

A. Tubal damage occurs with pelvic inflammatory disease, endometriosis, pelvic or abdominal surgery, especially for ectopic pregnancy or ruptured appendix, and intrauterine device use, but it is also found without any identifiable risk factor. Even if the tubal obstruction is documented, ensure that other infertility factors (p 82) are identified before considering corrective tuboplasty. Avoid surgery if there are concurrent conditions making conception unlikely. Investigate medical and psychological status as well to disclose conditions that might contraindicate pregnancy.

B. Conduct a general physical examination to rule out medical disorders. The pelvic examination should detect any objective evidence of adnexal distortion, induration, thickening, mass, cyst, or tenderness. Watch for deviation or fixation of the uterus or adnexal structures, suggesting the presence of adhesions. Uterosacral ligament nodularity is quite typical of endometriosis (p 190).

C. No form of surgical repair should be offered to an infertility patient without first evaluating her ovulatory, cer-

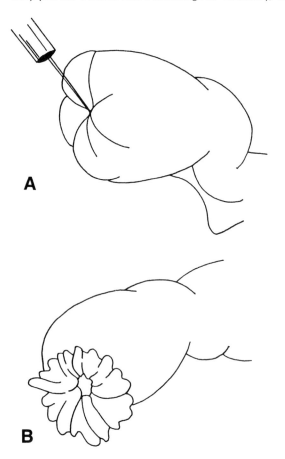

Figure 1 Fimbrioplasty for hydrosalpinx. The dimple in the clubbed tubal extremity, representing the point of closure, is probed and incised with a microelectrode (A) to reveal the residual fimbria (B), which can be sutured back to keep the distal tube open.

vical, and uterine anatomy and function. Also assess the male partner in depth (p 84). Hysterosalpingography is essential to define the site of tubal obstruction, although it may give only limited information, especially if the proximal end is occluded. Interpret with caution because tubal spasm can mislead. Thus, laparoscopy is required both to verify obstruction and to identify the nature of the disease process, its extent, and the sites involved. Laparoscopy facilitates planning and counseling.

D. Because severe pelvic adhesions or markedly distended tubes make success unlikely, consider in vitro fertilization (p 276) instead. Merely re-establishing tubal patency is inadequate to compensate for the damage to tubal anatomy, relationships (to the ovary), and function.

E. The site of obstruction is a critical consideration for planning the type of procedure. Expect the best results with peritubal adhesions affecting an otherwise normal tube. Simple lysis of these adhesions, perhaps even translaparoscopically, is sufficient (p 240). Midtubal obstruction, particularly if resulting from prior surgical sterilization, deserves special consideration (p 270).

F. Fimbrial clubbing is the most common form of distal tubal obstruction, the characteristic end result of chronic salpingitis and hydrosalpinx. Although patency can often be re-established by salpingostomy, only one-third achieve conception and ectopic pregnancy is common. The better preserved the fimbria, the better the prognosis. Therefore, discuss in vitro fertilization as an alternative if damage is severe. The corrective procedure involves mobilizing the distal end of the tube from the ovarian capsule and making an opening in the dimple formed where the original tubal ostium had been located (Fig. 1). Use magnification and meticulous microsurgical technique (see G). Postoperative hydrotubation may improve patency rates.

G. Proximal obstruction requires resection of the obstructed segment and tubocornual anastomosis. Microsurgical technique may yield success in two-thirds of cases. Good magnification is essential, usually with a dissecting microscope. Take care to handle tissues gently with constant irrigation, ensuring good hemostasis using a fine-needle diathermy electrode and meticulous tissue apposition with very fine nonreactive sutures. Intra-abdominal laser techniques may also prove beneficial in these cases. Consider referral to a center where special skills, facilities, and expertise can be provided.

H. Prevention of intra-abdominal adhesions and maintenance of patency are especially important in these cases. None of the practices in current use have been proved to be effective, although widely used. Corticosteroids, for example, are given for this purpose, although their real value is not known. Some instil dextran into the peritoneal cavity intraoperatively with the same objective. Close follow-up is important because ectopic pregnancy is such a serious risk. Re-evaluate in

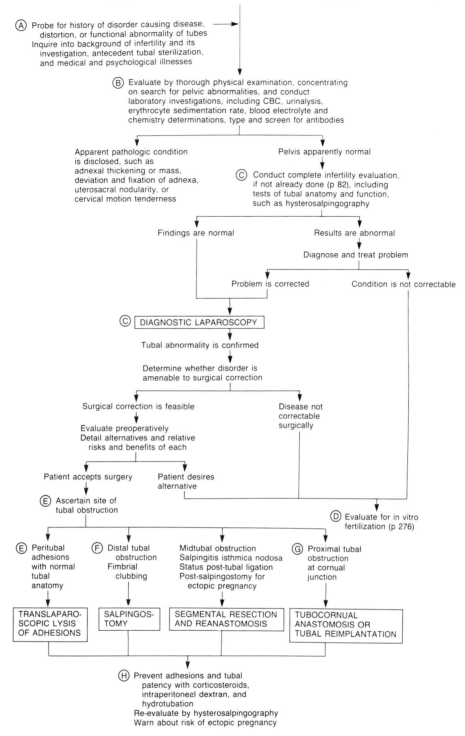

six months by hysterosalpingography to determine patency if conception does not occur.

References

Gomel V. Microsurgery in Female Infertility. Boston: Little, Brown & Co., 1983.

Margara RA. Tubal reanastomosis. In: Chamberlain G, Winston R (Editors). Tubal Infertility: Diagnosis and Treatment. Oxford: Blackwell Scientific, 1982.

McComb P. Microsurgical tubocornual anastomosis for occlusive cornual disease: Reproducible results without the need for tubouterine implantation. Fertil Steril 46:571, 1986.

Winston R. Reconstructive microsurgery at the lateral end of the fallopian tube. In: Chamberlain G, Winston R (Editors). Tubal Infertility: Diagnosis and Treatment. Oxford: Blackwell Scientific, 1982.

STERILIZATION COUNSELING

Max Borten, M.D., J.D.

A. It is important to evaluate the patient's psychosocial background, moral and religious attitudes, maturity, and comprehension of the significance of permanent sterilization. This should be done well in advance of undertaking an operation that is likely to interfere with fertility. Even for emergency surgery, it should be possible to ascertain the patient's desires and any constraints she feels must be imposed, within limits of safety. For a patient seeking voluntary sterilization, determine her reasons and explore her concerns and understanding of the consequences. Be sure to review alternatives in the context of prior contraceptive experience, especially as regards to side effects and failures, and give balanced information about relative risks and benefits of all relevant options applicable for the specific patient.

B. While there are no longer any real age and parity criteria for women seeking voluntary sterilization, be especially careful to counsel women of low parity or those who have unstable personal relationships because they are so much more likely to regret their decision in the future than others. The same applies for women whose libido or sexual satisfaction is marginal or poor and for any who are about to be sterilized at the same time they are undergoing pregnancy termination by induced abortion or cesarean section. Emotional instability, immaturity, personality disorder, sexual dysfunction, and a background of psychopathology are indices of potential problems, although they cannot always be considered to represent absolute contraindications against sterilization; when disclosed, the patient thus identified should be subjected to extensive assessment. Consider a formal psychiatric consultation before proceeding.

C. Very few women have any regrets about their sterilization operation. The procedure gives them newfound freedom from any concern about conception and averts the long-term, recurrent inconveniences, side effects, and risks of contraception. There are some who develop emotional difficulties as an apparent consequence of loss of fertility. Most likely to have such an adverse result are those who are young, have not satisfied their own perceived full reproductive needs (nulliparas or women of low parity), or do not fully comprehend that sterilization is permanent. Reactions are most likely to become manifest within the first two postoperative years. One has to be sure the patient understands that the operation is not reversible. She must be disabused of a false assumption that reversing it is safe, simple, and readily accom-

plished, or that the success of tubal reanastomosis can be relied on if she should change her mind in the near or distant future. The patient most likely to regret her decision, express dissatisfaction, or suffer an emotional reaction is one who has not been properly informed and counseled.

D. When counseling is done, try to discuss matters with both partners in a stable relationship. Detail the relative benefits and risks of all available sterilization procedures before their final decision is made. They should be aware that vasectomy for the male is simpler, quicker, less costly, and less hazardous than tubal sterilization for the female; since it is essentially a minor surgical procedure that can be done under local anesthesia, it does not ordinarily require hospitalization and its risks are negligible. Its irreversibility must be emphasized.

E. Discuss the technical aspects of sterilization procedures in some detail and provide information on risks and failure rates. Be sure the patient and her partner understand. Enter a comprehensive note in the record to that effect. The future potential for reversibility should not be a valid consideration for the patient's decision to proceed. Any woman who is uncertain about whether she might wish to conceive again at some time in the future should be counseled against being sterilized at this time. She should not be deluded into believing the operation can be easily and reliably reversed. Consultation with a psychiatrist or social worker may be in order. Ensure adequate contraception in the interim until a satisfactory and acceptable decision is made.

References

Kohn I. Counseling women who request sterilization: Psychodynamic issues and interventions. Soc Work Health Care 11:35, 1985.

Lachance D. In re Grady: The mentally retarded individual's right to choose sterilization. Am J Law Med 6:559, 1981.

Leader A, Galan N, George R, Taylor PJ. A comparison of definable traits in women requesting reversal of sterilization and women satisfied with sterilization. Am J Obstet Gynecol 145:198, 1983.

Lee HY. A 20-year experience with vaso-vasostomy. J Urol 136:413, 1986.

Taylor PJ, Freedman B, Wonnacott T, Brown S. Female sterilization: Can the woman who will seek reversal be identified prospectively? Clin Reprod Fertil 4:207, 1986.

PATIENT REQUESTING STERILIZATION

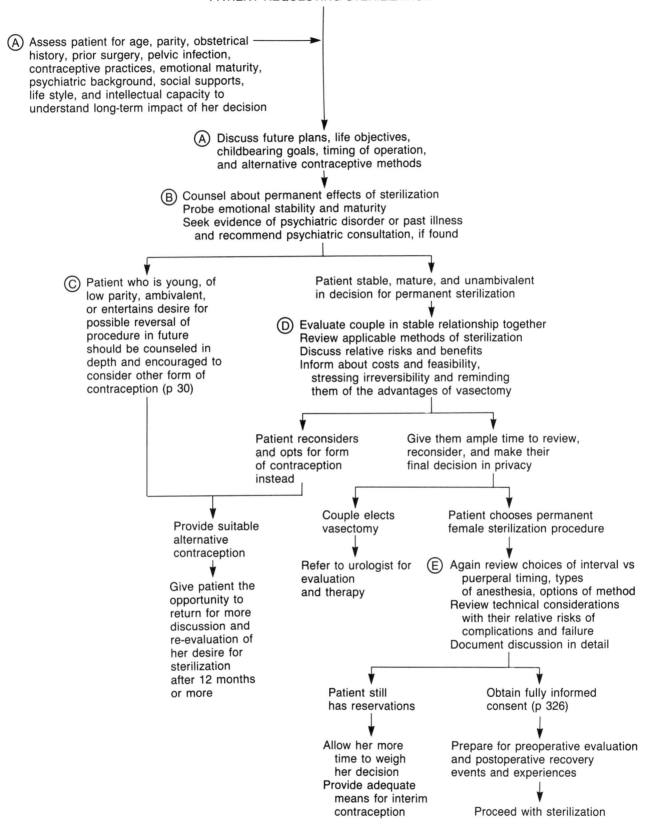

(A) Assess patient for age, parity, obstetrical history, prior surgery, pelvic infection, contraceptive practices, emotional maturity, psychiatric background, social supports, life style, and intellectual capacity to understand long-term impact of her decision

(A) Discuss future plans, life objectives, childbearing goals, timing of operation, and alternative contraceptive methods

(B) Counsel about permanent effects of sterilization
Probe emotional stability and maturity
Seek evidence of psychiatric disorder or past illness and recommend psychiatric consultation, if found

(C) Patient who is young, of low parity, ambivalent, or entertains desire for possible reversal of procedure in future should be counseled in depth and encouraged to consider other form of contraception (p 30)

Patient stable, mature, and unambivalent in decision for permanent sterilization

(D) Evaluate couple in stable relationship together
Review applicable methods of sterilization
Discuss relative risks and benefits
Inform about costs and feasibility, stressing irreversibility and reminding them of the advantages of vasectomy

Patient reconsiders and opts for form of contraception instead

Give them ample time to review, reconsider, and make their final decision in privacy

Provide suitable alternative contraception

Give patient the opportunity to return for more discussion and re-evaluation of her desire for sterilization after 12 months or more

Couple elects vasectomy

Patient chooses permanent female sterilization procedure

Refer to urologist for evaluation and therapy

(E) Again review choices of interval vs puerperal timing, types of anesthesia, options of method
Review technical considerations with their relative risks of complications and failure
Document discussion in detail

Patient still has reservations

Obtain fully informed consent (p 326)

Allow her more time to weigh her decision
Provide adequate means for interim contraception

Prepare for preoperative evaluation and postoperative recovery events and experiences

Proceed with sterilization

STERILIZATION

Max Borten, M.D., J.D.

A. Voluntary permanent sterilization has emerged as the most frequently used method for fertility control. It is now generally available to both men and women almost without any constraining selection factor as to age or obstetrical background. Nevertheless, not every woman requesting this procedure is a suitable candidate. Before undertaking a sterilization procedure, one must be familiar with the patient's medical, surgical, and sexual history. Details concerning previous contraceptive choices, failures, and side effects must be analyzed. Relative contraindications must be fully assessed due to the permanent nature of this procedure. In particular, alertness is required for potential problems in the patient's emotional background and psychosocial status (p 266).

B. A decision as to choice of the type of procedure to be performed cannot be made until after the patient has been fully informed about the available alternatives. Only then can she make an intelligent and informed decision about whether to proceed and which method she would prefer. One must highlight the beneficial as well as the negative aspects of the various techniques. Be especially careful not to allow one's personal bias to influence the

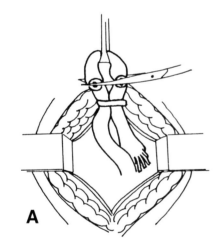

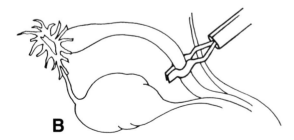

Figure 1 Sterilization by modified Pomeroy tubal ligation is done by grasping the midportion of the tube, ligating it once with an absorbable suture, and resecting the loop of tube above the ligature (A). Alternatively, translaparoscopic cauterization can be done using a bipolar electrode (B) to coagulate three progressively more distal midtubal segments.

patient unduly. She should be given not less than 72 hours to weigh her decision before the operation is performed.

C. Whereas puerperal sterilization was frequently practiced in the past, interval procedures performed six weeks or more after a delivery are more common at present and are clearly preferable. Interval sterilization has the advantage of improved safety and lower failure rates (p 308). Furthermore, postpartum sterilization operations are associated with technical difficulties not encountered at other times because the tubes are more friable, edematous, and larger as a consequence of gestational effects. Despite this shortcoming, the factors of convenience and firm patient desire and resolve weigh heavily in favor of the procedure being performed immediately after a delivery. It may be acceptable, therefore, if the decision has been made well in advance, the parturient is in stable condition (and the newborn infant appears healthy), and anesthesia is already in effect and adequate to permit the operation to be done safely.

D. Patients at risk of developing complications during or following a sterilization procedure must be counseled against it. More appropriate alternatives, such as vasectomy for the male partner or other contraceptive options, should be explored in depth. The benefits of a voluntary operative procedure must outweigh its risks by far before it can be recommended.

E. Closed laparoscopy is the most common technique used for sterilization. Open laparoscopy is an alternative method available for patients in whom closed endoscopy is relatively contraindicated because of a history of prior abdominal operations or a serious intraperitoneal infection. Bipolar electrocoagulation and Silastic ring mechanical obstruction of the tubes are the most frequent methods used today. Risk of serious bowel burns have relegated the use of unipolar electrocoagulation to the rare occasion in which neither of the other preferred methods is available. The high failure rate associated with the use of metal or plastic clips has prevented wider acceptance of this technique.

F. Minilaparotomy is the most frequent route utilized for postpartum sterilization. It can also be used for interval procedures. Pomeroy type tubal occlusion and resection continues to be the technique of choice when the surgical approach is elected (Fig. 1). Whereas the Irving and Uchida techniques yield more reliable results, their greater technical difficulty is accompanied by higher morbidity. Consider utililizing bipolar electrocoagulation or Silastic ring techniques in minilaparotomy sterilization. Fimbriectomy by way of a vaginal approach (posterior colpotomy) has fallen into disuse.

References

Borten M. Laparoscopic Complications: Prevention and Management. Toronto: B.C. Decker, 1986.

PATIENT BEING CONSIDERED FOR STERILIZATION

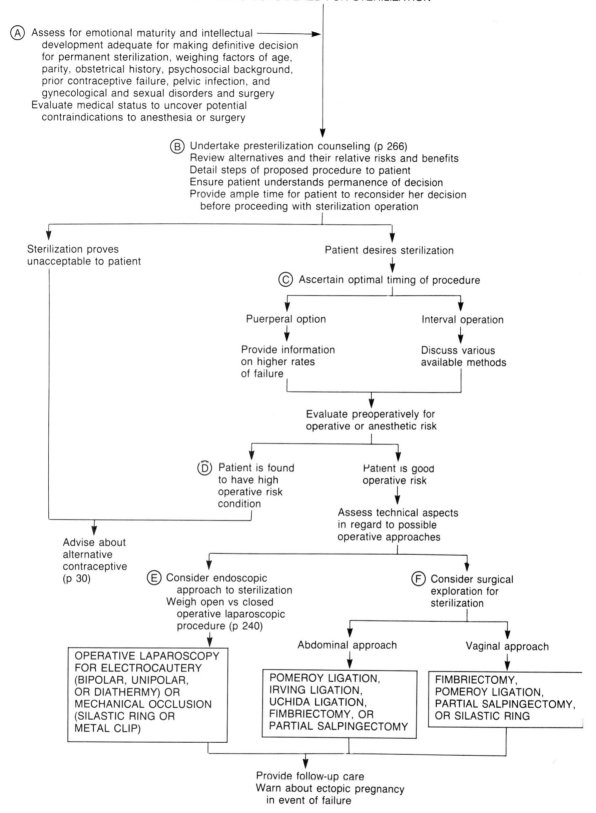

(A) Assess for emotional maturity and intellectual
development adequate for making definitive decision
for permanent sterilization, weighing factors of age,
parity, obstetrical history, psychosocial background,
prior contraceptive failure, pelvic infection, and
gynecological and sexual disorders and surgery
Evaluate medical status to uncover potential
contraindications to anesthesia or surgery

(B) Undertake presterilization counseling (p 266)
Review alternatives and their relative risks and benefits
Detail steps of proposed procedure to patient
Ensure patient understands permanence of decision
Provide ample time for patient to reconsider her decision
before proceeding with sterilization operation

Sterilization proves
unacceptable to patient

Patient desires sterilization

(C) Ascertain optimal timing of procedure

Puerperal option

Interval operation

Provide information
on higher rates
of failure

Discuss various
available methods

Evaluate preoperatively for
operative or anesthetic risk

(D) Patient is found
to have high
operative risk
condition

Patient is good
operative risk

Assess technical aspects
in regard to possible
operative approaches

Advise about
alternative
contraceptive
(p 30)

(E) Consider endoscopic
approach to sterilization
Weigh open vs closed
operative laparoscopic
procedure (p 240)

(F) Consider surgical
exploration for
sterilization

Abdominal approach

Vaginal approach

OPERATIVE LAPAROSCOPY
FOR ELECTROCAUTERY
(BIPOLAR, UNIPOLAR,
OR DIATHERMY) OR
MECHANICAL OCCLUSION
(SILASTIC RING OR
METAL CLIP)

POMEROY LIGATION,
IRVING LIGATION,
UCHIDA LIGATION,
FIMBRIECTOMY, OR
PARTIAL SALPINGECTOMY

FIMBRIECTOMY,
POMEROY LIGATION,
PARTIAL SALPINGECTOMY,
OR SILASTIC RING

Provide follow-up care
Warn about ectopic pregnancy
in event of failure

Chick PH, Frances M, Paterson PJ. A comprehensive review of
female sterilisation: Tubal occlusion methods. Clin Reprod
Fertil 3:81, 1985.
Cohen MM. Tubal sterilization in Manitoba. Can J Public Health
77:114, 1986.

Grubb GS, Peterson HB. Luteal phase pregnancy and tubal sterilization. Obstet Gynecol 66:784, 1985.
Vessey MP, Huggins G, Lawless M, Yeates D. Tubal sterilization:
Findings in a large prospective study. Br J Obstet Gynaecol
90:203, 1983.

TUBAL REANASTOMOSIS

Max Borten, M.D., J.D.

A. Midtubal obstruction is usually the consequence of an operation done at some time in the past for sterilization. While female sterilization is currently most often done by electrocoagulation, other forms of sterilization have enjoyed passing popularity in the past and their results may also be encountered, even though less often used today, including surgical resection and ligation or application of Silastic bands (Falope rings) and metal or plastic clips. The ampullary tubal segment can also become

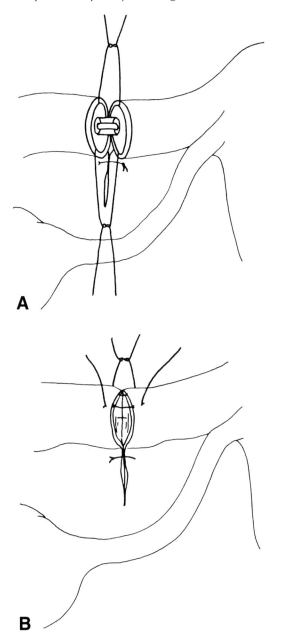

obstructed after a salpingostomy done for ectopic pregnancy; isthmic occlusion may be associated with salpingitis isthmica nodosa. Surgical correction is almost exclusively reserved for poststerilization cases. Full infertility investigation (p 82) must precede undertaking corrective repair, including identification of the site of the obstruction and any associated general medical disorder, local pelvic pathologic condition, or anatomic distortion (p 264). It is of obvious importance to ascertain that the male partner is fertile, whether or not he has previously sired any children, and that there are no previously unrecognized or newly developed female factors to prevent or interdict pregnancy.

B. Determine the technical feasibility of surgical end-to-end reanastomosis by examining the current status of the tubal segments on either side of the obstruction (or surgical interruption). Electrocauterization, when done vigorously with triple burns to ensure against failure (p 268), destroys a considerable portion of the tube, often leaving little salvageable tissue for the repair. By contrast, more viable tubal length is usually left after ligation techniques (such as Falope ring or the modified Pomeroy method) and the greatest usable length of all is left after clip occlusions. Hysterosalpingography demonstrates the residual proximal length, but it cannot show the distal segment. It is seldom of any real value except to show the absence of cornual obstruction (p 264). Only laparoscopy is capable of providing the necessary information about the distal stump. Bear in mind that, for postfulguration cases, residual damage to the endosalpinx and the extent of tubal impatency often probably extend well beyond that which is grossly observed to be destroyed; damage to the ciliated lining cells, for example, can extend as far as 2 cm in both directions. Thus, if there are no more than 2 cm remaining proximally, the only practical options that can be offered to the patient who wishes to have her reproductive potential restored are tubocornual anastomosis (p 264) or in vitro fertilization (p 276). If there are less than 3 cm left distally, the chances of the surgery successfully accomplishing patency with subsequent pregnancy are greatly diminished, although it may occasionally be worthwhile. The patient and her partner must be made aware of the poor prognosis so that she can choose knowledgeably.

C. Utilize meticulous microsurgical technique to perform end-to-end anastomosis (Fig. 1). Schedule the procedure during the proliferative phase of the menstrual cycle, inhibiting ovulation to enhance endosalpingeal growth and healing. Under good magnification and illumination, serially resect (in thin perpendicular slices) progressively away from the obstructed portion until the patent lumen is clearly identified. A fine probe facilitates identification. Dissect while irrigating to prevent unnecessary tissue damage and maintain hemostasis with a fine-needle electrode cautery. Reappose the mesosalpinx before proceeding. If the proximal and distal lumina are equal in diameter, the tubal walls can be readily approximated with size 7-0 or 8-0 polyglactic acid or

Figure 1 Tubal anastomosis requires resection of the damaged segment, followed by suturing the defect in the mesosalpinx. Then the tubal muscularis is reapposed with fine sutures over an intraluminal stint (A) and a re-enforcing serosal layer is applied (B).

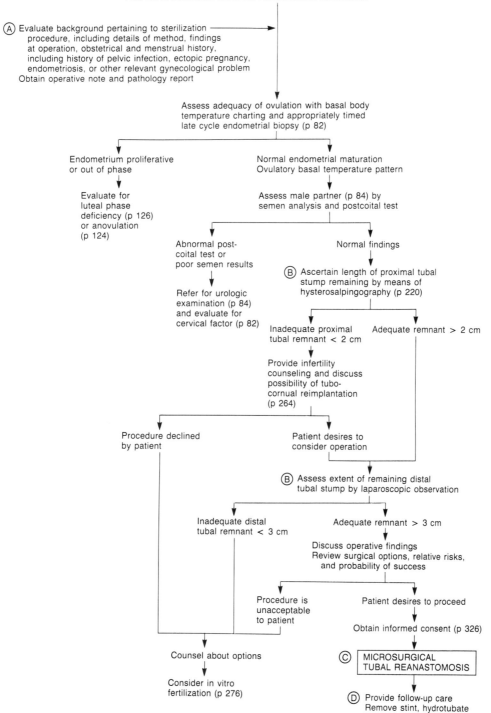

POSTSTERILIZATION PATIENT REQUESTING REVERSAL

Ⓐ Evaluate background pertaining to sterilization
procedure, including details of method, findings
at operation, obstetrical and menstrual history,
including history of pelvic infection, ectopic pregnancy,
endometriosis, or other relevant gynecological problem
Obtain operative note and pathology report

Assess adequacy of ovulation with basal body
temperature charting and appropriately timed
late cycle endometrial biopsy (p 82)

Endometrium proliferative
or out of phase

Normal endometrial maturation
Ovulatory basal temperature pattern

Evaluate for
luteal phase
deficiency (p 126)
or anovulation
(p 124)

Assess male partner (p 84) by
semen analysis and postcoital test

Abnormal post-
coital test or
poor semen results

Normal findings

Refer for urologic
examination (p 84)
and evaluate for
cervical factor (p 82)

Ⓑ Ascertain length of proximal tubal
stump remaining by means of
hysterosalpingography (p 220)

Inadequate proximal
tubal remnant < 2 cm

Adequate remnant > 2 cm

Provide infertility
counseling and discuss
possibility of tubo-
cornual reimplantation
(p 264)

Procedure declined
by patient

Patient desires to
consider operation

Ⓑ Assess extent of remaining distal
tubal stump by laparoscopic observation

Inadequate distal
tubal remnant < 3 cm

Adequate remnant > 3 cm

Discuss operative findings
Review surgical options, relative risks,
and probability of success

Procedure is
unacceptable
to patient

Patient desires to proceed

Obtain informed consent (p 326)

Counsel about options

Ⓒ | MICROSURGICAL TUBAL REANASTOMOSIS |

Consider in vitro
fertilization (p 276)

Ⓓ Provide follow-up care
Remove stint, hydrotubate

monofilament nylon sutures over a nylon stint. (The stint can be removed at once or during the next period postoperatively). A second, re-enforcing layer is then placed. If the distal lumen is larger than the proximal one, only open the distal stump enough to produce the size opening desired.

D. As for other forms of tuboplasty, close follow-up is essential. If the stint has been left in place, it is removed transcervically during the next period. Watch for pregnancy, being alert to the possibility of tubal implantation.

References

Divers WA Jr. Characteristics of women requesting reversal of sterilization. Fertil Steril 41:233, 1984.

Howard G. Who asks for vasectomy reversal and why? Br Med J 285:490, 1982.

Seiler JC. Factors influencing the outcome of microsurgical tubal ligation reversals. Am J Obstet Gynecol 146:292, 1983.

Spivak MM, Librach CL, Rosenthal DM. Microsurgical reversal of sterilization: A six-year study. Am J Obstet Gynecol 154:355, 1986.

VAGINAL RECONSTRUCTION

Emanuel A. Friedman, M.D., Sc.D.

A. Since the diagnosis of vaginal agenesis is seldom made before puberty or before intercourse is attempted, timing reconstructive surgery or a dilatation program to optimize the results is not always a problem. If the patient is very young or unlikely to have regular coitus, however, motivation may not be adequate to ensure success. Thus, the patient's age and sexual needs are important for deci-

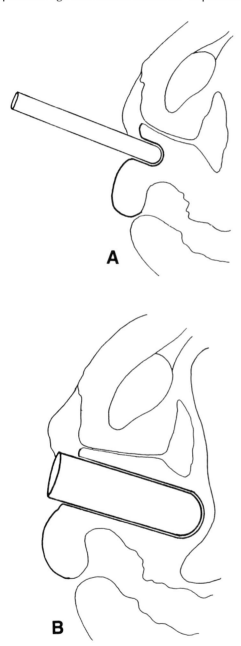

Figure 1 Formation of a neovagina. The McIndoe operation (A) requires careful blunt surgical dissection between bladder and rectum up to the peritoneal reflection and placement of a stint over which a reversed skin graft has been sewn. In the Frank method, external pressure is applied regularly by glass tube (B) or specially constructed bicycle seat to elongate perineal depression over time.

sions about both timing and type of procedure. A special exception is the teenager with vaginal agenesis and a normal uterus with functional endometrium. She can be expected to develop hematometra after menarche as a consequence of cyclic menstrual bleeding with progressively increasing periodic pain. The problem is readily correctable by establishing an adequate exit for drainage of the menstrual flow.

B. Vaginal agenesis frequently causes intense emotional problems, especially as related to the patient's sense of self-worth, sexuality, and fulfillment. She and her parents or partner deserve the benefit of intensive psychosocial assessment, counseling, and support plus full disclosure of information pertaining to her condition, the options available for correction, and the generally good prognosis for both anatomic results and functional satisfaction. In order to provide information concerning reproductive potential, the status of the uterus and tubes must be determined. Ovarian function is usually unaffected with vaginal agenesis, but the uterus is often (but not always) adversely involved.

C. While it is uncommon for there to be a functional uterus in these cases, if a normal uterus is present, surgical reconstruction of a neovagina with skin grafting is the method of choice. It not only provides an immediate pathway for menstrual outflow, but it offers an opportunity to enhance reproductive potential as well. The McIndoe procedure (see E), or some modification of it, is generally done under these circumstances. It may even prove successful in cases with cervical atresia (p 160), provided this additional problem is also dealt with appropriately.

D. In most women with vaginal agenesis, the uterus is either absent or rudimentary. Since the external genitalia are normally developed in these cases, there is usually a distal short vaginal pouch or dimple. For a strongly motivated patient, one might consider the long-term nonoperative program entailed in the Frank technique (see F). If rapid results are required, such as in anticipation of marriage, the surgical approach is more suitable.

E. The surgical procedure usually used for correcting congenital vaginal agenesis is the McIndoe technique (Fig. 1A). A transverse perineal incision is made and a space is created in the loose areolar tissue between the bladder and the rectum by careful sharp and blunt dissection. Special attention to the anatomic plane is needed to avoid damaging bladder or rectum. Meticulous hemostasis is also essential here before placement of a skin graft. If hemostasis is poor, consider merely allowing the vagina to epithelialize over a stint, bearing in mind that it takes much longer (months) to achieve the results possible with a graft. To proceed with grafting, take a large split-thickness skin segment by dermatome from the thigh or buttocks. The graft is shaped, trimmed, and sutured with its subdermis facing out over a plastic or glass mold. It is held in place for 10 to 14 days by means of a simple perineal T-binder. Continued use of a stint is needed to

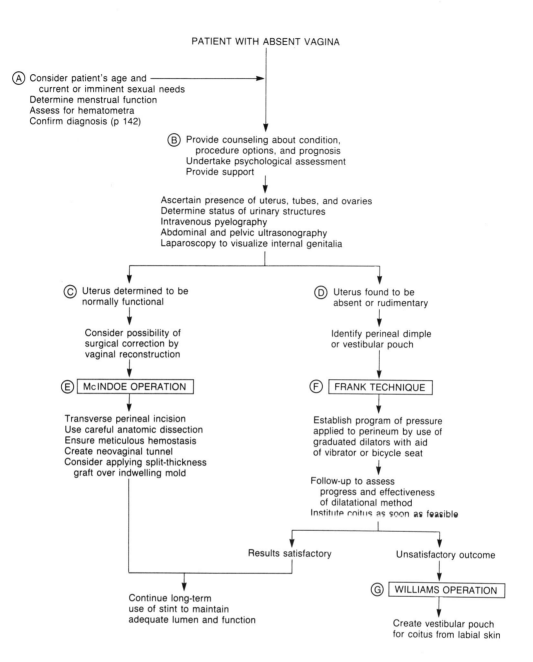

PATIENT WITH ABSENT VAGINA

Ⓐ Consider patient's age and
current or imminent sexual needs
Determine menstrual function
Assess for hematometra
Confirm diagnosis (p 142)

Ⓑ Provide counseling about condition,
procedure options, and prognosis
Undertake psychological assessment
Provide support

Ascertain presence of uterus, tubes, and ovaries
Determine status of urinary structures
Intravenous pyelography
Abdominal and pelvic ultrasonography
Laparoscopy to visualize internal genitalia

Ⓒ Uterus determined to be
normally functional

Ⓓ Uterus found to be
absent or rudimentary

Consider possibility of
surgical correction by
vaginal reconstruction

Identify perineal dimple
or vestibular pouch

Ⓔ McINDOE OPERATION

Ⓕ FRANK TECHNIQUE

Transverse perineal incision
Use careful anatomic dissection
Ensure meticulous hemostasis
Create neovaginal tunnel
Consider applying split-thickness
graft over indwelling mold

Establish program of pressure
applied to perineum by use of
graduated dilators with aid
of vibrator or bicycle seat

Follow-up to assess
progress and effectiveness
of dilatational method
Institute coitus as soon as feasible

Results satisfactory

Unsatisfactory outcome

Ⓖ WILLIAMS OPERATION

Continue long-term
use of stint to maintain
adequate lumen and function

Create vestibular pouch
for coitus from labial skin

prevent shortening or stenosis. Once the graft has taken and healing is complete, the patient may begin coital activity.

F. A well motivated patient can make effective use of dilators for progressively increasing vaginal length and diameter (Fig. 1B). A schedule of dilatation twice daily for 20 to 30 minutes is usually needed. A recently described bicycle seat arrangement is reported to be especially valuable. The direction and degree of pressure may have to be monitored to avoid injury.

G. For a postexenteration patient or a women in whom all other approaches have failed, one might consider a simple surgical procedure to form a vulvar pouch merely by joining the skin of the labia majora in the midline. A cavity for coitus is provided via the anterior introital opening. Although it does not function ideally, it may nonetheless serve the patient's needs.

References

Bates GW, Wiser WL. A technique for uterine conservation in adolescents with vaginal agenesis and a functional uterus. Obstet Gynecol 66:290, 1985.

Berek JS, Hacker NF, Lagasse LD, Smith ML. Delayed vaginal reconstruction in the fibrotic pelvis following radiation or previous reconstruction. Obstet Gynecol 61:743, 1983.

Lees DH, Singer A. Vaginal surgery for congenital abnormalities and acquired constrictions. Clin Obstet Gynecol 25:883, 1982.

Rock JA, Jones HW. Vaginal forms for dilatation and/or to maintain vaginal patency. Fertil Steril 42:187, 1984.

Smith MR. Vaginal aplasia: Therapeutic options. Am J Obstet Gynecol 146:488, 1983.

FISTULA REPAIR

Emanuel A. Friedman, M.D., Sc.D.

A. Vesicovaginal, ureterovaginal, or rectovaginal fistulas can occur from the trauma of obstetrical delivery, surgical procedure, or radiation. Difficult labor with forceful delivery is seldom a cause today, but radical surgery and intensive irradiation still contribute. Invasive cancer or severe chronic infection can also produce a fistula. A fistula can occur from routine gynecological surgery for benign disease, including simple total hysterectomy and vaginal plasty procedures. Careful dissection, identification of tissue planes, and hemostasis are all essential for avoiding this problem. Fistulas have also been reported to occur after hypogastric intra-arterial embolization to control pelvic bleeding. Fistulas associated with invasive cancer, radiation, foreign body, or infection, and those persisting after a failed attempt at surgical repair are not likely to be readily correctable by direct operative attack. A urinary or fecal diversion procedure must ordinarily be done first, followed by a long period during which the fistulous site can be brought to optimal condition of health and vascularity, devoid of infection. Fistulas resulting from intraoperative trauma to otherwise normal tissue are usually correctable by primary reparative surgery.

B. Visualize the site and extent of a ureterovaginal fistula by means of intravenous pyelography followed by cystoscopy with retrograde ureteral catheterization. Pack the vagina with clean dry gauze sponges and instill dilute methylene blue dye into the bladder. Blue staining of the gauze shows both the presence and the site of a vesico-vaginal fistula. Unless there is vesicoureteral reflux, dye should not be expected to be seen with a ureterovaginal fistula.

C. The technique for ureterovaginal fistula repair depends on the size of the tract and the extent of the damage. If the fistula is not too close to the bladder and the ureteral length is not compromised, undertake end-to-end reanastomosis over a ureteral splint. A fistula located near the ureterovesical junction is best implanted directly into the bladder with some degree of tunneling to support the anastomosis and prevent reflux. Ureteroureterostomy for implanting the end of one ureter into the side of the other can be done to preserve bilateral renal function if one ureter is so badly damaged that it is too short to reach the bladder. Ureteral implantation into an ileal loop is done if the bladder has to be removed in the course of anterior or total exenteration (p 256).

D. The vaginal approach is generally used for repairing a vesicovaginal fistula. Care must be taken to stay clear of the ureteral ostia, perhaps by preliminary retrograde ureteral catheterization to avoid inadvertent ureteral damage. A transabdominal attack may be needed to ensure adequate exposure for high vaginal fistulas and those that have been operated on previously. Debride the fistulous tract carefully and proceed to dissect all tissue layers. Ensure good hemostasis before closing in carefully apposed layers, without any tension on the sutures.

E. Rectovaginal fistulas can be readily diagnosed by gently inserting a fine probe into the vaginal opening while simultaneously feeling for the probe with a finger in the rectum. Take special care not to make a false passage in the tissues with the probe. Barium enema or sinogram obtained by injecting radiopaque dye directly into the tract discloses any ramifications in the tract.

F. Before undertaking fistula repair, consider diverting the fecal stream for three to four months by a colostomy. This is especially worthwhile if the fistula site is badly infected or the fistula has recurred after a surgical attempt to repair it. Bowel continuity can be restored later after the fistula has been successfully corrected.

G. Excise the fistulous tract out to healthy tissue and dissect the vagina well away from the rectal wall (Fig. 1). Maintain meticulous hemostasis. Close the bowel wall without tension in well approximated submucosal layers using absorbable sutures. Bring the levator ani fascia and muscles together in the midline to reconstruct the perineal integrity and interpose healthy vascular tissue between rectum and vagina. Then close the vaginal mucosa.

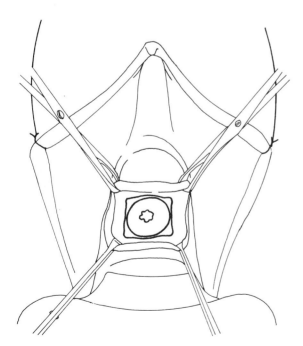

Figure 1 Fistula repair requires excision of the tract back to healthy, well vascularized tissue. Wide dissection and mobilization of the surrounding layers of the vaginal wall are necessary to ensure good healing. Meticulous hemostasis and closure are important.

References

Behnam K, Jarmolowski CR. Vesicovaginal fistula following hypogastric embolization for control of intractable pelvic hemorrhage. J Reprod Med 27:304, 1982.

Hoskins WJ, Park RC, Long R, et al. Repair of urinary tract fistulas

PATIENT WITH FISTULA UNDER CONSIDERATION FOR CORRECTION

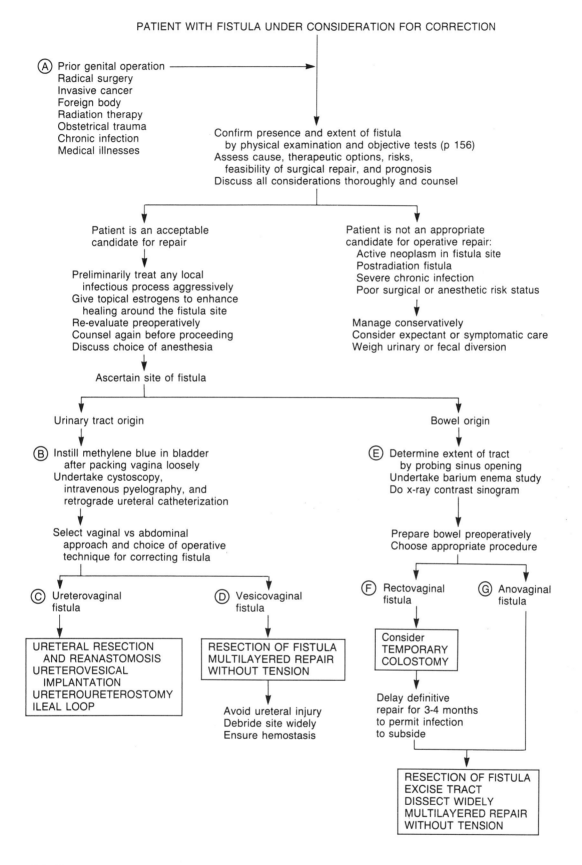

Ⓐ Prior genital operation
  Radical surgery
  Invasive cancer
  Foreign body
  Radiation therapy
  Obstetrical trauma
  Chronic infection
  Medical illnesses

Confirm presence and extent of fistula
  by physical examination and objective tests (p 156)
Assess cause, therapeutic options, risks,
  feasibility of surgical repair, and prognosis
Discuss all considerations thoroughly and counsel

Patient is an acceptable
candidate for repair

Patient is not an appropriate
candidate for operative repair:
  Active neoplasm in fistula site
  Postradiation fistula
  Severe chronic infection
  Poor surgical or anesthetic risk status

Preliminarily treat any local
  infectious process aggressively
Give topical estrogens to enhance
  healing around the fistula site
Re-evaluate preoperatively
Counsel again before proceeding
Discuss choice of anesthesia

Manage conservatively
Consider expectant or symptomatic care
Weigh urinary or fecal diversion

Ascertain site of fistula

Urinary tract origin

Bowel origin

Ⓑ Instill methylene blue in bladder
  after packing vagina loosely
Undertake cystoscopy,
  intravenous pyelography, and
  retrograde ureteral catheterization

Ⓔ Determine extent of tract
  by probing sinus opening
Undertake barium enema study
Do x-ray contrast sinogram

Select vaginal vs abdominal
  approach and choice of operative
  technique for correcting fistula

Prepare bowel preoperatively
Choose appropriate procedure

Ⓒ Ureterovaginal
  fistula

Ⓓ Vesicovaginal
  fistula

Ⓕ Rectovaginal
  fistula

Ⓖ Anovaginal
  fistula

URETERAL RESECTION
  AND REANASTOMOSIS
URETEROVESICAL
  IMPLANTATION
URETEROURETEROSTOMY
ILEAL LOOP

RESECTION OF FISTULA
MULTILAYERED REPAIR
WITHOUT TENSION

Consider
TEMPORARY
COLOSTOMY

Avoid ureteral injury
Debride site widely
Ensure hemostasis

Delay definitive
repair for 3-4 months
to permit infection
to subside

RESECTION OF FISTULA
EXCISE TRACT
DISSECT WIDELY
MULTILAYERED REPAIR
WITHOUT TENSION

with bulbocavernosus myocutaneous flaps. Obstet Gynecol 63:588, 1984.

Smith WG, Johnson GH. Vesicovaginal fistula repair: Revisited. Gynecol Oncol 9:303, 1980.

Symmonds RE. Incontinence: Vesical and urethral fistulas. Clin Obstet Gynecol 27:499, 1984.

White AJ, Buchsbaum HJ, Blythe JG, Lifshitz S. Use of bulbocavernosus muscle (Martius procedure) for repair of radiation-induced rectovaginal fistulas. Obstet Gynecol 60:114, 1982.

IN VITRO FERTILIZATION

Machelle M. Seibel, M.D.
Alexander M. Dlugi, M.D.

A. In vitro fertilization (IVF) was originally designed for use in infertile women with diseased or absent tubes as a means for bypassing the obstructed conduit. Experience has shown that it may be justified for other causes of infertility. However, its application may still be limited because the cost is prohibitively high and generally not covered by third-party insurance carriers. Moreover, results are imperfect at best, with successful pregnancy achieved and carried to viability in only 15 to 20 percent of the cases in centers with the greatest experience, volume, and technical skills.

B. It is essential to carry out a thorough infertility evaluation of a couple before resorting to IVF. This helps to uncover conditions that may prove readily correctable, thereby obviating the need for IVF. *Mycoplasma* cultures are generally obtained for two reasons: *Mycoplasma* infection is a treatable condition (although the proof that it is an important cause of infertility is as yet dubious) and it is important to eliminate the organism as a potential contaminator of the IVF incubator. Before beginning the IVF cycle, obtain a semen specimen for freezing. This is done in anticipation of transient impotence by the male partner who is called upon to perform essentially on command at the specific time when all is in readiness in regard to ovulation timing. The stress of the occasion may interfere with erection and ejaculation. Due to the severe emotional impact of IVF, it is essential to provide counseling for all participating couples by an especially knowledgeable, trained mental health worker from the outset.

C. Ovulation occurring spontaneously is certainly acceptable for IVF purposes, but it presents logistic problems in regard to optimal scheduling and mobilization of the resources and personnel needed for a successful procedure. Ovulation induction in a timely manner, therefore, is preferable. Superovulation to develop several follicles for simultaneous fertilization is the objective to be accomplished. Of the several drugs available today, clomiphene citrate and human menopausal gonadotropin are most frequently used in a regimen by which one or the other is given alone or both are given together or in sequence. Luteinizing hormone releasing hormone and follicle stimulating hormone (FSH) are alternative medications to help stimulate ovulation. Failure to achieve adequate follicle maturation in a given cycle makes it inappropriate to proceed with occyte retrieval; this deficiency prevails in about one-quarter of IVF attempts. Another problem is that in which ovulation takes place before oocyte retrieval can be done. This can be avoided by close monitoring for the luteinizing hormone (LH) surge that presages ovulation.

D. Oocytes are retrieved by aspirating the contents of mature graafian follicles with a long, fine needle. The most common approach thus far has been by laparoscopy and direct visualization of the sites for aspiration. A promising newly developed technique involves ultrasonographically-guided aspiration through the urinary bladder (transabdominally or transurethrally) or the posterior vaginal fornix. Aspiration is complemented by flushing the follicle to dislodge an adherent oocyte with its investing cumulus cells.

E. The aspirated follicular contents are examined microscopically to identify the oocytes that have been harvested. Washed semen treated to enhance capacitation of spermatozoa is mixed with the oocyte and incubated under ideal sterile laboratory conditions until fertilization and cleavage is observed to have occurred. For the 15 percent that fail to fertilize, one should consider undertaking renewed studies to disclose problems in the area of embryology and andrology. Poor results can be expected if the semen analysis shows low concentration of spermatozoa with poor motility and high proportion of abnormal forms. Newly evolving techniques for sperm separation may prove beneficial in such cases.

F. A patient who successfully conceives by IVF should be cared for in much the same way during the course of her pregnancy as any other pregnant woman. Although the incidence of congenital anomalies does not appear to be increased, one should be aware that there is an increased risk of fetal loss and premature delivery reported to be associated with pregnancies resulting from IVF. Current practice includes administration of natural progesterone ostensibly to help maintain the pregnancy even though it has not been shown to be effective by objective study.

References

Alper MM, Lee GS, Seibel MM, et al. The relationship of semen parameters to fertilization in patients participating in a program of in vitro fertilization. J In Vitro Fert Embryo Transfer 2:217, 1985.

Edwards RG, Fishel SB, Cohen J, et al. Factors influencing the success of in-vitro fertilization for alleviating human infertility. J In Vitro Fertil Embryo Transfer 1:3, 1984.

Jones HW Jr, Acosta AA, Andrews MC, et al. Three years of in vitro fertilization at Norfolk. Fertil Steril 42:826, 1984.

Seibel MM, Levin S. A new era in reproductive technology: The emotional stages of in vitro fertilization. J In Vitro Fertil Embryo Transfer, 4:135, 1987.

Taymor ML, Seibel MM, Oskowitz SP, et al. In vitro fertilization and embryo transfer: An individualized approach to ovulation induction. J In Vitro Fert Embryo Transfer 2:162, 1985.

INFERTILITY PATIENT CONSIDERED FOR IN VITRO FERTILIZATION

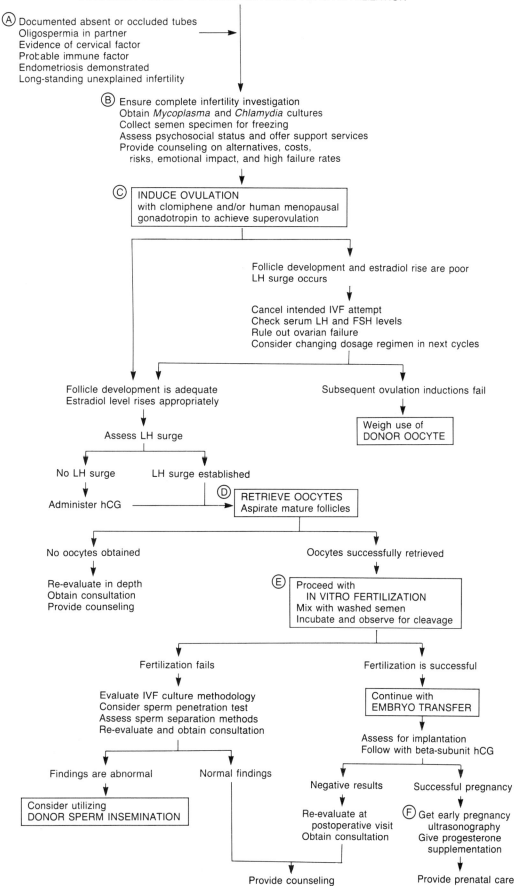

Ⓐ Documented absent or occluded tubes
Oligospermia in partner
Evidence of cervical factor
Probable immune factor
Endometriosis demonstrated
Long-standing unexplained infertility

Ⓑ Ensure complete infertility investigation
Obtain *Mycoplasma* and *Chlamydia* cultures
Collect semen specimen for freezing
Assess psychosocial status and offer support services
Provide counseling on alternatives, costs,
  risks, emotional impact, and high failure rates

Ⓒ INDUCE OVULATION
with clomiphene and/or human menopausal
gonadotropin to achieve superovulation

Follicle development and estradiol rise are poor
LH surge occurs

Cancel intended IVF attempt
Check serum LH and FSH levels
Rule out ovarian failure
Consider changing dosage regimen in next cycles

Follicle development is adequate
Estradiol level rises appropriately

Subsequent ovulation inductions fail

Weigh use of
DONOR OOCYTE

Assess LH surge

No LH surge   LH surge established

Administer hCG

Ⓓ RETRIEVE OOCYTES
Aspirate mature follicles

No oocytes obtained

Re-evaluate in depth
Obtain consultation
Provide counseling

Oocytes successfully retrieved

Ⓔ Proceed with
IN VITRO FERTILIZATION
Mix with washed semen
Incubate and observe for cleavage

Fertilization fails

Evaluate IVF culture methodology
Consider sperm penetration test
Assess sperm separation methods
Re-evaluate and obtain consultation

Fertilization is successful

Continue with
EMBRYO TRANSFER

Assess for implantation
Follow with beta-subunit hCG

Findings are abnormal   Normal findings

Consider utilizing
DONOR SPERM INSEMINATION

Negative results   Successful pregnancy

Re-evaluate at
postoperative visit
Obtain consultation

Ⓕ Get early pregnancy
ultrasonography
Give progesterone
supplementation

Provide counseling

Provide prenatal care

277

GAMETE INTRAFALLOPIAN TRANSFER

Alexander M. Dlugi, M.D.
Machelle M. Seibel, M.D.

A. A recently introduced procedure, gamete intrafallopian transfer (GIFT), affords a new method of conception for infertile couples. This technique was designed to provide a means for ensuring proper contact between oocyte and spermatozoa at the site where fertilization usually occurs, namely in the ampulla of the fallopian tube. GIFT involves collecting oocytes by laparoscopy or minilaparotomy (see C) and transferring them along with semen into the tube where fertilization may occur. It has the advantage of somewhat higher success rates than in vitro fertilization (IVF); it is also technically less difficult and does not require the same sophisticated laboratory support and resources. The theoretic possibility of tubal pregnancy has not been fully assessed yet. It differs from IVF (p 276) in several important ways. It requires an intact, patent, normally functional tube, although the fimbrial ovum pick-up mechanism is bypassed by the GIFT method. While the ova are harvested in the same way from intact mature graafian follicles, collected ova are not mixed with semen and incubated in vitro. Instead, they are placed into the tube along with an aliquot of washed sperm; they first come into contact with each other within the tubal lumen. As a consequence of the fact that fertilization can only occur within the patient, rather than in culture in the laboratory, this technique has found favor with those who hold there are insurmountable theologic constraints against other forms of fertilization aid. GIFT is applicable to a variety of infertility patients, such as those with minimal or mild endometriosis (p 190) whose inability to conceive appears to be based on some local factor related to a physical effect (adhesions perhaps affecting the ovum pick-up mechanism) or a biochemical one (histamines or prostaglandins produced in response to the foci of endometriosis). Couples with oligospermia or asthenospermia may also benefit by providing them the advantage of depositing adequate numbers of sperm within the tube. Similarly, those with immunologic factors as demonstrated by antisperm antibodies are good candidates because the adverse cervical factor is averted. A positive hamster sperm penetration assay is reassuring. Alternatively, consider an initial IVF cycle to show whether fertilization can occur; if implantation fails or the conception is blighted, this might then be followed by one or more GIFT cycles. Every potential candidate being considered for GIFT must understand that the method does not guarantee fertilization.

B. In order for GIFT to be considered, it is mandatory to ensure that the fallopian tubes are patent. This must be documented beforehand by hysterosalpingography (p 220) or prior chromotubation at the time of laparoscopy. Be especially alert for patients with a history of tubal disease because they may later prove to have peritubal disease even though it could not be detected before GIFT was undertaken. Some patients are found to have peritubal adhesions at the time of oocyte retrieval, a finding that generally precludes GIFT. If appropriately counseled for this, many couples agree in advance to convert the procedure to IVF.

C. Induction of multiple follicular maturation is carried out in the same manner as for IVF. Semen samples are collected several hours prior to the procedure, a prior specimen having been frozen in the event it is needed. The liquified semen is washed in special culture medium, centrifuged, and rewashed. Motile sperm are concentrated for use in the GIFT procedure. Oocytes are retrieved by needle aspiration of the follicles. The oocytes are also similarly washed. The transfer catheter is prepared under sterile conditions by sequential loading of culture medium, an air space, washed sperm, more air, the washed oocytes, and medium. The loaded catheter is inserted by way of the aspirating needle into the distal end of the tube where its contents are discharged. The best method for gamete transfer is still controversial. Some advocate laparoscopic placement, but this can be technically difficult and the carbon dioxide may be detrimental to ova or sperm. Therefore, others suggest it be done by minilaparotomy. The optimal number of oocytes to transfer is as yet unknown, but most recommend two per tube or perhaps three in one tube if the contralateral tube is surgically absent.

References

Asch RH, Balmaceda JP, Ellsworth LR, Wong PC. Preliminary experiences with gamete intrafallopian transfer (GIFT). Fertil Steril 45:366, 1986.

Corson SL, Batzer F, Eisenberg E, et al. Early experience with the GIFT procedure. J Reprod Med 31:219, 1986.

Guastella G, Comparetto G, Palermo R, et al. Gamete intrafallopian transfer in the treatment of infertility: The first series at the University of Palermo. Fertil Steril 46:417, 1986.

INFERTILITY PATIENT BEING CONSIDERED FOR GAMETE INTRAFALLOPIAN TRANSFER

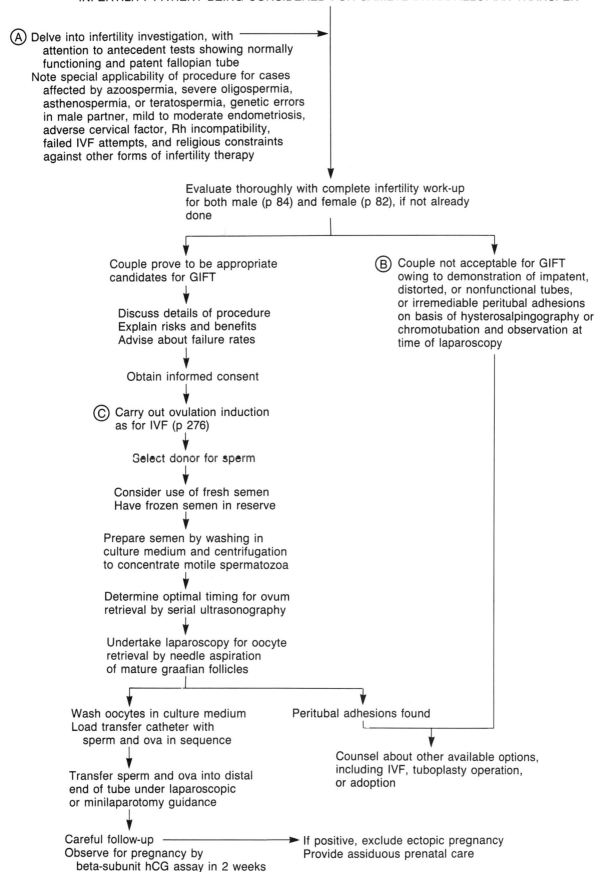

Ⓐ Delve into infertility investigation, with
    attention to antecedent tests showing normally
    functioning and patent fallopian tube
Note special applicability of procedure for cases
    affected by azoospermia, severe oligospermia,
    asthenospermia, or teratospermia, genetic errors
    in male partner, mild to moderate endometriosis,
    adverse cervical factor, Rh incompatibility,
    failed IVF attempts, and religious constraints
    against other forms of infertility therapy

Evaluate thoroughly with complete infertility work-up
    for both male (p 84) and female (p 82), if not already
    done

Couple prove to be appropriate
candidates for GIFT

Ⓑ Couple not acceptable for GIFT
    owing to demonstration of impatent,
    distorted, or nonfunctional tubes,
    or irremediable peritubal adhesions
    on basis of hysterosalpingography or
    chromotubation and observation at
    time of laparoscopy

Discuss details of procedure
Explain risks and benefits
Advise about failure rates

Obtain informed consent

Ⓒ Carry out ovulation induction
    as for IVF (p 276)

Select donor for sperm

Consider use of fresh semen
Have frozen semen in reserve

Prepare semen by washing in
culture medium and centrifugation
to concentrate motile spermatozoa

Determine optimal timing for ovum
retrieval by serial ultrasonography

Undertake laparoscopy for oocyte
retrieval by needle aspiration
of mature graafian follicles

Wash oocytes in culture medium
Load transfer catheter with
    sperm and ova in sequence

Peritubal adhesions found

Counsel about other available options,
    including IVF, tuboplasty operation,
    or adoption

Transfer sperm and ova into distal
end of tube under laparoscopic
or minilaparotomy guidance

Careful follow-up
Observe for pregnancy by
    beta-subunit hCG assay in 2 weeks

If positive, exclude ectopic pregnancy
Provide assiduous prenatal care

ARTIFICIAL INSEMINATION

Alexander M. Dlugi, M.D.
Machelle M. Seibel, M.D.

A. Artificial insemination by the patient's regular sexual partner (in the interest of brevity, the term "husband" will be used, understanding that marital status is not relevant) or by a donor is a technique widely used to help infertile couples whose problem is related to sperm number or quality, that is, azoospermia (no sperm), oligospermia (too few), asthenospermia (reduced motility), or teratospermia (abnormal forms). The donor method may also be indicated in other circumstances, such as for the male partner of a couple who has a proved chromosomal error or a known hereditary disorder such as Tay-Sachs disease, Huntington's disease, or hemophilia. It can also be considered in cases of severe Rh incompatibility if the husband is homozygous Rh-positive, utilizing semen from an Rh-negative donor.

B. Couples may not be appropriate candidates for artificial insemination for a variety of reasons. Of primary importance is a thorough infertility evaluation (p 82). This is critical to ensure optimal potential for the female partner if there may be some chance, albeit small, that the husband's sperm has some fertilizing capability. Counseling for the couple is very important to prepare them for the emotional impact of the procedure, especially if donor sperm is to be used. Other alternatives, such as in vitro fertilization (in the case of oligospermia) or adoption, should be explored. They must understand that failures and congenital anomalies occur (just as they do by natural fertilization).

C. The couple must sign a release form that allows the physician to perform the procedure, absolves the physician and staff from any resultant congenital anomalies, and requires the husband to recognize any children by donor artificial insemination as his own with full inheritance and support rights. A statement protecting the anonymity of the donor may or may not be included, but in any event the concept of anonymity is essential.

D. Selection of a donor requires a thorough history to screen out donors who are at potential risk for AIDS (p 122), who abuse parenteral drugs, have had multiple sexual partners, or who have a history of sexually transmitted diseases (p 112), including herpes. The physical examination should be detailed as well. Exclude the presence of a urethral discharge and genital warts or ulcers. A family history is particularly important to screen for recognized and suspected hereditary and familial disorders. A semen analysis must be performed. The first acceptable specimen should be cultured for gonorrhea, *Chlamydia trachomatis*, and *Mycoplasma*. Test blood for type and Rh factor, hepatitis B, syphilis, cytomegalovirus, and human immune deficiency virus. Screen for Tay-Sachs disease in Jewish donors and sickle cell trait in black donors. Chromosomal analysis of the donor is controversial and probably not necessary. Ideally, the donor should be matched as closely as possible in physical characteristics to the husband. The same donor should not be used for more than ten offspring in the interest of avoiding eugenic issues in a confined community.

E. The use of fresh semen has been associated with higher fecundity rates than encountered with frozen semen. Donors should be recultured for sexually transmitted pathogens at least every year, and probably every six months. The major risk of using fresh semen is the potential transmission of a recently acquired pathogenic organism. While fecundity rates using frozen semen may be lower than those using fresh semen, new freezing technology may lead to equivalent rates. Freezing semen has the theoretic advantage of facilitating use of banked culture-negative specimens.

F. The greatest single factor that underlies the success of artificial insemination donation is the timing of ovulation. Basal body temperature charting is a useful but somewhat crude method for assessing ovulation. The insemination is generally scheduled to be done on the day preceding the temperature rise as determined from the patterns of the foregoing several cycles. The use of kits for testing of urinary luteinizing hormone to detect the peak for a given cycle appears to be more precise, but it creates scheduling difficulties. Ultrasonographic monitoring of follicular development may be helpful. The number of inseminations required per cycle is controversial. If only temperature charting is used for timing, two inseminations (separated by 48 hours) are recommended. Otherwise, a single insemination per cycle is adequate.

References

Greenblatt RM, Handsfield HH, Sayers MH, Holmes KK. Screening therapeutic insemination donors for sexually transmitted diseases: Overview and recommendations. Fertil Steril 46:351, 1986.

Schwartz D, Mayaux MJ, Guihard-Moscato ML, et al. Abortion rates in A.I.D. and semen characteristics: A study of 1345 pregnancies. Andrologia 18:292, 1986.

Slovenko R. Sperm donation. Med Law 5:173, 1986.

Verp MS, Cohen MR, Simpson JL. Necessity of formal genetic screening in artificial insemination by donor. Obstet Gynecol 62:474, 1983.

INFERTILITY PATIENT BEING CONSIDERED FOR ARTIFICIAL INSEMINATION WITH DONOR SPERM

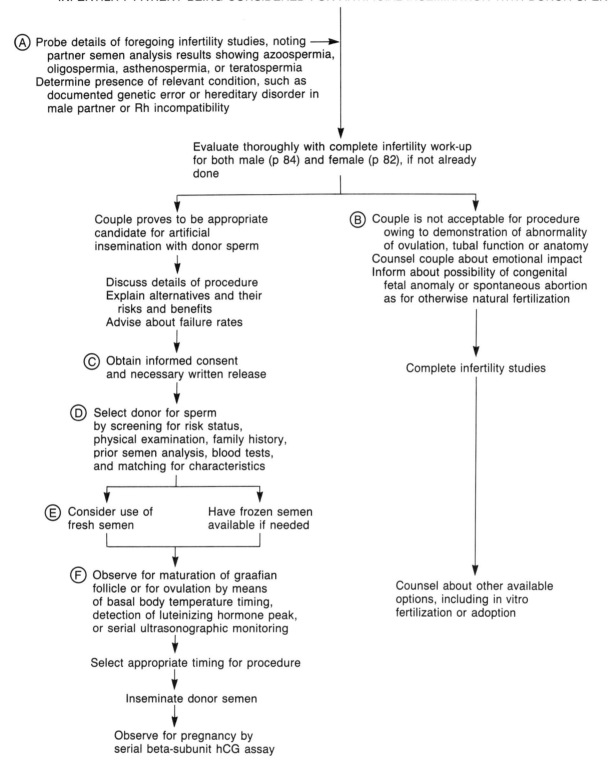

(A) Probe details of foregoing infertility studies, noting
partner semen analysis results showing azoospermia,
oligospermia, asthenospermia, or teratospermia
Determine presence of relevant condition, such as
documented genetic error or hereditary disorder in
male partner or Rh incompatibility

Evaluate thoroughly with complete infertility work-up
for both male (p 84) and female (p 82), if not already
done

Couple proves to be appropriate
candidate for artificial
insemination with donor sperm

(B) Couple is not acceptable for procedure
owing to demonstration of abnormality
of ovulation, tubal function or anatomy
Counsel couple about emotional impact
Inform about possibility of congenital
fetal anomaly or spontaneous abortion
as for otherwise natural fertilization

Discuss details of procedure
Explain alternatives and their
risks and benefits
Advise about failure rates

(C) Obtain informed consent
and necessary written release

(D) Select donor for sperm
by screening for risk status,
physical examination, family history,
prior semen analysis, blood tests,
and matching for characteristics

Complete infertility studies

(E) Consider use of
fresh semen

Have frozen semen
available if needed

(F) Observe for maturation of graafian
follicle or for ovulation by means
of basal body temperature timing,
detection of luteinizing hormone peak,
or serial ultrasonographic monitoring

Select appropriate timing for procedure

Counsel about other available
options, including in vitro
fertilization or adoption

Inseminate donor semen

Observe for pregnancy by
serial beta-subunit hCG assay

INTRAOPERATIVE HEMOSTASIS

Henry Klapholz, M.D.

A. Certain cases warrant special attention to hemostasis based on history, the type of operation being considered, or the kinds of hemorrhagic complications that can be anticipated. A detailed preoperative history is essential for evidence of prior surgical bleeding and easy bruisability. Inquire about exposure to prostaglandin synthetase inhibitors (including aspirin, naproxen, and ibuprofen), which have a lasting effect because of their anti-platelet action for the duration of life of the affected platelets (see B). For difficult dissections or radical surgery, type and cross match blood for intraoperative use and consider alerting skilled consultants for possible intraoperative aid.

B. Routine platelet smear, prothrombin time, and partial thromboplastin time are in order for all surgical patients. Any positive or suggestive history or finding demands a full coagulation profile. If surgery can be delayed, proceed to correct the defect encountered first. Platelet half-life is about two weeks under normal circumstances, after which platelets affected by aspirin, for example, can be expected to be replaced. Administer platelet transfusions (in 10 unit increments) or fresh frozen plasma, if surgery is urgent, to the patient with an intrinsic defect in either platelets or hepatic synthesis of clotting factors. If severe coagulopathy should develop in the course of a complex surgical procedure, the surgery may have to stop. Hemostasis under these circumstances may be accomplished by mass packing using large roll gauze packs (see F). If it is effective, it gives one time to correct the underlying coagulation disorder. The use of 1-deamino-8-D-arginine vasopressin (DDAVP) can correct an assortment of bleeding diatheses, including von Willebrand's disease, without having to resort to giving blood components.

C. Suspect an acute coagulopathy if uncontrollable oozing of blood begins during surgery. It may result when large volumes of blood are lost and replaced with stored citrated blood. To replenish the reduced clotting factors, give fresh frozen plasma intraoperatively after the diagnosis is made.

D. Bleeding from raw tissue surfaces may be uncontrollable with conventional sutures and clips, especially in the presence of inflammation or neoplasm. Direct pressure with a warm, saline-soaked pack applied for 10 to 20 minutes may provide the control needed unless a coagulation defect exists (see C). Microfibrillar collagen (Avitene) or Gelfoam may also be tried. Newer cryoprecipitate-thrombin glue preparations have recently been shown to be effective in venous and arterial bleeding. Bear in mind that these cannot be considered primary methods for hemostasis, but only serve as adjunctive measures.

E. Major arterial hemorrhage must be controlled either by direct ligation, taking care to avoid injury to adjacent structures (such as the ureter), or at a more proximal source. Internal iliac artery ligation (Fig. 1) reduces blood flow to the uterine artery to facilitate finding the mouth of the open vessel for ligation. It may even control the bleeding completely. Venous bleeding can also be slowed by this procedure if done bilaterally. The ovarian vessels are exposed, if necessary, cephalad to the infundibulopelvic ligament by careful retroperitoneal dissection, thereby identifying the ureter as it courses under the ovarian pedicle and over the bifurcation of the common iliac artery.

F. If bleeding is too massive or cannot be controlled by internal iliac artery ligation, try direct compression of the abdominal aorta just above the bifurcation. Another option is to place a large rubber dam in the pelvis and fill it tightly with a gauze head roll. Lead the end of the pack out through the vaginal fornix for purposes of removing it several days later. The pack can also be removed at a second laparotomy undertaken subsequently for completing the original surgery.

G. A bleeding pelvic vessel may be occluded by angiographically directed embolization. The angiographic catheter is threaded in retrograde fashion up the femoral artery into the hypogastric artery and then to the affected vessel identified by radiopaque contrast dye extravasation. Bleeding of 10 ml per hour or more may be visualized in this way. Gelfoam emboli or metal springs are then injected or vasopressin is infused through the catheter. If the hypogastric artery has already been ligated, this technique cannot be used because access is no longer possible.

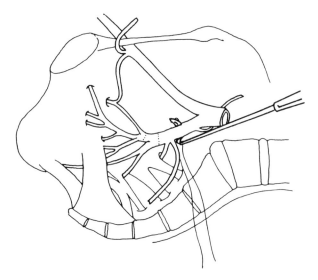

Figure 1 Ligation of the right internal iliac artery, sagittal view of the right hemipelvis, showing Deschamps aneurysm needle being advanced beneath vessel distal to superior gluteal branch. Other optional sites are also designated (broken lines).

References

Clarke-Pearson DL, Creasman WT. A clinical evaluation of absorbable polydioxanone ligating clips in abdominal and pelvic operations. Surg Gynecol Obstet 161:250, 1985.

PATIENT BEING PREPARED FOR MAJOR GYNECOLOGICAL SURGERY

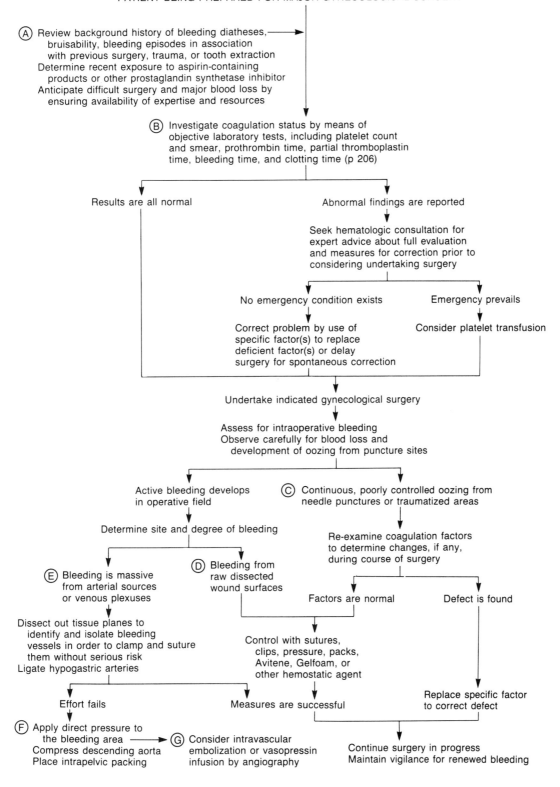

A Review background history of bleeding diatheses, bruisability, bleeding episodes in association with previous surgery, trauma, or tooth extraction
Determine recent exposure to aspirin-containing products or other prostaglandin synthetase inhibitor
Anticipate difficult surgery and major blood loss by ensuring availability of expertise and resources

B Investigate coagulation status by means of objective laboratory tests, including platelet count and smear, prothrombin time, partial thromboplastin time, bleeding time, and clotting time (p 206)

Results are all normal

Abnormal findings are reported

Seek hematologic consultation for expert advice about full evaluation and measures for correction prior to considering undertaking surgery

No emergency condition exists

Emergency prevails

Correct problem by use of specific factor(s) to replace deficient factor(s) or delay surgery for spontaneous correction

Consider platelet transfusion

Undertake indicated gynecological surgery

Assess for intraoperative bleeding
Observe carefully for blood loss and development of oozing from puncture sites

Active bleeding develops in operative field

C Continuous, poorly controlled oozing from needle punctures or traumatized areas

Determine site and degree of bleeding

Re-examine coagulation factors to determine changes, if any, during course of surgery

E Bleeding is massive from arterial sources or venous plexuses

D Bleeding from raw dissected wound surfaces

Factors are normal

Defect is found

Dissect out tissue planes to identify and isolate bleeding vessels in order to clamp and suture them without serious risk
Ligate hypogastric arteries

Control with sutures, clips, pressure, packs, Avitene, Gelfoam, or other hemostatic agent

Effort fails

Measures are successful

Replace specific factor to correct defect

F Apply direct pressure to the bleeding area
Compress descending aorta
Place intrapelvic packing

G Consider intravascular embolization or vasopressin infusion by angiography

Continue surgery in progress
Maintain vigilance for renewed bleeding

Kobrinsky NL, Israels ED, Gerrard JM, et al. Shortening of bleeding time by 1-deamino-8-D-arginine vasopressin in various bleeding disorders. Lancet 1:1145, 1984.
Marsden DE, Cavanagh D. Hemorrhagic shock in the gynecologic patients. Clin Obstet Gynecol 28:381, 1985.
Rousou JA, Engelman RM, Breyer RH. Fibrin glue: An effective hemostatic agent for nonsuturable intraoperative bleeding. Ann Thorac Surg 38:409, 1984.
Stone HH, Strom PR, Mullins RJ. Management of the major coagulopathy with onset during laparotomy. Ann Surg 197:532, 1983.

POSTOPERATIVE HEMOSTASIS

Henry Klapholz, M.D.

A. All postoperative gynecological patients must be observed carefully for bleeding, but certain patients deserve special attention because they are at increased risk of developing a bleeding problem. These include women with known or suspected coagulation problems (p 206), those whose surgery was difficult or complicated, those likely to heal poorly or perhaps dehisce (p 292), and those in whom intraoperative hemostasis (p 282) was suboptimal. They need intensive surveillance with frequent assessments of vital signs, examinations for signs of bleeding, and serial laboratory investigations for changing hematocrit and coagulation factors. Be alert to rising or persistently high pulse rate despite adequate hydration, because tachycardia generally precedes hypotension in the natural history of slowly evolving hypovolemic shock.

B. Bleeding from the abdominal incision is usually from a superficial vessel left unligated because it was not seen during closure, perhaps occluded by vasospasm. Such bleeding may also often be the first sign of a coagulopathy. Obtain prothrombin time, partial thromboplastin time, fibrinogen level, and platelet count. Examine the blood to ascertain if it clots. As soon as postoperative bleeding is detected, cross match blood for possible transfusion. A large bleeding vessel at the skin edge of the surgical wound can be controlled with a well placed Michel clip or suture.

C. Vaginal bleeding may actually represent intra-abdominal hemorrhage escaping through an open vaginal vault. It is important, therefore, to be alert to this possibility (see D). More often, however, large open vessels at the vaginal cuff edge are the source, sometimes even producing massive hemorrhage. Poorly placed mucosal sutures, especially at the lateral angles, can cause delayed bleeding.

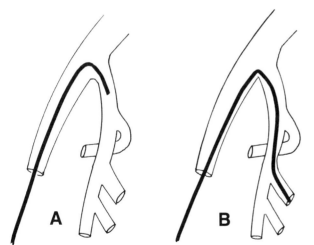

Figure 1 Angiographic embolization of uterine artery or other hypogastric arterial branches can be accomplished by retrograde advancement of a directable Ödman catheter by way of the femoral and external iliac arteries to the common iliac (A) and then in antegrade fashion into the internal iliac and uterine arteries (B) under direct fluoroscopic control.

Even well placed sutures of absorbable material (particularly catgut) may fail; this is not an uncommon complication in the presence of infection. Undertake a speculum examination with adequate exposure to identify the bleeding site. Counsel the patient that it may be necessary to undertake abdominal surgery to control the bleeding.

D. As with ruptured ectopic pregnancy (p 198), the presence of intraperitoneal blood can be signaled by shoulder pain from diaphragmatic irritation. Observe for distended loops of floating bowel, paralytic ileus, progressive abdominal pain, and deteriorating vital signs. Confirm intra-abdominal and large retroperitoneal blood by ultrasonography. Collections of 50 ml or more are easily seen in the cul-de-sac with sophisticated equipment. Perform paracentesis with an 18 gauge needle inserted into the flank or cul-de-sac to confirm the diagnosis. Peritoneal lavage with normal saline may be used to clarify the nature of the peritoneal contents.

E. Coagulopathy (p 208) may be corrected easily by the administration of specific factors found to be deficient. Use cryoprecipitate for fibrinogen deficiency and platelet concentrates for thrombocytopenia. Fresh frozen plasma carries less risk of hepatitis than cryoprecipitate and may also prove beneficial when required. Once the bleeding ceases, no further action need be taken, although close observation must be continued.

F. Small bleeding points in the subcutaneous tissue may sometimes be controlled with simple pressure, but a pressure dressing is of limited value in many cases. If bleeding continues, surgical exploration of the wound must be carried out with appropriate measures to find and control the bleeding vessels.

G. If the patient is stable and the estimated rate of blood loss is less than 250 ml per hour, consider angiography (Fig. 1) to identify the bleeding source and specifically occlude that vessel by transangiographic embolization (p 282). Angiography can detect extravasation of as little as 10 ml per hour. Rapid blood loss interdicts this technique, however, because it is neither sufficiently effective nor expeditious to satisfy emergency needs for hemostasis.

H. Heavy, rapid bleeding must be dealt with by direct surgical intervention. If any delay is anticipated, consider applying an antigravity garment (G-suit) until adequate fluid and blood can be replaced and the operating facilities and personnel fully mobilized. Proceed with ligation of the internal iliac arteries, resuturing of bleeding vessels, and pelvic compression with packing, as needed.

References

Cruikshank SH, Stoelk EM. Surgical control of pelvic hemorrhage: Bilateral hypogastric artery ligation and method of ovarian artery ligation. South Med J 78:539, 1985.

PATIENT SUSPECTED OF BLEEDING FOLLOWING GYNECOLOGICAL SURGERY

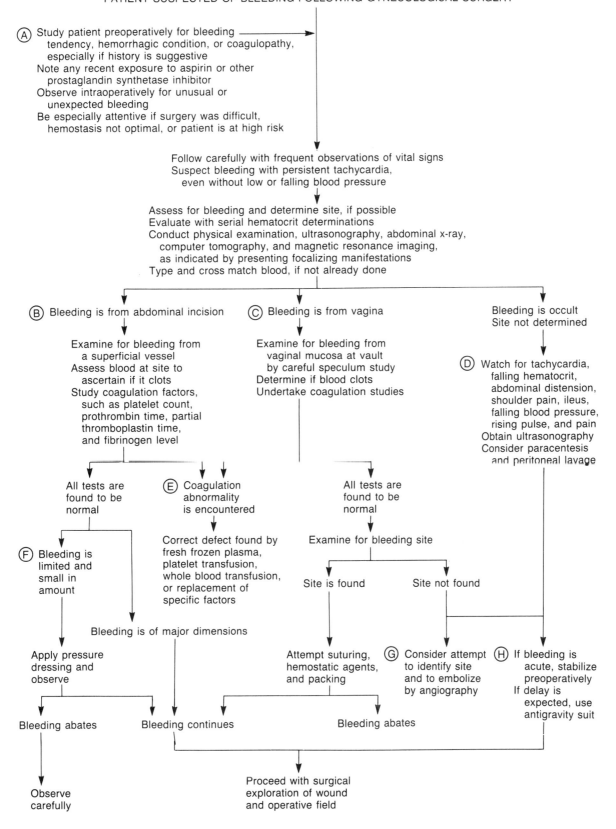

Ⓐ Study patient preoperatively for bleeding tendency, hemorrhagic condition, or coagulopathy, especially if history is suggestive
Note any recent exposure to aspirin or other prostaglandin synthetase inhibitor
Observe intraoperatively for unusual or unexpected bleeding
Be especially attentive if surgery was difficult, hemostasis not optimal, or patient is at high risk

Follow carefully with frequent observations of vital signs
Suspect bleeding with persistent tachycardia, even without low or falling blood pressure

Assess for bleeding and determine site, if possible
Evaluate with serial hematocrit determinations
Conduct physical examination, ultrasonography, abdominal x-ray, computer tomography, and magnetic resonance imaging, as indicated by presenting focalizing manifestations
Type and cross match blood, if not already done

Ⓑ Bleeding is from abdominal incision

Examine for bleeding from a superficial vessel
Assess blood at site to ascertain if it clots
Study coagulation factors, such as platelet count, prothrombin time, partial thromboplastin time, and fibrinogen level

Ⓒ Bleeding is from vagina

Examine for bleeding from vaginal mucosa at vault by careful speculum study
Determine if blood clots
Undertake coagulation studies

Bleeding is occult
Site not determined

Ⓓ Watch for tachycardia, falling hematocrit, abdominal distension, shoulder pain, ileus, falling blood pressure, rising pulse, and pain
Obtain ultrasonography
Consider paracentesis and peritoneal lavage

All tests are found to be normal

Ⓔ Coagulation abnormality is encountered

All tests are found to be normal
Examine for bleeding site

Ⓕ Bleeding is limited and small in amount

Correct defect found by fresh frozen plasma, platelet transfusion, whole blood transfusion, or replacement of specific factors

Site is found

Site not found

Apply pressure dressing and observe

Bleeding is of major dimensions

Attempt suturing, hemostatic agents, and packing

Ⓖ Consider attempt to identify site and to embolize by angiography

Ⓗ If bleeding is acute, stabilize preoperatively
If delay is expected, use antigravity suit

Bleeding abates

Bleeding continues

Bleeding abates

Observe carefully

Proceed with surgical exploration of wound and operative field

Davis SM. Antishock trousers: A collective review. J Emerg Med 4:145, 1986.
Dehaeck CM. Transcatheter embolization of pelvic vessels to stop intractable hemorrhage. Gynecol Oncol 24:9, 1986.
Ryan DW, Pridie AK, Johnston P, et al. The G-suit in controlling massive urological hemorrhage. Br J Urol 58:226, 1986.

POSTOPERATIVE FEVER

David B. Acker, M.D.

A. Be alert to intrinsic risk factors known to be associated with an increased incidence of postoperative infection, such as advanced age, obesity, cancer, debilitation due to chronic disease, immunosuppression, malnutrition, genetic predisposition to infection, poor hygiene, and low socioeconomic status. Operating in a contaminated field or failure to maintain strict aseptic surgical technique is also likely to contribute adversely. Infection is more likely to arise after certain procedures, including vaginal hysterectomy, vulvectomy, or abdominal hysterectomy following closely after cervical conization.

B. The use of disposable surgeon's gowns and operative drapes instead of those made of cloth may help decrease postoperative infection rates in both clean and contaminated cases. The nonwettable synthetic fabrics probably prevent skin bacteria from both patient and personnel gaining access to the surgical field. The common practice of preparing the operative area by shaving appears to yield more infections than clipping or cutting the hair, especially if it is done well before the procedure starts. Shaving causes innumerable microscopic skin cuts within which bacteria multiply. Therefore, if shaving the patient is felt to be necessary, it is much preferable to have it done just prior to the surgery, rather than the night before. Still better is elimination of the practice altogether, if acceptable, or substitution of some other method of hair removal. The gynecological surgeon must pay meticulous attention to the details of surgical technique. These include preventing contamination, using delicate anatomic dissection and gentle tissue handling, ensuring hemostasis, avoiding tissue damage, approximating tissue layers, closing dead space, and minimizing the amount of foreign material left in the wound.

C. The incidence of febrile morbidity following vaginal hysterectomy can be reduced if prophylactic antibiotics are given just prior to surgery. However, because no purpose is served if they are given for longer than a few hours after the procedure, a single dose given one hour prior to surgery generally suffices. The choice of antibiotic does not seem to matter in regard to efficacy, although those active against a broad spectrum of organisms are most frequently used.

D. The patient with postoperative fever should be evaluated in depth by undertaking a detailed study of the hospital record and system review, a thorough all-encompassing physical examination, and appropriate laboratory studies. Pay special attention to pre-existing risk factors, intercurrent infection, and known allergic reactions to any medications. Also note the type of surgery that was done and the anesthesia that was used. Consider any intraoperative complications that may have occurred, particularly aspiration, bowel, bladder, or ureteral injury, problems with hemostasis, need for transfusions, and drains. The physical examination helps disclose a pulmonary, abdominal, or pelvic source of the fever. Examine the wound site carefully and look for evidence of peripheral thrombophlebitis. Obtain complete blood count (CBC) with differential, blood cultures, and urinalysis at minimum, plus other laboratory studies and radiologic or ultrasonographic evaluations as indicated by the findings to elucidate the diagnosis and guide the treatment program.

E. One can expect the most expeditious response if a management regimen is designed to deal with a specific problem, provided the diagnosis has been correctly made. It is imperative, therefore, to identify the site of the infection and the offending organism, if possible. Once this is accomplished, treatment can be instituted with reasonable assurance of obtaining a good result quickly. It is clearly preferable under most circumstances to withhold antibiotics if the fever source has not been identified, except for serious cases of sepsis in which life or well-being is in jeopardy.

F. If the identified cause of infection has been properly and aggressively managed without success or if no cause can be found for continuing fever, consider the possibility of pelvic thrombophlebitis. Focalizing signs and symptoms are usually minimal and may even be nonexistent. Discontinuing all medications helps rule out a drug fever. Alternatively, a therapeutic trial of anticoagulation can be expected to produce dramatic defervescence in 24 to 48 hours if thrombophlebitis is the cause. If the fever persists, stop all treatment to allow the situation to become clarified and the focus of infection to become clinically manifest.

References

Altmeier WA. Sepsis in surgery. Arch Surg 117:107, 1982.

Cartwright PS, Pittaway DE, Jones HW, Entman SS. The use of prophylactic antibiotics in obstetrics and gynecology: A review. Obstet Gynecol Surv 39:537, 1984.

Hamod KA, Spence MR, King TM. Prophylactic antibiotics in vaginal hysterectomy: A review. Obstet Gynecol Surv 37:207, 1982.

Jones HW. Commentary on preoperative skin preparation: Shaving versus hair clipping. Obstet Gynecol Surv 40:316, 1985.

Sweet RL, Yonekura ML, Hill G, et al. Appropriate use of antibiotics in serious obstetric and gynecologic infections. Am J Obstet Gynecol 146:719, 1983.

PATIENT AT RISK FOR POSTOPERATIVE MORBIDITY

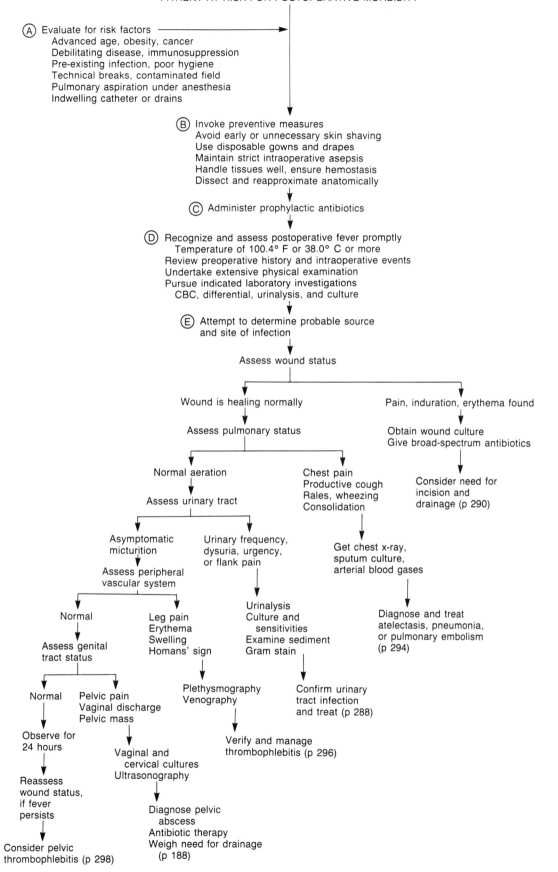

Ⓐ Evaluate for risk factors
   Advanced age, obesity, cancer
   Debilitating disease, immunosuppression
   Pre-existing infection, poor hygiene
   Technical breaks, contaminated field
   Pulmonary aspiration under anesthesia
   Indwelling catheter or drains

Ⓑ Invoke preventive measures
   Avoid early or unnecessary skin shaving
   Use disposable gowns and drapes
   Maintain strict intraoperative asepsis
   Handle tissues well, ensure hemostasis
   Dissect and reapproximate anatomically

Ⓒ Administer prophylactic antibiotics

Ⓓ Recognize and assess postoperative fever promptly
   Temperature of 100.4° F or 38.0° C or more
   Review preoperative history and intraoperative events
   Undertake extensive physical examination
   Pursue indicated laboratory investigations
   CBC, differential, urinalysis, and culture

Ⓔ Attempt to determine probable source
   and site of infection

Assess wound status

Wound is healing normally

Pain, induration, erythema found

Assess pulmonary status

Obtain wound culture
Give broad-spectrum antibiotics

Normal aeration

Chest pain
Productive cough
Rales, wheezing
Consolidation

Consider need for
incision and
drainage (p 290)

Assess urinary tract

Asymptomatic
micturition

Urinary frequency,
dysuria, urgency,
or flank pain

Get chest x-ray,
sputum culture,
arterial blood gases

Assess peripheral
vascular system

Normal

Leg pain
Erythema
Swelling
Homans' sign

Urinalysis
Culture and
   sensitivities
Examine sediment
Gram stain

Diagnose and treat
atelectasis, pneumonia,
or pulmonary embolism
(p 294)

Assess genital
tract status

Normal

Pelvic pain
Vaginal discharge
Pelvic mass

Plethysmography
Venography

Confirm urinary
tract infection
and treat (p 288)

Observe for
24 hours

Verify and manage
thrombophlebitis (p 296)

Reassess
wound status,
if fever
persists

Vaginal and
cervical cultures
Ultrasonography

Ⓕ Consider pelvic
thrombophlebitis (p 298)

Diagnose pelvic
   abscess
Antibiotic therapy
Weigh need for drainage
(p 188)

URINARY TRACT INFECTION

David B. Acker, M.D.

A. Symptoms may not be accurate indicators of the site of urinary tract infection. For example, frequency and dysuria can occur with upper tract infection while fever and flank pain are sometimes found with lower tract infection. Similarly, they do not always help distinguish urinary reflux or pyelonephritis.

B. Recurrent urinary tract infections appear in women with large bladder capacity or those who urinate infrequently. Bladder overdistension, which may disrupt the integrity of the urothelial lining, and urinary stasis enhance bacterial multiplication. Introital colonization with offending Gram-negative organisms (usually *E. coli*) also predisposes to recurrence. The fragile vaginal and urethral mucosa of the postmenopausal woman is particularly vulnerable.

C. Evaluation of the urinary sediment should be done with a freshly voided (preferably midstream clean catch) specimen. Plate for culture and centrifuge for sediment within 30 minutes; if this is not feasible, refrigerate the sediment. White blood cells and casts dissolve at high pH and crystal deposits obscure the examination. Tests of renal function and structure are done, if indicated. Excretory urography is seldom required because abnormalities disclosed by intravenous pyelography, such as pelvic mass, cystocele, stone, and urethral or bladder diverticulum, should be readily detectable by thorough physical examination, abdominal x-ray flat plate, ultrasonography, or voiding cystourethrogram.

D. Hospitalize sick patients with fever and gross pyuria. Obtain blood cultures, ultrasonographic study of the kidneys and renal function tests, as needed. Consult with a nephrologist or urologist if the response to parenteral antibiotics is not prompt. Confirm clinical recovery by urine cultures.

E. Select the initial therapy on the basis of the first Gram stained smear and modify it later according to the urine culture and sensitivity evaluation. Start with ampicillin (250 to 500 mg four times daily) or sulfisoxazole (Gantrisin, 1 to 2 g four times daily). Lower tract disease can be effectively treated with a single day of treatment. However, because one cannot be sure there is no upper tract involvement, give a full 10 to 14 day course. Relieve dysuria with phenazopyridine hydrochloride (Pyridium, 100 to 200 mg three times daily for two or more days), being sure to warn about orange discoloration of urine and sclerae. The patient should increase her fluid intake.

F. *Staphylococcus saprophyticus* frequently causes urinary tract infection in young sexually active women. It is a Novobiocin-resistant coagulase-negative organism with a longer generation time than Gram-negative rods. A colony count less than 100,000 per milliliter may, therefore, be significant with this organism. The infection is effectively treated with trimethoprim-sulfamethoxazole (Bactrim two tablets, containing 80 and 400 mg each, twice daily for 14 days).

G. Urethral syndrome consists of urinary tract infection symptoms without bacteriuria. It may represent urethral or paraurethral infection with fastidious bacteria (*Lactobacillus*, CO_2-dependent *Streptococcus*, or *Corynebacterium*). A trial of amoxicillin (500 mg every eight hours) or erythromycin (500 mg every six hours) for 10 to 14 days is warranted. Excretory urography is done for sterile pyuria to detect chronic pyelonephritis and papillary necrosis.

H. Good perineal hygiene may help decrease the number of urinary tract infections. Instruct patients in the proper technique for cleaning and drying the perineum by wiping from the vagina towards the anal area. Because sanitary pads may accumulate blood, fostering bacterial growth and contaminating the urethral meatus, they should be avoided. Topical antiseptic jelly may be used at the urethral meatus. Acidification of the urine (with cranberry juice, prune juice, or ascorbic acid 2 to 4 g per day) and a long course of antimicrobial agents (ampicillin, 500 mg twice daily or nitrofurantoin, 50 mg at bedtime supplemented with ascorbic acid for six months) are widely used. If sexual intercourse appears to trigger exacerbations, nitrofurantoin, 50 mg just before or after coitus, may be an effective prophylaxis.

References

Busch R, Huland H. Correlation of symptoms and results of direct bacterial localization in patients with urinary tract infections. J Urol 132:282, 1984.

Latham RH, Running K, Stamm WE. Urinary tract infections in young adult women caused by Staphylococcus saprophyticus. JAMA 250:3063, 1983.

Lieberman E, Macchia RJ. Excretory urography in women with urinary tract infection. J Urol 127:263, 1982.

Maskell R, Pead L, Sanderson RA. Fastidious bacteria and the urethral syndrome: A 2 year clinical and bacteriological study of 51 women. Lancet 2:1277, 1983.

Pfau A, Sacks T. The bacterial flora of the vaginal vestibule, urethra and vagina in premenopausal women with recurrent urinary tract infections. J Urol 126:630, 1981.

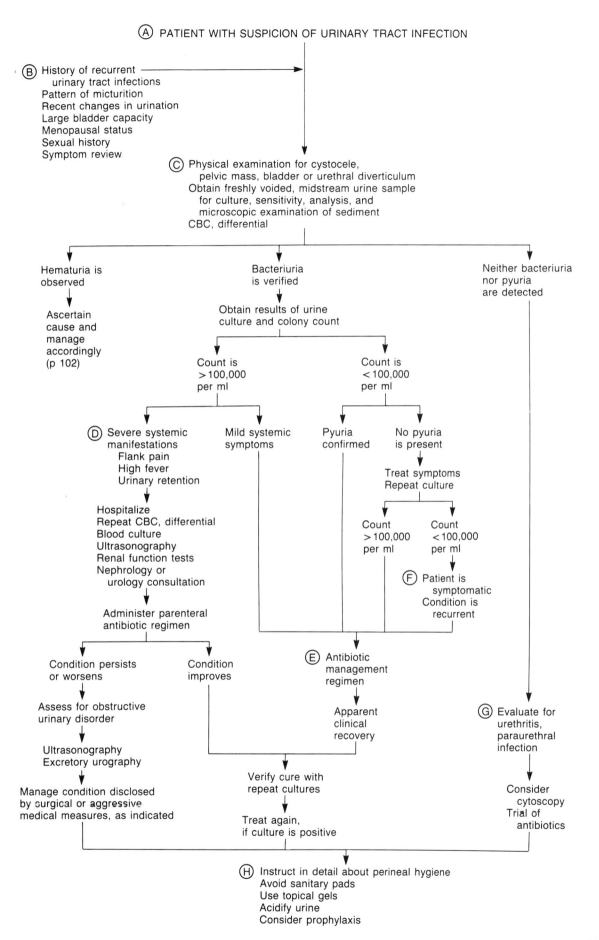

(A) PATIENT WITH SUSPICION OF URINARY TRACT INFECTION

(B) History of recurrent
    urinary tract infections
    Pattern of micturition
    Recent changes in urination
    Large bladder capacity
    Menopausal status
    Sexual history
    Symptom review

(C) Physical examination for cystocele,
    pelvic mass, bladder or urethral diverticulum
    Obtain freshly voided, midstream urine sample
    for culture, sensitivity, analysis, and
    microscopic examination of sediment
    CBC, differential

Hematuria is
observed

Ascertain
cause and
manage
accordingly
(p 102)

Bacteriuria
is verified

Obtain results of urine
culture and colony count

Count is
>100,000
per ml

Count is
<100,000
per ml

Neither bacteriuria
nor pyuria
are detected

(D) Severe systemic
    manifestations
      Flank pain
      High fever
      Urinary retention

Hospitalize
Repeat CBC, differential
Blood culture
Ultrasonography
Renal function tests
Nephrology or
  urology consultation

Administer parenteral
antibiotic regimen

Mild systemic
symptoms

Pyuria
confirmed

No pyuria
is present

Treat symptoms
Repeat culture

Count
>100,000
per ml

Count
<100,000
per ml

(F) Patient is
    symptomatic
    Condition is
    recurrent

Condition persists
or worsens

Condition
improves

Assess for obstructive
urinary disorder

Ultrasonography
Excretory urography

Manage condition disclosed
by surgical or aggressive
medical measures, as indicated

(E) Antibiotic
    management
    regimen

Apparent
clinical
recovery

Verify cure with
repeat cultures

Treat again,
if culture is positive

(G) Evaluate for
    urethritis,
    paraurethral
    infection

Consider
cytoscopy
Trial of
antibiotics

(H) Instruct in detail about perineal hygiene
    Avoid sanitary pads
    Use topical gels
    Acidify urine
    Consider prophylaxis

WOUND CARE

Lynn H. Galen, M.D.

A. Be alert to severe anemia, hypoalbuminemia, malnutrition, malabsorption, chronic debilitating illness, advanced age, cancer, diabetes mellitus, obesity, exposure to corticosteroids and immunosuppressive drugs, chronic cough, and obstructive pulmonary disease. Intraoperative contamination of the surgical field is critical to planning proper wound care. The greater the hazard of wound breakdown (p 292), the greater the need to take precautions.

B. The classification of wounds as clean, clean contaminated (involving bowel, urinary, or reproductive tract without gross spillage), and contaminated (exposure to frank pus or gross fecal material) is useful for weighing the potential for infection; the frequency increases from under 5 percent for clean wounds to over 25 percent for contaminated ones. Short-term administration of prophylactic antibiotics, limited to 24 hours or less beginning one to four hours preoperatively, is effective in reducing the incidence of wound infection and febrile morbidity in clean contaminated and contaminated cases.

C. Choose a suture material that causes minimal tissue reaction; select the size needed for maximum tensile strength to hold tissue layers in approximation without breaking, but minimize foreign body left in situ. Aim for the finest material necessary to ensure a stable and secure closure. One should be knowledgeable about the physical characteristics of various suture materials to be able to weigh relative tensile strength, absorbability (which reduces strength over time), elasticity, surface consistency (a factor that influences knot slippage), and wicking (enhancing bacterial transport). Avoid nonabsorbable suture in a contaminated wound, but bear in mind that infection accelerates enzymatic digestion. The slower disintegration and less tissue reaction of synthetic polyglycolic polymers favors their use over catgut; monofilament sutures resist bacterial colonization under these circumstances. Most wound dehiscences are associated with intact sutures pulling through the tissues. For strong wound closure, therefore, sutures should be placed well back from the cut tissue edge beyond the zone of expected lysis. Alternatively, use internal or full-thickness retention sutures (p 292).

D. The practice of applying wound dressings as a means of protecting the incision site from infection is of little documentable value after the first 24 hours following surgery because the dry wound is effectively sealed by this time. Sterile dressings help monitor drainage and perhaps provide some physical and emotional comfort to the patient. A draining wound requires continued dressing and attention to the reason for the drainage.

E. Skin sutures or staples are generally removed between three and six days postoperatively when healing has advanced sufficiently to hold the skin edges together. It is good practice to keep the wound edges approximated for an additional two to three weeks with adhesive strips to avoid minor separation, stretching, or widening of the scar.

F. Advise the patient to avoid vigorous physical activity that places undue stresses on the fascial repair, especially sudden strong movements or lifting heavy objects, for at least six weeks. This is recommended because the wound strength has reached only about one-third its final stage by then. Disruption of fascial integrity causes a ventral hernia to form.

G. Wound infection usually becomes manifest in five to seven days with the appearance of increased incisional pain, intermittent fever, leukocytosis, and differential shift to the left; the wound becomes erythematous and indurated, often with fluctuance and purulent drainage. When diagnosed, the infected wound must be opened and drained. Obtain smears and cultures and begin antibiotics based on preliminary identification of the type of offending organism. Debride the wound edges as needed; irrigate it with sterile saline solution; and pack it lightly with fine mesh or iodoform gauze. Subcutaneous fluid collection (hematoma or seroma) can be observed. If stable and not secondarily infected, it can be managed expectantly for absorption; if expanding or infected, drainage is indicated.

H. Wounds allowed to heal by secondary intent generally close spontaneously in two to six weeks if kept clean by periodic debridement and irrigations with hydrogen perioxide (half strength) or Betadine solution. The ventral hernia resulting from the residual fascial defect can be repaired at a later date, if necessary.

References

Eaglstein WH. Wound healing and aging. Dermatol Clin 4:481, 1986.

Polk HC Jr, Simpson CJ, Simmons BJ, Alexander JW. Guidelines for prevention of surgical wound infection. Arch Surg 118:1213, 1983.

Ruberg RL. Role of nutrition in wound healing. Surg Clin North Am 64:705, 1984.

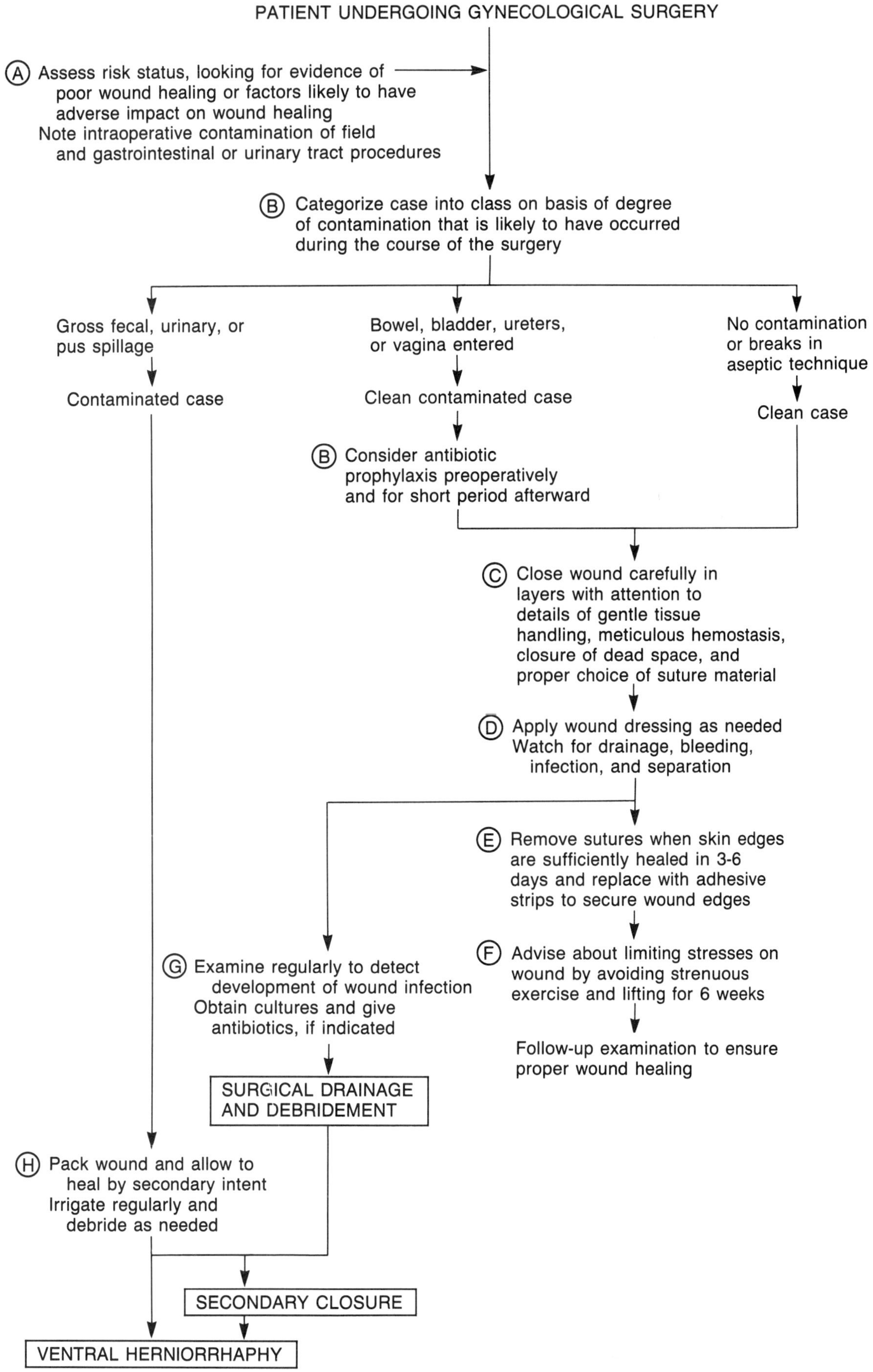

PATIENT UNDERGOING GYNECOLOGICAL SURGERY

(A) Assess risk status, looking for evidence of
poor wound healing or factors likely to have
adverse impact on wound healing
Note intraoperative contamination of field
and gastrointestinal or urinary tract procedures

(B) Categorize case into class on basis of degree
of contamination that is likely to have occurred
during the course of the surgery

Gross fecal, urinary, or
pus spillage

Bowel, bladder, ureters,
or vagina entered

No contamination
or breaks in
aseptic technique

Contaminated case

Clean contaminated case

Clean case

(B) Consider antibiotic
prophylaxis preoperatively
and for short period afterward

(C) Close wound carefully in
layers with attention to
details of gentle tissue
handling, meticulous hemostasis,
closure of dead space, and
proper choice of suture material

(D) Apply wound dressing as needed
Watch for drainage, bleeding,
infection, and separation

(E) Remove sutures when skin edges
are sufficiently healed in 3-6
days and replace with adhesive
strips to secure wound edges

(G) Examine regularly to detect
development of wound infection
Obtain cultures and give
antibiotics, if indicated

(F) Advise about limiting stresses on
wound by avoiding strenuous
exercise and lifting for 6 weeks

Follow-up examination to ensure
proper wound healing

SURGICAL DRAINAGE
AND DEBRIDEMENT

(H) Pack wound and allow to
heal by secondary intent
Irrigate regularly and
debride as needed

SECONDARY CLOSURE

VENTRAL HERNIORRHAPHY

DEHISCENCE

Lynn H. Galen, M.D.

A. Wound dehiscence, the disruption of the abdominal incision in all layers, is a serious postoperative complication demanding astute, expeditious diagnosis and aggressive management. The principal causes are stresses that exceed the tensile strength of the wound, including increased intra-abdominal pressure from gastric distension, coughing, or vomiting. In addition, the integrity of the fascial layers may have been compromised by a drain or stoma having been brought through the wound or by pressure necrosis from sutures applied too tightly. Systemic factors, including severe anemia, hypoproteinemia (albumen less than 0.3 mg per deciliter), obesity, vitamin deficiency, liver disease, uremia, advanced age, poor diabetic control, prior radiation to the region, wound infection, and hematoma, can interfere with healing and decrease the strength of the wound.

B. To avert wound dehiscence, consider measures for prevention. Correct malnutrition, hematologic deficiency, and active pulmonary disease, if possible. Anticipate intestinal distension and decompress by nasogastric tube. Avoid intraoperative wound contamination. Delay superficial wound closure for infected or contaminated cases. Use prophylactic antibiotics briefly when appropriate. Proper surgical technique is critical and should be closely supervised. When reapposing fascia, choose suture material for strength and durability. Place the sutures at least 1.5 cm from the fascial edge and 1.0 cm apart, with suture tension loose enough to prevent avascular necrosis and to accommodate expected postoperative abdominal distension. The Smead-Jones closure technique (subsurface retention sutures) gives added strength (Fig. 1). Careful hemostasis and gentle tissue handling are also important.

C. Only about one in ten wound dehiscences are due to technical factors, such as poorly placed, improperly tied, or broken sutures. Chromic catgut is more often associated with dehiscence than other suture material because of its rapid and unpredictable rate of dissolution. Be alert to risk factors and take special care to create a strong, secure closure.

D. Wound dehiscence may occur without forewarning, but it usually becomes clinically apparent between the fifth and eighth postoperative day. The patient frequently describes something giving way. Watch for a watery, serosanguineous drainage from the wound. Computer tomography or other lateral view imaging techniques may be useful for verifying the diagnosis. Whenever dehiscence is suspected, it is essential to proceed to explore the wound in an operating room to demonstrate whether the abdominal fascial layers are intact. A fascial disruption concealed beneath intact skin becomes manifest later as a ventral hernia.

E. Abdominal dehiscence is a surgical emergency. Place the patient in semi-Fowler's position to decrease abdominal pressure and cover the extruded bowel and omentum with moist sterile dressings. Insert a nasogastric tube to decompress the bowel. Start intravenous fluids and monitor vital signs. In the operating room under general anesthesia, the wound is thoroughly cleansed and debrided as needed. Aerobic and anaerobic cultures are taken and broad spectrum antibiotics begun. Minimize manipulation of the intestines, but try to replace them gently into the peritoneal cavity. Secondary closure after an evisceration is best accomplished using through and through sutures of a strong, nonabsorbable, nonreactive material. Apply the sutures 2 cm apart and incorporate at least 2 cm of fascia on either side of the incision. Skin may be closed if there is no evidence of infection. The ischemic effects of retention sutures may outweigh their prophylactic value. If used, they should be placed loosely and left in place for at least 10 to 14 days or until healing appears complete. Continue nasogastric decompression and intravenous hydration until bowel function returns to normal.

F. If surgery has to be delayed for purposes of stabilizing the patient, obtain cultures and try to reposit the bowel gently back into the abdomen, but do not persist. Apply packing softly and cover the wound with a large sterile plastic drape. If the patient's condition interdicts anesthesia or surgery, treat with an occlusive dressing and binder, recognizing that a ventral hernia is inevitable.

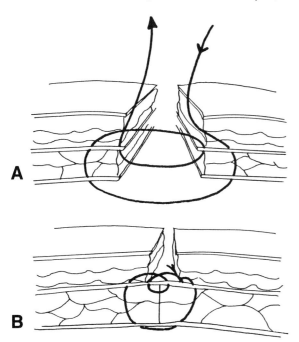

Figure 1 Smead-Jones suture technique for wound closure uses a double loop suture (A) to bring cut edges of fascial aponeurosis in apposition. When tied (B), it simultaneously supports the near fascial layer with a far re-enforcing layer of muscle and peritoneum.

References

Fagniez PL, Hay JM, Lacaine F, Thomsen C. Abdominal midline incision closure: A multicentric randomized prospective trial of 3,135 patients, comparing continuous vs interrupted polyglycolic acid sutures. Arch Surg 120:1351, 1985.

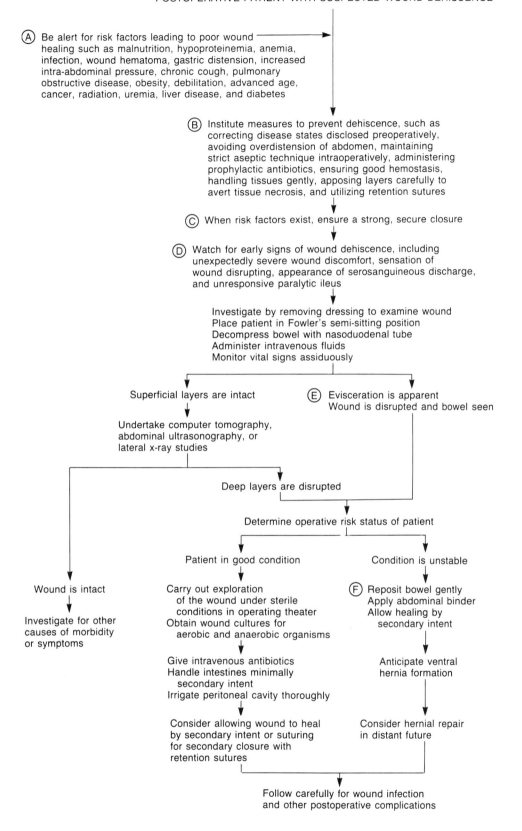

Ⓐ Be alert for risk factors leading to poor wound healing such as malnutrition, hypoproteinemia, anemia, infection, wound hematoma, gastric distension, increased intra-abdominal pressure, chronic cough, pulmonary obstructive disease, obesity, debilitation, advanced age, cancer, radiation, uremia, liver disease, and diabetes

Ⓑ Institute measures to prevent dehiscence, such as correcting disease states disclosed preoperatively, avoiding overdistension of abdomen, maintaining strict aseptic technique intraoperatively, administering prophylactic antibiotics, ensuring good hemostasis, handling tissues gently, apposing layers carefully to avert tissue necrosis, and utilizing retention sutures

Ⓒ When risk factors exist, ensure a strong, secure closure

Ⓓ Watch for early signs of wound dehiscence, including unexpectedly severe wound discomfort, sensation of wound disrupting, appearance of serosanguineous discharge, and unresponsive paralytic ileus

Investigate by removing dressing to examine wound
Place patient in Fowler's semi-sitting position
Decompress bowel with nasoduodenal tube
Administer intravenous fluids
Monitor vital signs assiduously

Superficial layers are intact

Ⓔ Evisceration is apparent
Wound is disrupted and bowel seen

Undertake computer tomography, abdominal ultrasonography, or lateral x-ray studies

Deep layers are disrupted

Determine operative risk status of patient

Wound is intact

Patient in good condition

Condition is unstable

Investigate for other causes of morbidity or symptoms

Carry out exploration of the wound under sterile conditions in operating theater
Obtain wound cultures for aerobic and anaerobic organisms

Ⓕ Reposit bowel gently
Apply abdominal binder
Allow healing by secondary intent

Give intravenous antibiotics
Handle intestines minimally secondary intent
Irrigate peritoneal cavity thoroughly

Anticipate ventral hernia formation

Consider allowing wound to heal by secondary intent or suturing for secondary closure with retention sutures

Consider hernial repair in distant future

Follow carefully for wound infection and other postoperative complications

Kenady DE. Management of abdominal wounds. Surg Clin North Am 64:803, 1984.
Morris DM. Preoperative management of patients with evisceration. Dis Colon Rectum 25:249, 1982.
Poole GV Jr. Mechanical factors in abdominal wound closure: The prevention of fascial dehiscence. Surgery 97:631, 1985.
Smith-Behn J, Arnold M, Might J. Use of computerized tomography of the abdominal wall in the diagnosis of partial postoperative wound dehiscence. Postgrad Med J 62:947, 1986.

PULMONARY EMBOLISM

Miguel Damien, M.D.

A. Nearly all pulmonary emboli arise from thrombi in deep leg veins, especially those above the knee, or in pelvic veins. The risk of embolism is greatest in the first few days after thrombus formation. It is essential, therefore, to prevent deep vein thrombosis or to treat it expeditiously.

B. The embolus obstructs the pulmonary arterial blood flow, yielding lung segments that are ventilated but not perfused. Reduction of alveolar surfactant begins after two to three hours and reaches its nadir by 12 to 15 hours. The absence of this surface-active lipoprotein, which is needed to maintain alveolar stability, leads to alveolar collapse. Clinical evidence of atelectasis may not be seen for 24 to 48 hours. Deep vein thrombosis is diagnosed in fewer than half the patients with pulmonary emboli. Embolism can even occur without symptoms. Sudden unexplained dyspnea is common and may be its only symptom. Pleuritic chest pain and hemoptysis reflect lung infarction, which seldom occurs. Secondary right ventricular cardiac ischemia produces severe substernal discomfort. Fever is seen with infection or infarction. Tachycardia is common. Pulmonary hypertension produces a split second heart sound. Atelectatic rales may be heard; friction rub or dullness is found only with infarction.

C. In most cases, arterial Po_2 is less than 80 mm Hg; hypocapnia is also often present with respiratory alkalosis. Leukocytosis and elevated erythrocyte sedimentation rate appear with infarction. The electrocardiogram is normal in most patients, but alterations reflecting acute pulmonary hypertension (right axis deviation and peaked P waves) and right ventricular strain (ST-T changes) may be seen. The chest x-ray film is seldom helpful, although a parenchymal infiltrate or pleural effusion may occur with infarction.

D. Definitive diagnosis of pulmonary embolism requires pulmonary perfusion and ventilation radiophotoscan and pulmonary angiography. A normal perfusion scan excludes the diagnosis, but a scan that reveals areas of decreased perfusion is not necessarily definitive. Perfusion defects can be caused by pneumonia, atelectasis, and pneumothorax. A ventilation scan is indicated for perfusion defects that are segmental in size or larger and for those appearing in radiolucent areas. A mismatch of good ventilation and poor perfusion is characteristic of vascular obstruction. If ventilation is also abnormal, pulmonary angiography is required. Small perfusion defects and those limited to areas of radiographic infiltration also require angiography.

E. Pulmonary angiography provides anatomic information about the pulmonary vasculature. There are two types of diagnostic findings: abrupt cutoff of a vessel at the point of complete embolic obstruction and, more commonly, a filling defect where the embolus occupies intraluminal space. Angiography in expert hands carries low mortality and morbidity, but it does entail more risk than the scan techniques. Nonetheless, angiography should be used for patients whose symptoms are severe, particularly since the hazards of therapy are substantial.

F. The treatment of pulmonary embolism must be rapid and aggressive, often in an intensive care setting. Give oxygen and maintain cardiac output and blood pressure with intravenous fluids. Inotropic drugs are sometimes required. Start anticoagulation immediately (p 20). Consider interruption of the inferior vena cava with a clip (placed surgically) or an umbrella filter (placed transvenously) as a preventive measure if there is a contraindication to heparin therapy in a critically ill patient in whom a recurrent embolus would likely prove fatal, if emboli recur despite anticoagulation, or if septic emboli continue to arise from below the level of the renal veins. Embolectomy may be essential in patients who have a massive embolus preventing adequate perfusion of the lungs and the left ventricle. Thrombolytic therapy with streptokinase or urokinase to hasten resolution of emboli is appropriate in patients with angiographically-proved life-threatening emboli; contraindications include internal bleeding, cerebrovascular accident within the past two months, or surgery within ten days.

References

Bartter T, Hollingsworth HM, Irwin RS, et al. Pulmonary embolism from a venous thrombus located below the knee. Arch Intern Med 147:373, 1987.

Bell WR. Pulmonary embolism: Progress and problems. Am J Med 72:181, 1982.

Cheely R, McCartney WH, Perry JR, et al. The role of noninvasive tests versus pulmonary angiography in the diagnosis of pulmonary embolism. Am J Med 70:17, 1981.

Kempczinski RF. Surgical prophylaxis of pulmonary embolism. Chest 89:384S, 1986.

Sasahara AA, Sharma GVRK, Barsamian EM, et al. Pulmonary thromboembolism: Diagnosis and treatment. JAMA 249:2945, 1983.

PATIENT WITH SUSPICION OF PULMONARY EMBOLISM

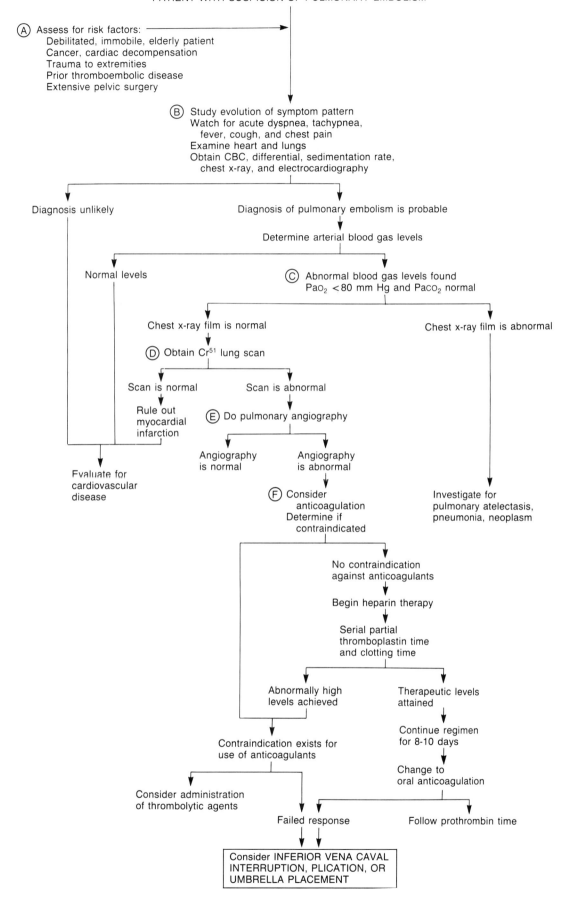

Ⓐ Assess for risk factors:
    Debilitated, immobile, elderly patient
    Cancer, cardiac decompensation
    Trauma to extremities
    Prior thromboembolic disease
    Extensive pelvic surgery

Ⓑ Study evolution of symptom pattern
    Watch for acute dyspnea, tachypnea,
      fever, cough, and chest pain
    Examine heart and lungs
    Obtain CBC, differential, sedimentation rate,
      chest x-ray, and electrocardiography

Diagnosis unlikely

Diagnosis of pulmonary embolism is probable

Determine arterial blood gas levels

Normal levels

Ⓒ Abnormal blood gas levels found
    $PaO_2 < 80$ mm Hg and $PaCO_2$ normal

Chest x-ray film is normal

Chest x-ray film is abnormal

Ⓓ Obtain Cr^{51} lung scan

Scan is normal

Scan is abnormal

Rule out myocardial infarction

Ⓔ Do pulmonary angiography

Angiography is normal

Angiography is abnormal

Evaluate for cardiovascular disease

Ⓕ Consider anticoagulation
Determine if contraindicated

Investigate for pulmonary atelectasis, pneumonia, neoplasm

No contraindication against anticoagulants

Begin heparin therapy

Serial partial thromboplastin time and clotting time

Abnormally high levels achieved

Therapeutic levels attained

Continue regimen for 8-10 days

Contraindication exists for use of anticoagulants

Change to oral anticoagulation

Consider administration of thrombolytic agents

Failed response

Follow prothrombin time

Consider INFERIOR VENA CAVAL INTERRUPTION, PLICATION, OR UMBRELLA PLACEMENT

295

PERIPHERAL THROMBOPHLEBITIS

David B. Acker, M.D.

A. Venous thromboembolic complications occur in one-third of postoperative patients suffering from gynecological malignancies and about one-quarter of those operated upon for benign disease. Risk factors include obesity, debilitation, prolonged surgical procedures, prolonged intravenous therapy, prior thrombophlebitis, malignancy (especially if advanced), and therapeutic irradiation within six weeks of surgery. Defective release of vascular plasminogen activator has been noted to be associated with both idiopathic and postoperative deep vein thrombosis and other thromboembolic complications. Preoperative activator level below 0.04 CTA (Committee on Thrombolytic Agents) units per milliliter serves to alert one to the problem.

B. Prophylactic measures aimed at reducing the incidence of thrombophlebitis include (1) pneumatic sleeves with automatic pump to provide 40 to 45 mm Hg pressure to the extremities for 12-second periods every minute beginning intraoperatively and continuing for five days, (2) low-dose heparin 5,000 units subcutaneously prior to surgery and 5,000 units subcutaneously twice daily for five days, (3) low molecular weight dextran to decrease platelet adhesiveness and increase peripheral perfusion, or (4) thromboembolic deterrent stockings (TED). Not all measures are applicable to all patients. Because the TED stockings are simple, effective, and have no known complications, however, they should be considered almost as a routine measure for all postoperative patients. Leg exercises and early ambulation are also important.

C. Although leg pain is common, deep venous thrombosis may be asymptomatic. Calf tenderness or pain at the back of the knee or calf upon dorsiflexion of the foot (Homans' sign) may be elicited even in the absence of subjective complaints. Impedance plethysmography, I^{125}-labeled fibrinogen uptake, Doppler ultrasonography, and venography are accurate methods of evaluation if thrombosis is suspected. Consider using noninvasive procedures regularly for high-risk patients.

D. Sheets of fibrin and soft thrombi form where the plastic catheter enters the vein. Infection here may lead to thrombosis and sepsis. Organisms found on the skin are commonly cultured from the catheter. Strict aseptic insertion technique is needed plus topical antibiotic at the entry site. Change the puncture site and the catheter every 48 hours. Initial therapeutic measures include elevating the extremity and applying warm compresses; they are almost always effective and generally suffice.

E. Postoperative thrombosis may sometimes occur in patients who have hyperactive platelets, increased coagulation proteins, a deficiency of plasma protease inhibitor antithrombin III, defective plasminogen, a deficiency of plasma protein C, or a circulating inhibitor of plasminogen activator. It is prudent to involve a consultant hematologist in the care of patients with a postoperative thrombotic complication.

F. Full heparinization should be administered promptly. Give a bolus of 12,000 units of heparin intravenously followed by 24,000 units every 24 hours by continuous infusion to prevent further clotting, thrombus propagation, or embolization. Partial thromboplastin time (PTT) should be maintained at two to three times the control value. Observe for signs of pulmonary embolism (p 294).

G. Any postoperative patient, even those successfully treated with prophylactic low-dose heparinization, may experience late deep venous thrombosis. The complication generally occurs within the first month, necessitating close outpatient follow-up.

H. After deep venous thrombosis, a postphlebitic syndrome may develop. Recanalization leaves the lumen patent, but destruction of the venous valves results in venous insufficiency. Stasis from this condition may cause induration and edema perhaps leading to ulceration. It is treated by elevating the leg and providing support in the form of elastic stockings.

References

Clarke-Pearson DL, Coleman RE, Synan IS, et al. Venous thromboembolism prophylaxis in gynecologic oncology: A prospective, controlled trial of low-dose heparin. Am J Obstet Gynecol 145:606, 1983.

Clarke-Pearson DL, Jelovsek FR, Creasman WT. Thromboembolism complicating surgery for cervical and uterine malignancy: Incidence, risk factors, and prophylaxis. Obstet Gynecol 61:87, 1983.

Gore M, Miller KE, Soong SJ, et al. Vascular plasminogen activator levels and thromboembolic disease in patients with gynecologic malignancies. Am J Obstet Gynecol 149:830, 1984.

Turner GM, Cole SE, Brooks JH. Efficacy of graduated compression stockings in prevention of deep vein thrombosis after major gynaecological surgery. Br J Obstet Gynaecol 91:588, 1984.

POSTOPERATIVE GYNECOLOGICAL PATIENT

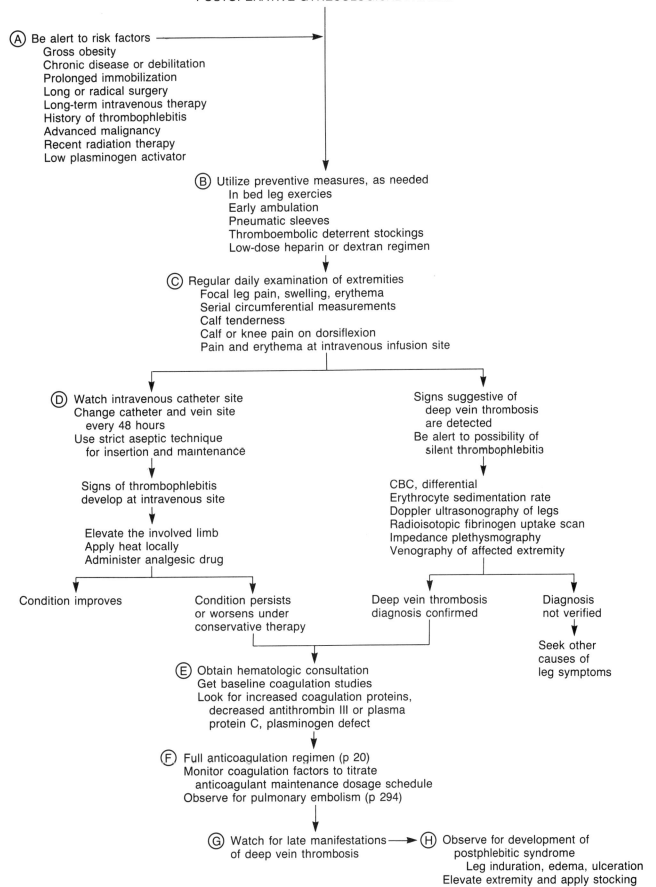

Ⓐ Be alert to risk factors
  Gross obesity
  Chronic disease or debilitation
  Prolonged immobilization
  Long or radical surgery
  Long-term intravenous therapy
  History of thrombophlebitis
  Advanced malignancy
  Recent radiation therapy
  Low plasminogen activator

Ⓑ Utilize preventive measures, as needed
    In bed leg exercises
    Early ambulation
    Pneumatic sleeves
    Thromboembolic deterrent stockings
    Low-dose heparin or dextran regimen

Ⓒ Regular daily examination of extremities
    Focal leg pain, swelling, erythema
    Serial circumferential measurements
    Calf tenderness
    Calf or knee pain on dorsiflexion
    Pain and erythema at intravenous infusion site

Ⓓ Watch intravenous catheter site
Change catheter and vein site
  every 48 hours
Use strict aseptic technique
  for insertion and maintenance

Signs of thrombophlebitis
develop at intravenous site

Elevate the involved limb
Apply heat locally
Administer analgesic drug

Signs suggestive of
deep vein thrombosis
are detected
Be alert to possibility of
silent thrombophlebitis

CBC, differential
Erythrocyte sedimentation rate
Doppler ultrasonography of legs
Radioisotopic fibrinogen uptake scan
Impedance plethysmography
Venography of affected extremity

Condition improves

Condition persists
or worsens under
conservative therapy

Deep vein thrombosis
diagnosis confirmed

Diagnosis
not verified

Seek other
causes of
leg symptoms

Ⓔ Obtain hematologic consultation
  Get baseline coagulation studies
  Look for increased coagulation proteins,
    decreased antithrombin III or plasma
    protein C, plasminogen defect

Ⓕ Full anticoagulation regimen (p 20)
  Monitor coagulation factors to titrate
    anticoagulant maintenance dosage schedule
  Observe for pulmonary embolism (p 294)

Ⓖ Watch for late manifestations ⟶ Ⓗ Observe for development of
  of deep vein thrombosis   postphlebitic syndrome
                                       Leg induration, edema, ulceration
                                     Elevate extremity and apply stocking

PELVIC THROMBOPHLEBITIS

Miguel Damien, M.D.

A. After major gynecological operations, patients are at increased risk for developing pelvic thrombophlebitis. This is especially the case for those who have undergone extensive surgery, such as radical cancer operations, or who were found to have active pelvic infection. Septic pelvic thrombophlebitis can arise as a consequence of septic abortion, severe salpingitis, and tubo-ovarian abscess and is particularly likely to occur postoperatively if surgery is undertaken during the acute phase of the infection. Venous thrombosis is promoted by circulatory stasis, intrinsic abnormality of or damage to the vessel walls, and alterations in the blood coagulation system. There is no reliable test for the hypercoagulability state except as applied to detecting the infrequent patient with antithrombin III, protein C or protein S deficiency, and cystinuria. The risk of venous thrombosis is best recognized by attention directed toward the clinical risk factors known to predispose a patient to the complication. These risk factors include obesity, advanced age, malignancy, radiation therapy, debilitation, and prolonged immobilization. Women with a history of prior venous thrombosis are at especially high risk of having recurrence following gynecological surgery.

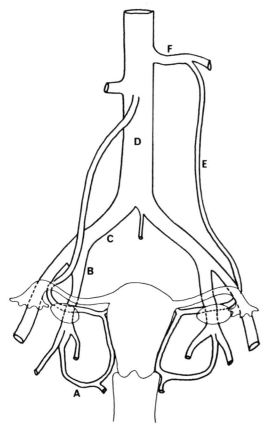

Figure 1 Venous drainage tributaries of the uterus and adnexa by the uterine veins (A) into the hypogastric (B) and common iliac veins (C) and inferior vena cava (D), as well as by way of the ovarian veins (E) into the renal vein (F) on the left and directly into the vena cava on the right.

B. The diagnosis of pelvic thrombophlebitis cannot ordinarily be made on the basis of specific signs and symptoms, although it is nearly always accompanied by fever that is unremitting and unresponsive to aggressive antibiotic therapy. Thus, its nonspecific manifestations mean that it is usually diagnosed following exclusion of other sources of fever. One should have a high index of suspicion for the condition among patients who fail to respond to a program of otherwise effective antimicrobial therapy. There are usually no physical findings to serve for identification markers. Patients with deep vein thrombosis of the lower extremities, diagnosed on the basis of its characteristic presenting clinical features (p 296), may have comitant pelvic thrombophlebitis. Nonetheless, anticoagulant treatment directed at the leg problem should be effective as prophylaxis against the development of pelvic thrombosis or as therapy for it. Watch for the rare phenomenon of paradoxical pulse in which the pulse rate does not rise in parallel with the temperature, as normally expected.

C. A common complication of radical surgery for gynecological malignancy is pelvic cellulitis. Brawny induration of the lateral pelvic tissues occurs, involving the parametria and broad ligaments. Thrombophlebitis develops in the large pelvic venous plexuses in and near these structures. Since this problem can be expected so often, it follows that prophylaxis with an anticoagulant regimen is called for whenever extensive dissection is done or is expected to be done. To this end, use of pneumatic boots and a course of low-dose heparin is warranted. There is a significant reduction in venous thrombosis and pulmonary embolism if heparin is given subcutaneously, in a dosage schedule of 5,000 units every 12 hours, commencing before surgery and continued until the patient is fully ambulatory. Early postoperative ambulation is the most important preventive measure. Intraoperative measures may be helpful in this regard. One should take special pains to use optimal surgical technique. This means all tissues must be handled minimally and with utmost gentleness; care must be taken to ensure optimal hemostasis; and one must skillfully avoid damaging the blood vessels within the pelvis.

D. Heparin therapy can be both diagnostic and therapeutic in patients with pelvic septic thrombophlebitis. A therapeutic program of continuous intravenous infusion of heparin is preferable to a regimen of intermittent heparin administration. Start with a bolus of 10,000 units and follow with a delivery system that provides 24,000 units per 24 hours. Monitor effectiveness by coagulation studies (partial thromboplastin time) and adjust accordingly, if needed (p 20). It may be necessary to consider supplementing antibiotic and anticoagulant therapy with inferior vena cava ligation (and even ovarian vein ligation) in patients with septic thrombophlebitis, especially if embolization has occurred to yield metastatic abscesses.

E. The vascular clots that form in the pelvic veins following gynecological surgery may gradually propagate along

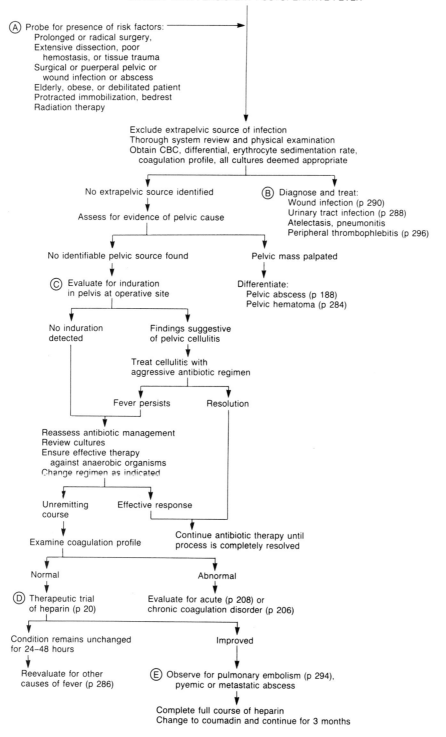

PATIENT WITH PERSISTENT POSTOPERATIVE FEVER

Ⓐ Probe for presence of risk factors:
   Prolonged or radical surgery,
   Extensive dissection, poor
      hemostasis, or tissue trauma
   Surgical or puerperal pelvic or
      wound infection or abscess
   Elderly, obese, or debilitated patient
   Protracted immobilization, bedrest
   Radiation therapy

Exclude extrapelvic source of infection
Thorough system review and physical examination
Obtain CBC, differential, erythrocyte sedimentation rate,
   coagulation profile, all cultures deemed appropriate

No extrapelvic source identified

Ⓑ Diagnose and treat:
   Wound infection (p 290)
   Urinary tract infection (p 288)
   Atelectasis, pneumonitis
   Peripheral thrombophlebitis (p 296)

Assess for evidence of pelvic cause

No identifiable pelvic source found

Pelvic mass palpated

Ⓒ Evaluate for induration
   in pelvis at operative site

Differentiate:
   Pelvic abscess (p 188)
   Pelvic hematoma (p 284)

No induration detected

Findings suggestive of pelvic cellulitis

Treat cellulitis with aggressive antibiotic regimen

Fever persists   Resolution

Reassess antibiotic management
Review cultures
Ensure effective therapy
   against anaerobic organisms
Change regimen as indicated

Unremitting course   Effective response

Examine coagulation profile

Continue antibiotic therapy until process is completely resolved

Normal   Abnormal

Ⓓ Therapeutic trial of heparin (p 20)

Evaluate for acute (p 208) or chronic coagulation disorder (p 206)

Condition remains unchanged for 24–48 hours

Improved

Reevaluate for other causes of fever (p 286)

Ⓔ Observe for pulmonary embolism (p 294), pyemic or metastatic abscess

Complete full course of heparin
Change to coumadin and continue for 3 months

the vessels if unchecked by anticoagulant treatment (Fig. 1). They may progress centrally to involve the common iliac, internal iliac, uterine, and ovarian veins. Even the inferior vena cava may be affected. The potentially fatal hazard of a large pulmonary embolus can result from such clot propagation. Septic embolization may also occur if infection is superimposed.

References

Angel JL, Knuppel RA. Computed tomography in diagnosis of puerperal ovarian vein thrombosis. Obstet Gynecol 63:61, 1984.

Cohen MB, Pernoll ML, Gevirtz CM, Kerstein MD. Septic pelvic thrombophlebitis: An update. Obstet Gynecol 62:83, 1983.

Duff P, Gibbs RS. Pelvic vein thrombophlebitis: Diagnostic dilemma and therapeutic challenge. Obstet Gynecol Surv 38:365, 1983.

Wille-Jorgensen P, Thorup J, Fischer A, et al. Heparin with and without graded compression stockings in the prevention of thromboembolic complications of major abdominal surgery: A randomized trial. Br J Surg 72:579, 1985.

VASOVAGAL REACTION

Vicki L. Heller, M.D.

A. Syncope is a common problem resulting from transient, acute diminution in blood flow to the brain and consequential loss of consciousness. The reduced tissue perfusion reflects a sudden fall in cardiac output. The intensity and duration of the symptoms parallel the degree of cerebral blood flow reduction. The typical common faint is a vasodepressor reaction. It can occur in response to any sudden pain or anxiety producing stimulus. It is a biphasic reaction characterized by a short initial period of anxiety and apprehension and then a vasodepressor phase. It usually begins with an intense sympathetic discharge often associated with palpitations and sensation of fear; although objective observations are seldom made during this time, cardiac output is generally increased along with increased heart rate, blood pressure, and peripheral resistance. This is followed by an overcompensatory parasympathetic hyperstimulation with loss of sympathetic tone, which results in increased vascular capacitance, hypotension, bradycardia, and decreased cardiac output. The patient experiences sweating, nausea, and decreased cerebral perfusion causing syncope. It is usually self limited and rapidly resolves with removal of the stimulus and application of conservative therapeutic measures. It must be differentiated from other cardiovascular events, such as cardiac arrhythmia or Stokes-Adams attack, and central nervous system events, such as seizure activity.

B. Anticipation of patients at risk is the first step in prevention. It is likely to happen to unprepared persons during procedures done under local anesthesia or without anesthesia. Under these circumstances, the precipitating event can be peritoneal irritation, visceral stretching, dilatation of the cervix, invoked uterine contraction, or acute pain. Careful description beforehand of the nature and degree of discomfort the patient should expect, the length of the procedure, and the availability of anesthesia or analgesia, if it proves to be needed, helps considerably to reduce the fear and the sense of helplessness and loss of control that predisposes to this reaction. Preoperative tranquilizer or analgesic medication serves to avert the response or reduce its intensity.

C. Most reactions are brief, lasting seconds to several minutes. Pallor, nausea, and sweating are the common early manifestations. Intestinal hypermotility occurs and sometimes vomiting as well. In addition, patients experience pupillary dilatation, hyperpnea, yawning, and bradycardia. Varying degrees of impaired sensorium are experienced, ranging from weakness, blurred vision, and confusion to overt syncope with loss of consciousness. Bradycardia to a rate of 50 to 60 per minute often persists for some time after the patient regains consciousness. Some complain of headache, confusion, weakness, and nervousness or anxiety. It is essential to give careful consideration to other causes of syncope, such as hemorrhage, perforation of a viscus, septic shock (p 202), cardiac arrhythmia, seizure, or stroke, especially if the patient fails to regain consciousness at once.

D. Immediate treatment consists of withdrawing the painful stimulus (in most instances, this consists of immediately withdrawing all surgical instruments and discontinuing the procedure) and placing the patient in the supine position. Autotransfusion can be promptly and easily accomplished by raising the patient's lower extremities and placing her in Trendelenburg position to improve cardiac return immediately. If there is insufficient improvement, compensation can be achieved by administering anticholinergic atropine, 0.4 mg parenterally. Subcutaneous or intramuscular injection is adequate in most circumstances, but in severe cases, it may be necessary to give the atropine intravenously to ensure absorption for a systemic effect. The patient should be observed several hours to ensure full recovery, increasing the time if necessary according to the severity of the episode and the rapidity of response. Lack of an effective and reasonably prompt response to therapy for vasovagal faint strongly suggests that some condition or factor other than cholinergic hyperstimulation is responsible for the loss of consciousness. Consider neurologic or cardiologic consultation for further assessment.

E. One may consider resuming the precipitating procedure only after the patient has completely recovered and a full discussion is carried out reviewing the condition and its causes. Undertake it again, if the patient agrees, with improved anesthesia, analgesia, and anxiolysis to avert recurrence. For example, paracervical block can be used in conjunction with intravenous sedation. To do less, risks a repetition of the episode.

References

Chi IC, Wilkens LR, Siemens AJ, Lippes J. Syncope and other vasovagal reactions at interval insertion of Lippes Loop D: Who is most vulnerable? Contraception 33:179, 1986.

Haddad RM, Sellers TD. Syncope as a symptom: A practical approach to etiologic diagnosis. Postgrad Med 79:48, 1986.

Henry JP. On the triggering mechanism of vasovagal syncope. Psychosom Med 46:91, 1984.

Zeigler MG, Echon C, Wilner KD, et al. Sympathetic withdrawal in the vasopressor (vasovagal) reaction. J Auton Nerv Syst 17:273, 1986.

PATIENT WITH ANTICIPATED OR DOCUMENTED SYNCOPAL ATTACK

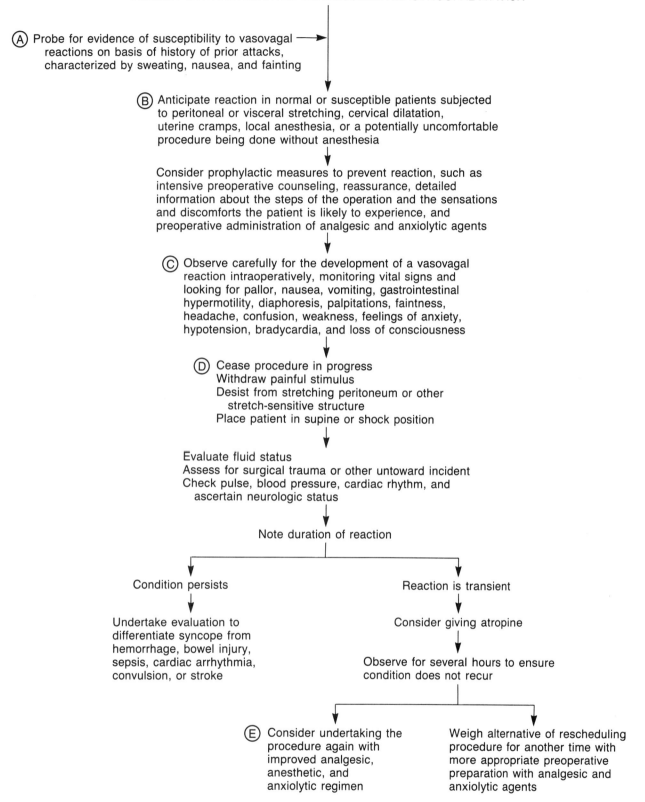

(A) Probe for evidence of susceptibility to vasovagal reactions on basis of history of prior attacks, characterized by sweating, nausea, and fainting

(B) Anticipate reaction in normal or susceptible patients subjected to peritoneal or visceral stretching, cervical dilatation, uterine cramps, local anesthesia, or a potentially uncomfortable procedure being done without anesthesia

Consider prophylactic measures to prevent reaction, such as intensive preoperative counseling, reassurance, detailed information about the steps of the operation and the sensations and discomforts the patient is likely to experience, and preoperative administration of analgesic and anxiolytic agents

(C) Observe carefully for the development of a vasovagal reaction intraoperatively, monitoring vital signs and looking for pallor, nausea, vomiting, gastrointestinal hypermotility, diaphoresis, palpitations, faintness, headache, confusion, weakness, feelings of anxiety, hypotension, bradycardia, and loss of consciousness

(D) Cease procedure in progress
Withdraw painful stimulus
Desist from stretching peritoneum or other
    stretch-sensitive structure
Place patient in supine or shock position

Evaluate fluid status
Assess for surgical trauma or other untoward incident
Check pulse, blood pressure, cardiac rhythm, and
    ascertain neurologic status

Note duration of reaction

Condition persists

Undertake evaluation to differentiate syncope from hemorrhage, bowel injury, sepsis, cardiac arrhythmia, convulsion, or stroke

Reaction is transient

Consider giving atropine

Observe for several hours to ensure condition does not recur

(E) Consider undertaking the procedure again with improved analgesic, anesthetic, and anxiolytic regimen

Weigh alternative of rescheduling procedure for another time with more appropriate preoperative preparation with analgesic and anxiolytic agents

COMPLICATIONS OF UTERINE CURETTAGE

Eric D. Lichter, M.D.

A. Cervical dilatation and endometrial curettage (p 230) are very common gynecological operations done for a variety of compelling reasons. They are done so often and are so relatively safe that clinicians sometimes lose sight of the fact that they can be associated with a number of potentially serious complications. These complications can usually be avoided or minimized by gentleness and control. Be alert to risk factors, such as cervical stenosis (p 160), endometrial cancer (p 178), pregnancy (p 196), and uterine anteflexion or retroflexion. In the course of preoperative counseling, one must inform the patient of the material risks involved (p 328), including perforation, infection, bleeding, bowel injury, and even the possibility that hysterectomy may be required.

B. To minimize the operative risk, preliminary examination must be done, preferably under suitable anesthesia, to determine the size, consistency, shape, and position of the uterus, especially noting antefexion or retroflexion, softening, irregularity, fixation, or evidence of atrophy or malformation. Sounding is generally done to measure the depth of the cavity and its axial direction. It should be remembered that sounding may not be innocuous. Although perforation can occur at any step in the procedure, the narrow bore of the sound makes it especially likely to cause this complication (Fig. 1). Therefore, the sound (and other instruments as well) must be introduced with negligible force, supporting and controlling the hand holding it so that it does not advance suddenly. If resistance is met because the canal is stenosed, special care must be taken to avoid perforation. Similarly, the cervix is dilated slowly with graduated rigid dilators. The tapered Pratt type is preferred. If not done slowly, dilatation may cause fracture or laceration of the cervical stroma, possibly leading to bleeding, infection, or cervical incompetence with midtrimester abortion in subsequent pregnancy. When it is necessary to achieve much dilatation, such as for inducing a late abortion (p 234), consider using natural or synthetic laminaria, which effect safer dilatation by hygroscopic expansion.

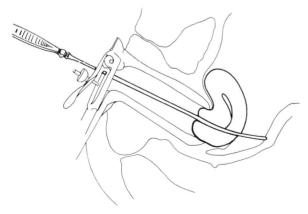

Figure 1 Perforation of the posterior wall of cervix or lower uterine segment of a sharply anteflexed uterus by the uterine sound.

C. The diagnosis of uterine perforation is generally apparent when the perforating instrument is felt to pass more deeply than the original sounding had shown the uterine fundus to be. Once this is recognized, do not reconfirm the perforation by additional probing since this practice may enlarge the channel or create new ones, magnifying the damage. Prompt diagnosis may avoid further injury to nearby structures. Most uterine perforations in the course of diagnostic dilatation and curettage cause no significant clinical problems. They can be managed simply by observing the patient for a few hours to ensure hemodynamic stability and absence of evidence of intraperitoneal manifestations. Midline perforations are usually uncomplicated, but those directed laterally are much more likely to cause vascular injury with retroperitoneal bleeding and hematoma formation. Perforation occurring with a suction curette, especially one of large caliber (12 mm diameter or more), exposes bowel to serious injury as well. Not only is it possible to injure bowel serosa directly, but a loop of bowel or omentum can be readily drawn down through the uterine tear to become herniated in the myometrial wall, uterine cavity, or even externally into the vagina. A large perforation of this kind generally requires operative intervention for direct inspection of the entire bowel and repair of visceral and uterine injuries. If bowel lumen has been entered, primary repair or segmental resection and repair should be done with lavage of the peritoneal cavity to reduce contamination and appropriate drainage. Colostomy is seldom needed. Lateral uterine or cervical perforation accompanied by evidence of retroperitoneal bleeding makes exploration necessary. Internal iliac artery ligation and ureteral dissection may have to be done. If bleeding cannot be controlled, hysterectomy is required.

D. Laparoscopy is reserved for cases in which postoperative observation suggests intraperitoneal bleeding from a perforation on the basis of physical findings or falling serial hematocrit levels. If active bleeding is seen and the site is accessible, usually at the fundus or posterior wall, consider attempting to accomplish hemostasis translaparoscopically. If the bleeding is not too brisk, apply electrocoagulation (either unipolar to selected points or bipolar to tissue held in the forceps), being very careful to avoid burning other tissues. Microfibrillar collagen (Avitene) can also be placed on the site in pledget form, applying pressure through a secondary puncture to ensure effectiveness.

References

Ben-Baruch G, Menczer J, Frenkel Y, Serr DM. Laparoscopy in the management of uterine perforation. J Reprod Med 27:72, 1982.

Grimes DA. Diagnostic dilatation and curettage: A reappraisal. Am J Obstet Gynecol 142:1, 1982.

PATIENT UNDERGOING UTERINE CURETTAGE

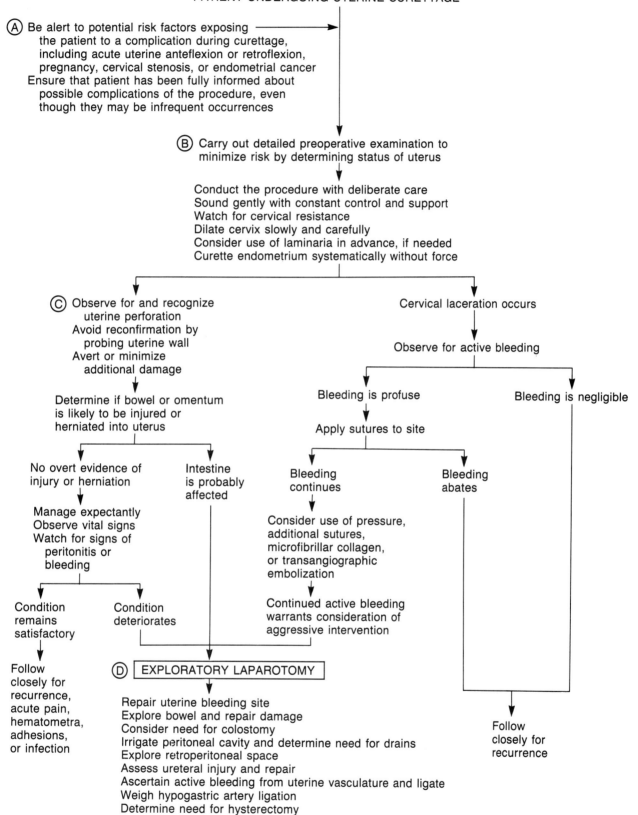

Ⓐ Be alert to potential risk factors exposing
    the patient to a complication during curettage,
    including acute uterine anteflexion or retroflexion,
    pregnancy, cervical stenosis, or endometrial cancer
Ensure that patient has been fully informed about
    possible complications of the procedure, even
    though they may be infrequent occurrences

Ⓑ Carry out detailed preoperative examination to
    minimize risk by determining status of uterus

Conduct the procedure with deliberate care
Sound gently with constant control and support
Watch for cervical resistance
Dilate cervix slowly and carefully
Consider use of laminaria in advance, if needed
Curette endometrium systematically without force

Ⓒ Observe for and recognize
    uterine perforation
Avoid reconfirmation by
    probing uterine wall
Avert or minimize
    additional damage

Cervical laceration occurs

Observe for active bleeding

Bleeding is profuse

Bleeding is negligible

Determine if bowel or omentum
is likely to be injured or
herniated into uterus

Apply sutures to site

No overt evidence of
injury or herniation

Intestine
is probably
affected

Bleeding
continues

Bleeding
abates

Manage expectantly
Observe vital signs
Watch for signs of
peritonitis or
bleeding

Consider use of pressure,
additional sutures,
microfibrillar collagen,
or transangiographic
embolization

Condition
remains
satisfactory

Condition
deteriorates

Continued active bleeding
warrants consideration of
aggressive intervention

Follow
closely for
recurrence,
acute pain,
hematometra,
adhesions,
or infection

Ⓓ EXPLORATORY LAPAROTOMY

Repair uterine bleeding site
Explore bowel and repair damage
Consider need for colostomy
Irrigate peritoneal cavity and determine need for drains
Explore retroperitoneal space
Assess ureteral injury and repair
Ascertain active bleeding from uterine vasculature and ligate
Weigh hypogastric artery ligation
Determine need for hysterectomy

Follow
closely for
recurrence

Lothrop JC. Perforation of the uterus at dilatation and curettage.
    In: Nichols DH, Anderson GW (Editors). Clinical Problems,
    Injuries and Complications of Gynecologic Surgery. Balti-
more: Williams & Wilkins, 1984.
Smith JJ, Schulman H. Current dilatation and curettage practice:
    A need for revision. Obstet Gynecol 65:516, 1985.

FAILED ABORTION

Vicki L. Heller, M.D.

A. Induced abortion procedures (p 234) are almost always successful in achieving their objective of terminating the pregnancy and evacuating the uterus completely. However, they may fail under certain circumstances. One should be alert to these circumstances so as to be able to take special precautions to avoid this problem. Although it is not always possible to prevent it, the effort to do so is important because it may have untoward emotional impact on the patient and liability implications for the operator. The most common reason for failed abortion is undertaking the procedure at a time when the conceptus is small and easily missed. Thus, menstrual extraction, which is generally done very shortly after the first missed period, carries the highest risk of failure. Be particularly aware that failure can also occur in cases with a poorly palpable uterus, stenotic cervix, or uterine malformation because these conditions make evacuation difficult.

B. Whenever the operation does not yield easily recognizable fetoplacental tissues, use histopathologic study to ensure that chorionic villi can be identified and that the amount of gestational tissue is compatible with the uterine size and pregnancy duration. Floating the tissue in saline is often sufficient for the purpose of grossly visualizing the gestational sac, fronds of villi, and fetal parts. Only by being certain about the nature and quantity of the tissues removed can one logically rule out ectopic pregnancy (p 198), although very rare coexistent intrauterine and extrauterine pregnancies do occur. Moreover, it may still be possible to leave behind a separate intact sac of a twin gestation, particularly if it is implanted in another uterine horn. For the late abortion with advanced fetal development, be sure to look for the major anatomic components of the fetus, particularly the calvarium, to ensure against leaving retained parts which may serve as a nidus for infection and cause subinvolution, cramps, and bleeding. Intraoperative ultrasonographic scanning may help in this assessment.

C. If technical difficulties are encountered, reconsider the clinical situation, weighing the risks of proceeding against the benefit of postponing the procedure to provide the opportunity to improve anesthesia and mobilize emergency care resources and additional supportive and consultative personnel, if they should prove to be needed. For example, if the abortion is being done with local anesthesia at a free-standing surgical unit, it could be rescheduled for general anesthesia in a hospital setting under laparoscopic surveillance. This relocation might be called for on an emergency basis in the event of a uterine perforation (p 302), especially if it is a lateral perforation or associated with signs of intraperitoneal bleeding. Laparoscopic guidance is essential for complet-

ing an abortion in which the uterus has been perforated. This applies whether or not bleeding is occurring. It may also prove useful in cases with cervical stenosis, uterine malposition, malformation, or leiomyomas.

D. Unrecognized failed abortion is gratifyingly rare if precautionary measures are taken to ensure the presence of a gestational sac and adequate placental tissue at the time of the procedure (see A). However, since it is not always possible to be certain, patients should be advised about the possibility and encouraged to seek follow-up care to detect it. Alert them to the significance of continuation of the manifestations of pregnancy, such as nausea, vomiting, breast engorgement and tenderness, fatigue, urinary frequency, and constipation. Such symptoms should subside progressively over several days following the procedure. If they do not do so within the first week, the patient should be told to return. The same applies for continued vaginal bleeding, which suggests incomplete evacuation, but deserves the same attention. Even in the absence of persistent symptoms, the histologic observation that no chorionic villi are seen in the evacuated tissue mandates contacting the patient so that she can be assessed for ectopic pregnancy and managed accordingly.

E. Many women who find themselves still pregnant after an attempted induced abortion attempt to change their mind about their original decision to terminate the pregnancy. If they wish to continue the pregnancy, that decision should be supported. They need counseling to help overcome concerns about the potentially adverse impact of the procedure on the fetus. Reassure them that while the risk of premature delivery and infection is increased after dilatation and evacuation (and there may be a teratogenic risk from fetal exposure to prostaglandin), successful pregnancies can occur. Good prenatal care is important.

References

Fakih MH, Barnea ER, Yarkoni S, DeCherney AH. The value of real time ultrasonography in first trimester termination. Contraception 33:533, 1986.

Fielding WL, Lee SY, Borten M, Friedman EA. Continued pregnancy after failed first-trimester abortion. Obstet Gynecol 63:421, 1984.

Kaunitz AM, Rovira EZ, Grimes DA, Schulz KF. Abortions that fail. Obstet Gynecol 66:533, 1985.

Munsick RA. Clinical test for placenta in 300 consecutive menstrual aspirations. Obstet Gynecol 60:738, 1982.

Tchabo JG. Use of contact hysteroscopy in evaluating postpartum bleeding and incomplete abortion. J Reprod Med 29:749, 1984.

PATIENT UNDERGOING INDUCED ABORTION

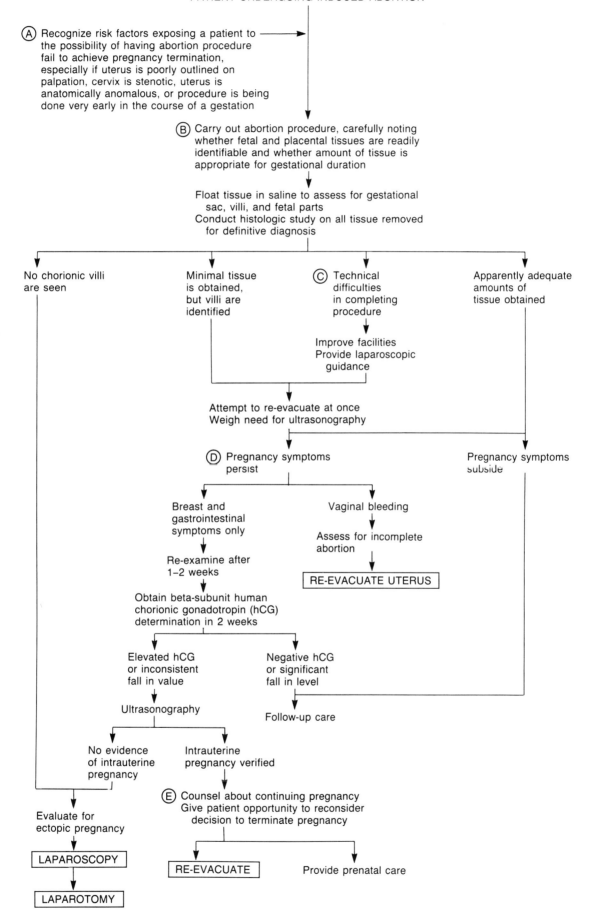

Ⓐ Recognize risk factors exposing a patient to
the possibility of having abortion procedure
fail to achieve pregnancy termination,
especially if uterus is poorly outlined on
palpation, cervix is stenotic, uterus is
anatomically anomalous, or procedure is being
done very early in the course of a gestation

Ⓑ Carry out abortion procedure, carefully noting
whether fetal and placental tissues are readily
identifiable and whether amount of tissue is
appropriate for gestational duration

Float tissue in saline to assess for gestational
sac, villi, and fetal parts
Conduct histologic study on all tissue removed
for definitive diagnosis

No chorionic villi
are seen

Minimal tissue
is obtained,
but villi are
identified

Ⓒ Technical
difficulties
in completing
procedure

Apparently adequate
amounts of
tissue obtained

Improve facilities
Provide laparoscopic
guidance

Attempt to re-evacuate at once
Weigh need for ultrasonography

Ⓓ Pregnancy symptoms
persist

Pregnancy symptoms
subside

Breast and
gastrointestinal
symptoms only

Vaginal bleeding

Assess for incomplete
abortion

RE-EVACUATE UTERUS

Re-examine after
1–2 weeks

Obtain beta-subunit human
chorionic gonadotropin (hCG)
determination in 2 weeks

Elevated hCG
or inconsistent
fall in value

Negative hCG
or significant
fall in level

Ultrasonography

Follow-up care

No evidence
of intrauterine
pregnancy

Intrauterine
pregnancy verified

Evaluate for
ectopic pregnancy

Ⓔ Counsel about continuing pregnancy
Give patient opportunity to reconsider
decision to terminate pregnancy

LAPAROSCOPY

RE-EVACUATE

Provide prenatal care

LAPAROTOMY

SEPTIC ABORTION

Vicki L. Heller, M.D.

A. Septic abortion is an important cause of major infection, shock, and mortality in the gynecological patient. Prior to the era of legalized abortion, pregnancy terminations were done under suboptimal circumstances with poor technique, frequently resulting in significant damage to the reproductive tract and bowel with severe, potentially fatal peritonitis. Fortunately, this sequence is rare today, although still possible. Most septic abortions develop spontaneously. It should be suspected in any woman whose pregnancy is complicated by high fever, uterine cramps, and pelvic tenderness. A purulent or foul cervical discharge is seen late in the course. Sometimes, the only symptoms are nonspecific, resembling flu or viral gastroenteritis, especially when associated with an intrauterine device (p 90). A high index of suspicion is essential in such cases to ensure early diagnosis and successful therapy.

B. Patients can be separated into treatment categories by the degree of illness. Evaluate immediately for imminent or overt septic shock (p 202), manifest by cardiovascular instability, clammy skin, tachycardia or bradycardia, hypotension, extreme leukocytosis or leukopenia, and acute abdominal signs. Begin appropriate fluid resuscitation using one or more large bore intravenous access routes. Provide an airway and adequate oxygenation. Monitor with central venous pressure or Swan-Ganz catheter. Watch for changing mental status and peritoneal signs.

C. Obtain complete blood count (CBC), leukocyte differential, erythrocyte sediment rate, and coagulation screen. Type and cross match blood. Culture the cervix, urine, and blood. Cervical cultures are not always helpful for identification of uterine organisms, although sexually transmitted infection (p 112) and group B streptococci can usually be reliably detected this way. Occasionally, acute gonorrhea (p 116) can be diagnosed and treated, sparing the patient from having to have an otherwise salvageable pregnancy evacuated. More useful bacteriologic information is obtained by blood and urine cultures. Special methods have been proposed for obtaining uterine cultures, but they have not been proved effective as yet. Amniocentesis is sometimes helpful when the diagnosis is unclear if bacteria are seen or the culture is positive, although treatment must precede identification of the offending organisms.

D. Choose high-dose broad-spectrum antibiotics effective against the type of organisms usually found in such cases, namely anaerobes, Gram-negative bacilli, and streptococci. Once adequate serum levels are achieved, proceed to uterine evacuation in the stable patient. One can begin giving antibiotics that are excreted by the kidneys, but be sure to check for azotemia (by assessing blood urea nitrogen and creatinine) before continuing. Nephrotoxic drugs must be avoided in cases with possible renal failure. In the unstable patient, consider immediate evacuation of the uterus, if feasible.

E. Prior to any kind of surgery, assure adequate coagulation function. Transfuse blood, if needed. Evaluate and treat disseminated intravascular coagulation (p 208). Abdominal upright or decubitus radiography may reveal peritoneal gas, indicating perforation of a viscus. This requires emergency laparotomy to assess for bowel, uterine, and vascular damage. It may be necessary to consider hysterectomy for a severely infected uterus. Bowel damage may require repair or colostomy. Drainage is important through separate stab wounds (p 36).

F. The gravid septic uterus is especially susceptible to damage during an instrumental evacuation procedure. In addition to perforation, ablation of the endometrial basal layers may occur, leading to Asherman's syndrome (p 168). In general, suction evacuation is safer than sharp curettage. Consider using prostaglandins instead for emptying the uterus in an advanced pregnancy. Diagnose perforation promptly (p 302) and manage aggressively. Laparoscopic guidance may prove helpful.

G. Monitor closely after evacuation for signs of coagulopathy, hypovolemia, septic pelvic thrombophlebitis, embolization, and renal failure. Weigh the need for dialysis, heparinization, and use of glucocorticoids.

References

Cavanagh D, Rao PS, Roberts WS. Septic shock in the gynecologic patient. Clin Obstet Gynecol 28:355, 1985.

Rackow EC, Weil MH. Recent trends in diagnosis and management of septic shock. Curr Surg 40:181, 1983.

Richards A, Lachman E, Pitsoe SB, Moodley J. The incidence of major abdominal surgery after septic abortion: An indicator of complications due to illegal abortions. S Afr Med J 68:799, 1985.

Rotimi VO, Abudu OO. Anaerobes and septic abortion. Afr J Med Sci 15:41, 1986.

PATIENT SUSPECTED OF EXPERIENCING SEPTIC ABORTION

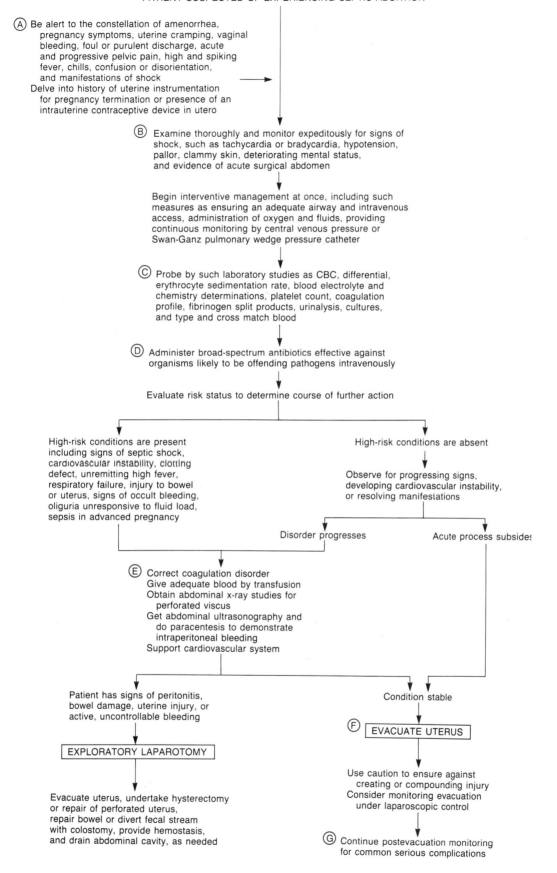

(A) Be alert to the constellation of amenorrhea,
pregnancy symptoms, uterine cramping, vaginal
bleeding, foul or purulent discharge, acute
and progressive pelvic pain, high and spiking
fever, chills, confusion or disorientation,
and manifestations of shock
Delve into history of uterine instrumentation
for pregnancy termination or presence of an
intrauterine contraceptive device in utero

(B) Examine thoroughly and monitor expeditously for signs of
shock, such as tachycardia or bradycardia, hypotension,
pallor, clammy skin, deteriorating mental status,
and evidence of acute surgical abdomen

Begin interventive management at once, including such
measures as ensuring an adequate airway and intravenous
access, administration of oxygen and fluids, providing
continuous monitoring by central venous pressure or
Swan-Ganz pulmonary wedge pressure catheter

(C) Probe by such laboratory studies as CBC, differential,
erythrocyte sedimentation rate, blood electrolyte and
chemistry determinations, platelet count, coagulation
profile, fibrinogen split products, urinalysis, cultures,
and type and cross match blood

(D) Administer broad-spectrum antibiotics effective against
organisms likely to be offending pathogens intravenously

Evaluate risk status to determine course of further action

High-risk conditions are present
including signs of septic shock,
cardiovascular instability, clotting
defect, unremitting high fever,
respiratory failure, injury to bowel
or uterus, signs of occult bleeding,
oliguria unresponsive to fluid load,
sepsis in advanced pregnancy

High-risk conditions are absent

Observe for progressing signs,
developing cardiovascular instability,
or resolving manifestations

Disorder progresses   Acute process subsides

(E) Correct coagulation disorder
Give adequate blood by transfusion
Obtain abdominal x-ray studies for
perforated viscus
Get abdominal ultrasonography and
do paracentesis to demonstrate
intraperitoneal bleeding
Support cardiovascular system

Patient has signs of peritonitis,
bowel damage, uterine injury, or
active, uncontrollable bleeding

Condition stable

(F) | EVACUATE UTERUS |

| EXPLORATORY LAPAROTOMY |

Use caution to ensure against
creating or compounding injury
Consider monitoring evacuation
under laparoscopic control

Evacuate uterus, undertake hysterectomy
or repair of perforated uterus,
repair bowel or divert fecal stream
with colostomy, provide hemostasis,
and drain abdominal cavity, as needed

(G) Continue postevacuation monitoring
for common serious complications

POSTSTERILIZATION PREGNANCY

Max Borten, M.D., J.D.

A. Unplanned gestation following sterilization should be considered a serious complication of this procedure. Its occurrence has social, medical, and legal implications affecting the patient and physician alike. Sterilization failure occurs in approximately two to ten women for every 1,000 operations. As more sterilizations are performed, one can reasonably expect an increase in the absolute number of pregnancies as a consequence of failure of the procedure to achieve its objective. Thus, one must always be alert for pregnancy in a patient who presents with signs and symptoms suggesting pregnancy, including amenorrhea or irregular uterine bleeding, nausea, vomiting, and breast tenderness, even though she has previously been sterilized.

B. Poststerilization pregnancy may result from technical (operator error) or true method (recanalization) failure. The technical type includes luteal phase pregnancy (that is, undertaking the procedure late in a menstrual cycle when fertilization may already have occurred yet is still undiagnosable) and misidentification of pelvic structures (operating on the round ligament rather than the tube). True method failure is related to reopening the lumen of the proximal tubal stump by fistula formation during the postoperative healing process or at a later date. Try to obtain details of the sterilization method from the patient; alternatively, if she is uninformed, consider contacting the physician who performed the procedure to obtain a full report of the operative procedure and findings.

C. Because pregnancy is one of the most serious late complications of a sterilization operation, determination of the beta-subunit human chorionic gonadotropin (hCG) must be carried out on any poststerilization patient who experiences symptoms compatible with pregnancy. This very sensitive test tends to be quite adequate as a first step in diagnosing or ruling out gestation. Less sensitive pregnancy tests are only of value in this regard if they are positive; a negative test cannot be relied upon to rule out pregnancy definitively. Early identification of this condition is essential to alert one to begin evaluation for ectopic gestation before it becomes a threat to health and life (see D). One must not wait for advanced symptoms, such as abdominal and pelvic pain, vaginal bleeding, or evidence of hemodynamic instability, before embarking on a thorough diagnostic work-up (p 198).

D. A positive beta-subunit hCG assay disclosed in a previously sterilized patient should be considered a matter of great concern for the physician. Whereas technical sterilization failure is usually associated with intrauterine gestation, a pregnancy in a sterilized patient must be assumed to be in an ectopic implantation site until proved otherwise. The common occurrence of ectopic pregnancy in these patients warrants maintaining a high index of suspicion at all times. Patients must be clearly informed of the seriousness of this condition and admonished that a thorough evaluation is mandatory rather than just desirable.

E. Poststerilization ectopic pregnancies tend to be located in the distal tubal stump. This is especially the case for recanalized tubes because spermatozoa reach the ovum by way of the fistula in the proximal stump, but the zygote is picked up and transported by the functional fimbria of the distal stump. The large capacity of the tubal ampulla enables the gestation to progress longer than it would if implanted elsewhere. This is accompanied by a higher level of circulating beta-subunit hCG, thus diminishing the significance of a large serum concentration of hCG as a marker of normal gestation. Ultrasonographic identification of the gestational sac within the uterine cavity is often the only reliable means for excluding eccyesis in these cases.

F. Laparoscopic evaluation of the previously sterilized pregnant patient must be undertaken promptly in the absence of ultrasonographic confirmation of an intrauterine gestation. If the woman desires to preserve the normally implanted pregnancy, avoid using a uterine mobilizer (the intrauterine probe, usually an insufflator) during diagnostic laparoscopy. In the event the patient does not wish to retain the unplanned pregnancy, uterine curettage should precede the endoscopic evaluation.

References

Ayers JWT, Johnson RS, Ansbacher R, et al. Sterilization failures with bipolar tubal cautery. Fertil Steril 42:526, 1984.

Borten M. Laparoscopic Complications: Prevention and Management. Toronto: B.C. Decker, 1986.

Loffer FD, Pent D. Pregnancy after laparoscopic sterilization. Obstet Gynecol 55:643, 1980.

McCausland A. Endosalpingiosis ("endosalpingoblastosis") following laparoscopic tubal coagulation as an etiologic factor in ectopic pregnancy. Am J Obstet Gynecol 143:12, 1982.

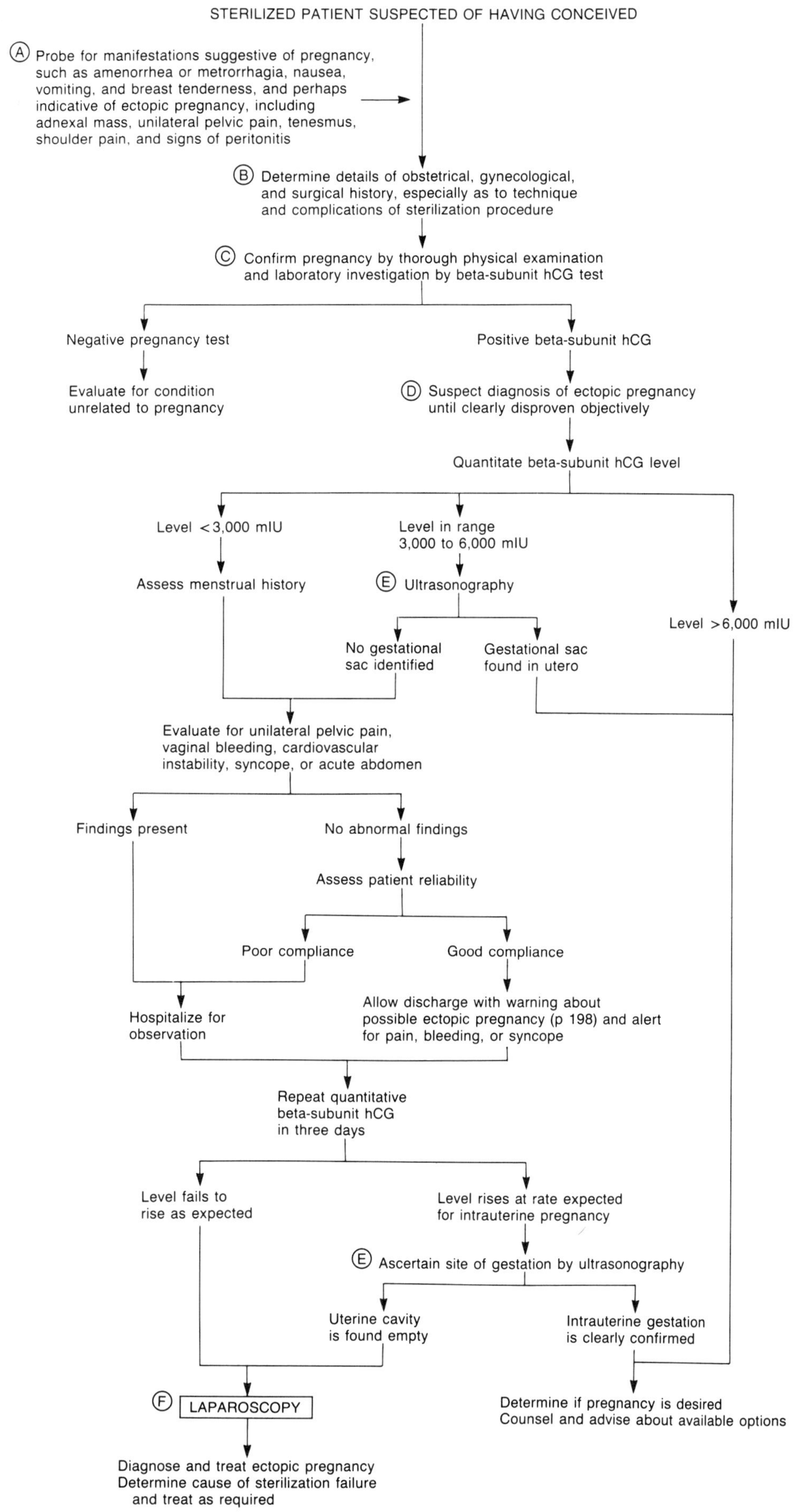

STERILIZED PATIENT SUSPECTED OF HAVING CONCEIVED

(A) Probe for manifestations suggestive of pregnancy,
such as amenorrhea or metrorrhagia, nausea,
vomiting, and breast tenderness, and perhaps
indicative of ectopic pregnancy, including
adnexal mass, unilateral pelvic pain, tenesmus,
shoulder pain, and signs of peritonitis

(B) Determine details of obstetrical, gynecological,
and surgical history, especially as to technique
and complications of sterilization procedure

(C) Confirm pregnancy by thorough physical examination
and laboratory investigation by beta-subunit hCG test

Negative pregnancy test

Positive beta-subunit hCG

Evaluate for condition
unrelated to pregnancy

(D) Suspect diagnosis of ectopic pregnancy
until clearly disproven objectively

Quantitate beta-subunit hCG level

Level <3,000 mIU

Level in range
3,000 to 6,000 mIU

Assess menstrual history

(E) Ultrasonography

Level >6,000 mIU

No gestational
sac identified

Gestational sac
found in utero

Evaluate for unilateral pelvic pain,
vaginal bleeding, cardiovascular
instability, syncope, or acute abdomen

Findings present

No abnormal findings

Assess patient reliability

Poor compliance

Good compliance

Hospitalize for
observation

Allow discharge with warning about
possible ectopic pregnancy (p 198) and alert
for pain, bleeding, or syncope

Repeat quantitative
beta-subunit hCG
in three days

Level fails to
rise as expected

Level rises at rate expected
for intrauterine pregnancy

(E) Ascertain site of gestation by ultrasonography

Uterine cavity
is found empty

Intrauterine gestation
is clearly confirmed

(F) LAPAROSCOPY

Determine if pregnancy is desired
Counsel and advise about available options

Diagnose and treat ectopic pregnancy
Determine cause of sterilization failure
and treat as required

LAPAROSCOPIC COMPLICATIONS

Max Borten, M.D., J.D.

A. Even in the best hands, laparoscopy can be associated with a range of unavoidable complications. These can be minimized by astute awareness of the conditions that make them likely to occur and by early recognition and expeditious management to reduce their impact. Similar to other surgical procedures, laparoscopy should not be undertaken when the anticipated risks are greater than the benefits that can be expected from its use. Risk factors have to be evaluated for each individual patient. When a laparoscopy is undertaken in a patient who exhibits a relative contraindication, it is essential to ensure that the surgeon is able to deal appropriately with any complication that may arise. Alternatively, appropriate consultants must be readily available.

B. Extraperitoneal insufflation of the distending gas can occur into the anterior abdominal wall (in subcutaneous, supra- or subfascial, or properitoneal sites) or retroperitoneally. A distinctive sign of subcutaneous accumulation of gas is the sensation of crepitation obtained by palpating the abdominal wall. Subfascial extraperitoneal insufflation creates a properitoneal emphysema that may preclude adequate visualization of the pelvic organs. Instilling and aspirating saline solution (syringe test) is the most accurate means for ensuring proper placement of the Verres needle (p 224). When encountered, emphysema can sometimes be decompressed, if needed to aid visualization; if not, it can be expected to subside spontaneously with time.

C. Peripheral blood pressure can fall acutely during gas insufflation to create or maintain the pneumoperitoneum. It may lead to a shock-like state and, if unchecked, can even result eventually in cardiac arrest. The severe hypotension is attributed to compression of the inferior vena cava by enhanced intra-abdominal pressure with consequent decrease in venous return. Prompt correction and recovery can be seen immediately following decompression of the abdomen by evacuation of the insufflated carbon dioxide. Maintaining the intraperitoneal pressure below 20 mm Hg is the single most important measure for preventing the appearance of acute hypotension.

D. Vascular injuries complicating a laparoscopic procedure range from minor bleeding from superficial vessels at or near the incision site to massive hemorrhage from lacerations of the major retroperitoneal vessels. If blood is aspirated by the syringe test (p 224), it identifies intravascular placement of the Verres needle. Under this circumstance, the penetrating instrument should be left in place to identify the site of injury by visualizing it through a second laparoscopic puncture or at laparotomy. If this complication is promptly recognized, gas insufflation will not be done, thus averting potentially catastrophic intravascular gas embolization. Identification of major vessel laceration mandates exploratory laparotomy to achieve hemostasis. Concealed retroperitoneal hemorrhage may result in hematoma formation and progress to hemorrhagic shock.

E. Damage to the gastrointestinal tract at the time of laparoscopy can result in serious postoperative complications. Injuries produced with the Verres needle, if small, not extended (by manipulation of the needle), and unaccompanied by bleeding, are usually associated with uneventful recovery. The seriousness of sharp laparoscopic trocar lacerations are in direct proportion to their size and depth. Tissue damage may range from a pinpoint hole produced by the trocar tip to one as large as the full diameter of the instrument. Burns may occur from arcing sparks or direct contact thermal damage during electrocoagulation procedures. Intraoperative recognition of these types of gastrointestinal tract trauma demands exploratory laparotomy and repair.

F. Recovery of urine through the Verres needle indicates that the needle has entered the urinary bladder. The incidence of injury to the urinary tract during laparoscopy is small. The most common underlying condition predisposing the patient to bladder injury by the Verres needle or the laparoscopic trocar is a distended bladder. Consequently, the most important precaution a laparoscopist can take to prevent this type of complication is to ensure that the urinary bladder is empty immediately prior to surgery. Most bladder injuries can be treated expectantly by continuous transurethral or suprapubic bladder gravity drainage for three to five days.

References

Borten M. Laparoscopic Complications: Prevention and Management. Toronto: B.C. Decker, 1986.

Peterson HB, DeStefano F, Rubin GL, et al. Deaths attributable to tubal sterilization in the United States. Am J Obstet Gynecol 146:131, 1981.

Peterson HB, Greenspan JR, Ory HW. Death following puncture of the aorta during laparoscopic sterilization. Obstet Gynecol 59:133, 1982.

Yacoub OF, Cardona I, Coveler LA, Dodson MG. Carbon dioxide embolism during laparoscopy. Anesthesiol 57:533, 1982.

PATIENT UNDERGOING LAPAROSCOPY

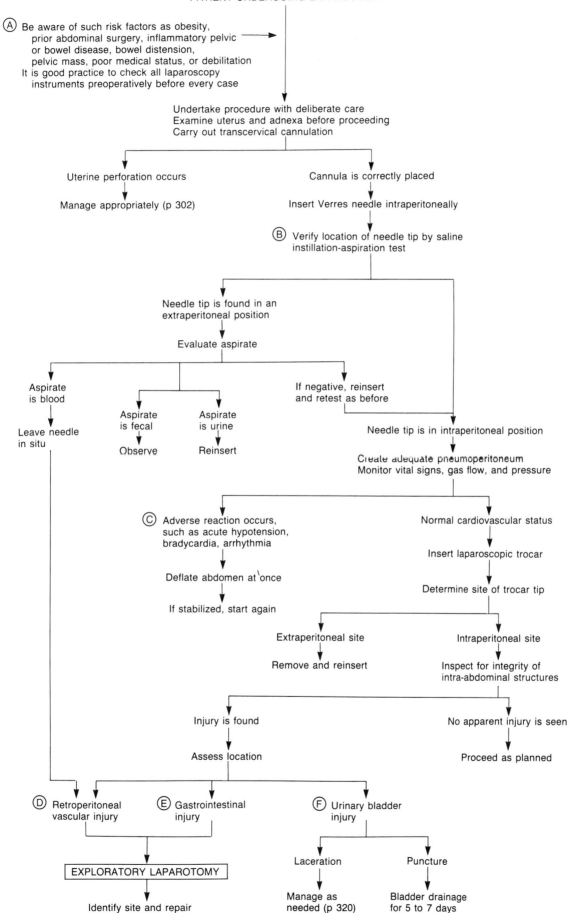

Ⓐ Be aware of such risk factors as obesity,
    prior abdominal surgery, inflammatory pelvic
    or bowel disease, bowel distension,
    pelvic mass, poor medical status, or debilitation
It is good practice to check all laparoscopy
    instruments preoperatively before every case

Undertake procedure with deliberate care
Examine uterus and adnexa before proceeding
Carry out transcervical cannulation

Uterine perforation occurs

Manage appropriately (p 302)

Cannula is correctly placed

Insert Verres needle intraperitoneally

Ⓑ Verify location of needle tip by saline
    instillation-aspiration test

Needle tip is found in an
extraperitoneal position

Evaluate aspirate

Aspirate
is blood

Leave needle
in situ

Aspirate
is fecal

Observe

Aspirate
is urine

Reinsert

If negative, reinsert
and retest as before

Needle tip is in intraperitoneal position

Create adequate pneumoperitoneum
Monitor vital signs, gas flow, and pressure

Ⓒ Adverse reaction occurs,
    such as acute hypotension,
    bradycardia, arrhythmia

Deflate abdomen at once

If stabilized, start again

Normal cardiovascular status

Insert laparoscopic trocar

Determine site of trocar tip

Extraperitoneal site

Remove and reinsert

Intraperitoneal site

Inspect for integrity of
intra-abdominal structures

Injury is found

Assess location

No apparent injury is seen

Proceed as planned

Ⓓ Retroperitoneal
    vascular injury

Ⓔ Gastrointestinal
    injury

Ⓕ Urinary bladder
    injury

EXPLORATORY LAPAROTOMY

Identify site and repair

Laceration

Manage as
needed (p 320)

Puncture

Bladder drainage
for 5 to 7 days

COMPLICATIONS OF VAGINAL HYSTERECTOMY

David S. Chapin, M.D.

A. A carefully planned, skillfully executed vaginal hysterectomy done in a patient with clear-cut indications and no complicating features is seldom associated with significant problems. Nonetheless, even under optimal circumstances in skilled hands, technical difficulties can be encountered and complications, such as hemorrhage, tissue damage, and infection, can arise. Risk factors that increase the hazard include prior pelvic surgery, infection, endometriosis, or an enlarged or distorted uterus. Most intraoperative problems in the course of vaginal hysterectomy can be prevented by ensuring good exposure and hemostasis to visualize the structures being dissected. Only by being knowledgeable about the anatomy and taking appropriate pains to identify planes and tissues can such complications be avoided.

B. The intraoperative complication of hemorrhage is usually all too apparent, although gynecological surgeons frequently underestimate blood loss. Assessment by sponge or pad count or, more objectively, by serial blood volume measurements or monitoring observations of cardiovascular status is useful for indicating when blood loss is excessive and replacement by transfusion is needed. This applies especially if bleeding is concealed. It can happen, for example, if a vascular pedicle retracts out of the operative field and its ligature slips. Carefully secure all such severed pedicles by anchoring with suture ligatures, doubly ligating them, and not applying any traction that might loosen or dislodge the ligature. If traction is really needed for exposure, place a holding suture for this purpose distal to the critical vascular ligatures. The sources of the active bleeding must be clearly identified. Placing clamps or sutures blindly to control hemorrhage risks serious damage to important structures in the vicinity, such as bladder, ureters, or bowel. Packing is unreliable and nearly always ineffective. Expeditious laparotomy is generally needed under these circumstances to find the open vessels and safely ligate them at the bleeding site or more proximally (p 282).

C. Bladder injury occurs most often because the initial step requiring dissection to separate the bladder from the anterior cervix is not done in the proper avascular plane. Cutting into the bladder musculature can be recognized by the bleeding it invokes. Entering the bladder lumen is readily recognized by its characteristic urothelial lining and the presence of urine. If in doubt, place dye in the bladder. Once verified, ensure that the ureteral ostia are unaffected and repair the defect (p 320). Uneventful healing can be expected; unrecognized injuries are more likely to cause future problems.

D. Ureteral injury is seldom recognized during vaginal hysterectomy, although the ureters are often at risk. Damage can usually be avoided by appreciating where the ureters are likely to be coursing and giving those sites wide berth. Clamps for resecting vessels and ligaments should be applied close to the cervix under vision. Blind clamping or suturing for bleeding is interdicted (see B). If there is concern that a ureter has been clamped, sutured, cut, or kinked, intraoperative excretory urography may be helpful. Urologic consultation may be prudent. Evaluation and management can be done at once if the problem is recognized or at a later time, if it is not (p 322).

E. Bowel damage may occur if loops of intestine are adherent in the cul-de-sac. Attempts to enter the peritoneum posteriorly may inadvertently injure the adjacent bowel at this location. Similarly, if bowel is adherent to the uterus or adnexa, and unrecognized, it can be damaged in the course of the vaginal hysterectomy. Although rare, this serious complication can be appreciated by smelling fecal odor or seeing liquid fecal material in the operative field. Management requires laparotomy for repair or colostomy (p 318).

F. Overzealous trimming of excess vaginal mucosa can result in an excessively narrowed vagina. It is better to err on the side of leaving too much than too little. The complication may require using lateral relaxing incisions and long-term vaginal packing or stints, analogous to vaginal reconstruction (p 272).

G. Infection, especially involving the vaginal cuff, occurs less often than in the past because prophylactic antibiotics are so effective. Nonetheless, it is still encountered. Watch for persistent fever and leukocytosis. Examine vaginally and rectally to verify induration and detect serous or pus collection above the vault. Drainage and antibiotic therapy are in order.

References

Cruikshank SH. Avoiding ureteral injury during total vaginal hysterectomy. South Med J 78:1447, 1985.

Dicker RC, Greenspan JR, Strauss LT, et al. Complications of abdominal and vaginal hysterectomy among women of reproductive age in the United States: The collaborative review of sterilization. Am J Obstet Gynecol 144:841, 1982.

Ledger WJ. Current problems in antibiotic treatment in obstetrics and gynecology. Rev Infect Dis 4:5679, 1985.

Scotto V, Sbiroli C. Cefoxitin single dose prophylaxis and/or T-tube suction drainage for vaginal and abdominal hysterectomy: Prospective randomized trial on 155 patients. Clin Exp Obstet Gynecol 12:75, 1985.

PATIENT UNDERGOING VAGINAL HYSTERECTOMY

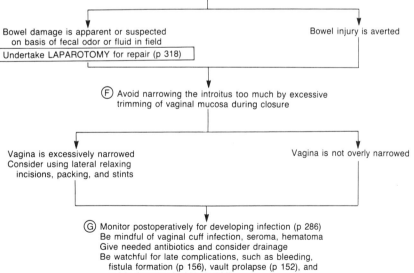

(A) Review indications for procedure, concurrent or past medical conditions, and any complicating factors ⟶ likely to cause technical difficulties

Undertake preoperative physical examination and laboratory studies to ensure optimal condition before proceeding
Administer prophylactic antibiotics in brief regimen

(B) Undertake operation under optimal circumstances
Dissect in correct planes, handle tissues gently, and pay special attention to careful hemostasis
Watch blood loss, assessing periodically by sponge and pad counts or serial blood volume determinations, monitoring cardiovascular status
Secure vascular pedicles and avoid traction on them

Hemorrhage is recognized
Transfuse to replace blood loss
Identify active bleeding sites
Dissect near bladder, ureters, and bowel to ensure against injury

Consider resorting to ABDOMINAL LAPAROTOMY if bleeding site out of reach or hemorrhage is uncontrollable

Intraoperative bleeding is not excessive

(C) Observe for bladder injury when separating bladder from cervix

Bladder injury is disclosed or suspected during course of surgery
Verify by instilling dye in bladder

Do cystoscopy to identify ureteral proximity and REPAIR as required (p 320)

No bladder injury is encountered

(D) Be alert for ureteral damage during division of uterine pedicles
Avoid blind clamping and suturing

Obtain intravenous pyelography if injury is suspected

Catheterize ureter and proceed to evaluate and REPAIR (p 322)

Ureteral damage does not occur

(E) Look for bowel trauma while dissecting cul-de-sac
Watch for adherent intestinal loops

Bowel damage is apparent or suspected on basis of fecal odor or fluid in field
Undertake LAPAROTOMY for repair (p 318)

Bowel injury is averted

(F) Avoid narrowing the introitus too much by excessive trimming of vaginal mucosa during closure

Vagina is excessively narrowed
Consider using lateral relaxing incisions, packing, and stints

Vagina is not overly narrowed

(G) Monitor postoperatively for developing infection (p 286)
Be mindful of vaginal cuff infection, seroma, hematoma
Give needed antibiotics and consider drainage
Be watchful for late complications, such as bleeding, fistula formation (p 156), vault prolapse (p 152), and pelvic thrombophlebitis (p 298)

313

COMPLICATIONS OF ABDOMINAL HYSTERECTOMY

David S. Chapin, M.D.

A. To a large extent, the complications associated with abdominal hysterectomy and the factors leading to them are similar to those seen with vaginal hysterectomy (p 312). To these can be added the complications associated with an abdominal incision (p 290). While good exposure tends to be easier to achieve by the abdominal route, the fact that more difficult procedures are done abdominally than vaginally is counterbalancing. Intraoperative complications can be expected in the presence of anatomic distortion from cancer, infection, endometriosis, or extensive adhesions. Careful, skillful, and meticulous dissection is required to prevent damage to gastrointestinal, urologic, or vascular structures, although such injury may be unavoidable even when the dissection is carried out optimally. It is important to recognize when the limits of one's technical capabilities are being exceeded; prudence and good judgement dictate seeking intraoperative consultation or, if unavailable, desisting in the patient's best interests before irreparable damage is done.

B. The ureter is most often injured adjacent to the cervix where it passes posteriorly to the uterine vessels or under the infundibulopelvic ligament where it crosses the bifurcation of the common iliac artery. Care must be taken when applying clamps or sutures to the uterine or ovarian vessels in these locations to avoid such damage. Isolate these vascular pedicles from surrounding tissue, when possible, to ensure against injury. If necessary, dissect the ureter along its retroperitoneal pathway from the pelvic brim to the tunnel under the uterine vessels, subjacent to the posterior leaf of the broad ligament. This dissection is critical if ureteral injury is recognized or suspected (p 322). Another option for tracing the ureter intraoperatively is to incise the dome of the bladder and pass a catheter in retrograde fashion up the ureter toward the renal pelvis. Consider urological consultation and evaluation as required.

C. Bowel serosa is not uncommonly injured in the course of surgery. If repaired when recognized, it should cause no subsequent problems. Penetrating injury to the lumen, while less frequent, is more serious because of the risk of severe infection from fecal spillage and fistula formation. Primary repair is generally done, although extensive injury and contamination may require temporary colostomy and drainage, delaying repair until a more optimal time (p 318). Unrecognized bowel injuries are the most perilous.

D. Damage to the bladder can occur when the bladder is advanced off the anterior wall of the cervix. Take care to ensure the dissection is being done in the correct plane. The loose areolar tissue should ordinarily give way without bleeding. Sharp dissection under vision is optimal, especially if the tissues are indurated or distorted. While blunt dissection is often acceptable, advancing the bladder with a gauze sponge may cause damage if the bladder is adherent. Confirm the injury by observing leakage of dye placed in the bladder. Primary repair and drainage (p 320) is usually satisfactory.

E. Postoperative infections are relatively infrequent following abdominal hysterectomy, although not unexpected in view of the clean contaminated nature of the procedure (p 290) due to exposure to the vaginal flora which cannot be eradicated. Evaluation should seek the source and causative organisms by thorough physical examination and appropriate cultures (p 286). Infection of the vaginal cuff is recognized by induration and tenderness on vaginal examination. Rectal palpation helps detect a seroma or abscess collection above the vaginal vault for drainage. Leaving a drain in place postoperatively prevents such collections from accumulating (p 36). If diagnosed, infection of the vaginal cuff is treated with antibiotics effective against Gram-negative and anaerobic organisms, the common pathogens encountered in these cases. Metronidazole and clindamycin, for example, are usually effective.

F. Vault granulations are quite commonly seen postoperatively, especially in cases in which the vaginal mucosa was left open. Patients may complain of some bleeding, discharge, or odor as a consequence. Granulations should be biopsied before treatment to diagnose prolapse of tubal fimbria (if the tubes were not surgically removed).

G. Vault prolapse is a particularly problematic late complication of hysterectomy (p 154). It requires deliberate evaluation and skilled care for correction.

References

Dicker RC, Greenspan JR, Strauss LT, et al. Complications of abdominal and vaginal hysterectomy among women of reproductive age in the United States: The collaborative review of sterilization. Am J Obstet Gynecol 144:841, 1982.

Dowling RA, Corriere JN Jr, Sandler CM. Iatrogenic ureteral injury. J Urol 135:912, 1986.

Krebs HB. Intestinal injury in gynecological surgery: A ten-year experience. Am J Obstet Gynecol 155:509, 1986.

Wetchler SJ, Hurt WG. A technique for surgical correction of fallopian tube prolapse. Obstet Gynecol 67:747, 1986.

PATIENT UNDERGOING ABDOMINAL HYSTERECTOMY

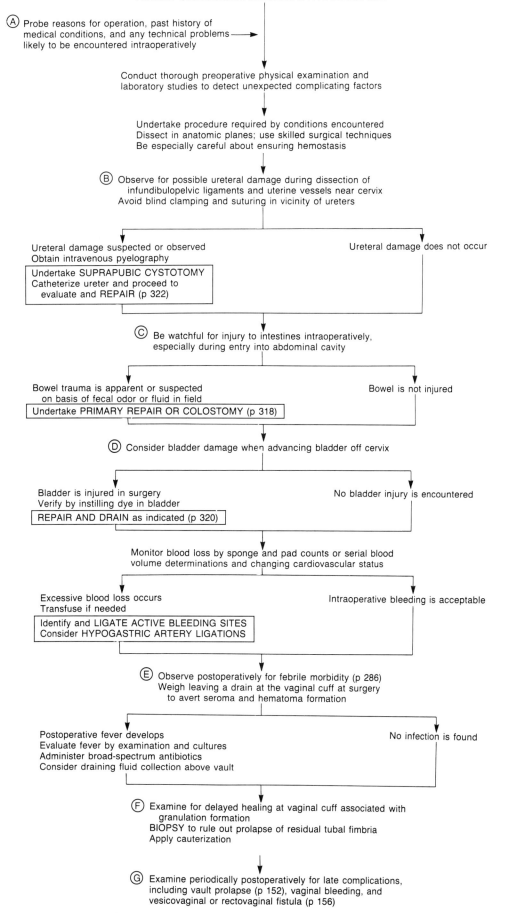

Ⓐ Probe reasons for operation, past history of
   medical conditions, and any technical problems ⟶
   likely to be encountered intraoperatively

Conduct thorough preoperative physical examination and
laboratory studies to detect unexpected complicating factors

Undertake procedure required by conditions encountered
Dissect in anatomic planes; use skilled surgical techniques
Be especially careful about ensuring hemostasis

Ⓑ Observe for possible ureteral damage during dissection of
   infundibulopelvic ligaments and uterine vessels near cervix
   Avoid blind clamping and suturing in vicinity of ureters

Ureteral damage suspected or observed   Ureteral damage does not occur
Obtain intravenous pyelography

Undertake SUPRAPUBIC CYSTOTOMY
Catheterize ureter and proceed to
  evaluate and REPAIR (p 322)

Ⓒ Be watchful for injury to intestines intraoperatively,
   especially during entry into abdominal cavity

Bowel trauma is apparent or suspected   Bowel is not injured
on basis of fecal odor or fluid in field
Undertake PRIMARY REPAIR OR COLOSTOMY (p 318)

Ⓓ Consider bladder damage when advancing bladder off cervix

Bladder is injured in surgery   No bladder injury is encountered
Verify by instilling dye in bladder
REPAIR AND DRAIN as indicated (p 320)

Monitor blood loss by sponge and pad counts or serial blood
volume determinations and changing cardiovascular status

Excessive blood loss occurs   Intraoperative bleeding is acceptable
Transfuse if needed
Identify and LIGATE ACTIVE BLEEDING SITES
Consider HYPOGASTRIC ARTERY LIGATIONS

Ⓔ Observe postoperatively for febrile morbidity (p 286)
   Weigh leaving a drain at the vaginal cuff at surgery
   to avert seroma and hematoma formation

Postoperative fever develops   No infection is found
Evaluate fever by examination and cultures
Administer broad-spectrum antibiotics
Consider draining fluid collection above vault

Ⓕ Examine for delayed healing at vaginal cuff associated with
   granulation formation
   BIOPSY to rule out prolapse of residual tubal fimbria
   Apply cauterization

Ⓖ Examine periodically postoperatively for late complications,
   including vault prolapse (p 152), vaginal bleeding, and
   vesicovaginal or rectovaginal fistula (p 156)

COMPLICATIONS OF VAGINAL PLASTY

David S. Chapin, M.D.

A. In addition to problems related to advanced age and medical conditions, bleeding, infection, and poor healing may occur in patients undergoing vaginal plasty (p 258). Atrophic changes take place in the vaginal mucosa of the postmenopausal woman who has not had the benefit of long-term estrogen replacement (p 28). This reduces vascularization so the operative field is relatively bloodless; but the effect is of dubious advantage because the resulting diminution of tissue perfusion also interferes with good healing. Patients whose operation was done for uterine prolapse (p 152) or urinary stress incontinence (p 98), therefore, may find their symptoms unrelieved by the surgery. Recurrence is an especially common complication among women who present with aggravating factors, such as chronic cough, obstructive pulmonary disease, and obesity. They deserve preoperative counseling and recommendations about stopping cigarette smoking, losing weight, and treating bronchitis and bronchial asthma. Eradicate infection in the operative site. Treat necrosis of dependent tissues, especially at the distal extremity of a protruding cystocele or prolapsed uterus, with reposition, pessary support, and topical antibiotics and estrogens. Plan the surgery to take known adverse factors into account. Urethropexy alone or in combination with vaginal plasty, for example, is more likely to be successful than vaginal plasty by itself in high risk cases with stress incontinence.

B. Both anterior colporrhaphy and urethropexy elevate the urethrovesical angle and restrict the urethral lumen somewhat. As a consequence, urinary retention is common (p 104). The indwelling gravity drainage urinary catheter is generally left in place for five to seven days and then withdrawn after a short period of bladder retraining (allowing it to fill and periodically emptying it to encourage bladder tone). Most patients void spontaneously within the first 24 hours, but in some the catheter has to be replaced to avoid repeated catheterizations. Return of bladder function is more easily assessed if a suprapubic drain is used instead of a urethral catheter. In nearly all cases, the symptom abates in time, but care must be taken to detect and treat secondary urinary tract infection.

C. Intraoperative hemostasis is important to ensure against hematoma formation. Take special measures during dissection of the fascia and mucosa to clamp and ligate all active bleeding points. Do not rely on vaginal packing to provide the necessary hemostasis, although such packing is useful for keeping dead space occluded, thereby preventing serous collections from forming. Examine the postoperative patient who develops vaginal bleeding, under anesthesia if necessary, to locate the source and ligate it. If the cut mucosal edge is bleeding, simple absorbable sutures may suffice, but if active bleeding is emanating from the depth of the repair or a hematoma has developed and is not yet under control, consider exploring the field.

D. Bladder injury is infrequently encountered in vaginal plasty procedures unless accompanied by vaginal hysterectomy (p 312). Careful anterior vaginal wall dissection generally avoids this complication, although it can still occur, especially in a patient who has had previous surgery, trauma, infection, or radiation in this area. Recognizing the damage is critical because if it is properly repaired, it almost always heals without difficulty. Verify with dye placed in the bladder. Check cystoscopically to ensure that the injury does not involve the ureteral ostia. Repair the defect in layers. Urethral injury can occur as well, especially during urethropexy if the sutures intended for the paraurethral tissues are placed too medially. Avascular bladder neck or urethral necrosis is a rare but serious complication resulting from having compressed the angle excessively. It is encountered after a sling operation in which the sling is drawn up too tightly.

E. Damage to the bowel is also uncommon, but it may occur during the posterior vaginal wall dissection or in the course of opening the sac of an enterocele. Rectal or anal injury during posterior colpoperineorrhaphy requires meticulous closure with re-enforcement to ensure against fistula formation. Small bowel damage in enterocele correction demands laparotomy for repair or for enterostomy (p 318).

F. Avoid trimming too much vaginal mucosa in a vaginal plasty operation or the resulting vagina will be too narrow for satisfactory coital function. Levator muscle fascia must also not be approximated too tightly and the perineal body not built up too high for the same reason. These technical problems can be corrrected, although they usually require another surgical procedure.

References

Hofmeister FJ. Pelvic anatomy of the ureter in relation to surgery performed through the vagina. Clin Obstet Gynecol 25:821, 1982.

Leach GE, Zimmern P, Staskin D, et al. Surgery for genital prolapse. Semin Urol 4:43, 1986.

Maulik TG. Kinked ureter with unilateral obstructive uropathy complicating Burch colposuspension. J Urol 130:135, 1983.

Nichols DH, Randall CL. Vaginal Surgery. 2nd ed. Baltimore: Williams & Wilkins, 1983.

Williams JK, Ingram JM, Welden SW. Management of noncongenital vaginal stenosis and distortion by the bicycle seat stool pressure technique. Am J Obstet Gynecol 150:166, 1984.

PATIENT UNDERGOING VAGINAL PLASTY PROCEDURE

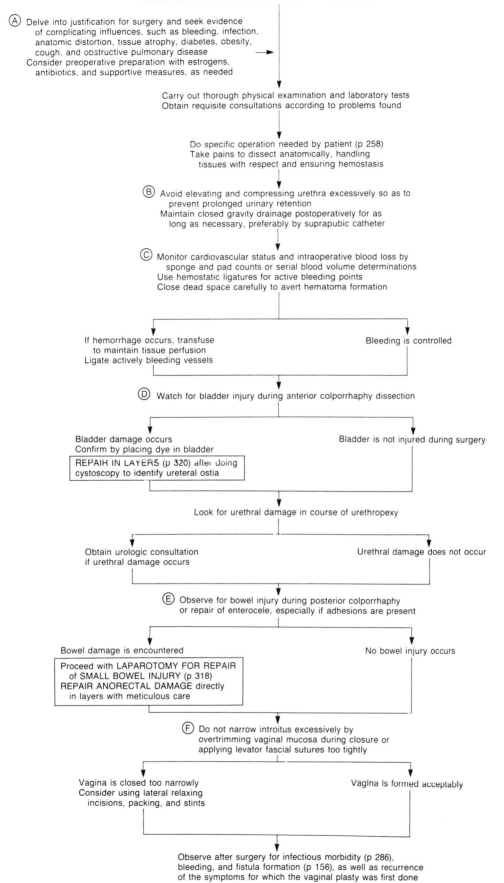

Ⓐ Delve into justification for surgery and seek evidence
   of complicating influences, such as bleeding, infection,
   anatomic distortion, tissue atrophy, diabetes, obesity,
   cough, and obstructive pulmonary disease
   Consider preoperative preparation with estrogens,
   antibiotics, and supportive measures, as needed

Carry out thorough physical examination and laboratory tests
Obtain requisite consultations according to problems found

Do specific operation needed by patient (p 258)
Take pains to dissect anatomically, handling
tissues with respect and ensuring hemostasis

Ⓑ Avoid elevating and compressing urethra excessively so as to
   prevent prolonged urinary retention
   Maintain closed gravity drainage postoperatively for as
   long as necessary, preferably by suprapubic catheter

Ⓒ Monitor cardiovascular status and intraoperative blood loss by
   sponge and pad counts or serial blood volume determinations
   Use hemostatic ligatures for active bleeding points
   Close dead space carefully to avert hematoma formation

If hemorrhage occurs, transfuse   Bleeding is controlled
to maintain tissue perfusion
Ligate actively bleeding vessels

Ⓓ Watch for bladder injury during anterior colporrhaphy dissection

Bladder damage occurs   Bladder is not injured during surgery
Confirm by placing dye in bladder
REPAIR IN LAYERS (p 320) after doing
cystoscopy to identify ureteral ostia

Look for urethral damage in course of urethropexy

Obtain urologic consultation   Urethral damage does not occur
if urethral damage occurs

Ⓔ Observe for bowel injury during posterior colporrhaphy
   or repair of enterocele, especially if adhesions are present

Bowel damage is encountered   No bowel injury occurs
Proceed with LAPAROTOMY FOR REPAIR
of SMALL BOWEL INJURY (p 318)
REPAIR ANORECTAL DAMAGE directly
in layers with meticulous care

Ⓕ Do not narrow introitus excessively by
   overtrimming vaginal mucosa during closure or
   applying levator fascial sutures too tightly

Vagina is closed too narrowly   Vagina is formed acceptably
Consider using lateral relaxing
incisions, packing, and stints

Observe after surgery for infectious morbidity (p 286),
bleeding, and fistula formation (p 156), as well as recurrence
of the symptoms for which the vaginal plasty was first done

317

BOWEL INJURY

Eric D. Lichter, M.D.

A. Both small and large intestines are exposed to potential damage in the course of gynecological surgery whether performed by the abdominal or vaginal route and whether done by open surgical exploration or translaparoscopically. If loops of bowel are adherent to the parietal peritoneum, they risk being traumatized at the time the abdominal cavity is entered through a laparotomy incision (p 242) as the overlying peritoneum is cut. Similarly, injury by Verres needle or trocar can occur during the initial blind steps of a laparoscopic procedure (p 224). If the problem is anticipated, it can be averted by utilizing the open Hasson type of approach, which addresses the matter of underlying bowel by dissecting into the peritoneal cavity under vision before inserting the laparoscope. In the course of vaginal hysterectomy (p 248), opening the cul-de-sac of Douglas exposes bowel fixed in this region to the same hazard. Bowel wall is also at risk from thermal burns when electrocauterization is being done, for tubal sterilization, for example (p 268), either by direct contact effect or as a result of arcing. Be alert to the increased potential for bowel damage in patients with predisposing intra-abdominal diseases, such as cancer, endometriosis, inflammatory bowel disease, chronic salpingitis, and prior radiation. If thus forewarned, undertake thorough bowel preparation in advance (p 18) to reduce bacterial flora and diminish the risk of serious infection if the bowel lumen is entered and its contents are spilled intraperitoneally.

B. The technique for closure of injured small intestine depends on the extent and depth of the damage. Nonpenetrating serosal lacerations are merely re-enforced with sutures. Full-thickness lacerations can be repaired in two layers as a primary procedure (Fig. 1). To avoid constricting the luminal diameter, close the laceration perpendicularly to the long axis of the bowel. The first row of sutures encompasses all tissue layers and the second tier re-enforces the first with nonabsorbable mattress sutures. If damage is extensive, it may be necessary to resect one or more loops of bowel with end-to-end

anastomosis. Drain the site through a separate stab wound (p 36).

C. Large intestinal damage is also repaired by perpendicular closure in two layers (see B) with drainage. If prior bowel preparation has been adequate, the repair procedure is secure, and there has not been any gross fecal contamination of the operative field, it is not necessary to divert the fecal stream by means of colostomy. A double-barrel colostomy is made under any other circumstances, exteriorizing a proximal loop of colon (usually transverse colon) through an upper quadrant incision distant from the primary operative incision.

D. Management of a thermal bowel burn depends on its extent. Injuries limited to 1 cm or less can be followed expectantly without any effort to repair it surgically unless symptoms arise. Usually, the course is entirely benign, requiring no further care. However, between three and seven days after the injury, the patient may begin to develop manifestations suggesting the need for intervention, including fever, nausea, anorexia, and lower abdominal pain. Physical examination discloses signs of paralytic ileus or beginning peritonitis. Surgical exploration and repair is called for under these circumstances. Thermal injuries more extensive than 1 cm mandate exploration without delay once they are recognized. Burns are treated by wide segmental resection of the affected loop of intestine. It is important to resect well beyond the portion identified visually as having been burned because it is recognized that the damage extends both proximally and distally much further than can be seen grossly. Colostomy is usually needed for a colon burn (see C). Small intestinal damage can usually be repaired directly.

E. Postoperative care should include measures to keep the bowel decompressed while it is healing and until intestinal peristaltic function is re-established, using nasogastric or preferably nasoduodenal catheter suction. Give broad-spectrum antibiotics intraoperatively if there has been peritoneal contamination by spillage of bowel content, and continue the antibiotics postoperatively as well. In such a contaminated case, it is preferable to leave the skin and subcutaneous layers open, or alternatively to drain the subcutaneous space, to prevent wound infection (p 290).

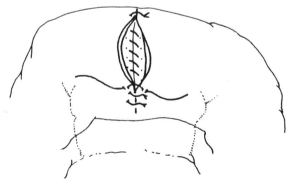

Figure 1 Suturing a bowel laceration in two layers, orienting the repair transversely to prevent constriction of the luminal diameter. The first layer is closed with continuous absorbable suture, while the remaining outer muscularis and serosa are carefully apposed with interrupted horizontal mattress (Lembert) sutures of nonabsorbable material.

References

Gray AJ, Copeland GP. Small bowel perforation following vacuum suction drainage. J R Coll Surg 30:324, 1985.

Imoedemhe DA, Ezimokhai M, Okpere EE, Aboh IF. Intestinal injuries following induced abortion. Int J Gynaecol Obstet 22:303, 1984.

Krebs HB. Intestinal injury in gynecologic surgery: A ten-year experience. Am J Obstet Gynecol 155:509, 1986.

Paloyan D. Intestinal problems in gynecologic surgery. In: Sciarra JJ (Editor). Gynecology and Obstetrics. Philadelphia: Harper & Row, 1986.

PATIENT SUSPECTED OF EXPERIENCING INTRAOPERATIVE BOWEL INJURY

Ⓐ Be alert to factors predisposing to damage to
intestines during abdominal or vaginal surgery
or laparoscopy, such as dense adhesions, peritonitis,
endometriosis, severe pelvic inflammatory disease,
inflammatory bowel disease, antecedent abdominal
radiation therapy, extensive carcinomatosis, and
extensive dissection or radical surgery

Weigh benefits of preoperative bowel preparation (p 18)
Take precautions to avert bowel damage during procedure by
   ensuring good exposure and carrying out careful dissection
Consider open laparoscopy if risk factors warrant

Bowel injury is suspected by identification of liquid fecal
   material or flatus in operative field
Bowel damage is verified by inspection of entire intestinal tract
Ascertain extent, depth, and type of trauma

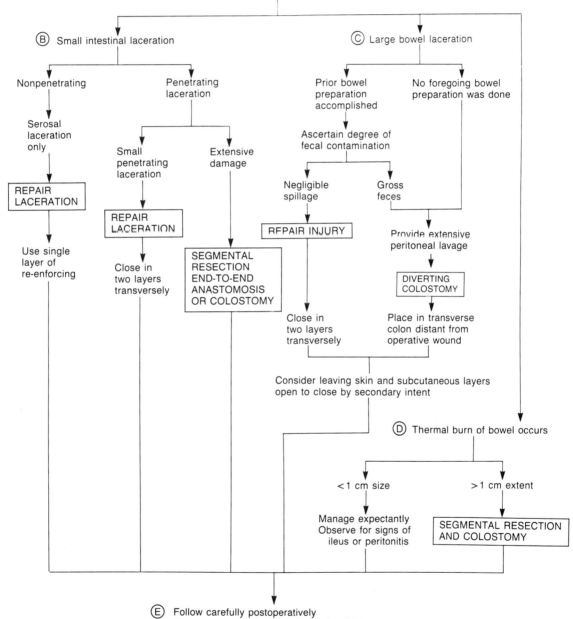

Ⓑ Small intestinal laceration

Nonpenetrating

Serosal
laceration
only

REPAIR
LACERATION

Use single
layer of
re-enforcing

Penetrating
laceration

Small
penetrating
laceration

REPAIR
LACERATION

Close in
two layers
transversely

Extensive
damage

SEGMENTAL
RESECTION
END-TO-END
ANASTOMOSIS
OR COLOSTOMY

Ⓒ Large bowel laceration

Prior bowel
preparation
accomplished

Ascertain degree of
fecal contamination

Negligible
spillage

REPAIR INJURY

Close in
two layers
transversely

Gross
feces

Provide extensive
peritoneal lavage

DIVERTING
COLOSTOMY

Place in transverse
colon distant from
operative wound

No foregoing bowel
preparation was done

Consider leaving skin and subcutaneous layers
open to close by secondary intent

Ⓓ Thermal burn of bowel occurs

<1 cm size

Manage expectantly
Observe for signs of
ileus or peritonitis

>1 cm extent

SEGMENTAL RESECTION
AND COLOSTOMY

Ⓔ Follow carefully postoperatively
Decompress bowel with nasoduodenal tube
Administer broad-spectrum antibiotic regimen
Watch for and manage wound infections aggressively (p 290)

BLADDER INJURY

Balmookoot Balgobin, M.D.

A. The anatomic proximity of the bladder to the gynecological operative field exposes it to considerable risk of damage. This risk is magnified by prior pelvic surgery, radiation, and infection, or distorted anatomic relations from cancer, endometriosis, inflammatory bowel disease, and chronic salpingitis. The risk is especially high with radical hysterectomy from direct physical injury, denervation, and devascularization. Detailed knowledge of the anatomy is essential in order to avoid injury or, if damage is unavoidable, to recognize when injury has occurred so that it can be repaired promptly and correctly.

B. Bladder trauma can generally be averted by careful, delicate, deliberate intraoperative dissection in the correct tissue planes. When the bladder is being advanced off the anterior cervix during total abdominal (p 246) or vaginal hysterectomy (p 248), one risks entering the bladder wall musculature if the correct plane is not found and developed. This is associated with bleeding, which is a signal to desist. Sharp dissection under visualization with good lighting and exposure is helpful in preventing or correcting this technical error. Another frequent site of potential bladder injury is at the dome when the abdominal incision (p 242) is being made. It is good practice to open the peritoneum first at the cephalic end of a vertical incision, taking care to avoid bowel damage (p 318). Visualize the bladder pole and note where the obliterated lateral umbilical arteries converge with the midline urachus at the apex of the bladder. The peritoneum can then be opened in a caudal direction without risk of bladder injury. If it is necessary to cross the urachus, ligate the cut ends in the event its embryologic canal is still patent.

C. Recognizing a bladder injury is paramount. If recognized, it is usually readily reparable and heals without problems. Unrecognized injuries cause potentially serious problems, namely fistula formation and morbidity (p 156). Large injuries are easily appreciated; smaller ones are less apparent. Whenever bladder damage is suspected, verify it by placing dye in the bladder and observing whether any appears in the operative field. This usually entails instilling 300 ml dilute methylene blue solution through an indwelling urethral catheter placed preoperatively; alternatively, inject the dye directly through the bladder wall for this purpose. Once diagnosed, ascertain if the ureteral ostia are involved by opening the bladder dome for exposure or by cystoscopy.

D. Most bladder injuries heal uneventfully if repaired at the time of the damage. The technique of the repair is not as critical as for bowel repair, but careful reapposition of the cut edges is prudent. Use absorbable sutures in two layers to provide a watertight hemostatic closure of the injured site as well as the dome incision, if made (Fig. 1). When complete, test the repair by instilling dye again. Retroperitoneal drainage is generally superfluous, but urethral or suprapubic drainage of the bladder lumen is important to prevent any tension on the repair. Maintain continuous drainage for seven to ten days at minimum.

E. If the injury occurs at or near the ureterovesical junctions, seek urologic consultation for advice on optimal management. Primary closure may be feasible, but it may be necessary to consider other options, such as division and reimplantation or other procedures applicable for use in cases with ureteral injury (p 322). If primary closure can be achieved, it may require three layers of absorbable sutures plus a peritoneal or omental graft. Alternatively, long-term drainage may be preferred to permit maximum healing of the vesicovaginal fistula that can be expected to form. Repair can then be undertaken at a more appropriate time.

F. Bladder injury that is identified postoperatively requires investigation to differentiate it from ureteral injury. Acute or progressive manifestations of fever and pain warrant exploration for urinary inspissation into tissues. The site should be identified and drained. Primary repair, while sometimes possible, is seldom appropriate to undertake because the concurrent inflammatory reaction or overt infection makes healing unlikely. It is preferable, therefore, to drain the site retroperitoneally and drain the bladder transurethrally or suprapubically; postpone repair for several months until the tissues are in more optimal condition for the repair.

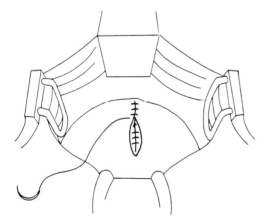

Figure 1 Bladder injury is closed in two layers, using interrupted or continuous sutures of delayed absorbable material. The first layer inverts the mucosa and the second reapposes the cut muscularis to re-enforce the repair.

References

Alonso Gorrea M, Fernandez Zuazu J, Mompo Sanchis JA, et al. Spontaneous healing of uretero-vesico-vaginal fistulas. Eur Urol 11:341, 1985.

Bissada NK, McDonald D. Management of giant vesicovaginal and vesicourethrovaginal fistulas. J Urol 130:1073, 1983.

Guerriero WG. Operative injury to the lower urinary tract. Urol Clin North Am 12:339, 1985.

Symmonds RE. Incontinence: Vesical and urethral fistulas. Clin Obstet Gynecol 27:449, 1984.

Zimmern P, Schmidbauer CP, Leach GE, et al. Vesicovaginal and urethrovaginal fistulae. Semin Urol 4:24, 1986.

PATIENT SUSPECTED OF EXPERIENCING INTRAOPERATIVE BLADDER INJURY

Ⓐ Review background of patient in regard to conditions that might place her at special risk for bladder damage intraoperatively, including severe distortion by obstetrical or other trauma, cesarean sections, vaginal or pelvic surgery, radiation therapy, inflammatory processes, and cancer, or technical problems during surgery, such as poor exposure, active bleeding, poor tissue planes, and extensive dissection or radical surgery in the vicinity

Ⓑ Use preventive measures to avert bladder damage, including anatomic dissection in carefully defined and well-identified tissue planes, using an indwelling catheter as a guide and the obliterated umbilical arteries and urachus as landmarks

Ⓒ Suspect bladder injury by appearance of urine in the operative field or blood in the urinary drainage
Confirm bladder damage by instilling dye into the bladder and observing it appear in the surgical site
Determine site of injury, extent, and proximity to the ureteral ostia by way of cystotomy or cystoscopy

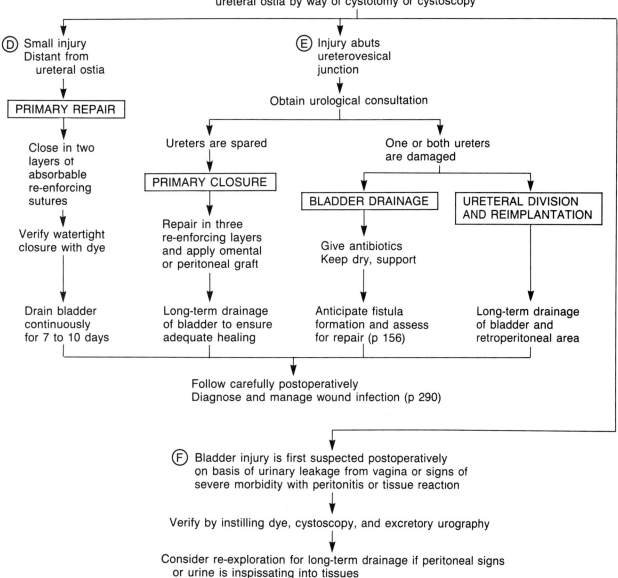

Ⓓ Small injury
Distant from
ureteral ostia

PRIMARY REPAIR

Close in two layers of absorbable re-enforcing sutures

Verify watertight closure with dye

Drain bladder continuously for 7 to 10 days

Ⓔ Injury abuts ureterovesical junction

Obtain urological consultation

Ureters are spared

PRIMARY CLOSURE

Repair in three re-enforcing layers and apply omental or peritoneal graft

Long-term drainage of bladder to ensure adequate healing

One or both ureters are damaged

BLADDER DRAINAGE

Give antibiotics
Keep dry, support

Anticipate fistula formation and assess for repair (p 156)

URETERAL DIVISION AND REIMPLANTATION

Long-term drainage of bladder and retroperitoneal area

Follow carefully postoperatively
Diagnose and manage wound infection (p 290)

Ⓕ Bladder injury is first suspected postoperatively on basis of urinary leakage from vagina or signs of severe morbidity with peritonitis or tissue reaction

Verify by instilling dye, cystoscopy, and excretory urography

Consider re-exploration for long-term drainage if peritoneal signs or urine is inspissating into tissues
Manage as fistula, if flow is exteriorized (p 156)

URETERAL INJURY

Balmookoot Balgobin, M.D.

A. There are three sites at which the ureter is at special hazard during gynecological surgery: adjacent to the cervix posteriorly to the uterine vessels, at the bifurcation of the common iliac artery dorsad to the infundibulo-pelvic ligament, and in the posterior leaf of the broad ligament. The risk of injury is enhanced if the anatomy is distorted by malformation or disease, such as acute or chronic infection, cancer, leiomyomas, endometriosis, or retroperitoneal mass. Even in its normal anatomic site, the risk of injuring the ureter is increased considerably by poor exposure and suboptimal operative technique.

B. To avoid ureteral injury, carefully dissect the anatomic planes and maintain good hemostasis. It is essential to have detailed knowledge of the pelvic anatomy and the relationships of the ureters to gynecological structures. If distortion of these relationships is anticipated, obtain excretory urography beforehand to identify the course of the ureters relative to the pelvic organs. Stress the need for oblique or lateral radiographic views to show anterior ureteral displacement by a retroperitoneal process. Intra-operatively, in the course of hysterectomy, take special care to place clamps and sutures as close to the cervix as feasible. When dividing the infundibulopelvic liga-ment, be sure it is clear of the ureter; if necessary, open the peritoneum over the iliac vessels and trace the path of the ureter caudad. Place clamps and sutures for hemostasis under vision, never blindly.

C. To verify ureteral injury intraoperatively, inject indigo carmine intravenously. The dye appears in the operative field if the ureter has been severed, but it is not seen if the ureter is clamped, ligated, or kinked. The lumen has to be cannulated for this purpose. This can be accom-plished by inserting a ureteral catheter by way of the bladder (through a cystotomy incision in the dome or by cystoscopy) or through an incision in the ureter at the pelvic brim. Methylene blue instilled in the bladder only demonstrates bladder injury (p 320) if there is reflux into the ureters.

D. Postoperatively, suspect ureteral injury in a febrile patient with flank pain. Urine inspissation in tissues generates considerable systemic response. Obstruction may be silent and lead to kidney atrophy, but it is often associated with manifestations of pyelonephritis. Urinary discharge from the vagina raises the specter of fistula formation (p 156). Azotemia from bilateral obstruction is a serious matter demanding intervention urgently. In most other circumstances, ureteral damage discovered postoperatively should be managed conservatively. Verify the damage by intravenous and retrograde pyelography. Urologic consultation is essential. An attempt to bypass the obstruction or defect by catheterization is useful. If successful, the catheter can be left in place to give the ureter the opportunity to heal without further surgery. If temporary bypass is not possible, consider nephros-tomy for a totally obstructed ureter or re-exploration for definitive repair.

E. The type and timing of repair depends on the type of damage and when it is diagnosed. Corrective repair is best done at the time of the original injury. Later, infec-tion and induration makes an attempt to repair less likely to succeed. It will be necessary to delay repair for weeks or even months until the tissues are in optimal condition. Immediate primary repair can be done for a fresh partial transection, using fine interrupted absorbable sutures to reappose the cut edges longitudinally over a ureteral stint. An indwelling catheter and a retroperitoneal drain are necessary. Obstruction by kinking or sutures requires dissection and exploration of the ureteral pathway to release the offending sutures. Transection near the blad-der requires ureterovesical anastomosis with tunneling to prevent reflux. This may necessitate mobilizing the bladder and fixing it cephalad (by psoas hitch) (Fig. 1A) or creating a bladder flap (Boari flap) to accommodate the ureteral anastomosis without tension. Higher tran-section can sometimes be corrected by end-to-end anastomosis, the juxtaposing lumina having been en-larged first by oblique or fishmouth revision (Fig. 1B,C). If a large segment of ureter is lost or damaged, however, consider use of a bridging ileal conduit, tran-sureteroureterostomy (anastomosis to the opposite ure-ter), renal autotransplantation (to the pelvis), or urinary diversion procedure.

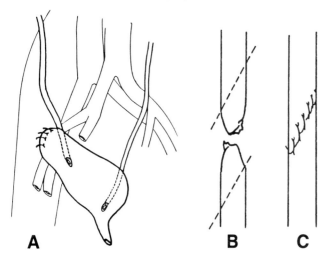

Figure 1 Psoas hitch (A) involves advancing the bladder and at-taching it to the psoas major muscle and implanting the severed and shortened ureter into the bladder after tunneling in the bladder wall. Repair of ureteral injury by resecting the damaged portion at an an-gle (B) and reapproximating the cut edges carefully with a single layer of fine interrupted delayed absorbable sutures (C) over an indwel-ling ureteral stint to ensure good healing of the end-to-end anasto-mosis. Angled closure prevents stricture.

References

Dowling RA, Correire JN Jr, Sandler CM. Iatrogenic ureteral in-jury. J Urol 135:912, 1986.

Harshman MW, Pollack HM, Banner MP, Wein AJ. Conservative management of ureteral obstruction secondary to suture en-trapment. J Urol 127:121, 1982.

PATIENT SUSPECTED OF EXPERIENCING INTRAOPERATIVE URETERAL INJURY

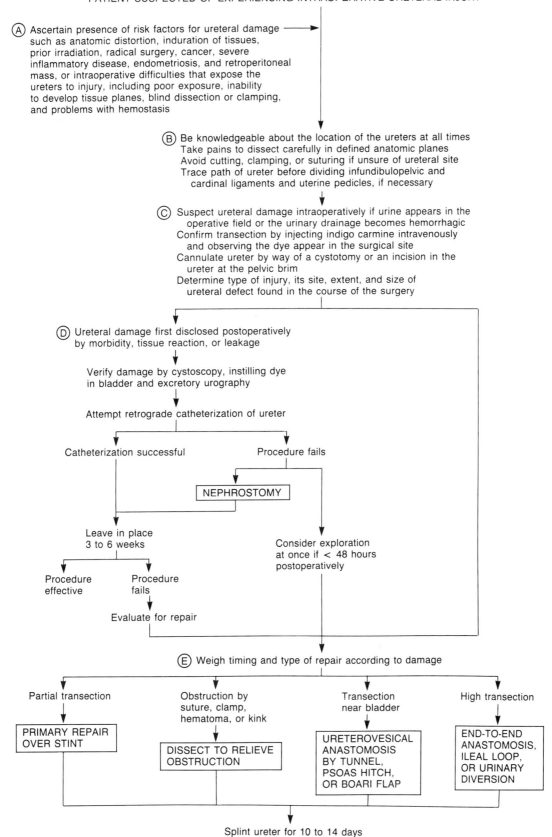

(A) Ascertain presence of risk factors for ureteral damage such as anatomic distortion, induration of tissues, prior irradiation, radical surgery, cancer, severe inflammatory disease, endometriosis, and retroperitoneal mass, or intraoperative difficulties that expose the ureters to injury, including poor exposure, inability to develop tissue planes, blind dissection or clamping, and problems with hemostasis

(B) Be knowledgeable about the location of the ureters at all times
Take pains to dissect carefully in defined anatomic planes
Avoid cutting, clamping, or suturing if unsure of ureteral site
Trace path of ureter before dividing infundibulopelvic and cardinal ligaments and uterine pedicles, if necessary

(C) Suspect ureteral damage intraoperatively if urine appears in the operative field or the urinary drainage becomes hemorrhagic
Confirm transection by injecting indigo carmine intravenously and observing the dye appear in the surgical site
Cannulate ureter by way of a cystotomy or an incision in the ureter at the pelvic brim
Determine type of injury, its site, extent, and size of ureteral defect found in the course of the surgery

(D) Ureteral damage first disclosed postoperatively by morbidity, tissue reaction, or leakage

Verify damage by cystoscopy, instilling dye in bladder and excretory urography

Attempt retrograde catheterization of ureter

Catheterization successful

Procedure fails

NEPHROSTOMY

Leave in place 3 to 6 weeks

Consider exploration at once if < 48 hours postoperatively

Procedure effective

Procedure fails

Evaluate for repair

(E) Weigh timing and type of repair according to damage

Partial transection

PRIMARY REPAIR OVER STINT

Obstruction by suture, clamp, hematoma, or kink

DISSECT TO RELIEVE OBSTRUCTION

Transection near bladder

URETEROVESICAL ANASTOMOSIS BY TUNNEL, PSOAS HITCH, OR BOARI FLAP

High transection

END-TO-END ANASTOMOSIS, ILEAL LOOP, OR URINARY DIVERSION

Splint ureter for 10 to 14 days
Follow carefully postoperatively

Winslow PH, Kreger R, Ebbeson B, Oster E. Conservative management of electrical burn injury of ureter secondary to laparoscopy. Urology 27:60, 1986.

Witters S, Cornelissen M, Vereecken R. Iatrogenic ureteral injury: Aggressive or conservative treatment. Am J Obstet Gynecol 155:582, 1986.

QUALITY ASSURANCE

Catherine T. Alvarez, R.N.

A. Health care providers are dedicated to the highest quality medical care for the patient as an individual within the context of her family environment and societal structure. Standards of practice must be examined continually, not only to verify that acceptable care is being rendered, but that improved quality is fostered and that hospital bed and operating facility utilization is appropriate to satisfy cost containment needs. The latter is increasingly relevant to hospital activities as regulatory and fiscal constraints are being imposed. Quality assurance programs require some formal mechanism for providing ongoing objective assessments of patient care activities within a department or institution. These entail data collection by trained, qualified reviewers who can function autonomously to audit all medical activities. The information derived in this way should serve to identify chronic problems in need of correction.

B. Specific cases should be automatically assessed on the basis of an adverse outcome, such as death or complication. In addition, routine audit is appropriate for every major surgical procedure. The retrospective evaluation of the completed patient record includes ascertaining completeness, accuracy, and suitability of documentation with regard to rationale for the procedure, acceptable preoperative history, physical examination, and laboratory investigations as indicated, adequate assessment of risk-benefit relationship, informed consent, appropriateness of procedure, and timely recognition of the developing complication and its correct evaluation and management, including seeking consultation when indicated.

C. To establish a functional audit system that will not be considered challenging and counterproductive necessitates staff understanding and cooperation. This requires prior and continuing education and participatory involvement of practitioners, administrators, and nurses during the planning and formative stages, as well as subsequently (perhaps on a rotational basis).

D. It is important for the audit and data collection team to be independent of the clinical service unit in order to ensure objectivity. In the absence of such autonomy and empowering authority pertaining to record access and detailed analysis, it could not function in a satisfactory manner to accomplish its aims of reviewing cases, assessing and establishing quality and standards of conduct, determining allocation of clinical responsibility, identifying and reporting deficiencies, and disseminating collected information in a meaningful way. A written protocol is needed, stating the guiding principles and goals, the organizational plan, pathways of responsibilities, and transmission of information in clear and unambiguous terms. A procedure manual is especially useful for regular operational activities. Provide well defined, long-term leadership with consistent coordination and supervision, ample full-time personnel (according to the case load), designated workspace, support, and operational budget.

E. Auditing records is a skilled and labor intensive activity. Personnel must be trained in this difficult task and supervised on an ongoing basis to guarantee accuracy, completeness, and consistency in the application of the rules for case selection and evaluation. Only if the data collection and audit processes are reliable and uniform can the information generated be considered valid and useful.

F. One of the most important aspects of a quality assurance program is the identification of cases requiring close attention based on possible error in diagnosis, inappropriate procedure, inept operative performance, delayed diagnosis or response to a complication, or some other type of substandard action. If specific guidelines are established, trained auditors should uncover nearly all of the cases in which these problems may be found. These selected cases are then reviewed in detail to determine if the management was acceptable, marginally justifiable, or unacceptable. Those deemed not fully acceptable are referred in turn to the authorized department chairman for review with the responsible clinicians. Such individuals, if chronically identified, should be expected to improve their performance in the future or jeopardize their practice privileges by having constraints imposed. They should have the opportunity to seek formal redress if they feel such constraints are inappropriate.

References

Clemenhagen C, Champagne F. Quality assurance as part of program evaluation: Guidelines for managers and clinical department heads. Qual Rev Bull 383:387, 1986.

Donabedian A. Criteria and standards for quality assessment and monitoring. Qual Rev Bull 12:99, 1986.

Hepburn PF. Self assessment. Br J Hosp Med 35:129, 1986.

Holroyd BR, Knopp R, Kallsen G. Medical control: Quality assurance in prehospital care. JAMA 256:1027, 1986.

Kahn J. Quality assurance professionals: A national profile. Dimens Health Serv 63:14, 1984.

Warner AM. Education for roles and responsibilities in quality assurance: Physician leadership. Qual Rev Bull 11:111, 1985.

REQUIREMENT FOR QUALITY ASSURANCE IN GYNECOLOGICAL CARE

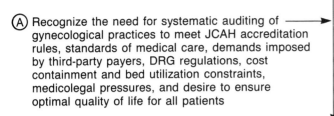

Ⓐ Recognize the need for systematic auditing of gynecological practices to meet JCAH accreditation rules, standards of medical care, demands imposed by third-party payers, DRG regulations, cost containment and bed utilization constraints, medicolegal pressures, and desire to ensure optimal quality of life for all patients

Ⓑ Collect baseline information for individual physicians and for the department staff collectively pertaining to rates of mortality, morbidity, complications, and frequencies of major procedures, reviewing records for completeness, accuracy, rationale for and acceptability of admission and procedure, timeliness and astuteness of care, and errors in diagnosis

Ⓒ Educate and motivate medical and nursing staff as to objectives of quality assurance program, discussing requirements and justification for undertaking and supporting it, and ensuring their involvement, active participation, and full cooperation

Ⓓ Establish independent organization for audit and data collection, unrelated to clinical service personnel and with authority to establish written protocols for reviewing and evaluating case records, objectively investigating and reporting disclosed problems, and assigning responsibility for substandard practice, with long-term leadership, adequate personnel, and resources

Ⓔ Hire and train personnel and ensure ongoing supervision to maintain reliable consistency in case selection and in application of criteria for evaluation

Appoint participants from among medical and nursing staffs to function on rotational basis as formal reviewers of cases designated by the audit team

Medical-nursing committee and audit group help design and modify operations for case finding and screening, record keeping, data analysis, and periodic reporting

Ⓕ Cases are flagged by trained auditors for review by medical-nursing committee on basis of documentable shortcomings as determined by formally established criteria

Committee reviews identified cases
Responsibility specified
Minutes or actions are recorded
Data are collected and collective results reported back to staff

Specific problems reported to department chairman for direct discussion with responsible physician or nurse and appropriate action, if called for because of chronicity, in form of limitation of privileges or imposition of supervisory or educational program

Ensure availability of a grievance process with mechanism for judicial review

325

INFORMED CONSENT PRINCIPLES

Max Borten, M.D., J.D.

A. No diagnostic or therapeutic procedure can ordinarily be done unless the patient has first given her full consent. The doctrine of informed consent is based on the premise that all adults of sound mind have the right to determine what shall be done to their bodies. Neither the state nor another individual has the right to compel a person to undergo any procedure or therapy. To undertake any operation without appropriate informed consent risks liability for medical negligence or battery.

B. There are special emergency situations when consent may be implied to exist. Consent will generally be acknowledged in law if the patient's life is at stake and it is just not possible to obtain consent from the patient herself or some other authorized person. It is advisable to notify the hospital administrator on call before proceeding, however. Under emergency conditions in which informed consent cannot be obtained prior to surgery either from the patient or a close family member, a statement acknowledging the emergency care should be obtained from the patient as soon afterwards as possible. Bear in mind that the effects of general anesthesia and sedation may persist for some time insofar as her recall and decision making thought processes are concerned.

C. In law, a "fiduciary relationship" is said to exist between a physician and his or her patient. This implies a mutual sense of trust and confidence such that each party owes the other a positive obligation to disclose all relevant facts. The nature of the patient's condition and the proposed therapy, therefore, must be explained to her in plain language. Full disclosure requires a description of alternative options along with their comparative benefits and risks. Furthermore, one must provide information on the prognosis in the event the condition is allowed to go untreated.

D. Physicians are all supposed to possess basic knowledge and skills. Each has an inherent obligation to keep up to date and to have the same knowledge as other physicians practicing under like circumstances. If one fails to meet the standard of required knowledge, this will constitute a liability distinct from that due to the failure to disclose. Merely because one is unaware of the potential risks of a procedure does not mean that the duty to inform the patient is in any way diminished or excused.

E. Details about the risks that have to be disclosed to any given patient or for any particular procedure are still unclear. It is recognized that full disclosure of risks to some patients may be harmful to them. If the physician chooses not to inform the patient fully under these circumstances, he or she is exercising the privilege to withhold disclosure. This is a privilege that is subordinate to the duty to disclose. If this privilege to withhold disclosure cannot be clearly substantiated, any material risk must be discussed with the patient. For guidance in this regard, one should consider a risk to be material if it is likely that a reasonable person would deem it important for deciding about whether or not to have the operation under consideration. One should be aware that the privilege to withhold disclosure cannot be considered applicable just because knowledge about a given risk might cause the patient to refuse permission for a procedure that the physician feels she needs.

F. It is good practice to review as many options as one can anticipate will or may have to be exercised in the course of a procedure before undertaking it. Even when this is done, however, unforeseen situations may arise requiring action for which specific permission was not obtained preoperatively. Without such prior informed consent, one can usually justify extending the surgical procedure. This applies especially if certain criteria are met: If one could not have been reasonably expected to have diagnosed the condition before surgery; if the additional surgery is carried out through the same incision; if it is well justified on the basis of good medical practice; and if the patient has not specifically prohibited it. Moreover, it is usually only applicable if the patient is not awake and there is no responsible surrogate to give permission.

G. One must document the informed consent process clearly. Preprinted operative consent forms cannot be relied upon as sufficient for this purpose. A general authorization that gives blanket permission for the physician to exercise judgment is not necessarily valid unless there is an emergency problem demanding intervention. Enter a hand written note in the patient's chart unambiguously stating that the patient is aware of her condition, and that she has been fully informed about the procedure, its risks, and alternatives. It is especially wise to list those potential complications that were specifically discussed. It is self-evident (but deserves emphasis nonetheless) that the note should conclude with a statement about whether the patient comprehends the information discussed and consents to operative measures about to be undertaken.

References

Fineberg KS, Peters JD, Willson JR, Kroll DA. Obstetrics/Gynecology and the Law. Ann Arbor: Health Administration Press, 1984.

Keeton WP, Dobbs DB, Keeton RE, Owen DG. Prosser and Keeton on the Law of Torts. St. Paul: West Publishing, 1984.

King JH. The Law of Medical Malpractice in a Nutshell. St. Paul: West Publishing, 1977.

Rozovsky FA. Consent to Treatment: A Practical Guide. Boston: Little, Brown, 1984.

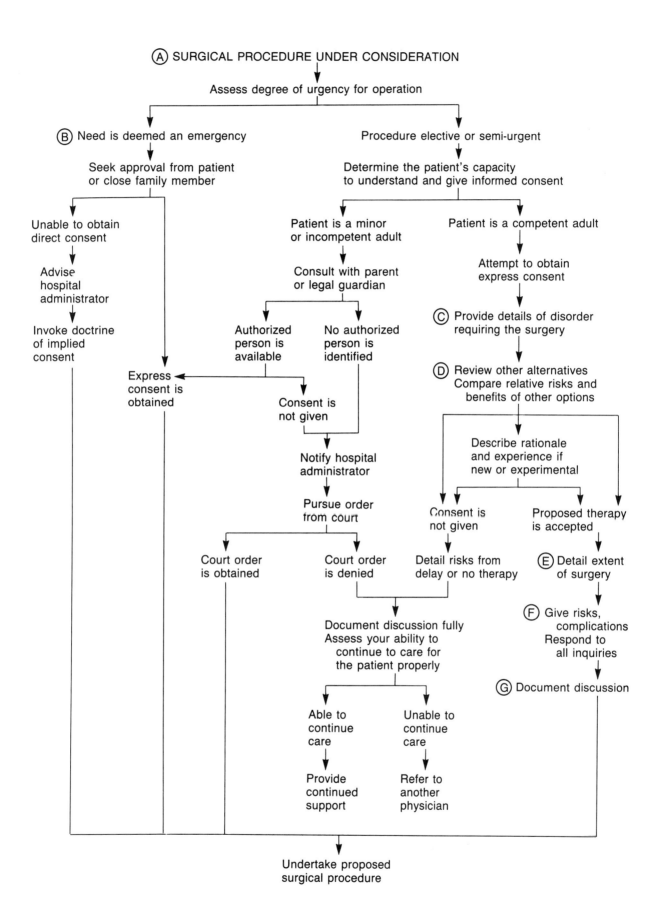

A SURGICAL PROCEDURE UNDER CONSIDERATION

Assess degree of urgency for operation

B Need is deemed an emergency

Seek approval from patient
or close family member

Unable to obtain
direct consent

Advise
hospital
administrator

Invoke doctrine
of implied
consent

Procedure elective or semi-urgent

Determine the patient's capacity
to understand and give informed consent

Patient is a minor
or incompetent adult

Consult with parent
or legal guardian

Authorized
person is
available

No authorized
person is
identified

Express
consent is
obtained

Consent is
not given

Notify hospital
administrator

Pursue order
from court

Court order
is obtained

Court order
is denied

Detail risks from
delay or no therapy

Document discussion fully
Assess your ability to
continue to care for
the patient properly

Able to
continue
care

Unable to
continue
care

Provide
continued
support

Refer to
another
physician

Patient is a competent adult

Attempt to obtain
express consent

C Provide details of disorder
requiring the surgery

D Review other alternatives
Compare relative risks and
benefits of other options

Describe rationale
and experience if
new or experimental

Consent is
not given

Proposed therapy
is accepted

E Detail extent
of surgery

F Give risks,
complications
Respond to
all inquiries

G Document discussion

Undertake proposed
surgical procedure

CONSENT FOR CURETTAGE

Max Borten, M.D., J.D.

A. Cervical dilatation and endometrial curettage (p 230) is done for a wide diversity of conditions and is, therefore, one of the most common gynecological operations performed. Because it is short in duration, seldom associated with serious complications, and generally classified as a minor procedure, it has received little attention. It should be emphasized that the procedure is far from totally innocuous (see E) and it is not always necessarily beneficial or even fully justified. Moreover, it is a frequent source of medicolegal questions. As more emphasis is placed on the socioeconomic implications of all surgical practices, dilatation and curettage is rapidly becoming a standard office procedure. Principles of informed consent relevant to this operation when it is performed in a hospital environment are equally applicable to it when done in an office setting.

B. Progress in gynecological endocrinology has resulted in the development of a number of pharmacologic modalities that can be effectively utilized in lieu of surgery to help normalize uterine function. Estrogen supplementation and progestin replacement, for example, have been used quite successfully to avoid operative intervention in a variety of conditions, such as anovulatory bleeding (p 124) and luteal phase deficiency (p 126).

C. Some of the technical aspects of dilatation and curettage have slowly evolved in recent years so that what was once almost exclusively a hospital based operation is now often safely and efficiently done as an ambulatory office procedure. In the past, it usually required general anesthesia; it is now frequently carried out under local anesthesia, specifically paracervical block, although intravenous analgesic supplementation may sometimes be needed. Unless inappropriate for a given patient because of known or expected complicating factors, these alternative options should be discussed and offered to help ensure that she can make an informed decision.

D. The physician has not discharged full responsibility by simply providing pertinent information to the patient. It is imperative to assess whether she has understood and assimilated what she has been told. It is not sufficient to believe this to be the case; instead, one must try to assess the degree of knowledge of the facts she has acquired by eliciting it from her as they apply to her particular case. The patient should be given ample opportunity to ask questions and to weigh her decision carefully. This means delaying the procedure for a minimum of several days between the initial discussion and the final preoperative assessment. At the time of this reassessment and before the informed consent is signed, she should be allowed to reconsider and encouraged to ask any additional questions she may have.

E. Discussion of the material risks associated with any surgical procedure includes transmitting information about those hazards which occur often or are serious enough to be material to the patient's decision to have the procedure. For dilatation and curettage, they include the possibility of a localized infection, specifically endometritis, or a more disseminated infection, such as salpingitis leading to pelvic peritonitis; excessive bleeding, which may require transfusions of blood or blood products and, rarely, even hysterectomy; perforation of the cervix or uterine wall with associated damage to surrounding pelvic or abdominal structures, including bowel; and inability to complete the intended procedure as planned, perhaps necessitating additional surgery in the future.

F. The currently accepted standard of practice is to perform nearly all dilatation and curettage procedures as a same day admission, that is, the patient is not admitted for evaluation and care the night before surgery and is not expected to remain in the hospital more than a few hours after the procedure, barring complications. Use of short-acting anesthetics ensures that patients are able and ready to be discharged soon after the operation. Nonetheless, one must inform the patient of the possibility that overnight (or even longer) hospitalization will be needed if the circumstances require (for example, for observation in the event of a uterine perforation). Similarly, she should be told that intravenous antibiotic therapy might prove to be necessary, and if it were required, it would prolong her hospitalization.

References

Grimes DA. Diagnostic dilatation and curettage: A reappraisal. Am J Obstet Gynecol 142:1, 1982.

Lathrop JC. Perforation of uterus at dilatation and curettage. In: Nichols DH (Editor). Problems, Injuries and Complications of Gynecologic Surgery. Baltimore: Williams & Wilkins, 1983.

Rozovsky FA. Consent to treatment: A Practical Guide. Boston: Little, Brown, 1984.

Smith JJ, Schulman H. Current dilation and curettage practice: A need for revision. Obstet Gynecol 65:516, 1985.

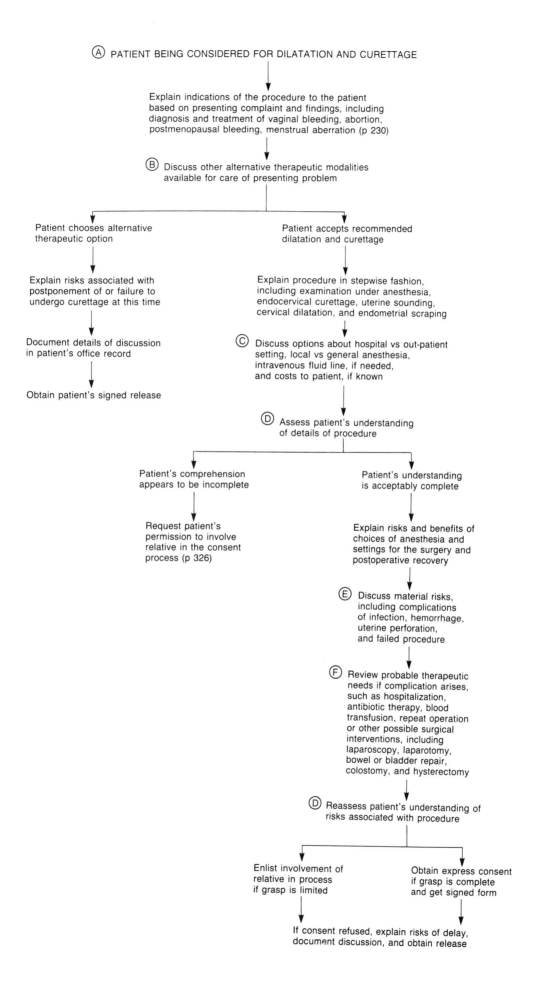

Ⓐ PATIENT BEING CONSIDERED FOR DILATATION AND CURETTAGE

Explain indications of the procedure to the patient based on presenting complaint and findings, including diagnosis and treatment of vaginal bleeding, abortion, postmenopausal bleeding, menstrual aberration (p 230)

Ⓑ Discuss other alternative therapeutic modalities available for care of presenting problem

Patient chooses alternative therapeutic option

Explain risks associated with postponement of or failure to undergo curettage at this time

Document details of discussion in patient's office record

Obtain patient's signed release

Patient accepts recommended dilatation and curettage

Explain procedure in stepwise fashion, including examination under anesthesia, endocervical curettage, uterine sounding, cervical dilatation, and endometrial scraping

Ⓒ Discuss options about hospital vs out-patient setting, local vs general anesthesia, intravenous fluid line, if needed, and costs to patient, if known

Ⓓ Assess patient's understanding of details of procedure

Patient's comprehension appears to be incomplete

Request patient's permission to involve relative in the consent process (p 326)

Patient's understanding is acceptably complete

Explain risks and benefits of choices of anesthesia and settings for the surgery and postoperative recovery

Ⓔ Discuss material risks, including complications of infection, hemorrhage, uterine perforation, and failed procedure

Ⓕ Review probable therapeutic needs if complication arises, such as hospitalization, antibiotic therapy, blood transfusion, repeat operation or other possible surgical interventions, including laparoscopy, laparotomy, bowel or bladder repair, colostomy, and hysterectomy

Ⓓ Reassess patient's understanding of risks associated with procedure

Enlist involvement of relative in process if grasp is limited

Obtain express consent if grasp is complete and get signed form

If consent refused, explain risks of delay, document discussion, and obtain release

329

CONSENT FOR LAPAROSCOPY

Max Borten, M.D., J.D.

A. Over the last decade, laparoscopy has become one of the most common gynecological procedures performed in this country. Diagnostic evaluations (p 224), sterilization (p 266), and other operative procedures (p 240) have been increasingly performed transendoscopically. Although the growing popularity of gynecological laparoscopy attests to its value and safety, one must never assume that the patient is sufficiently familiar with it and its risks as to obviate the need for instruction and counsel. The procedure should be discussed in detail (see C); advantages and limitations must be freely reviewed with the patient; alternative options and their relative benefits and risks deserve equal consideration.

B. There are many advantages to laparoscopy, but its most outstanding feature is the direct benefit accrued to the patient herself in regard to achieving limited objectives with considerably less morbidity or other adverse effects of laparotomy done for the same purpose. It is thus essential to weigh the risk-to-benefit equation when recommending the procedure. Safety is stressed above all. Bear in mind that a relative contraindication, which may be irrelevant for the young, healthy woman undergoing an elective procedure, such as sterilization, may become an absolute contraindication for another patient. Whenever such clear-cut contraindications are present, alternative modalities must be employed in lieu of endoscopy.

C. The detailed explanation of the procedure must include an exposition of the anesthetic modality selected and its expected effects. Inform the patient about the need for creating a pneumoperitoneum before the laparoscope is inserted. Discuss the probability of an auxiliary trocar puncture; if operative laparoscopy is anticipated, advise about the possibility of several ancillary punctures. Tell her about plans to utilize either closed or open laparoscopic technique. Remember to provide details of what she may expect immediately following the operation, explaining the recovery phase thoroughly.

D. It may at times be impossible for a lay person to absorb and comprehend the medical aspects of laparoscopy. Be sure that the patient understands the indication for the procedure, alternatives to it (if such other options are available), an overview of the technical aspects, and the possible complications that may follow as a consequence of the anesthesia and the operation. A common error is to assume the patient understands everything she is told at once. One must assess and reassesss the patient's comprehension to ensure a proper informed consent is obtained. When in doubt, the patient should be given sufficient time to think and ask questions. Only then is it proper to proceed.

E. Each laparoscopist has personal preferences in regard to performing the operation. If contraindications are determined to exist, discuss and counsel about alternative modes of accomplishing the desired goal. Take the patient's desires for a given anesthetic modality into account whenever possible within the constraints of appropriateness and safety. It is also important to discuss what she is likely to experience in the immediate postoperative period. Give her information concerning the first and second postoperative days. This should be done at the time one is obtaining the informed consent rather than postoperatively prior to discharging the patient home. Her ability to understand and retain information at the later time may be affected by the residual anesthetic impact.

F. Before the patient consents to laparoscopy, she must be informed about the complications associated with the procedure. In addition to the most common risks known to occur, the physician has a duty to apprise her of any risk that is material to her in particular and which it is reasonable to believe she will take into account in making a decision. Complications that may result from the blind insertion of the Verres needle and the sharp laparoscopic trocar should always be mentioned. If vascular injury, laceration of a loop of intestine, or urinary tract damage occurs, it will require extended hospitalization for observation and additional corrective surgical procedures when indicated. One must inform the patient about what steps would have to be taken in the event a complication arises in regard to investigative assessment, observation, exploratory intervention, and reparative operations.

References

Borten M. Laparoscopic Complications: Prevention and Management. Toronto: B.C. Decker, 1986.

Cunnanan RG, Courey NG, Lippes J. Laparoscopic findings in patients with pelvic pain. Am J Obstet Gynecol 146:389, 1983.

Dubuisson JB, Aubriot FX, Cardone V. Laparoscopic salpingectomy for tubal pregnancy. Fertil Steril 47:225, 1987.

Penfield AJ. How to prevent complications of open laparoscopy. J Reprod Med 30:660, 1985.

Rozovsky FA. Consent to Treatment: A Practical Guide. Boston: Little, Brown, 1984.

PATIENT BEING CONSIDERED FOR LAPAROSCOPY

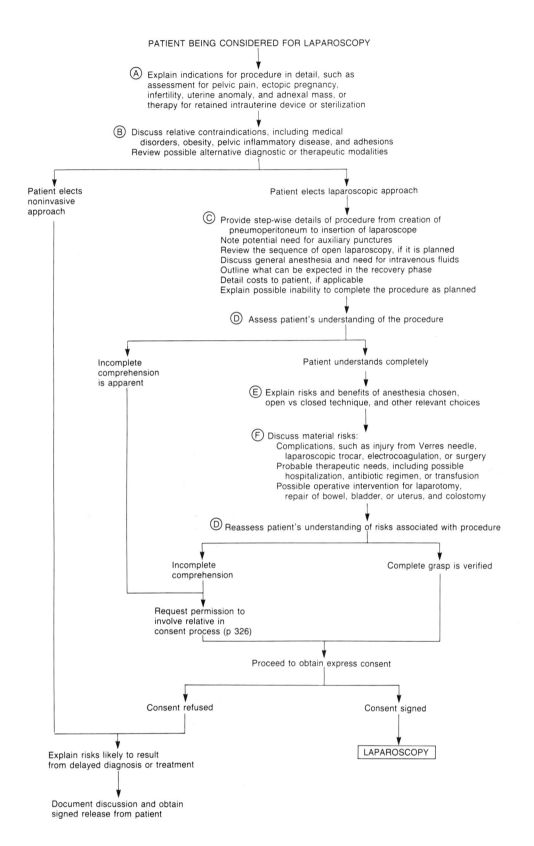

Ⓐ Explain indications for procedure in detail, such as
   assessment for pelvic pain, ectopic pregnancy,
   infertility, uterine anomaly, and adnexal mass, or
   therapy for retained intrauterine device or sterilization

Ⓑ Discuss relative contraindications, including medical
   disorders, obesity, pelvic inflammatory disease, and adhesions
   Review possible alternative diagnostic or therapeutic modalities

Patient elects
noninvasive
approach

Patient elects laparoscopic approach

Ⓒ Provide step-wise details of procedure from creation of
   pneumoperitoneum to insertion of laparoscope
   Note potential need for auxiliary punctures
   Review the sequence of open laparoscopy, if it is planned
   Discuss general anesthesia and need for intravenous fluids
   Outline what can be expected in the recovery phase
   Detail costs to patient, if applicable
   Explain possible inability to complete the procedure as planned

Ⓓ Assess patient's understanding of the procedure

Incomplete
comprehension
is apparent

Patient understands completely

Ⓔ Explain risks and benefits of anesthesia chosen,
   open vs closed technique, and other relevant choices

Ⓕ Discuss material risks:
   Complications, such as injury from Verres needle,
      laparoscopic trocar, electrocoagulation, or surgery
   Probable therapeutic needs, including possible
      hospitalization, antibiotic regimen, or transfusion
   Possible operative intervention for laparotomy,
      repair of bowel, bladder, or uterus, and colostomy

Ⓓ Reassess patient's understanding of risks associated with procedure

Incomplete
comprehension

Complete grasp is verified

Request permission to
involve relative in
consent process (p 326)

Proceed to obtain express consent

Consent refused

Consent signed

Explain risks likely to result
from delayed diagnosis or treatment

LAPAROSCOPY

Document discussion and obtain
signed release from patient

CONSENT FOR HYSTERECTOMY

Max Borten, M.D., J.D.

A. The first step one should generally take in the discussion preceding a recommendation for hysterectomy is a review of the probable diagnosis and the rationale upon which the recommendation is based. Use simple, easily comprehensible language, avoiding technical medical terminology. Prepared pictures are often helpful in facilitating understanding. It is imperative for the physician to be certain that the patient (and her significant other, if such individual is an active participant in the decision making process) understands the indications for the operation and what the surgery is intended to accomplish. The explanation must include a thorough discussion about alternative therapeutic approaches, if any exist. In the patient with a fibroid uterus, for instance, discuss the option of myomectomy, if it is appropriate to consider it. If it is not appropriate, the reasons the option is not correct for this particular patient should be disclosed. The patient must be given the opportunity to choose between the proposed procedure and other treatments, including expectancy, not just between accepting and rejecting one specific recommendation. Give her ample time to ask questions and to weigh her decision in depth.

B. An integral part of the informed consent process is an explanation of the details of the procedure. Among surgical procedures, hysterectomy is perhaps the one most often associated with misconceptions in the lay population. There is much confusion as to the distinction between total and subtotal extirpation of the uterus. Whereas a subtotal hysterectomy signifies supracervical resection of the uterine fundus to a gynecologist, it is generally interpreted by the uninformed as one in which the tubes and ovaries are left in place. Concomitant removal of tubes and ovaries should be specifically discussed, if anticipated. The choice of route of surgery, vaginal versus abdominal, while heavily influenced by the personal preference of the operator and the nature of the disease, should take into account the patient's desires, if possible. This also applies to the type of incision chosen, that is, subumbilical midline vertical as opposed to low transverse incision. When constraints exist making a particular route or type of incision strongly indicated rather than just preferred, the patient should be counseled accordingly.

C. No less important is the need to discuss the socioeconomic aspects of the decision to undergo a major surgical procedure, such as hysterectomy. These include the prudence of obtaining a second surgical opinion, the expected length of hospitalization, the anticipated period of convalescence, the contemplated duration of recuperation before the patient will be able to return to her routine activities (such as household responsibility, exercise, and work), and the expected cost of the operation when pertinent. Assess whether the patient actually understands the potential impact on her economic and physical status.

D. Explaining the procedure should not be limited to the technical aspects of surgery. One must discuss the choice of anesthesia, ensuring that the patient understands that the final decision will be made by the anesthesiologist after his or her own preoperative evaluation. It is also important to inform the patient about what she can expect during the recovery period, extending from immediate postoperatively to the long-term recuperative process.

E. The patient must be informed about all common and potentially serious complications associated with the hysterectomy. The discussion should extend to all material facts relevant to the patient's decision making process. At minimum, it should include postoperative infection, excessive bleeding (intraoperative as well as postoperative), the potential need for transfusion of blood or blood products, traumatic injury to urinary and gastrointestinal tracts, and their potential sequelae. If the course should prove to be complicated, the patient has to be aware that extended hospitalization and even additional surgery may become necessary.

F. It is essential for the physician to assess the patient's understanding of the shared information continuously. The informed consent process must be a dialogue between physician and patient. Encourage her to ask questions and make her feel at ease when doing so by soliciting responses and avoiding haste.

References

Dicker RC, Greenspan JR, Strauss LT, et al. Complications of abdominal and vaginal hysterectomy among women of reproductive age in the United States: The collaborative review of sterilization. Am J Obstet Gynecol 144:841, 1982.

Easterday CL, Grimes DA, Riggs JA. Hysterectomy in the United States. Obstet Gynecol 62:203, 1983.

Ryan M, Dennerstein L. Hysterectomy and tubal ligation. Adv Psychosom Med 15:180, 1986.

Webb C. Professional and lay support for hysterectomy patients. J Adv Nurs 11:167, 1986.

PATIENT BEING CONSIDERED FOR HYSTERECTOMY

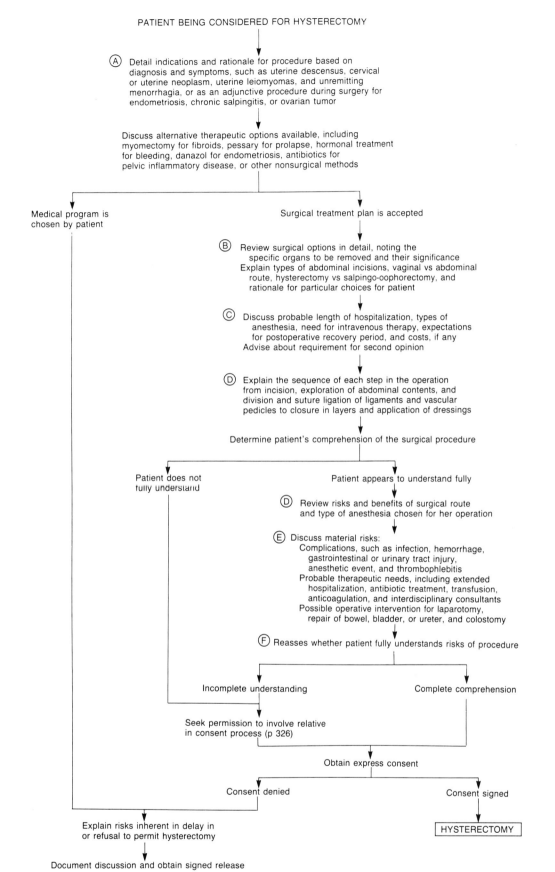

Ⓐ Detail indications and rationale for procedure based on
diagnosis and symptoms, such as uterine descensus, cervical
or uterine neoplasm, uterine leiomyomas, and unremitting
menorrhagia, or as an adjunctive procedure during surgery for
endometriosis, chronic salpingitis, or ovarian tumor

Discuss alternative therapeutic options available, including
myomectomy for fibroids, pessary for prolapse, hormonal treatment
for bleeding, danazol for endometriosis, antibiotics for
pelvic inflammatory disease, or other nonsurgical methods

Medical program is
chosen by patient

Surgical treatment plan is accepted

Ⓑ Review surgical options in detail, noting the
specific organs to be removed and their significance
Explain types of abdominal incisions, vaginal vs abdominal
route, hysterectomy vs salpingo-oophorectomy, and
rationale for particular choices for patient

Ⓒ Discuss probable length of hospitalization, types of
anesthesia, need for intravenous therapy, expectations
for postoperative recovery period, and costs, if any
Advise about requirement for second opinion

Ⓓ Explain the sequence of each step in the operation
from incision, exploration of abdominal contents, and
division and suture ligation of ligaments and vascular
pedicles to closure in layers and application of dressings

Determine patient's comprehension of the surgical procedure

Patient does not
fully understand

Patient appears to understand fully

Ⓓ Review risks and benefits of surgical route
and type of anesthesia chosen for her operation

Ⓔ Discuss material risks:
Complications, such as infection, hemorrhage,
gastrointestinal or urinary tract injury,
anesthetic event, and thrombophlebitis
Probable therapeutic needs, including extended
hospitalization, antibiotic treatment, transfusion,
anticoagulation, and interdisciplinary consultants
Possible operative intervention for laparotomy,
repair of bowel, bladder, or ureter, and colostomy

Ⓕ Reasses whether patient fully understands risks of procedure

Incomplete understanding

Complete comprehension

Seek permission to involve relative
in consent process (p 326)

Obtain express consent

Consent denied

Consent signed

Explain risks inherent in delay in
or refusal to permit hysterectomy

HYSTERECTOMY

Document discussion and obtain signed release

CONSENT FOR ADNEXAL MASS EXPLORATION

Max Borten, M.D., J.D.

A. The doctrine of informed consent imposes on the physician the duty to advise the patient of the nature and risks associated with the proposed therapy. In the case of an anticipated exploratory laparotomy for an adnexal mass (p 184), the surgeon may be confronted by a difficult dilemma. Whereas in most other conditions one can predict what the definitive treatment will be within narrow limits, the same cannot be said for a woman who presents with a pathologic adnexal condition. Quite often, the patient is brought to surgery with a nonspecific, generic diagnosis of adnexal mass that will not be more clearly defined until well into the operation (see C).

B. The extent of one's discussion about alternative therapeutic modalities for a patient with an adnexal mass is influenced by her age and future reproductive needs. For the perimenopausal and postmenopausal woman, the suspicion of a neoplasm makes prompt action essential and exploratory surgery (including laparoscopy or laparotomy) just about the only possible avenues of action. For the young woman of reproductive age, this limitation need not apply. Unless a diagnosis of a condition mandating intervention (such as dermoid cyst, large ovarian mass, or bleeding corpus luteum) can be firmly established, one should always review consideration of other alternative approaches to reduce the risk of compromising future fertility by hasty and unduly aggressive surgery.

C. Initially, inform the patient about the most likely diagnosis and probable therapy. The explanation should include the technical aspects of the procedure, what to expect in the immediate postoperative period, probable length of hospitalization, and expected course of long-term convalescence. Of particular importance in these circumstances is explaining to the patient that there is always the possibility that the original plan of management may have to be altered or extended if the circumstances require (see D and F).

D. The uncertainty that surrounds surgical therapy for an adnexal mass is never more evident than when the preoperative diagnosis is not firmly established. Because of the long-term consequences, which can directly affect the reproductive capabilities of the patient, informed consent for adnexal surgery must include a discussion concerning the possible management options that may be called for in the event unexpected findings are encountered. The patient should be made aware that even the most conservative approach in the best of hands may require extirpation of part or all of the adnexa.

E. Similar to the risks associated with other major gynecological procedures, there are hazards of unexpected postoperative infection, intraoperative or postoperative hemorrhage, and inadvertent injury to the gastrointestinal or urinary tract. These potential complications must be discussed with the patient when informed consent is being obtained. In addition, the therapeutic steps that will have to be taken in the event these complications arise should be explained to the patient. It is equally important to inform her of the probable prolongation of hospitalization under these conditions.

F. It is generally inadvisable to perform surgery beyond the confines of the specific informed consent one has obtained preoperatively. Nonetheless, the traditional rule of law is that a surgeon may extend an operation to remedy any abnormal or diseased condition discovered in the area of the original incision whenever professional judgment dictates that such extension is required to carry out the correct surgical procedure. Furthermore, if a later operation might unduly endanger the patient's life or health and it is impracticable to obtain the consent of the patient (who is under general anesthesia, for example) or the patient's family, it is considered justifiable for the surgeon to extend the operation beyond that originally planned. Extreme caution is in order when applying this doctrine, however. It is not a substitute for the required preoperative informed consent. Because one cannot always predict what will be encountered at the time of surgery for adnexal disease, the discussion leading to patient consent for this type of operation must range widely to include the variety of findings most likely to be encountered and the spectrum of probable procedures.

References

Krebs HB. Intestinal injury in gynecologic surgery: A ten-year experience. Am J Obstet Gynecol 155:509, 1986.

Rozovsky FA. Consent to Treatment: A Practical Guide. Boston: Little, Brown, 1984.

Wharton LR. Surgery of benign adnexal disease: Endometriosis, residuals of inflammatory and granulomatous diseases, and ureteral injury. In: Ridley JH (Editor). Gynecologic Surgery: Errors, Safeguards, Salvage. 2nd ed. Baltimore: Williams & Wilkins, 1981.

PATIENT BEING CONSIDERED FOR EXPLORATORY LAPAROTOMY FOR ADNEXAL MASS

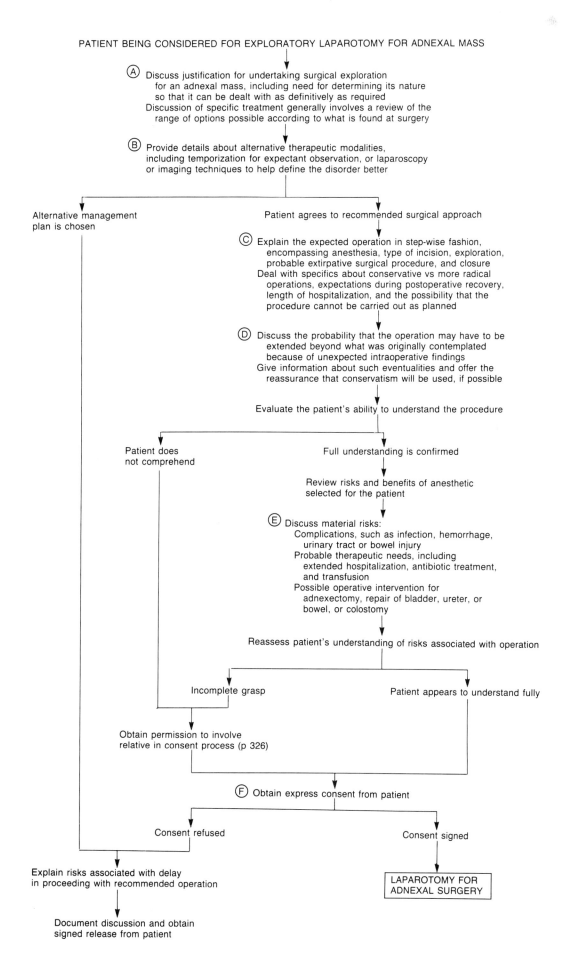

Ⓐ Discuss justification for undertaking surgical exploration
for an adnexal mass, including need for determining its nature
so that it can be dealt with as definitively as required
Discussion of specific treatment generally involves a review of the
range of options possible according to what is found at surgery

Ⓑ Provide details about alternative therapeutic modalities,
including temporization for expectant observation, or laparoscopy
or imaging techniques to help define the disorder better

Alternative management
plan is chosen

Patient agrees to recommended surgical approach

Ⓒ Explain the expected operation in step-wise fashion,
encompassing anesthesia, type of incision, exploration,
probable extirpative surgical procedure, and closure
Deal with specifics about conservative vs more radical
operations, expectations during postoperative recovery,
length of hospitalization, and the possibility that the
procedure cannot be carried out as planned

Ⓓ Discuss the probability that the operation may have to be
extended beyond what was originally contemplated
because of unexpected intraoperative findings
Give information about such eventualities and offer the
reassurance that conservatism will be used, if possible

Evaluate the patient's ability to understand the procedure

Patient does
not comprehend

Full understanding is confirmed

Review risks and benefits of anesthetic
selected for the patient

Ⓔ Discuss material risks:
Complications, such as infection, hemorrhage,
urinary tract or bowel injury
Probable therapeutic needs, including
extended hospitalization, antibiotic treatment,
and transfusion
Possible operative intervention for
adnexectomy, repair of bladder, ureter, or
bowel, or colostomy

Reassess patient's understanding of risks associated with operation

Incomplete grasp

Patient appears to understand fully

Obtain permission to involve
relative in consent process (p 326)

Ⓕ Obtain express consent from patient

Consent refused

Consent signed

Explain risks associated with delay
in proceeding with recommended operation

LAPAROTOMY FOR
ADNEXAL SURGERY

Document discussion and obtain
signed release from patient

PREVENTIVE RISK MANAGEMENT

Max Borten, M.D., J.D.

A. It is generally accepted that surgery is accompanied by certain unavoidable risks. One must, therefore, conduct a detailed discussion with every patient well in advance of a contemplated operation, if at all possible. This gives her ample opportunity to consider all options and, if desired, seek other opinions. Review the nature of the patient's condition with her as well as the various alternatives and their relative risks and benefits. Documentation is critical. If a complication should actually occur, advise the patient fully about it. Be frank and forthright about the possible cause, if known, and maintain accurate, detailed and timely records including treatment regimen, consultations, and all discussions with her and her family. Failing to make such notes in the patient's medical chart or inserting inaccurate or self-serving information may prove counterproductive.

B. It is always good practice to document the patient's status in the hospital chart, including facts, probable diagnosis, and plan. A skimpy, inaccurate, illegible or otherwise poorly maintained record may support an unjustified malpractice claim, while a well-detailed one reflects good care and caring. Be sure to date, time, and sign every note entered in the medical chart. Record all relevant facts promptly and accurately. Delaying an entry risks error or omission. Avoid statements that are contradictory or contrary to facts. Supervisory physicians in an academic environment are responsible to read, correct, and countersign notes by housestaff and students to show that they are overseeing the care being rendered by those they are supervising.

C. Clearly document the problem for which a consultant is being called and the rationale for the request. Be sure to tell the patient beforehand about the issues that need resolution and why other physicians have to become involved in her care. It is more than common courtesy and professional respect to introduce the consultant to the patient and to remain in attendance, if possible. This show of interest maintains and enforces the doctor-patient relationship, bolsters the patient's confidence, and may allay her fears somewhat.

D. Turning the responsibility of care over to another physician requires the patient's specific acknowledgement and agreement. Document the transfer of responsibility in the record and formally advise the nursing staff. Whether or not a consulting physician is to take over the care, the primary physician should review the consultant's findings and recommendations with her. To avoid conflicting messages and confusing information, keep the number of people explaining the management plan to an absolute minimum. Advise ancillary personnel accordingly. While it is not mandatory to follow the consultant's recommendations to the letter, one is well advised to have substantive arguments for not doing so and to document the reasons for choosing an alternative plan of management.

E. Management plans should be spelled out in the patient's record. This applies most especially if there has been a complication or untoward event. Be as objective as possible in describing events, observations, tests, and treatment. Give the rationale for a particular examination, drug or intervention, elaborating the logic of the decisions. An honest error in judgment usually proves to be supportable if adequate and appropriate diagnostic methods were used to arrive at that judgment.

F. Objectivity is essential for the contents of the discharge summary. Avoid including conjectural statements or opinions that can be interpreted as intended to be self-serving. Limit the material to a factual account of the events that transpired during the course of the hospital stay. Incorporate only information that can be found in the medical record. If the record is incomplete, ensure that missing reports (or official copies) are found and included. Missing notes can be appended as addenda, properly dated to show they were added afterwards. No record should be altered, although one can indicate an erroneous entry by a marginal note, signed and dated in an appropriate manner.

G. Preventive risk management requires that all complications be reported and analyzed in depth. This is best done as soon as possible after the complication is discovered. This ensures that recollection of events is still fresh in the mind of the participants. Be forthright with the risk management coordinator (or legal counsel) about the most likely causes of the complication. Re-evaluate your decisions and work closely with your hospital's peer review or quality control unit.

References

Lewis SM. Ob/Gyn Malpractice. New York: John Wiley & Sons, 1986.

Southwick AF. The Law of Hospital and Health Care Administration. Ann Arbor: Health Administration Press, 1978.

Waltz JR, Inbau FE. Medical Jurisprudence: New York: Macmillan, 1971.

PATIENT WITH COMPLICATION FROM A PROCEDURE

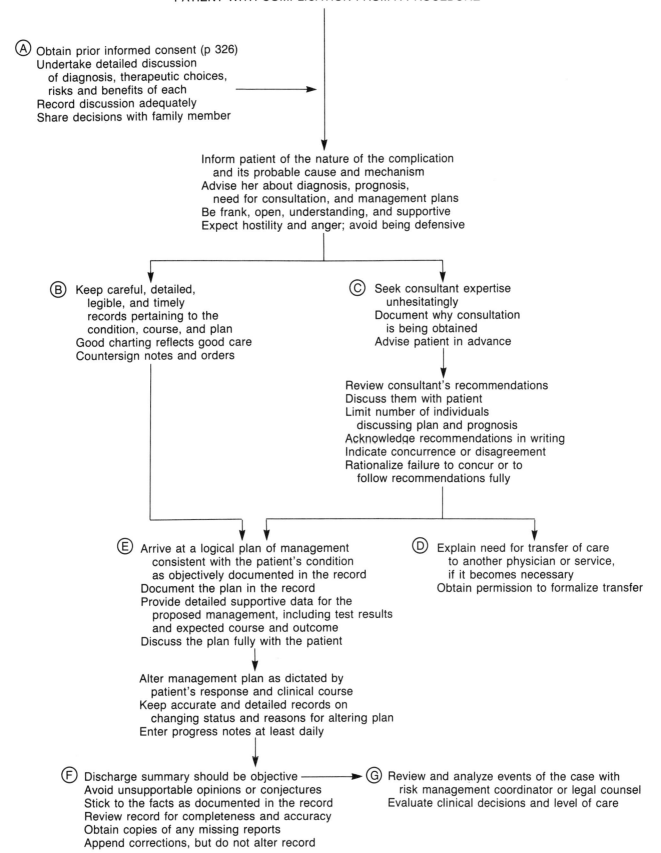

Ⓐ Obtain prior informed consent (p 326)
   Undertake detailed discussion
      of diagnosis, therapeutic choices,
      risks and benefits of each
   Record discussion adequately
   Share decisions with family member

Inform patient of the nature of the complication
   and its probable cause and mechanism
Advise her about diagnosis, prognosis,
   need for consultation, and management plans
Be frank, open, understanding, and supportive
Expect hostility and anger; avoid being defensive

Ⓑ Keep careful, detailed,
      legible, and timely
      records pertaining to the
      condition, course, and plan
   Good charting reflects good care
   Countersign notes and orders

Ⓒ Seek consultant expertise
      unhesitatingly
   Document why consultation
      is being obtained
   Advise patient in advance

Review consultant's recommendations
Discuss them with patient
Limit number of individuals
   discussing plan and prognosis
Acknowledge recommendations in writing
Indicate concurrence or disagreement
Rationalize failure to concur or to
   follow recommendations fully

Ⓔ Arrive at a logical plan of management
      consistent with the patient's condition
      as objectively documented in the record
   Document the plan in the record
   Provide detailed supportive data for the
      proposed management, including test results
      and expected course and outcome
   Discuss the plan fully with the patient

Ⓓ Explain need for transfer of care
      to another physician or service,
      if it becomes necessary
   Obtain permission to formalize transfer

Alter management plan as dictated by
   patient's response and clinical course
Keep accurate and detailed records on
   changing status and reasons for altering plan
Enter progress notes at least daily

Ⓕ Discharge summary should be objective
   Avoid unsupportable opinions or conjectures
   Stick to the facts as documented in the record
   Review record for completeness and accuracy
   Obtain copies of any missing reports
   Append corrections, but do not alter record

Ⓖ Review and analyze events of the case with
      risk management coordinator or legal counsel
   Evaluate clinical decisions and level of care

DELINEATION OF PRIVILEGES

Max Borten, M.D., J.D.

A. The practice of medicine involves the representation to the public by a physician that he or she possesses that knowledge and those skills that can aid in the prevention, diagnosis, and treatment of diseases to which human beings are subjected. To protect the public and foster professionalism, states have instituted the process of licensing. States are entitled to limit admission to a profession, with the privileges pertaining to the practice of that profession, to those who can prove their competence to practice. To that effect, they require an applicant to have pursued and completed a prescribed course of studies in a satisfactory manner and to have taken and passed a variety of state-approved examinations. While states differ in their specific requirements, they all require formal application and satisfactory demonstration of medical education and some form of documented competency testing. In addition, more states are demanding evidence of continuing education for periodic renewal of licensure to practice.

B. The regulations adopted by a state need not be internally uniform with respect to all methods and systems of practice nor consistent with other states. Some activities may be exempted from the regulations and others subjected to especially constrictive regulations. This differential practice is acceptable as long as it is not imposed arbitrarily or unreasonably. No physician has an absolute vested right to practice method. A conditional right is given instead which is subordinate to the police power of the state to protect and preserve the public health. State relicensure regulations are designed to help provide a mechanism by which the quality of health care providers can be assessed, although the control of quality is seldom fully exercised. In addition to continuing education requirements, some states are introducing investigations based on required reporting of liability cases and restriction of hospital privileges.

C. A hospital may be held liable for its failure to exercise reasonable care in selecting and retaining employees. Such duty has been extended to require a hospital to apply due care in conferring and renewing staff privileges to self-employed physicians who may not be hospital employees or its agents. Hospital liability for negligent failure to properly screen or evaluate physicians seeking or holding staff privileges could probably be supported on the theory of vicarious liability or corporate liability. Thus, the hospital has a positive requirement to ensure that all who apply to practice within its walls are qualified and competent before privileges are granted and that they remain competent while continuing to practice.

D. Hospitals have a legal obligation to monitor the quality of care rendered in their institutions (p 324). Of additional relevance are the physician's attributes of ethics, honesty, and interpersonal dealings as well as continuing education. As a result of such quality assurance surveillance, the institution can curtail or revoke staff privileges of physicians who are shown to provide substandard care to patients. These actions cannot be taken arbitrarily. They require documentation and substantiation.

E. Hospitals must afford staff physicians some formal due process mechanism to permit them to redress their grievances, such as the opportunity to answer the charges upon which the constraining measures rest. Minimal due process with respect to staff appointments and renewals includes the opportunity for a formal hearing preceded by appropriate notice, a written statement of the charges or reasons for the denial of appointment or reappointment, the right to call witnesses on behalf of the physician, the right to cross examine the hospital's witnesses, and the right to have a written statement summarizing the decision and the basis for the decision as formulated by the hearing committee.

F. It is imperative for the medical profession to police itself and protect patients from physicians impaired on the basis of drugs, alcohol, physical or emotional disease, or debilitation. State regulatory groups, medical societies, and hospital peer review bodies must identify, discipline, and encourage treatment and rehabilitation of the disabled physician. Early identification prevents exposing patients to risk while simultaneously increasing the possibility of effectively rehabilitating the affected physician.

References

Annas GJ, Glantz LH, Katz BF. The Rights of Doctors, Nurses and Allied Health Professionals. Cambridge, MA: Ballinger, 1981.

Clemenhagen C. Credentialing procedures need strengthening. Dimens Health Serv 63:4, 1986.

Parfrey PS, Gillespie M, McManamon PJ, Fisher R. Audit of the Medical Audit Committee. Can Med Assoc J 135:205, 1986.

Wadlington W, Waltz JR, Dworkin RD. Law and Medicine: Cases and Materials. Mineola, NY: The Foundation Press, 1980.

PHYSICIAN SEEKING GYNECOLOGICAL PRACTICE PRIVILEGES

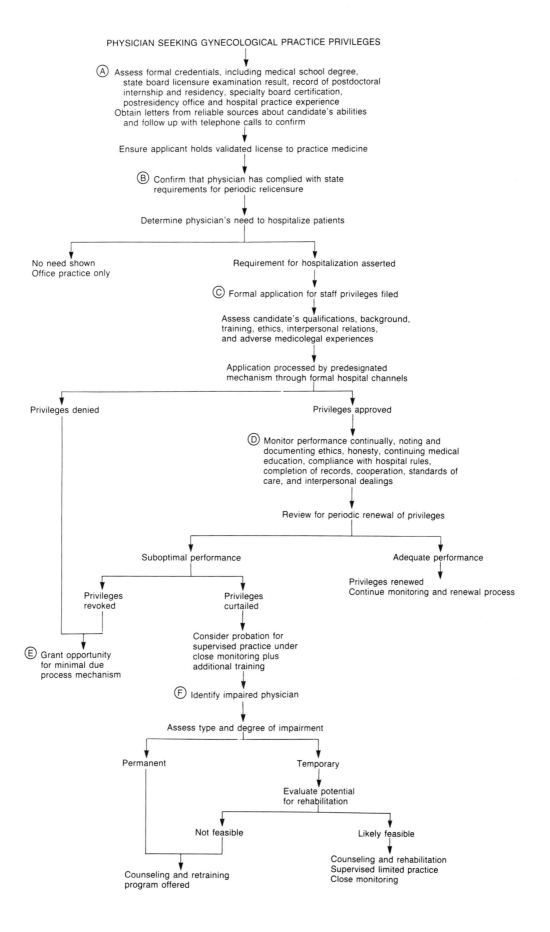

Ⓐ Assess formal credentials, including medical school degree,
state board licensure examination result, record of postdoctoral
internship and residency, specialty board certification,
postresidency office and hospital practice experience
Obtain letters from reliable sources about candidate's abilities
and follow up with telephone calls to confirm

Ensure applicant holds validated license to practice medicine

Ⓑ Confirm that physician has complied with state
requirements for periodic relicensure

Determine physician's need to hospitalize patients

No need shown
Office practice only

Requirement for hospitalization asserted

Ⓒ Formal application for staff privileges filed

Assess candidate's qualifications, background,
training, ethics, interpersonal relations,
and adverse medicolegal experiences

Application processed by predesignated
mechanism through formal hospital channels

Privileges denied

Privileges approved

Ⓓ Monitor performance continually, noting and
documenting ethics, honesty, continuing medical
education, compliance with hospital rules,
completion of records, cooperation, standards of
care, and interpersonal dealings

Review for periodic renewal of privileges

Suboptimal performance

Adequate performance

Privileges renewed
Continue monitoring and renewal process

Privileges
revoked

Privileges
curtailed

Consider probation for
supervised practice under
close monitoring plus
additional training

Ⓔ Grant opportunity
for minimal due
process mechanism

Ⓕ Identify impaired physician

Assess type and degree of impairment

Permanent

Temporary

Evaluate potential
for rehabilitation

Not feasible

Likely feasible

Counseling and retraining
program offered

Counseling and rehabilitation
Supervised limited practice
Close monitoring

RECORD REQUEST PROCEDURE

Max Borten, M.D., J.D.

A. When faced with a request from a patient or any third party for medical records or information about a patient, one should insist on first getting the patient's written consent for disclosure. In general, a physician cannot lawfully disclose information obtained in the course of a professional doctor-patient relationship without the patient's consent. This restrictive guiding principle does not hold, however, if the physician recognizes that there is a serious danger to the patient or to others. In fact, under such circumstances, one may actually have an overriding obligation to disclose the information to prevent harm. In case of doubt, consult knowledgeable counsel. Ordinarily, if the patient's written release is not forthcoming, information contained in the medical record and the record itself can only be released in response to a court order.

B. A physician receives information relating to a patient's health in a confidential capacity. There is, thus, an express or implied agreement by the physician not to disclose such information to anyone unless the patient authorizes or requests such disclosure. Unless she formally consents otherwise, the patient has the unlimited privilege to refuse to disclose and to prevent anyone else from disclosing all communications between herself and her physician. A patient's claim of confidentiality is considered to be waived, however, when the patient puts her medical condition at issue by filing suit against the physician. Once this occurs, therefore, the physician is free to discuss the patient's care with his or her defense counsel without the patient's written authorization.

C. Although the physician actually owns the patient's medical records in the eyes of the law, there is nonetheless an obligation for the physician to grant the patient or her authorized agent the opportunity to read them. This obligation derives from the confidence and trust inherent in the fiduciary nature of the doctor-patient relationship (see p 342). It means the physician is expected to reveal to the patient any information that is clearly in her best interests. The right to gain access to a record is granted by statute in some areas. It may be given to the patient or her representative; alternatively, it may be limited to her attorney unless the patient can substantiate her need to see the records. One risks a charge of concealing information fraudulently if one refuses access to records to an authorized attorney.

D. The malpractice liability insurance carrier is obligated to provide the physician the services of competent counsel in the event a suit is filed or anticipated. Even though the defense counsel is usually appointed by the carrier, his or her loyalty should be undivided and directed toward representing only the interest of the physician. One should avail oneself of these services well in advance of trial participation to review details of the case while such details are still fresh in mind. Involve the hospital's risk management officer and legal counsel as well to help coordinate activities and reduce redundancy. Discuss the issues freely with the reassurance that the exchange will be held strictly confidential within the context of the attorney-client relationship which is analogous to the privileged nature of doctor-patient communications.

E. If copies of the medical records have been requested by a patient's attorney, these records and any related reports, correspondence or billing data should be gathered together and safely locked away. This ensures against any alterations being made or any items becoming lost or misfiled. Be especially careful to avoid making any changes, even if it is clear that there has been an erroneous entry. It is almost impossible to mount a satisfactory defense in a case, no matter how fine the care or blameless the physician, if the medical record has been altered. Once brought to light, the altered medical record will be interpreted as an admission of negligence. Along the same lines, make no new entries either, because they have a tendency to be viewed as self-serving. Nevertheless, if information that might be important to the case is recalled, it should not be ignored; ask for professional aid from legal counsel about how to handle and document this new material.

F. Do not discuss the case or any of its details with anyone but the risk management officer and your counsel. This exclusion encompasses one's own colleagues or other personnel, even if they are principals in the case. The desire to talk about the case is understandable, but it should be resisted because it may cause more harm than good in giving the appearance of collusion and in perhaps disseminating undesirable information. Any communications received should be referred directly to the defense attorney who is handling and coordinating the case. Be especially circumspect to avoid any correspondence or direct contact with the patient or her attorney.

References

Annas GJ, Glantz LH, Katz BF. The Rights of Doctors, Nurses and Allied Health Professionals. Cambridge: Ballinger, 1981.

Fineberg KS, Peters JD, Willson JR, Kroll DA. Obstetrics/Gynecology and the Law. Ann Arbor: Michigan Health Administration Press, 1984.

Southwick AF. The Law of Hospital and Health Care Administration. Ann Arbor: Health Administration Press, 1978.

Wadlington W, Waltz JR, Dworkin RB. Law and Medicine: Cases and Materials. Mineola: Foundation Press, 1980.

COPY OF RECORD REQUESTED BY ATTORNEY

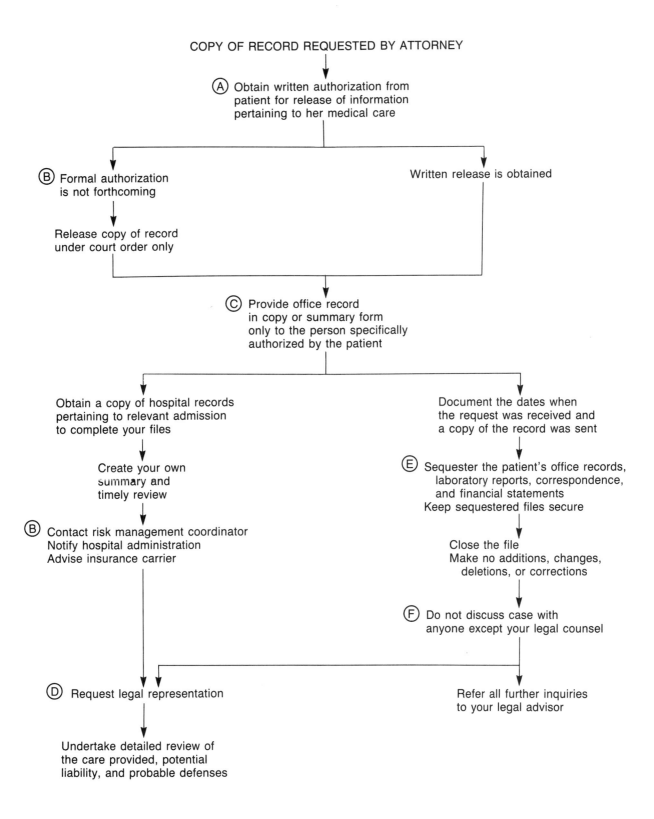

(A) Obtain written authorization from patient for release of information pertaining to her medical care

(B) Formal authorization is not forthcoming

Written release is obtained

Release copy of record under court order only

(C) Provide office record in copy or summary form only to the person specifically authorized by the patient

Obtain a copy of hospital records pertaining to relevant admission to complete your files

Document the dates when the request was received and a copy of the record was sent

Create your own summary and timely review

(E) Sequester the patient's office records, laboratory reports, correspondence, and financial statements
Keep sequestered files secure

(B) Contact risk management coordinator
Notify hospital administration
Advise insurance carrier

Close the file
Make no additions, changes, deletions, or corrections

(F) Do not discuss case with anyone except your legal counsel

(D) Request legal representation

Refer all further inquiries to your legal advisor

Undertake detailed review of the care provided, potential liability, and probable defenses

NEGLIGENCE

Max Borten, M.D., J.D.

A. In medical malpractice litigation, cases stand or fall most commonly on the basis of the allegation of negligence. Several independent elements must be considered in determining whether there is true liability due to negligence: Did the physician have a duty to the patient? What was the standard of care owed to the patient? Did the physician violate that duty of care? Was the patient harmed as a consequence of the physician's conduct? Was the physician's conduct the proximate cause of the harm to the patient?

B. In order to hold a physician (defendant) liable for medical malpractice, the patient (plaintiff) must first establish that a doctor-patient relationship (duty of care) existed. The nature of the physician's duty is based on the legal obligation (contract) imposed on anyone who undertakes to enter such a relationship. Once a physician consents to treat a patient, he or she has a duty to use reasonable care and diligence in carrying out the treatment program. The law holds a physician responsible for an injury resulting from a deficiency of the requisite skill and knowledge or the failure to exercise reasonable care.

C. Although a general or family practitioner is held to the minimal standard of care applicable to all reasonably careful and prudent physicians, a specialist is required to practice at a higher level, namely at the level of the standards of the specialist practicing in that field anywhere. This uniform standard, now in force almost without exception throughout the United States, signifies that all gynecologists are expected to be knowledgeable about those advances made in the discipline in recent years that are generally accepted and widely incorporated into practice patterns.

D. A special situation may exist when it can be inferred from the weight of circumstantial evidence that the physician's negligence is likely to have caused harm to the patient. This falls under the doctrine of *res ipsa loquitur*. It is invoked in cases with complications that are not usually encountered unless there actually has been some form of negligence. Generally, it is determined that no other factors can be found that might have contributed to the bad result. The alleged substandard act must fall within the scope of the physician's responsibility to the patient. Contrary to most other cases in which the plaintiff has

to prove negligence, the burden of proof shifts to the defendant to establish lack of culpability whenever this principle is applied.

E. It is necessary for the plaintiff to show that the physician's action or omission was the actual cause of the adverse outcome. If it can be shown that the damage would have occurred even if the care had been optimal, then the physician's conduct cannot be faulted as the cause.

F. If the physician's conduct has been established as the actual cause of the plaintiff's injury, it becomes necessary for the plaintiff to show that the defendant's act was its proximate (or legal) cause. Liability extends to that damage which could be foreseen to result from the negligent act. Thus, the defendant could be held liable for any later ensuing harm if it can be shown that he or she should have known that the adverse effect of the damage might be aggravated by someone else's negligent acts.

G. It is sometimes possible to mount a defense in a malpractice litigation based on contributory negligence and assumption of risk by the patient herself. This applies if some proportion of the damage can be shown to be attributable to some action or failure to act by the patient, particularly if she did not follow clearly stated recommendations such as follow-up examinations or prompt reporting of warning symptoms. The principle of comparative negligence, in which the relative fractions of negligence attributable to the several parties involved in the case are taken into account in assigning responsibility, is widely accepted. Recovery for damages in such cases is reduced accordingly to the degree of negligence for which the patient is determined to be responsible.

References

Fineberg KS, Peters JD, Willson JR, Kroll DA. Obstetrics/Gynecology and the Law. Ann Arbor: Health Administration Press, 1984.

Keeton WP, Dobbs DB, Keeton RE, Owen DG. Prosser and Keeton on the Law of Torts. St Paul: West Publishing, 1984.

King JH. The Law of Medical Malpractice in a Nutshell. St Paul: West Publishing, 1977.

Louisell DW, Williams H. Medical Malpractice. New York: Matthew Bender, 1986.

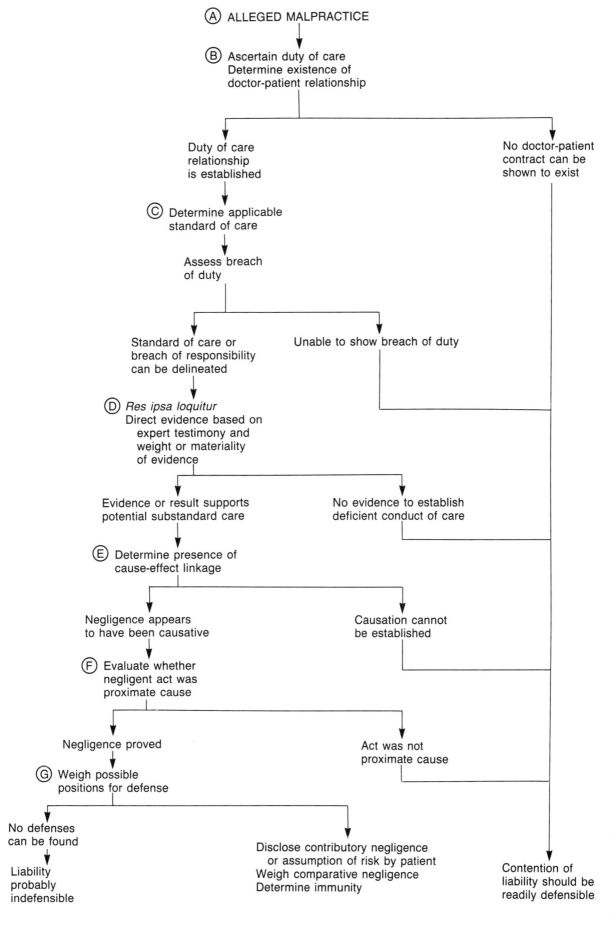

(A) ALLEGED MALPRACTICE

(B) Ascertain duty of care
Determine existence of
doctor-patient relationship

Duty of care
relationship
is established

No doctor-patient
contract can be
shown to exist

(C) Determine applicable
standard of care

Assess breach
of duty

Standard of care or
breach of responsibility
can be delineated

Unable to show breach of duty

(D) *Res ipsa loquitur*
Direct evidence based on
expert testimony and
weight or materiality
of evidence

Evidence or result supports
potential substandard care

No evidence to establish
deficient conduct of care

(E) Determine presence of
cause-effect linkage

Negligence appears
to have been causative

Causation cannot
be established

(F) Evaluate whether
negligent act was
proximate cause

Negligence proved

Act was not
proximate cause

(G) Weigh possible
positions for defense

No defenses
can be found

Liability
probably
indefensible

Disclose contributory negligence
or assumption of risk by patient
Weigh comparative negligence
Determine immunity

Contention of
liability should be
readily defensible